THE BOOK OF THE
FORMER PROPHETS

The Book of the
FORMER PROPHETS

✺ ✺ ✺

THOMAS W. MANN

CASCADE *Books* • Eugene, Oregon

THE BOOK OF THE FORMER PROPHETS

Copyright © 2011 Thomas W. Mann. All rights reserved. Except for brief quotations in critical publications or reviews, no part of this book may be reproduced in any manner without prior written permission from the publisher. Write: Permissions, Wipf and Stock Publishers, 199 W. 8th Ave., Eugene, OR 97401.

Cascade Books
An Imprint of Wipf and Stock Publishers
199 W. 8th Ave., Suite 3
Eugene, OR 97401

www.wipfandstock.com

ISBN 13: 978-1-60608-669-8

Cataloging-in-Publication data:

Mann, Thomas W. (Thomas Wingate), 1944–

The book of the Former Prophets / Thomas W. Mann.

ISBN 13: 978-1-60608-669-8

xii + 444 p. ; 23 cm. Includes bibliographical references and indexes.

1. Bible. O.T. Former Prophets—Criticism, interpretation, etc.. 2. Narration in the Bible. 3. Deuteronomistic history (Biblical criticism). 4. Bible. O.T. Joshua—Criticism, interpretation, etc. 5. O. T. Judges—Criticism, interpretation, etc.. 6. Bible. O.T. Samuel—Criticism, interpretation, etc. 7. Bible. O. T. Kings—Criticism, interpretation, etc.. I. Title.

BS1286.5 M4 2011

Manufactured in the U.S.A.

In honor of Mary Elizabeth Mann

and all Peace Corps Volunteers

who make this world a better place.

Contents

List of Excursuses ❋ *viii*
List of Figures ❋ *viii*
Preface ❋ *ix*
Abbreviations ❋ *xi*

Introduction ❋ 1
ONE Joshua ❋ 13
TWO Judges ❋ 50
THREE Ruth ❋ 94
FOUR 1 Samuel ❋ 107
FIVE 2 Samuel ❋ 171
SIX 1 Kings ❋ 243
SIVEN 2 Kings ❋ 318

Summary and Conclusion ❋ 380

Glossary ❋ *415*
Bibliography ❋ *417*
Scripture Index ❋ *425*

List of Excursuses

Excursus 1: The Treaty Model of God ✳ 16
Excursus 2: Disobedience and Disaster ✳ 32
Excursus 3: Yahweh and the "Other Gods" ✳ 57
Excursus 4: "According to the Word of the Lord" ✳ 285
Excursus 5: The Clash of Storm Deities ✳ 289
Excursus 6: The Assyrian Menace ✳ 352
Excursus 7: The Vassal's Dilemma ✳ 356

List of Figures

Figure 1: Families of Saul and David ✳ 176
Figure 2: David's Children ✳ 201
Figure 3: House of Omri ✳ 319
Figure 4: House of Jehu ✳ 347
Figure 5: House of Josiah ✳ 376

Preface

I HOPE THAT THIS book will be helpful to students at the college and graduate levels, the latter in Seminaries or Divinity Schools and in doctoral programs. I also hope that the book will be informative to any general reader interested in understanding more fully a major document in the faith traditions of Judaism and Christianity, as well as a story that has informed the self-understanding of North Americans beginning with those colonists who first came to this country from Europe. To aid the reader in seeing parallels with their own history I have occasionally inserted brief quotations from various sources on numerous topics ranging from video games to the war in Iraq. I have also provided a number of Excursuses on various subjects that occur repeatedly, as well as genealogies or similar information on key figures and their families. Finally, there is a brief glossary of key terms.

Sometimes I will refer to verses in the text as, for example, v. 46b or 46a. For readers unfamiliar with scholarly biblical citations, a and b refer generally to the first and second parts of a verse. Sometimes the NRSV will print part b with a separate indentation, for example in 1 Kgs 2:46, with part b beginning with "So the kingdom." In this case, the Hebrew text has an indentation also. At other times, it is not obvious to the English reader where the break comes (it is indicated in Hebrew by a superscript symbol). E.g., in the previous verse (45), the division comes after "blessed." In the following verse (3:1), the division comes after "Egypt," at the semicolon, which often, but by no means always, may indicate a and b. (I use a similar system occasionally to cite pages in a scholarly book that has dual columns of text, e.g., p. 45a or 45b.)

All quotations of the biblical text are from the New Revised Standard Version, using the HarperCollins Study Bible edition, unless otherwise indicated. When I provide my own translation, I will so indicate with the abbreviation "AT," for "author's translation." At times I will give the Hebrew word in question in transliteration. My system is informally phonetic, for example, using *v* for the soft *b*, as in *yashav* (where the Hebrew more technically is *yashab*). Those who know Hebrew should have little trouble determining the root word in question. I use a single quotation mark (‘) to represent the silent letter '*ayin*, and the reverse single quotation mark (’) to represent the letter *'alef*.

Although you can read this book without consulting the Bible, your understanding and appreciation for the considerable artistic, historical, and religious merits of the biblical text will be enhanced by reading the two together, in whatever order you decide. Many readers may want to skip the footnotes in order to follow the narrative thread more smoothly. The notes take up interpretive issues in more detail, including the opinions of other scholars, comparative texts, and explanations of my own arguments. When there are extensive footnotes (e.g., on 1 Kings 16–19) the reader might benefit from reading the text at least in whole paragraphs and then consulting the footnotes, in order to keep the thread of the narrative and commentary. Other scholars will, I trust, recognize my inability to consult all of the commentaries on each of the biblical books, not to mention separate monographs and journal articles. (One scholar alone—J. P. Fokkelman—has written close to twenty-five hundred pages limited largely to 1 and 2 Samuel!) Had I attempted to do so, it would have taken another lifetime.

I thank Anne Herndon for plowing through the whole thing in rough form and providing numerous helpful suggestions for which the reader can be grateful. I thank my sister-in-law, Marta Weigle, for suggesting readings about the sixteenth- and seventeenth-century Spanish involvement in the American Southwest. I thank David Gunn and Pat Miller for their endorsements, and Pat also for his encouragement of my written work that goes back many years. Both of them endorsed the precedent for this book—*The Book of the Torah*—and I am delighted to have their names together again on the back cover.

Abbreviations

ANET	*Ancient Near Eastern Tests Relating to the Old Testament.* Edited by James B. Pritchard. 3rd ed. Princeton: Princeton University, 1969
AT	Author's translation
DtrH	a variant of numerous abbreviations designating the Deuteronomistic historian
LXX	Septuagint, the ancient Greek version of the Hebrew Bible, translated around 250 BCE in Alexandria, Egypt
MT	Masoretic Text, the Hebrew text with the accompanying diacritical marks that indicate vocalization, punctuation, etc.
NRSV	New Revised Standard Version of the Bible
RSV	Revised Standard Version of the Bible
YHWH	The "Tetragrammaton" representing the consonants in the personal name of God, Yahweh (see glossary)

Abbreviations of Biblical Books Cited:

Gen	Genesis
Exod	Exodus
Lev	Leviticus
Num	Numbers
Deut	Deuteronomy
Josh	Joshua
Judg	Judges
1–2 Sam	1–2 Samuel
1–2 Kgs	1–2 Kings
1–2 Chr	1–2 Chronicles
Neh	Nehemiah
Ps	Psalms
Prov	Proverbs
Eccl	Ecclesiastes
Song	Song of Songs
Isa	Isaiah
Jer	Jeremiah
Lam	Lamentations
Ezek	Ezekiel
Hos	Hosea
Mic	Micah
Mal	Malachi
Matt	Matthew
Rom	Romans
Jas	James
Rev	Revelation

Introduction

In my senior year of college I took an advanced course in the Hebrew Bible that concentrated on the Former Prophets, the biblical books of Joshua through 2 Kings. The professor was Bernard Boyd, a legendary lecturer who had captivated me, like so many others, and converted me from a pre-med major to a religion major, much to the puzzlement of my friends. At the outset of this course, which had only a handful of students, Prof. Boyd presented each of us with a box of crayons. We then spent the rest of that session coloring in our Bibles, an activity that may seem more appropriate to kindergarten than an advanced college course. But the coloring was solidly academic: we were marking the various literary sources that the editors used in putting together the Former Prophets. Each source had a different color side bar or underline. I still have the Bible, and still find it helpful, even though the designation of many texts has changed in the scholarly community. The Deuteronomic editor was marked with red. In Samuel, the "Early Source" was marked in yellow, the "Late Source" in blue, and so on. A recent study of the Former Prophets uses a very similar technique, only with fonts and lines instead of colors.[1]

Most people read the narrative portions of the Bible as straightforward, seamless accounts, without even thinking about *who* might have written a particular story, *when* they were writing, and for *whom* (or *against* whom). Whether it's Genesis or Judges (or for that matter, John), many people read the stories without considering the identity of both author and audience, not to mention the moment in Israelite history that might have shaped the author's writing. Similarly, most people do not stop to consider the possibility that a particular biblical story is not simply the work of a single author but, in fact, may contain the words of two or more authors. Yet anyone who has taken a college course like "Bible 101," or read scholarly works on the Bible, or has encountered "biblical criticism" in a Sunday school or synagogue class, knows that our very notion of what an "author" is does not fit with the writers of biblical narratives. We know that William Faulkner wrote

1. Campbell and O'Brien, *Unfolding*.

the novel *Go Down, Moses*, but whoever wrote the *biblical* story of Moses is anonymous.[2] Indeed, *all* of the stories in the Hebrew Bible are anonymous. Even the titles of the books were supplied by later readers, and no book has a copyright page with author's name, date, and place of publication. Even the word "book" is misleading, in that the original biblical documents were scrolls without "pages."

Students in Bible 101 would learn that, in fact, biblical narratives are invariably the product of numerous "authors," often reflecting different points of view from different times. There are many resources that describe the process whereby the biblical books came to be, and we shall not go into great detail about the process here.[3] However, it is crucial to acknowledge that biblical narratives are the result of such a process. The final *product*—that is, the current text contained in contemporary versions of the Bible, like the New Revised Standard Version—is a *composite* document put together by numerous writers over a long period of time. You could think of biblical narratives as a literary montage. As a graphic art form, a montage is a hodgepodge of various bits and pieces ranging from pictures to symbols to abstract designs, often glued together. Imagine a *group* of artists putting together a single montage. They would bring to the composition what suits their own individual interpretation of how the final product should look, what it should "say" to the observer. Although the group might agree on an overall theme, they might also choose pictures or designs that either complement or clash with one another. Think how different the style and content might be between just two contributors—Norman Rockwell and Pablo Picasso! Moreover, if there *is* no prior agreement, the components of the final product might seem ironic or even completely incompatible.

Like the Pentateuch that precedes it, the Former Prophets is a literary montage.[4] In academic discourse, the Former Prophets is part of a work called the "Deuteronomistic history." The academic title derives from the connection between the book of Deuteronomy and the books that follow it. That is, many of the issues, themes, and images, and much of the literary style, that dominates Deuteronomy also appears to be shared by at least one of the writers who put together the Former Prophets.

---

2. The popular notion that Moses wrote the Pentateuch (Genesis through Deuteronomy) has no basis in Scripture. The "book" that Moses writes according to Deut 31:9, 24, most likely refers at most to chaps. 12–26. Otherwise, Moses writes a hymnic poem that we call the "Song of Moses," Deut 31:22; chap. 32. It would be awkward indeed to explain how Moses wrote about his own death (Deuteronomy 34)!

3. For one example, see Friedman, *Who Wrote the Bible?*

4. This present book is a sequel to my earlier work on the Pentateuch, *Book of the Torah*. Robert Alter has also used the metaphor of a montage in this sense; see *Art*, 140. Perhaps we could phrase Alter's emphasis in terms of an artful montage rather than an awkward hodgepodge. He recognizes that the biblical authors were "editing and splicing . . . antecedent literary materials," but the purpose was to reveal "two different dimensions of his subject" (cf. 181). He also uses the term "collage" (Alter, *David Story*, ix) instead of "a stringing together of virtually independent sources." Halpern, *First Historians*, 219, thinks of "a patchwork of sources."

One could say that the Former Prophets originally had a preface, which is the book of Deuteronomy.[5] Rather late in Israel's history, however, some of the "composers" separated Deuteronomy from the Former Prophets to form the Pentateuch, also called the Torah (Genesis–Deuteronomy). The Former Prophets is so named to distinguish the books of Joshua through Kings from the books of the "Latter Prophets" (sometimes called the "Writing Prophets"), i.e., the books named for various prophets (e.g. Jeremiah, Amos, etc.). The canon of the Hebrew Bible thus contains three parts: the Torah (Genesis through Deuteronomy), the prophets (Joshua through Malachi), and the Writings. The Hebrew word *torah* is often translated as "law," even though *the* Torah clearly includes stories and many other literary genres. One can already see the first two parts of the eventual canon in the New Testament phrase "the Law and the Prophets" (e.g., Matt 7:12; Luke 16:16; Rom 3:21).

In short, when we consider the writers of biblical stories we often need to think not only of authors but also of editors. An editor revises an existing work, making changes as needed, correcting what seem to be mistakes, adapting the material to the editor's own understanding. We also use the word "editorial" to refer to a newspaper column that does not claim to report news neutrally but represents an editor's opinion about an issue. That is, an editorial is biased in accordance with the editor's views, and may well be polemical, directly or implicitly arguing against a different view. Biblical stories often are literary montages that reflect just such an editorial process. (Biblical scholars use the terms "redactor" and "redaction" synonymously with "editor" and "edition.") The editors compiled their montage by combining a variety of sources and literary genres into a single narrative—historical annals, legends, folktales, laws, poems, songs, and administrative lists, to name a few.[6]

To take one example, in 1 Samuel there is a story about how Saul came to be anointed the ruler of Israel. He was out looking for some lost donkeys and went to a seer for help in finding them. Saul was surprised when the seer threw a big party in his honor, and even more surprised when the seer (who proved to be the prophet Samuel) announced that God had appointed him the ruler who would save Israel from their enemies (1 Sam 9:1—10:8). There is barely a hint of anything wrong with Saul or the appointment of a ruler in this story.[7] But the reader has already read 1 Samuel 8, in which the people *demand* a king, and God condemns their demand as a rejection of God's own sovereignty. The original author of the "lost donkeys" story clearly thinks that a human king is needed, and that God has initiated the anointing of Saul, much the way God had appointed Moses to liberate

---

5. The editor known as the Deuteronomistic Historian probably composed chaps. 1–4 as an introduction to the history as a whole as well as the book. The original, groundbreaking study of the Deuteronomistic History was done by Noth in 1943, now translated as *The Deuteronomistic History*.

6. For an annotated bibliography of those sources used by the Deuteronomistic Historian see Halpern, *First Historians*, 207–18.

7. Certainly this is true for general readers, even though some scholars see rather subtle criticisms of Saul in the story, e.g., Alter, *Art*, 60–61.

the Hebrews from Egypt. The author of the "demand for a king" story thinks just the opposite: human monarchy inevitably subverts divine sovereignty, and God appoints Saul only grudgingly. As Alter says regarding another story, "the joining of the two accounts leaves us swaying in the dynamic interplay between two theologies, two conceptions of kingship and history."[8]

The example illustrates how there are two voices to be heard. They are arguing with each other, and at stake is a profound theological question: what is the nature of divine sovereignty, and how does it relate to human political institutions? If we hear the two distinct voices in the text, we acknowledge the tension between them, rather than trying to make the two say the same thing (scholars call the latter "harmonizing"). And, more importantly, we join the *process* of interpretation that the voices reflect: we consider what divine sovereignty means for us, and how we should understand our own political institutions and leaders in relationship to that sovereignty (or if at all!). In fact, it is remarkable that, whoever spliced the two stories together, did not simply remove the offending one, or edit out any conflicting view. Rather, conflicting views co-exist, as if the editors want their readers to engage in the discussion.[9]

A rabbi once told me a joke about a Jewish man who was stranded on a desert island. After many months, a ship appeared and sent a boat to rescue him. When the pilot of the boat arrived on shore, he saw that the stranded man had built two synagogues. When he asked him why *two* synagogues, the man pointed to one of them and said "To that one I don't go." He was used to arguing about religion, and needed two synagogues in order to have one with which he did not agree. The biblical canon (both Jewish and Christian) is the product of a very long process of interpretation and argumentation in which various authors and editors express their views, sometimes even contradicting one another. Part of the richness of the text is this very multiplicity of voices. The text is polyphonic, not monophonic. At stake is nothing less that intellectual and spiritual honesty. When we acknowledge the multiple and even conflicting voices in the text we affirm the "multifaceted truth" that the text represents.[10] Indeed, we affirm that truth *is* multifaceted.

---

8. Ibid., 152, referring to David in 1 Samuel 16 and 17. More generally on duplicate accounts, see his chap. 5. In some ways, the books of Chronicles offer a parallel account to much of 1 Samuel through 2 Kings, but the focus is radically different, essentially reduced to "the story of the Jerusalem temple" (Campbell, *Joshua to Chronicles*, 117). Notoriously, incidents like David's adultery with Bathsheba are omitted. We will only refer to Chronicles on rare occasions.

9 As Smith, *Memoirs*, 6, puts it, overall the Bible's aim is not to present "a single version of the past" but an "ongoing dialogue" about "different versions of the past." Different authors *remember* the past differently. Cf. Halpern, *First Historians*, 230: "Inconsistency in the text stems from sources, from a reverence toward them that transcends [the Deuteronomistic Historian's] central themes." That is, the Deuteronomistic Historian does not carelessly *sacrifice* history for ideology. "Antiquarian interest mottled theological interest as much as the reverse" (242).

10. The phrase is Alter's, *Art*, 140. Alter argues that we must recognize multiple authorship when it is present (19) but also not allow rigid critical methods to blind us to the art (21).

Like editorials in newspapers, the biblical narratives also reflect the times in which the editors lived. Part of the meaning of a text may come from the historical *context* in which it is written. Again, however, *unlike* newspaper editorials, there is no date at the top of the page, no byline, and no title (*Jerusalem Times*) to tell us where and when the editor is working. An editor writing about Joshua (c. 1250 BCE) might be living in the sixth century, say, 550 BCE (yes, that's seven hundred years later!). If so, then the editor's situation may be radically different from that of the story. Joshua leads the occupation of the land of Canaan; the editor would be writing at a time when Israel had lost the land in military defeat and the editor might be among the exiles in Babylon. In fact, many scholars think that my example is precisely the situation of at least one of the editors of the Former Prophets. In 721 BCE the northern realm of Israel fell to the Assyrians, who hauled off many Israelites into exile. In 587 BCE the southern realm of Judah suffered the same disaster, now perpetrated by the Babylonians, who destroyed Jerusalem—in particular, the palace and temple—and carried away the king and prominent citizens to exile.

American history isn't even long enough to match a seven-hundred-year gap, but let's consider a much smaller gap. Imagine how differently a historian writing a history of America might conclude his work if he was writing at two different times: first, in 1961, a few months after the inauguration of John F. Kennedy as President, when the White House was called Camelot and Kennedy had summoned Americans to join in pursuing a "new frontier," and, second, in 1974, just thirteen years later, when Kennedy had been assassinated, then Martin Luther King, Jr., and then Kennedy's brother, Robert, and after the shame and horror of the Vietnam War had divided the country (arguably the only war America had lost), and Camelot had descended into the petty disgraces of Watergate. After the assassination of Robert Kennedy, the novelist John Updike is said to have lamented "that God might have withdrawn His blessing from America."[11] That is precisely the anxiety that haunts the Former Prophets, especially in its exilic edition.

How, then, do scholars determine the date of a biblical editor? It is a complicated process, and the results are often highly debated. Nevertheless, there are clues in texts that hint at the context of the editor. Again to draw an analogy with American history, imagine finding a history of the American Revolution purportedly written close to the event, in which the historian criticizes owners of inns for "discriminating" against "African-Americans." We would see immediately that the account clearly was anachronistic, for such racial segregation did not become a major issue until the twentieth century, long after the even worse racial oppression of slavery was over, and the term "African-American" would not have made sense to anyone in the eighteenth century, for it was coined

---

11. The quote comes from Norman Mailer's *Miami and the Siege of Chicago*, as cited in Christopher Hitchens, "Master of Conventions," *Atlantic*, September 2008, 113.

as part of the racial justice movement in the twentieth.

To take an example from the book of Joshua, Joshua gives a kind of valedictory speech in which he warns against disobedience to "all that is written in the book of the law of Moses." The punishment for such disobedience, he warns, will be that "you shall perish quickly from the good land that [God] has given you" (Josh 23:16). It is quite possible that the editor is describing a situation that has already happened—the Babylonian exile. Through the words of Joshua the editor is saying to the current audience, "Joshua told us so." Moreover, the phrase "book of the law of Moses" most likely refers to some form of the book of Deuteronomy, and appears at critical places in the Former Prophets (e.g. Deut 31:24; Josh 1:8; 24:26). In particular, the alleged rediscovery of this book prompts a massive attempt at national renaissance under the young King Josiah in the late seventh century (2 Kings 22–23). The connection between Joshua 23 and Josiah raises another possibility for dating: the text could come from the time of Josiah's reform, rather than roughly fifty years later. In that case, Joshua's warning would function to reinforce Josiah's reform movement, in which the same warning is read from "the book of the law" (2 Kgs 22:8, 16). So Joshua's valedictory address is really addressing the people of Josiah's time, urging them to support Josiah's religious, political, and economic changes. In other words, the editor of Joshua 23 is engaging in polemic, warning those who would oppose Josiah's policies that they are a threat to national security. (It would not be the last time that politics would involve such a ploy!) Thus an exilic and a Josianic setting for an author would indeed be much like the hypothetical American historian above, before and after 1961, at the moment when a "new frontier" opened up, or at a time when disaster had closed the frontier.

Yet there is at least one more possibility: the author could be writing shortly after the fall of the *northern* realm of Israel in 721 BCE.[12] Also, only a few years later, King Hezekiah ascended to the throne in Judah and mounted a national reform movement similar to the later Josiah's.[13] Accordingly, the editor of Joshua 23 could be writing at this time, using Joshua's valedictory address to explain the fall of the North and, at the same time, to bolster Hezekiah's reform. Indeed, one editor of 2 Kings explained the fall of the North precisely this way: "this happened because the people of Israel had sinned against the Lord their God" (2 Kgs 17:7).

Thus there are at least three possible dates for the editor responsible for Joshua 23: the Babylonian Exile (c. 550 BCE), the time of Josiah (c. 640), and Hezekiah (c. 700). In fact, there are scholars who would defend each of these

---

12. There was a brief united monarchy under David and Solomon, but North and South split up during the reign of Solomon's son, Rehoboam. Often the name "Israel" refers to the whole, united entity, but sometimes it refers only to the Northern segment.

13. One indication of subsequent editions under Hezekiah and then Josiah are the summary notices praising them. Hezekiah was so good that "there was no one like him among all the kings of Judah after him" (2 Kgs 18:5), yet when we get to Josiah, "Before him there was no king like him" (2 Kgs 23:24).

dates, as well as later or earlier dates. If we think of a Deuteronomistic History more broadly, there are those who have argued for a single editor working in the exile, and those who argue for several editors working during the times of Hezekiah and Josiah, as well as the exile.[14] My own conclusion is that there are at least three stages of writing involved: stories from various older sources, a Josianic edition, and an Exilic edition.

At this point you might be thinking (regarding Joshua 23), what about the possibility that Joshua said it after all, and that the text preserves his words from roughly 1250 BCE? That is extremely unlikely—some would say, impossible. There are too many similarities to literature that is clearly seventh century (some of it non-Israelite literature) to allow for a thirteenth-century date. (Note again the analogy of language from American history above.) That does not mean that there are no texts in the Former Prophets that are quite old; clearly, there some that precede any of the major editions. But the relatively late date of the editions (Hezekian, Josianic, Exilic) suggests that the "Deuteronomistic History" is simply not "history" in the sense that we use that term. Again, editors certainly used historical sources—they sometimes refer to them, e.g. the "Book of Jashar" (Josh 10:13; 2 Sam 1:18); the "Book of the Chronicles of the Kings" (1 Kgs 14:19). Nevertheless, much of the Deuteronomistic History is more like historical *fiction* than history. Some scholars would even drop the adjective "historical" altogether. For example, Thomas Römer argues that the picture of the Solomonic empire is "a complete fiction," and that the period of the Judges is "nothing other than a literary invention."[15] Nevertheless, he can also say that the work of the exilic Deuteronomists is "the first attempt to create a comprehensive *history* of Israel and Judah."[16] J. P. Fokkelman puts it another way, speaking of 1 and 2 Samuel: "the David of the narrative, however fictionally portrayed, is not fictitious."[17]

As Robert Alter has written, "fiction was the principal means which the biblical authors had at their disposal for realizing history."[18] Any history worth its salt is far more than a list of facts. The

---

14. The possibility of exile was real at least as early as the eighth century BCE. Thus a reference to exile could be a realistic warning about a future possibility, as well as an anachronism reflecting an author's situation. As Halpern, *First Historians*, 172, says, "the threat of exile is pale evidence for exilic authorship."

15. Römer, *So-Called Deuteronomistic History*, 99, 136.

16. Ibid., 114 (italics added).

17. Fokkelman, *King David*, 424.

18. Alter, *Art*, 32 (the chapter title is "Sacred History and the Beginnings of Prose Fiction"). More fully, he says "It is perhaps less historicized fiction than fictionalized history—history in which the feeling and the meaning of events are concretely realized through the technical resources of prose fiction" (41; cf. 156; more recently *David Story*, xvii). Cf. Campbell, *Of Prophets*, 119–20: "The endeavor is not to create a fictive theology, but to discern in the traditions embodying the past the deeper meaning and significance obscurely shrouded in them." On the other hand, Halpern, *First Historians*, 13, recognizes the fictive quality in the Former Prophets (and all history), but insists that "Much of the literature in question is antiquarian in its intent. . . . We must approach it not as fiction, and not as romance, but as historiography." Indeed, he concludes that the Deuteronomistic Historian "sits squarely in the mainstream of narrative history, from Herodotus to the present" (234; cf. 241–44, and 267 and notes regarding Alter and others). See also Gottwald, *Politics*, 13–14.

historian also inevitably must *interpret* those facts: why did certain things happen, what is the significance of the event, what led up to the event and what are the ramifications? So any history is to some extent historical fiction. The word "fiction," after all, derives from the Latin word meaning "to form." A historian gives shape to the past. That is certainly what we see in the Deuteronomistic History: writers, editors, and redactors giving shape to the past in literary form. They shape the past in order to speak to the present, and the remarkable dimension of Scripture is that the text has continued to speak to people's present down to this day. Accordingly, our reading of the book of Joshua will begin with an example from American religious history.

It is a fact that the united monarchy under David and Solomon broke apart under Solomon's son, Rehoboam. Most likely, the reasons for this split were political and economic: ancient tribal loyalties compounded by a royal policy of using forced laborers funded by taxes that disproportionately burdened the North, a policy that Rehoboam recklessly continued. For the editor, however, the reason for the split was God's displeasure over *Solomon's* numerous foreign wives and the introduction of "other gods" than the traditional God of Israel.[19] The narrative holds these two together. The imposition of a theological interpretation *addressed directly to the reader* here and elsewhere is quite overt; more often, it is indirect and subtle. In any case, we need to read the overall Deuteronomistic History having in mind that, at any given point, the editor may well "have an agenda" that is more than reportorial.

We began with the observation that most people who *haven't* taken "Bible 101" read the biblical narratives without any awareness of the process that produced the present text. Here we come full circle, in a sense. It's the old problem involving the forest and the trees. In looking at the process that produced the Former Prophets, we are looking at the trees. But if we *only* look at the trees, we will not see the forest. Both, in fact, are lovely. In biblical scholarship, interpretation that focuses on the present canonical text is called "synchronic." Interpretation that focuses on the process that produced the text is called "diachronic." To switch metaphors, synchronic interpretation follows the thread of the narrative, as it were, whereas diachronic looks at where that thread is not seamless but spliced together.[20]

Alongside the diachronic studies of the Former Prophets (and other biblical texts), there is a growing interest in a synchronic reading. What does the text say in the form that we have it now? What are the literary themes and motifs that appear throughout the narrative? What theological issues does it raise? How can we appreciate the artistry of the whole? Looking at the text synchronically pre-

---

19. The historical reasons appear in 1 Kgs 12:1–14; the theological interpretation appears in 1 Kgs 12:15 (with preceding texts for both). For another example, see Campbell, *Of Prophets*, 118–19, where he concludes that the anointing of David (1 Sam 16:1–13) "never happened" but "was not simply creative fiction," for "elements existed which could legitimate its plausibility."

20. I have discussed this interpretive issue with respect to the Pentateuch in the introduction to *The Book of the Torah*.

vents our reading it *only* as editorial opinion speaking to the specific time of the editor. In fact, sometimes diachronic studies seem to reduce the text to a kind of historical allegory in which, say, a figure like Joshua is merely a stand-in for Josiah, and what the text says depends totally on the *historical context* of the year 638 BCE. It is possible to see the Exile lurking around every corner. How do we square such an interpretation with countless readers who have found the text meaningful *without* knowing its historical setting?

Some scholars, of course, affirm the value of *both* the diachronic and the synchronic approaches, which is what this present study attempts to do. Campbell puts it succinctly in his book *Joshua to Chronicles*: "We are not obliged to choose between these two . . . ; we can read the present text as it is (synchronic), while remaining aware of the potential process of its development (diachronic). In such a case, the final author . . . makes the entire text their own."[21] A *combination* of the two methods provides the most complete reading. In a sense, "the final author" wins in that she has the last word. The final author says that we must in some way read one text along with another, even if the two texts were written three hundred years apart in very different situations. To do otherwise—to read the text only *one* way—would not adequately acknowledge

---

21. Campbell, *From Joshua to Chronicles*, 79. Campbell also suggests that the different voices in these texts may well offer alternative ways for a storyteller to tell the story. Cf. Smith, *Memoirs*, 161: "the Bible's fuller understanding requires recognizing both its synchronic and diachronic dimensions, brought together into some sort of dialogue."

the process that produced *both* the trees *and* the forest. As McKenzie says, "Those who search for sources must be careful not to obscure the unity of the work," and "those who study the creativity of the [Deuteronomist] must in turn not lose sight of the conclusions of older literary critics regarding the sources."[22] To return to a previous metaphor, to read the text without acknowledging its composite nature is like looking at a montage and not recognizing how different are the pieces from Picasso and Rockwell; but to read the text without seeing the whole is to miss the artistry of the finished work (even if we do not know who the "final artist" was who placed the pieces side by side). As Robert Alter has so eloquently said, the multiplicity of literary sources produces a "composite artistry" that has it own esthetic and spiritual integrity.[23] The whole is greater than the sum of its parts.

This study will emphasize the synchronic approach without, I hope, failing to give the diachronic its due. The very title—"The Book of the Former Prophets"—recognizes the ecclesial process in which the books of Joshua through Kings were separated from the book of Deuteronomy, thereby making that book the conclusion of the Pentateuch or Torah. By beginning with Joshua, this study does not begin at the beginning of the original Deuteronomistic History (although I will often refer to Deuteronomy). Similarly, I include the book of Ruth, which is not considered to be part

---

22. McKenzie, "Deuteronomistic History," 167b.

23. Alter, *Art*, where the phrase is the title of chap. 8.

of the Deuteronomistic History, and, in the Hebrew Bible, is not in the Former Prophets but in that section called the "Writings."[24] Nevertheless, I will also often listen to the different voices that make up the text. There is an irony in acknowledging and honoring the multiplicity of voices, in that one voice (the Deuteronomist) does not really like what the others say, even when allowing them to say it. We will encounter this voice over and over again, as well as voices that seem to call it into question. We can summarize it this way: there shall be only one God, one land, one sanctuary, and one people. Any voice that disagrees with this is heterodox, a word which literally means "other opinion." This insistence on unity is the voice we will call "orthodox," which means "correct opinion," and therein lies the problem! Orthodoxy begs some questions: what if you live outside the land? What if you are not a full-blooded Israelite, and what does that mean anyway? What if (like the Jewish man above) you want to build *two* synagogues—but also *attend* them? What if you think that there are multiple ways of representing the divine?

The Former Prophets was so named because the figure of the prophet plays a major role, especially in the books of Samuel and Kings, but also because the theological and ethical world-view of the prophets pervades the narrative as a whole. On the one hand, the prophets affirmed the traditional identity of Israel as God's "chosen people." On the other hand, they had no reservations in criticizing Israel for failing to live up to the responsibilities of that calling. Amos puts it succinctly, representing the words of God: "You only have I known of all the families of the earth; therefore I will punish you for all your iniquities" (3:2). As one theologian has said, the prophets "had a lover's quarrel with their country."[25] True patriotism was not grounded in an absolute love of country, but in an absolute love of God. True patriotism was not an unconditional devotion—"Israel, love it or leave it." Rather, patriotism involved calling the nation to account when need be.

In the summer of 2008, a sermon by the minister of Senator Barack Obama's church, the Rev. Jeremiah Wright, inflamed many people because of these lines: "The government wants us to sing God bless America? No, no, no. Not God bless America. God damn America." For many Americans, the very words "God damn America," under *any* circumstances, seem unpatriotic, if not downright treasonous, but they happen to be fully within the covenantal tradition that runs throughout the Former Prophets. In Wright's sermon the word "damn" is simply another word for "curse" *in its biblical sense*, i.e., as the opposite of blessing. From Joshua to the end of the books of Kings, we hear the echo of the words of Moses in Deuteronomy: "I call heaven and earth to witness against you

---

24. I am following the Septuagint (and Christian) tradition in which Ruth appears between Judges and 1 Samuel because that is its narrative setting "in the days when the judges ruled" (1:1).

25. William Sloane Coffin used the phrase in a sermon the date and title of which I cannot remember but at a time in the 1970s when he was highly critical of the Vietnam War. See the anthology of his various sayings in *Credo*, especially "Patriotism," 75–86.

today that I have set before you life and death, blessings and curses. Choose life so that you and your descendants may live, loving the Lord your God, obeying him, and holding fast to him; for that means life to you and length of days, so that you may live in the land that the Lord swore to give to your ancestors" (30:19-20). Wright was fully in the prophetic tradition in condemning America for a long history of injustice, beginning with the enslavement of Africans and the genocide of Native Americans, "for killing innocent people, for treating her citizens for less than human [*sic*]."[26] So he rightly said that "God damn America" is "in the Bible."

Anyone who is uncomfortable with the notion that God might curse a nation as well as bless it should not read the Former Prophets, because that is the premise behind the whole narrative. If we want to invoke God's blessing, we must be willing to endure God's curse. As the passage from John Winthrop at the beginning of the next chapter shows, the same premise has informed a religious understanding of America from the outset. Obviously, Updike is operating on that premise in the quotation above—what if God has withdrawn God's blessing? What if it is more appropriate, at certain times, to say "God curse America" instead of "God bless America"? Directed at ancient Israel, that is the anxious question that pervades the Former Prophets.

By now it should be clear that you are not about to read a narrative that will hold you in suspense until you find out how it ends—it ends in disaster. The Babylonian Exile was an enormous rift in ancient Israel's history and identity, forcing the people to rethink who they had been before and who they might be in the future, or even if there *was* a future awaiting them. The Former Prophets as a whole is one answer to those questions. We will look more thoroughly at the answers at the conclusion of this study, but from the very first page of Joshua it will be clear what *might* happen—if Israel disobeys God's commandments, they will be destroyed. By the time we get to the beginnings of the northern realm, warning will have become doom, telling us of the outcome some two hundred years before the fall of the North in 721 BCE (1 Kgs 14:15-16). In some ways, the editors are like those annoying people who, on the way out of a film, tell those waiting to go in how the film ends. This foreknowledge suggests that the purpose of the editors—especially the *exilic* editors—is not to present us with a thriller (even though many individual stories may be thrilling to read). They are not interested in keeping us on the edge of our seats. They are writing a commentary on Israel's history, not simply reporting Israel's history. They are concerned to show how and why the story ends the way it does, and they are quite willing to sacrifice narrative suspense to make their point. The result will increasingly seem to put the characters in a hopeless situation—no matter what they or their descendants do, the outcome will be the same. But does the

---

26. There is a striking parallel in the comment by Tran, *Vietnam War*, 234, regarding America's attitude toward Vietnamese: "it rendered the stranger less than human."

Former Prophets pose its exilic audience in a hopeless situation also? That question, to which we shall return at the end, has no easy answers. One thing is clear, however: Israel did not come to an end. Out of the exile emerged a people now called the Jews who, one would have to say almost miraculously, not only survived but thrived, a community that exists to this day thousands of years after Babylon crumbled into dust.

ONE

Joshua

THE BOOK OF JOSHUA is a complex combination of texts reflecting quite different literary and theological interests put together over a long period of time, immediately illustrative of the editorial process in the Former Prophets that we have outlined in the Introduction. There are exciting stories that all biblically literate children will recognize, like the defeat of Jericho, when the ear-splitting noise of trumpets makes its walls fall down, a story immortalized in the Negro Spiritual, "Joshua Fought the Battle of Jericho." But then there are geographical survey lists that offer an antidote to insomnia. There are stories of the peaceful assimilation of "Canaanites" within the people of Israel; but then there are stories of Israelite genocide that raise the specter of "ethnic cleansing," revealing a barbaric people and a gruesome God.

Despite the complexity, we can sketch the compositional stages in general terms.[1] Most likely there was an original assembly of conquest stories about entering the land, perhaps limited to the places of Jericho, Ai, and Gibeon (appearing loosely in chap. 2, some of chap. 6, and most of chaps. 8–10, ignoring brief editorial insertions). To the conquest stories someone added a group of texts that portray some of the events in terms of religious ritual. For example, 6:3–20 describes the fall of Jericho as a liturgical stratagem; most of chaps. 3–5 describes crossing the Jordan as ritual, perhaps associated with liturgical reenactments at the place called Gilgal.[2] There are covenant renewal ceremonies in 8:30–35 and chap. 24. Another perspective appears in chap. 11 with its focus on events in the Northern parts of the land.

Yet another stage appears in speeches typical of the Deuteronomist, interpreting the events within the theology of that movement (e.g., most of chap. 1; 2:10–11; 3:7–8, etc.)—indeed, framing the book by preface and epilog (chap. 1 and chaps. 23–24). At some stage the geological survey material was incorporated by the addition of chs. 14–21.

---

1. The following reflects the analysis of Campbell and O'Brien, *Unfolding*, 101–64 (cf. Weinfeld, *Deuteronomic School*, 50). See also Römer, *So-Called Deuteronomistic History*, especially 81–90, 133–36.

2. Judg 5:9; 10:6; 14:6; cf. 3:19; 1 Sam 7:16; 10:8; Hos 12:11; Amos 4:4.

Other concerns appear in smaller literary units (e.g., the East Jordan tribes in 1:12–18; 22:9–34).

Some scholars see the figure of Joshua as a model for King Josiah—that is, parts of the book of Joshua were composed or edited to serve as a kind of historical pattern for Josiah's national and religious revival. Since that revival included an attempt to reunite "all Israel" under one king with territory extending to Israel's original boundaries, what better way to promote the king than to associate him with Israel's "founding father" of the "conquest"? It would be something like a history of the United States written in 1933 in such a way that George Washington looked a lot like Franklin D. Roosevelt and Washington's policies a lot like the New Deal. Numerous parallels between the two figures suggest such a relationship: covenant renewal and honoring the "book of the Torah";[3] keeping the Passover festival;[4] opposition to "Canaanite" religion.[5]

The final product juxtaposes sociological and theological tensions without resolving them, offering a mirror to readers who are willing to be as honest about their own society and its history as were the biblical editors. Much of what appears in Joshua is not pretty. For Americans, an analogy would be reading a book like *A People's History of the United States* by Howard Zinn, who hangs out our dirty laundry alongside all the pretty garments of our childhood education (Plymouth Rock, Washington crossing the Delaware, "winning" the West, Southern plantation "gentility").

The theological perspective that dominates Joshua is precisely what we see in a famous speech from American religious history, a speech clearly based on the biblical covenant tradition. Indeed, the speaker, John Winthrop, speaks from a situation identical to that of the character of Joshua—about to enter the Promised Land:

> *Thus stands the cause betweene God and us. Wee are entered into Covenant with him for this worke . . . We have hereupon besought him of favour and blessing: Now if the Lord shall please to heare us, and bring us in peace to the place wee desire, then hath he ratified this Covenant and sealed our Commission [and] will expect a strickt performance of the Articles contained in it, but if wee shall neglect the observacion of these Articles which are the ends wee have propounded, and dissembling with our God, shall fall to embrace this present world and prosecute our carnall intencions seeking greate things for our selves and our posterity, the Lord will surely breake out in wrathe against us, be revenged of such a perjured people and make us know the price of the breache of such a Covenant . . .*

---

3. 2 Kgs 22:8–13; 23:2–3 and Josh 1:7; 8:32; 23:6–7; 24:26; cf. Deut 17:14–20.

4. 2 Kgs 23:21–23; Josh 5:10–12.

5. 2 Kings 23; Josh 23:7, 16; 24:14–24. See Nelson, "Josiah"; Sweeney, *King Josiah*, 25–26, 133–35, 173; Smith, *Memoirs*, 23. Coote, *Joshua*, 555–80, argues that the Josianic reforms provide the most substantial context for the book.

> *[Then the blessing shall] be turned into Cursses upon us till wee be consumed out of the good land whither wee are goeing . . . If our heartes shall turne away soe that wee will not obey, but shall be seduced and worship . . . other Gods, our pleasures, and proffitts, and serve them; it is propounded unto us this day, wee shall surely perishe out of the good Land whither wee passe over this vast Sea to possesse it.*
> —John Winthrop, "A Modell of Christian Charity." Written On Boarde the Arbella, On the Attlantick Ocean, Anno 1630[6]

"Going by the Book" (Chap. 1)

The book of Joshua begins "after the death of Moses," whose presence dominated the Pentateuchal narrative from Exodus through Deuteronomy. The setting is something like the day before D-Day, as Israel stands on the East Bank of the Jordan River, looking into the land occupied by the enemy generally called "the Canaanites." Before the story of the initial battle, however, the editors have provided a series of pep talks, first by God to Joshua, then by Joshua, then by the tribes whom Joshua has addressed.[7]

Filling Moses' shoes is a daunting task. The concluding paragraph of the book of Deuteronomy says, "Never since has there arisen a prophet in Israel like Moses, whom the Lord knew face to face. He was unequaled for all the signs and wonders that the Lord sent him to perform . . . and for all the mighty deeds and all the terrifying displays of power that Moses performed in the sight of all Israel (34:10–12). Now God addresses a new leader, but the difference between the two appears in their titles: Moses, "the servant of the Lord," and Joshua, "the assistant of Moses." Moses enjoyed an intimacy with God that no successor could match.[8] Another, and more important, indication of the difference is the way in which Moses continues to be the mediator between Joshua (and Israel) and God—not in his person, but in his words. Moses did what God said; Joshua is to do what Moses said God said. It is true that God talks to Joshua also, but part of what God says is that Joshua is to follow the words of Moses, that is, "the law that my servant Moses commanded you" (v. 7). That law, of course, is contained in "this *book* of the law," by which the author means the book of Deuteronomy.[9] Indeed, when God says "*this* book of the law" it is almost as if God is *handing* Joshua a copy.

The opening speech focuses on two "ways," the geographical way that has led to the current setting (vv. 1–6), then the theological "way of Torah" that Joshua must follow (vv. 7–9). Both ways require that Joshua "be strong and very courageous," but two different kinds of

---

6. Winthrop, "A Model." A printed copy appears in Bellah, *Individualism and Commitment*, 22–27, and in numerous other anthologies.

7. See Weinfeld, *Deuteronomic School*, 45–51, on the literary genre of "the Military Oration."

8. Only at the end of the book, and posthumously, will Joshua assume the title of "servant of the Lord" (24:29)

9. How *much* of the book depends on complex issues involving the dating of the authors of Joshua and of Deuteronomy.

battles are involved—taking the land and remaining faithful. It is as if the editor wants to emphasize the spiritual strength that must accompany Joshua's military strength. The book of the Torah is the manual that Joshua is to meditate on day and night, resembling the assignment that Deuteronomy makes for Israel's later kings (Deut 17:18–19); the Torah provides the blueprint for success. It is encouraging that God promises to "be with" Joshua, as God was with Moses, but that presence alone will not be sufficient for victory. Rather, Joshua (and, again, Israel as a whole) must walk the straight and narrow path, looking neither to the left or the right, that path being the way of Torah.

Excursus 1: The Treaty Model of God

My use of the term "manual" can be misleading in that it might suggest a simple list of rules to follow. In fact, many people have understood the "Torah" in this way, partly because the word often is translated as "law"—the "book of the law" or "the law of Moses."[10] The basic meaning is "guidance" or "instruction," but especially when used to describe a document like Deuteronomy that shapes a people's ethos, the word *torah* would be much closer to our word "constitution" in its political sense. Another translation would be "polity" from the Greek word *politeia* rather than "law" from *nomos*. S. Dean McBride, Jr. in particular has emphasized the important distinction between the two.[11] "Polity" refers to the "social order" spelled out in the document; "law" refers to specific ordinances or rules that the document contains.[12] There is no doubt that Deuteronomy contains laws (concentrated in 12:2—25:16), but the laws are contained in a framework that grounds them in the people's history (the Exodus experience in particular) and in their relationship to God (cf. Deut 5:1–6). Much of the framework of Deuteronomy contains hortatory exhortations to the civic responsibility that the polity requires, as well as procedures that will enact the constitution and insure its transmission to future generations (e.g., 26:16—31:29). The laws are the specific requirements that govern the entire range of the people's life as a community. Obeying the laws is no more important than remembering the history—indeed, it is less so, because forgetting their history easily *leads to* disobedience. The people's *mythos* (its narrative identity) grounds its *ethos* (its way of living in society).

In Israel's polity, the relationship with God is understood as a "covenant."

---

10. Christians may have a bias against "law" deriving from disputes over its interpretation in various Gospel stories and in the arguments of Paul involving ecclesiastical controversies.

11. McBride, "Polity of the Covenant People," 17. In "Essence of Orthodoxy," 139, he also refers to "the book of the Torah" as "Israel's unique national constitution." In "Deuteronomy," 109, in addition to "polity" he uses the terms "constitutional blueprint" and "comprehensive social charter." See also his introduction and notes to Deuteronomy in the HarperCollins edition of the NRSV Bible. Weinfeld, *Deuteronomic School*, 170–71, says that for the Deuteronomist the Torah "was the ideal legal constitution for a monarchic regieme." Cf. also Miller, *Ten Commandments*, 6–7.

12. McBride, "Polity of the Covenant People," 21.

The Hebrew word (*berit*) can also be translated as "treaty." The language is diplomatic as well as political. Our understanding of Israel's covenant theology is enhanced by a comparison with treaty documents from ancient Near Eastern nations—i.e., treaties between two nations or rulers.[13] Israel adapted the language and formalities of such treaties as a model for construing the people's relationship to the divine. God is the suzerain, or to use the frequent (male) term, Israel's "king" (more inclusively, Israel's "sovereign"). The people are the vassal, i.e., God's "servants." The treaty model is one among numerous possibilities for construing a relationship with God. In this model, the vassal owes its allegiance to the suzerain because of the suzerain's protection of the vassal in the past, including the suzerain's "saving" the vassal from enemies (again, the liberation from Pharaoh of Egypt). The most important stipulation is the demand for absolute fidelity to the suzerain, prohibiting any such treaty agreements with other rulers who would thereby compete for the people's allegiance and alter the social order. Treaties often refer to this allegiance as "loving" the suzerain. Such "love" refers more to covenant loyalty than to an emotion:

> You [the vassal] shall love Assurbanipal [the suzerain] . . . king of Assyria, your lord, as yourself. You shall hearken to whatever he says and do whatever he commands, and you shall not seek any other king or other lord against him. This treaty . . . you shall speak to your sons and grandsons, your seed and you seed's seed which shall be born in the future.[14]

Such covenant love is the heart of Israel's relationship with God (compare the language in Deut 6:4–7). Thus the "love of God" so central to Western religions has it roots here.[15]

The suzerain's continuing protection of the vassal depends on the vassal's loyalty. Obedience to the stipulations (or requirements) of the treaty will assure the suzerain's protection; failure to obey will lead to punishment. The two options often appear in the form of blessings or curses (e.g., Deuteronomy 28), but also are incorporated in the historical exhortations (e.g., Deuteronomy 8). Just as human overlords would punish rebellious vassals who switched allegiance to "other lords," so Yahweh[16] will punish Israel when they switch allegiance to "other gods."[17] Indeed, the model of covenantal reward and punishment is widely assumed not only in the Former Prophets but also in the writing Prophets.[18]

The abiding truth of the covenant model is its insistence on absolute allegiance to God, over against any contenders, whether gods in the theistic sense or those powers which are socio-economic

---

13. There is a vast literature on this subject. For examples of ancient Near Eastern texts, see *ANET*, 199–206, 531–41.

14. Quoted in Römer, *So-Called Deuteronomistic History*, 75, citing the study of Younger on Assyrian annals. For an informative review of covenants, treaties, and the political meaning of love, see Kugel, *How to Read the Bible*, 243–47, 348–50, 353–55.

15. The groundbreaking study of this is by Moran, "Love of God." Cf. also Weinfeld, *Deuteronomic School*, 81, among other scholars. Cf. Matt 22:36–40; Mark 12:28–34; Luke 10:25–28.

16. See the glossary (below) on the divine name *Yahweh*. Here is a good example of when knowing the personal name helps to understand the contrast with other "gods."

17. On the identity of these "other gods" see Excursus 4. The annals of the Assyrian overlords in the ninth century BCE record their devastating punishment of vassal kings who broke the terms of their treaties and rebelled against them.

18. For the classic formulation in the Former Prophets, see 2 Kgs 17:5–8; in the prophets cf. Jer 34:13–17; Hos 2:2–13; Amos 4:6–12. On this "merit system," see Excursus 2.

or political.[19] This model is potentially subversive of *any* power that would claim ultimate authority (e.g., a human king of Israel or a foreign power like Assyria—not to mention contemporary powers).[20] For contemporary readers, the phrase "other gods" may make little sense in *theistic* terms, but it makes a great deal of sense in terms of what one values above all else and for what one is willing to sacrifice everything.[21] The quotation from John Winthrop at the outset of this chapter shows how the covenant language of ancient Israel could apply to English settlers in America in the 17th century. The "other gods" who threaten to "seduce" the settlers are not gods in the usual sense; they are "our pleasures and our profits"—in short, materialism, greed, and wealth.[22] Hundreds of years later, we can hear an echo of Winthrop's terms in the admission of a man named Brian: "'I was operating as if *a certain value* was of the utmost importance to me. Perhaps it was success. Perhaps it was fear of failure, but I was extremely success-oriented, to the point where everything would be *sacrificed* for the job, the career, the company.'"[23]

We shall return to the implications of Israel's polity again and again for it undergirds much of the editorializing in the Former Prophets, especially that of editors from the Deuteronomic tradition. To anticipate, some of the most important implications will involve political relationships between Israel and other peoples (or between Israel's rulers and other rulers), social relationships with non-Israelites (especially marriage), and worship practices. Above all, an ongoing issue will be the challenge to Yahweh's absolute suzerainty by competitors—i.e., other gods (see Excursus 4).

To return to the opening passage in Josh 1:1–9, it is also a fitting introduction to the entire narrative that stretches to the end of 2 Kings. There is the promise of God's gracious presence, but there is the command to obey the Torah. The combination of promise and command poses a tension that Israel will test again and again: what happens if Israel is *disobedient*? Will God withdraw the promise of presence if Israel does *not* follow the Torah, does not live "by the book"? If obedience produces success, will disobedience produce failure? In fact, will God then annul the covenant? It does not require much meditation on the book of the Torah to know that disobedience will have dire consequences, as the curses of the covenant with God reveal (Deuteronomy 28:15–68). But the same book also gives glimpses of a "merciful God" whose grace continues *despite* disobedience (Deut 4:30–31; 30:1–10). To

---

19. See my discussion of Deuteronomy 7 in Mann, *Deuteronomy*, 62–69.

20. Römer, *So-Called Deuteronomic History*, 81, suggests that the "Deuteronomic law code of the seventh century" was modeled on an Assyrian treaty, but in acknowledging God as Israel's only sovereign, "may also reveal a subversive or polemical intention" directed at Assyrian power.

21. The theologian Paul Tillich used the term "ultimate concern." That which is one's ultimate concern functionally is one's god. See Tillich, *Dynamics of Faith*, 1–4.

22. See McBride, "Yoke," especially 306, and his discussion of "radical monotheism." On the other hand, Winthrop was among those who often demonized the Native Americans (see below).

23. One of the interviewees in Bellah, *Habits*, 5 (italics added). This book, and its companion book of primary readings, is one of the most perceptive investigations of the role of covenantal language and identity in American experience. Note especially 28–35.

the bitter end of the story, the tension between judgment and mercy will pose great risks for Israel, and also a great dilemma for God.

The introductory speech has already named the prize that awaits: the Promised Land. The next passage raises other questions that will persist throughout the narrative: what are the boundaries of the Promised Land, who constitutes "Israel," and what space is the sacred center? The boundaries are sketched in v. 4—the Negev desert to the South, Lebanon to the North, the Euphrates River to the East, and, of course, the Mediterranean on the West. But some tribes will possess land on the *East* bank of the Jordan ("trans-Jordan"). Is that also the Promised Land, and are they part of "Israel"? The apparent answer to both questions is yes, but the answers will be challenged after the events projected in vv. 12–18 take place (13:8–33; chap. 22). Moreover, the boundaries of v. 4 are idealistic and never materialized, at least with respect to the Euphrates. Eventually, the Promised Land will shrink, and throughout the narrative divisions will occur that belie the apparent unity of the people. Already the point-of-view that sees the East bank land as "*beyond* the Jordan" presupposes the *West* bank as the real land, implying that trans-Jordan is "the other side of the tracks."[24] As we will see in chapter 22, the primary concern will revolve around the question: Can there be more than one shrine that is the unifying sacred space of the community? This question will become a major issue in the narrative, especially after the construction of the Jerusalem temple (1 Kings 8).

Two Boy Scouts and a Lady of the Night (Chap. 2)

The story of Rahab and the spies is one of those stories that parents are likely to skip over when reading the Bible to children. Whores are not the role models we want to present as heroines. The biblical authors, however, were not so squeamish. They did not cover up the apparent folly of two young scouts who were ordered to survey the land but made a beeline for a brothel. In fact, the story is not really so much about them as it is about Rahab, and her occupation is crucial to the significance of her actions.

The scouts are described as "young men" or "youths" (v. 23), probably teenagers, and their behavior betrays their ineptitude at espionage. You can almost see it happening: the two neophytes out on their first great adventure as spies, and, as soon as they enter the city gate—behold, the red light district! They look at each other and grin, and one says to the other, "Jacob, how many shekels did you bring?" Of course, the author does not say explicitly that they sought out Rahab for her services, but he tells us that they "lay down there," highly suggestive language, if also ambiguous. In any event, the young scouts begin to look like bumbling fools when they have to risk their lives—and their mission—to the madam of the house; they seem more like Barney Fife than James Bond. Instead of reconnoitering the city, they must hide under the flax on Rahab's flat roof, escape by the rope she provides,

---

24. Feiler, *Walking the Bible*, 353; cf. Hawk, *Joshua*, 16.

hide for three days, and then flee back to Joshua. Their "surveillance report" relies totally on what the prostitute has told them.

But this is Rahab's story, not a spy story, which is why we never learn the names of the scouts or even the king. In terms of literary genre, it is both folk tale and etiology. It is a trickster tale of how a lowly but wise woman duped Israelite "intelligence" as well as the king of her city.[25] But in its context the story is also an explanation of how and why the Canaanite family of a prostitute ended up living among the people of God. Originally the story was probably independent of the fall of Jericho sequel in chap. 6, and not completely consistent with it.[26] Its position here—even before the people have crossed over the Jordan—sets a major theme for what follows: already Israel is *not* "going by the book" of the Torah.

When the scouts swear an oath to protect Rahab's family, they are breaking a commandment of God. According to the ideology of warfare, there were to be no such agreements with the Canaanites, indeed, no survivors. They are subject to the "ban." As Deuteronomy puts it, "you must utterly destroy them. Make no covenant with them and show them no mercy."[27] However reasonable the spies' agreement with Rahab may seem to us, "it is an illegal covenant according to the rules governing the war of occupation, the law of YHWH."[28] This same commandment will factor largely in the story of the Gibeonites (chap. 9). In fact, Rahab's fear of such treatment is based on what she has heard (v. 10), and anticipates Joshua's command in 6:17 and its execution in 6:21. In the end, all the inhabitants of Jericho are slaughtered, "both men and women, young and old" —even livestock (6:21), a grisly precedent for more to follow (8:25 [twelve thousand slaughtered!]; 10:28–40; 11:11, 14, 20). Although the numbers in such casualty figures are highly exaggerated,[29] such passages present some of the most reprehensible parts of the Bible, ultimately assuming an understanding of God that is clearly unacceptable to virtually all contemporary people of faith (whether Jewish, Christian, Muslim, or other). On the other hand, these stories that seem to describe what we call "ethnic cleansing" hold a mirror to our own history and culture.

Generally, there are two basic types of the "ban" (*herem*). The NRSV often translates the word with "devote to destruction," which may seem like a bizarre understanding of "devotion," but actually points to the religious meaning in one type. Here the ban is a sacrifice by the Israelite military leader, an offering to God in exchange for God's defeat of the enemy. This type presumes that God, in fact, values human sacrifices—indeed, in this version of the ban humans are of ultimate value, far more than material things. So, as Niditch puts it, "Paradoxically, the ban

---

25. For other examples, see Bird, "The Harlot."

26. Cf. Nelson, *Joshua*, 41, who points out that the survival of Rahab's family in their city-wall house is incompatible with the collapse of the entire wall in 6:20.

27. Deut 7:2; cf. 20:15–18; Exod 34:11–16.

28. Gunn, "Joshua and Judges," 108.

29. McNutt, *Reconstructing*, 110, notes that "the population for the whole of Palestine . . . in 1000 B.C.E. has been estimated at about 150,000."

as sacrifice may be viewed as admitting of more respect for the value of human life than other war ideologies."[30] In the second type, the ban is not a sacrifice but an act of justice.[31] Again, this may seem a bizarre notion of justice, but here it simply means that, according to the religious and moral criteria of those who enact the ban (whether God or humans or both), those subject to the ban *deserve* it—it is punitive. The reason could be worshipping "other gods," i.e., the *wrong* gods in the author's view, or behavior deemed immoral or sinful. In the sacrificial type, the enemy has ultimate value as a holy offering to God; in the punitive type the enemy is sub-human and ultimately offensive to God. The ban is God's insistence on purity, and those banned are seen as "an infectious fungus," a "monster worthy of destruction," "a 'Gook,' an Infidel, an 'Other,' not of human stock."[32] The term "Gook" derives from the way in which Americans referred to North Vietnamese (not just soldiers, but everyone), thus already hinting at why the biblical ban may point uncomfortably to the unsuspecting reader.[33] So we are faced with an act of religious devotion that involves human sacrifice, or a punitive act that demonizes ones opponents. Choose your poison!

Although both types of the ban appear in the Deuteronomic history, the Deuteronomic school emphasized the punitive (or perhaps even better, "purgative"). "The Deuteronomic writers, supporters of the Josianic reform, consider the ban a means of rooting out what they believe to be impure, sinful forces damaging to the solid and pure relationship between Israel and God."[34] The reason that Deuteronomy gives for the ban is not military or even political but religious. If the Canaanites remain they will seduce Israelites into following "other gods," which would invoke God's wrath and lead to Israel's destruction (Deut 7:4). This is the voice of relentless orthodoxy; sometimes, of fanaticism. It will sound again and more fully at the end of Joshua, there as a warning about the peoples who are left. The xenophobia of the "ban" is rooted in insecurity. The "violent language is typical for a minority group which is afraid to lose either its identity or its power."[35] Here is a precedent for what we call a "witch hunt," with 17th century Salem, Massachusetts the prime illustration.[36] (More contemporary ex-

---

30. Nidtich, *War*, 50. Gottwald, *Politics*, 62, translates the ban with "ritual destruction." Examples of the ban as sacrifice are Num 21:2–3; Judg 11:30; 1 Sam 7:9–10; 13:12. The *herem* was also practiced by other peoples, prominently the Moabites.

31. Nidtich, *War*, chap. 2.

32. Ibid., 95; cf. 77 ("a monster, unclean and diseased"). For examples from American history, see below.

33. See Tran, *Vietnam War*, 234: with regard to the Vietnamese, America "rendered the stranger less than human."

34. Nidtich, *War*, 56; cf. 75–76.

35. Ibid.,74; cf. Römer, *So-Called Deuteronomistic History*, 63, who suggests that the "ban" really reflects the situation of an editor in the Persian period (sixth century), when the fear of assimilation was prominent (cf. Ezra 9–10; Nehemiah 13). Similarly, Campbell and O'Brien, *Unfolding*, 104, suggest that the "'extermination'" passages are late (although "no less appalling"). Römer, *So-Called Deuteronomistic History*, 131, argues that the very laws on warfare in Deuteronomy 20 stem from the exilic editors, when such laws were totally useless, as "a 'legal' introduction to the conquest stories."

36. Nidtich, *War*, 57, uses the term to describe the Deuteronomic reforms. For the literal precedent, see 2 Kgs 23:24 and 1 Sam 28:3 (the "medium" there is often called "the witch of Endor").

amples abound).[37] In fact, some scholars argue that the ban in Deuteronomic texts "could only have been created at the writing-desk and does not reflect any real circumstances."[38] In other words, the stories of ethnic cleansing are at least highly exaggerated, if not simply fictional (see below on Jericho).[39]

Nevertheless, here in the Jericho story we come up against one of the most repugnant aspects of Israelite religion (one could say of all religions). Even if the story of Rahab and Jericho is completely fictional,[40] we would still have a theology of genocide, a divine sanctioning of mass murder. Clearly, the resulting picture of God is unconscionable. Here religion becomes evil. I once had a Sunday school teacher come to me frantically on Sunday morning saying, "The lesson is on Jericho. What should I do? I don't believe in a God who orders human slaughter." "Then tell the children just that," I said. "Tell them that you do not think God is like this. Tell them that here is a place where we have to reject what the Bible says as theologically wrong." Indeed, to make such an interpretive judgment is to engage in that process—that *argument*—of competing voices that is present in the text itself.

But, despite its horrors, we would be wise to read the story (at what age, is another matter), and for three reasons. First, here is a good example of how the Bible "tells all." The Bible generally does not hide the questionable—even damnable—traits of its characters, including God. In fact, the theological problem is compounded in that there is no explicit authorial indication that God's genocidal orders *are* damnable. Still, it is healthy for us to be forced to look at what is ugly and brutal in such stories because *our own history* is full of such brutality. Contemporary examples—often involving religious ideology—are all too abundant (the genocide of Native Americans in our own "New Canaan" [a town name in Connecticut]; the Holocaust of European Jews; machete tribal massacres in Rwanda; "ethnic cleansing" in Bosnia;

---

37. In the United States, one thinks of white supremacist groups, who propose getting rid of all Jews, African Americans, and homosexuals. In Nigeria the tension is between Muslims and Christians. Muslims are generally wealthier than Christians, who are in the minority. According to a recent study, one Christian minister, "like many others of his faith, felt that Muslims were trying to wipe out Christians by converting them through marriage." The minister identifies the problem as "'scriptural,'" perhaps thinking of passages like the intermarriage prohibitions in question. "So he and the other elders decided to punish the women. 'If a woman gets caught with a Muslim man' [he] said, 'she must be forcibly brought back.'" The decree resulted in "vigilante violence" on both sides. See Griswold, "God's Country," 42.

38. Weinfeld, *Deuteronomic School*, 167; cf. Niditch, *War*, 74.

39. Remarkably, two ancient Near Eastern kings declared that they had annihilated Israel: Mernepthah in the thirteenth century and Mesha in the ninth century. Clearly they were both wrong! The latter says "Israel utterly perished forever" and boasts that he "killed the entire population" of one city," men and women, having "devoted" them to his god (i.e., the biblical "ban," *ḥerem*). For the translation see Dearman, *Studies*, 97–98, or *ANET*, 320. For the Merneptah text, see *ANET*, 376–78.

40. At the time of the story, Jericho was at best an insignificant village, and the older city was already in ruins. The annals of ancient Near Eastern kings typically employ exaggerated claims of conquests. For a summary, with parallels to the book of Joshua, see Römer, *So-called Deuteronomistic History*, 83–86.

the "killing fields" of Cambodia; the "disappeared" in Guatemala; sectarian mass murders in Iraq). If these stories prompt us to engage in our own critical self-examination of both our religions and cultures, they will have provided a worthwhile service.[41]

> *The quotation from John Winthrop at the head of this chapter, often celebrated for its rich contribution to the formation of American religious identity, needs to be balanced with the following, from Winthrop's contemporary colonist, William Bradford, and his History of Plymouth Plantation, regarding the massacre of Pequot Native Americans, who were burned alive: "It was a fearful sight to see them thus frying in the fyer, and the streams of blood quenching the same, and horrible was the stincke and sente there of, but the victory seemed a sweet sacrifice, and they [i.e., the English colonists] gave the prayers thereof to God, who had wrought so wonderfully for them, thus to inclose their enemise in their hands, and gave them so speedy a victory over so proud and insulting an enimie."[42]*

> *The slaughter [at My Lai, Vietnam] was conducted in March 1968, by platoons of American soldiers who shot and abused more than 300 victims—mainly women, children and elderly peasants—in a murderous frenzy.[43]*

> *Q: You killed men, women, and children? A: Yes. Q: You were ordered to do so? A: Yes [from a Viet-Nam era court martial][44]*

> *I accompanied a South Vietnamese battalion to a village the Vietcong had raided the previous night. Dangling from the trees and poles in the village center were the village chief, his wife, and their twelve children, the males, including a baby, with their genitals cut off and stuffed into their mouths, the females with their breasts cut off.[45]*

> *We must act with vindictive earnestness against the Sioux, even to their extermination, men, women, and children"*
> —William Tecumseh Sherman[46]

---

41. "The power of the Bible is largely that it gives an unvarnished picture of human nature and of the dynamics of history, and also of religion and the things that people do in its name" (Collins, "The Bible and Legitimation of Violence," 6).

42. The quotation (widely available) is from Cook, "Thanksgiving"; or Zinn, *A People's History*, 15.

43. *Winston-Salem Journal*, August 31, 2009, A8 (quoting the *New York Times*, August 28, 2009).

44. O'Brien, *In the Lake*, 261–63. For further examples, equally as difficult to read, see also Tran, *Vietnam War*, 35–48. The book is an extended examination of how America has denied much of the reality of the war.

45. Siemon-Netto, *Acquittal of God*, 34, who argues that such an atrocity was "government policy," in contrast to the illegal acts committed at My Lai (35).

46. O'Brien, *In the Lake*, 260.

> *In the summer of 1885 Geronimo attacked settlements within several miles of Fort Bayard and Silver City. Cowboy, hunter, and guide James H. Cook claimed that the Apaches killed "sixteen in all . . . several of them being women and children. One or two of the children were tortured to death by being hung up on spikes outside their houses."*[47]
>
> *From the infant in its cradle to the feeble old man, no one was spared; the crusaders slaughtered all the inhabitants without distinction.*[48]

Second, the portrayal of a massive blitzkrieg "conquest" from outside the land is, in fact, almost certainly fictional.[49] As Coote states, "Most scholars now think that the people of Israel were indigenous to Palestine, and were not outsiders."[50] More ambiguously, "Israel" quite likely emerged from groups both inside and outside of Canaan, the latter reflected in the Exodus traditions, however much that picture is inflated.[51] Such an emergence would reflect a peaceful process of social developments rather than warfare. Other scholars argue for an historical nugget behind the story of "conquest" in which good does, in fact, conquer evil. In this reading, a small group of "Israelites" who experienced the Exodus infiltrate the land and rally support for a "peasant's revolt" against an oppressive ruling class.[52] The "conquest" was really a type of sociological and political *revolution* that subverted and destroyed a feudal system. Rahab would represent the native underclass who saw in the Israelites a chance for freedom. The overlords would be those Canaanite kings who appear in the story (2:3; 5:1; 8:1; 9:1; ch.12, etc.). Joshua would resemble a contemporary revolutionary hero like Che Guevara (and more successful!). The story would then provide a "theology of liberation," a continuation of the Exodus story with its overthrow of Pharaoh—precisely what Rahab describes (2:10)! Such a reading would make the story far more palatable, although it would not remove the theological problem of a God who commands genocide.[53]

---

47. Weigle and White, *Lore of New Mexico*, 289.

48. Nigg, *Heretics*, 191, on the Church's thirteenth-century suppression of Albigensians. For more examples from Europe and Australia, see Campbell and O'Brien, *Unfolding*, 102.

49. For an excellent summary of the issue, see Kugel, *How to Read the Bible*, chap. 22, especially 374–85; and McNutt, *Reconstructing*, 53–63, on the various "models" of the settlement. Cf. also Niditch, *War*, 52–55; Niditch, *Judges*, 6–8; Newman, "Rahab," 171.

50. Coote, *Book of Joshua*, 557; cf. also 575. According to Coote and other scholars, "Canaanites" in Joshua represent actual or potential opponents to the reforms of Josiah in the seventh century, and the story intends to terrorize them into submission (577 and n. 24 for other scholars).

51. E.g., Smith, *Memoirs*, 22; McNutt, *Reconstructing*, 57–59, reviews this perspective.

52. For a succinct description of this reading see Newman, "Rahab," 170–72.

53. Gottwald, a major proponent of the social revolution theory, suggests that the "ban" was, in fact, a "selective expulsion and annihilation of kings and upper classes . . . with the aim of buttressing the egalitarian mechanisms of Israelite society . . . for the peasant economy" (*Tribes of*

A third reason for us to read the story of Rahab is that she represents an *alternative* to the merciless orthodoxy that demands extermination. Here, over against texts like Deut 7:1–5, 17–26, Israel *does* make a covenant with Canaanites, Israel *does* show mercy. Against the brutality of war, the story juxtaposes the beauty of an inclusive community. In terms of American films, the combination is something like splicing together the films *How the West Was Won* with *Dances with Wolves*. Already the tension posed in chap. 1 is tested. Israel has broken the law of the Torah, and gone unpunished. Such immunity will not always be the case (chap. 7), but here the *curse* of the law is withheld. Moreover, in the Rahab story the "conquest" of Canaan involves collusion between Canaanites and Israelites. Israel takes the city in part because of the cooperation of a native inhabitant. One who is a Canaanite joins in the fight against the Canaanite king. The story implies a complex social interaction that confounds a simple "good guys/bad guys" dichotomy. As a prostitute, and a woman, Rahab is at the very bottom of the social hierarchy, "the lowest of the low."[54] Certainly, she is far removed from the aristocratic ladies of Jericho's court. However we may understand the historical situation behind such a story, Rahab would be part of the peasantry, representing an oppressed group having more in common with the "Israelites" than the "Canaanites"—in fact, an example of just how fluid those two terms are.[55] As an oppressed person, Rahab could empathize with the way Black slaves in America identified with "Joshua's *avenging* army" when they sang "Joshua Fought the Battle of Jericho."[56] In any event, "Israel" now includes a family of "Canaanites" (6:25). Jewish legend goes one better: Rahab marries Joshua![57] The Rahab story is a classic example of how the personal trumps the political, how a human being gives a name and a face to the "enemy." Because of this person, a strict application of the Torah must be relaxed and "Israel" must include a Canaanite family.[58]

Whatever may stand behind the story historically, Israel's "outsider" status is crucial to the meaning of the present narrative. Indeed, much of the irony of the story in Joshua (and Judges) hangs on the interplay between outsiders and insiders, as we shall see. Here in the Rahab story, already the line between friend and enemy breaks down,

---

Yahweh, 550). For a recent assessment of this approach, see McNutt, *Reconstructing*, 54–56.

54. Bird, "The Harlot," 121. For more recent studies of Rahab as prostitute see Coote, *Book of Joshua*, 592. Coote points out that prostitution was usually the result of indebtedness, making Rahab a representative of those poor people relieved of their debt in the administration of king Josiah (presumably based on Deuteronomy 15).

55. Niditch, *Judges*, 39, puts it well: "For the biblical writers, all such terms, like 'Canaanite' itself, connote the oxymoron 'foreign natives.'"

56. Mathews, *Religion in the Old South*, 219 (italics added). The reference is to sermons about Joshua's defense of the Gibeonites but surely would apply to Jericho also (cf. 217). Mathews describes how such sermons allowed the slaves to vent their anger without risking punishment.

57. Matthew goes one better still: Rahab is numbered in the genealogy of Jesus (Matt 1:5). Cf. Jas 2:25.

58. Thus, if Joshua serves as a model for king Josiah and his reforms, one could also argue that the Rahab story *subverts* the xenophobia of the reforms.

however small the fracture. Rahab is supposed to be someone who is literally "God damned." Only when we see her this way can we begin to see the irony of her story. By her actions, Rahab destroys the stereotype of the "infidel." The book of Proverbs warns that a young man who seeks a prostitute is "like a bird rushing into a snare, not knowing that it will cost him his life" (7:23). Yet Rahab rescued the hapless scouts and *saved* their lives. In a sense, Rahab resembles a faithful Israelite more than a "pagan" Canaanite. In describing how her people "melt" in fear before the Israelites, she declares "Yahweh your God is indeed God in heaven above and on earth below" (2:11, Author's Translation—hereafter AT). Her theological *credo* echoes the Deuteronomic editor (cf. Deut 3:24, 4:39), who no doubt wants us to see her as a devout convert. Moreover, her trust in Israel's God is "with all her life" (Deut 6:5) for, by becoming a traitor to Jericho's king, she is *risking* her life.[59] In the underlying story, however, it is not her theology that saves her; it is her deed (later Judaism will call it a *mitzvah*, "commandment"). In fact, here is another irony in the story: this woman who was, by religious standards, sinful, and by ethnic standards, an outsider, is saved because of her moral integrity. Rahab exhibits "kindness," or "steadfast love" (*ḥesed*). Such "loyalty" is the glue of communal bonds. "Since I have dealt kindly with you, swear to me by the Lord that you will deal kindly with my family," she says, thereby exhibiting what the prophet Micah pronounced as what God most wants from human beings (Mic 6:8). In the Rahab story, human kindness (*ḥesed*) overcomes inhuman killing (*ḥerem*, see below).

The Deuteronomistic insertion of 2:10–11 deserves further comment. Perhaps it was a face-saving addition to show that Rahab was really an Israelite at heart—that is, someone who believed in the God of Israel. But the effect is profound. Rahab the harlot does not seduce the young men, as harlots stereotypically do (again, Prov 7:6–23). But she also does not seduce Israel into worshipping other gods. Indeed, she praises *Yahweh's* universal sovereignty. So Rahab defies the stereotype of both harlot and Canaanite on the two levels we have outlined—common human kindness (morality) and confessional orthodoxy (theology). She is a good woman (occupation notwithstanding) who "praises the Lord"! Thus she represents a moral and religious complexity and ambiguity apparently beyond the imagination of the Torah (Deut 7:1–6). Rahab forces a reinterpretation and loosening of the law and the development of a "situational ethic."

Protecting one family from the slaughter of an entire city is, on the surface, a miniscule departure from the policy of genocide, but given the personal prominence of Rahab in the plot, the story as a whole produces a profoundly subversive effect.[60] In the present text, her story precedes the annihilation of

---

59. Cf. Miller, *Ten Commandments*, 30.

60. The Gospel of Matthew might have such subversion in mind when it includes Rahab within the genealogy of the Messiah (Matt 1:5). Similarly, with Rahab a harlot enters the realm of God (Mat 21:31; cf. Heb 11:31; Jas 2:25). Here we may also think of the Jewish proverb, "to save one life is to save the world."

Jericho, inviting us to focus on and celebrate her survival, instead of the fate of the city's other inhabitants. Thus the voice that speaks in her story overrides the voice of relentless orthodoxy and its exclusive nationalism. Although there are many differences, her story anticipates that of Ruth the Moabite, in which human kindness will trump ethnic divisions and intermarriage will counter segregation.

> *I do think it is important for the African-American community, in its diversity, to stay true to one core aspect of the African-American experience, which is we know what it's like to be on the outside. If we ever lost that, then I think we're in trouble. Then I think we've lost our way.*
>
> —President Barack O'Bama[61]

Passages (Chaps. 3–5)

A number of years ago there was a popular book called *Passages*, by Gail Sheehy. Sheehy explored the studies of psychologists who had outlined the various stages or passages that an individual goes through in a lifetime, from birth to death. Anthropologists call these stages "rites of passage," some of the primary ones being puberty, marriage and parenthood, retirement, etc. Various religious rituals mark such passages, such as the Bar or Bat Mitzvah for Jewish adolescents, and Confirmation for their Christian counterparts. Indeed, Hinduism has taken the rites of passage and worked out a religious path for one's entire life. Yet another term for such passages is liminality, a word derived from the Latin for "threshold," and related to the word for "boundary." Passing through a stage of life is a liminal experience.

Not only individuals, but also entire peoples can have liminal experiences. Chapters 3–5 of Joshua describe a critical passage of Israel: crossing the Jordan River and entering the land of Canaan. In fact, the Hebrew word for "cross over" or "pass over" is used some twenty-five times in 3:1—5:1 alone. The Jordan River is no Mississippi, and merely crossing it would not make for much of a story. In fact, one could easily skip from 3:1, where the Israelites set up camp before crossing, to 6:1 where the conquest of Jericho really begins, and not miss a thing. But whoever added most of what intervenes (3:2—5:15) wanted to highlight the religious *significance* of this crossing. One might compare George Washington's crossing the Delaware, and Emanuel Gottlieb Leutze's painting by that name which evokes the heroic nature of that event. In fact, the exaltation of Joshua (3:7; 4:14) along with the miraculous river crossing and imminent conquest has its parallels in the stories of numerous ancient hero figures.[62] In Joshua 3–5 the result is a blend of narrative and liturgy.[63] In this story, Israel not only crosses a geographical boundary, but a spiritual one as well. In crossing the threshold, a new people emerges on the other side

---

61. Speaking to the NAACP convention, as quoted by Robinson, "The New Reality," A6.

62. See Römer, *So-Called Deuteronomistic History*, 134, and the reference to John Van Seters.

63. Compare a similar blend in the story of Israel leaving Egypt and the first Passover (Exod 12:1—13:16).

with a new identity. The transition represents a major fulfillment of past hopes, but also an unfolding horizon that is full of both promise and danger.

Much of the symbolism that characterizes the passage over the Jordan appears in a combination that we can call Egypt-Wilderness-Canaan or Exodus-Wandering-Settlement, the former suggesting geography, the latter, the experience. The authors accomplish the connections with numerous references or allusions to the language of previous stories:

> The ark of the covenant guides the people across (3:3–4)
> *The ark guides the people on their wilderness journey (Num 10:33–36)*
> Joshua orders the people to be sanctified before the crossing (3:5)
> *Moses orders the people to be sanctified before receiving the Ten Commandments (Exod 19:10)*
> God exalts Joshua as a leader and commander like Moses (3:7; 4:14)
> *Moses is exalted after the defeat of Pharaoh's troops (Exod 14:30–31)*
> Stones from the Jordan provide a "sign" and "memorial" for future generations (4:5–7)
> *The Passover ritual provides a "sign" and "memorial" (Exod 12:14, 26–27; 13:8, 14)*
> The date of the crossing is noted (4:19; 5:10)
> *The date of the Exodus is noted (Exod 12:2, 40–41; cf. 19:1; Num 10:11–12)*
> The river is dammed and the people cross on dry ground (3:13, 16–17; 4:7, 22–24), with explicit comparison to the Exodus (4:23)
> *The people escape from Egypt on dry ground through the Red Sea (Sea of Reeds) (Exod 14:16, 21–22, 29)*
> The second generation of men (those who survived the wilderness) is circumcised (5:2)
> *The first generation is circumcised (Exod 12:48; note also the "disgrace of Egypt," Josh 5:9)*
> The Passover is celebrated for the first time in the land (5:10–12)
> *The first Passover looks ahead to celebration in the land (Exod 12:25)*
> The Canaanites and other peoples melt in fear of Israel's onslaught (5:1)
> *The Canaanites and other peoples melt in fear of Israel's onslaught (Exod 15:14–16)*
> The commander of God's Hosts appears to Joshua (Josh 5:13–15)
> *God appears to Moses (Exod 3:1–6)*

The Exodus-Wilderness-Settlement allusions serve to illustrate Israel's passage into Canaan as the completion of a long process of divine promise and fulfillment that stretches back to Abraham and Sarah (Gen 12:1–3), the original recipients of the promise of the land. More immediately, the triangulation of Exodus-Wilderness-Settlement validates the identity of the God of Israel. In numerous settings, God has promised to "bring out," to "bring up," and to "bring in," that is, to bring out Israel from Egypt, to bring them up through the wilderness, and to bring them in to the land of Canaan.[64] Liberation from servitude to

---

64. Gen 15:13–14; Exod 3:7–12; cf. Deut 8:7, 14; 26:8–9.

Pharaoh in the land of Egypt has had this trajectory that leads to servitude to God in the land of Canaan, which is God's fief (cf. Lev 25:23). The covenant community is to be a landed community, which is to say, a nation (*goy*).[65] God is "the Lord (*'adon*) of all the earth" (or "land"; 3:11, 14). This is a God who can dry up the Red Sea and stop up the Jordan River, who can make manna fall from heaven and crops grow from the ground.

To borrow a term from the business world, Israel's passage from wilderness to Canaan is a major event in God's *vita*—one of the "mighty acts" that defines who God is. Just so, this passage is a major event in Israel's identity as well. In fact, the difficulty of separating narrative and liturgy is one of the reasons why it is sometimes difficult to follow the plot of chaps. 3–4. In other words, the story of Israel's crossing is loaded with the language of a ritual re-enactment of that story. The story gives us a rite of passage in two senses: the liminal experience, and the ceremonial language that *memorializes* that experience. To use the terms of anthropologists, the story combines myth and ritual.

By "myth" I do not mean a story that is not true (the common misunderstanding of that word); I mean a story that is "foundational" for a people's identity. The story of Israel's passage into Canaan here resembles the (North) American foundation myth of the Pilgrims' passage across the Atlantic to the "New World" (founding towns like "New *Canaan*") or, in a far different sense, the foundation myth of African-Americans whose ancestors came to the New World via the "Middle Passage" of slave ships. These stories of passage are fundamental to the identity of these peoples. In the Jordan crossing, the key image is that of the stones from the river that provide "a memorial forever" (4:7). The place is named Gilgal, which means "a circle of stones."[66] Gilgal is Israel's Stonehenge, but in this case we have the story behind the stones.

The origin of the ceremonial stones causes much of the confusion in the narrative. The people seem to cross the river two times (4:1, 8, 11). There seem to be two sets of stones, those carried to the bank (4:3), and those erected on the river bottom (4:9), the function of the latter being hard to determine! It is also difficult to imagine how long it would take for forty thousand people to cross (4:13), not to mention how the priests could hold up the ark that long (and the people are warned to stay about a kilometer away from the ark [3:4]!). But, again, the narrators are not so much intent on rendering a plausible series of events as they are in conveying how momentous the crossing is. The foundational quality of the story appears in the symbolism of the twelve stones representing the twelve tribes of Israel. The stones are to serve a catechetical function. "When your children ask in time to come, 'What do these stones mean to you?'" the stones will be a "memorial," that is, a concrete reminder. Subsequent generations can make a pilgrimage to Gilgal and show their children these stones, much the

---

65. The word *goy* is particularly associated with the possession of geographical territory (sometimes in contrast to the word *ʿam*, "people").

66. The etymology in 5:9 is more a play on words.

way contemporary Americans take their children to Plymouth Rock, or the spot where Washington crossed the Delaware. The purpose of such a memorial is not simply to be an historical marker; rather, a memorial functions to maintain the continuing ethos of the people by inculcating in each generation the sense that *they* were there at the founding, as well (cf. Deuteronomy 26).

The memorial function of the stones, in other words, is similar to the function of the reenactment of the festival of Passover—the spiritual self-identification of each participant as someone who has experienced God's liberation: "*We* were Pharaoh's slaves in Egypt" (Deut 6:21). It is fitting, therefore, that the story of the crossing leads to the celebration of Passover (5:10-12). Indeed, the original Passover story looks forward to this celebration in the land (Exod 12:25). "Passover" derives from a different Hebrew word than "pass (cross) over," yet both of the ceremonies are the reenactment of liminal experiences—the one remembering the night before leaving Egypt, the other remembering the day of entering the land.[67] Moreover, the foundational quality of the crossing story also appears in the ceremony of circumcision (5:2-7). Circumcision is the most definitive rite of passage for the male Jew. Usually, of course, it is performed shortly after birth. Although the narrator does not tell us why, we learn that no males had been circumcised since the people left Egypt. The importance of this note, however, is that a whole new generation stands on the west bank of the Jordan: all the males who left Egypt have died (along with females, as well), a punishment for their *refusal* to enter the land out of fear (Numbers 13-14).[68]

The celebration of circumcision and Passover tie together the two central covenant traditions of Israel—the promise of Canaan to the ancestors (Gen 12:7; 15:18; 17:2, 8), and the Sinai covenant in its association with the Exodus (Deut 16:1-6). In fact, entering Canaan is the completion of God's promise of liberation in the Exodus story (Exod 3:7-8; 12:25). Israel's identity as a "wandering Aramean" is over (Deut 26:5). The Abram who went down into Egypt has indeed become a great nation, and now has come home. Israel celebrates the transition in eating the first "produce"[69] of the land, just as Moses had commanded (Deuteronomy 26). As if on cue, the manna that has sustained them in the wilderness ceases. The taste of the newly roasted grain is the taste of freedom.

Two texts frame the celebrations of circumcision and Passover—5:1 and 5:13-15. Both texts return to the military campaign ahead and the assault on Jericho. In 5:1 all the kings of the Amorites and Canaanites hear about Israel's

---

67. Note also the parallel between the "hasty" crossing of the river (Josh 4:10) and the hasty eating of bread (Exod 12:11). Cf. Num 9:1-10 where the Passover is celebrated at the departure from Sinai and the beginning of the wilderness journey. See my article, "Passover."

68. The story in Numbers parallels Joshua 2 in that the denouement follows a spy story (Num 13:1-30). Cf. also Deut 1:19-40. Joshua, of course, is one exception to the mass mortality of the wilderness generation (the other being Caleb, Num 14:24).

69. Only here (5:12) is the root ʿabar, normally meaning "cross over," used to refer to agricultural "produce," perhaps a way of emphasizing the rite of passage involved.

crossing the Jordan and how the river was cut off, and they melt in fear, precisely the response that Rahab had reported earlier (2:11). Four other coalitions will not be so passive, but eventually Israel will defeat them (9:1; 10:1; 11:1). Israel now stands prepared to accomplish what the "warriors" before them failed to do (5:6). The foundational myth is complete, as Nelson puts it: "a story of transition from a past time of promise to a present time of fulfillment, a journey from desert chaos to landed order, from Moses to Joshua, from desert manna to the produce of land . . . from outside the land to inside it."[70]

Jericho, the Finale: "The Walls Come a' Tumblin' Down" (Chap. 6)

The narrative now returns to the assault on Jericho, but the fall of the city is as much a result of a military parade as combat. Here, as elsewhere, God acts as commander in chief, issuing a strategy to Joshua who then relays the orders to the warriors. The plan for Jericho expands the military significance of the ark processional in crossing the Jordan, revealing God to be the "Lord of all the land/earth" over against Israel's enemies (3:10–13; 4:23–24; 5:1). With a great fanfare of trumpets, the warriors march around the city with the ark in tow. Here the ark functions as a kind of military palladium mediating the presence and power of the "Lord of hosts" (cf. Num 10:35–36).

Like many folk tales, the story is highly repetitive, giving us the details of the plan and its execution five times for the seven-day pattern. On the final day, the troops shout a resounding battle cry and the walls "come a-tumblin' down," as the old Spiritual puts it. Joshua has declared the city to be "devoted to the Lord for destruction" (ḥerem). Rahab's fears are about to be realized (2:13). As I have already insisted above, there is no way for us to condone such religiously sanctioned genocide. But the Rahab story has already softened the portrayal of the "ban" because she and her family are spared, an "illegal" act of mercy that is fulfilled in 6:22–25. Now Joshua's orders foreshadow a kind of reverse irony in the ban. Joshua declares that all booty is part of the ban—it constitutes "devoted things" (the root ḥerem appears four times in 6:18). If anyone covets the "devoted things" and keeps them, he will bring "trouble" upon the Israelites—*they* will become subject to the ban, as if they were Canaanites. That is precisely what happens in the next story—The Treasure of Trouble Valley.

The Treasure of Trouble Valley (Chap. 7)

The conquest of Jericho went off without a hitch, but the initial assault on Ai proves disastrous for the Israelites. The author gives the reason for the defeat in the first verse: Achan, one of the warriors, disobeyed the prohibition against taking the spoils of war for himself, thereby invoking God's wrath. The sequel in which the Israelites successfully conquer Ai (8:1–29) could stand on its own.[71] With the Achan story as an in-

---

70. Nelson, *Joshua*, 68.

71. All one need do is delete the phrase "as before" in 8:6–7; see Campbell and O'Brien, *Unfolding*, 126.

troduction, however, the initial defeat at Ai shows how disobedience to God's command leads to disaster, just as eradicating the perpetrator of disobedience leads to victory.

Excursus 2: Disobedience and Disaster

As we have already noted in Excursus 1, covenant theology correlated disaster with disobedience, especially as spelled out in the covenant curses. Even without a covenant (or treaty) framework, however, such a correlation was assumed throughout the ancient Near East (and, arguably, down to this day). In the Ai story, the disaster is a military defeat, something that we will see over and over. In fact, the Former Prophets will end with such a defeat writ large. Moreover, other disasters usually were attributed to God, including events in nature such as famine or drought (e.g., Amos 4:6–11). Even disease came under the umbrella of assumed divine punishment. Thus a character from 1 Kgs 17:17–18 says that the reason for the mortal illness of her son is "to bring my sin to remembrance." The consequences of disobedience can even take on cosmic proportions affecting the land, animals, and "even the fish of the sea" (Hos 4:1–3). There is an assumption of historical causation operative here that many contemporary people do not hold—at least, not so explicitly![72] To us war is the result of political policies, foolhardiness, national aggrandizement, long-standing ethnic feuds, etc. Often the *victims* of warfare are entirely innocent of wrongdoing, so that to say to them "You must have sinned for this to have happened" would be obscene. The same applies to illness such as cancer, diabetes, or heart disease, etc. It would take a complete lack of sympathy to say to someone "You have cancer because you have sinned."[73] Such correlations, however, were simply part of the biblical worldview. Sometimes the author's insistence on the correlation seems to be nothing short of an obsession. As Nelson puts it with regard to one's king's evaluation, "The need to make these connections between sin and disaster is so strong that the narrator simply ignores the question of how Zimri could have had much opportunity for apostasy in his seven-day reign."[74] It must have been a devilishly busy week!

One Hebrew word (*ra'ah*) illustrates the correlation. The word is often translated as "evil" when referring to human wrongdoing; on the other hand, it is often translated as "calamity" or "disaster" when attributed to God's punishment, probably to evade any notions

---

72. A line from a song in *The Sound of Music*, of all things, illustrates the pervasiveness of such thinking, only in reverse. Maria sings to her newfound love, the captain, explaining her good fortune in finding him because "somewhere in my youth or childhood, I must have done something good." Also, insurance policies continue to speak of natural disasters as "acts of God," and people sometimes explain calamities like car accidents or hurricanes as part of God's inscrutable "plan." Clergy and political leaders sometimes pray for rain in the midst of drought on the assumption that God has willfully withheld rain (cf. again Amos 4:7).

73. However, there are also certain advocates of mind-body spirituality who would ask a person, "What did you do to cause your cancer?" Jesus deals with the origins of illness in John 9.

74. Nelson, *First and Second Kings*, 102, on 1 Kgs 16:8–20.

that God causes moral evil. Sometimes it is clear that human *ra'ah* has the consequence of divine *ra'ah*, but we will encounter numerous times when the division of cause and effect is far from clear. Indeed, there will be times when it seems as if divine *ra'ah* causes *human ra'ah*.[75] Such incidents will raise very difficult theological and ethical questions that ultimately are beyond the scope of this study. I introduce the issue briefly here near the outset, with regard to the failed battle at Ai, as a way of recognizing an interpretive problem that we will face repeatedly.

In a sense, one could lay part of the blame for what happens initially at Ai at Joshua's feet. Normally soldiers could keep the spoils of war for themselves (Deut 20:14-18).[76] The law specifically applies to distant towns "which are not towns of the nations here" (i.e., in Canaan).[77] Canaanite cites are different: there "anything that breathes" must die, meaning that livestock may not be kept as part of the spoils. But the law does not specifically say that objects like gold and silver are also banned (in fact "devoted things" are not mentioned).[78] Why does Joshua declare the booty of Jericho to be under the ban? That is, why is the booty here not simply the ordinary "spoils" rather than "devoted things"? Joshua says that all the precious metal objects must be put "into the treasury of the Lord" (whatever that is). But that simply begs the question, and the ambiguity does not end with 6:18-19. In 8:2 God tells Joshua that the soldiers *may* keep the spoil of Ai "*and its livestock*." Similarly, later Joshua will tell the East-Jordan tribes that they may keep both livestock and precious metals that they have gained from battles within Canaan (22:8). The inconsistencies in applying the law are enough to call for a Supreme Court decision! One can see how a soldier like Achan might plead ignorance, or at least confusion, but, as we shall see, he does not opt for such a legal excuse.[79]

As with Jericho, Joshua sends spies to reconnoiter the city of Ai. They report that taking the city will be a cinch, requiring only a relatively small force. But the Israelite troops are roundly defeated and retreat. Then "the hearts of the people melted and turned to water" (v .5). Ironically, their fear is precisely that of the Canaanites as previously expressed by Rahab and kings (2:11; 5:1), and threatens a recurrence of the aborted conquest of Israel's past (cf. Number 13-14; Deut 1:22-40, especially v. 8).

---

75. For example, God sends an "evil spirit" to torment poor king Saul (1 Sam 16:14). David's "evil" in committing adultery with Bathsheba leads to the "evil" that God will "raise up" within his family (e.g., his son's rape of his own sister Tamar, then Absalom's murder of the rapist, etc), 2 Sam 12:1, 11. Here (as often) the NRSV and other translations can hide the connections especially with *ra'ah*, which is used in v. 1 ("displeased" for "was evil in the eyes of") and v. 12 ("trouble" for "evil"). See the discussion of each of these stories.

76. Cf. 2:33-34; 3:7; Num 31:7-12 (all places outside Canaan).

77. Note that "here" gives away the author's point of view as already in the land!

78. In Deut 7:25, taking silver and gold is prohibited, but there the metals are the veneer of idols that are banned.

79. Of course, it may be that the storyteller is unaware of the Deuteronomic law.

Wary of complete destruction, Joshua and the community elders perform a ritual of repentance (tearing their clothes). Unaware of Achan's disobedience, Joshua pleads with God to spare the people. The similarities between his speech and that of Moses in previous situations (the golden calf, the aborted conquest), suggest the seriousness of the crisis—Israel stands at the brink of annihilation.[80] Joshua points out the incongruity of God's bringing them across the Jordan only to let them perish in the land. He also is not above implying that God's own reputation is at stake (v. 9).

Now God informs Joshua of the sin that has created the crisis. The Israelites have "transgressed my covenant" and now *they* "have become a thing devoted for destruction themselves" (vv. 11–12). Just as their liquefied hearts make them like the Canaanites, so does their subjection to the ban. Suddenly the roles of conqueror and enemy are reversed. The only way out of this trouble is to find the culprit (probably by casting lots) and put him to death. Otherwise, God will be with them no more (v. 12; contrast 1:5, 9). When the lot finally falls to Achan, Joshua's demand for a confession seems almost touching ("my son," v. 19). As we have seen, Achan might rightly plead ignorance, or at least confusion, over the law. God says that Achan has taken from the "devoted things" (v. 11), whereas Achan says that he has taken from the "spoil" (v. 21) and does not mention the "devoted things." But the rest of his admission is clearly self-incriminating; he acknowledges that he is the sinner. So there is no mercy for Achan, or for his family—all of them are stoned to death, their corpses burned and covered with a pile of rocks.

To us, this horrific execution of an entire family for the sin of the father seems as barbaric as the ban itself (whether applied to Canaanites or Israelites). We need not condone the practice, however, to see the logic that leads to it. The stealing and possession of the "devoted things" threatens to contaminate the entire community. The offense and its antidote closely resemble the Torah prescriptions for dealing with a heretical city (Deut 13:12–18). There is a peculiar notion of fault here that understands it as a kind of communicable disease, the course of which can be stopped only by totally eliminating the source. The spoil is an "abomination," and everything that comes in contact with it *becomes* an abomination (Deut 7:25–26). Then, as the Torah says, disaster will come upon "moist and dry alike" (29:19). The correlation is a grisly version of the old proverb about one rotten apple spoiling the barrel. The principle behind this notion of "calamity" (or "evil") was common to ancient peoples: the guilt of an individual can lead to the suffering of an entire people. In fact, the Deuteronomic editors of Kings will employ this principle in interpreting the fateful results of the sin of individual kings, to the point of *national* calamity (especially King Jeroboam of Israel, e.g., 1 Kgs 14:16).[81]

---

80. See Exod 32:11–14; Num 13:13–19; Deut 9:18–19, 25–29.

81. See also 2 Sam 21:1–14 where famine results from the "blood-guilt on Saul." The problem of corporate suffering for an individual's wrongdoing will appear repeatedly—sometimes within a family, sometimes for the entire nation.

Here, to prevent the contamination and subsequent annihilation of the entire people, it is necessary to annihilate the perpetrators, to "single them out from all the tribes of Israel for calamity" (Deut 29:21; 13:12–18). In his pre-battle speech at Jericho, Joshua had warned against precisely the "trouble" that Achan has caused (6:18). Now the calamity is memorialized in the name of Achan's grave: "Trouble Valley" (v. 26). The heap of stones that marks the grave serves as a constant warning "to this day" (cf. Deut 13:16), a grim contrast to the stones that commemorated the crossing of the Jordan (4:3–7).

> *In 1553 the heretic Servetus was burned at the stake in Geneva. John Calvin was among those who condemned him, although Calvin pleaded for a more humane form of execution. "Calvin shared a conviction with many other theologians in the sixteenth century (both Catholic and Protestant) that heresy was not just a matter of poor judgment or wrong belief that threatened the soul of the heretic, but was a threat to the faith and life of the entire church, and as such even more dangerous than plague or famine."*[82]

The Achan story is full of reversals and ironies, especially considering its literary context. The defeat at Ai is the flip side of the victory at Jericho. At Jericho, the outsiders (Rahab and her family) became insiders (admitted into the community of Israel); at Ai, the insiders (Achan and family) become outsiders (victims of the ban). A Canaanite whore is spared from the ban because of her righteous deed; an Israelite blue blood (note the family tree, v. 1) is subjected to the ban because of his transgression. There are also outright contradictions. Achan breaks the covenant (7:11) and he and family are put to death. Disobedience results in punishment, not only for Achan, but also for the soldiers killed and potentially all Israel. Rahab and family are spared contrary to Deut 20:16–17, resulting in a breach of covenant (Deut 7:2), yet Joshua and Israel remain unscathed. Punishment does *not* follow disobedience. The inconsistencies in applying the Torah regulations on spoils of war call into question the clarity of the Torah itself, as well as Joshua's thinking and even God's judgment. The inconsistencies, of course, are partly due to the collection of originally unconnected stories and traditions. Nevertheless, the result is a picture that is far more ambiguous than a simple rewards and punishment scenario, and, once again, the distinction between Israelite and Canaanite is blurred.

With Achan and his family removed, the conquest of Ai now can move forward again (8:1–29). God summons Joshua with the familiar words "do not fear or be dismayed" (cf. 1:9), then acts as commander in chief by providing the battle plan. The ambush succeeds and Ai's troops are destroyed along with the entire population of the city. The conclusion of the story provides an ironic echo of the preceding calamity: Joshua

---

We will look at the problem at various times, and in the summary and conclusion of this book.

82. Stroup, *Calvin*, 9. Of course, Servetus's *family* was not burned along with him!

executes the king of Ai and covers his body with a heap of stones, precisely the fate of Achan (7:26).

Now that calamity has turned to victory, maybe it's time for a revival service. Or, to use the language of the narrator, it's time to get back to the book of the Torah and a renewal of the covenant that binds together Israel and God (8:30–35). In fact, the Torah requires such a ceremony, and at the location here—the adjoining hills of Ebal and Gerizim that loom over the town of Shechem (Deut 27:2–8). The position of the revival here has multiple functions. Although the Torah seems to require a ceremony immediately after entering the land (like the one with the stones in chaps. 3–5), clearly the narrator sees Joshua's ritual as a fulfillment of the Torah's prescription, even if a bit delayed. Retrospectively, covenant renewal also offers the hope of God's renewed blessing, in contrast to the "calamity" of the Achan story. Prospectively, renewing the covenant with God will have an ironic dimension in that the next story shows Israel (including Joshua) as *breaking* a stipulation of that covenant by making a covenant with the Gibeonites. Finally, covenant renewal here anticipates the conclusion of the book with another covenant ceremony at Shechem (chap. 24).

Joshua builds an altar on Mt. Ebal and offers sacrifices. He writes on the stones of the altar "a copy of the law of Moses," assembles "all Israel—alien as well as citizen" with half on Mt. Ebal and half on Mt. Gerizim and the ark in between, and then reads "all the words of the law, blessings and curses, according to all that is written in the book of the law." Moreover, just as the covenant reaffirms the polity of Israel, so the building of an altar in the land represents a political claim to sovereignty, much as did Abraham's (Gen 12:7, albeit with far less warrant). Similarly, the ark reappears as the unifying palladium that led the people into the land.

The situation of this covenant renewal is reminiscent of the restoration following the incident of the golden calf that almost brought an end to Israel (Deut 10:1–5). For the narrator, Joshua's action not only follows the words of Moses, it also may foreshadow the much later covenant renewal under King Josiah, when the book of the law is *rediscovered*, triggering a national religious revival (2 Kings 22–23). Going by the book is critical to the people's continuing existence in the land, a point emphasized by virtually reducing "the words of the law" to "blessings and curses." In its literary location, this reiteration of the orthodox position seems to suggest that "calamity" is still a threat if Israel is not obedient to the covenant. But for the moment, the Deuteronomic dream of Israel reappears. As Hawk puts it, "a flawed and irresolute Israel gives way to an Israel that binds itself wholeheartedly to God and to the words of Moses."[83] The altar inscribed with the Torah combines ritual and law in a physical expression of the unity of Israel under the sovereignty of God.[84]

83. Hawk, *Joshua*, 132.

84. We needn't assume that some sense of such unity is a complete fiction, however, even for the period of the judges. As Gottwald, *Politics*, 75, says, "the traditionists do correctly identify a commonality in the populations of Israel and Judah that entailed shared sociocultural and re-

On the other hand, the participants in Joshua's ceremony seem to reflect the ambiguity that has developed in the preceding stories concerning the distinction between "Israelites" and "Canaanites." When Joshua assembles "all Israel," the assembly includes "*alien* as well as citizen" (vv. 33, 35). An alien is a non-Israelite who is virtually a permanent resident (as opposed to a "foreigner" who is simply there temporarily for business). The distinction would be something like someone who has come into the United States from another country and has a "green card" in contrast to a temporary visitor who has a visa. The green card allows the alien certain legal rights—to hold a job, to receive government benefits—that a "foreigner" would have only temporarily, or not at all. Within Israelite culture, an "alien" is virtually identical to a "citizen" *under the law*. In fact, the famous Golden Rule refers specifically to this equitability: "The alien who resides with you shall be to you as a citizen among you; you shall love the alien as yourself, for you were aliens in the land of Egypt" (Lev 19:33–34; cf. 24:22).[85]

The inclusion of aliens in Joshua's covenant ceremony immediately raises yet another irony involving "outsider"/ "insider." Of course, the *narrator* assumes the point-of-view of a native inhabitant. But the Israelites in the story are in effect *still* aliens who are coming into the land inhabited by Canaanites—indeed, they are alien invaders! So who can be an "alien" vis-à-vis an Israelite? The irony of this question is at the heart of the next story, the ruse of the Gibeonites.

Trick and Treaty (Chap. 9)

No sooner have Joshua and the people renewed their covenant with God than they are forced to break it. They break it by *making* a covenant with the Gibeonites, a group within the Hivites who are to be destroyed (Deut 7:1–2). Although the introductory verses lead us to expect a massive military onslaught from "all the kings" and peoples of Canaan (vv. 1–2), what follows instead is a motley group of apparently weary foreigners waving a white flag. In negotiating a treaty, they prove the adage that the pen is mightier than the sword.

As we noted briefly in Excursus 1, making treaties with parties other than the suzerain normally is prohibited. Here the contemporary reader may well wonder what is wrong with signing a peace treaty with another people (the same puzzlement will arise from the prohibition of "inter-faith" marriages).[86] Again the treaty model provides an answer: treaties with other parties create a divided loyalty and are likely to foster sedition, if not already be a *result* of sedition. In religious terms, sedition is "apostasy" (the original Greek word means "revolt" or "rebellion"), and sedition is at the bottom of the slippery slope

---

ligious traditions and practices that ran deeper than the political 'union' accomplished under David and Solomon."

85. Cf. Lev 24:22. Note that an alien also may participate in the Passover celebration as long as the males are circumcised (Exod 12:48–49), and the alien benefits from the Sabbath commandment (Exod 20:10). For special protections, see Exod 22:21; Deut 24:17–21.

86. We will not discuss the marriage prohibition at length until we look at the dynamics in the reign of king Solomon, 1 Kings 11. For political treaties in the later monarchy, see Excursus 7.

of seduction—the way in which another people's culture entices Israel into prohibited acts (Deut 20:18). Apparently this is why treaties with indigenous peoples are prohibited, but with far-away people allowed (Deut 20:15). In fact, the Gibeonites are shrewdly taking advantage of one of the rules of warfare in Deut 20:10–11. However horrific the practice of *ḥerem* would be, at least the protocol requires Israel to offer "terms of peace" to a faraway city instead of decimating it. The terms, however, are that the city become Israel's slaves (which is what happens below).

> The somber act of reading the Requerimiento, [was] demanded by Spanish law before a conquistador could legally commence hostilities and take slaves . . . This surreal, nine-hundred-word manifesto drawn up by legalists at the Spanish court about 1512 was at once an invitation to submit peaceably and a declaration of war.[87]

It is possible to see in the Gibeonite story a situation familiar from the annals of imperialistic kings, in which a city surrenders to the king and becomes a vassal, rather than fight a losing battle. In this case Joshua would appear to be like such kings (and a prototype for King Josiah). On the other hand, the story has numerous ironies that blur such a picture. Joshua the Conquerer seems more like Joshua the Confused; the white flag of surrender is part of the disguise of deceit; and the victors of war are at the same times victims of a hoax.

87. Kessell, *Spain in the Southwest*, 31.

The juxtaposition of 9:1–2 and the following story suggests a study in different reactions. The kings assemble to fight Israel when they hear "this"—but what is the referent? One would think it is the defeat of Ai and execution of its king (that is the Gibeonites' reference, v. 3). Yet the immediate context suggests that the kings are reacting to Israel's covenant revival service. One effect of inserting the covenant ceremony here is to affirm the saying "united we stand." The author emphasizes the totality of the people by listing the officials (v. 33): "and the women, and the little ones, and the aliens who resided among them" (v. 35). A unified people, gathered together in sacred space around their holy ark, in accordance with the Torah of Moses, which represents the words of God, is, the author suggests, intimidating and invincible. Chapter 9 presents two reactions: hostility by "all the kings who were beyond the Jordan," and appeasement by the Gibeonites. The differing fates of those who react to Israel as enemy and those who react as friend (or at least *would-be* friend) will dramatically play out in the following chapters.

The Gibeonites are a people who live inside the land of Canaan, but pretend to live outside. Their pretension is rooted in fear. They know about the God of Israel and Israel's policy of genocide. They even seem to know the Torah regulation in which God allows for peace treaties with far-away folks but decrees annihilation for the indigenous Canaanites. They have heard about Jericho, although they carefully do not mention that in order not to give away their location. When they say "We are your servants" they are submitting to vassalage under Israel (cf. 1 Kgs 16:7).

And they are masters at deception. For their little drama of deceit, the Gibeonite representatives dress up in costumes of ragged clothes and carry props of moldy bread and broken beverage containers, as if they have been on a long journey from their faraway home.

The Israelite officials fall for it and Joshua signs a peace treaty, handing out pens as if it's a wonderful day. Instead of asking God for guidance, they proceed to eat the Gibeonites' moldy bread (v. 14)! The gluttony is ironic: in stuffing their mouths they neglect to "consult the mouth of Yahweh" (AT). Of course, Joshua discovers the deception, but by then it is too late. An oath sworn in the name of God must stand, even if the oath *disobeys* what God has said. The Gibeonites do not escape unconditionally, however. Joshua curses them and sentences them as a people to perpetual service, precisely what they had claimed to be, although merely in deference (vv. 8, 11, 22).[88] Joshua's decree conforms to the Torah regulation of Deut 20:11. As "hewers of wood and drawers of water," the Gibeonites are second-class citizens. But their service is for the sanctuary, presumably for sacrifices.[89] The Gibeonites are the altar guild! These outsiders, you might say, are "devoted" to the sacristy rather than to destruction; the hexed become sextons. Not only do they survive as part of Israel (however subservient); they work at the very heart of Israelite faith.

In the end, the way the author tells the Gibeonite story creates a "revisionist" opinion over against the orthodox. The orthodox is: follow the rules, looking neither to the left or the right, as God tells Joshua at the outset (1:7). Loyalty to God and country demand obedience. All Canaanites are infidels. Exterminate them. Show no mercy. Onward, Israelite soldiers. One God, one people, one land!

But then there's the story of the Gibeonites with all its complex irony. *They* seem to follow the Torah more than the Israelites. *They* acknowledge the power of Israel's God (v. 9) whom Israel ignores, using virtually the same words of praise as Rahab (2:10). Like the kings of the Amorites (5:1) they have heard of Israel's triumphs, but they see opportunity where the others saw only doom; and unlike the kings who later hear of Israel (9:1; 11:1–5), they opt for peace rather than war. The Gibeonites are deceptive, yet rewarded. They are accursed, yet they are blessed with life and citizenship. They are menial laborers, but their work is sacred. Readers who know the story of Jacob will see some parallels with the Gibeonites. "Israel" is the namesake of Jacob (Gen 32:28). The Gibeonites succeed by deception, and it was Jacob whom God rewarded despite his deceit of father and brother. The Gibeonites enjoy mercy and grace without meriting it, just like Israel, of whom God has said, "I do not love you because you are mighty and righteous, but simply because I love you" (Deut 7:7–8, AT). Indeed, for both,

---

88. The Hebrew word translated "servant" in vv. 8 and 11 and "slave" in v. 22 is the same.

89. The reference to a "house" of God may be anachronistic. Note that v. 26 only refers to an altar. In 22:19 there is a reference to the "tabernacle," i.e., to the tent shrine (cf. Exodus 25–31). See also below on 24:26 ("sanctuary of the Lord"). Otherwise, we do not hear of such a house until the one at Shiloh mentioned in 1 Samuel 1 (and even the existence of such a structure will be ignored or denied in 2 Samuel 7).

the Torah demands complete annihilation, yet both find a reprieve (for Israel, cf. Deuteronomy 9–10).[90] Another detail also hints at Israel's experience of grace. The props that the Gibeonites use (worn out clothing) make them look like what Israel *would* have looked like had God not cared for them in the wilderness (Deut 8:4; 29:5).[91] But next to the words that speak of God's grace to Israel, God also condemns the Canaanites to death (Deut 7:1–6). As we have seen, Israel cannot obey those words of God because they have sworn an oath to God to protect the very people they are supposed to destroy.

In short, the story of the Gibeonites raises difficult and irresolvable questions about identity: who is "Israel," who is a "Canaanite," and who is God? Once again things are not neat and tidy. Indeed, the ironic shifts in identity are almost comical: the insiders who pretend to be outsiders become part of the new insiders who were outsiders! What it means to be "all Israel" has changed dramatically. The story illustrates the ambiguity of going by the book, of what it means to obey God and follow the law. The law presupposed the opposites of native and foreigner, pious and pagan, blessed and cursed. There was no precedent for natives who praised the Lord and passed the peace! New experience demands flexibility in living under the law rather that an inflexible orthodoxy.[92]

A Treaty Fulfilled (Chap. 10)

Immediately circumstances put the Israelite treaty with the Gibeonites to the test. In terms of ancient international legal protocol, Israel is the suzerain to Gibeon, who is the vassal. In exchange for the vassal's servitude, the suzerain is obligated to protect the vassal from hostile forces. Now, alarmed by Israel's destruction of Ai and collaboration with Gibeon (here portrayed as a powerful city), a coalition of kings led by Adonizedek of Jerusalem lays siege to the city. Responding to the Gibeonite's plea for help, Joshua and his troops counterattack. It is God, the Holy Warrior, however, who leads the battle, throwing the coalition into a panic so that they become easy targets (cf. Exod 14:24–25). In fact, God bombards the hapless soldiers with hailstones of lethal proportions, killing all the more. Even cosmic forces act on Israel's behalf when the daily cycle of sun and moon pauses—the first "daylight savings time"—to allow for complete vindication (v. 13).[93]

In the face of defeat, the five kings prove to be cowards. Rather than rallying the troops they flee and hide in a cave.

---

90. Cf. Polzin, *Moses*, 120.
91. Cf. ibid., 119; Hawk, *Joshua*, 140.
92. Cf. Polzin, *Moses*, 82, 124–26.
93. The Hebrew in vv. 12–13 is ambiguous. Cf. Hab 3:10. Just as the treaty relationship accords with ancient Near Eastern custom, so does the action of God as warrior. In the annals of Assyrian kings, the deities go before the human troops, instilling terror and panic in the enemy and fighting against them, and the kings narrate their military victories in a way similar to much of chap. 10. Indeed, there is a striking parallel to 10:11 (hailstones) in the annals of Sargon, who boasts of his god Adad: "With a bursting cloud and hail stones he cut off the remainder [of the enemy]." See my study, *Divine Presence*, 246, 202–3. For a more recent study, see Younger, *Ancient Conquest Accounts*.

The Israelites find them, and Joshua has them sealed inside until he can finish the destruction of their forces. Joshua then brings the kings out, humiliates them by having his generals stand on their necks, executes them, and impales their bodies on stakes, one of the more grisly aspects of ancient warfare intended to instill terror, no doubt successfully (cf. the contemporary examples above). But Joshua takes care to remove their bodies from public view by the end of the day in accordance with the Torah (Deut 21:22–23). The Israelites then proceed to conquer and annihilate seven cities. While the list is not completely consistent with the preceding narrative, the overall effect is a sequence involving the defeat of armies, kings, and cities.

These victories now lead to a sweeping conclusion (vv. 40–43), emphasizing the totality of Israel's dominance. Joshua has "defeated the whole land" with "all their kings" and "destroyed all that breathed." Joshua has acted in obedience to "all that God had commanded Moses," and God has rewarded that obedience by fighting for Israel. As a conclusion to chaps. 1–12, however, vv. 40–43 represent an idealistic ideology that the preceding stories refute, for beginning with Rahab and ending with Gibeon, Joshua has *not* done all that God commanded Moses, as we have seen. Once again, the reader is likely to respond to the "party line" of vv. 40–43 with a smile of bemused skepticism.

Moreover, it immediately becomes clear that it is the southern portion of Canaan that Joshua had conquered, for now yet another coalition of northern kings attacks, led by Jabin of Hazor (11:1–5). It is "a great army, in number like the sand on the seashore," but their fate is predictably that of their predecessors: defeat and annihilation of kings, armies, and cities—everyone who breathed (vv. 10–15). Now the narrator repeats the claim that the *whole* land belongs to Israel—even the land of the giants (Anakim; cf. Num 13:28, 33; Deut 1:28; 3:11). So "the land had rest from war"—at least, for now. But here again success is less than ideal. Almost hidden in the claim of total victory is the aside (v. 22) that Joshua did not, in fact, conquer the Anakim in the coastal plain, including the cities of Gaza, Ashdod, and Gath, the last being the later home town of one rather famous giant by the name of Goliath (1 Samuel 17). There are, in fact, more battles ahead, and, ironically, with the very giants who thwarted Israel's first foray into the land (Deut 1:26–28). The first half of the book then concludes with a summary list of conquered kings (chap. 12).

The preceding stories present dramatic contrasts between two types of "Canaanites": those individuals (Rahab) or groups (Gibeonites) who acknowledge the power of Israel's God and make a bid for peace are spared and in some way become part of "Israel." Those kings and groups that challenge Israel's incursions into the land and fight against Joshua are defeated and utterly destroyed. In the end, the relations between Israelites and Canaanites corresponds more closely to God's promises to the Ancestors—"those who bless you, I will bless; those who curse you, I will curse" (e.g., Gen 12:3)—and less like God's demands in the

Torah—"make no covenant with them and show them no mercy" (Deut 7:2).[94]

Dividing Up the Pie (Chaps. 13–21)

The second half of the book (chaps. 13–22) now turns to the partitioning and assignment of the land to the various tribes of Israel.[95] Included are two incidents that represent the fulfillment of decisions that Moses had previously made: the land grant to Caleb (14:6–15), who, along with Joshua, is the only survivor of the wilderness generation because he did not join in the infamous revolt at Kadesh-barnea (Num 14:1–25); and the land grant to the daughters of Zelophehad, a rare instance of gender equality (17:3–6; Num 27:1–12). The benefactors of these land grants represent a subtle replay of the irony seen in figures like Rahab and even the Gibeonites in contrast to Achan. Caleb is identified as a "Kennizite," which questions the ethnic consistency of Israel, and the Zelophehad daughters (along with Achsah, Caleb's daughter), as women, question the exclusive right of males to inheritance. On the other hand, the privileged Josephites come across as selfish and ignoble (17:14–18; cf. Achan). As before, the idiosyncrasy of the characters defies any rigid categories of who is a true Israelite, and, in effect, confirms the makeup of Israel as defined in the covenant ceremony in 8:35.[96]

There are proportionately more references to the fulfillment of Moses' orders in this section of the book than in any other. This sense of completion comes to a head at the conclusion of the section dealing with the East Jordan tribes. There is another sweeping claim that God has given to Israel "all the land that he swore to their ancestors" and "rest" from their enemies (as in 11:23). Indeed, "Not one of all the good promises that the Lord had made to the house of Israel had failed; all came to pass" (21:43–45).

Yet much of the intervening material belies the claim of all promises fulfilled. In fact, the opening lines (13:1) state that "very much of the land still remains to be possessed," followed by a list of daunting size. Similar exclusions will appear later (v. 13; 15:63; 16:10; 17:12–13) and in one Joshua lectures the people regarding their "slackness" (18:3–10). The geographical details of the distribution may seem enough to put even a surveyor to sleep, but the ironic contradiction between the sweeping claims and the acknowledged exclusions links this part of the book with the first part in terms of both peoples (Rahab) and land (Gibeonites and their cities). Moreover, as Hawk shows, careful analysis of the geographical details reveals a subtle tendency in which the ideal of clear borders dissolves into com-

---

94. Again, reading the text in the context of the Josianic reform, some scholars see in the two groups those who submit to Josianic rule and those who resist (e.g., Coote, *Book of Joshua*, 625–26).

95. Ibid., 658, suggests that three different modes of land redistribution are at work here: monarchy, village, and tribe. The configurations here reflect the Josianic reform as well as older patterns. McNutt, *Reconstructing*, 75, represents the general view that chaps. 13–19 "reflect the situation during the monarchic period, and thus their value for determining the original settlement patterns of the Iron Age I highlands is limited."

96. Polzin, *Moses*, 130; Hawk, *Joshua*, 192.

plicated ambiguities.⁹⁷ In combination, the clash between bombastic hyperbole and the embarrassing facts approaches the sardonic humor of political satire, however unintended. The voice that declares "Mission Accomplished" has tried to "spin" the facts (to use a contemporary term), but it sounds a lot like a little horn blaring big things (Dan 7:8–10).

Altar of Contention (Chap. 22)

The section on land distribution concludes with the settlement of the East Jordan tribe (chap. 22). At the beginning of the book, they had sworn agreement with their allotment and vowed death to anyone who would "rebel" against Moses' words (1:12–18). Ironically, the other tribes now accuse them of precisely that offense and threaten them with that punishment.

The story begins otherwise with Joshua's praise for the Eastern tribes' loyalty and obedience, concluding with an exhortation to continue in such faithfulness, couched in the language of covenant love (vv. 1–6; cf. Deut 6:4–5). In the process of leaving Canaan and moving to their lands, however, the Eastern tribes stop to erect an altar "at the frontier," that is, at the boundary marked by the Jordan River, but on the West bank. The Western tribes hear of this and immediately gather to make war with their Eastern counterparts. The tribes are scarcely settled when a "civil war" threatens.

It may seem ironic that people would make war over an altar, but history is full of such religious squabbles, often leading to unbelievable violence. Here the issue is not so much the altar itself as what each side thinks it represents in terms of the unity of "Israel." The narrator implicitly poses the problem by distinguishing between the Western tribes as "the Israelites" and the Eastern tribes by their specific names (Reubenites, Gadites, and half-tribe of Manasseh [the other half is Western]). The implication is that the Eastern tribes are not really a part of "all Israel," that their geographical separation outside Canaan spells their social ostracizing by the "true" Israel—in a word, that living outside Canaan makes them *outsiders*. As Polzin observes, the previous section explored the relationship between those who "lived *in* Israel but were not fully *of* Israel"; chap. 22 explores the relationship between those who are "in some sense *of* Israel, but did not live *in* Israel."⁹⁸ Whenever this section was written, it does not take much imagination to see how significant this story could be for those 6th century exiles who will consider themselves Israelites (or "Jews").⁹⁹

Fortunately, warfare remains only a threat and diplomacy saves the day. The Israelites send a priest and tribal representatives of "the whole congregation of the Lord" to the Easterners and state

---

97. Hawk, *Joshua*, 223; Polzin, *Moses*, 131–32.

98. Polzin, *Moses*, 134.

99. As Gunn says, "Joshua and Judges," 112, "Israelite and Canaanite share the same fate. Neither deserves the Land." Römer, *So-Called Deuteronomic History*, 176, argues that much of Joshua 22 reflects the postexilic situation and the question of the legitimacy of being an Israelite (or now a Jew) who lives outside the land of Israel (e.g., those exiles who remained in Babylon). We will return to this in the summary and conclusion of this book.

their accusation: they see the construction of the altar as "treachery," apostasy, and "rebellion." They liken the rebellion to the infamously disastrous one at Peor (Numbers 25) and the more recent one of Achan (chap. 7). The language of their indictment echoes the warnings of the Torah: "turning away" by one element will mean disaster for the "whole congregation" (Deut 7:4; 29:19). Awkwardly, the language also reinforces the appearance of alienation by referring to the East bank territory as "your land" and the West bank as "the Lord's land." The delegation even hints that the East Jordan region is ritually "unclean" (i.e., impure; v. 19).[100] Finally, the indictment includes the charge that the Easterners' altar poses a rival to "the altar of the Lord our God" and the tabernacle (at Shiloh).[101] To the Westerners, the illegitimate altar represents disobedience to the Torah's insistence that there be only *one* sanctuary and one altar (e.g., Deut 12:2–14, especially vv. 13–14).[102] In short, the Westerners fear that an alternate altar will undermine the covenant unity affirmed in the revival service of 8:30–35.

The Easterners respond with precisely the fear of ostracism that the language of the narrator and the characters reflects. They praise Yahweh as "God of gods" (cf. Deut 10:17).[103] They claim that they have not constructed the altar as a rival to the one in Canaan; theirs is only a "copy" of that one. Their altar is not even for sacrifices. In fact, it really isn't an "altar" at all; it is more like the stones erected to commemorate the crossing of the Jordan in chap. 4, only here the marker functions to confirm that that boundary does not divide "all Israel." Instead of a divider, the marker is a "witness" to the *unity* of the two.

The Easterners' argument sounds suspiciously clever and contrived, but the Westerners accept the explanation. Yet the story does not end without some ambiguity. On the one hand, the tribes are united by faith in one God and recognition of one sanctuary; on the other hand, the narrator reports that the "Israelites" withdraw from war, and the "Reubenites and Gadites" remain in their land. The Easterners call the marker "Witness," testifying that "Yahweh is God," but the question remains as to whether or not they are truly living in "the *land* of Yahweh" (AT)! Can there be more than one legitimate holy place? Is it possible to live outside the *land* of Israel and still *be* Israel? These questions will haunt Israel to the end of the Former Prophets and beyond.

Benediction or Malediction? (Chap. 23)

The authors have punctuated the narrative with lengthy speeches delivered by Israel's leaders in critical situations. Just as Joshua began with such speeches (chap. 1), so it ends with them (chaps. 23–24). Subsequent books will have the same punctuation (e.g., 1 Samuel 12; 1

---

100. Cf. Lev 18:24–28 and Ezra 9:11.

101. The only reference to the tabernacle in Joshua. See Exodus 25–31.

102. The centralization of worship in the Jerusalem temple was a hallmark of the Deuteronomic reforms under Josiah and becomes a primary criterion of fidelity in the books of Kings.

103. Three divine names are involved here: *Yahweh*, *El*, and *Elohim*. See Excursus 4.

Kgs 2:1–9; 8:22–53). This structural element is a fitting continuation of the book of Deuteronomy, for the setting of that entire book is the imminent death of Moses and the people's imminent entrance into Canaan, and the book itself is largely a very long sermon by Moses. Now it is Joshua's turn.

Chapter 23 picks up where 13:1 left off: Joshua is old and nearing death.[104] God has given rest to Israel from all their enemies, and now Joshua assembles "all Israel"—with specific reference to leaders—and summarizes the conquest stories from the preceding chapters. God has fought for the people, and they have received their "inheritance." Here Joshua emphasizes that some nations still remain, and that God will defeat them also, but victory depends on Israel's obedience. In a sense, the editor here is saying that the declaration in 11:23—"Mission accomplished"—is qualified.[105] The speech harks back to Joshua's opening exhortation to observe "all that is written in the book of the law of Moses" (v. 6; cf. 1:7). Moreover, the conditionality of Israel's possession of the land, which had receded from prominence since chap. 1, reappears. Now, however, Joshua narrows the content of Torah observance to the prohibition of "mixing" with the remaining Canaanites by intermarriage (vv. 7, 12). The ban is specifically linked with the warning that such liaisons will lead to apostasy—the worship of other gods. Indeed, it is this outcome that makes intermarriage taboo, precisely as outlined in the Torah (Deut 7:3–4). Such intermarriages will occur again and again; indeed, King David will marry a descendant of those Geshurites who still remain (13:2; 2 Sam 3:3)! But there will be more notorious examples: Samson and Delilah (a Philistine); Solomon and his many foreign wives;[106] Ahab and Jezebel (a Phoenician, see below), and such marriages almost certainly stand behind the author's concern in chap. 23. As we saw at the outset with the Jericho massacre, the danger *for Israel* that would result from intermarriage stands behind the various references to genocide.

The orthodox extremism that demands "ethnic cleansing" is grounded in both theology and ethics, strange as it may seem. Theologically, the rigidity derives from an uncompromising absolute allegiance to God as the Lord of the covenant; "pledging allegiance" to any other god will lead to disaster (see Excursus 1). Ethically, the rigidity derives from an insistence on the correlation of *who* God is with *Israel's* communal identity and *how* the people ought to live—forgetting who God is will lead to corporate amnesia and social injustice. The story of God's liberating Israel from slavery is fundamental to an ethos that insures justice for the aliens within Israel (and widows and orphans; e.g., Exod 22:21–22). Marrying someone who does not share this story can lead to a loss of identity and therefore the loss of justice.

---

104. A deathbed setting is also intrinsic to the delivering of personal testaments, including blessings and curses—e.g., with Jacob, Genesis 27; and Genesis 48–49.

105. For similar qualifications, see the discussion of Judges 1–2.

106. We will look at some of the historical and political dimensions of such royal marriages in 1 Kings 11.

We can anticipate one infamous intermarriage as an example—Ahab and Jezebel. King Ahab married the Phoenician Jezebel, who (quite understandably) wanted her own sanctuary devoted to her own god, Baal (1 Kgs 16:29-32). She and Ahab also wanted a particular vineyard, and she orchestrated the murder of the vineyard owner in order to get it (1 Kings 21). Here to the orthodox is a perfect example of what could happen when the Israelites intermarry. If one's allegiance is not to God, whose covenant demands "justice and only justice" (Deut 16:20), then the primary sanction for ethical behavior is lost. So, we might say, relativism ("one god is as good as another") leads to depravity. And since God will *punish* injustice, as the covenant states and the prophets repeatedly warned, intermarriage became a threat to national security. In hindsight (the Exile), warnings like Joshua 23 may have been an editor's way of saying "I told you so"! Clearly the extreme of "ethnic cleansing" is morally reprehensible, but the other side of the spectrum has its own dangers, a wishy-washy pluralism that undermines the ethos of the community and breeds injustice and national disaster. As we read through the Former Prophets we must recognize the tension between the orthodox and the heterodox positions, acknowledging that both have strengths and weaknesses, and perhaps the way of Torah lies somewhere in between.

To return to Joshua's speech, worshipping other gods is the most serious theological expression of the failure to "love" God. Undivided allegiance to God will determine whether or not God will complete the conquest of those remaining nations. If, instead, those nations remain, then "they shall be a snare and a trap for you, a scourge on your sides, and thorns in your eyes, until you perish from this good land that the Lord your God has given you" (v. 13). This warning foreshadows the entire narrative that follows.

Joshua is posing the alternative possibilities of blessing or curse, much as Moses does in Deuteronomy 28-29 (cf. also 31:1-6). Israel now enjoys the blessing—God has done "all the good things" that God had promised. Only the future—and Israel's obedience or disobedience—will determine whether or not blessing or curse awaits. Joshua's dire warning is not oracular, however; that is, it does not spell inevitable doom. Instead, the warning is prophetic, not, again, in the sense of prediction, but in the sense of a critical challenge. We, at least, know that the warning proved to be all too accurate. But the characters in the story do not know that. They are not prescient. They are called to be responsible. It is within their ability to know and keep God's words (Deut 30:11-14).

Reprise (Chap. 24)

The concluding chapter serves as an expansion of Joshua's preceding speech. One critical addition, however, is that the people now face a decision of how to respond to Joshua's speech by swearing an oath. In short, chap. 24 constitutes a covenant renewal ceremony, similar to but more extensive than the one in 8:30-35. Both are fulfillments of prescriptions in the Torah (Deut 27:1-13).

The ceremony here, of course, is more definitive than the previous one because now Israel stands in possession of the land (despite exceptions). In a sense, Joshua 24 represents a formal completion of the covenant process that began in Deuteronomy, where the people's assent is reported but not explicitly spoken, as it is here in vv. 16–21 (cf. Deut 26:16–18). What better way to conclude the book that traces Israel's settlement in the land of promise than to have Israel reaffirm *its* promise of allegiance to the God who gave the land?

Joshua emphasizes the significance of the moment by telling Israel's story beginning with the Ancestral Saga of Genesis. Such a recitation of the suzerain's gracious acts often stood at the beginning of a political treaty, demonstrating why the vassal owed allegiance to the suzerain. Here the story stretches back to the ancestor Terah (Abraham's father) who lived "beyond the Jordan" (Gen 11:27–32). Since 1:6, this is the only time in the book where the settlement in the land appears within such a broad horizon. The perspective provides two sharp contrasts with Joshua's audience: not only did Terah live outside the land of Canaan; he also "served other gods." Joshua then summarizes the stories of the Ancestors, the Exodus (dwelling on the defeat of Pharaoh's troops at "the Great Sea"), a brief mention of the wilderness period, the defeat of hostile Amorites "on the other side of the Jordan" (i.e., the East), along with Balak of Moab, concluding with the victory over the Canaanites represented only by Jericho.

Now comes the hour of decision, as it were. The center of covenant theology appears at the nexus of historical recitation and communal response. The connection (v. 14) seems deceptively simple (one word in Hebrew: *weʿatta*, "and now"), but what follows will be determinative for Israel's future, so the appropriate translation is "now *therefore*" (cf. Exod 19:5). "Now therefore revere the Lord and serve him in sincerity and in faithfulness; put away the gods that your ancestors served beyond the River and in Egypt, and serve the Lord." It is remarkable that the phrase "(other) gods" appears nowhere else in Joshua other than 23:7; 16 and here (vv. 2, 14–16, 20, 23 [the last two "foreign gods"]). The prohibition against serving other gods constitutes the first of the Ten Commandments (Exod 20:3; Deut 5:7) and appears repeatedly in the Torah (e.g., Deut 6:14; 7:4). The prohibition is the negative side of the central, positive commandment of Israel's covenant with God—"love the Lord your God." Again Joshua poses the alternative in terms of Israel's ancestors: "choose this day whom you shall serve," the gods of the ancestors or Yahweh (v. 15). In effect, the choice will either reverse Israel's entire history as a people, or insure their *future* as a people—i.e., as the people of God. By implication, serving other gods (here including "the gods of the Amorites") will have the result already outlined in 23:15–16: Israel once again will dwell "beyond the River," "beyond the Euphrates." Israel will end up where their ancestors began. The Psalmist will say "by the rivers of Babylon" (Ps 137:8).[107]

---

107. That is where we will begin the summary and conclusion.

Who are these other gods? The gods of Terah (Abraham's father) are never mentioned in Genesis. One could read the brief notices about him as implying that Israel's God was his god, but historically that would not be possible. Presumably the gods in mind in Joshua 24 would be the gods common to the area of ancient Mesopotamia ("Ur of the Chaldeans," Gen 11:28). The implication that the Israelites of Joshua's time still serve these gods (24:14) is inexplicable in terms of the rest of the book. The gods of Canaan, on the other hand, are well known to us from both the Hebrew Bible and extra-biblical sources. Since these gods are only hypothetical attractions here, and become major figures in the editorial framework of Judges, we will postpone discussing them until then (Excursus 4).

The people now respond to the recitation with a little summary of their own, and then a resounding acclamation: "we also will serve the Lord, for he is our God." The ceremony would be neat and tidy if we could move on to v. 25 and the making of a covenant document, but a jolting passage intervenes. Joshua's first response to the people's acclamation is not to say, "We've got a deal," but more like "You don't really know what you're saying!" "You *cannot* serve the Lord," he says, because God is "jealous," unforgiving, and punitive. The denial seems to contradict the notion that, in fact, Israel *can* serve God—that, as the Torah puts it, God's word is "in your mouth, and in your heart, to do it" (Deut 30:14, AT). It is possible that the author of v. 19 has in mind the people's subsequent history, which proved all too confirming of Joshua's warning.[108] However, we can more likely take the warning to refer not to incapability of the will but as a hyperbolic emphasis on the critical nature of the decision and the severe consequences of failure.

Undaunted by Joshua's severity, the people persist in their vow: "Yahweh our God we will serve, and him we will obey" (v. 24, AT; cf. Exod 24:7). With this, Joshua proceeds to the actual writing of a covenant, and writes the words "in the book of the law of God."[109] In compliance with the Torah's instructions, he erects a large stone "in the sanctuary[110] of the Lord," and declares that the stone will function as a "witness." The stone witnesses both to "the words of the Lord," apparently referring to Joshua's speech as *prophetic* speech (v. 2; "thus says the Lord"), and to the people's vow. Disobedience will not go unnoticed.

Now, at Joshua's death, the narrator finally grants him the exalted status

---

108. The prophets often portray Israel's stubbornness in a similar way; cf. 2 Kgs 17:13–14; Isa 6:9–10.

109. It is not clear whether the reference is to a separate covenant document or to an addendum to the book of the law of Moses; it is probably the former, however, given Deut 12:32.

110. This is the only occurrence of the word *miqdash* in the book of Joshua. It would be anachronistic to refer to a structure like a temple. The first such structure was at Shiloh (1 Sam 1:3; 3:3). Here the word may simply have its etymological meaning—"place of holiness," or "sacred place." There are deep pitfalls in this passage for the later narrative, for sacred trees and stone pillars are anathema to the Deuteronomic school (cf. Deut 16:21–22), commemorative stones like those in the Jordan notwithstanding. The issue does not become explicit until later, but here we can note again the editorial refusal to delete embarrassing details.

formerly reserved for Moses: he is "the servant of the Lord" (v. 29; cf. 1:1). Tying the book to the end of Genesis, the Israelites bury the bones of Joseph at Shechem in the plot that Jacob had bought (Gen 35:18–20; 50:25). Jacob (= "Israel") has now come home to the land of the promise. Thus the editors have stitched together the Former Prophets and the Pentateuch. As the book of the Torah of Moses ends with Moses' death outside the land, the first book of the Former Prophets ends with Joshua's death inside the land. "Israel served the Lord all the days of Joshua, and all the days of the elders who outlived Joshua and had known all the work that the Lord did for Israel" (v. 31). Yet the book ends with an implied question: will they *still* serve the Lord in the days to come?

TWO

Judges

THE CANONICAL MOVEMENT FROM the book of Joshua to Judges and then to Ruth and Samuel suggests the political developments that preoccupy the books: from a unified people under a single leader (Joshua), to increasingly disintegrated tribal relations and no single leader (Judges), to another single leader (Samuel and then King Saul) and (temporarily) social cohesion (1 Samuel).[1] Historically, the tribal period was probably far more ambiguous sociologically.[2] The book consists of stories of "judges" and their exploits, many of which no doubt existed independently prior to being collected and arranged, certainly prior to the first Deuteronomic edition (the latter being quite limited).[3] It would be preferable to translate the word for "judge" here as simply "leader," or perhaps "chieftain," for they are primarily military or political figures.[4] Seen individually, and without the theological framing (see below), many of the stories also exhibit traits of epic literature in which heroes (and, here, heroines) are "social bandits" who fight for the oppressed against the powerful, much like the legendary Robin Hood.[5] These include Othniel, Ehud, Deborah, Gideon, Abimelech, and Jepthah (along with other "minor" judges)—most of chapters 3–12. A second collection of stories that exhibit much less editing appears in chapters 13–21—the stories of Samson and several other less-well-known stories.

Much of the editing of the original stories in 3:7—13:1 consists of theologi-

---

1. Even Ruth, with its apparent detachment from political matters, ties in with the story of David in the end—indeed, David has the last word (4:22).

2. See McNutt, *Reconstructing*, 75: "Nowhere in this material . . . do we find an explanation of how the notion of tribe was conceptualized, what the composition of tribes was, how the tribes related to one another on economic and political levels, or the structure of society in general."

3. See Campbell and O'Brien, *Unfolding*, 165–214; Römer, *So-Called Deuteronomistic History*, 91; Niditch, *Judges*, 3–13.

4. Niditch, *Judges*, 1–3, notes that "judging" involves political decision making (note especially 4:4–5). The root word (*shofet*) figures prominently also in the stories in 1 Samuel of Israel's move from "judges" to a king. See McNutt, *Reconstructing*, 98–100, for sociological analysis.

5. Niditch, *Judges*, 3. Sometimes the contemporary term "tribal war lord" would seem to apply.

cal frames that interpret the stories and, as we shall see, attempt to induce the *reader* to frame them accordingly. The frames largely follow a paradigmatic circle of sin, punishment, cry for help, and deliverance, spelled out initially in chap. 2. The stories in chaps. 17–21 apparently needed little editorial comment, quite capable themselves in revealing the horrors of chaos and anarchy. However, there is one motif that recurs four times and concludes the book: "In those days there was no king in Israel; all the people did what was right in their own eyes" (21:25; cf. 17:5; 18:1; 19:1). Scholars disagree about the meaning of this statement. Is it a libertarian's dream or a royalist's nightmare? Similarly, does the anarchy in the concluding chapters point to the need for monarchy? The answer may turn on one's view of the monarchy itself, which, as we shall see, involved its own deep tensions and ambiguities, including civil war.[6] One thing that it is safe to say is that by the end of the book no deliverer has appeared who is able to provide permanent security from external foes or unity within various tribal and kinship groups. In a sense then, the book of Judges ends without a judge, setting the stage for Samuel.[7]

Some scholars argue that, overall, Judges represents a polemic against the Northern tribes, who prove incapable of governing themselves, and, more particularly, against the future figure of Saul, Israel's first king, who will trace his lineage back to the town of Gibeah and the tribe of Benjamin, both of whom are responsible for the gang-rape story in ch.19 (cf. 1 Sam 9:1; 10:26). Presumably, such a polemic would point toward Judah and the Davidic monarchy as the legitimate rulers, thus supporting the national revival of King Josiah. Similarly, the shrines of the later Northern realm, Dan and Bethel, come under suspicion (Judges 18; 21:15–24).[8] On the other hand, some scholars argue for an underlying collection of "deliverer stories" that "was *not* used by the royal scribes at the time of Josiah" precisely because they were Northern heroes.[9] In fact, Saul will later unite the tribes in defeating the Ammonites, and thereby "deliver" the town of Jabesh-gilead, which could suggest that the Judges stories ultimately serve to promote him![10] Whether or not we can infer an ideological agenda behind the stories, both individually and collectively they have an integrity of their own.

How the West Was Lost (1:1—3:11)

In Joshua, an introduction "laid down the law" that was to be followed without deviation, but the ensuing stories in various ways showed how the law was

---

6. Cf. Linafelt, *Ruth*, 80, and see the conclusion to our discussion of Ruth.

7. The Christian canon has placed Ruth after Judges because it is set "in the days when the judges ruled" (1:1).

8. Sweeney, *King Josiah of Judah*, 112–13, 120–21, 123, 174; see 1 Kgs 12:25–33.

9. Römer, *So-Called Deuteronomic History*, 91 (italics added), 137–38. He argues that the exilic Deuteronomists changed the stories into the cyclical sin/punishment episodes, and most of chaps. 13–21 are "post-Deuteronomistic," as late as the Hellenistic period. Thus the scholarly dating of some of the stories ranges from about 1250 BCE to 400 BCE!

10. See the discussion of 1 Samuel 11 below.

not followed and yet Israel survived, indeed, prospered. In Judges, there are two introductory units, one showing the increasing failure of Israel to take all of the land (ch.1) and the other outlining Israel's failure to follow God completely (2:1—3:6). Part of the second introduction (2:11–19) explains *why* the conquest was incomplete and leads us to expect a series of hero stories that follow a predictable (indeed, predicted) good-guys-bad-guys scenario, but the ensuing stories in various ways show increasingly ambiguous circumstances and heroes of questionable character. The cycle of stories then begins at 3:7.

The opening incidents sound a lot like the military victories reported in the book of Joshua (including the "ban" [ḥerem], 1:7). In fact, this section is a retelling of numerous incidents first reported in Joshua 14–19, but here with a bias toward Judah and against the Northern tribes.[11] The opening scene introduces a note of horror that foreshadows much of the book: Judah (the tribe) defeats ten thousand Canaanites and mutilates their king, cutting off his fingers and big toes (what *he* had done to *his* enemies; cf. 7:25; 8:6). Readers might as well steel themselves now. In the following chapters, the atrocities will only increase: beheadings, a woman and her father burned alive, whipping with thorns and briers, gang rape, impaled victims, more dismemberment, and a man's skull split open with a tent peg. A rough count of casualties cited in the book (and clearly hyperbolic) adds up to about one hundred fifty thousand.[12] Here again, Israel's historians did not whitewash their past. The grisly brutality is hardly limited to ancient peoples.

> *Consider the report of a Vietnam veteran quoted in* Time Magazine, *24 May 2004, p. 50: "'I knew guys in Vietnam with dried ears and penises hanging from their dog tags.'" The article concerned the current warfare in Iraq. In 2004 Islamic guerillas assaulted a convoy of American support staff, killed the occupants of the vehicle and set it afire; then a mob pulled out the charred bodies and dismembered them. In May, 2004, it was disclosed that American troops had systematically tortured, sexually assaulted, and even murdered Iraqi prisoners in the Abu Ghraib camp. In response, an Islamic terrorist group beheaded a civilian American captive and published a video of the execution.*

Next Judah appears to take the city of Jerusalem; the settlement of Debir introduces us to the first "judge," Othniel (1:11–15; 3:7–11); Judah takes Gaza and Ashkelon. But already by v. 19 it is clear (as it already was in Joshua) that victory is by no means total, for some of the inhabitants have superior weaponry (iron chariots), a factor that will continue to frustrate Israelite hopes of domination and security. Against such armament,

---

11. For example, the incident involving Caleb and Othniel in Judg 1:11–15 is a duplicate of Josh 15:13–19. On the other hand, there are no repeats of prominent stories like Jericho or Ai.

12. As we have noted before, according to McNutt, *Reconstructing*, 110, "the population for the whole of Palestine . . . in 1000 BCE has been estimated at about 150,000," remarkably identical to the sum of casualties cited here!

Judah cannot complete the campaign even though God is with them! Indeed, previously God had promised victory *despite* those chariots (Josh 17:18), so their failure here is one of trust in God's empowerment over against human power. In retrospect, were the Israelite warriors as assertive as was Achsah in acquiring springs in her land (despite *her* status as acquisition; 1:11–15), they would have fared much better. Similarly, Jebusites remain in Jerusalem (due to the fault of Benjamin).[13]

When the story turns to the northern campaigns (v. 21), an initial victory against Bethel echoes the story of Jericho in Joshua, complete with an informer who is spared (as there, contrary to the law of holy war in Deut 20:16–18). But here the Canaanite informer goes on to build a new city, thus preserving Canaanite culture.[14] Then the incomplete conquests reach a crescendo in vv. 27–36. The concluding notice about the Danites even shows them *retreating* in the face of Amorite pressure. Everywhere pockets of "Canaanites" remain, and the Israelites "live among" them (vv. 27, 29–30, 32–33, 35), albeit sometimes as taskmasters. Overall, it's as if many of the Canaanites resemble the Gibeonites but without a ruse or covenant (Josh 9:7, 16, 22; 9:10). As in Joshua, this blending of Israelite and Canaanite has ominous implications if the warnings of Deuteronomy and Joshua are recalled (Deut 7:1–6; Josh 23:1–14). As in Joshua, then, we find that the sweeping claim to have conquered "all the land" is far from accurate. The *reason* for the incomplete occupation was not addressed in the book of Joshua, except for the implication that Israel was militarily incapable (e.g., 13:13; 15:63; 16:10; except for 23:13, on which see below). A similar implication seems to govern Judges 1. Here there is no explicit theological criticism, as there will be later. Israel's successes and failures simply reflect the way political and military power shifts back and forth.[15]

Chapter 2 consists of three units, the appearance of "the angel of the Lord," a notice of Joshua's death along with his whole generation, and then an overt editorial statement that provides a theological prologue for the rest of the book. The author of the first unit offers a new answer to the question of the incomplete conquest. The angel appears to the people, recounts God's gracious acts and covenant with them, and then roundly condemns them for not keeping their part. Near the beginning of Joshua, such a divine messenger came to fight

---

13. Gunn and Fewell, *Narrative*, 159–62. The opposite reaction to armor will appear in the courage of David and his trust in God over against Goliath's superior weaponry (2 Samuel 17).

14. See Webb, *Book of Judges*, 94–95, who notes the contrast with the "lord of Bezeq's" execution in vv. 4–7.

15. Niditch, *Judges*, 42–43, suggests that chap. 1 and chaps. 17–21 represent the "humanist" voice, "whose central theme is that power comes and goes, for the mighty fall" (39). In Deuteronomy 7, the most important Torah statement about the occupation, Moses says that God will deliberately leave some of the nations in Canaan, and Israel will only gradually eliminate them, "otherwise the wild animals would become too numerous for you" (v. 22; cf. Exod 23:29). The strategy is ambiguous. (Does it mean that there would otherwise be fewer Canaanites and more Israelites for the beasts to eat, or that fewer Canaanites would mean fewer hunters to keep the beasts in check?) Nevertheless, this part of God's plan is ignored by the authors of Judg 2:3, 21–23 and 3:1–2.

for Israel (Josh 5:13–15);[16] here the messenger has a message of accusation and warning. The Israelites have done what they ought not to have done, namely, covenanted with the Canaanites, and they have not done what they ought to have done, destroyed the Canaanite's altars (v. 2; Deut 7:1–5). The agreement to show "kindness" to the Bethel informant (2:24) is covenantal, albeit with only one person, but nothing has been said about altars. Nevertheless, because of Israel's disobedience, God will not drive out the Canaanites completely; they will continue to be Israel's enemies and their gods a snare (2:3). The Deuteronomic editor already anticipated this situation in Joshua's farewell speech (Josh 23:13). The juxtaposition of 2:1–5 with chap. 1 is awkward, projecting the incomplete occupation into the future as if it has not already happened, and on grounds of largely unsubstantiated accusations. In context, however, this unit seems to comment on the religious *consequences* of the incomplete occupation, consequences that will produce a vicious cycle: Canaanites "among them," therefore Canaanite altars among them, therefore God's judgment, therefore continued Canaanite opposition. No wonder the unit ends with the people weeping.

The next passage (2:6–10) provides a transition from the generation of Joshua to a new generation, harking back to the time before Joshua's death. His generation had seen "the great work that God had done," but, inexplicably, the generation after him knows nothing of it. Somehow the "elders" (v. 7) have failed to inculcate the faith in their children, producing a fatal communal amnesia that takes the place of historical memory, the transmission of which is the responsibility of worship.[17] The generational transition here echoes the language used at the beginning of Exodus (Exod 1:6–8), but ironically there Israel's troubles began because the *Pharaoh* did not know *Joseph*. Israel's ignorance here does not bode well for covenant loyalty.

> *From the very start of European settlement in New England, colonists were warned that God was disappointed in them, so they should improve not just their individual ethics but their collective social behavior. Indeed, only six years after the Arbella brought John Winthrop to Massachusetts, a Congregationalist minister was lamenting the lost golden age of the colony, asking parishioners, "Are all [God]s kindnesses forgotten? all your promises forgotten?"*[18]

The next unit (2:11–23) presents a foreshadowing of repetitive disobedience that contrasts with the preceding generation's faithfulness. The stories of the judges that begin in 3:7 will generally follow the pattern outlined here: Israel does

---

16. Josh 5:13–15. Note the presence of the angel also in Exod 23:20, 23 with reference to the occupation of the land.

17. See Ps 78:1–8; Josh 4:4–7; Exod 12:24–27; Deut 5:15; 8:2; 16:3, 12; 24:18, etc.

18. Fallows, "How America Can Rise Again," 41–42 (brackets original), citing Sacvan Bercovitch, *American Jeremiad*. The reference to John Winthrop is to his classic sermon quoted at the outset of the chapter on Joshua. The word *Jeremiad* refers to a fiery, judgmental sermon, and comes from the name of the biblical prophet Jeremiah.

evil (sometimes specifically by worshipping the Canaanite gods, "Baal and the Astartes," v. 13, see further below), God is incensed and punishes them by means of enemies, but then sends a deliverer who rescues them, but Israel does not "listen" to the judges (implicitly to their teaching), instead returning to apostasy. In the following stories, Israel will "cry" to God, but here God's deliverance comes simply out of compassionate hearing of their "groaning" under persecution and oppression. The divine "pity" and Israel's suffering closely resemble the situation in which God initiated freeing Israel's ancestors from Egyptian oppression (cf. Exod 2:24; 3:9). *Without* the framework here, each story would be something like a "mini-exodus" of liberation from oppressors, perhaps the original intent. *With* the framework, however, the narrator insists that the people's oppression is punishment for sin.

Here Israel's disobedience also leads to an explicit reason why nations remain: it is *God's* doing. This reason expands on the "snare" of 2:3. The Canaanites in their midst will be a "test" of Israel's obedience, a test that they will most often fail (2:22–23). In fact, here the test is also *retrospective* to the time of *Joshua*, and why *he* could not attain complete victory.[19] In a sense, there is also a test for God, who faces the dilemma of reconciling the covenantal promise to give the land to Israel with the punitive threat of an incomplete conquest—in effect, producing a tension between grace and justice. The resolution here in 2:21–23 presents a kind of compromise expressed in the incomplete occupation of the land—it is because of Israel's persistent evil. Thus "the non-fulfillment of the promise is acknowledged but Yahweh is vindicated."[20] One way to solve the problem of an unfulfilled promise is to redefine the promise.[21]

Before the stories of the judges begin, yet another transition passage (3:1–6) reiterates the nations who are left, Israel's intermarriage with them and worshipping their gods. The unit also suggests a third reason for the lingering presence of enemies: each generation has to learn the art of warfare, and for that, enemies are required. It's as if the remaining enemies serve as the "boot camp" for neophyte Israelite warriors.[22] Ignoring this reason, vv. 4–6 reiterate the "test" explanation and emphasize again Israel's disobedience, now in terms of the kind of intermarriage that was expressly forbidden in the Torah (v. 6; cf. Exod 34:6; Deut 7:3).

In short, the editorial interpretations of the failed conquest in 2:1—3:6 suggest that Joshua's warnings at the end of his life were all too prescient: Israel has succumbed to Canaanite intermarriage and worshipping other gods (cf. Josh 23:7, 12, 16; 24:14–28). The effect is to make the following stories illustrations of the theological framework in which everything turns on covenant disobedience, divine punishment, and divine grace. In the first story (3:7–11),

---

19. Note the pluperfect tense in the NRSV of v. 23.

20. Webb, *Book of Judges*, 122; also 105, 114–16.

21. Cf. Weinfeld, *Deuteronomic School*, 22, who notes that when one "word of God" fails for the Deuteronomist, "then a second word of God appears."

22. Niditch, *Judges*, 55, sees the training explanation as typical of "the bardic ideology of war."

Israel does evil by worshipping other gods, God gives Israel over to "serve" the enemy king, Israel cries for help, God sends Othniel to rescue them, and there is rest for forty years. Stripped of theological commentary, there is little *to* the story other than that simple sequence. Though subsequent stories will be far more detailed, the editor's interest *here* is not primarily in presenting an accurate historical report of the events; rather, he wants to reiterate how in every case his theological *interpretation* reveals each incident to be typical rather than distinctive. For the reader, the result could be a plodding predictability were it not for the brilliantly colorful characters and plots. The cumulative effect, however, will be that the whole book raises over and over again a central theme of the Former Prophets: disobedience brings punishment and defeat, saved only by grace. But will that grace always continue?

The typology outlined in 2:11–19 and illustrated in the Othniel story shows how "editorial" theology has prejudiced the "news" of the reporter. This heavy-handed judgment is unprecedented in the Former Prophets.[23] To be sure, the opening chapter of Joshua laid out the ideal of covenant obedience, and the following stories illustrated how difficult it was to enact that ideal. There if the editors spoke, it was largely through the mouths of their characters (e.g., 1:1–9; chaps. 23–24), with occasional brief editorial commentary (4:14; 21:43–45).

But here the editor is speaking directly to the reader—and in advance of the events—to show *how to interpret* the following stories. Events that apparently could stand on their own—political and military oppression, liberation—here are *caused* by religious deviance, as the author understands it. Thus God is really the one in control, using Israel's enemies as "the rod of my anger," as Isaiah will later describe the Assyrians (Isa 10:5). The theology here is by no means unique to Israel. In the 9th century Mesha Inscription, the Moabite king Mesha claims that Omri, the king of Israel, "oppressed Moab for many days because Kemosh [the god of Moab] was angry with his country," but then Kemosh appointed Mesha to overthrow Israel.[24] (Turn about is fair play!) The editors of Judges have simply imposed this same theology as the framework of the individual stories—indeed, *it undergirds the entire Former Prophets*. In the prophetic tradition, this understanding of causation extends beyond military defeats to famine, drought, and disease (e.g., Amos 4:6–11), and, of course, it is part of the curses of covenantal theology (Deuteronomy 28; see also Excursus 1). Apostasy is the lead cause, and lies at the heart of the editor's entire historiography. "Doing evil in the sight of the Lord" by "worshipping the Baals" (2:11), expressed in various ways, will mark the Former Prophets from here to the end. The kings of later Israel will be judged by this criterion, and almost all found lack-

---

23. See the comments of Gottwald, *Politics*, 33–34 on the "metadiscourse" of the moralizing editor versus the "discourse" of the historical narrative especially regarding what appears as true or false Yahweh worship.

24. For the inscription, see *ANET*, 320–21 ("The Moabite Stone") or, more recently, Dearman, *Studies*, 97–98. The inscription presents the Moabite perspective on the events reported in 2 Kings 3.

ing. For the southern kingdom of Judah, the impetus will come from Solomon who "does evil" by marrying numerous "foreign" wives and worshipping their gods (1 Kgs 11:1–8); for the northern kingdom of Israel, the culprit will be Jeroboam, who constructs "golden calves" and establishes illicit sanctuaries and sacramental objects. Eventually, the fate of Judah will be the same as that of Israel: "sin . . . [will] cut it off and destroy it from the face of the earth" (1 Kgs 13:33–34). Or, at least, the time will come when it will *seem* that such complete annihilation has occurred.

Excursus 3: Yahweh and the "Other Gods"

In the framework of the Judges stories, then, we are encountering for the first time the programmatic editorial *evaluation* of the characters *addressed to the reader* as an explicit moral lesson, stated in terms of covenant obedience or disobedience. Such a pattern will reappear in the books of Kings and frame the accounts of each king's tenure. As we noted in the Introduction, much of the language and theology of such editorial "moralizing" reflects the ideology of the Deuteronomic "movement" that led to religious reforms hundreds of years after the time of the judges. In particular, the reforms under Hezekiah (2 Kgs 18:1–8) and Josiah (2 Kgs 22:4–24) banned numerous practices that before were considered acceptable (see below).[25] An analogy would be the way Luther banned indulgences as part of the Protestant Reformation. Much of the book of Deuteronomy was produced by the same groups that promoted the reforms. In other words, major portions of Deuteronomy were composed around the time of the reforms rather than literally spoken by Moses some six hundred years before. Thus the book and the reforms function together as legislation and implementation, commandment and obedience. To use again an analogy from American history, it would be as if the New Deal reforms of Franklin Roosevelt were based on legislation supposedly composed by George Washington. What Moses has ordered (on divine authority), Hezekiah and Josiah will (finally) enact, many previous kings being negligent or, worse, deliberately lawless.

The connection between command and obedience functions within the Former Prophets much as the connection between prophecy and fulfillment: a prediction is made at one point and later on it comes true. For example, after Joshua destroyed Jericho, he placed a curse on anyone who would rebuild it, saying that it would be "at the cost of his firstborn" (Josh 6:26). Sure enough, when a man named Hiel rebuilds the city, some five hundred years later, he sacrifices his firstborn son as a macabre cornerstone dedication (1 Kgs 16:34). The prophecy is fulfilled (albeit with a twist).[26] Indeed, the editor says so explicitly: "according to the word of the Lord,

---

25. For a brief overview, see Smith, *Memoirs*, 21–25, 37–38, who argues that the various practices (described in 2 Kgs 21:3–7) became heterodox only under the reforms of Hezekiah and Josiah (roughly 700–600 BCE).

26. The fulfillment assumes that the builder *sacrifices* his firstborn, which is not apparent in Josh 6:26.

which he spoke by Joshua son of Nun." Similarly, in Deuteronomy Moses forbids the construction of a "sacred pole" (or ʾasherah; Deut 16:21–22) and Josiah, having dusted off his Torah (as it were), obediently destroys the ʾasherah that disobedient kings have placed in the temple (2 Kgs 22:10–13; 23:6). The law is followed. This reciprocity of promise and fulfillment appears even more explicitly in the books of Kings. It is fair to say that *the* most important commandment to obey is the worship of Yahweh alone, thereby *not* worshipping "other gods" (Deut 7:1–4).[27] Similarly, the most serious prediction is the divine curse that will follow upon disobedience to that commandment—national disaster (Deut 7:4). Together the combination of commandment and implementation, prophecy and fulfillment, provide the foundation for how the Deuteronomic editors interpret Israel's history. That interpretation is nowhere more explicit than in the introduction and framework of the book of Judges.

While it is not our purpose to explore fully the historical situation that may lie behind the text of the Former Prophets, we cannot adequately read the narrative without appreciating the editorial perspective. The introduction emphasizes Israel's disobedience by referring repeatedly to the worship of "other gods" (2:11, 17, 19; 3:6), sometimes naming the god Baal and goddesses Astarte or Asherah (2:11, 13; 3:7). However, *outside* the editorial introduction and framing of individual stories (see above and 8:33; 10:6, 10), there is only one clear incident of worshipping "other gods" in the entire book[28] Most scholars would agree that the picture of rampant and perpetual worship of "other gods" is anachronistic, and, in fact, may well be an exaggeration even for the editor's own time. In particular, conflicts over the worship of Baal did not become significant until the 9th century, and even then probably reflect the religious affiliations of the royal court more than the ordinary Israelite. The same can be said for making covenants and intermarrying with Canaanites (2:2; 3:5); although that certainly happens in Judges[29] it does not really become a serious theological issue until the time of Solomon (cf. 1 Kings 11) and especially the marriage of Ahab and Jezebel, who was a fervent Baal devotee (1 Kings 17—2 Kings 10).[30] It is as if, in editing the stories in Judges, the editor had in mind the example of that notorious couple.

Here we will simply sketch the religious background of the dominant divine figure in the narrative, Yahweh, the God of Israel, with respect to the "other gods" of Canaan, focusing on three: Yahweh and El, Yahweh and Baal, and Yahweh and Asherah.[31]

Yahweh and El: Much of our knowledge about those "other gods" comes from a remarkable collection of cuneiform texts from the late fourteenth century BCE from the ancient city of Ugarit, near the Mediterranean coast in what is

---

27. See Excursus 1.

28. Cf. Tigay, "Israelite Religion," 194 n. 122: "In contrast to the recurrent national polytheism of the framework, the older parts of Judges mention the worship of other gods only in 5:18a [*sic*, read 5:8a]; 6:25–32 (the latter limited to one town); and perhaps 9:4, 46 (in Shechem)."

29. Gideon and Samson marry Canaanites. The repeated comment that the "Canaanites lived among them" in chap. 1 may imply intermarriage more generally.

30. We will look more closely at the intermarriage prohibition when we get to 1 Kings 11.

31. On the following, see Smith, *Early History*; Smith, *Origins*, especially chap. 7; *Memoirs*, 54–56, 106–23; and the excellent survey in Kugel, *How to Read the Bible*, 417–35: "The Other Gods of Canaan"; Miller, *Israelite Religion*, chap. 1 ("God and the Gods") and chap. 2, especially the sections on orthodoxy/heterodoxy; Miller, *Ten Commandments*, 19–47; Gottwald, *Politics*, 209; McBride, "The Essence of Orthodoxy," especially 134, 145–47.

now Syria.[32] We do not see the kind of mythological stories about the gods in the Hebrew Bible that we see in Ugaritic literature,[33] and there are significant differences in *how* the gods are portrayed.[34] Nevertheless, there are many similarities between Yahweh and El.

In Ugaritic mythology, El is the head of the pantheon and presides over the "council" of gods.[35] The word *'el* can mean simply "god" or it can be a personal name, El (something like our "god" and "God"). There is no doubt that ancient Israelites worshipped El. Often El was not only the "high god" of mythology but also the personal god of a family, referred to as "the God of my father," who cared for and guided the family.[36] Indeed, the very name "Israel" is an El name ("El reigns").[37] Abraham uses the title "El Elyon" (Gen 14:22; "God Most High") and Jacob names the place where he encounters God "Beth-El," i.e., "House of El." Even Yahweh uses the self-referent of "El Shadday" (Gen 35:11; traditionally "God Almighty" but probably "God of the Mountain"). *Translating* the word *'el* as "God," rather than *transliterating* it as "El" tends to hide the personality behind the title, thereby obscuring the fact that El and Yahweh originally were two separate deities. (The obfuscation resembles that with rendering the Hebrew consonants YHWH as "the Lord" instead of "Yahweh"—see the Glossary). Thus, early in Israel's history, some Israelites worshipped the "other god" El, even though later generations would not remember El's original independence.

Yahweh's self-referent as El becomes developmentally significant in the Exodus story. There Yahweh says explicitly that *before* the Exodus he was known *only* as El Shadday (6:2–3), even though the name Yahweh obviously appears repeatedly in the book of Genesis. This text seems to reflect a process in which the separate deities El and Yahweh merged into one, with some group who experienced the Exodus being behind the merger.[38] However, it is

32. The texts include myths, epics, and liturgical and administrative documents. Especially interesting to biblical scholars have been the myths about Baal, El, Anat, and Athirat (Asherah), along with the gods of chaos, Yam (Sea) and Mot (Death). There are also epic texts about figures named Keret and Aqhat. While these texts are enormously informative, one must remember that they predate most biblical texts by at least four hundred years. How the Ugaritic theology and anthropology might have developed in that time we cannot know.

33. Cf. Pardee, *Ritual and Cult,* 236: "there are only traces of polytheism visible in the Hebrew Bible in contrast with the full-blown Ugaritic polytheism." For some major exceptions, see below on Psalm 82 and Deut 32:8–9; see also Gen 6:1–4. Also the cosmic battle between Yahweh and the chaos monster sometimes approaches mythical status (as conflict between divine powers); cf. Isa 27:1; 51:9. However, Israel almost always adapts such myth to apply it to Israel's history (e.g., Isa 51:10–11 where the defeat of the sea dragon results in Israel's release from exile; see further in the discussion of 1 Kings 19).

34. For example, there are Ugaritic stories about Baal having sexual intercourse with a cow, and El getting falling-down drunk at a party. However, Wyatt, *Religious Texts,* 405 warns that those who see El's behavior here as shameful "import an alien ethic (indeed an absurdly moralistic posturing) . . . and misconstrue the symbolic parameters of this kind of mythology." Cf. Smith, *Early History,* 203–4.

35. Smith, *Origins,* 78, points out that Israelite theology used the council model for construing divine community rather than a familial model, whereas at Ugarit there were both (i.e., El as father of other gods). Only in an earlier stage might Israelite theology have seen El as the father of Yahweh (again, Deut 32:8).

36. El names are prominent in the ancestral stories of Genesis. Cf. Smith, *Memoirs,* 22; Miller, *Religion of Ancient Israel,* 62–63.

37. Traditionally interpreted as "he who strives with God" (Gen 32:28). On "El reigns," see Gottwald, *Politics,* 18.

38. This exodus tradition is consistent with various texts (including Judg 5:4) that point to

also quite possible that El originally was the God of the Exodus story, as some texts indicate.[39] There are a few passages that suggest that Israelites once understood El as the head of the council of gods, precisely as he is in the Ugaritic texts (e.g., Psalm 82),[40] and Yahweh appears as a subordinate:

> When Elyon apportioned the nations,
> when he divided humankind,
> He fixed the boundaries of the
>   peoples,
> according to the number of the
>   gods;
> Yahweh's portion was his people,
> Jacob, his allotted inheritance.
>
> (Deut 32:8, AT)

Here there is the clear vestige of a kind of pantheon involving the senior deity, El, a junior deity, Yahweh, and other deities as well. Reading this text is like looking back in time, back to a time when Israel (Jacob) clearly believed in "other gods," believed that the God El had determined their destiny, even as they confessed that the God Yahweh was appointed as their "patron" deity.[41] Eventually the figure of El was fused with that of Yahweh, an easy transition since 'el could mean "god" to begin with. Thus "worshipping El" was the same as "worshipping God," leaving primarily the figure of Baal as God's chief competitor.

Yahweh and Baal: As one scholar suggests, "in premonarchic Israel, Baal worship was considered a legitimate practice."[42] Nevertheless, there is no officially sanctioned use of the name Baal in the Hebrew Bible, as there is for El. Looking ahead, there is the story of Gideon's father, who has an "altar of Baal" (Judg 6:25). Yet this is the only clear instance in Judges in which the worship of Baal plays an important role in a story.[43]

In Ugaritic mythology, Baal is something of an upstart and a storm god, among other attributes—i.e., his power is manifested in thunder and lightning, clouds and rain. As the one who brought the seasonal rains, Baal was a fertility deity, making life itself possible. Just as there are similarities between Yahweh and El, so there are between Yahweh and Baal, in that Yahweh also is a storm deity, providing the rain, and thus fertility. Baal is the "Cloud Rider," just as God "rides upon the clouds" (Ps 68:4; cf. Ps 18:10; 104:3). Baal lives on his holy mountain Tsaphon, just as Yahweh inhabits the holy mountain of Zion, also called Tsaphon.[44] And Baal is a warrior, again as storm god, using his lightning as a weapon, just like Yahweh (Ps 18:14). We will see an example of such meteorological language used to describe Yahweh's

---

the area south of Canaan as the origin of belief in Yahweh.

39. Num 23:8, 19, 22, 23; 24:4, 8, 16 (three also with Yahweh). See, among others, Smith, *Origins*, 146–47.

40. Literally, "El has taken his place in the divine council; in the midst of the gods he holds judgment . . . You are gods, sons of El Elyon," whereupon El condemns them to mortal status. This is a good example of how polytheism was adapted by Israel, especially in a concern for social justice (vv. 2–4).

41. Smith, *Memoirs*, 109, notes that the poem also reflects later developments when it refers to the "no-gods" whom Israel worshipped (32:17) and describes Yahweh as the "only god " (v. 39). That latter verse sounds very much like Second Isaiah (e.g., 43:10–13).

42. Smith, *Memoirs*, 25.

43. Furthermore, there is no reference to Baal in Joshua, and in 1 Samuel there are only two isolated references (7:4 and 12:10). Other than *baal* in personal names, there are no references to Baal in 2 Samuel.

44. Cf. Ps 48:3, "far north" = Ṣaphon, transliterating both terms literally; prior to Zion, Yahweh dwelled for a time at Sinai/Horeb, the "mountain of God" (e.g., Exod 3:1; 19:2). In fact, Sinai may have originally been Yahweh's home, helping also to explain the meaning of *El Shadday* as "El of the Mountain."

theophany (appearance) in Judges 5:4–5, 20–21 (the Song of Deborah). Much of the conflict between the two deities seems to derive from their very similarity, leading to the question "Who is better at providing rain, and thus fertility?" This is the question to which we will return when we look at the stories in 1 Kings 17–19. Furthermore, just as ʾel can be a word for "god," so baal can be a word for "lord" or "husband," as well as the personal name Baal.[45] Thus people might address Yahweh as "my baal" meaning simply "my Lord," but obviously producing considerable confusion.[46] Here again is a point of potential contention that we will see more fully later: who is Israel's true "husband"? The metaphor includes the use of "adultery" or even "prostitution" as an expression for apostasy ("infidelity").[47] Corresponding to such "adultery" is Yahweh's "jealousy" as the cuckolded husband, to pursue the analogy.[48]

Yahweh and Asherah (or *"the ʾasherah"*): Asherah is a Canaanite goddess mentioned in the plural in 3:7. Here, however, the word seems to be an editorial error for "Astartes" (as in 2:13), or simply functioning as a generic term for goddesses (parallel "the baals").[49] Moreover, ʾasherah can refer not only to the goddess but to an object used in worship, which the NRSV often translates as a "sacred pole," as in the story about Gideon's father in 6:25–26, 30. Sometimes it is difficult to tell if a text is referring to the deity or the object. In fact, some scholars argue that the goddess was not a significant figure in Israel's history, and that the "pole" was the real problem.[50] The object was wooden[51] and probably represented a stylized tree, presumably the mythical "tree of life," and thus (like Baal) was connected with fertility, as was the goddess herself. As an object, apparently the ʾasherah could also be associated with

---

45. I am using the transliteration *baal* even though technically it would be *baʿal*. Many personal names incorporate the name of a god (like "Isra-el," see above). Such names *may* provide evidence of the *worship* of the respective deity, but there is much room for ambiguity. Consider many contemporary names based on originally Hebrew names—the parents of a boy named Jonathan may not even be aware that the name contains a nickname (originally *Yah*) for *Yahweh*. Moreover, *baal* can be simply a title for Yahweh (or *any* god) meaning "lord." Thus king Saul, a devout Yahwist, named one son for Yahweh (Jonathan) and another with *baal* (Ishbaal, 1 Chr 8:33). King David, also a devout Yahwist, used *three* divine names (or titles) for his sons: Adonijah (*J/Yah*, short for *Yahweh*), Eliada (*El*), and Beeliada (*baal*). See Miller, *Religion of Ancient Israel*, 245 n. 105; Smith, *Early History*, 45. Fearing that such names with *baal* represented heterodoxy, the editors at times replaced *baal* with the word *bosheth*, meaning "shame"!

46. See Hos 2:16 where the prophet envisions a time when Israel will call God "husband" (using the word ʾ*ish*, "man") but no longer Baal. The metaphor of "husband" represents a different construal of the relationship with God than *covenant* lord (suzerain).

47. This use is apparent in Judg 2:17 where Israel "lusted after other gods." The word for "lusted" often is translated as "prostituted (herself)" (cf. 8:33). The metaphor presents all sorts of problems, not the least of which is the danger of misogynism.

48. See McBride, "The Essence of Orthodoxy," 147.

49. The plural for Baals or Asherahs refers to multiple places where the deities would be worshipped, as in Baal-Gad or Baal-Hazor, etc. (see above on El names). See Miller, *Religion of Ancient Israel*, 32; Smith, *Early History*, 128. The Baal/Astarte pairing occurs elsewhere only rarely (Judg 10:6; 1 Sam 7:4; 12:10).

50. See Smith, *Early History*, 125–33, who concludes that the symbol is the only problem (the only clear reference to the deity is 1 Kgs 18:19), and again probably a mistake for Astarte, who was a far more prominent goddess from the area of Sidon (Jezebel's home). Cf. also Smith's *Memoirs*, 112.

51. Thus Deut 16:21 says, "you shall not *plant* any tree as a sacred pole," referring to installing an ʾ*asherah*.

other deities as well, including Yahweh (see below). ʾAsherahs were probably particularly appealing to women, both because of the goddess and because of concerns over fertility and general well-being.[52] Families often had shrines in their homes equipped with ʾasherahs and other objects used for worship. There are references to "household gods" (teraphim), figurines probably representing deceased ancestors,[53] as well as "ephods," often used for divination.[54] In a story in Judg 17:1–6 a family has a fully equipped shrine consisting of an "idol," an ephod, teraphim, probably an altar for sacrifice, and an in-house priest. Similar to the ʾasherahs were other objects called "pillars," made of stone, looking something like a contemporary tomb stone (with a rounded top; a more technical term would be "stela"). At various times in Israel's history, Israelites used such objects in their worship of *Yahweh* without thinking that they were "doing evil." Abraham built an altar at the site of a sacred oak tree at Shechem (Gen 12:6). Jacob erected a stone "pillar" and sanctified it with a libation (Gen 28:18–22)—even calling it "God's house"![55] The menorah used in contemporary Judaism originated in the lampstand in the tabernacle, which was a symbolic representation of the "tree of life" (Exod 25:31–40).[56] There is even a celebrated extra-biblical text dating to the 8th century that refers to Yahweh and "his ʾasherah," a find that has generated enormous scholarly debate, needless to say.[57] There is even a book entitled *Did God Have a Wife?*[58]

The use of such images ("idols")[59] in worship presented two theological

---

52. Women seem particularly connected to Asherah: 1Kgs 15:13; 18:19; 2 Kgs 23:7b; Miller, *Religion of Ancient Israel*, 35–40; Smith, *Memoirs*, 22.

53. Judg 17:5; 18:14, 18, 24. David (or at least his wife Michal) has "an idol" (teraphim) in his house (1 Sam 19:13) as does Rachel (Gen 31:30–35), although they play a comical role in both stories, and thus perhaps are ridiculed. See Smith, *Memoirs*, 24–25; Miller, *Religion of Ancient Israel*, 56.

54. Judg 17:5. It is not clear exactly what an ephod was. It is a priestly vestment (Exodus 28) but may have a different construction elsewhere; it can be used quite legitimately for divining God's will, as in the stories of David (e.g., 1 Sam 30:7, where the priest Ahimelech is involved). See Miller, *Religion of Ancient Israel*, 67 and n. 111.

55. It is possible that the editors let such stories stand because they were before the prohibitions of the Sinai covenant.

56. Cf. Meyers, *Tabernacle Menorah*.

57. Again, part of the debate is whether ʾasherah refers to an object or to the goddess by that name (or both). Those who see the goddess involved understand her to be Yahweh's "consort" or wife, a relationship that otherwise seems totally absent from biblical theology. Cf. Coogan, "Canaanite Origins," 118–20; McCarter, "Religion of the Monarchy," 143–49. Miller, *Religion of Ancient Israel*, 35, agrees that the ʾasherah in question was "a cult object of Yahweh marking his presence, in other words, a hypostatization of Yahweh," but not the goddess Asherah as consort. (*Hypostatization* refers to the way in which an aspect of the deity represents the reality of that deity, who may otherwise be ineffable or transcendent. Examples include "wisdom," "face," "name," and "word.") In fact, Miller argues that "there was no worship of a separate goddess Asherah in Israel" but that "the asherah in some fashion could be acceptable even to a radical Yahwist like Jehu" (*Religion of Ancient Israel*, 35; referring to the fanatical reformer of 2 Kings 9–10). Similarly, see Smith, *Early History*, 130. Note also another goddess, the "Queen of Heaven," who is popular as late as the time of Jeremiah (7:18; 44:15–16).

58. By William Dever. See the previous note.

59. Note that the translation "idol" is already prejudiced because of its long history as a pejorative term, whereas a translation such as "image" might not be. Contemporary Catholics can speak reverently of an "image" of the Virgin Mary but would not use the term "idol" (although some sixteenth-century reformers did!). The same holds true for the Christian Orthodox use of icons, making it difficult for the Orthodox to identify

dangers: idolatry and apostasy. Israel's covenant theology was thoroughly aniconic, i.e., prohibiting the use of any kind of physical object as a representation of God—the second of the Ten Commandments (Deut 5:8–10).[60] Even in the elaborate sanctuaries of the wilderness Tabernacle and the later temple, there was no statue of any kind—Yahweh was believed to be "enthroned upon the cherubim" above the ark, but still invisible. Even if a worshipper only intended to use an ʾasherah as a visible means to point to the invisible Yahweh (or perhaps to represent Yahweh's blessing of fertility), it was easy to confuse the two. Of course, one could see the same danger in the ark, but the descriptions of it consistently imply God's invisibility.[61] Moreover, since an ʾasherah obviously could be misunderstood as representing the *goddess* Asherah, the danger of idolatry was compounded with that of apostasy. Consequently, the Deuteronomic reformers of the 7th Century banned both ʾasherahs and "pillars" from worship.[62]

To summarize: on the one hand, the Deuteronomic insistence that ancient Israel always considered only the worship of one God as legitimate is definitely anachronistic, for early in Israel's history Yahweh was a deity recognized along with others, particularly El. On the other hand, the editorial picture of early Israel's constant and widespread polytheism—worshipping "other gods"—is almost certainly overdrawn, even given some notable instances. In addition, some of the practices that the Deuteronomists consider heretical were probably not so considered by the people at the time. In other words, the framework of Judges condemns the Israelites for a chronic disobedience that most likely did not happen, or for practices that most people considered perfectly acceptable at the time. Thus the sharp contrast between "Israelite religion" and "Canaanite religion" that so motivates the editor of the Former Prophets did not exist at the time in which the stories take place, or at least the situation was far more blurred than the stereotype would allow.[63] Some scholars would even speak of an early Israelite "polytheism" that allowed for far more

---

with an "aniconic" Christianity! (Niditch, *Judges*, 105, uses "icon" to refer to Gideon's ephod and to Micah's "iconic representations," which are "not idols," 181. On the latter, see the discussion of 17:3 below.) This is why I use the term "sacramental" to refer to such images or their use, recognizing that they functioned as visible means to an invisible grace, to borrow one definition of the term.

60. Much of Deuteronomy 4 is a lively sermon elaborating on the reasons for banning images, primarily that Israel *heard* God's voice but did not *see* God when receiving the Ten Commandments.

61. In some ancient texts, the ark, with its uncanny numinous power, seems to come close to idolatry (e.g., Num 10:35–36), which is why the Deuteronomists emphasized that the ark's holiness came from its function as a container for the covenant document (cf. 1 Kgs 8:9).

62. Deut 16:21; 7:5; 12:3. One unfortunate result of such biblical injunctions, arguably, has been to taint any religious appreciation for natural subjects like trees with the smell of paganism. Thus Jeremiah's ridicule of those who use a tree or a stone as an idol (2:27) has no room for perhaps the loveliest line from Ugaritic poetry, where Baal says that he has a "Word of tree and whisper of stone" (for the text see Parker, "The Baal Cycle," 110). For contemporary poetry, see my *God of Dirt*, 27–34, and the discussion of Martin Buber's classic phenomenological essay on a tree as a "thou."

63. Coogan, "Canaanite Origins," 115, sees "Israelite religion . . . as a subset of Canaanite religion." Dever, "Contribution of Archaeology," 215, quotes Halpern's comment: "'Israelite religion did not import Canaanite. Israel's religion was a Canaanite religion.'" While this certainly applies to the worship of El, or the use of ʾasherahs, the origins of Yahweh seem to lie *outside* of Canaan, as we have seen.

flexibility than the Deuteronomic reforms would tolerate.[64] Sometimes the line between orthodoxy and heterodoxy was far more ambiguous than the Deuteronomists would have us believe.[65] We must also remember that an editor writing even in the 9th century was some three hundred years removed from the time of the judges (in the 7th century, it would be half a millennium!). Again, the Deuteronomic editors were convinced that the vicissitudes of Israel's history, from the outset, were directly linked by cause and effect to the people's fidelity or infidelity to Yahweh, and in Judges they have employed that theology in explaining events that may well have had nothing to do with the identity of the gods.

Remarkably, the direct intervention of God within the stories themselves is relatively rare. At the outset the angel lectures the entire people (10:10–16), but Gideon is the only judge to whom God (or an angel) talks, often giving orders. While the narrator may tell us that God "raised up" a deliverer, only Gideon benefits from a direct commissioning (6:11–24). To be sure, the angel announces Samson's destiny to his mother (chap. 13), but never to Samson himself. In chs.17–21, God speaks only in response to questions, apparently through divination with the ark (20:18, 23, 28).[66] Perhaps by that point God is as speechless as we are.

Similarly, the editorial preface in 2:11–19 gives the impression that God is in control of events, but the reported activity of God in the surrounding stories is relatively sparse (outside the frames). God fights by panicking the enemy (Judg 4:15) or (somewhat mysteriously) in "star-wars" fashion (5:4–5, 20). In another mode, "the spirit of the Lord" sometimes possesses a judge, giving him the power to do his work (Othniel, Gideon, Jephthah, Samson),[67] but there is no indication that the judge is *aware* of this possession as we are, and even here it is the *judge* who acts directly. Otherwise, over extended sections of narrative, God says and does nothing, and there is no "servant of the Lord" with a stature like Moses or Joshua to speak authoritatively *for* God.[68] In the editorial comment at the end of the Abimelech story (9:56–

---

64. Again, Deut 32:8 is a good example, reflecting a stage at which El and Yahweh had not been collapsed into one. For recent studies see Smith, *Early History* and Penchansky, *Twilight of the Gods*; Miller, *Religion of Ancient Israel*, chap. 1. In contrast, Tigay, "Israelite Religion," 178, argues from archaeological (written) evidence "that there was not much polytheism of any kind" from the eighth century to 587. Moreover, references to polytheism before the eighth century "come from the same type of historiographic literature that has proven so hard to follow for the eighth century and following" (180; referring to Deuteronomic editorials).

65. Miller, *Religion of Ancient Israel*, 46–61, has a helpful discussion of these terms. A similar diversity was probably the norm in the exilic period. "The priestly-deuteronomistic/prophetic version of what exilic Yahwism was is only that: a version," according to Susan Akerman as quoted by Gottwald, *Politics*, 274 n. 56.

66. This is the only reference to the ark in Judges.

67. Respectively Judg 6:34; 11:29; 13:15 (plus three other times). Cf. 1 Sam 10:6 and 16:13–14. With Saul, the experience will include "spirit possession," or a "prophetic frenzy."

68. The sole exception is the appearance of a prophet in 6:7–10.

57), the author tells us that the preceding events are due to God's punishment, but there was no direct involvement of God reported in the story. The same kind of providential guidance appears with the Samson story (14:4). Yet the only "acts of God" there are to empower Samson for his own personal liberation or simply to quench his thirst (15:14–20; 16:30). Even more troublesome, the defeat of the tribe of Benjamin in the civil war that rages near the end of the book is attributed to God, along with the slaughter of over twenty-five thousand people (20:35). Otherwise, human beings act on their own, an independence that will spell disaster by the end.

As we saw at the outset, the office of "judge" is far different from our modern figure robed in black and sitting in a courtroom. Although some judicial function may be intended (i.e., arbitrating disputes; teaching the law; cf. Deborah, 4:4–5), the primary role of the judge in these stories is to be the deliverer of Israel. Otherwise, "judging" means fighting, and the judge is a warrior. As we move through the stories, we will increasingly see in retrospect how Othniel is the model or paradigm, the judge who does everything right, the perfect savior (correspondingly, the villain here is a classic also, named "Cushan Double-Wickedness"!). Othniel works only "inside the box" of 2:11–19. We already know of his military success, and his marriage to a blue-blood Calebite, Achsah (1:11–15). Despite her subjection as the property of males, her demand for fertile land models a form of female independence and initiative that will dis-

appear later in the book.[69] Moreover, as the son-in-law of Caleb, who, along with Joshua, was the only surviving Israelite of the wilderness generation, Othniel represents that part of the *new* generation that *does* know the Lord (contrast 2:10). Othniel also just happens to be a Southerner, not a Northerner.

The following stories, however, will not follow a neat and tidy pattern. Other judges will increasingly muddy the pattern—or more fittingly, *bloody* it—throwing into question the integrity of the office. If we think of a verb paradigm, Othniel is it, and the other judges increasingly appear as "irregular" verbs, until we get to Samson, who hardly "judges" at all, and then the horrible conclusion of the book (chs.17–21), when there are *no* judges—and no king—in Israel. The editorial in 2:11–23 leads us to expect a cyclical plot, but overall the plot is a spiral with a plummeting trajectory.

Murder in the Outhouse (3:12–30)

The Ehud story is a bawdy tale involving "bathroom language." Ehud is left-handed and devises a special sword that he hides under his clothes on his right hip (and not in the belt, as usual). The detail is significant because it means that Ehud can reach for his sword without causing immediate suspicion.[70] He comes to Eglon, the Moabite King who is oppressing Israel, at first as a submissive envoy,

---

69. See Schneider, *Judges*, 17.

70. The left-handedness may be suggestive of abnormality, but Halpern concludes that left-handed warriors were specially trained (*First Historians*, 40–45). Niditch, *Judges*, 57, suggests that left-handedness is also an example of the "marginal" social status of the judges.

bearing tribute (i.e., a tax payment), but after handing over the money and taking his leave, he returns, announcing that he has "a message [word] from God for you." Eglon dismisses his courtiers as if to facilitate hearing this word, then apparently heads for the "bathroom" to relieve himself (NRSV "cool roof chamber").[71] The word for "seat" used with royalty normally means "throne," but here (v. 20) refers to the potty. (Compare the English idiom "sitting on the throne" as a euphemism for using a toilet.) Such is the author's scatological view of Moabite royalty! But Ehud indiscreetly barges right in and Eglon stands up, literally caught with his pants down. Ehud then delivers not a "word" but a sword thrust in the belly, and a fat belly it is. With scurrilous humor, the author portrays Eglon as so fat that Ehud's sword can go in hilt and all and still not protrude.[72] Adding insult to injury, Eglon loses control of his bowels and he "messes his britches," as it were. Then Ehud locks the king in the bathroom so that it will appear that he is, in fact, relieving himself in the usual sense. When Eglon's servants arrive, that is precisely what they assume, so they wait politely outside the door, thinking that the king is taking an unusually long time to read the newspaper. Finally, they unlock the door and find Eglon dead on the floor. The one whom God had "strengthened," God's messenger now has slain. After the assassination, the battle and Israel's victory seem almost anticlimactic, and certainly far less colorful (vv. 26–30).

Eglon is the first enemy king to receive any dramatic attention, and the author seems to relish the opportunity. The name "Eglon" is a pun on the word for calf, perhaps implying the *fatted* calf of sacrifice. Far from a powerful, royal figure, Eglon appears as an obese, undignified fool whose throne is a toilet. Instead of a commander in chief in the field, we see him as a helpless, unarmed weakling caught with his pants down, lying dead in his own excrement. Much of Judges will have to do with a political critique of monarchs (both real and would-be), often satirically, and Eglon is only the first in a line of kings or military leaders to be so ridiculed. On the other hand, Ehud's brutal assassination raises ethical questions about God's appointee. He may be a deliverer, but he is no diplomat. Here the agent that God uses to subdue Israel's enemy makes us wonder if the means justify the end. Ehud sees his assassination as "the word of God," but the narrator never reports any such word. In justifying his action, Ehud in effect takes the Lord's name in vain. Perhaps it is not insignificant that in this episode the Spirit does not come upon the deliverer.

Women's Liberation (4:1—5:31)

The Ehud story described a Moabite king whom we could call "his royal lowness." The next story portrays an

---

71. For the logistics here, see Halpern, *First Historian*, ch. 3. Niditch, *Judges*, 54, n. v, retains the NRSV reading but recognizes that of Halpern and others. There is considerable ambiguity, including how Ehud escapes, Houdini-fashion, from the locked room!

72. Alter, *Art*, 39, suggests that "there is something hideously sexual" about the thrust (i.e., penetration), along with other sexual allusions. So also Niditch, *Judges*, 57–58.

Israelite general (Barak) who is helpless without a female prophetess (Deborah) and a Canaanite general (Sisera) who dies by the hand of a woman (Jael). The resourcefulness of these women, and in some cases their treachery, will echo later in an unnamed woman of Thebez and in Delilah (9:53–54; ch.16; cf. already Achsah in 1:11–15). Their role stands over against women who are victimized (Jephthah's daughter, 11:29–40; the Levite's concubine, ch.19). But the story of Deborah and Jael is one of women's liberation—i.e., women as liberators, not the liberation of women.

The rod of God's anger in this case is King Jabin of Hazor, in the northern part of Israel.[73] Jabin has a monopoly in iron chariots enabling his control over the rich agricultural plain. For twenty years Jabin oppresses the Israelites "cruelly," though we are not told how (v. 3). Deborah appears as both prophetess and judge. As prophetess, she summons Barak and delivers an oracle declaring liberation from the Canaanites. She orders Barak to gather his troops at Mount Tabor, promising that God will give Sisera into his hand. Barak, however, appears reluctant to act on his own, saying that he won't go if Deborah won't go with him—her presence will guarantee victory.[74] "Barak" means "Flash" (as in lightning), but Deborah will provide the spark (or, to mix metaphors, the "sting,"

since "Deborah" means "bee"). She consents, but then changes the promise: God sold the Israelites into the hand of King Jabin (v. 2), but now "the Lord will sell Sisera into the hand of a woman" (v. 9). One would assume that the woman is Deborah (the "woman prophetess," v. 4, AT), but there is a surprise in store. At any rate, there will be no medal of honor for Barak.

Of course, the one who really leads the charge is God, who "goes before" the Israelites as their vanguard, throwing them into a panic (4:14–15).[75] The enemies are totally annihilated, and Sisera abandons his chariot and flees on foot. Now comes the gory part. Sisera comes to the tent of one Jael, a Kenite related to the later in-laws of Moses, but not an Israelite (v. 17; cf. 1:16). Apparently Sisera assumes that Jael will grant him sanctuary, because "there was peace between King Jabin of Hazor and the clan of Heber the Kenite." Jael does indeed invite him in as an honored guest, reassuring him that he has nothing to fear. There is even a hint of seduction. A relieved Sisera asks for water. She gives him milk, then covers the cowering general with a blanket. It's as if she has fed him warm milk and cookies and tucked him in for the night.

The scene is a comical satire of this Canaanite warlord and king. He has fled for his life, sought protection from a woman, and now is hiding under a blanket. Like a child playing hide-and-seek, he says, "If anyone comes, don't tell them I'm here," as if that big lump under

---

73. Unless we are dealing with two kings by the same name (not all that unlikely) this account ignores the death of Jabin in Josh 11:1, 10. Cf. Halpern, *First Historians,* 90; Campbell, *From Joshua to Chronicles,* 87.

74. Niditch, *Judges,* 65, argues that this recognition typifies epic literature and is not a sign of cowardice.

75. The divine vanguard motif is prominent in accounts of warfare in the ancient Near East and a primary subject in my study *Divine Presence.*

the blanket was invisible. Then he falls asleep. But now the satire turns ugly, for Jael takes a tent peg and a hammer and drives the tent peg into his head, "and," the text says laconically, "he died." Just then Barak arrives in hot pursuit, only to find his prey "lying dead, with the tent peg in his temple." "So," the story concludes, "on that day God subdued King Jabin of Canaan," and the Israelites press their victory until he too is dead.

Now a poetic celebration—"The Song of Deborah"—caps off the prose narrative, much the way the "Song of Miriam" closes the story of Israel's escape from Egypt (Exodus 14–15).[76] The poem is a triumph song in praise of God, who is portrayed as a storm deity coming from the region of southern trans-Jordan (vv. 4–5). The description fits with the battle account in vv. 20–21, where a rain-swollen stream sweeps away the enemy and the stars fight against them (cf. Josh 10:12–14; Exod 15:4–5). The poem also reveals a picture of "Israel" divided rather than united, with some tribes bravely joining the fray and others holding back (vv. 14–18), a motif of dissent that will increase in subsequent stories (also the southern tribes of Simeon and Judah are not mentioned). Finally, like the prose account, the poem focuses on the grisly death of Sisera and the ironic role of women. In parallel with Deborah, the "mother" of Israel (v. 7) there is the mother of Sisera, eagerly waiting for her son to bring home the spoils of war. She wonders why he tarries, and her ladies in waiting reply that he must be taking time to rape "a girl or two," little knowing that instead two women have brought about the death of her son.[77] She dreams of a new dress, embroidered and dyed, while her son lies dead under a rug that has become his shroud, stained with his blood. "So perish all your enemies, O Lord," sings the poet. After all the violence, we too are ready for the rest that comes (v. 31).

Jael with her hammer and tent peg is as lethal—and brutal—as Ehud with his sword, again raising ethical questions. Jael does not claim to be God's messenger, but the prophetess who *speaks* for God predicted her action (if not the method). In murdering Jabin's general, Jael has violated the peace between her husband and the King. Moreover, the sanctuary of a beduin tent is renowned as a place where even enemies are safe from harm. That's what the 23rd Psalm is all about—"you prepare a table before me in the presence of my enemies." Yet here the peace treaty is a sham and the sanctuary becomes an execution chamber. The narrator addresses none of these issues overtly. He simply tells the gruesome tale and leaves the reader to raise any questions. The story, therefore, includes multiple ironies. In the midst of a patriarchal culture

---

76. The poems in Exodus 15 and Judges 5 may be some of the earliest literature of ancient Israel. Some scholars think that Judges 5 hints at the obscure process whereby Yahweh became the chief God of Israel (note especially vv. 4–5). See Smith, *Origins*, 145.

77. The words for "a girl or two" are unique utilizations of the root meaning "womb," as Schneider points out (*Judges*, 96), thus almost suggesting an obscene colloquialism. The irony is compounded when we realize that Jael's act of murder has clearly erotic overtones: she penetrates Sisera and he falls dead "between her legs" (5:27); cf. Niditch, *Judges*, 81. For the complexities involving the hospitality custom here, see Matthews, *Judges and Ruth*, 68–73.

(and in warfare, nonetheless), it is women who provide liberation for Israel—Deborah's handholding of Barak, Jael's "man-handling" of Sisera. On the other hand, Jael's act defies decency (as in the Geneva Conventions) and her treachery is almost enough to make us sympathetic with one of the "villains."

Gideon: The Diffident Deliverer (Chaps. 6–8)

The story of Gideon is the longest and most detailed so far, expanding on the various parts of the cyclic typology: Israel's evil, oppression, and cry (6:1–6); the sending of a deliverer, including the gift of the Spirit (6:7–40); the liberation followed by rest (7:1–28). Like a horde of locusts, the Midianites and Amalekites, "people of the east," are harassing Israelite farmers, driving them from their fields and destroying their crops and livestock. Ironically, these enemies are doing to Israel what Israel is supposed to be doing to the native inhabitants—claiming "squatters' rights." But when Israel cries to God, they get a lecture before they get liberation.

God sends an unnamed prophet with a fiery sermon, reminiscent of the angel's address in 2:1–5. Only here in Judges is there a reference to a prophet. The prophet recalls Israel's exodus from Egypt and deliverance from "all who oppressed you," including the native Canaanites, implying a total victory such as in Joshua 21:43. Yet Israel's allegiance to God has failed, for they now "pay reverence to the gods of the Amorites, in whose land you live." This accusation is, in effect, an expansion of the charge of "doing evil" in v. 1. The substance of the charge will be verified in retrospect as the story progresses, in that Gideon's family will appear as Baal worshippers, the only place in the book (outside the framing passages) where Baal is mentioned.[78]

First, however, God has to find a deliverer, and that proves to be far more complicated than in previous incidents. God dispatches an angel (soon fused with God, v. 16), who finds Gideon "beating out wheat in the wine press, to hide it from the Midianites." One would normally beat out wheat in the open, allowing the wind to carry away the chaff, but Gideon has resorted to a concealed method for fear of being seen and perhaps losing his wheat to the oppressors. Such diffidence does not bode well for this deliverer, whom the angel nonetheless addresses as a "mighty warrior." Gideon immediately questions the rest of the angel's greeting, the statement that "the Lord is with you." "If God is with us," he says, "then why are all these bad things happening?" Apparently Gideon was busy in the winepress when the prophet gave his sermon, for Gideon seems to know nothing of Israel's "evil" (much less his family's culpability!). In fact, he turns the language of the prophetic indictment of Israel into an indictment of God: "where are all [God's] wonderful deeds that our ancestors recounted to us, saying, 'Did not the Lord bring us up from Egypt?' But now the

---

78. The name Baal occurs eleven times in the book, five times in framing passages, and all the rest in the Gideon story. Ironically, the story ends with the Israelites returning to the worship of Baal (8:33).

Lord has cast us off, and given us into the hand of Midian" (6:13; cf. vv. 8–9).

The angel seems to be as hard of hearing as Gideon. Just as it has not registered with Gideon that he is a "mighty warrior," so the angel continues as if Gideon has not posed his question: "Go in this might of yours and deliver Israel from the hand of Midian; I hereby commission you."[79] But Gideon remains unconvinced. He can't deliver Israel because his clan is the weakest in the tribe of Manasseh, and he himself—far from being mighty—is the runt of the clan. "But,'" God counters, "I will be with you, and you shall strike down the Midianites, every one of them." If Hebrew had italics, the text would probably italicize "with": "but I will be *with* you," repeating the initial greeting, with a tone suggesting "I've already *told* you the source of your strength!" At this point Gideon surely must be trying the Lord's patience, for now he demands a "sign" that it is truly God who is speaking to him (apparently the divine nature of the "messenger" is not obvious).[80] So Gideon runs home, prepares some sacrificial foods, returns and places them before the angel, whereupon the angel extends his staff and zaps the foods, then instantly vanishes. Now "Gideon perceived that it was the angel of the Lord" (v. 22). In fact, his doubt turns to fear, because he has "seen the angel of the Lord face to face," an encounter that reputedly brings death.[81] But God assures him that he will live, and Gideon builds an altar to God.

Now God puts Gideon to work, but his first assignment is not political deliverance, it is liturgical revolution, corresponding to the prophet's indictment in vv. 7–10. Here we learn *how* the Israelites have paid "reverence to the gods of the Amorites," for Gideon's own father has an "altar of Baal" and a "sacred pole," i.e., an ʾ*asherah* (see Excursus 3 above).[82] God orders Gideon to destroy his father's altar and pole. Gideon obeys—but, as with winnowing the wheat, he conceals his act from discovery, in this case, under cover of darkness. There he was afraid of the Midianites; here he is afraid of his family, but Joash comes to his son's defense when the outraged townspeople demand that he be put to death. Here the author introduces a wordplay that will recur again: "Will you contend for Baal?" The Hebrew word for "contend" is *rib* (pronounced *reev*). As a play on Joash's challenge, Gideon acquires a nickname—Jerubbaal, which is said to mean, "let Baal contend [against him]." Joash's challenge includes the ironic parallel: "will you save him?" (AT), which, of course, is what *gods* are supposed to

---

79. Here the author begins to switch back and forth from angel to God, suggesting their interchangeability.

80. At times angels seem to *look* like ordinary humans, e.g., Gen 18:1–15.

81. Cf. Gen 32:30; Exod 33:11–23; 19:21; 24:10–11 (the first and last being exceptions that prove the rule).

82. Gideon's father also seems to own what may well be a sacred tree ("the oak of Ophrah," 6:1) the very place where the angel appears and where Gideon brings his first sacrifice. There is an unintended irony here in that the artificial tree (ʾ*asherah*) is destroyed but the real tree goes undisturbed. Cf. the "oak of Moreh" at Shechem (Gen 12:6–7), including a theophany and altar building (also Josh 24:26). On the tree symbolism, see Hiebert, *Yahwist's Landscape*, 107–10.

do for humans.[83] Indeed, Joash seems to have acquired the zeal of a sudden convert, for he threatens any Baal devotees with death (v. 31). The dual name Jerubbaal introduces an ambiguity, however: is the deliverer the "namesake" of Baal or of God?

We should note the remarkable reticence of the editors here. Joash's cultic apostasy and Gideon's response seem to be the most explicit examples so far of what the Torah forbids and demands, respectively. Yet the editor does not even say, "as it is written in the Torah of Moses," or some such reference. Of course, if the framework of 2:11–23 and the lecture in 6:7–10 have done their work, the editor needn't rub it in. Historically, however, the situation may well illustrate the fluidity of Israelite religion prior to the rule of Deuteronomic orthodoxy. Although it is possible that an early conflict between Baal worshippers (defended by Gideon's family) and Yahwists is in the picture, more likely Gideon's family were Yahwists who used the *baal* title for Yahweh, which the later editor mistook for the god Baal. The same kind of misreading may be functioning when Gideon constructs an "ephod," using it as a sacramental object in the worship of Yahweh (see below, 8:26). Miller puts the potential for confusion well: "Gideon's father bore the Yahwistic name Joash but is depicted as having set up a Baal altar. Gideon, who set up an altar to Yahweh and tore down the Baal altar of his father, had a Baal name, Jerubbaal . . . !"[84]

Now it would appear that all is ready for battle with the Midianites and Amalekites, who mass their forces in the valley of Jezreel. And now "the spirit of the Lord took possession of Gideon" (to resume the typology; literally "clothed" him) and he sounds the trumpet, summoning the Israelites to arms (four tribes). But wait, Gideon isn't really ready, Spirit or no. He has yet another test for God! Now, rather impudently, he wants to confirm that God will deliver Israel, that God's word is trustworthy. He lays out a fleece of wool, and suggests that God make dew to fall only on the fleece, not on the surrounding ground. Sure enough, the next morning, his wish is fulfilled. Then, begging God not to be angry, he has one *more* test, to reverse the fleece miracle, so there is dew on the ground and not on the fleece. And so it is. God is as versatile as God is patient.

Why all of these questions, signs and tests? Gideon is a diffident deliverer. He does not at first understand that he *is* a mighty warrior, *because* God is with him, all appearances notwithstanding. Vocation is empowerment. In the same way, he does not understand that *God* is trustworthy, that the deliverance God has done in the past is the earnest of God's deliverance in the present. But there is another dimension to Gideon's diffidence that involves more than his attitude as a character in a story. Gideon's reluctance mirrors that of Moses, who also needed reassurance and some signs (Exod 3:1—4:9).

---

83. Isaiah 44:9–20 (an exilic text) presents a satire on the construction of idols and the pathetic appeal of the artisan for the god's salvation (v. 17).

84. Miller, *Religion of Ancient Israel*, 67.

Similarly, there are allusions to the figures of Elijah (the miraculously ignited sacrifice) and Jacob (seeing God face to face).[85] These allusions set up expectations, as Olson suggests: "Will Gideon be the one to end Israel's oppression, like Moses, to defeat the Baal cults of Canaan, like Elijah, or even to wrestle a blessing from God, like Jacob?"[86] In retrospect we shall see that the author has set us up for much disappointment.

The diffident deliverer will soon appear winsome in comparison to the ruthless warrior who emerges in the midst of battle. But before he can commence fighting, God has a little test as well. God doesn't want Gideon to have a large army, because then, when they are victorious, they might take all the credit, ignoring God, the "commander in chief." So Gideon orders all of the potential soldiers who are "fearful and trembling" to return home (in accordance with the Torah, by the way—Deut 20:5–8). But the army is still too large (thirty-two "thousand"[87]), and God suggests a way of reduction involving how the soldiers drink from a stream; God chooses the ones who lap like a dog rather than the ones who cup the water in their hands.[88]

The final contingent will be infinitesimal compared to the enemy who is "thick as locusts," with its camels "countless as the sand on the seashore" (7:12).

Now God gives the order to "attack the camp," but immediately offers Gideon a way to confirm once again that the victory will be God's (by now, God knows the man, after all). Gideon, true to form, accepts, and sneaks up to the camp in the night. After overhearing an enemy soldier reporting a nightmare about defeat, and an interpretation by another soldier who designates Gideon as the victor, the deliverer is finally ready to deliver: "the Lord has given the army of Midian into our hand" (7:15).

Gideon employs an ingenious battle plan that rivals the conquest of Jericho by military band (cf. Josh 6:5; Judg 3:27). Each soldier has a trumpet and an empty jar with a torch inside and the soldiers surround the Midianite camp at night. At Gideon's signal, they blow their trumpets and smash the jars, thus producing a kind of "sound and light" show worthy of July 4. The trumpet blasts and eerie flames wreak havoc in the Midianite camp, driving them into a panic, as the sound of three hundred trumpets well might do to the mightiest of warriors who have been sound asleep. In their confusion and in the dark, the Midianites fight among themselves, then run for their lives.

Up to this point, Gideon's tactics resemble non-violent disruption more than armed resistance—there has been no mention of Israelite soldiers even having weapons. Gideon almost seems like a Gandhi. But now a bloodbath replaces the relatively peaceful victory

---

85. Cf. 1 Kgs 18:20–40 and Gen 32:30. On the reluctance to accept a commission, cf. 1 Sam 9:21; Isa 6:5; Jer 1:6.

86. Olson, *Judges*, 797a.

87. The word for "thousand" when referring to troops more likely means something like "platoon" or "squad" with perhaps as few as ten soldiers, but here, at least, the translation "thousand" simply enhances the author's point.

88. Although the test is puzzling, it may be that God chooses the lappers because they have their heads down to the water and therefore cannot see the enemy approaching, thereby making them less fit for battle but by the same token enhancing God's credit as commander (cf. v. 2).

(7:23—8:21). After all, the non-violent rout of the Midianites has already delivered Israel—the enemy has fled out of the land, returning to the trans-Jordan. But Gideon is not satisfied with that. He now musters more troops from several tribes and the forces from Ephraim join the fray, capturing and beheading two of the Midianite captains, and delivering their heads to Gideon. However, the Ephraimites complain that Gideon only summoned them as an afterthought, and Gideon deftly appeases them by praising their contribution to the battle (8:1–3). Still, Gideon pushes on, even though his troops are "exhausted and famished" (8:4). He captures two Midianite kings and kills them. All told, there are over one hundred twenty thousand enemy dead (8:10). When the two kings confess that they themselves had killed the brothers of Gideon (an otherwise unreported incident, 8:19), it becomes clear that Gideon is now motivated by personal revenge more than political redemption. Indeed, the rest of his actions are equally brutal. He punishes the officials of Succoth and Penuel (*Israelite* towns) because they refused to give him food: "So he took the elders of the city and he took thorns of the wilderness and briers and with them he trampled the people of Succoth. He also broke down the tower of Penuel, and killed the men of the city" (8:16–17). Ironically, Penuel was the place where Jacob wrestled with the angel and gained the new name of Israel.

The diffident deliverer has become a homicidal avenger. God's intention was to use the least number of soldiers possible, and even then (assuming it was God's idea), to give them the victory without "firing a shot," as it were. But Gideon is out for blood. Not content with the small band of musicians, he calls out all the troops from four tribes, and they are armed with far more than trumpets and torches. Moreover, there is an ominous implication in Gideon's battle cry: "'For the Lord *and for Gideon*'" (7:18). Not only has Gideon abandoned God's plan of a small force; he also has claimed equal footing with God, as if the troops are fighting for *him*. So much for God getting all the credit. And the troops foreshadow the coming violence when they supplement the cry: "A *sword* for the Lord and for Gideon'" (7:20).[89]

This exaltation of Gideon comes to a head in the aftermath of victory. The Israelites say to him, "Rule over us, you and your son and your grandson also; for you have delivered us out of the hand of Midian" (8:22-23). There was a foreshadowing of this request already when the Midianite kings said that Gideon and his brothers "resembled the sons of a king" (8:18). It would be difficult to overestimate the significance of the request for a human ruler (here the word for "rule" is *mashal*, not the more precise word, *malak*, but still hereditary monarchy is in view).[90] To the end of the Former Prophets, the relationship between human leader and divine

---

89. The contemporary organization called the Gideons uses the symbol of a pitcher and torch as its logo, and apparently sees Gideon as a model for spreading the gospel to the world, making one wonder if they have read the full story with its strange combination of diffidence and aggression.

90. Roberts, "In Defense of the Monarchy," 381, points out that Gideon's rejection of kingship "appears to have been more the rejection of a title than of the substance behind that title."

sovereign will be a dominant theme. Theologically, the issue will turn on the tension between the practical need for a human leader for order and security over against the possibility that such a human figure will rob God of God's exclusive sovereignty (e.g., 1 Samuel 8–9). Yet another problem with an established monarchy, of course, concerns how the monarch is selected. So far, God has appointed Israel's leaders in *ad hoc* situations. Here the people's representatives want to appoint their leader, and in proposing dynastic succession, they propose an *institution* that will replace the spontaneity of "charismatic" leaders (i.e., those "clothed with the spirit"). One could read the overall story without this incident (i.e., vv. 22–27), which may suggest an "anti-monarchy" editorial addition. We already see the tension in the story of Gideon, where Israel needs a deliverer, but the deliverer acts in a way that challenges God's will.

Still, Gideon refuses. Gideon's refusal points to the central theological issue: "I will not rule over you, and my son will not rule over you; the Lord will rule over you" (8:23). In Israel's covenant relationship with God, God is, in fact, the "king," or better, the suzerain, and Israel is the vassal. Israel is God's fiefdom, and God's rule extends beyond the people of Israel to include other nations. As the Exodus victory song puts it: "the Lord will reign forever and ever" (Exod 15:18). This is why the "love" of Israel for God is fundamentally *allegiance* to God, and God demands that that allegiance be exclusive (Deut 6:4–5; see Excursus 1). For Israel also to pledge allegiance to a human king creates a troubling ambiguity. Despite Gideon's refusal, the problem will appear again immediately in the story of Abimelech.

Gideon refuses the crown but immediately dons a chasuble, as it were—that is, a priestly vestment. Gideon collects the gold earrings captured from the enemy and makes an ephod. In official lore, at least, the ephod was a kind of vest worn by the priest, and attached to it was a breastplate containing a set of sacred dice that were used for divination (Exodus 28:6–30). Elsewhere the ephod seems also to be under priestly control, although others use it with a priest at hand (David, 1 Sam 30:7).[91] Gideon won't be a prince, but he *will* be a priest (cf. below at 17:5). Indeed, the juxtaposition of his "No" to kingship and his request for the earrings (v. 24) suggests that he has an alternative to power in mind, showing where the request for a king can lead. His self-investiture stands over against those who are invested from *God's* initiative (cf. 1 Sam 2.28). The author seems to understand the ephod as an even more radical departure, however, because he says that "all Israel prostituted themselves to it," and "it became a snare to Gideon and to his family" (8:28). The language repeats that of the angelic sermon in 2:17 and 2:3 respectively, using the sexual metaphor to talk about theological infidelity. "Prostituting" oneself means shifting one's allegiance to another god, most likely the male deity Baal. Or the offense may be that the ephod becomes an idol, even if Yahwistic. Gideon may have meant the ephod to be a means to

---

91. The exact nature of the ephod remains unclear, including its relationship to the "linen ephod" (1 Sam 2:18; 22:18; 2 Sam 6:14).

worship *Yahweh*, but, in the narrator's view, it became the *object* of worship.[92]

There is nothing in the text, however, that justifies the claim that Baal is involved. Indeed, that would be highly ironic since it was precisely an altar of Baal that Gideon destroyed, and later we learn that it was only after the death of Gideon that Israel turned again to the Baals (8:33). Presumably, Gideon considered his ephod an expression of his faith in God. It would not be the first (or last) time that such a move easily merged with idolatry, as in the case of Aaron's infamous golden calf (also constructed from earrings; Exod 32:2–4). The same blurring of image and other gods appears in the Ten Commandments (Deut 5:7–9). (An ephod will figure prominently in the chaos of the closing chapters of Judges.)

The cycle concludes with the typical reference to rest from war, followed by the notice of Gideon's death. With Gideon, the character of the judge is far more complex than the figure in the cyclic typology. The diffident deliverer who became the homicidal avenger, in the end, has become the heretical judge, albeit unintentionally.

Abimelech: The Man Who Would Be King (Chap. 9)

Abimelech's very name—"my father is king"—repeats the questions about a human king raised at the end of the Gideon episode. True, the "father" could refer to God, but in context one suspects it refers to Gideon—and raises the question as to why Gideon *chose* the name in the first place. In fact, at the conclusion of the Gideon story, the narrator tells us that Israel forgot God and "did not exhibit loyalty to the house of Jerubbaal." Here again is the paring of God and king, but even more suggestive is the explicit reference to "loyalty" and the phrase "the *house* of Jerubbaal," which normally would indicate a *dynasty* stemming from Gideon (exactly what the people requested in 8:22). The mature Gideon refused kingship, but the young father named his son as the heir apparent to a throne.

Abimelech is the man who *would* be king, if his father would not. He suggests to his mother's clan in Shechem that it would be better to have *one* son of Jerubbaal ruling over them than seventy (Gideon was nothing if not prolific). The narrator has already told us that Abimelech is the son of a concubine, that is, a female servant who, though legally a wife, is of secondary status in the harem (8:31).[93] Moreover, it appears that she is a Canaanite, not an Israelite, which means that Gideon has disobeyed the orthodox prohibition of intermarriage. Retrospectively, the suggestion of illegitimacy continues in that Shechem is the place where Joshua held his great covenant affirmation ceremony (Joshua 24), but now it has become the place where Israel is "prostituting" itself to "Covenant Baal" (8:33; NRSV "Baal-berith," literally "Baal of the Covenant"). After the fall of the Northern Kingdom of Israel in 701 BCE readers would have appreciated the irony of this story in which an upstart pretender to the throne

---

92. The turn of phrase is Carolyn Pressler's as quoted in Miller, *Ten Commandments*, 56.

93. On this problem, cf. the story of Ishmael: Genesis 16 and especially Gen 20:8–10.

ends up destroying the very city that was ostensibly founded by the northern rebel King Jeroboam as the capital of his upstart realm (1 Kgs 12:25).

Abimelech's kinfolk convince "the lords of Shechem" that he is *their* "brother" more than he is brother to Gideon's other sons. They fund a band of thugs to support him, and he promptly murders all but one of those sons, whereupon the lords proclaim Abimelech king "by the oak of the pillar of Shechem," which now supplants, as it were, "the oak at Ophrah" (9:6; 6:11).

Having escaped the mass fratricide, Gideon's surviving (and youngest) son, stands on the top of Mt. Gerizim and delivers a stinging allegorical satire. The trees decide that they want to "anoint a king over themselves." (Here is the first occurrence of the word "anoint" that is the root of the word "Messiah." Later in the Former Prophets, of course, just who is the Lord's messiah and what that means will be a major focus, but here the term is almost incidental.) Several worthy candidates refuse the nomination—the olive tree, the fig tree, and the grape vine—each prized for its luscious fruit. Why should they cease bearing fruit in order to be king of the trees? So the trees resort to the bramble, a plant that pricks and entangles those who haplessly walk into it. It's as if the trees choose poison ivy, or even worse, Kudzu. Jotham then ends his parable with a curse: "let fire come out of the bramble and devour the cedars of Lebanon." A mere vine will be the downfall of a mighty forest. In the expanded interpretation, the curse invokes the mutual self-destruction of both the trees and the bramble, i.e., of both the "lords of Shechem" and Abimelech. With the language of a devouring fire, the parable ends very much like a prophetic oracle of judgment: "I will send a fire on the house of Hazael, and it shall devour the strongholds of Ben-hadad" (Amos 1:4; cf. 1:7, 10, 12, 14; 2:5, etc.). However, despite the overall negative tone, the parable does suggest the possibility of monarchy providing "refuge" *if* the relationship between monarch and people is "in good faith."[94] But if not, then the monarch will turn into a forest fire (v. 15)! Abimelech's murderous rise to power clearly does not qualify as good faith, as Jotham proceeds to emphasize (9:18).

The narrator tells us that Abimelech "ruled" over Israel three years, but the word really means something like "acted as commandant." Now in an ironic twist of the cyclic typology, instead of sending the spirit to a deliverer, God sends an *evil* spirit to the villain (9:22). This theological ploy apparently explains the otherwise puzzling turn of events in which the lords of Shechem suddenly oppose Abimelech by acting as highway robbers.[95] They shift their loyalty to a newcomer in town, one Gaal ben Abed, who himself would be king. His name means "loathsome son of a slave," a name not indicative of parental affection, and resembling none other than Abimelech, son of a slave woman (v. 18). Yet, inflamed by too much wine consumed in the temple of his god, Gaal has

---

94. Niditch, *Judges*, 116.

95. The same explanation appears for the bizarre behavior of the later king Saul, 1 Sam 16:14–16, where we will look at the "evil spirit" more carefully.

the audacity to challenge the pedigree of Abimelech—*he* isn't a true Shechemite, says this loathsome newcomer! The mayor of Shechem, Zebul, hears of the plot and informs Abimelech, presenting a plan to ambush Gaal and Co. when they come out of the town. Abimelech and Zebul together rout the rebels, and the next day they kill everyone in the city and raze it to the ground, leaving only the temple complex. The lords and ladies flee to the temple, but Abimelech sets it afire and kills them all (cf. the end of Samson's story, 16:30). Fire indeed has come out of the bramble and devoured the forest. But the rest of the parable now comes into play. Having destroyed the tower of Shechem, Abimelech now besieges the tower of another town, Thebez, seeking to burn it down also. "But a certain woman threw an upper millstone on Abimelech's head, and crushed his skull" (9:53). It seems to be another Sisera-and-Jael end, but Abimelech has enough strength left in him to ask his armor bearer to run him through, "so people will not say about me, 'A woman killed him'" (a fate *worse* than death itself for an epic hero).[96]

The narrator now explicitly draws a theological conclusion to the story: "Thus God returned to Abimelech the evil he committed against his father in killing his seventy brothers; and God also made all the evil of the people of Shechem return on their heads, and on them came the curse of Jotham son of Jerubbaal" (9:56–57, AT). This judgment was already noted as the purpose for sending the evil spirit: "so it would come about that the violence done to the seventy sons of Jerubbaal and their blood would return to Abimelech their brother . . . and to the lords of Shechem" (9:24, AT). The narrator tells us that God is the agent behind the story, "turning" events in accordance with the "wheels of justice"; or we can look at the story apart from such divine causation and say "what goes around comes around." For the biblical author, the two are inseparable, however—simply two ways of saying the same thing. There is a proverb for one and for the other: "The perverse get what their ways deserve"; "will [God] not repay all according to their deeds?" (Prov 14:14; 24:12).[97]

Interlude (Chap. 10)

Following two judges with only brief notices (10:1–5), the narrator provides an interlude in vv. 6–18 separating the extensive stories of Gideon and Abimelech from that of Jepthah. At first sight the interlude follows the cyclic typology, but there are significant differences. Israel's apostasy is illustrated with gods, gods, and more gods in v. 6—along with the Baals and Astartes, five occurrences of "the gods of X." Yahweh's agents of punishment now are the Philistines on the coast and the Ammonites in trans-Jordan, producing a vise grip of oppression that includes virtually all of Israel (Judah and Benjamin in the south; Ephraim in the north). When Israel cries

---

96. Niditch, *Judges*, 118.

97. We will return to the topic of divine causation when we look at the fall of the house of Eli, the fate of king Saul, Absalom's rebellion, and king Rehoboam's revolt, among other examples. See also the discussion in the Summary and Conclusion of this volume.

out now, it is a cry of confession as well as distress: "we have sinned against you." God responds with another summary recitation of saving deeds, from Egypt to Canaan, contrasted with Israel's disobedience, then vows that "I will deliver you no more." God has had enough. If the Israelites want to worship other gods, let *those* gods deliver them. In turn, the people reiterate their confession, and even repent by putting away the foreign gods and worshiping Yahweh, so God relents. But God's relenting is as reluctant as the people's repentance is unreliable. There may be a sense here in which God resents being repeatedly used, only to be abandoned again, yet cannot bear to see Israel suffer.[98]

The stage is set for the next deliverer, but immediately another difference from the typology appears: the narrator does not tell us that *God* raises up a deliverer; rather, "the commanders of the people of Gilead" do, with the pledge that "he shall be head over all the inhabitants of Gilead." Once again, a human leader will be exalted, and without explicit divine initiative. To be sure, the people do not say that Jepthah will be *king*, as with Abimelech. They are looking primarily for a *military* leader, or, to use the term that will soon appear, a "chief" (11:6).[99] But we are left to wonder if such a chief will aspire to even greater things.

Jephthah: Piety for Politics (11:1—12:7)

The opening line of the story presents a mixed picture. On the one hand, Jepthah is a mighty warrior, as was Gideon; on the other hand, he is the son of a prostitute, albeit engendered by Gilead. "Gilead" here is the eponymic individual who gave his name to both tribe and geographical region.[100] Ostracized by Gideon's legitimate sons, Jephthah flees away and gathers together a band of "outlaws" (literally "worthless men," as with Abimelech's gang, 9:4) who live by raiding. Desperate for a warlord, the elders of Gilead (here the region) couldn't care less about Jephthah's inferior family status. Jephthah accuses *them* of ostracizing him as well, but accepts their newfound appreciation for him, as well as the role of their "commander" and "head." Jephthah bases his acceptance on the condition that God will provide victory, and the people make their vow with God as witness.

So far, then, *human* initiative, appointment, and commissioning take precedence. Jepthah not only accepts the role as "commander," essentially what the "deliverer" is, but also welcomes the more exalted status of "head." Here the deliverer's artful negotiations seem more concerned to insure that the *elders* "deliver" on their election of him as head; then *he* tells *God* what is hap-

---

98. Cf. Polzin, *Moses*, 177–78; Webb, *Book of Judges*, 48; Campbell and O'Brien, *Unfolding*, 168; Campbell, *From Joshua to Chronicles*, 94.

99. "Commander" in NRSV, but not the same Hebrew word as in 10:18. "Head" seems to be a higher rank, and probably more political than military—a tribal "chief." Cf. Webb, *Judges*, 74.

100. More precisely, Gilead is a grandson of Manasseh, who, of course, is also the patron of one of the traditional twelve tribes of Israel. So Gilead as a tribe is really a subgroup within Manasseh, here especially that "half-tribe of Manasseh" that lives beyond the Jordan (Josh 1:12; 13:8–13). To further confuse things, Gilead is sometimes used as an alternate to Gad.

pening. In a sense, he and God are in the same boat: both have been rejected but then suddenly invited back when trouble appears.

Turning to the enemy, at first the mighty warrior attempts some diplomacy, something lacking especially in characters like Ehud. He sends ambassadors to the Ammonite king, asking why he is attacking Gilead. The king responds that Israel took his land (here conflated with that of Moab) when they came up from Egypt. The king demands its peaceful return. Jephthah responds with a little historical lesson. Israel never took the land of Moab or Edom, but circumvented both. They did fight against and defeat King Sihon of the Amorites, because he attacked them, and Israel occupied their land, precisely the territory that the Ammonite king claims. Also conflating Ammon with Moab, Jephthah then recognizes the legitimate territory of Ammon as that given by the god Chemosh (or "Kemosh"), basically south and east of the land that Ammon now claims. Thus it is Ammon, and not Israel, that is the aggressor. Finally, Jephthah the judge appeals to the *chief* justice, as it were: "let the Lord, who is judge, decide [lit. "judge"] today for the Israelites or for the Ammonites" (v. 27). Just as he did in negotiating with the elders of Gilead (11:9), so in his negotiating with Ammon, Jephthah trusts that God will decide the issue (albeit without prior consultation), and in Jepthah's favor. Here the negotiations end.

Now we return to the cyclic typology with the first indication that God, in fact, *has* chosen Jephthah and will give him victory, for "the spirit of the Lord" comes upon him. But before Jephthah draws his sword, he makes an apparently pious vow that unfortunately also proves to be tragically stupid. If God will give him victory, he will offer up as a sacrifice "the one coming out who comes out of the doors of my house to meet me when I return unharmed" (v. 31, AT). Jepthtah proceeds to defeat the Ammonites in a battle reported only briefly, then returns home, only to see his daughter—and only child—coming out to meet him dancing for joy. The situation is strangely like that of Sisera's mother in Judges 5, whom we see fantasizing over the return of her hero, not knowing that he is dead; here the daughter comes out to greet the returning hero, not knowing that her celebration seals her own death. For in ancient Israelite religion, a vow once made to God cannot be withdrawn.[101] Even Jephthah's daughter acknowledges the truth of that belief, and, after giving her two months to mourn her premature death, Jepthtah keeps his vow.[102]

Jephthah's vow was not only rash, it was unnecessary. The Spirit had already come upon him, but apparently that wasn't enough to assure him of victory. He wanted to make a deal. He made conditional what was already unconditional. He insisted on bargaining for what was already given. The gesture of the oath does not reveal piety; it reveals anxiety

---

101. The irrevocability of a vow is also involved in the story of the Gibeonites in Joshua 9. Niditch, *Judges*, 133, also notes that the story reflects a male culture in which "keeping one's word" is highly esteemed, however "troubling" the results here.

102. For the ambiguity of the story and how it can produce numerous readings, see Gunn and Fewell, *Narrative*, 112–19.

and distrust. Ironically, the oath sworn to God results in taking God's name in vain, for now he must commit one of the most abhorrent acts prohibited by the Torah—infanticide (Deut 12:31; 18:10). The *personal* tragedy of Jephthah's foolish vow becomes the focus of the narrative, not the *political* deliverance of Gilead. Moreover, just as self-interest conflicted his role as deliverer, so here Jephthah acts as if his daughter is the "cause" of "trouble" for *him*, an example of male arrogance that will recur later in the book.

Now Jephthah's victory leads to inter-tribal strife. The Ephraimites are offended that they were not invited to the war, the same complaint that they lodged against Gideon, who resolved the conflict without a fight. Jephthah claims that he called them, but got no answer, so went ahead on his own. He does not seem to wait for a response, but attacks the Ephraimites (the very ones that most likely suffered under the Philistines, 10.7). Indeed, he exploits the difference in regional pronunciation to determine the enemy who is to die, thereby giving us the word "shibboleth." Thus the career of Jephthah ends with a civil war in which the unity of the tribes of Israel is shattered. Unfortunately, such tribal strife is only a sign of worse things to come. The story ends with the formula of Jephthah's judgeship over "Israel," but he is still "the Gileadite."

Thus Jepthah joins a growing list of judges who show poor judgment—Ehud, the brutal assassin, and Gideon, the idolater. Although the spirit of God comes upon him, enabling him to deliver Israel, everywhere else in the story Jephthah *invokes* God for his own political gain, but the narrator never says that God agrees with those goals.[103] To some extent Jephthah seems to *use* God for political gain the same way that fickle Israel uses God for rescue—but then, God is using Jephthah too! In the end, the deliverer paradoxically brings death to Israel and to his own house.

Samson: The Playboy Judge (Chaps. 13–16)

After the brief reports of three other minor judges, the story of Samson begins (chaps. 13–16). If anyone breaks the mold of the judge, it is Samson. At times his story seems like a farce, were it not for the violence. Samson is a combination of Rambo, Paul Bunyan, and Cassanova, all rolled into one. Although a remnant of the cyclic pattern appears at the beginning, little else fits the picture of previous deliverers. There is no outcry from Israel, no appointment of Samson (except prenatal). The spirit of the Lord will come into play, but Samson will use the accompanying power more to protect himself than to win battles. In fact, it is never really clear that Samson delivers Israel from the oppression of the Philistines; at one point, his conflicts with the enemy threaten to make things *worse* (15:9–11). In the end, he will win personal revenge against the "lords of the Philistines," and, in the process, a kind of theological victory for God, but the Philistine threat will be far from over.

---

103. Thus the overall theme of the story concerns "the tendency to accommodate religion to political norms" (Webb, *Book of Judges*, 74).

The story of Samson begins with a familiar "type scene" known as an annunciation. The wife of a man named Manoah, of the tribe of Dan, is barren, and the angel of God comes to her with the news that she will have a child. He will be a "Nazirite to God," a member of a religious order requiring strict abstinence not only from wine and other alcoholic drinks, but from all products of grapes. The Nazirite also had to let his hair grow uncut until renouncing his vows, and the Nazirite was prohibited from coming near a corpse. Contact with a corpse would render the Nazirite ritually impure and require stringent purification rituals.[104] As a prenatal preparation, the angel forbids the mother-to-be herself from drinking wine or eating anything impure. The angel then concludes the annunciation in saying that Samson "shall begin to deliver Israel from the hand of the Philistines." Perhaps the angel should have used italics when saying "begin."

A rather humorous series of conversations follows in which Manoah's wife (never named) reports the angelic visitation to him. Manaoh does not listen well, however, for he then asks God what they are to do concerning their child. The angel again appears to his wife in his absence, and she decides to bring the two together. Manaoh repeats his question: what is the child to do? The angel says, in effect, "I've already told your wife." So Manaoh invites the visitor to lunch, but the angel declines, suggesting that Manaoh instead make a burnt offering to God (here we learn that Manaoh did not recognize the visitor as an angel).[105] Only when the offering is burning and the angel ascends to heaven in the flame does Manoah fully understand who it is. Then he says that they will die because they have seen God, but, as his wife wisely points out, why would God accept the offering much less promise a child if God had come to kill them? The story concludes with the birth of the child, his growth and blessing by God, and the first stirrings of the spirit of God in him.

With the invocation of the Spirit, one might expect an act of deliverance from the Philistines at this point. But instead of delivering, Samson is philandering—and with the enemy! He is infatuated with a Philistine woman. So intense is his attraction that he demands of his parents, "get her for me as my wife." His parents ask why can't he find a nice girl from their own people? Why marry among those "uncircumcised Philistines," a reference to their ritual impurity vis-à-vis Israel's customs. But Samson wants this woman only, literally "because she is right in my eyes" (14:3), foreshadowing the major theme of the concluding portion of the book (17:6 etc). Samson's choice could evoke the judgmental comment about intermarriage in 3:6, but there is no editorial criticism here. In fact, juxtaposed to the expression of Samson's will, the narrator now tells us that all of this is really according to *God's* will—one of those rare authorial commentaries that informs us of what the characters themselves do not know—"this was from the Lord," i.e., "a pretext to act against the Philistines,"

---

104. See Num 6:1–21. Samuel will be a prominent Nazirite as well.

105. Cf. with Gideon, 6:11–22.

who, as if *we* don't know, had dominion over Israel at the time. Samson's romance with the Philistine woman is, indeed, a bizarre way for God to work, especially since it breaks the very prohibition of intermarriage that God has issued in Deuteronomy (Deut 7:3).

Samson now goes with Mom and Dad to the town of Timnah, in search of his wife, but the betrothal is intertwined with a strange incident in which Samson kills an attacking lion and later eats some honey from a beehive in the carcass. Samson does not tell his parents about killing the lion, nor where he got the honey that they ate also. Moreover, it is when the lion attacks that the Spirit of the Lord rushes on him, enabling him to do to the lion what the lion would have done to him—tear it apart with his bare hands. Here Samson is very much the folk hero, along the lines of a Paul Bunyan or a Davy Crockett. The Spirit has delivered Samson from the lion, but so far this has nothing to do with liberation from the Philistines. It is also somewhat suspicious that Samson is wandering around in the vineyards of the town, since he's not to have anything to do with grapes, and that he touches the corpse of the lion, since he's not to touch the corpse at least of another human (and that will happen soon enough!). It is not that he has broken his vows, but he seems to be testing the limits.

Now the lion and honey come into play at Samson's wedding feast, literally a "drinking occasion" (and we're not talking about Baptist punch). Samson poses a riddle to his Philistine hosts, along with a wager that they cannot decipher it: "Out of the eater came something to eat. Out of the strong came something sweet." Samson has a way with words, after all. At first the Philistines cannot unravel the riddle, but in desperation they threaten Samson's new bride and her family with being burned alive if she will not help them. The wedding festivities have turned into terror.

Samson's wife, understandably frightened, cries and whines and begs Samson to tell her the solution to the riddle. Why, I haven't even told Mom and Dad, he says, but then gives in. The men of the town then present Samson with the solution to the riddle, and Samson responds with another bit of verse: "If you had not plowed with my heifer, you would not have found out my riddle." (His wife has now been threatened with immolation by her friends and called a promiscuous cow by her husband.) Now again the Spirit of the Lord rushes on Samson, with the result that he goes to Ashkelon, a major Philistine city, and kills thirty men, takes their clothing, and gives it in payment to the men of Timnah. *Now* the Nazirite has touched *thirty* corpses. Samson then stomps back to Mom and Dad's, and his bride goes to the best man!

After a while, Samson tries to see his wife again in a visit to her house, but her father refuses him entry. Samson then says that this wrong gives him the license to "do mischief to the Philistines without blame." In a wild prank, Samson attaches flaming torches to three hundred foxes and drives them into the field, vineyards, and olive groves of the Philistines, destroying them. It is an act of vandalism, not to mention animal cruelty. The Philistines respond by burning to death Samson's wife and father, as if they were involved. In turn, Samson avenges their deaths by inflicting "a great slaughter" on the Philistines.

In retaliation, the Philistines raid a Judahite town of Lehi, seeking to find Samson and capture him. The people of Judah find Samson first and complain: "Do you not know that the Philistines are rulers over us?" Then they add, "What then have you done to us?" As Niditch suggests, "An avenging Wildman is a difficult sort of hero to deal with, even for the community he champions."[106] Samson replies with "they did it to me first." The Judahites say that they have come to bind him and hand him over, and Samson agrees, on condition that they will not strike him themselves. How the portrait of the judge-redeemer has changed! Here the oppressed people seem resigned to accepting their oppressors as their "rulers," and instead of following their hero into battle with the enemy, they *hand him over* to the enemy.

With this "binding" of Samson, a repetitive series of incidents follows in which he loosens the bands and retaliates, leading ultimately to his death. Although there is only the faintest of hints so far (14:11), Samson apparently is a very strong man, and not easily bound. That is particularly true when the spirit of the Lord rushes on him, as it does again now for the third time. The ropes pop like straw and Samson then uses an animal jaw bone to kill a thousand Philistines. God again comes to his aid when Samson is thirsty after all that killing, as well as giving a little self-congratulatory speech.

So God opens a well and Samson drinks and is revived. The story seems to come to an abrupt end with the formula number of days that Samson judged Israel, but there is more.

We now learn first hand of Samson's unusual strength. He consorts with a prostitute in a Philistine city. The Philistines hear that he is there, and wait to ambush him when he leaves in the morning. But Samson "lay only until midnight," went to the city gate, pulled up the posts out of the ground and sauntered off with them on his shoulders to Hebron—an uphill climb of some forty miles! Then Samson falls in love again, unfortunately with a woman—Delilah—who is far from loyal to him and easily bribed. She is the quintessential "seductive and dangerous foreign woman,"[107] and she accepts the Philistines' offer of a lot of money if she will find out the source of Samson's great strength.

The story is well known and follows the typical three/four pattern of a folk tale. Given Samson's playboy habits, the story almost looks like a game of "Bondage and Discipline." Three times Samson pretends to give away his secret, only to break the bonds that his scheming wife has tied on him. But the fourth time, Delilah whines and pouts so effectively, accusing Samson of not *really* loving her, that he discloses the true source of his strength: "A razor has never come upon my head; for I have been a Nazirite to God from my mother's womb. If my head were shaved, then my strength would leave me; I would become weak, and be like anyone else." Far from being

---

106. Niditch, *Judges*, 159.

107. Ibid., 167.

moved by Samson's religious vocation, Delilah betrays him to the Philistines. The scene in which she lulls him to sleep in her lap, then has someone shave his head, reminds us of her more brutal counterpart, Jael, but here it is the ostensible hero, not the villain, who is lured to his death.

Earlier, after the jawbone massacre, Samson had appealed to God for water, referring to himself as "your servant." Now is the only time that he refers to his status as a Nazirite, and, ironically, once his hair is cut, he is a Nazirite no longer (cf. Num 6:13–20). A haircut is a sign of the return to secular status over against holiness, to civilized society over against raw nature.[108] The moment he ceases to be a Nazirite, God leaves him (16:20). Now the Philistines can prevail, so they seize him, gouge out his eyes, shackle him, and hitch him to a mill stone. Symbolically, the mighty hero is emasculated, forced to perform a woman's work.[109] "But," the narrator tells us, "the hair of his head began to grow again."

The lords of the Philistines gather together for a religious festival of sacrifice to their god, Dagon, who, they say, "has given Samson our enemy into our hand." The language, of course, ironically reflects that of the cyclic pattern; the Philistines do not know that "this was from the Lord" (14:4). They make the mistake of carrying their ridicule of Samson too far. They bring him to the temple, thronged with thousands of celebrants, including "all the lords of the Philistines," and make him perform for their entertainment. Samson, however, manages to get his hands on the pillars of the temple. "Then Samson called to the Lord and said, 'Lord God, remember me and strengthen me only this once, O God, so that with this one act of revenge I may pay back the Philistines for my two eyes.'" Then he pulls down the pillars and the temple collapses on him and all the worshippers of Dagon, killing more that he had managed to kill in all his other exploits (16:30).

Has Samson delivered Israel? At the end, there is the formula that he "judged" Israel, but in what sense? Early in the story, his father had asked God "what is to be the boy's rule of life?" (13:12). The word for rule here is *mishpat*, often meaning "justice" and based on the same root as the word for judge. But Samson leads an *unruly* life. He shows no consciousness of his calling as a Nazirite, except for thinking that long hair made him a Superman. He shows no interest in liberating Israel. He never leads fellow Israelites in battle. His interests are exclusively personal, not political, motivated by lust and revenge. His mind is pretty much below his belt. The one time he calls himself the "servant" of the Lord, it is to get a drink of water and escape his enemies. At his death, it is true, he takes "the lords of the Philistines" with him, and perhaps this suggests a kind of deliverance for Israel, but it remains unclear if the "rule" of the Philistines (15:11) is over, and still it is revenge for the loss of his eyes (16:29).[110] The Philistines are one of those people

---

108. Ibid., 170.

109. Ibid., 171, citing Job 31:10 and Isa 47:2–3.

110. Samson's victims thus resemble the "lords of the Tower of Shechem" destroyed by Abimelech, 9:46.

whom God left to "test" Israel (3:3), and it will not be long before we see the lords of the Philistines back in action, along with their god Dagon (1 Sam 5:1–5).[111] Perhaps all of this suggests that the Samson stories are much closer to the type of epic hero tales than with other judges. His personal conflicts with the Philistines would delight any readers for whom "Philistine" signifies the enemy "Other" paradigmatically, but the stories do not bear the stamp of the deliverer or liberator that an editor imposed on all the stories at the outset (2:16, 18; cf. 3:9).[112]

We are also left to ponder the role of God in all of this. Beginning with Samson's illicit marriage, the narrator tells us that everything "is from the Lord" as a "pretext to act against the Philistines" (14:4). Three times the spirit of God rushes upon Samson, once to fight off a lion, and two times to exact revenge. After Samson loses his hair, and thus symbolically ceases to be a Nazirite, God leaves him (16:20), but apparently again provides the strength needed to destroy the temple. It is almost as if in these stories we see a kind of primitive level of spiritual power that provides physical strength but without any social dimension or function, or at least where such a function seems incidental. Yet another unique feature of these stories is how, in the end, there seems to be a contest between God and the *gods* of Canaan, in this case, represented by Dagon. Ironically, at his death, Samson fulfills the command of the Torah to "tear down their altars" (Deut 7:5)—and just when sacrifices are being offered—but there is no indication that there is a religious motivation at work. The fall of the temple is symbolically the fall of Dagon as well, but God has had to stoop unusually low for this semblance of deliverance.

Chaos (Chaps. 17–21)

The book concludes with five chapters in which Israel descends into chaos. Politically, this chaos appears in a recurring motif that also closes the book: "in those days there was no king in Israel; all the people did what was right in their own eyes" (17.6; 18.1; 19.1; 21.24). Scholars differ widely on how to read this refrain, from a neutral description—"in the old days things were different"[113]—to a judgmental condemnation that also has an anti-Northern bias.[114] Taken by itself, the statement could refer to a kind of democratic ethos that *requires* no king, a social order of which even locusts are capable (Prov 30.27); but in context, the statement refers to a situation of increasing social *disorder* where human decency is abandoned and human depravity runs out of control.[115] These chapters do not

---

111. In the 1 Samuel story, the statue of Dagon falls to the ground. But the Philistines will kill the first king, Saul, and not until the realm of David will they be subdued (2 Sam 8:1).

112. See Niditch, *Judges*, 154–55: "Samson is a complex, epic-style hero who would be incomplete without flaws," and whose subversive acts might fit with the "peasant revolt" model of the conquest. Overall, "the author seeks to portray him positively" (172).

113. Niditch (ibid., 182) sees these chapters (along with chap. 1) as expressive of the "humanist" voice whose major theme is the vacillations of power in various social and political situations.

114. See the introduction to this chapter.

115. Gunn and Fewell, *Narrative*, suggest another possible reading: the absence of a king

even have a deliverer, nor do they conform to the previous cyclic pattern of Judges in any way. Part of the reason is that here there is no external threat to Israel, although there is plenty of evil, some of it inflicted *by* Israel on innocent natives. The threats are internal: barbarism and inter-tribal war.

In my judgment, the placement of the refrain points to editorial work that frames earlier stories: first immediately after the story of the home shrine (17:6);[116] two others tacked on to the beginning of separate incidents (18:1; 19:1);[117] and a final one to conclude the whole collection and the book itself (21:25), setting the stage for the rise of Samuel and then the first king, Saul.[118] When everyone does what is right in his or her own eyes, individual "autonomy" reigns—literally, "self-law"—the result being anarchy. Such autonomy is precisely what the Torah warns against (Deut 12:8). In effect, doing what is right in one's own eyes functions as the counterpart to the earlier "doing what is evil in the eyes of the Lord." This does not necessarily mean that the refrain evokes a king as the only answer to anarchy. Even under David, a civil war between North and South took the lives of twenty thousand (2 Sam 18:7); and in the North, sectarian violence led to massacres (e.g., 2 Kings 9–10). One might simply conclude that a *judge* is necessary for civil order, as long as the judge authentically represents Yahweh's will, as does Samuel (by and large).[119]

Micah and the Levite (Chaps. 17–18)

The first story of Micah and the Levite is intertwined with the story of how the tribe of Dan came to occupy its territory.[120] Micah, an Ephraimite, confesses to his mother that he was the thief who had stolen her money, a sizeable sum of eleven hundred pieces of silver. Rather than criticizing her son, the woman invokes a blessing upon him, and, perhaps to insure the blessing, piously vows to give all of the money to God "to make a hewn icon and a cast icon" (v. 3).[121]

---

is referring to God, who "might as well not have existed." Polzin, *David*, 74–75 suggests yet another: the contrast is "between Israelites doing what was right in their own eyes and Israelites having to do what was right in their kings' eyes," the latter turning out to be "as bad as the first."

116. Here it is possible that the refrain could simply mean, "that's the way things were then," along the lines of Niditch's neutral reading (see above) and indicative of religious practices later prohibited, but the placement easily suggests another reading, more in tune with those prohibitions themselves.

117. Thus 18:1 clearly has *two* introductory phrases with "in those days," the second being typical of epic stories about "the days of yore," the first being editorial. Also 19:1 has two introductory phrases: "And it was in those days, and there was no king in Israel, and there was a man, a Levite" (AT), where again the "no king" clause seems editorial. On the syntax, see Niditch, *Judges*, 14–15, although she does not comment on the apparent doublets at 18:1 and 19:1.

118. Note again how the editorial conclusion of Ruth ties in the monarchy of David, 4:17–22.

119. See 1 Sam 7:12–17 and 8:1–4. There the debate becomes whether a judge or a king best serves Israel's needs.

120. For a detailed analysis of this story, see Mueller, *Micah Story*.

121. The translation of Niditch, *Judges*, 172. There may be two figurines, one wooden and one metal, or one employing both media (181). Niditch emphasizes that the "objects are not idols but iconic representations that allow

Dishonesty seems to run in the family, for when Micah's mother pays a silversmith to make the image she gives him only *two* hundred pieces of silver. It's an image on the cheap. Micah installs the image in his house, then decides to expand on his religious equipment by making an ephod and *teraphim*, that is, a vestment (see regarding Gideon above) and another type of sacramental object.[122] Micah now has a "shrine" (literally, "house of God or gods"), and to round off his little home chapel he installs one of his sons as a priest—and the narrator introduces the first "there was no king" motif. Micah is among those who "did what was right in their own eyes."

Remarkably, there is no acknowledgment here (including by the narrator) that Micah and Mom have committed the kind of "heresy" that the later Deuteronomists will condemn. Images, of course, are explicitly prohibited in the Torah (whether images of God or of other gods) especially in the Ten Commandments (Exod 20:4; Deut 5:8; cf. 4:16–25). Moreover, Micah's home shrine would make a sterling example of the kind of uncontrolled local religious practices that led to their prohibition and the centralization of worship in the Jerusalem temple (Deut 12:8–9). To put it another way, here is a story that seems to reflect religious practices that only later would be considered unorthodox.[123] The only hints of criticism here appear in the "no king" motif and perhaps in more subtle ways. The mother's wish for a blessing ironically uses exactly the same words as a Deuteronomic *curse* on those who do construct such an image.[124] Also, after the image is made, the author no longer uses the longer name "Micayahu" ("Who is like Yahweh?").[125] By name "Micah" is now "godless."

Apparently, Micah soon replaces his son as priest with someone who has ecclesiastical credentials—a wandering Levite from Bethlehem.[126] This Levite is off seeking "to live wherever I can find a place," and accepts Micah's invitation to be the priest of his homemade chapel, apparently with image, ephod, dice, and all. Micah provides room and board and an annual salary. Now, he thinks, he will surely be blessed with prosperity, having a priest in tow.

The narrator now moves to the story of the tribe of Dan, introducing it with the "no king" motif (18:1). Like the Levite, the Danites are seeking "a territory to live in."[127] Like Joshua with

worshipers to focus upon the deity." Smith, "Idolatry," 53, provides a trenchant comment on "idolatry": "'No one has ever worshiped an idol. Some have worshiped God in the form of an idol; that is what idols are for'" (he is quoting an earlier remark he made). He also suggests that "*Theologies are conceptual images of God*" (56, italics original). The later Deuteronomist would make no such equivocation.

122. The *teraphim* likely were connected with the veneration of family ancestors. See Miller, *Religion of Ancient Israel*, 72, citing the work of van der Toorn. See Excursus 3.

123. See Excursus 3: and Smith, *Origins*, 142.

124. The Hebrew words in 17:3 are translated as "[who makes an] idol or casts an image" in the curse in Deut 27:15.

125. Cf. Mueller, *Micah Story*, 53.

126. Some scholars think that the two priests are one and the same, since Micah says that the Levite is "like a son to me." Presumably the priest is the same as the one named in 18:30.

127. The statement in v. 1 about no allotted territory seems inconsistent with previous references. See Josh 19:47 and note that in Judg 1:34

Jericho, they send out spies to reconnoiter the land, and the spies just happen to come upon the house of Micah, where they stay. They recognize the Levite's southern accent (perhaps he says "yall"), and when they find out how he got there and what he was doing, they jump at the opportunity to benefit from his crystal ball. They ask about the success of their mission, and the priest replies: "Go in peace. The mission you are on is under the eye of the Lord." Presumably, this is a benediction, but proverbial wisdom hints that it could be a *malediction*: "human ways are under the eyes of the Lord, and he examines all their paths. / The iniquities of the wicked ensnare them, and they are caught in the toils of their sin" (Prov 5:21–22).[128]

The Danites proceed in their mission, and come to the town of Laish. "They observed the people who were there living securely . . . , quiet and unsuspecting, lacking nothing on earth, and possessing wealth." Although some of the Hebrew here is unclear, the description of the town as a kind of idyllic community, peaceful and prosperous, is apparent. Obscured in translation, the word *betaḥ* recurs four times (NRSV "securely," "unsuspecting" vv. 7, 10, 27). Far from being a threat to the Danites, or anyone else, these people seem to know no enemy, and their naiveté is soon to have tragic consequences, because they live in the *territory* that the Danites want. But the spies say to their comrades: "God has indeed given it into your hands." Ironically, the narrator (and then the spies) describe the land as "a place where there is no lack of anything on earth," making it look very much like the description of the land promised to Israel in the Torah—"a land where you will lack nothing" (Deut 8:9). Laish *looks* the way the land of Israel is supposed to look, only it is in the "wrong" hands.

Now the spies report Micah's religious equipment, and the Danites decide that they would like to have the equipment and the priest for themselves, so they send a company of six hundred soldiers to confiscate them. The company is a ridiculously large number, and Micah must watch as his precious chapel is denuded. Not to be outdone, however, he musters some of his neighbors to pursue and challenge the Danites, complaining that he has nothing left now that they have taken "my gods that I made, and the priest." The Danites warn him that they include some "hot-tempered fellows" who will kill Micah and his family, so Micah desists.

Now we see that *all* of the Danites seem to be "hot-tempered"—in fact, ruthless murderers. They attack Laish, kill the residents and burn the city. Ironically, the narrator tells us that "there was no *deliverer*" for the victims, whom the narrator again describes as "quiet and unsuspecting." It is as if we see what it would have been like if *Israel* had no deliverers like Othniel, Deborah, Gideon, and the rest. Throughout the so-called "conquest" stories, contemporary readers have had ample reasons to recoil at the savagery and even genocide of Israel's attacks on the native inhabitants. Here,

---

the Danites have no territory because they are repulsed by the Amorites. Now they will pick on someone less than their own size.

128. Cf. Polzin, *Moses*, 198, who observes that the Hebrew word for "under the eye of" is ambiguous and can be positive or negative.

precisely because of the bucolic description of the "Canaanites," the treachery seems both poignant and appalling.[129]

The story concludes with the rebuilding of the city and renaming it for the tribal ancestor, Dan. The Danites also "set up the image for themselves," and we learn that none other than a grandson of Moses provided the priestly family "until the time the land went into captivity." Here is a rare, explicit reference to the time that is no doubt in the past of the narrator, that time after the fall of the Northern Kingdom of Israel in 721 BCE. Some scholars see the preceding story as an implied critique of the Northern Kingdom, whose apostate king, Jeroboam, installed golden calves as gods in the capital, Shechem, and in Dan (1 Kgs 12:28).[130] Irrespective of any such implication, the story is clearly a "foundation legend" telling the story of how the sanctuary came to be.[131] The reference to the exile of Northern Israel turns the legend into irony. The Danites located their territory and annihilated an innocent community in order to seize it; their descendants will *lose* their territory and be exiled from it. In a final aside, the narrator refers to "the house of God" at Shiloh and the time of its existence to date the duration of the shrine at Dan. Especially with the preceding allusion to exile, the reference could be a signal from an editor familiar with Shiloh's history, including the way in which Jeremiah would use the destruction of Shiloh to illustrate God's refusal to be present when there was "wickedness" (Jer 7:12), a condition that will become apparent already below, in 21:19–24.[132] By association, Dan's days are numbered even as it is founded.

As one scholar has observed, chaps. 17–18 present a kind of "morality tale" in which the characters break eight of the Ten Commandments (making an image, dishonoring a mother, taking God's name in vain, killing, lying, and coveting.)[133] This is what happens when everyone "does what is right in her own eyes" and there is no central authority which will enforce the law. But lawlessness is mild here compared to what happens next.

The Levite's Concubine: Rape, Murder, and Mayhem (Chaps. 19–21)

> *One clothing store displays "battered and bloody mannequins posing as upscale assault victims." In Rapper Eminem's recent album, Relapse, he sings: "'See whore, you're the kinda girl that I'd assault and rape.'"*[134]

---

129. Niditch, *Judges*, 183, notes that at least there is no "self-righteous justification" as in Deuteronomy and Joshua.

130. Presumably this polemic against the northern part of Israel (as opposed to Judah) reflects a wider pattern in that the geographical movement from Othniel on is increasingly toward the north—and disaster (cf. chap. 1). However, Niditch, *Judges*, 184, points out that the evocation of Moses (despite some textual variants) makes such a critique unlikely.

131. For other examples of such stories, see Gen 12:6–7; 28:10–22.

132. Note especially 1 Sam 2:11–36. The Philistines probably destroyed Shiloh in the battle recounted in 1 Samuel 4.

133. Mueller, *Micah Story*, 3, 14, 35.

134. Goodman, "Equal Rites Awards 2009," A9.

There is probably no story in the Bible that can match the horror of the closing story in Judges. Even people familiar with the Bible often do not know this story, because it is not likely to appear in Church School curricula, or even in sermons, much less does it provide an inspiring "memory verse." This story is by far the most terrible among several "texts of terror" that illustrate misogyny in its most barbaric form.[135] Like the stories of genocide in Joshua, however, we must not ignore this story of violence against a woman because that violence is still very much a part of our own world. Consider another example from American culture: "The video world is especially hostile toward women—games often include rape scenes, prostitution, full nudity and disembodied body parts . . . Revenge is a common feature, and the stories foster the notion that violence as payback is justifiable."[136]

The story begins with another occurrence of the "no king" motif. A Levite and his concubine, or subordinate wife, have a marital spat and the woman goes home to her father.[137] After four months, the Levite seeks reconciliation, suggesting that *he* is the one who owes an apology, so he travels to his wife's home. His father-in-law welcomes him, in fact, wines and dines him for five days, continually thwarting his departure. Presumably, the father is reluctant to lose his daughter again. But finally the Levite has had enough, and he sets out for his own home with his wife and a servant. As night draws nigh, the servant suggests that they spend the night in Jebus (Jerusalem), but the Levite refuses, saying that he doesn't want to be among "foreigners" but with those who "belong to the people of Israel." Ironically, in the previous story, a foreign town, Laish, was a peaceful community, but annihilated by Israelites; here, an Israelite fears a foreign town, but finds unbelievable hostility in an Israelite town.

They head on to the town of Gibeah, and the Levite proceeds to the square where he sits and waits for someone to offer them hospitality for the night, as was the custom. No one does so until an old man appears and invites them to his home, saying, "Peace be to you. I will care for all your wants." But as they are enjoying themselves over dinner, "the men of the city, a perverse lot, surround the house." Literally, these men are "sons of the Devil," as it were, invoking an obscure figure of the underworld named Belial (he will become one of Milton's fallen angels). They pound on the door and demand of the host that he send out the Levite so that they may "know" him. The euphemism refers to sexual intercourse, in this case, male homosexual rape.[138] The host refuses, and instead, he

---

135. See Trible, *Texts of Terror*.

136. Herzfeld, "Games," 22–23. Almost certainly the biblical author does *not* intend this story of rape and murder as "entertainment."

137. A textual variant to v. 2 suggests that the woman has "prostituted herself." That could be an interpretive description since desertion of a marriage by the wife was equated with adultery; at worse, it could be an attempt to "blame the victim."

138. There are strong similarities to the story of Lot and his daughters in Genesis 19. Such stories are often used to condemn male homosexuality in general, but that is a misuse, because the subject is rape, not mutually affirming intimacy. It makes no more sense to condemn homosexual sex on the basis of this story than it does to con-

offers his virgin daughter and the Levite's concubine! "Do to them what seems good in your eyes," he says (AT), ironically echoing the "no king" motif. The host is willing to subject "their" women, but not another man, for sexual violation. When the townsmen persist, the host (or the Levite) brings out the concubine. The subject of the verb is ambiguous, but in either case, both men make the concubine available. Then the townsmen "wantonly raped her, and abused her all through the night until the morning."

In the morning, the Levite finds his wife lying on the doorstep. "Get up," he says, "we are going." His callousness only compounds the brutality of the rapists, but it cannot affect *her* because she is dead. So the Levite puts her body on a donkey and returns home. Then he takes a knife and dismembers her into twelve pieces and sends a body part to each of the twelve tribes of Israel with a message: "Has such a thing ever happened since the day that the Israelites came up from the land of Egypt until this day? Consider it, take counsel, and speak out" (19:30).

Now, for the first and only time in Judges, "all the Israelites" gather together as a "congregation assembled in one body before the Lord," as "the congregation of the people of God" (20:1–2).[139] They interrogate the Levite, who summarizes what has happened in terms that exaggerate the threat to himself, conveniently omitting the damning part of his complicity in the rape of his concubine. In fact, his accusation against "the lords of Gibeah" is an outright lie (20:5) that dangerously politicizes the incident. As Schneider says, "The irony is that the Levite man demanded that the Israelites go to war on account of the woman whom he had done nothing to help and whose situation he had caused in the first place."[140] Moreover, personal revenge—which increasingly has preempted political redemption—now becomes a *national* obsession.

Outraged by the rape, "*all* the people" rise up "as *one*" and vow to avenge Gibeah "'for all the disgrace that they have done to Israel.' So *all* of the men of Israel gathered against the city, *united as one*" (vv. 8–11). Again we confront an irony: the only time all of the tribes unite to do *anything* it is to attack one of their own, and they do so as God's "congregation"! The purpose seems appropriate—to "purge the evil from Israel."[141] Initially, of course, the intention is to execute the rapists themselves, but the Levite's account has implicated the *tribe* of Benjamin as well (20:4, 10, 12). But the tribe of Benjamin, which includes the town of Gibeah, refuses to hand over the rapists, and, instead, mounts an opposing armed force of sharp-shooters.[142]

---

demn *heterosexual* sex because of the rape of the concubine.

139. The latter phrase is my translation, reflecting the common root *qhl* for assembly or congregation. The last reference to such a gathering was in the covenant ceremony in Josh 8:30–35 (cf. v. 35). Cf. 21:13 where "congregation" is from another root.

140. Schneider, *Judges*, 268.

141. The phrase "purge the evil" appears frequently in Deuteronomy, e.g., 22:21, 22, 23, where vv. 25–27 come closest to the situation of rape in our story.

142. The left-handed slingshot soldiers among the Benjamites were renowned for their accuracy (v. 16; cf. with Ehud, whose weapon, of course, is a sword, 3:15).

The result is civil war with eleven tribes against one. The irony is apparent when the question about who will lead the battle (Judah, 18:18) is exactly the same that was asked in 1:1 about attacking the *Canaanites*.

The Israelites consult with God (apparently using the ark, v. 27, the only reference in Judges), who three times encourages them to attack the Benjamites (strangely, the first two assaults result in defeat!). Finally, the Israelites succeed, or rather, God does, for the narrator says "the Lord defeated Benjamin before Israel" (20:35; cf. 21:15), thereby *excluding* Benjamin from the people. The Israelites then do to Gibeah what they had done to *Canaanite* cities in Joshua—subject it to the "ban," killing all the people and even the animals (20:48), setting on fire "the remaining towns." Benjamin and its environs must have looked like Atlanta and its environs after Sherman's infamous march.

The reaction of the Israelites continues the misogyny of the story. Having just killed apparently all the Benjamite women (but not the men, as it turns out), the Israelites are worried for those poor men who are left without a "pool" of wives! There is compassion for *them*. And since there exists a previous oath (never explained) prohibiting giving wives to Benjamites from the other eleven tribes (21:1, 18), the possibility of genocide appears all too real. But not to worry, because on investigating into the tribal constituency of the troops, it appears that the men of Jabesh-gilead did not answer the call to battle. Here, then, is a solution: the Israelites promptly murder the inhabitants of the town, "including the women and the little ones" (21:10)—*except* for the *virgin* women, whom they now provide to the men of Benjamin for wives. With this, "the whole congregation" sends a proclamation of peace to the Benjamites!

But there are not enough wives still. What to do now? More misogyny—the elders of the congregation suggest that the remaining Benjamite bachelors sneak up on the vintage festival at Shiloh, and, when the women come out to dance, seize them and kidnap them. It's something like raiding an old-time camp revival meeting! If the father or brothers of the women complain, simply say to them, "Be nice, there weren't enough women for our Benjamites, and think of it this way—you don't have to feel guilty for giving your daughters' hands in marriage." But we never hear from the fathers or brothers. A story that began with rape in effect ends with rape, and no man—father, brother, husband (and priest!), or host—seems to care.

"In those days there was no king in Israel; all the people did what was right in their own eyes." In her commentary, Niditch emphasizes that "Judges does *not* end with chaos; it ends with wholeness, reconciliation, rehabilitation, and peace, made possible in men's eyes through the taking of women."[143] After all, the tribe of Benjamin is saved from annihilation and reunited with Israel, healing a "breach" that the narrator rather unfairly blames on God (21:14). The Benjamites rebuild their ruined cities (21:23). One could add that the return of the tribes "to their inheritances" (v. 24, AT) restores them to

---

143. Niditch, *Judges*, 211 (italics added).

the apparently congenial state that they enjoyed at Joshua's death, albeit without a leader (Josh 24:28; Judg 2:6).[144] But the cost is enormous. The title of Niditch's closing chapter includes the phrase "'the Traffic in Women,'" suggesting the callous, misogynistic exploitation of women by means of sexual abuse, rape, and commercialization. Thus the peace that comes at the end is *at the expense of* women. They are sacrificed on the altar of national unity.

Overall the negative connotations of the "no-king" refrain remain compelling. "All the people did what was right in their own eyes." We have seen what can happen when some of them do precisely that (19:24). The judges started with the bare story of Othniel who fit the deliverer mold perfectly, but immediately with the subsequent judges, problems and complications arose. Ehud's act of deliverance was a brutal assassination coupled with a kind of religious sarcasm. Deborah's victory was marred because of the brutal murder of Sisera by Jael and tribal defections. Gideon's deeds involved unnecessary and unsanctioned violence, tribal jealousy, and a son, Abimelech, who raised the problem of illegitimate pretenders to royalty. Jepthah's careless piety resulted in the horror of child sacrifice, and his victory was marred by inter-tribal strife. Samson was only incidentally a deliverer, so bent on personal pleasure and revenge. Following Samson there is no pretension of judges, only incidents of unprovoked massacre, sadistic sexual abuse, and inter-tribal bloodshed, ending in a peace that may be heaven for men but hell for women. A friend of mine has suggested a musical analogy—Ravel's *Bolero*, which begins in quiet, mellifluous harmony, but gradually grows more intense and unrestrained until the cacophony of loud blasts at the end.[145] What social order will emerge beyond families and tribes (21:24)? Can "all the Israelites assemble as a congregation like a single individual" once more (20:1, AT), and under what conditions? Will new judges arise? Or will a genuine monarchy arise to fill the void, and what are the criteria of genuineness? In the Torah, the criteria are clear, centering in the king's continual *study* of Torah (Deut 17:14–20), and this model reappeared in the commissioning of Joshua (Josh 1:7–8). However, Jotham's fable reminds us that royalty in and of itself is not necessarily a wise political move—it is all too easy to crown a bramble bush.

---

144. On the other hand, the reference to "tribes and families" may point to the *lack* of integration, perhaps in contrast to the assembled congregation of 20:1.

145. Robert Sacks, a tutor at St. John's College, Santa Fe, New Mexico. Cf. Schneider, *Judges*, xii: instead of repeated cycles, the book demonstrates "a degenerative progression; each cycle shows a generation beginning yet lower on the scale of legitimate behavior regarding the Israelites' relationship to their deity than the previous generation had."

THREE

Ruth

The Fidelity of an Infidel

JEWISH READERS OF THE Former Prophets traditionally would not include the book of Ruth, for it is not *part* of the Former Prophets in the Hebrew Bible. There the book occurs among the Writings, the third part of the Tanak.[1] The Christian canon, however, following the ancient Greek Septuagint, inserts the book in between Judges and 1 Samuel, for the obvious reason that the opening line poses the narrative setting "in the days when the judges ruled." Moreover, the conclusion of the story places Ruth within the ancestry of the future King David, making the story part of his "family history."[2] In our day, such a connection would be perfectly suited for the background promotion of, say, a Presidential candidate.[3] Like much of the Former Prophets, however, various *historical* settings (of both author and audience) provide various angles of interpretation, ranging from a time contemporaneous with David to hundreds of years later, in the post-exilic period (see below).[4]

Coming after the horror of the book of Judges, the book of Ruth is best described by the name of one of its central characters—Naomi, which means "My Pleasantness."[5] That at one point she will call herself Mara, "Bitter," but then become Naomi again also suggests something of the plot. This is above all a pleasant tale of family devotion, compassion, and love. The key theme is "fidelity," "faithfulness," or "kindness," various translations of the Hebrew word *ḥesed*. We have seen that word before, and the accompanying behavior, in the

---

1. The acronym for *Torah, Nevi'im, Ketuvim* ("Torah, prophets, and writings," cf. the New Testament phrase, "the law and the prophets").

2. Linafelt, "Ruth," xx, 80–81, suggests that the author of Ruth composed it "as a connector between Judges and Samuel," implying an ironic ambivalence regarding the reign of David and the monarchy. See below on chap. 4.

3. One can imagine a film version screened at the nominating convention for David Jesseson (i.e., "son of Jesse"), showing the family background of "the next president of the United States."

4. For a review of these possibilities, see Farmer, *Ruth*, 895–96.

5. One could also translate "sweetness" (cf. the NRSV at 2 Sam 23:1; Ps 81:2), in the sense in which Jonathan Edwards could talk about the "sweetness" of God (cf. Austin, *Beauty*, 19).

story of Rahab, the prostitute of Jericho: "since I have dealt *kindly* with you, swear to me by the Lord that you in turn will deal *kindly* with my family" (Josh 2:2). But no reader of the rest of Joshua or of Judges would choose kindness as the major theme of those books! Here, in Ruth, kindness is like the proverbial "balm in Gilead."

A comparison between Ruth and Judges, of course, is suggested not only by the setting but also by the phrase "a certain man of Bethlehem of Judah," which may echo the beginning of the horror story of the Levite's concubine ("there was a young man of Bethlehem in Judah," Judg 17:7). Also, the name of Naomi's husband, Elimelech, means "my God is king," reminding us of the chaos when "there was no king in Israel," but also pointing to the central theological question that has already arisen in the story of Gideon (Judg 8:23): how does a human king fit with God's sovereignty (cf. 1 Samuel 8)?

Even more unusual compared to Judges, the central characters of Ruth are women. Again, in Joshua and Judges we have occasionally seen women in positive roles, even leadership positions. In addition to Rahab, there were Achsah and Deborah. But there were also more ambiguous characters like the bloody Jael and the devious Delilah, and in the end the story disintegrated into the horror of rape, murder, and forced marriage (the Levite's concubine, the virgin girls of Jabesh-gilead)—women as helpless victims. Here, in Ruth, women are the primary protagonists and the models of faith (with a little help from a man), and some of their words are as familiar as the cross-stitch hanging on the kitchen wall: "wither thou goest, I shall go." The book begins and ends with reference to men (Elimelech and David), but in between "a man's world tells a woman's story."[6]

The prominence of women also points to another idiosyncrasy—the absence of God. Only once in this story does God say or do anything (i.e., at the end, when Ruth gets pregnant, 4:13). God does not speak to Ruth or any other characters; God does not act in any observable way to advance the plot of the story. The only active agents are human agents. Of course, Naomi will interpret events in her life (both good and bad), as signs of God's activity (1:13, 20–21), and God's blessing will be invoked (1:8; 2:4, 12, 19, 20; 3:10) or proclaimed (2:20; 3:14), but never does the author *tell* us that God has *arranged* things to happen. Compared to Joshua and Judges, where God occasionally orders people around, directly intervenes, or secretly controls events (e.g., Samson, Judg 14:4), here God is completely off the stage. Redemption happens here not because God enacts it or even *sends* a redeemer, but because human beings act with "fidelity" and, again, "kindness." Campbell puts it well: "God is present in this story where responsible human beings act as God to one another."[7]

While the canonical context of the book may not substantively alter our

---

6. Trible, *Rhetoric,* 166. For other studies of Ruth by women see Kates, *Reading Ruth.*

7. Campbell, *Ruth,* 138; cf. Trible, *Rhetoric,* 195; Farmer, *Ruth,* 922, 931, 945; Linafelt, "Ruth," xvi–xvii, 27–28, 78 ("If there is someone acting throughout the story from behind the scenes or in the shadows [including 4:13], we must conclude that it is Ruth.").

reading of its major theme, the significance of that theme is enhanced. Ruth is a Moabite, an ethnic identity repeatedly emphasized throughout the story. Moab represents an ambivalent role within the nations surrounding Israel. Moab is a descendant of Abraham's nephew, Lot, but the product of a night of drunken incest initiated by his *daughters* (Gen 19:30–38), a licentious reputation later confirmed by the behavior of their descendants (Num 25:1–2). Moab appears as Israel's enemy throughout Israel's history (from the wilderness period to the Exile), and sometimes succumbed to Israelite expansion.[8] In Deuteronomy Moab is supposed to have received an inviolable gift of land from God just as did Israel (Deut 2:9), yet Moabites are prohibited from membership within the Israelite "assembly" (Deut 23:3), a ban (along with intermarriage) that post-exilic Israel attempted to enforce (Neh 13:1).[9] Ezra puts it in terms that seem racist to us: "the holy seed" of Israel should not "mix itself" with people like the Moabites, a miscegenation that leads to "infidelity" (9:1–2, AT). The *historical* context of Ruth could well be in that latter period, serving as an antidote to the radical exclusivity of Ezra and Nehemiah (and a kind of companion to the book of Jonah). But we have often heard the voice of such exclusivity in the immediately preceding books (Deut 7:3; Josh 23:12), and, of course, we know that that voice sometimes went unheeded (cf. Gideon; Samson; the people in general, Judg 3:5–6). In short, although the Moabites were not a people subject to the holy war ban, they were sufficiently qualified as "outsiders" to merit the label of infidel. But, as we have seen before (e.g., Rahab), the Torah had not wrestled with the problem of what to do with an infidel who is the model of fidelity—and a woman to boot. A "good Moabite" was as unthinkable as a "good Samaritan" in Jesus' day.

> *When Jews hate Muslims for their religion, when gays scorn straights for their sexual orientation, when blacks beat a white teenager for the color of his skin, it suggests people too dense to understand the moral of their own story, the meaning of their own passages. The minority is no more righteous in its hate than the majority is.*[10]

Famine to Harvest (Chap. 1)

The story opens with a series of disasters worthy of the book of Job. A famine in the land of Judah drives Elimelech and family to the neighboring country of Moab, but then Elimelech dies, and soon his sons follow him, leaving the widow and mother—Naomi—in a foreign land. She is not alone, however, for she still has her two daughters-in-law, Moabite women that her sons had married, named Orpah and Ruth. The sons seemed not to have known the danger

---

8. Numbers 22–24; Judges 3:12–29; 2 Samuel 8; cf. the oracles against Moab in Isaiah 15–16; Jeremiah 48. Moab is accused of conniving with the Babylonians against Judah (Jer 27:1–11).

9. Cf. Neh 13:23–27. The post-exilic restrictions included the demand that Israelites divorce Moabite spouses (Ezra 9–10).

10. Pitts, "Brutal Act of Bigotry," A19, referring to the vicious beating of a white teenager by a group of blacks because he was dating a black girl.

of "the women of Moab" (Num 25:1; cf. again Ezra 9:2).

Naomi's return to Judah dominates the next section, as the root for "return" occurs twelve times in vv. 6–22 (including "go / bring / turn back"). The word links together the actions of Naomi, her daughters-in-law, and God (as perceived by Naomi), but often denotes spiritual more than geographical movement (the Hebrew word can mean "repent," "change," and "restore"). Throughout the book the author often employs puns and double-entendres in ways that may reveal connections or irony or create deliberate ambiguity. In fact, the motivations of the characters often are open to multiple interpretations, ranging from self-interest to magnanimity, naïveté to shrewd manipulation.[11]

The three women have already set out to return to Judah, but Naomi stops, suggesting that her daughters-in-law return to Moab. There they would have the protection of their own families. So Naomi dismisses them with a benediction and the first occurrence of the key word "kindness": "may the Lord deal kindly with you, as you have dealt with the dead and with me" (v. 8). This reciprocity between kindness offered and kindness received will mark the rest of the story. Here, Naomi's benediction includes the hope for new husbands for her daughters-in-law, contrasted with the hopelessness of *her* marrying again and having more sons for them. Naomi's invocation of God's kindness on her daughters-in-law is ironic, for she then declares that her life is "bitter" "because the hand of the Lord has turned against me."

Orpah heeds Naomi's advice, but Ruth *clings* to her and refuses to *leave* (vv. 14, 16). As examples of word play, the word for "cling" can refer to marriage, along with "leaving" one's parents (Gen 2:24), suggesting that the relationship between her and Naomi replaces that of spouses and kin.[12] "Cling" is used in 2:8 for "keep close," tying together Ruth's meeting with Boaz, and he praises her for *leaving* her own family (2:11). Once again Naomi dismisses Ruth, saying that Orpah has returned "to her people and to her gods," so now she should return also. But Ruth expresses her commitment in one of the most beautiful soliloquies in the Bible:

> Where you go, I will go;
> > where you lodge, I will lodge;
> your people shall be my people,
> and your God my God.

In a real sense, Ruth's words express a "conversion" of the Moabite into an Israelite. Indeed, she exemplifies three of the key ideals of Israelite faith: one land, one people, one God. She then invokes upon herself a curse if she should allow even death to separate her from Naomi. Ruth's fidelity is all the more striking and unorthodox in that she commits

---

11. Linafelt, "Ruth," emphasizes such ambiguity, which he says cannot be finally resolved. For example, in the next episode, Naomi seems to dismiss her daughters-in-law in a kindly way, but one could also infer that she would just as soon have done with them. For a similar earlier reading, see Fewell and Gunn, *Compromising Redemption*.

12. For different readings of this relationship, ranging from lesbian to friendship, see Kates, *Reading Ruth*, and compare the debate over Jonathan and David (see below on 1 Samuel 18–20).

herself to an aging woman rather than the search for another man.[13]

Faced with such devotion, Naomi relents, and the two continue their journey to Bethlehem. There the women of the village greet them, recognizing Naomi, but she identifies herself not by her real name but by the alias "Mara"—not "Pleasant" but "Bitter," because, she says, "the Almighty has dealt bitterly with me. I went away full, but the Lord has brought me back empty." Moreover, she says, God has "oppressed" her and "brought calamity" upon her. The language is as harsh as the alleged treatment, reminiscent of the oppression and bitterness wreaked upon the Hebrew slaves in Egypt (Exod 1:11, 14).

The return to Bethlehem, however, ends on a promising note: it is "the beginning of barley harvest," suggesting that the famine is over. Coincidently, Naomi and Ruth have come home for Thanksgiving! The promise inherent in the harvest already suggests that Naomi's bitterness, though understandable, may prove to be exaggerated. It is true that she is bereft of husband and sons, and thus, in her culture, without security. Widows were among the most vulnerable, including the orphan and the stranger.[14] But she is not *completely* empty—above all, she has the fidelity of Ruth—and now the story that began in famine has turned to harvest, a reversal of the original irony in that Bethlehem means "home of food" (vv. 1, 22). As for Ruth herself, this homecoming has special significance because Bethlehem is now her *adopted* home. Yet for both women, questions remain: will Thanksgiving prove to be more than a meal? Can the emptiness in Naomi's *heart* be filled, and will *Bethlehem* adopt the stranger? In short, Ruth has made a radical act of trust—"your people shall be my people, and your God my God"—but will both people and God "return" the gesture?

Bringing in the Sheaves (Chap. 2)

The next section begins with a juxtaposition of two key factors in the narrative: circumstance and initiative. The combination of the two will prove to be serendipitous. Naomi has a wealthy kinsman from Elimelech's family named Boaz, living in Bethlehem, and thus potential support. Ruth volunteers to provide food by gleaning in the local fields and "just so happens" to choose the field of Boaz. This is the stuff of both romance and redemption.

Our first impression of Boaz appears in his first words: he approaches the workers in his field with the greeting "the Lord be with you." Here is a boss with a warm heart and genuine piety. The workers respond in kind: "May the Lord bless you," foreshadowing precisely what is about to happen. Apparently Boaz already has his eye on Ruth, and he asks who she "belongs to," reflecting the patriarchal culture in which a woman belongs to her father or husband. Correspondingly, the worker identifies her not by her name but by her ethnic background and family attachment: "she is the Moabite who came back with Naomi from the country of Moab."

As one of the destitute—widow, orphan, stranger—Ruth is exercising her

---

13. Cf. Trible, *Rhetoric*, 173.
14. Exod 22:22; Deut 10:18; 24:19.

right to glean in the fields, that is, collect the leftovers from the harvest, whatever the workers have dropped in the field.[15] This is ancient Israel's version of "workfare," a system that imposes a limit on the rights of property owners in order to guarantee the more basic universal right to food. Moreover, Boaz immediately ensures that Ruth receives special treatment. He addresses her as "my daughter," a phrase both patriarchal and protective, and suggesting that she may well be "adopted" after all. He instructs her to stay in his field, working alongside the other women, and assures her that she will not be bothered by any young men who may have their eye on her themselves. Ruth humbly bows in gratitude, asking "why have I found favor in your sight," even though she is a foreigner? Her question already shows that her hope at the beginning of the day of "finding favor" has indeed been fulfilled.

Boaz now reveals that he apparently has been asking around and has learned of her situation—in particular, what she has done for Naomi, "and how you left your father and mother and your native land and came to a people that you did not know before" (v. 11). Her pilgrimage sounds very much like the mission given to Abram at the beginning of Israel's history ("go from your country and your kindred and your father's house to the land that I will show you"—Gen 12:1). But there is a difference: Abram set out in response to a divine charge and in search of a promised blessing, whereas Ruth set out with no such commission, accompanying a mother-in-law who was *returning* home "empty" and feeling, if anything, *cursed* by God. Ruth's faith is all the more compelling because it is *without* "the assurance of things hoped for" (Heb 11:1). Boaz concludes his commendation of Ruth with another invocation of reciprocity: "May the Lord reward you for your deeds, and may you have a full reward from the Lord, the God of Israel, under whose wings you have come for refuge!" (v. 12). But, as we shall see, God's wings in effect will be Boaz's arms.

Boaz's care for Ruth continues throughout the day. He invites her to eat lunch with him and his field hands, heaping her plate so full that she has plenty of leftovers.[16] Then Boaz instructs the young male workers to let Ruth glean even before the grain is cut, and to drop some sheaves deliberately for her to gather. At the end of the day, Ruth returns to Naomi with a full basket as well as a full belly. When she shares her bounty she also begins to fill the emptiness that Naomi had felt.

When Ruth reports all that has happened, Naomi confirms the invocation of Boaz's workers—"Blessed be the man who took notice of you" (v. 19). But there is more: she discovers that Ruth's benefactor is none other than Boaz, and now Naomi identifies Boaz's potential role as "nearest kin" (v. 20). The word also means "redeemer," referring to the right and responsibility of a relative to provide protection and sustenance to someone in Ruth's position, namely, widowed and without her own extended family.[17] In this situation, the kinship link

---

15. Lev 19:9; 23:22; Deut 24:19.

16. The word for "satisfied" in vv. 14 and 18 also means "full."

17. However, Ruth's situation does not fit neatly with any of the various biblical regulations on redemption, but may be loosely connected

is patrilineal, i.e., connecting Elimelech and his sons with Boaz. With this news, Naomi extends her invocation: "Blessed be he by the Lord, whose kindness has not forsaken the living or the dead." Here is the second occurrence of the keyword "kindness," probably referring to that of Boaz,[18] but the ambiguity of referent again illustrates how human actions are the way in which God acts.[19] The reference suggests a shift in Naomi's feelings in that she is capable of thinking of God once again as the source of blessing.

Compromising Positions (Chap. 3)

This chapter is fraught with ambiguity, ultimately insoluble. Various interpretations of the actions and motivations of the characters are possible. Ruth might be manipulated by a controlling Naomi, or she might be a savvy, assertive woman who knows how to get what she wants. Boaz could be a dullard who needs to be shown what to do, or biased against Moabite women and needing some ethnic "consciousness-raising," or a victim of entrapment befuddled by too much alcohol and forced into a "shotgun wedding."[20]

Presumably, the two women could get by for the rest of their lives living on the more than ample gleanings from Boaz's field. But that would be subsistence living, at best. Naomi wants more security for Ruth, and she devises a plan to get it. She suggests that Ruth take the initiative with Boaz. More specifically, she tells Ruth to get herself all dolled up and put herself in a compromising position in a midnight rendezvous. With the harvest over, Boaz will be working at the threshing floor, apparently until bedtime. Ruth is to lie in wait until Boaz beds down, then "uncover the place of his feet and lie down" (AT). Boaz—Naomi assures her—will see to the rest. Ruth waits in the dark until Boaz has finished his work, had his dinner, and is "in a contented mood." Then she sneaks up on him, uncovers "the place of his feet," and lies down.

But here the ambiguity of language frustrates the reader's desire for accuracy, which is to say the extent of intimacy involved. The incident is full of possible double entendres. "Feet" can be literal or a euphemism for genitals (and "the place of his feet" [vv. 4, 7, AT] is doubly ambiguous—the spot under his feet or the location of his genitals?).[21] As in English, to sleep ("lie down") is one thing, to "sleep with" is something quite different. The Hebrew word "know" can refer to recognition or copulation (compare "have intercourse with" meaning "converse with" or "have sex with"), and what the characters know is a leitmotif in the scene. "Uncover" sometimes is used for sexual activity (Lev 18:6–19), but not here *if* 'feet' simply means 'feet.' It is as if the author is winking all the time, but we're not sure why. Those who revel in the steamy novels and films of contem-

---

with the levirate marriage possibility; cf. Farmer, *Ruth*, 921b.

18. It is possible to understand the referent for "whose" to be God, but one would expect "blessed be God."

19. Cf. Gunn and Fewell, *Narrative*, 157: "divine and human action are often indistinguishable."

20. See Farmer, *Ruth*, 924, and references.

21. The Hebrew letter *mem* at the beginning of the word means "place of." Note the similarity in "place of his head" in 1 Kgs 19:6.

porary Western culture will no doubt be enormously disappointed. Those who think the Bible is too "holy" to contain a "sex scene" may be shocked. Neither the prurient nor the prudish can claim certainty.

At midnight, Boaz is startled awake (literally "trembled" or "shuddered"), perhaps by a dream (or a sudden rush of cool air!), and lo and behold, there *is* a dream lying "at the place of his feet" (AT). Here within his grasp is the fulfillment of a universal male fantasy! In the dark, Boaz asks who she is, and *we* are in the dark yet again as to the exact meaning of what now transpires.[22] She says, "I am Ruth, your servant; spread your cloak over your servant, for you are next-of-kin." Most likely (but, again, not certainly), Ruth is not simply offering Boaz a "roll in the hay," as it were. She is asking him to marry her. She is not simply propositioning him; she is proposing to him. She is also not waiting for Boaz to take charge (3:4). At this point Boaz has several options: he can take advantage of her sexually, or he can accuse her of sexual impropriety and have her punished. He chooses another way: he ignores the proposition and attends to the proposal. His response is rich in nuances. He invokes God's blessing on her as the return for this superior instance of "loyalty" (again, *ḥesed*). In doing so, he recognizes her gesture for the act of integrity that it is—not a wanton, sexual adventure motivated purely by pleasure or self-interest, but a courageous if desperate attempt to secure for herself and for Naomi the family protection that they need, and, at the same time, to make it possible for her to bear children that will continue the family line of her deceased husband. So Boaz promises that he will "do for you all that you ask, for all the assembly of my people know that you are a worthy woman" (v. 11). With this, Ruth's vow to Naomi—"your people shall be my people"—is reciprocated. Naomi's people affirm her integrity, using the same word that was used to describe Boaz at the outset (v. 2, "prominent," here "worthy"—and "strong" might be better).

Boaz's role here as potential "redeemer" is central as well. In fact, when Ruth says to him, "spread your cloak over your servant," she is literally saying "spread your *wings* over your servant," thereby in effect equating Boaz's protection with what *he* had described as *God's* protection (2:12). Here is perhaps the clearest indication of the theology of redemption that pervades the story: human actions are *"co-operative"* with God's will and blessing in such a way that those actions *are* God's actions.[23] This is how God acts in this story. As the popular saying goes, here God "has no hands but our hands."

But there is a hitch: Boaz is *not* the closest relative to Elimelech; there is another. Before Boaz can commit to honor Ruth's request, he must ensure

---

22. See Farmer, *Ruth*, 927–30, for a helpful overview of the complexities and various solutions. One ambiguity is the connection between redemption of the family property (see 4:3) and marriage, which would be redemption from the plight of widowhood.

23. See above, n. 7. More generally, alternative expressions include "concursive operation," and "double agency." See Russell, "God Who Acts," 45; Johnson, "God's Ordering," 30; Allen, *Christian Belief*, 172; Barbour, *Religion in an Age of Science*, 249. There will be numerous examples of this in the rest of the Former Prophets, often where God's part is much more explicit.

that the other relative does not want to exercise his right and responsibility to be the redeemer. So, Boaz sends Ruth away (while it is still dark, to protect her from scandal), but he does not send her away empty. She goes with his promise of redemption, and also with a hefty supply of the barley, reporting his previously unnoted comment, "Do not go back to your mother-in-law empty-handed." Thus this section concludes with a complete reversal of the opening scene ("the Lord has brought me back empty," 1:21).

All in the Family (Chap. 4)

In ancient Israel, the city gate was the "courtroom." When legal matters needed to be settled, here is where the litigants and "jury" would gather. In a coincidence resembling that at the beginning of chap. 2, Boaz goes to the gate and it just so happens that at that moment who should walk by but that more closely related redeemer. Literally, Boaz addresses him as "So-and-so" (NRSV "friend"), suggesting already that his identity will not be important. Now Boaz proves to be as shrewd as both Naomi and Ruth. He announces something heretofore unknown to us, that Naomi has inherited land and wants to sell it.[24] The closest relative has first dibs on such transactions, and Boaz offers it to his fellow kinsman. The man promptly accepts the offer, but then Boaz adds a codicil: when the man acquires the field, he also acquires "Ruth the Moabite" as a wife "to maintain the dead man's name on his inheritance." We do not know for sure how accurate Boaz's claim is, i.e., if the redeemer is legally bound to take both land *and* widow.[25] Nor do we know if he emphasizes "the Moabite" to turn the other man off or simply to be above board. But in any event, the kinsman balks, and Boaz concludes the transaction.

At last, Ruth and Boaz are to become one. But the bargaining certainly puts a damper on the romantic conclusion and brings out the stark ambivalence in Ruth's presentation. On the one hand, she is a woman of remarkable integrity, resourcefulness, and courage; on the other hand, her marriage to Boaz illustrates the inferior status of women in a patriarchal culture in that she is completely absent from the proceedings. Although we know her desire to marry Boaz, she has no voice here. She is tied to the estate of her deceased husband, and her marriage is linked to a real estate transaction (even if she is not mere "property" here).[26] She does not

---

24. Like so many other circumstances in the story, the exact meaning of the customs and transactions here are ambiguous, including Naomi's ownership of the land, which seems to conflict with her earlier depiction as without resources. Linafelt, "Ruth," 67, even raises the possibility that Boaz is lying about Naomi's land as a bluff to dissuade the redeemer from getting Ruth. As Farmer, *Ruth*, 933a, suggests, "none of the solutions suggested by interpreters can make complete sense of the text as it now stands."

25. Here is another complex interpretive problem. The original Hebrew text of v. 5 says "*I* acquire the dead man's widow," which may indicate that Boaz is informing the would-be purchaser that Boaz intends eventually to father a son to take Mahlon's name, who later could reclaim his father's property. See Farmer, *Ruth*, 936–37; Linafelt, "Ruth," 68.

26. Farmer, *Ruth*, 938, and Sakenfeld, *Ruth*, 73, point out the unusual use of language here, which does not support a purely commercial understanding of Ruth as wife.

reappear until 4:13, and then only as a secondary reference.

The elders witness the proceedings, then add their own blessing:

> Then all the people who were at the gate, along with the elders, said, "We are witnesses. May the Lord make the woman who is coming into your house like Rachel and Leah, who together built up the house of Israel. May you produce children in Ephrathah and bestow a name in Bethlehem; and, through the children that the Lord will give you by this young woman, may your house be like the house of Perez, whom Tamar bore to Judah.

Here Israel's ancestors are invoked, the two wives of Jacob who are, in effect, the "mothers" of Israel (i.e., the twelve eponymous tribes). The circumstances of their childbearing in some ways resemble Ruth's. On Jacob's wedding night, supposedly with the beautiful Rachel, her father, Laban, exploited the darkness of the tent and replaced her with her homely sister Leah. Jacob didn't realize that he had been tricked until the next morning (cf. Boaz's midnight encounter, 3:8). After Rachel also became Jacob's wife, the two sisters fiercely competed for the top childbearing award, employing their servants as surrogate mothers when necessary (Gen 29:21—30:24). Leah became the matriarch of Judah and the Southern tribes, Rachel the matriarch of the Northern tribes. Thus they "built up the house of Israel."[27]

Finally, Ruth's situation is compared to an illicit relationship that produced a son—the story of Tamar (Genesis 38). She was the widowed daughter-in-law of Judah who held back another of his sons from the levirate custom of providing a child through Tamar. Not to be outdone, she pretended to be a prostitute, solicited Judah, and had a child by *him*, one Perez, who stands at the root of David's family tree. Just as the people wish for Ruth to be as prolific as Rachel and Leah, so they wish fecundity for Boaz: "may your house be like the house of Perez" (v. 12), and the book ends by tracing the genealogy of Perez up to his far more famous relative, King David. Of course, one would have expected the "house" to be that of Mahlon, Ruth's deceased husband (v. 5), so, in a sense, Boaz is "grafted in" as father.

No sooner is the blessing pronounced than (nine months later) it is fulfilled (v. 13). In one verse Ruth is married, impregnated, and gives birth. Here God finally does enter the story in that God "gave her pregnancy" (v. 13, AT), that (or the denial thereof) being one of God's procreative functions, as the story of Rachel and Leah demonstrates.[28] But still Ruth does not speak. As Levine says, "Her feelings for her son and husband, and her sense of belonging in Israel are never addressed."[29] It is as if, having born a son, Ruth disappears. Indeed, the women of the village turn their attention to Naomi and her grandson, and their

---

27. A similar phrase appears in the levirate ordinance, Deut 25:9, which would be more fitting for the Tamar story that follows.

28. Gen 29:31; 30:2, 22; cf. 1 Sam 1:5–6, 19–20.

29. Levine, "Ruth," 90. Cf. Linafelt, "Ruth," 77, who adds that we don't even know if Ruth *wanted* children!

hope that he will be "renowned in Israel." Although they praise Ruth's worth to Naomi far above male offspring ("more to you [Naomi] than seven sons"), *Naomi* takes the role of the child's mother and the women say "A son has been born *to Naomi,*" and name him Obed. "He became the father of Jesse, the father of David." The blessing also reminds us of the location of the story, in Ephrathah of Bethlehem (cf. 1:2). One can hear echoes of the prophecy of Micah (itself *after* the time of David), continuing what will be known as the Messianic hope: "But you, O Bethlehem of Ephrathah, who are one of the little clans of Judah, from you shall come forth for me one who is to rule in Israel, whose origin is from of old, from ancient days" (Mic 5:2).

So the book ends with a political dimension, a promotion of the Davidic dynasty with its origins in the tribe of Judah. Soon this connection will come into play when the ancestor of Obed becomes God's anointed ("Messiah"; 1 Samuel 16). Since the book opens with the setting "in the days when the judges ruled (or judged)," and closes with the name of David, the personal story of the characters is framed by the larger story that will dominate the next two books—the transition from judges to a king. That the king designated is David, and not Israel's first king, Saul, is, of course, required by the genealogy, but it already foreshadows the favoritism that David will enjoy (both human and divine).

One could argue that the Davidic politics at the end is typical of a patriarchal culture in which the woman's significance is reduced to her function as a "breeder" for kings. "Long before David is even born, strong women put forth their strength so that he may become king!"[30] On the other hand, beneath the cultural and political cooption of Ruth there are some subversive tendencies at work. In a sense, "Compromising Positions" applies not just to the threshing floor scene but to the whole book.[31] In fact, Linafelt suggests that the connection to the preceding book of Judges and the following books of Samuel may well indicate an ironic reading of the references to David as well (especially 2 Samuel 11–12): "Decentralized chaos gives way to centralized bureaucracy and exploitation, with its own fair share of murder, rape and kidnapping."[32] Thus Naomi and Ruth present a brief, shining moment that, tragically, men will turn to darkness.

In other ways, Exum has summarized the remarkable role reversals implied especially by 4:13–17: "Naomi holds the following symbolic positions: husband to Ruth, wife to Ruth, mother to Ruth, wife to Boaz, father to Obed, and Mother to Obed."[33] Similarly, Ruth becomes the heroine despite her status as a foreigner with a scandalous ancestry, and the hero who marries this infidel has the incestuous Tamar as his grandmother. When read in the context

30. Jobling, *I Samuel*, 174; cf. Linafelt, "Ruth," 79.

31. Cf. the title of Fewell and Gunn, *Compromising Redemption*.

32. Linafelt, "Ruth," 80–81.

33. Exum, *Plotted*, 171. Much of this derives from the implications of Naomi being called the mother in v. 17: not only does Naomi replace Ruth, but normally the birth formula would refer to the father, not the grandmother. Exum shows also how the roles of Ruth and Boaz exhibit such reversals.

of post-exilic Israel, which we discussed at the outset, Ruth is a *counter*-cultural figure and the book is "a subversive parable that was written specifically to undermine the authority of the priests who were trying to 'purify' Israel by ostracizing foreign women."[34] Moreover, now the family tree of David—the anointed—itself includes such foreign women and sexual impropriety. The Gospel of Matthew goes further in tracing the genealogy of Jesus, including not only Tamar but also the tradition that Boaz was the son of none other than Rahab, that other infamous foreign woman and prostitute who, like Ruth, exhibited kindness (*ḥesed*).[35] So there is a lot of dirty linen hanging on the family line of the Messiah.

Without ignoring the ideological appropriation of the story of Ruth, one could see the political connection more positively as exemplary of the way in which personal, family stories are tied to a community's social wellbeing. The private and the public are linked interdependently. The family is not simply an isolated kinship of individuals, but part of the larger society, in many ways responsible for the community's wellbeing, and vice versa. The mutuality appears in the unusual naming of the child not by the mother but by the village women, reminding us of the proverb "it takes a village to raise a child." Conversely, good families contribute to the common good. Thus the blessing incorporates the word "house" four times. Here and elsewhere the word does not refer only to a physical structure but to a household, and, at the same time, to future generations of the family. The book began with the death of Naomi's sons and the apparent end of Naomi's and Ruth's family; it ends with the birth of a son (to both, in a sense), projecting innumerable offspring.

In yet another sense, "house" can refer to a political dynasty, a meaning that becomes crucial in the stories of Saul and David soon to come (e.g., 2 Sam 3:1; 7:15–16). Traced for generations, the later "house of David" is an outgrowth of the "house of Perez." (Along the lines indicated above, one could also loosely say that David's "house" has a "house of ill repute" in its ancestry [Tamar, Rahab]!) In short, Ruth's entering Boaz's house is inseparable from the role she plays in the development of the "house of Israel." In narrative terms, the story of the family participates in and influences the "community of memory"—for us, not only the Former Prophets but ultimately the entire Bible and the various religious traditions that followed.[36]

Finally, the quotation from Micah referring to the Davidic connection stands alongside another: "[God] has told you, O mortal, what is good; and what does the Lord require of you but to do justice, and to love kindness, and to walk humbly with your God?" (6:8). This affirmation of goodness, and of the responsibilities of a relationship with the source of all be-

---

34. Farmer, *Ruth*, 902.

35. Joshua 2; Matt 1:1–17, also with an explicit reference to Uriah, the victim of David as the messianic murderer of 2 Samuel 11. See my essay called "Four Ladies of Ill Repute," in *To Taste and See*, 7–13.

36. Cf. Berlin, "Ruth and the Continuity of Israel," 260. See Bellah, *Habits of the Heart,* for an extended discussion of this topic with respect to American religious traditions.

ing, could apply to virtually any religion (and, for that matter, an ethos that is not explicitly religious). Just as it described Rahab, so it describes Ruth. In the end, the book of Ruth is a story of human kindness, modeled primarily by women, although Boaz figures prominently as well. In fact, even the kindness of Boaz is a *response* to the initiative of Naomi and Ruth. Boaz does not ride in on a white horse and sweep the fainting damsel out of distress. The story contains dramatic reversals: from emptiness to fullness, bitterness to sweetness, barrenness to parenthood, lament to thanksgiving, and foreigner to family. Here human refuge stands for God's refuge, human redemption represents divine redemption, and the fidelity of a female infidel provides a model for what the community of Israel *can* be if kindness is in its heart.

> *One day the South will recognize its real heroes . . . They will be old, oppressed, battered Negro women, symbolized in a seventy-two-year-old woman in Montgomery, Alabama, who rose up with a sense of dignity and with her people decided not to ride segregated buses, and who responded with ungrammatical profundity to one who inquired about her weariness: "My feets is tired, but my soul is at rest." . . . They were in reality standing up for what is best in the American dream and for the most sacred values in our Judaeo-Christian heritage.*[37]

---

37. King, "*Letter*," 94.

FOUR

1 Samuel

LIST OF MAJOR CHARACTERS:

Ahimelech, great-grandson of Eli, head priest at Nob, site of massacre by Saul

Abiathar, priest, sole survivor of the Nob massacre; priest to David; later banned to Anathoth in deference to Zadok

Abigail, wife of Nabal who became wife of David after Nabal's death

Achish, Philistine king of Gath, employs David as a mercenary

David, Israel's second king, a Judahite (Southerner)

Doeg, servant of Saul, informant against Ahimelech, agent for Saul's massacre of Nob priests

Hannah, mother of Samuel

Hophni, corrupt priest, son of Eli, killed by Philistines

Jonathan, son of Saul, close friend of David

Michal, daughter of Saul, given to David as wife

Nabal, "Fool," husband of Abigail, who rejects David's request for hospitality

Phineas, corrupt priest, son of Eli, killed by Philistines, father of Ichabod

Saul, Israel's first king, a Benjamite (Northerner)

The book of 1 Samuel presents the reader with a rich potpourri of narrative characters and subjects: an infertile woman who gives birth to a national leader, a supernatural box that topples an idol and causes a plague, a man who searches for a donkey and finds a crown, another a king caught with his pants down, gory scenes involving mutilated and dismembered bodies, a God who has both a good and an evil spirit, a "witch" who is far from wicked, and, of course, "David and Goliath." Above all, it is a story about a powerful prophet of authoritarian strictness, a king whose fall evokes Greek or Shakespearean tragedies, and a young man whose calculating aspirations to power are inextricably mingled with piety and divine providence.[1]

---

1. For an insightful exploration of the role

A broad outline of the literary ingredients of 1 Samuel includes stories about the priestly family of Eli and the rise of Samuel (chaps. 1–3), along with an "ark narrative" (chaps. 4–7); stories about the first king, Saul (chaps. 8–15); and the rise of David (chaps. 16–30, extending to 2 Samuel 5). Within this outline, however, there are numerous editorial connections that combine originally independent literary strands. This textual history is evident in numerous doublets, i.e., duplicate versions of the same incident: Saul's appointment as king, Saul's offense and rejection, David's introduction to Saul's court, David preserving Saul's life, etc. Similarly, numerous inconsistencies or contradictions indicate the presence of separate if not competitive accounts. Moreover, there are numerous problems with the Hebrew text that require correction based on the Greek translation.

There is general agreement that most of 1 Samuel derives from sources prior to the Deuteronomic historian of the Josianic era (or Hezekian).[2] The combination of originally independent stories, along with editorial arrangement and commentary produces a wide range of opinions, especially on the origin of the monarchy. The monarchy was a major watershed in Israel's history politically, sociologically, and theologically. Opinions in the text range from approval of the institution as a gracious gift of God for Israel's protection, to disapproval of the institution as Israel's "wicked" rejection of God's sovereignty. The controversy is compounded by the sad story of Saul's failed leadership and his premature death, accompanied by the adventures of David and his ultimate succession to the throne. Throughout the stories of Saul and David, the menace of the Philistines is a critical factor in the events. Several questions stand behind the narrative: Why did Samuel come to be God's prophetic mediator? Why did the monarchy arise and how should one interpret it theologically? Was David's succession to the throne, instead of Saul's son Jonathan, the result of foul play on David's part? Why did God nullify a permanent dynasty for Saul? The last question can be coupled with another when we reach 2 Samuel 7: Why did God *affirm* a dynasty—indeed, an eternal one—for David?

The various voices that speak in these stories often represent ideological agendas, primarily those of priestly, prophetic, and political interests. More than anywhere before in the Former Prophets, we can detect the ways in which editors have given their shape to the older stories which they included within the composition. The reader should occasionally step back and ask, Who stands to benefit politically from the way this story is told?—recognizing that the beneficiary may not be one of the characters, but someone at a later time. Nevertheless, the two books of Samuel are far from mere ideology; they contain some of the most exquisite

---

of fate in Saul's story, and the Shakespearean similarities, see Gunn, *Fate*, especially 116–20 on Shakespeare.

2. Campbell and O'Brien, *Unfolding*, 24–31, argue for a basic substratum that they call the "Prophetic Record," which ultimately runs through 2 Kings 10. This document came out of the northern prophetic circle of Elisha. Previously, McCarter, *I Samuel*, 21, argued for "a prophetic history," accepted in a qualified way by Birch, *Samuel*, 956.

narrative art in the Bible. After all is said about editors, political agendas, and historical background, what remains are simply wonderful stories. The concluding sentence from Robert Alter's remarkable book, *The Art of Biblical Narrative*, rightly invites us to *enjoy* these stories however much we may analyze them critically: "Subsequent religious tradition has by and large encouraged us to take the Bible seriously rather than to enjoy it, but the paradoxical truth of the matter may well be that by learning to enjoy the biblical stories more fully as stories, we shall also come to see more clearly what they mean to tell us about God, man, and the perilously momentous realm of History."[3]

God "Brings Low, and Also Exalts" (Chaps. 1–3)

There are two canonical contexts for the book of 1 Samuel. In the Christian Bible the book follows Ruth; in the Jewish Bible, it follows Judges. The latter ended with the notation "In those days there was no king in Israel; all the people did what was right in their own eyes." The former ends with a genealogical reference to David, the king whose name will become synonymous with God's "anointed" (Messiah). Thus, as radically different in subject and tone as Ruth and Judges are, they both connect with 1 Samuel in focusing our attention on the rise of a monarchy in ancient Israel. Samuel will be the first of a long line of prophets who are "king makers and king breakers" (indeed, Samuel himself will be both).

First Samuel connects with Judges also in that Samuel is the *last* of the judges. A premature epilog tells us that Samuel "judged Israel all the days of his life" (7:15), employing a literary notice familiar from Judges.[4] Similarly, 13:1 presents an incomplete date for Saul's reign that reflects the literary formula used for the reigns of subsequent monarchs. Thus one could say that the book of Judges really ends—and the books of Kings really begin—at 13:1.[5] Like Samson before him, Samuel is born of a barren mother who dedicates him as a Nazirite—a long-haired teetotaler—but any resemblance ends there (Judg 13:5–7; 1 Sam 1:11). Samuel did what a judge is supposed to do: he "administered justice" in Israel (7:17). It seems that God saved the best for last.

On the other hand, first Samuel connects with Ruth also in that a personal and familial problem resolves in a way that proves to be political and historical. Though their stories have made them famous, obscure women in their faithfulness are the agents of redemption both for themselves and, more importantly to the larger narrative, for Israel (Ruth, Naomi, Hannah). As Brueggemann puts it, "Israel never separates intimate family joy from public destiny."[6] The same will be true for intimate family pain.

First Samuel begins with a familiar type-scene: a barren woman's desperate effort to have a child. Readers of Genesis will recognize the problem that drove characters like Sarah and Rachel and, to

---

3. Alter, *Art*, 189.

4. Judg 10:2–3; 12:7–14; 15:20; 16:31.

5. The Greek version titles 1 Samuel through 2 Kings as 1 through 4 Kingdoms.

6. *Samuel*, 17.

some extent, the book of Ruth (there, the *loss* of children [1:5; cf. 4:10–11]). The emotional pain of childlessness was compounded by the belief that it was God who directly controlled conception (v. 5). Hannah has no children, unlike her rival wife (the culture allowing multiple wives), who seems to delight in her procreative superiority. In fact, she seems to reserve her taunting of Hannah for their annual pilgrimage to worship (v. 7; cf. Ps 15:1–3)! To his credit, Hannah's husband Elkanah expresses his love for her, notwithstanding the cultural stigma—in fact, he favors her over the rival Penninah (vv. 5, 8), which probably did not help the family dynamics. However, his arrogant suggestion that having him as husband is better than having ten sons shows that he cannot truly understand the affect of childlessness on a woman, and Hannah persists in her hope.[7]

Now at their annual pilgrimage Hannah prays fervently for a son. The priest, Eli, confuses her mumbling lips with that of a drunkard, and chastises her accordingly. When Hannah explains her behavior and the substance of her prayer, Eli reverses himself and pronounces a blessing over her. When he says "may the Lord establish his word" (v. 23) the story is already looking far beyond the immediate situation to Samuel's role as prophet (3:19—4:1; 15:11). In no time at all, Hannah is pregnant. God has remembered her as she asked (vv. 11, 19). Correspondingly, Hannah remembers the vow that she made: she gives her son back to God, dedicating him as a Nazirite to remain in God's presence forever (vv. 11, 22). Ironically, the woman falsely accused of drunkenness faithfully commits her son to alcoholic abstinence. Her motivation may well go beyond personal fulfillment and piety to politics, in that placing her son in apprenticeship to the priest Eli places him at the seat of power.[8]

Though etymologically inaccurate,[9] she names him "Samuel" to recognize the mutual giving—divine and human—that marks his birth (v. 20). The more significant play on words involves the name Saul, which means "asked." Eli said "may God grant to you the asking you have asked," and in v. 28, Hannah says "I have made him asked [i.e. lent him] to the Lord; all the days he lives he is asked to the Lord" (v. 17, 28, AT). The one who is asked for here (Samuel) will later replace the one who blessed the asking (Eli), and will be asked to supply a king (cf. 12:13), and will appoint "Asked" (Saul) for the job.[10]

Sacerdotal[11] language and concerns appear throughout the story of Samuel's birth and into the following chapters. There is obviously a temple at Shiloh, although 2:22–25 reverts to the traditional "tent of meeting," and a later editor will insist that Solomon built the first temple (cf. 2 Sam 7:6; 1 Kgs 8:16). Soon we will hear about the temple furniture, especially the lamp and the "ark

---

7. See Hackett, "1 and 2 Samuel," 95b, and Fokkelman, *Vow and Desire*, 29–30, who sees Elkanah's "why" questions as reproachful.

8. Some see even more, with Hannah deliberately reacting to misogyny and political corruption; so Jobling, *I Samuel*, 133–34.

9. "Samuel" comes from the words "name" and "El."

10. The word "asked" appears similarly elsewhere, e.g., 10:22; 12:13; 17:56.

11. See the glossary.

of God" (3:3), the latter familiar from the Jordan crossing story (Joshua 3–5). Eli and his sons are the priests at the temple. Finally, sacrifice plays a major role (as it will throughout the book). Elkanah observes an annual family sacrifice at the temple. Moreover, Hannah's gesture of giving up her son is itself a kind of sacrifice (a correlation sharply evidenced by v. 25), and a consecration recognizing the first-born as God's gift (Exod 13:1-2; 22:29b). Indeed, her gift is forever, even though Nazirites normally have a limited time of service. Her pious generosity will soon highlight the blasphemous greed of the priests, who will misuse "the first part of every offering" (2:29, AT). Hannah would have made a far better priest, had it been allowed!

The name Hannah means "grace," and the narrative pauses now for her to sing praise to God for the gracious gift of her child. Typologically this is a victory song that goes far beyond Hannah's personal life in talking about triumph over enemies, even given the reference to barrenness in v. 5. The hymn has a revolutionary fervor, celebrating God's championing of the humble over the arrogant, the feeble over the mighty, and the poor over the rich (compare the Magnificat of Mary in Luke 1:46b-55). In its context, the hymn could easily allude to the downfall of Eli's priestly dynasty, soon to be announced, but other mighty ones will fall throughout the book (not the least of whom will be Israel's first king, Saul). The "seat" or "throne" that Eli so prominently occupies (1:9) is to be inherited by a usurper (2:8),[12] and Samuel does not come from a priestly family.[13] Hannah ends with an invocation of divine blessing to God's king, and frames the song with the word "horn," a metaphor for power or strength: "my horn is exalted in the Lord," the Lord "will exalt the horn of his anointed" (AT), again tying together the birth of Samuel and the rise of monarchy. As we shall see, Hannah's hymn combined with a very similar victory hymn of David at the end of the 2 Samuel (chap. 22) provides a frame of the entire story, focusing on the theme of v. 7b: God "brings low, and also exalts" (AT).[14]

Literary juxtaposition now vividly contrasts the increasing priestly service of the growing Samuel to the corruption of Eli's sons. From 2:11 to the end of chap. 3, an editor has inserted affirmations of Samuel's ministry that alternate antiphonally with denunciations of Eli & Sons (indicated by italics):

Samuel remains with Eli, "to minister to the Lord" (2:11).

The sons engage in ritual impropriety driven by greed and sexual immorality driven by lust. Normally, priests live off of the sacrificial offerings of the people. Strict rules govern what part of a sacrifice goes to God, to the priests, and to the people. Basically, the priests are not supposed to get any well-marbled

---

12. The Hebrew word can simply mean "seat" but most often means "throne" (cf. 4:13, 18).

13. The editor tells us that Elkanah is an Ephraimite (1:1), whereas in 1 Chr 6:26 Samuel has a priestly lineage which would put him among the caretakers of the ark (Num 3:29–31). If the editor responsible for 1 Sam 1:1 is deliberately ignoring that tradition, he may want to indicate the revolutionary character of Samuel's priestly role. Jobling, *1 Samuel*, remarks that Samuel "arrogates to himself priestly functions."

14. On the framing, see Birch, *1 and 2 Samuel*, 980 and n. 27.

steak. As Leviticus puts it, "All fat is the Lord's" (3:16). Indeed, *anyone* who eats the fat "shall be cut off from his people" (Lev 7:25). Yet Eli's sons obtain their meat without burning the fat—indeed, when it is still raw—thus treating the sacrifices to God "with contempt" (2:12-17). Moreover, they may be taking more than their share (v. 12), thus treating the *people* with contempt.

But Samuel ministers to God and wears the priestly vestment of an ephod and "grew up in the presence of the Lord" (2:18, 21).

Eli's sons also abuse their office by having sex with the women who served at the sanctuary entrance.[15] At the very moment when Eli accused Hannah of sin, his "worthless" sons may well have been philandering outside the door (and Eli had implied that *Hannah* was "worthless"!).[16] The offense combines ritual defilement with sexual licentiousness. Not only are the priests apparently committing adultery, but sexual relations render them ritually "unclean" until the evening (Lev 15:18), so any work done before that would defile the sanctuary and warrant excommunication (Lev 21:3). Eli warns them of committing unpardonable sin, but they will not listen. In fact, in v. 25b the narrator says that Eli's sons are morally and spiritually deaf "because it pleased the Lord to kill them" (AT). Here is an example of the narrator presuming to know what God wants and explicitly informing the reader in direct speech. The language is strong: "to take delight, or pleasure in." Elsewhere, we are told that God does *not* take delight in the death of a sinner, but prefers repentance (Ezek 18:23). Here God is of a different mind. The short sentence anticipates the longer oracle to come (vv. 27–36) and raises enormous theological and philosophical issues involving the nature of human freedom and divine sovereignty, none of which seem to trouble the author. Human stubbornness and divine willfulness stand in juxtaposition, but clearly the latter is in control, which is to say that history is Providentially driven. We will look at this issue more carefully later, when the divided mind of God is even more apparent.[17] After the next antiphon, an oracle will tell us more about the fate of the house of Eli.

But Samuel "continued to grow both in stature and in favor with the Lord and with the people" (2:26).

With the sinfulness of Eli's sons thoroughly uncovered, the stage is set for a hellfire sermon delivered by an unknown "man of God" who appears out of nowhere (2:27–36), but most likely out of the commentator's imagination. The title "man of God" applies to numerous individuals ranging from men (Moses, Deut 33:1) to angels (Judg 13:6), and is used most often for prophetic figures like Elijah and Elisha, including Samuel himself (1 Sam 9:6). The content and tone of the speech suggests the Deuteronomic editor who is fond of such diatribes.[18] A prophetic messenger formula leads

---

15. What this service entails is not clear here or elsewhere (Exod 38:8).

16 NRSV "scoundrels" in v. 12 is the masculine equivalent to the same Hebrew words used in 1:16 for "worthless." The Hebrew of v. 12a literally says "Sons of Eli sons of worthlessness."

17. We have already seen such commentary regarding Samson (Judg 14:4). See below on the oracle in chap. 2 and on 16:14.

18. Cf. Josh 24:1–15; Judg 2:1–5; 1 Kgs 13:1–3.

to a historical review, then an indictment and the threat of punishment. Retrospectively, the gluttony of Eli's sons mirrors those who are condemned in Hannah's song, as does their begging for bread (2:36 and 2:5).

In the context of the ensuing narrative, the speech has a prophecy/fulfillment function, combined with a sign, predicting what will soon take place in chap. 4 (v. 34; cf. 1 Kgs 13:3)—the death of Eli and his sons. But the speech also refers far ahead to Saul's massacre of the Shiloh priests, survived only by Abiathar (22:6–23). Further still, the speech predicts changes in the priesthood by which Eli's offspring, Abiathar, will, under Solomon, be supplanted by his colleague, Zadok, the latter thereby founding a dominant priestly line or dynasty that, the author avers, will be eternal.[19] The fulfillment of the prophecy is reported retrospectively in 1 Kgs 2:27, 35. Of course, God had said that about *Eli's* family (2:30), so an eternal promise can prove to be ephemeral, indeed. Finally, there is yet another reference to God's "anointed," anticipating the monarchy to come.

Is the oracle simply clairvoyant or prescient—telling what will happen in the future—or is it "fatal," i.e. deterministic—*determining* what will happen in the future?[20] Often the answer will not be obvious. The comment in 2:25b has suggested that God *causes* the deafness of Eli's sons, thus determining their fate. Again, the editor does not engage in philosophy; clearly what is about to happen (indeed, what will happen years from now) is according to God's will, but the characters also will seem to bring about their own end out of sheer cussedness (for Eli's sons). Birch puts it subtly: "the death Hophni and Phinehas *bring upon themselves* is *from God* because God will not rescue them from the *consequences of their own sin.*"[21]

But "*the boy Samuel was ministering to the Lord under Eli*" (3:1), *and wearing that vestment (ephod) that originally belonged to Eli's ancestors (2:18, 28).*

The antiphon introduces the story of Samuel's appointment as God's representative (chap. 3). Heroic figures often have stories about their vocation. Samuel's takes place in the temple.[22] Hannah, of course, has dedicated him to God, but so far God has not said a word in return. In fact God has not spoken directly at all. The editor emphasizes that silence with the preface to Samuel's appointment: "The word of the Lord was rare in those days; visions were not widespread." All of that is about to change. The rarity of visions is juxtaposed to the near blindness of Eli (v. 2), who couldn't have seen a vision if there were one! Just so, the flickering lamp might suggest the dark

---

19. As Campbell and O'Brien put it, "Priestly quarrels are a quagmire, and this is a priestly quarrel," *Unfolding*, 225a.

20. For an earlier example, cf. Gen 25:21–23. Weinfeld, *Deuteronomic School*, 15, suggests for the Deuteronomist God's word "is conceived as an 'acting force which begets future events' rather than a mantic word of God which merely reveals the future" (quoting I. Seeligmann).

21. Birch, *1 and 2 Samuel*, 989 (italics added). Still, v. 25b seems to suggest that God controls even the ability of human listening, and thus human behavior that would result from it. See below on God's "evil spirit" and Saul, 16:14.

22. Cf. the stories of Jesus at the temple (Luke 2:22–40—dedication; and vv. 41–51—child prodigy; cf. v. 52 there with 1 Sam 3:19—4:1).

state of where things are at this point in the narrative.[23]

Samuel is sleeping "where the ark of God was" suggesting closeness to the presence of God. God calls his name twice, but Samuel thinks it is Eli. In folklore fashion the pattern repeats two more times. Samuel's auditory acuity is the negative mirror of Eli's visual deterioration, although Samuel does not *understand* what he is hearing until Eli realizes that God is the source of the voice. Now God is fully present ("stood there," v. 10).[24] When Samuel repeats the words, "Speak, for your servant is listening," the correspondence between God and agent is established. Samuel now knows God because God's word is revealed to him. This is the primary function of prophets—to listen to the word of God. It is also the source of their authority, as suggested by the conclusion in 3:21—4:1, where the correlation between God's word and Samuel's word is confirmed. Samuel is a "trustworthy prophet," "trustworthy" being a word based on the root for our word "amen" sometimes translated as "believe in," as with Moses (Exod 14:31; 19:9). In fact, Samuel is the first recipient of God's revealed word who comes close to matching the intimacy enjoyed by Moses (e.g., Deut 34:10–12). Samuel is the last of the judges (see below), but no other judges were called prophets.[25] Samuel will function as priest, judge, and prophet, but his prophetic role is foremost.

23. Fokkelman, *Vow and Desire*, 160–61.

24. This is a motif in other appearances (Gen 28:13; Exod 34:5).

25. The only prophet in Judges appears out of nowhere to deliver God's indictment against Israel's apostasy (6:7–10; note the similarities with 1 Sam 2:27–36 and 7:3–17).

The vision simply confirms the indictment already delivered by the "man of God" to Eli, adding that God is about to fulfill it. Again the priestly focus appears: no sacrifices by Eli and sons will expiate their iniquity. *Their* vocation, in effect, is rescinded, even as Samuel's is initiated. Shiloh's significance as a sacrificial sanctuary now shifts to become the place of God's continuing revelations to Samuel; correspondingly, Samuel's role as prophet transcends his role as priest, and his authority extends beyond Shiloh: "The word of Samuel came to all Israel" (4:1a). From here on out, direct speech from God now will be mediated almost exclusively through the prophet; thus the prophet enjoys a monopoly on the word of God—as does, thereby, the author.

"The Hand of the Lord" (Chaps. 4–7)

The role of the ark now takes center stage in the conflict with the Philistines (last seen in the exploits of Samson). Whatever the origin of the "ark narrative" that follows, in their present setting chaps. 4–7 function as the fulfillment of the prophecy of doom in chap. 2. Along with the authorial observation about God's will in 2:25b and the preceding oracle, the following story will raise another serious question: does God determine the *means* by which God's will is accomplished, or are human beings alone responsible for the means? In what follows, the means includes warfare, death, and plague, not only of Eli and sons, but also of thousands of both Israelites and Philistines. But if God is not responsible for the means as well as the end, in what sense is God's will involved in the events that ensue? From the broadest perspective, we could ask this question of the entire Former Prophets, but, again we must infer the question from the narrative; the author does not raise the question explicitly.[26]

When Israel loses a battle, the elders decide to bring in the big gun, as it were. As a portable shrine, the ark can function as an iconic representation of God's presence in warfare. In ancient Near Eastern religion, the gods often appear in battle, fighting for their devotees. We have already seen such incidents before (Josh 5:13–14; 10:14, 42; 23:3, 10, etc.). Here the author reiterates the military imagery—"the ark of the covenant of the Lord of hosts, who is enthroned on the cherubim" (4:4). The "hosts" are God's heavenly "forces" who scatter the enemies of Israel in battle.[27] Other ancient peoples sometimes used standards or emblems as physical representations of their gods who formed the vanguard of the battle.[28] For Israel, the ark could function as such an emblem. But—and here is the rub—God must be willing to be present; otherwise the ark is just a box, something into which God will not be put (cf. Exod 25:22)![29]

The Israelites bring the ark from Shiloh to the military camp, accompanied by an earthshaking war cry, such as destroyed the walls of Jericho (Josh 6:5, 20). At first intimidated, the Philistines acknowledge the threat: "Gods have come into the camp" (v. 7). They exhibit their somewhat confused knowledge of Israel's history in associating the threat with the plagues inflicted on the Egyptians (but it was in Egypt, not "in the wilderness").[30] The fear of plague will prove to be well-founded, but the Philistines overcome their dismay and rally, winning the battle, capturing the ark, and killing Eli's sons. Now the story focuses on the horrible moment when Eli hears the news. The messenger saves the worst for last (reflecting Eli's concerns): "the ark of God has been captured." At this, Eli tumbles off his seat, breaks his neck, and dies. Samuel's vision has become real, and an editor gives an epitaph identifying Eli's role as that of a judge (4:18b).

The capture of the ark is a devastating reversal both militarily and theologically. Nothing in the preceding oracle or vision prepared for this surprise. Clearly, God is *not* with Israel. If anything, God seems to be on the side of the Philistines.

---

26. Cf. Fokkelman, *Vow and Desire,* 209: "The defeat of Israel is purely the result of a divine decree and entirely the realization of the oracle of doom." But Eli's sons "could have averted a catastrophe if only they had . . . [Fokkelman's ellipsis]," 239.

27. Cf. Num 10:35–36; Ps 68:1, 17–18. The word for "host" also means "army." The English word comes from the Latin *hostis* ("enemy"), not *hospes* ("host/guest"). The heavenly host is God's armed services, and is *not* hospitable. Note that the "us" in Gen 1:26 also refers to the heavenly council.

28. See my study, *Divine Presence,* 74–76, and the pictures at 265–68.

29. The ark's portability extends to its use in liturgical processions, in which worshippers celebrated God's victories (cf. Ps 68:17, 24–27; Psalm 24 [although the ark is not specifically mentioned here, it almost certainly is part of the procession]). The ark liturgy will be part of David's rise to power (2 Samuel 6; cf. Ps 132:1–8).

30. They could have cited the more appropriate analogy of plague in Egypt due to the acquisition of Sarah by Pharaoh, albeit with Abraham's complicity (Gen 12:17).

Now the words of Hannah's song attain a deeper irony: "The Lord! His adversaries shall be shattered" (2:10). But it is the Israelite troops who are shattered, indeed, who seem to be God's enemy. As we have seen before, the threat of such a reversal runs throughout the Former Prophets, and will reach its deepest level at the end. Phineas's now widowed wife gives birth to a son and names him "Ichabod," saying "The glory has departed from Israel." One can doubt the verisimilitude of the story in that the narrator renders a woman's deep personal anguish secondary to institutional concerns, such that the loss of her husband and imminently her own life are nothing compared to the loss of the ark! But the name reflects the close association between God's presence and God's glory, here connected to the ark (cf. Exod 40:34-35). Significantly, we could translate "the glory has gone into exile,"[31] which would present a deep resonance for readers who were in *the* Exile (post 587 BCE).

Given the common ancient Near Eastern concept of warfare, Israel's defeat could be explained as *God's* defeat. After all, if an army was defeated, it stood to reason that the god who was the *vanguard* of the army had failed. The enemy's god was the victor. On the other hand, one could explain defeat another way by saying that the god of the defeated was *punishing* them, using the enemy as "the rod of my anger," as Isaiah will put it (10:5—a virtual leitmotif for the Former Prophets). The sins of Eli's sons imply such a connection, and the oracle of the "man of God" and Samuel's vision confirm it. Now the story of the ark's return in 5:1—7:2 will dispel any lingering doubts about God's superiority.

The scene switches from the Israelite temple at Shiloh to the Philistine temple at Ashdod—the temple of the god Dagon. The human battle is over and decided; now the divine battle begins. The Philistines place the captured ark next to the statue of Dagon, no doubt as a trophy. In fact, the capture of such an emblem of a deity in warfare was a way of representing the victory of one's own deity.[32] But the next morning the victors find their god Dagon lying facedown on the floor in front of the ark, as if Dagon is paying homage. They replace the poor fellow, only to come back the next day and find Dagon not only in obeisance but also with head and hands dismembered. Thus the story of Dagon's humiliation is deeply ironic, as well as humorous—in effect, a satire against Philistine political and theological power. The severed hands of Dagon symbolize his powerlessness over against "the hand of the Lord," a motif that recurs throughout this episode (vv. 6, 7, 9, 11; 7:13).[33] Just as Israel's expectations over

---

31. The opening chapters of Ezekiel contain an elaborate vision of the departure of God's glory from the temple correlated with Israel's exile to Babylon.

32. See my *Divine Presence*, 68-69, 214-18; Miller and Roberts, *Hand of the Lord*, 10-11. The situation with the ark is precisely that described in the Mesha Inscription of the ninth century, in which the Moabite king boasts of defeating Israel and capturing some kind of vessels or other objects (the word is uncertain) "of Yahweh," and dragging "them before Kemosh," the god of Moab. See *ANET*, 320, and, more recently, Dearman, *Studies*, 98. The text provides background for 2 Kings 3.

33. See the appropriately titled *The Hand of the Lord: A Reassessment of the "Ark Narrative" of 1 Samuel*, by Miller and Roberts, especially 48.

the ark were turned upside down, so are those of their enemies. The Philistines' victory becomes their downfall, and the God of Israel usurps Dagon's temple.[34]

Now God strikes them with the plague that they had feared (5:6). The tables are turned, indicated by the word play on the root *kbd*—here, "heavy," before, the base of the name Ichabod. God's glory has returned (cf. also below on 6:5). Just as the elders of Israel had sent for the ark, the lords of the Philistines ask what they should do with it. Inexplicably, the citizens of Gath say bring it on, whereupon they too succumb to plague. The Ekronites are not so gullible, and they insist on sending the ark back to Israel.

The ark is tossed around like a hot potato for seven months until the Philistine religious establishment is called in and asked what should be done (an awkward notice, given that a solution already appeared in v. 11). But the return of the ark here focuses on what kind of "guilt offering" should accompany it (v. 3). The answer is a kind of reverse voodoo by which gold representations of tumors and mice,[35] it is hoped, will "give glory to the God of Israel," prompting God to lighten the hand that had struck them (v. 5). In effect, the solution is to *return* the glory that had departed (4:22). The Philistines are determined not to repeat the mistake of those hard hearted Egyptians. In the process, like the Egyptians, they are despoiled of their gold (Exod 3:22; 12:36).

The Philistines construct a container to hold the gold offerings and place it next to the ark on a cart. They yoke the cart to two milking cows that have never been yoked before. The cows would not normally leave their calves, unless compelled by some unnatural power, and, untrained, they are free to go the way the ark tells them to go. This notion, in fact, reflects an understanding of the ark as a kind of pathfinder empowered by the presence of God (and related to its function as vanguard; cf. Num 10:33; Josh 3:3–4). Moreover, the *return* of a deity's emblem to its home could represent the reversal of the punishment that allowed for its capture. Sure enough, the ark makes a beeline for Beth-shemesh, just as the Philistines had hoped, proving that the hand of God was indeed behind all of their trouble.

The citizens of Beth-shemesh rejoice over the return of the ark, and promptly offer up the hapless cows as a sacrifice of thanksgiving (hungry calves notwithstanding). The author refers to the still-extant stone which marks the spot and serves as a reminder ("witness," v. 18).[36] Then a strange incident beclouds the otherwise happy resolution. God kills seventy people of one family for some kind of offense. One alternate reading appears in the NRSV footnote: "because they looked into" the ark.[37] We know

---

34. See ibid., 44–46, regarding the mythological battle between gods.

35. The Greek text refers to mice coming off of ships docked on the Mediterranean coast of Philistia, which could explain the plague. However, some scholars continue to associate the plague with hemorrhoids, which provides some scatological humor to the story.

36. Cf. 7:12 and Josh 7:26; 22:27; 24:27.

37. The NRSV of v. 19a is based on the Greek text and implies that the family is punished for not joining in the celebration. The footnote (u) reflects the Hebrew text. McCarter (*I Samuel*, 131, 136) concludes on text-critical grounds that originally the problem concerned the absence

from a later story that even touching the ark can lead to death (2 Sam 6:7). Like the temple itself, the ark is a numinous, holy object, and in ancient thought holiness was charged with dangerous power, something like the way we would think of a radioactive substance (cf. v. 20—"this *holy* God").[38]

A contemporary film in the "Indiana Jones" series is illustrative here—*Raiders of the Lost Ark*. In the film, Nazis have discovered the long lost ark and intend to use its alleged power as a secret weapon against the Allies. In the climactic scene, Indiana Jones and his damsel in distress, Marion, are caught in their attempt to outwit the Nazis. The Nazis tie them up inside a cave and then proceed to open the ark. Jones warns Marion to keep her eyes closed and not to look no matter what happens. The head Nazi looks into the ark and a whirlwind swirls out of it, filling the cave with a thunderous noise. At that point the flesh of the man's head melts like wax, right down to the skull. Indiana Jones, after all, is an archaeologist who knows his stuff. In fact, we can understand the message of the film to be analogous to the biblical story: the power of the Nazis—whose uniform belt buckles said "God is with us"—proved to be helpless against the power of God. They too could ask the question that concludes the theological thrust of the biblical story: "'Who is able to stand before the Lord, this holy God?'"[39]

Now the citizens of Beth-shemesh are as reluctant to keep the ark as were the Philistines, and they send it to yet another town, Kiriath-jearim (surprisingly, not back to Shiloh, but perhaps because the Elide priests there are dead!). There the ark will reside under the keeping of Levitical priests for twenty years, when it will make its final journey to Jerusalem.

The story now focuses on Samuel's role as judge as well as priest (7:3–17). With Eli and sons dead, Samuel is the de facto ruler. Samuel gives a little speech calling for repentance as the path that will lead to victory over the Philistines. The language is clearly Deuteronomic: "returning to the Lord with all your heart," abandoning "foreign gods," and pledging exclusive allegiance to God (vv. 1–4).[40] However, the charge of worshipping "foreign gods" and "the Baals and Astartes" seems more appropriate to the book of Judges than here.[41] There has been no reference to such apostasy in 1

---

of authorized Levitical priests (v. 15 being an addition to correct the problem, and the phrase "looked into" an attempt at explanation). Note that v. 15 must be read in the pluperfect to make chronological sense; still v. 15b repeats part of 14b. Polzin (*Samuel*, 65) retains "looked into," as does Fokkelman, *Vow and Desire*, 289, who concludes that the incident remains "gruesome and bewildering."

38. Cf. Exod 19:12 where God has Moses warn the people not to even "touch the edge of the mountain" unbidden, lest they die, and not to move forward "to look" (v. 21) or else God will "break out against them" (v. 24, using the same word as 2 Sam 6:8). In Numbers 16, people unauthorized to offer incense are swallowed up by a fissure in the ground!

39. Cf. Miller and Roberts, *Hand of the Lord*, 59.

40. On repentance (literally "return") cf. Deut 4:30; 30:10 and 1 Kgs 8:48.

41. And even there we saw it to be highly inflated: Josh 24:14–15; Judg 2:1–5; 10:10–16. On the other hand, Polzin, *Samuel*, 59, suggests that this verse demonstrates the validity of the Philistines' earlier reference to Israel's gods (4:7–8), i.e., that the ark functioned as an "idol." Cf. also Birch, *1 and 2 Samuel*, 1017–19.

Samuel, and all of the offenses have been ascribed to Eli and sons, not to the people. If anything, the people spoke *against* the offenses (2:16). Thus the charge of idolatry seems like a retro-explanation. Nevertheless, the editor tells us that the people comply with Samuel's command. Samuel calls for a prayer service at which the people make libations, fast, and confess their sin; thus "Samuel judged the people of Israel at Mizpah" (vv. 5–6).

Repentance has not boosted the people's courage, however, so they plead with Samuel to pray continually for God's salvation from the Philistines. Samuel sacrifices a lamb, cries out to God, and God answers with a thunderous voice that throws the enemy into a panic.[42] Now God has done precisely what Hannah's song had proclaimed (2:10). Again, "the hand of the Lord" has been at work, and, in fact, "was against the Philistines all the days of Samuel" (v. 13). The unit concludes with a summary of Samuel's role as a circuit Judge, his administration of justice, and construction of an altar in his home town.[43] Ramah has now replaced Shiloh. As the conclusion to the preceding ark story, Samuel's work here is to restore "genuine religion," which "is not the magical belief in, nor manipulation using, objects," such as the ark, "but the full and sincere submission to the one God, and Him alone."[44]

We are at a critical point in the narrative, for in the next scene the people will ask Samuel to supply them with a king. Looking back, the request will seem inexplicable. After all, God the Holy Warrior has routed the Philistines and the ark has come back to a proper home. Samuel, God's prophetic mediator, has served admirably, solidifying the judicial system and reinstating authentic ritual. Thus Samuel is the ideal ruler: "the prophet is also priest, warrior, judge and governor," demonstrating "the sufficiency and theological propriety of non-royal leadership."[45] With peace and security "all the days of Samuel," what more could Israel want?

"A King to Judge" (Chap. 8)

A verse or two can make all the difference. If the summary in 7:15 sounded like an epilog, 8:1–2 seems to confirm the end of Samuel's career: "When Samuel became old, he made his sons judges over Israel" (but he takes a long time to die—25:1). This move to hereditary succession raises the specter of Abimelech and the disastrous outcome of his brief reign as king (Judges 9).[46] Moreover, the elders reveal that the sons do not continue their father's judicial work, but

---

42. Thunder is a metaphor for God's voice (cf. Exod 19:19; Psalm 29), and part of a storm deity's weaponry; cf. Ps 18:13–14. On the "confusion," cf. Josh 10:10; Judg 4:15.

43. Thus 7:3–17 closely resembles the typical pattern in the Judges stories, as outlined by Jobling, *1 Samuel*, 51–52.

44. Fokkelman, *Vow and Desire*, 314.

45. McCarter, *1 Samuel*, 99, 150; cf. Birch, *1 and 2 Samuel*, 960. So also Polzin, *Samuel*, 79, who again sees a message addressed to the exiles—they must abandon the monarchy itself.

46. Surprisingly, throughout these passages, there is no reference to the stories of Gideon and Abimelech, especially since the latter contains the scathing ridicule of the very institution of monarchy (Jotham's fable, Judg 9:8–15). For a recent survey of various historical and sociological interpretations of dynastic succession see McNutt, *Reconstructing*, chap. 4, especially 132–34.

pervert justice by seeking to fill their pockets with bribes. They look a lot like the two sons of Eli, greed being the bond that unites them. So up to this point we have two fathers who have produced unrighteous sons, even though one of the fathers (Samuel) is God's answer to the first's problem. As priests, one set of sons corrupted the sacerdotal system in breach of canon law; as judges, the other set has perverted the judicial system in breach of civil law (cf. Deut 16:19). Herein lies an answer to the question "What more could Israel want?" They want someone to replace Samuel, now that he has grown old. His sons obviously will not fill the bill. Samuel's promoting them as successors, combined with their irresponsibility, has produced a leadership vacuum, the final prop in setting the stage for Israel's request for a king.

To anticipate the complex composition, we can sketch the separate literary strands that the editors pieced together to produce the inauguration of monarchy (the key word is *melek*). The request for a king arises out of two different contexts—military leadership and judicial leadership. Some of the material clearly affirms the need for a king without reservation or criticism; some clearly opposes the very notion of a human king, condemning it as evil.[47] On the one hand, God initiates the monarchy graciously; on the other hand, God gives in to it grudgingly. The reader should be prepared for numerous inconsistencies, contradictions, and illogical shifts in the reported speech of the characters and in the flow of the plot. Although some voices dominate over others, the canonical narrative makes no attempt to harmonize these ambiguities, much less to stifle them. Indeed, the ambiguities in the narrative reflect the deep ambiguity of the main issue (and it is a perennial human issue)—what form of government Israel should have—for which there is no unambiguous resolution. At least two original literary strands are present, along with editorial insertions.[48]

- **Scenario A** (8:1–5, 21–22; 10:20–24): Because of the corruption of Samuel's sons in perverting justice, the elders of Israel request a king (*melek*) to "judge us" (NRSV "govern"). Possibly God responds without condemning the request, and Samuel selects Saul by a process of elimination using lots (which, in effect, means God's determination). The people then shout "'Long live the king (*melek*)!'"

---

47. Not surprisingly, scholarly opinions mirror the conflict of biblical voices. Polzin, *Samuel*, 224 takes the extreme position throughout his book that for the Deuteronomic Historian, "kingship, despite all its glories, constituted for Israel communal suicide." The only way exilic Israel can return to the land is "kingless." "Once Israel rejects God by demanding a king (8:7), it will take the rest of the History to describe the slow and painful process of God rejecting Israel" (213). Contrast Roberts, "In Defense of the Monarchy," 381, who emphasizes the Deuteronomist's inclusion of conflicting opinions, some in favor of the monarchy (e.g., the failure of Samuel's sons) and argues that despite the "imperialistic" aspects of the Davidic empire, it provides "the base of the great prophetic visions of universal peace," including the hope for a Messiah (387, 378). Similarly, Halpern, *First Historians*, 219, says the Deuteronomic Historian "sees monarchy ... as the nation's life's breath." "DtrH positively wheezes with royalism."

48. In the following, Scenario A corresponds roughly to Campbell and O'Brien's "prophetic" strand, and B to their "assembly" strand, *Unfolding*, 217b–18a, 233b, 242a.

Add 8:6 and there is a relatively mild condemnation.

- **Scenario B** (9:1—10:16; 11:1–11, 15): The monarchy is God's response to the people's cry for help, with the purpose of *saving* Israel from "the hand of the Philistines" (contrast 7:13, where the Philistines are subdued "all the days of Samuel").[49] The language is very similar to that of Moses' call to be Israel's leader in saving them from Pharaoh (Exod 2:23–25; 3:7–10). On God's orders, and in private, Samuel anoints an unsuspecting Saul to be "ruler (*nagid*) over my people Israel" (9:16).[50] This account is attached to the story of Saul's initial exploit against the Ammonites, which sounds like a Judges deliverance story, with the spirit-possessed Saul providing *salvation* (NRSV "deliverance"; 11:9). The conclusion, in which the people make Saul king (*melek*), could have been originally independent, but now functions as Saul's *public* inauguration.[51]

- Expansions of the anti-monarchical position appear in the rest of chaps. 8 and 12, the latter condemning the monarchy as "wickedness" and "evil" totally inconsistent with God's saving history with Israel.[52]

Thus one could actually propose at least three variations on Saul's appointment: the donkey story, the lottery story, and the Ammonite story.[53] It is possible that the elders' request was composed to tie in with one or more of these, or that it was yet another independent account, concluding with 11:15. In any event, and despite the intricacies of composition, the product remains an admirable literary achievement with a defined structure marked by the pairing of a report of an assembly followed by a story, alternating from an anti-monarchy to a pro-monarchy opinion.[54]

A Assembly: request for a king, anti-monarchy: 8:1–22
   B Story: private anointing of Saul, pro-monarchy: 9:1—10:16
A Assembly: public presentation, anti-monarchy: 10:17–27
   B Story: Saul's first campaign, pro-monarchy: chap. 11
A Assembly: Samuel's valedictory address, anti-monarchy: chap. 12

---

49. Or this scenario may reflect the situation as Samuel comes into his old age, thus leaving a vacuum in leadership to defend against the Philistines (his sons apparently are not so qualified).

50. The word *nagid*, sometimes translated "prince," almost exclusively refers to someone who is designated to become king, something like our "president elect."

51. That Saul fights the Ammonites (not the Philistines), that Saul's militant spirit possession resembles that of the judges (contrast 9:6 where the phenomenon is prophetic), and that v. 15 is a second inauguration using the word *melek* are all reasons why one might see here an originally independent story.

52. Note that 12:12 ascribes the people's request to their fear of the Ammonites, which is inconsistent with 8:4 as well as the Ammonite story, where Saul's king-elect status seems to be presupposed (11:12–13). However, such a request fits with the "cry" of Israel in 9:16.

53. Campbell, *From Joshua to Chronicles*, 179, suggests as many as five variant traditions.

54. See Childs, *Introduction*, 277–78; also Fokkelman, *Vow and Desire*, 533, who is adapting the study of McCarthy. Fokkelman also points out how three stories about Saul are framed by chaps. 8 and 12.

The editor has carefully presented both sides of the argument, while at the same time framing the structure with the anti-monarchy pieces, thus giving that position predominance. The composite artistry is aptly described by Campbell and O'Brien: "a classic specimen of Israel's theological processes, expressing critical reflection in story, juxtaposing differing traditions, drawing on new material to update views, and often blending the whole into a final text of remarkable artistry and elegance."[55]

Even with the notice about Samuel's sons, one could say that the request for a king represents a failure of trust in God, i.e., that *God* will again send the Spirit to motivate a leader when the need arises, as God has done with previous judges.[56] Instead, the elders ask *Samuel* to appoint a leader. In effect, what they ask for here is what they get in Scenario B, but, by positioning their request here, the editor has made it difficult for the reader to see God's action there apart from an anti-monarchy ideology. Moreover, at Samuel's passing, Israel might need a new Samuel, but not necessarily a king. Even though the words "to govern" in v. 5 literally mean "to judge," the use of the crucial word *melek* signals a radical departure from the order previously ensured by judges. Thus the phrase "a king to judge" catches the critical transition from one form of leader to another (i.e., in reverse). While the order of judges was unique to Israel (as the editor seems to think), the people want a king to be "like other nations." The phrase is telling, because Israel's calling is not to keep up with the Joneses, as it were. God has elected Israel to be a "special people," whose merit resides in God's unmerited love, not in national might, and whose ethos is supposed to reflect nothing less than the holiness of God.[57] Can Israel be God's "special people" and "like the nations" under a king? The answer is not obvious. Indeed, one need only contrast the implied "No" here with the text in Deuteronomy where God, in fact, grants the request for a king "like all the nations" without a hint of condemnation (Deut 17:14–20)!

The response from God and Samuel is at once personal, theological, and political. Samuel is "displeased" (more literally "it was evil in his eyes"), apparently because the request seems like a rejection of him as well as his sons. At least, that is God's reading of Samuel's attitude, but God says that the request is a denial of *God's* sovereignty—"they have rejected me from being king over them." The critique here resembles that of Gideon, who declined a request to be ruler, saying that only God was Israel's ruler (Judg 8:23; however, the word there is *mashal*). God identifies Israel's abandonment as typical of Israel's behavior from the Exodus to the present, and compares it to "serving other gods," a favorite phrase of Deuteronomic theology. In other words, the request for a king is equated with theological treason, the most profound breach of covenant. Nevertheless, God decides to grant their request, and instructs a very reluctant

---

55. *Unfolding*, 229b. Cf. Halpern, *First Historians*, 231.

56. This is the point made later in 12:6–12; cf. Judg 3:10; 6:34; 11:29; 14:6.

57. Cf. Exod 19:4–6; Lev 18:24–27; Deut 7:1–6.

Samuel so to do.⁵⁸ God then tells Samuel to inform the people of "the judgment (or justice) of the king,"⁵⁹ (AT), i.e., the governmental and juridical consequences of the political choice they are making.

The monarchy will be far different from the order of judges, affecting the traditional social structures of family, clan, and tribe. State centered religion, with its royal palace and temple, will replace family centered religion (or at least attempt to), with its household shrines or village "high places," the "lord of all the earth" (Ps 97:5) overshadowing the "God of the ancestors." Power will shift from tribal and inter-tribal authorities to a central authority, and the monarchy will impose permanent administrative and organizational institutions, such as a standing army rather than a militia. The king will conscript citizens to perform agricultural and household work for the king's benefit. He will seize private property by royal "eminent domain," partly to reward his cronies. Funding the various royal projects will entail the imposition of a tax and even conscripted labor. Overall, the monarchy will institute a sociological system based on political ties and economic interests, over against the traditional ties of family, tribe, and land.⁶⁰ In other words, historically the monarchy is about money more than monotheism, no doubt complete with pro-monarchy "lobbyists"!⁶¹ The monarchy will differ also when it comes to a king's successor, for hereditary monarchy will rival the mode of God's selection of judges (though not completely, thanks to the prophets). Indeed, the problem with hereditary leadership is already apparent in Samuel's sons, and his promotion of them prompts the elders' request.⁶²

Samuel emphasizes the oppressive severity of the king's power by concluding "in that day you will cry out because of your king," but God will not answer them (v. 18). The word for "cry out" here refers to a distress call—an SOS. Israel has uttered this cry before when oppressed by foreign rulers or military enemies, paradigmatically in the Exodus story (Exod 2:23), but also in the Judges stories (Judg 6:2). Indeed, it is this cry to which God responds in Scenario B (9:16). But here Samuel says that they will cry out because of their *own* king. The author, of course, knows that such has been the case as of the time of his writing, and there are numerous examples of this cry elsewhere (notably 1 Kgs 12:4). Elementally, the distress call

---

58. Polzin, *Samuel*, 83, argues that Samuel is a "stubborn and self-interested judge" who repeatedly delays following through with God's decision and does *not* report to the people all of God's words, especially God's acquiescence despite feelings about rejection (8:7–9). Of course, the omission could be explained as well by redactional activity (e.g., the insertion of vv. 11–18). The repetitions in vv. 9 and 21–22 ("all the words," "listen to their voice") suggest editorial seams. Cf. the similar ambiguities in Exod 19:3–8, 25.

59. The recurring root *shafat*, as in v. 4.

60. The critique here is similar to the "law of the king" in Deut 17:14–20, there primarily emphasizing too much money and too many wives, no doubt with Solomon as the chief offender.

61. For a sketch of the socioeconomic factors, see Birch, *1 and 2 Samuel*, 1023: "vested economic and political power interests stood to gain more than simply relief from Philistine pressure."

62. Jobling (*1 Samuel*, 62) suggests that blaming Samuel is a way to obfuscate the contradiction between God's offering the choice of a king in Deuteronomy 17 and God's reluctance or outright repugnance here.

signifies the total abandonment of the king's major responsibility—to protect the weak—and undermines the bedrock of Israel's covenantal understanding of social justice—the very reason for their request.[63] There is no mention here of royal offenses involving worship places or other gods, those being the primary offenses that the Deuteronomic historian continually condemns in the books of Kings. Nevertheless, the people insist on having a king, and add insult to injury in saying "[to] fight our battles" (v. 20). To which God could reply "though I am their supreme commander," a role prominently played in the previous chapters ("the hand of the Lord" in the ark story, God's victory over the Philistines in 7:10). God says as much later in 10:19.

Having heard the dire warnings, it is amazing that the people insist on having a king after all. By the same token, we could see God's acquiescence here as more punitive than resigned, an understandable response to the insult of rejection. "You want a king, OK, I'll *give* you a king such as will make you wish you had never asked." Fokkelman even suggests that God's attitude here has "a masochistic touch"![64] A comparable situation appears in the wilderness story when the people crave meat (having lived on vegetarian manna seemingly forever). God criticizes their complaint by saying "you have rejected the Lord who is among you," then warns them that they will have to eat meat for so long it "will come out of your nostrils"![65] Just so, they may become "fed up" with the monarchy.

The heavy editorializing here (and even more so in chap. 12) against the monarchy makes it difficult for the reader to weigh the pros and cons objectively. There is no editorial voice speaking for the monarchy in the same way and with the same depth as the opposition. The latter speaks most loudly in long speeches delivered by Samuel in chaps. 8 and 12 (cf. Joshua in Joshua 23–24). The voices in defense of the monarchy appear only implicitly in narrative (e.g., 8:1–3; scenario B). For example, none of the elders in chap. 8 is allowed a voice to counter the objections raised by Samuel. No voice says "Yes, but . . ." Those who ask for a king likely would not agree that the request is evil, or that it necessarily entails rejecting God as the ultimate sovereign, but they do not speak.[66] Had they done so, they might

---

63. Exod 22:21–24; cf. Isa 5:7; Mic 3:1–4. On the king's role in the judicial system, see McNutt, *Reconstructing*, 174–76.

64. Fokkelman, *Vow and Desire*, 337. Cf. Hos 13:10–11: to Israel's request for "a king and rulers" God says, "I gave you a king in my anger, and I took him away in my wrath," referring to king Hoshea.

65. Num 11:18–20. The key word "reject" is the same as in 1 Sam 8:7. Moreover, the rejection is not just the demand for meat but the deeper rebellion expressed in the words "Why did we ever leave Egypt?" i.e., questioning God's act of salvation itself. The rejection in 1 Sam 8:7 almost seems to refer to this kind of story when v. 8 compares it to how Israel has behaved ever since God "brought them up out of Egypt." Fokkelman (ibid.) goes even further in suggesting that God's ultimate "rejection" of Saul results from the people's rejection of God here.

66. See Roberts, "In Defense of the Monarchy," 383: "many biblical writers, including Dtr [the Deuteronomist], did not share the view of Gideon and Samuel that the choice of a human king implies the rejection of Yahweh," and comparison of other ancient Near Eastern examples of monarchy shows that such a view "is anything but self-evident."

have pointed out that most incidents of God's salvation of Israel from its enemies involve, in some way, a human agent—beginning at least as early as Moses, and continuing with Joshua and the judges, then Samuel and (soon to be) Saul.[67] Paradigmatically, God's operation in the world occurs through the *co*-operation of such an agent (who can be as ostensibly insignificant as Hannah).[68] The questions, then, are what type of leader best fits Israel's situation and how is Israel to discern who that leader is? In fact, all but the fiercest opposition had to come to terms with the monarchy, and did so, developing, as we shall see, a full-blown royal theology.[69]

There would be important historical factors that led to the perceived need for a monarchy.[70] One could pose the question of the monarchy in a dialectic involving judges versus kings, charismatic leadership versus hereditary, a volunteer militia versus a standing army, serendipitous divine involvement versus the stability of divinely ordained institutions, local and regional government versus centralized or "federal" government. Those who favor the monarchy might recall the chaos at the end of Judges, exemplified in the phrase, "there was no king in Israel; people did what was right in their own eyes." On the other hand, anti-monarchists might want to read that statement differently, i.e., that when there was no monarchy the people could exercise their "unalienable rights" to pursue "life, liberty, and happiness," to quote the Declaration of Independence. In fact, numerous scholars emphasize the tendency toward egalitarianism on one side, and a hierarchical system on the other, with the latter suppressive of minorities—especially women.[71] But local power figures can be just as domineering—and unjust—as centralized ones (one need only think of the American civil rights movement and how federal actions were required to put an end to school segregation, voting rights abuses, and other injustices). Or

67. Note the way in which two literary sources in Exodus 3 emphasize the two sides of salvation, one from God (vv. 7–8), the other by means of Moses (vv. 9–10). An exception would be God's mysterious power ("hand") at work in the ark story (although even there one might see the ark as a surrogate agent!). Another incident close to unmediated divine action is God's rout of the Philistines in 7:10, yet even here God is responding to Samuel's ritual intercession, and the militia takes over in v. 11. Even Israel's return from exile, as prophesied by Second Isaiah (Isaiah 40–55), assumes the agency of the Persian ruler Cyrus, who is called God's "anointed" (Isa 45:1)! As Birch, *1 and 2 Samuel*, 959, puts it, "God's will is usually brought to pass through human events and personalities." However, he suggests that the ark story contradicts the notion "that God has no power to act in the world apart from human agency" (1007).

68. On cooperation see more fully the discussion in on 9:16; 17:31–47; 2 Sam 17:14; 1 Kgs 12:15.

69. Even so, "The texts that come out of the royal cult betray no indication that the presence of a human king compromises the position of the divine king," Roberts, "In Defense of the Monarchy," 384.

70. For a recent survey of the issues, see McNutt, *Reconstructing*, chap. 4 and especially 123–24.

71. See Hackett, "1 and 2 Samuel," 91–101, as well as the article there on the other books in the Former Prophets. Roberts, "In Defense of the Monarchy," 386, suggests that the monarchy "probably offered the powerless the first effective check against the oppression of powerful local leaders that they had experienced in a long time." There are benefits to a "federal" system!

to use an analogy from ancient Greek history, we could note how "the plays of Aeschylus" (fifth century BCE) proposed "for people to transfer their social allegiance from tribes to states, ceding justice to the rule of law . . . and not merely tribal vengeance."[72]

To take one example: the Philistine threat, already in view in Joshua, and frequent in Judges (e.g., 1:19), seemed to be resolved at the end of ch.7, but it appears again in no time and, in fact, will be the death of Israel's first king. Can Israel survive such a threat relying on a volunteer militia, with only some tribes participating (cf. Judg 5:14-18), summoned by a leader whose own authority relies on the unpredictable movement of God's Spirit? And how does one know with certainty whom the Spirit has designated, or who might be an imposter? Or, in fact, does such a threat require the efficiency of a centralized command, a standing army, and weaponry ready for deployment?[73]

At the heart of the issue of the monarchy is this question fundamental to virtually all communities that consider themselves in some way "under God": What type of leader can be most effective in faithfully representing God's will for a peaceful and just society, and how is that leader to be identified? Needless to say, when we use the term "anointed"— or the transliteration "Messiah," or its Greek equivalent, *Christos*—this question extends far beyond the confines of the Former Prophets. Moreover, *how* the sovereignty of God is related to the sovereignty of human rulers is a fundamental dimension of the issue, and scarcely limited to ancient times.[74]

Lost Donkeys, Newfound King (Chaps. 9–11)

In the present text, Samuel has dismissed the people without following through with God's instructions (it is not even clear that he has informed the people of God's acquiescence).[75] With the editorial critique of the monarchy as a frame, the narrative turns to the folktale of how Saul became the first king. Again, without the frame, we could read this story and see

---

72. Hay, "Of Storytellers," W9. Just as intriguing when comparing the stories in Judges 17–21 is his comment regarding the *Iliad*, which "shows us a world before nation-states, when blood feuds led to conflict and grievances (e.g., the abduction of a woman) to war."

73. Cf. Roberts, "In Defense of the Monarchy": "The transition to royal rule took place in Israel because the old system was no longer working," referring specifically to the Philistines and Ammonites. Cf. also his quotation from G. Buccellati on 388 n. 2: "the monarchy was the institution which best met the political exigencies of the Israelites at a given time." Cf. also Miller, *Religion of Ancient Israel*, 11–12, 87; Birch, *1 and 2 Samuel*, 957; Gottwald, *Politics*, 173–75.

74. This is clearly the case in numerous New Testament passages in which the attribution of titles like "king" and "lord" to Jesus creates enormous conflicts with human authorities. With roots already in the Exodus covenant tradition, one can see here the precedent for theological issues stretching down to contemporary times. See the comments of Birch, *1 and 2 Samuel*, 1031. In terms of American history, the way in which presidents have appealed to religion to support their programs and policies is only one example within the larger issue of "civil religion."

75. Cf. Birch, *1 and 2 Samuel*, 1028–29, following Polzin, *Samuel*, 85–88. Of course, as Birch notes, the postponement makes room for the following story of the secret anointing of Saul, which would be anticlimactic if Samuel had already held a public inauguration.

nothing obviously wrong with Israel's having a king.⁷⁶ His father sends him on a search and rescue mission for some lost donkeys. When he fails to find them, he wants to turn back, but his servant suggests that they go into the nearby town and consult with a "man of God," who, for a shekel, will tell them where to look. "Perhaps he can tell us about the journey on which we have set out," he says. Little does he know that this journey will lead to far more than lost *donkeys*. The author tells us that those who are called "prophets" once were called "seers," a role more similar to our notion of a fortune teller than to the political role of the biblical prophets. Probably in the original version of this story, that was more descriptive of the character who became Samuel in the retelling. Saul learns that Samuel can be found at a "shrine"⁷⁷ where he will be performing a sacrifice. His informer says that no one "will eat until he comes, since he must bless the sacrifice" (v. 13). Such a blessing is otherwise unknown in the Hebrew Bible,⁷⁸ suggesting Samuel's idiosyncratic prerogative, which will eventually be the undoing of Saul, as we shall see.

The author now takes us back to the previous day, when God revealed to Samuel that God was sending a man whom Samuel should anoint to be king-elect (*nagid*) over Israel: "He shall save my people from *the hand of the Philistines*; for I have seen the suffering of my people, because their outcry has come to me" (v. 16). As noted before, this commissioning clearly echoes that of Moses in his mission to save Israel from "*the hand of the Egyptians*" (Exod 3:7–10). In effect, Saul will become the extension of "*the hand of the Lord*" that acted alone in the ark narrative, administering God's salvation just as Samuel administers God's word (3:19–21). Again, salvation is literally a co-operation of God and human agent, as it was with Moses. The commissioning here clearly has no negative dimensions, is initiated by God in response to Israel's suffering, and presumes a situation of Philistine oppression that contradicts the previous statement that "the hand of the Lord was against the Philistines all the days of Samuel," so that they "were subdued" and posed no threat to Israel (7:13).

Now the author returns us to the present and the arrival of Saul. God says to Samuel, "Here is the man who shall muster my people."⁷⁹ When Saul and Samuel meet, Samuel invites him to the sacrificial meal, adding that in the morning he "will tell you all that is on your mind." But the latter does not refer to the *donkeys*, for Samuel immediately tells Saul that they should *not* be on his mind, for they have been found, then

---

76. So also Birch, *1 and 2 Samuel*, 1036. However, some scholars see subtle signs of Saul's deficiencies; e.g., Alter, *Art*, 60–61. See below on Saul's Benjamite connection and selection by lot.

77. Or "high place," the type of shrine that the Deuteronomic editors will rail against later in the Former Prophets (e.g., 1 Kgs 12:31–32; 14:23; 15:14, etc.).

78. McCarter, *I Samuel*, 177.

79. NRSV "rule"; McCarter (*I Samuel*, 179) translates with "muster"; the word can also be used for "assembly," and probably focuses on military leadership. Fokkelman (*Vow and Desire*, 396–97) emphasizes a different possibility, translating "curb" and "bridle"; similarly Polzin, (*Samuel*, 94) with the stronger "hinder, imprison." One would think such hindrance would be against the Philistines!

adds another mysterious comment, "On whom is all Israel's desire fixed, if not on you and on all your ancestral house?" (v. 20). Saul counters that he comes from the lowliest of families within "the tribe of Benjamin," and rightly asks why Samuel is speaking to him in this way. Here, and again in the lottery story that follows (10:20–24), Saul's self-deprecation acknowledges the way in which God tends to choose people of little status for big roles.[80] We will see the same phenomenon at work with the young David. Given what *we* know from the book of Judges, Saul also could have registered his disapproval of the horrors associated with his tribe and his home town of Gibeah (Judges 19–21—the Levite's concubine, civil war, mass rape). But neither the characters nor the narrator make any such explicit connection, leaving the readers to make the associations themselves, and draw any conclusions.[81]

Samuel does not answer Saul's question; instead, he takes him to the banquet and seats him at the head of the table, the honored position, and orders the chef to present Saul with the cut of meat normally enjoyed only by the priests. Saul will receive a similar gift in 10:4 (bread designated for priests), both instances reflecting the ecclesiastical dimensions of a monarch.[82] Moreover, here is the first of several critical moments in Saul's life that are associated with sacrifice (13:8–15; ch.15; perhaps 28:24). The next morning Samuel sends Saul's servant on ahead so that "I may make known to you the word of God." Then he anoints Saul as prince and informs him of God's commission to save Israel "from *the hand of their enemies* all around" (10:1). As in the call of Moses,[83] Saul receives a series of signs to verify its authenticity (10:2–8):

- Saul will hear about the recovery of the donkeys
- he will encounter pilgrims heading to the sanctuary at Bethel, who will give Saul some of the bread they are carrying for sacrifice
- he will come to a town "where the Philistine garrison is," where he "will meet a band of prophets"—a "band" in both senses of the English word, for they are playing instruments—caught up in a "prophetic frenzy." The latter could be translated as "prophesying like crazy," referring to the animated state of ecstasy (the "whirling dervish" of Islam could serve as an analogy, or other "charismatic" behavior)

---

80. The insignificance, and even incompetence, of those whom God calls is evident in Moses (Exod 3:11—4:17), Gideon (Judg 6:13), and Jeremiah (Jer 1:6), among others. The literary pattern here is a "call narrative." See the helpful excursus by Birch, *1 and 2 Samuel*, 1040–42.

81. The associations include the towns of Jabesh-Gilead and Shiloh (Judg 21:8–25; 1 Samuel 11; 31:11–13) and what happened there. Some interpreters see these associations in Judges as anticipating Saul's kingship and ascribing "guilt by association." As Sweeney suggests (*King Josiah*, 121), "after all, what kind of a king could come from a city like Gibeah or a tribe like Benjamin?" Cf. Fokkelman, *Vow and Desire*, 403. If the Judges allusions intend to demean Saul, the same associations in chap. 11 seem to redeem him! See below.

82. See McCarter, *I Samuel*, 180–81. On the other hand, Saul's priestly status does not protect him from the consequences of performing a sacrifice in disobedience to Samuel, as we shall see.

83. Exod 3:12; 4:8–9; cf. Judg 6:17 with Gideon; Jer 1:4–10 with Jeremiah.

- Saul too will be possessed by the spirit of the Lord, join in the prophetic ecstasy, and "be turned into a different person"

All of these signs are assurances that "God is with you." In fact, the entire donkey story exhibits the way in which Hebrew narrative often combines apparently insignificant, everyday activities with a sense of inscrutable divine presence guiding historical events. In this tale Saul is simply a youth looking for lost donkeys, but God is looking for a king, so Saul's searching fuses with God's searching until the two meet in the figure of Samuel, who is far more than a seer. Saul's father has sent him after the donkeys; God has sent him to Samuel (v. 16). The subtlety of divine providence here appears in such detail as the serendipitous discovery of a coin by Saul's servant, which makes the continuation of their search possible (9:8).[84] Samuel then gives conflicting instructions that will prove to be Saul's downfall: he tells Saul to "do whatever you see fit to do," but then says for Saul to wait seven days for him at Gilgal where Samuel will offer a sacrifice "and show you what you shall do" (10:7-8). Perhaps Samuel should have added the elliptical warning, "Or else." Is Saul a free agent or the prophet's pupil?

All of the signs come true, although the author only describes the prophetic ecstasy and that "God gave him another heart." Saul will have another episode of such ecstasy later (19:19-24), both connected to the proverbial question, "Is Saul also among the prophets?"[85] The result of this type of spirit possession does not involve his role as a deliverer from the Philistines, as it soon will (11:6). Perhaps prophetic interests saw this incident as another example of royal subordination—the prince becomes a prophet—and familial disruption—Saul has a new "father" as does the member of a religious order.[86] Saul finally returns home, having had quite an adventure indeed. But when asked about the trip, Saul reports on the donkeys and says nothing about "the matter of the kingship." That he reports to his uncle and not his father is a familial (and patriarchal) way of suggesting the radical change in his life.

The sequel to the donkey story (9:1—10:16) appears most clearly in Saul's first victory over the Philistines and the unhappy conclusion to Samuel's instructions to wait seven days at Gilgal (13:2-15). There are numerous interruptions of that sequence:

- Saul's selection by tribal lottery at Mizpah in 10:17-27a
- Saul's first military victory (but against the Ammonites, not the Philistines) in 10:27b—11:13, with vague similarities in the donkey story[87]

---

84. See McCarter, *I Samuel*, 185; Alter, *David Story*, 48: "Look, I happen to have at hand a quarter of a shekel"; Fokkelman, *Crossing Fates*, 125.

85. Only in the latter text does Samuel seem to be associated with such prophecy. For another example, see Num 11:16-30;

86. Cf. Fokkelman, *Vow and Desire*, 429-30; cf. Second Kings 2:9-12 where Elijah is the "father" for a band of prophets. Jobling suggests that there is a "father/surrogate son" pattern in the entire book (*I Samuel*, 110-25).

87. Compare Saul's mission of "deliverance" (or "salvation") in 9:16 and 10:1 with 11:9; Saul's spirit possession in 10:6, 10 with 11:6, the latter *as deliverer*, not ecstatic prophet.

- brief notices about Saul's critics (10:26–27a; 11:12–13)
- acclamation as king at Gilgal, 11:14–15 (*before* the prearranged meeting at Gilgal)
- chap. 12, Samuel's (premature) farewell address

Thus there are three incidents in which Saul is appointed, two military victories, and two gatherings at Gilgal. Yet the editor has arranged all of these literary strands in such a way that they work together, if not without bumps on the way.

In an abrupt literary shift, Samuel now gathers the people to Mizpah, and, as prophet ("thus says the Lord") announces God's word of judgment, condemning the request for a king as a rejection of God, much like what we have seen in chap. 8 (10:17–19; cf. Judg 6:7–10). For this author, *God* is the one who "saves" Israel, and no human king is necessary. Then follows immediately the independent account (vv. 20–24) of Saul's selection by lot (and therefore, divine direction), a process of elimination from tribes to families and finally to Saul. But the candidate is missing, and yet another divination determines that he has curiously "hidden among the gear."[88] A hiding hero does not inspire confidence, perhaps another hint at Saul's problems to come.[89] Yet Samuel notes his heroic stature, "head and shoulders taller than any of them," a promising beginning, it would seem. Now, in this public acclamation, the people shout "Long live the king!"

We can see in retrospect how the editor responsible for the judgment oracle in vv. 18–19 has soured both the preceding donkey story and the following lottery story. The language of rejection combines with that of chap. 8, framing the donkey story and leading into the lottery story. Moreover, that story in itself may imply a negative evaluation of Saul, in that lottery selection elsewhere singles out culprits.[90] The association could easily imply that "throwing the dice" will produce a loser rather than a winner!

Samuel informs the people of "the rights and duties of the kingship," otherwise unexplained (from 8:10–16 we know the rights, but none of the duties), then dismisses them. Saul heads home, accompanied by volunteer warriors "whose hearts God had touched," just as God had touched Saul's. A brief notice about Saul's critics links the preceding

---

88. McCarter's translation (*I Samuel*, 193).

89. Or is the hiding a sign of humility? Numerous readings are possible. Saul's hiding may simply be another way of putting the typical diffidence in 9:21 (cf. Birch, *1 and 2 Samuel*, 1050). For Fokkelman, *Vow and Desire*, 447, Saul's reluctance is far worse: he "attempts to withdraw from his election," foreshadowing what is to come. For Campbell and O'Brien (*Unfolding*, 242a) here is an awkwardness resulting from editorial composition: the man empowered by the spirit with a "new heart" is not likely to hide among the gear (10:9–10, 22), nor are God and Samuel likely to act as if Saul has not already been chosen and anointed.

90. Other culprits are Achan and Jonathan (Joshua 7; 1 Sam 14:38–44). See McCarter, *I Samuel*, 195–96, who also notes how the expected punishment following the indictment in v. 19a leads instead into the request for a king and the lottery story, making "the gift of the king a kind of punishment." So also Fokkelman, *Vow and Desire*, 443–44. For Polzin, *Samuel*, 104, the lottery associations make Saul "a personification of kingship's sinfulness." On the other hand, Birch, *1 and 2 Samuel*, 1047–48, concludes that "this account is very positive" apart from vv. 18–19.

and following episodes with its rejoinder in 11:12–13. The link includes the key word "save," tying together Saul's mission (9:16) with his first military engagement against the Ammonites and their sadistic king, Nahash (10:27—11:13).

Nahash is brutalizing two Israelite tribes, and has gouged out the right eye of everyone except a group of men who have escaped to Jabesh-gilead.[91] No reason for Nahash's torture is given; probably it terrorizes the populace, forcing them to pay tribute to Nahash. But Nahash's cruelty knows no bounds. He besieges Jabesh-gilead, and even when the people offer to become his servants (or "slaves"), he says that the eye gouging will continue. His intent is to "put disgrace upon all Israel."[92] The focus is on Nahash's oppression and the Israelite's slim hope that someone might come "to save us" (v. 3).[93] Needless to say, Saul is the one.

When messengers from Jabesh-Gilead come to Gibeah and report what has happened, both Saul and the Holy Spirit get to work: "the spirit of God came upon Saul in power . . . and his anger was greatly kindled" (v. 6). Fortunately for the victims, *this* possession does *not* produce prophetic ecstasy but military leadership, much as in Judges. Saul musters thousands of Israelites (not without a bit of coercion), and they send a message to Jabesh-gilead: the next day they will have "deliverance" (or "salvation"). After Saul's victory, some want to execute those who had questioned Saul's capabilities (10:27), although here the question is posed as "Shall Saul reign (*melek*) over us?" (11:12).[94] But Saul declines any punishment—the day of God's "deliverance" is a day for celebrating. The key root *melek* in the question ties in with vv. 14–15, when Samuel emerges again and calls for a renewal of the kingship at Gilgal (see below on "renew"). Saul has now proved his capability of fulfilling the mission for which he was anointed, so now *the people* make him king *"in the presence of* the Lord" (AT). God's prophetic word finds completion in the *vox populi*. In fact, Saul does not really become king *de facto* until this moment, for Samuel anointed him as "prince" (king-elect), the people said "Long live the king," but only here does Saul actually *become* king, and it is the people (not God or Samuel) who effect it.[95] (Once again a sacrifice is involved,

---

91. Accepting the textual tradition represented in the NRSV of 10:27b (note the space; this half verse did not appear in the RSV) and the phrase "About a month later" in 11:1. Without that text, Nahash's eye-gouging would be only a threat; moreover, the citizens' request for a treaty would be without apparent cause. Cogan and Tadmor, *II Kings*, 318, suggest that blinding one eye of captives probably maintained their usefulness as slaves!

92. This is a key word in the David and Goliath story later (= "reproach," "defy," e.g., 17:25–27).

93. Were it not after the fact, this hope, and the weeping in v. 4, might be the "cry" reported in 9:16 (just so, 12:12).

94. Assuming the standard emendation. Otherwise the quotation is a statement—"Saul shall rule over us."

95. So McCarter, *I Samuel*, 205; Alter, *David Story*, 63–64. Retrospectively, the agent may reflect the reluctance of God and Samuel in chap. 8. However, this combination results from redactional composition. Originally, there may have been an independent story about Saul's popular acclamation as king after a victory, in which the monarchy was a legitimate extension of the role of "judge" (similar to what Gideon refused, Judg 8:22–23). See McCarter, *I Samuel*, 206–7, and below, on 8:5, 20.

but we still await the pre-arranged sacrifice at Gilgal from 10:8.)

Although the narrator does not make any explicit connections to the horrors reported in the closing chapters of Judges (19–21), numerous parallels in 1 Samuel 11 reveal a kind of resolution to that time "when there was no king in Israel." To review, Saul's home town, Gibeah in the tribe of Benjamin, was where the horrible rape and dismemberment of the Levite's concubine took place. The other tribes almost annihilated the Benjamites (Judg 20:48), save for some warriors. But that left the Benjamites threatened with extinction. To obtain the necessary women for breeding (that's what it was!), the other tribes singled out the town of Jabesh-gilead for not joining them in the civil war, annihilating the town ("including the women and the little ones," Judg 21:10) save for the requisite number of virgin women. But there were not enough virgins there, so the wifeless Benjamite survivors kidnapped women from the town of Shiloh ("in the land of Canaan").

In the light of those associations, Saul's accomplishment is not only military; it is also political in that he has reunited these formerly hostile factions. Under him, the Israelites act "as one" (specifying both Israel and Judah, 11:7–8) against a foreign enemy, whereas before they had acted "as one" against Benjamin (Judg 20:8). Saul has redeemed the reputation of his home town Gibeah, whose "scoundrels" had started the whole mess (Judg 20:13), wisely excusing the "scoundrels" who oppose him (11:27, 12–13, AT)—a good king *can* come from Gibeah! Saul has also brought some recompense to the town of Jabesh-gilead for the wrong done to them in the past. Here it may refer to the rift that threatens to divide Saul's supporters from his opponents. As Fokkelman puts it, "The action of the charismatic deliverer Saul, judge-and-king, heals the nation."[96]

In his call for renewal, Samuel now seems to be promoting the monarchy of which he was so critical, and which he will soon reject again.[97] What, then, does "renewal" mean? There are numerous answers, ranging from "inaugurate" to "repair." The word "renew" usually refers to restoring something that is broken. The reference could be to the potential political rift that Saul squelched, but perhaps the most cogent reading is that of Fokkelman, who sees 11:14–15 not only as the conclusion of chap. 11 but as the introduction to chap. 12.[98] What Samuel means by "renew" is more like

---

96. Fokkelman, *Vow and Desire*, 477; also 470–76. This, he says, is why the Ammonite victory belongs where it is even before Saul's commissioned battle with the Philistines. Thus interpretations of the stories in Judges as anti-Saul do not adequately consider how his role as redeemer in the Ammonite story could redeem *him*!

97. Polzin, *Samuel*, 108–17, 119, offers a very different reading of chap. 11, using the present Hebrew text without the addition of 10:27b and reading 11:12 as "Saul shall be king over us." The parallels with Judges 19 and Saul's success as a deliverer in the Judges mode suggest that the people reverse their request for a king, having realized that a judge will do, but Samuel overrules the request and reestablishes Saul's monarchy, contrary to God's wishes, in a rather sinister grab for power and control. For critique, see Fokkelman, *Vow and Desire*, 478; more briefly Alter, *David Story*, 63 n. 12. In any reading, the Samuel who before and after resists the monarchy here insists on it!

98. Fokkelman, *Vow and Desire*, 487–90.

"correct," and refers to the monarchy, not just to Saul. It is time, says Samuel, to rethink this whole thing, and that is what he does in his long-winded speech in chap. 12. "For him renewal consists of his having to abandon the exclusive or pure doctrine of Yahweh's kingship, and his now being called to formulate an inclusive doctrine uniting the monarchy of Saul and that of God."[99]

Samuel's Maledictory Address (Chap. 12)

Samuel now delivers his valedictory address, but it seems more of a malediction than a benediction. Presumably, this speech is delivered to the gathering at Gilgal, with Saul himself a prominent member of the audience. Significantly, Samuel did not crown the king in 11:15 (the people did), but he is center stage now—indeed, he says "*I* have set a king over you." From Samuel's point of view (that is, the *prophetic* point of view), he has appointed the king, and he will now provide his interpretation of what the monarchy involves. In 11:15 the narrator assigned the deed to the people, but here all the talking goes to Samuel.[100] In this speech, all of Samuel's ambivalence sounds again. In fact, the narrator has told us that the people made Saul king, and Samuel acknowledges that they have "chosen" him (v. 13), but Samuel also says that *he* has appointed the king (v. 1), and that God has appointed the king (v. 13). The combination produces "a form of creative tension which is a close reflection of the dilemma" at the very heart of the monarchy.[101]

Much of the speech is similar to the farewell address of Joshua in Joshua 23–24 reflecting the concerns of the Deuteronomic school. The opening assumes Samuel's old age, reminding us of 8:1–3, but here Samuel refers to his sons without any indication of their previous troublemaking. He and the people affirm that Samuel has acted with integrity, including *not* taking bribes (vv. 3–5)! In fact, Samuel's honesty in *not* taking from the people contrasts, retrospectively, with the "ways of the king" in 8:11–18, where the king takes everything he can get his hands on. Samuel then summarizes the history of God's "saving deeds," alluding to the ancestors in Genesis, then focusing on the Exodus and the period of the judges. In a manner similar to 10:17–18, he contrasts God's gracious acts with Israel's disobedience, echoing the cycle familiar from Judges: forgetting God, the sin of serving "the Baals and Astartes," God's punishment through oppressors, repentance, and rescue (cf. Judg 10:10–16).

Now the speech suddenly jumps to the recent oppression of King Nahash and claims that it was Israel's reason for wanting a king (v. 12), which is inconsistent with any of the reasons stated before. However, perhaps the main intent is to show that God's previous provision of deliverers (judges) was all that Israel needed, similar to the implicit criticism in 8:5, 20—a king (*melek*) "to judge us" (AT) "and fight our battles." As there,

---

99. Ibid., 490. Birch, *1 and 2 Samuel*, 1064–65, holds a similar view: "old values (covenant) can embrace new forms and realities (kingship)," so Samuel "challenges king and people to renewed covenant obedience."

100. Fokkelman, *Vow and Desire*, 488.

101. Ibid., 492.

Samuel equates the request with a denial that *God* is their true king. To demonstrate God's anger, as well as his own authority, Samuel arranges for a thunderstorm in an unlikely time of year (vv. 17–18, something like a blizzard in August in Florida; cf. 7:10). The rest of the speech ties together God's reluctant provision of a king with traditional Deuteronomic covenant theology, to which the king, like everyone else, is subject: the demand for absolute loyalty to God, obedience to God's commandments, serving God "with all your heart," not turning aside to "useless things," that is, the chaos of lawlessness and idolatry.[102] Samuel then concludes with the promise of blessing for obedience and the warning of curse for disobedience: "if you still do wickedly, you shall be swept away, both you and your king" (v. 25).[103] The speech exemplifies the tension between hope and the fear that runs throughout the Former Prophets—the hope that God "will not cast away his people," and the fear that God will do just that. Seen from the perspective of the end of the Former Prophets, it is the admonition that Israel and most of Israel's kings failed to heed.

Chapter 12 thus presents a reflection on the role of the prophet in the new era of the monarchy, especially considering that Saul is standing there listening to all this! In effect, Samuel's speech sketches the compromise position in which the monarchy is grudgingly accepted even though it threatens the absolute sovereignty of God. Although the king will hold titular political power, the prophet will continue to be the people's primary mediator with God, interceding for them when they go astray, so that they "may not die" (v. 19)—exactly the role that the people asked Samuel to perform in 7:8–10. Moreover, the prophet will continue to "instruct" the people "in the good and the right way." The word for "instruct" derives from the root word for *torah*, i.e., law, instruction, guidance. The prophet thus will continue in the role of Moses—precisely as Moses had suggested (Deut 18:15–18), an ongoing reminder of Israel's covenant responsibilities. The prophet, then, will be "the moral conscience of the kingdom,"[104] a role that will often put him at odds with the king when the king fails in his responsibility to execute justice. Samuel's speech here sets the precedent for many encounters between prophet and king that follow, not the least of which immediately in chap. 13. Of course, the problem with power, whether royal or prophetic, is that it is always subject to abuse, and, arguably, we see that potential become a reality in the next few chapters.

Desperate Disobedience (Chaps. 13–15)

Chapter 13 opens with a formula that is typical of the books of Kings, marking somewhat awkwardly (and incompletely) the official beginning of Saul's reign. Saul's *resumé* here is virtually empty, possibly an editor's opinion about his accomplishments.[105] Then the first engagement

---

102. The word for "useless things" often means chaos, as well as being connected with idolatry. See Gen 1:2, where it has cosmic dimensions; also Isa 24:10; 34:11; 45:18–19.

103. Cf. Deut 29:19.

104. McCarter, *I Samuel*, 219.

105. So Jobling, *I Samuel*, 79–80.

with the Philistines begins when Saul's son Jonathan assassinates a Philistine official, initiating Israel's revolt.[106] This story originally connected directly with the conclusion of the donkey story, for here Saul finally engages the Philistines (9:16) and goes to his appointment with Samuel at Gilgal (10:8)—and to his doom.

Saul rallies his troops at Gilgal. The reported size of the Philistine force is typically hyperbolic ("like the sand on the seashore for multitude"), and the Israelites are overwhelmed with fear, many of them hiding in every nook and cranny and even fleeing across the Jordan River. Even those that stay with Saul at Gilgal are "trembling." But, as instructed, Saul is waiting for Samuel to come and show him what to do (10:8). In the context, it seems that Saul is waiting for his military orders, as if Samuel is the commander-in-chief. He waits the required seven days, all the while watching one after another of his soldiers slip away. In desperation at losing his troops, Saul goes ahead with the sacrifice, and even before the fire has cooled Samuel shows up at last, but too late. In fact, his timing is suspiciously coincidental, for he arrives at the moment *after* the burnt offering but *before* the "offerings of well-being" (vv. 9–10). It is as if he has been hiding behind a tree, looking at the calendar and his watch, waiting to pounce on Saul the very moment that *Saul* has grown tired of waiting. Samuel is shocked that Saul has not waited for him, and Saul defends his decision by reporting the continual desertion of his troops, Samuel's delay, and the Philistine's imminent assault. He also apparently sees the sacrifice as necessary to entreat God's favor before the battle, a precedent set by Samuel (7:9–10—distress cry, sacrifice by Samuel and appeal to God, God's victory over the Philistines). So, he says, "I got hold of myself, and offered the burnt offering" (v. 13, AT).

One can read the expression "got hold of myself" in quite different ways. The NRSV says "forced myself," suggesting, perhaps, that Saul knows he is doing something wrong but proceeds anyway. Yet the general meaning of the fairly rare word has to do with controlling emotions, e.g., anger (Esth 5:10) or affection (Gen 43:31; 45:1). Sometimes the word is used synonymously with "keep still" and "hold one's peace" (Isa 42:14; 64:12). So here Saul may mean that he resisted a growing panic (v. 11b), got control of himself, and did what he thought he had to do as a military commander. If that is the case, then the reaction of Samuel seems all the more exaggerated, if not devious. Instead of blaming himself for being late, he blames Saul for not waiting.

Saul seems to have performed adequately as military commander so far. Indeed, when the spirit came upon him (11:6), he did what he saw fit to do— exactly as Samuel had suggested almost in the same breath when telling him to wait at Gilgal (10:7–8). However, he succumbs to a prophetic understanding of obedience that is unwaveringly strict. Samuel is livid that Saul has "not kept the orders of Yahweh your God" (AT),

---

106. Here reading the first part of v. 3 as "Jonathan killed the Philistine prefect who was in Gibeah, and the Philistines were told, 'The Hebrews have revolted.'" Cf. McCarter, *I Samuel*, 224. Jonathan is introduced as if we already know him (cf. 14:1; 13:2).

i.e., not waiting for seven days, down to the very minute. As God's spokesperson, Samuel's orders are God's orders (cf. again 3:19—4:1), so disobedience to him is disobedience to God.[107] Samuel clearly is not one of those who indulge in "situation ethics." A more sympathetic response might have been for Samuel to say, "Well, I see that there were extenuating circumstances, and sometimes rules are made to be broken. You acted in the best interest of your troops, and with genuine piety toward God. After all, you can offer the sacrifice just as well as I." Indeed, Samuel has already treated Saul as if he were a priest; see above on 9:24; 10:3,[108] and lay people could perform a sacrifice as well.[109] But that is not Samuel's attitude toward his orders or his privileged position (perhaps already hinted in 9:13). An order is an order. Failure to follow orders is tantamount to treason. In breaking the "commandment of the Lord" (which frames Samuel's speech) Saul is already at fault for the very rebellion that Samuel forbade in 12:14 (perhaps one reason why Samuel's "farewell speech" is there and not later). Therefore, the punishment is severe: Saul's kingdom could have lasted "forever," but not so now. In other words, there will be no *dynasty* of the "house of Saul" consisting of one of his sons and subsequent male heirs. Ironically, just as ritual disobedience was the ruin of Eli's sons, so here it is the ruin of Israel's first king. Thus Saul's fate is identical to that of the "house of Eli" (2:30)—forever is a short time! Instead, God has "sought out a man after his own heart; and Yahweh has ordered that he shall be ruler over his people" (v. 14, AT). Broken orders result in a new order.[110] If we follow the chronology from the donkey story to here, Saul has had only one week of governing before failing his performance review!

Whereas Samuel is relentless in his condemnation of Saul's alleged fault, one cannot help but sympathize with Saul's dilemma. Should he do what seems fit to do, or wait for the prophet to tell him what to do? Samuel has issued contradictory orders that are impossible to follow. On the one hand, his encouragement of Saul's freedom of action undermines the authority that the prophet is supposed to hold over the king, thus subverting what God had intended; on the other hand, he exercises that authority in making Saul wait for instructions. Samuel has set up Saul for inevitable failure. In short, Samuel is as much at fault as Saul, if not more

---

107. The nature of Saul's alleged offense, other than not waiting, is not clear. See Gunn, *Fate*, chap. 2; Jobling, *I Samuel*, 251; Bodner, *I Samuel*, 121; Fokkelman, *Crossing Fates*, 36, 44, (but "did not completely trust in God," 73), ("acting *bona fide*" but it is a "façade," 95). Birch, *1 and 2 Samuel*, 1071-73 suggests a conflict over the sacral roles of prophet and king.

108. According to Lev 1:1–9, the layperson participates by presenting, laying hands on, and slaughtering, the animal; the priests manipulate the blood and burn the animal. But the relative dating of such laws and the incident here is difficult to determine. Moreover, neither Samuel nor Saul comes from priestly family lines (1:1; contra 2 Chr 6:26), so Samuel cannot throw stones, as it were. The offense comes down simply to not doing *exactly* what Samuel said to do, which was to wait for Samuel to tell him what to do, even though he had also told Saul to do whatever he wanted!

109. Usually the head of household would perform the sacrifice. See Miller, *Religion of Ancient Israel*, 69.

110. Cf. McCarter, *I Samuel*, 228, who uses the word "appointment" to express the play on words.

so, and Saul's alleged offense seems like a peccadillo, condemned by a legalistic, self-righteous Samuel.[111] Furthermore, in the present text sequence, Samuel declares the nullification of Saul's potential dynasty at the very moment that Saul is scrambling to retain his troops and engage the Philistines in battle. The prophet's timing could be demoralizing, at the least, even unintentionally aiding the enemy, at the worst—something like dressing down Gen. Eisenhower on the night before D-Day.

Here we see the first instance of how Israel's prophets assumed the divinely given authority to subvert the normal process of royal succession. The assumption that one knows God's will and speaks for God entails enormous political power when the assumption is shared by the people—a phenomenon attested throughout history. Moreover, here is the first indication of a Davidic bias that will increasingly seek to demonstrate why David became the legitimate replacement for Saul, ordained by God. Those who opposed dynastic kingship faced daunting contradictions in Saul and David. Moreover, even in the Deuteronomic law of the king (Deut 17:14–20), God grants the need for a king, "like other nations," without criticism, and even assumes that the monarchy will be hereditary (v. 20b), and there is no mention of a role for the prophet; but God withdraws the dynastic possibility from Saul; but God will promise dynastic succession to David (2 Samuel 7); but (much later) God will often terminate dynasties in the North. The overriding question, then, is how the everlasting covenant with Saul could be annulled in favor of an everlasting covenant with David. Though the answer does not come in full until later, it will be: "because God can change his mind about Saul but not about David!"[112] Although we will soon know David to be the heir apparent, the canonical 1 Samuel ends where Judges ended—with no king in Israel—thereby creating a time in between judgeship and fully dynastic kingship.[113]

Despite his rejection, Saul honorably continues with the mission God has placed on him.[114] Even so, the editors hardly pause to acknowledge Saul's victory—which, of course, they attribute solely to God, 14:23—before presenting the story of Saul's potentially tragic oath

---

111. If we focus on the present text, this negative picture of Samuel applies whether or not 10:7–8 resulted from editorial juxtaposition or a single author's artistic rendering. Polzin (*Samuel*, 107), who champions the latter, argues that Samuel's failure also includes his "foolishly push[ing] Saul" to become a prophet as well as a king, thereby illegitimately inflating the role God had granted to the king. But this interpretation seems to ascribe to Samuel the ability to control the very divine spirit that inspires Saul (10:6–8), or we must include God in the error. Campbell and O'Brien (*Unfolding*, 241a) opt for the editorial explanation, in which v. 8 was added to an originally independent story of inspiration that led directly to Saul's military success in chap. 11, connecting with 11:6, but now also connecting with 13:8: "We have here an example of the practice of preserving variant traditions, offering alternative versions for storytelling."

112. Jobling, *I Samuel*, 99–100.

113. Ibid., 109.

114. Campbell and O'Brien, *Unfolding*, 255a, see an older story behind the "Prophetic Record," in which Samuel merely rebukes Saul without the speech about rejection, concluding with a reconciliation (v. 31). This might also explain why Saul does not respond to Samuel, but proceeds with fighting the Philistines as if nothing has happened.

(14:24–46). Other notices of Saul's success (14:47–48, 52, see below) are few and far between. In short, the overall editorial bias is overwhelmingly inimical to Saul, something that was evident implicitly by the placement of chap. 8. The reader must strain to look at Saul objectively, to see his strengths as well as his weaknesses. Looking ahead, the reverse will be true of David, even though the two at times exhibit the same traits. To take one detail, in rejecting the proposed punishment of his critics ("worthless fellows," 11:12–13), Saul shows wise leadership, and his theology is appropriately orthodox in attributing the victory to God—just as David will do with some "worthless fellows" in 30:22–25.

Aside from the anti-Saul bias, one must admire the clever ways in which the editors have stitched together 7:3—13:15. God's victory over the Philistines and Samuel's administration of justice make the following request for a king seem to be unnecessary,[115] but the notice about Samuel's sons raises the question about his successor. The position of chap. 8 implies that the donkey story is the *way* God *grudgingly* answers the request for a king. Samuel's admonition at the end of the donkey story for Saul to wait seven days at Gilgal is not resolved until 13:8–15a. The introduction to the lottery story functions much like chap. 8, making the lottery selection also seem like God's *reluctant* acquiescence. The first notice about Saul's critics waits for resolution until after the Nahash incident. The acclamation at Gilgal appears as a "renewal." Chapter 12 reinforces the anti-monarchy position, and prepares for Saul's failure to keep God's commandments (12:14, 15; 13:13; 15:24). The next Gilgal story, of course, resolves the seven-day wait. Throughout, the key word "king" (*melek*) appears numerous times. Similarly, the key word "save" (or "deliver") connects the donkey story with the lottery introduction, Saul's critics, and the Nahash story. The word "spirit" connects the donkey story with the Nahash story. In short, there are numerous stitches that take originally independent stories or editorials and create the impression of an integral narrative that flows in such a way as to keep the reader looking forward to some resolution.

Saul's Strategic Blunder (13:15b—14:52)

The preparations for war with the Philistines resume in 13:15b, then pause again while the author tells us of the Philistine's monopoly on weapons as well as metal agricultural tools.[116] Amazingly, no Israelite soldier other than Saul and Jonathan has a sword or spear, but the author does not tell us how they would be able to fight; in fact, the following battle contradicts this (14:20). Though we are still expecting Saul to launch his attack, the narrator turns to an episode in which Jonathan is the sole hero (14:1–15). At the onset of this episode, Saul is behind the scenes, accompanied

---

115. Despite some contradictions later—7:13 versus 9:16.

116. There is a redundancy in 13:2 and v. 16, as well as some confusion in 13:2–4. There seem to be three or four different beginnings in 13:2, 5, 15b, and 14:1. Similarly, Saul has 2,000 men at 13:2, 600 at v. 15b and 14:2, and 10,000 at 14:24. The opening "one day" at 14:1 also suggests an independent story, yet v. 11 ties in with 13:6.

by none other than the priest Ahijah—doomed royal and priestly lines keeping company (v. 3; cf. 2:30–31).

Jonathan and armor bearer brazenly approach a Philistine garrison, and Jonathan poses a test to elicit a "sign" from God about their success or failure. The sign shows that, indeed, God has given the Philistines "into the hand of Israel," and the two stalwart Israelites kill a score of the enemy. Their victory produces an enormous "panic" among the Philistines (the last phrase could be translated "panic of God," or "god-awful panic"; the root appears three times in v. 15). Ironically, the Philistines had ridiculed the Hebrews for "coming out of the holes where they have hidden themselves" (14:11, referring back to 13:6; see below on "Hebrews"), but it is the Philistines who are now "trembling" just as the Israelites had before (14:15; 13:7). Such is the seismic effect of Jonathan's feat that the earth quakes!

Saul's lookouts observe the tumult among the Philistines, and Saul discovers that Jonathan is missing. Saul asks the priest (who accompanies the troops, 14:3) to divine God's intent, but, inexplicably, does not wait for a reply, and launches into the fray.[117] The Israelites are strengthened when some Hebrews, who had been with the Philistines, switch sides. ("Hebrew" is a term often heard from foreigners like Philistines when referring to Israelites. The term can refer to a sociological group only loosely connected with Israel. Here they seem to have in effect answered Saul's appeal in 13:3 to join with the Israelites.) Victory seems to be in hand, but then the battle spreads to the hill country of Ephraim (v. 23), and now another flaw in Saul's leadership emerges.

One could dismiss Saul's disobedience to Samuel with the Gilgal sacrifice as trivial, if not, in fact, warranted, but here there is a rash lack of judgment that could lead to disaster. Saul lays a curse on anyone who eats before he is "avenged on my enemies" (v. 24). There are two problems here: one, Saul acts as if the Philistines have offended him personally rather than menaced the people of God, supposedly the beneficiaries of his calling (9:16–17; echoes of Samson!); two, the oath is stupid. What commander would make his troops fast under these circumstances? The second problem grows more ominous when we learn that Jonathan has not heard the oath (was he still away?—cf. v. 17), and, coming upon a honeycomb from which the rest of the soldiers have abstained, he eats some honey. Immediately "his eyes brightened," not a surprising result from an ingestion of sugar! When told of Saul's oath, Jonathan criticizes it as troubling the land by starving the soldiers.

The problem of enforced hunger now deepens. With the battle won, the troops are even more "faint" (vv. 31, 28), so they "flew upon the spoil," including numerous animals which they promptly slaughtered and ate, and not "well done"

---

117. In the context of Saul's not waiting for Samuel, this could imply a pattern of behavior! The Hebrew text refers to the ark, the Greek text refers to the ephod—the latter already mentioned in v. 3, and more likely, given the instruction to "withdraw your hand," itself ambiguously inconclusive. But the ark apparently was lodged at Kiriath-Yearim at this time (1 Sam 6:21; 2 Sam 6:1–2). Later, when Saul is desperate for a word from God, there will be none (chap. 28).

or even "rare" but raw, i.e., "with the blood"—steak tartare. However unappetizing this may seem to us, eating meat with the blood was absolutely prohibited in Israelite dietary law, indeed, a restriction supposedly issued as early as the time of Noah. The blood represented the life of the animal, given by God, and anyone who ate the blood would be "cut off from the people."[118] So Saul condemns the act as treacherous, and arranges for a proper (i.e., "kosher") slaughter, building an altar on the spot. But the treachery is really Saul's. His impulsive oath has threatened the life of his own son, making Saul the greatest risk to his own dynasty.

When Saul seeks to resume the battle, a priest wisely advises a consultation with God by means of the sacred dice (Urim and Thummim, meaning something like "thumbs up" and "thumbs down"). They get no response, indicating to Saul that "sin has arisen today." Saul calls for another roll of the dice, designating the troops on one side and he and Jonathan on the other. The dice indicate the two of them, and a final throw points to Jonathan. Jonathan admits to his snack of honey, and Saul declares that, in fact, he will die. The dice seem to be strangely loaded, however, selecting the least guilty, who did not know of the oath, instead of the more guilty, who issued it.[119] The whole situation is sadly reminiscent of Jepthah's tragically ill-conceived oath leading to the execution of his daughter (Judges 11). But the people will not have it, for Jonathan "has worked with God today." "So the people ransomed Jonathan, and he did not die" (v. 45). The supreme commander had issued an order that *required* insubordination. With this, the Israelites and the Philistines withdraw to their respective territories, and the reader is left to question if Saul is the best man for the job after all.

An editor now provides a kind of summary of Saul's military successes and a list of his family members (14:47–52). Were we to judge Saul's achievements on v. 47 alone, he would make for an outstanding military leader.[120] In fact, Saul's victories and opponents in v. 47 here are virtually the same as those of David much later (2 Sam 8:6, 12, 14), but described with far more reticence (and without mention of God's involvement). The passage fits here in that it refers back to the Ammonites (Nahash) and the Philistine battle, but it is out of place in that the Amalekite story follows in chap. 15.[121] In effect, this notice is sandwiched in between Saul's problematic behavior in chap. 14 and chap. 15, making it a thin filling indeed! The concluding v. 52 suggests how persistent the Philistine menace was—"*all* the days of Saul"—just the opposite of that reported for Samuel (7:13). Despite Saul's

---

118. Gen 9:4; cf. Lev 17:10–14; Deut 12:23. The carnivorous feast apparently occurred "that day" (v. 31), meaning, "before it is evening" (v. 24).

119. Polzin, *Samuel*, 138.

120. Fokkelman, *Crossing Fates*, 81–82, notes that Saul's assertiveness here "is in complete contrast with the unprepared peasant boy of 1 Sam. 9–10" and thus "an undermining of the negative image in 13:2—14:46."

121. Verse 47 literally says "Saul took the kingship over Israel; he fought . . . ," a less smooth transition than the NRSV translation. Similarly, 15:1a seems like an unnecessary reminder.

successes, we know now that he will not completely fulfill his original mission against this enemy (9:16), which raises the question, who will?

Rejection (Chap. 15)

The story about Saul's engagement with the Amalekites and their King Agag in 15:1–35 is a kind of parallel to the story about Saul's previous offense in that once again an allegedly illicit sacrifice is involved, here concerning the rules of warfare—"holy war," to be precise. We have discussed the phenomenon of such warfare in the book of Joshua (the Jericho story). Samuel transmits the message from God: the Israelites are to "utterly destroy" the Amalekites because they once had attacked those who had escaped from Egypt. This is a punitive "ban" (*ḥerem*) fulfilling God's decree at the time (Exod 17:8–13; Deut 25:17–19) and including men, women, children, and all livestock. We are back in the horror of genocide, and a horrible understanding of God, even though for the narrator the order is simply the background for the story.

The Israelites besiege the city and allow the Kenites who live there to flee, because they "showed kindness" to Israel when they came out of Egypt.[122] They then decimate the city, destroying every human being but one—King Agag. They also keep as spoil the best of the livestock "and all that was valuable," destroying only what seemed worthless. God apparently has been watching, and Samuel immediately hears God's word of judgment: "I regret that I made Saul king for he has turned back from following me, and has not carried out my commands" (v. 10)—in other words, Saul has done precisely what Samuel warned against in his farewell speech (cf. 12:14–15, 20–21). But God does not say what the result might be. When Samuel goes to find Saul, he discovers that Saul is far from remorseful—he has "set up a monument for himself" (v. 12)! Moreover, when they meet, Saul greets Samuel and says "I have carried out the command of the Lord." Samuel asks why, then, does he hear "this bleating of sheep." To Samuel, Saul and the entire army seem to have committed the sin of Achan (Joshua 7), but there is no suggestion of concealment. On the contrary, we could take Saul seriously in his explanation, in which case it would be a misunderstanding of *when* the sacrifices were to be made.[123] Either option is possible. Saul's lack of character here comes out more when he seems to blame the mistake on the people ("*the people* spared the best of the sheep and the cattle," v. 15).

We would not expect Samuel to be forgiving, and we are not surprised. Reminding Saul once again that he is the king, anointed and commissioned by God, Samuel demands to know why Saul disobeyed "the voice of the Lord." Saul simply repeats his explanation insisting that he *has* accomplished his mission, and he has brought Agag and the best of

---

122. On the Kenites, see Judg 1:16 (the tent-peg murderer, Jael, was a Kenite). Sparing the Kenites here resembles sparing Rahab in Joshua 6 for her "kindness" (*ḥesed*).

123. As Gunn notes, *Fate*, 47, 15:21 begins with "and" in Hebrew, suggesting that Saul's explanation of saving the best for the sacrifice could be honest (even if, again, a misunderstanding). Niditch (*War*, 62) suggests that Saul also misunderstands what *type* of sacrifice is appropriate (i.e., *not* one for the celebrants to partake of for food).

the spoil for sacrifice. Saul's fault seems to lie in his presumption of *interpreting* how God's word should be executed.[124] At this, Samuel waxes poetic, producing a prophetic criticism of sacrifice as inferior to obedience: "to obey is better than sacrifice."[125] Rebellion is as offensive as divination, stubbornness as idolatry (cf. 12:14). Then comes the verdict: "Because you have rejected the word of the Lord, he has also rejected you from being king." The very language used to describe the people's "rejection" of God's sovereignty in requesting a king (8:7; 10:19), now describes *God's* rejection *of* that king. The judgment goes further than the Gilgal incident. There it was the continuation of Saul's *dynasty* that God cancelled; here, it is Saul's own standing as king. Here again the political power assumed by the prophet is astounding, for we did not hear of God's rejection of Saul from God, we only hear it from Samuel, who thereby is *himself interpreting* the meaning and significance of God's change of mind, even though God's own words will soon confirm Samuel's interpretation (16:1).

Saul finally admits his sin, but the excuse he offers is pathetic: "I feared the people and obeyed *their* voice" (v. 24). Not only does this ignore Saul's own participation in the deed ("Saul *and* the people," v. 9), and reveal a weakness that is fatal to effective leadership, it also shows how deaf Saul is to *God's* voice (or, again, how he misunderstands it). Samuel ignores Saul's appeal for pardon, repeating God's rejection, and as he turns to leave, Saul grabs his robe, tearing it. Samuel declares the gesture to be a sign—just so God "has torn the kingdom of Israel from you" and "given it to a neighbor of yours, who is better than you" (v. 28). Those are stinging words, and we will soon find out who this other "man" (13:14) or "neighbor" is. Ironically, Samuel concludes by saying that God never has a change of mind (Hebrew *naḥam*), meaning that the verdict against Saul is irrevocable, but contradicting God's own words in v. 11 ("regret") and the narrator's immediately again in 15:35 ("was sorry").[126] Samuel changes his mind upon Saul's second confession (v. 30) by returning with Saul to publicly "honor" him in worship.[127] But the narrator has the last word: "the Lord was sorry that he had made Saul king over Israel." A divine change of mind is precisely what is about to produce a change of kings.

The story has a gruesome ending. Samuel summons King Agag, who is bound "in fetters," and who says, "Would death have been as bitter as this?"[128] It would have been more honorable to die in battle than tied up helpless. Samuel will finish the job that he sees as required by God, and cuts Agag to shreds "before

---

124. Jobling, *I Samuel*, 86; so also Gunn, *Fate*, 48.

125. For classic prophetic critiques of sacrifice, see Isa 1:11; Jer 7:21–23; Hos 6:6; Amos 5:21–24.

126. An alternative is to see v. 29 as referring to God's election of *David* (Birch, *1 and 2 Samuel*, 1090, following Fretheim).

127. Verse 31, contrast v. 26; the word "return" often means "repent." Cf. Polzin, *Samuel*, 143.

128. Following McCarter, *I Samuel*, 260-64 (there is considerable textual confusion here). The text seems too uncertain to read into it a broader authorial commentary about repentance and forgiveness, as Polzin reads it (*Samuel*, 144); he reads the MT in v. 32 (NRSV note y; so also Alter, *David Story*, 93). Here again Polzin has in mind an exilic audience.

the Lord." Supposedly, God is pleased to watch this butchering. Yet, as with many of the stories in Joshua and Judges, the reader is confronted with enormous moral ambiguity. Listening to and obeying the voice of God is surely at the heart of faith, but what if that voice demands actions that, by every humane measure, are *inhumane*. Modern readers would quite likely think *more* of Saul if he had not only spared Agag, but also refused to kill innocent civilians. Presumably, Agag himself had committed atrocities (v. 33), but the Amalekites are annihilated for offenses that their *ancestors* committed. Who, then, are the real "sinners" in this story (v. 18)—the Amalekites or the Israelite soldiers? Even to ask the question is to take a point of view outside the narrator's presuppositions. Again, the dilemma is one that we have observed before (e.g., Jericho). All we can do is to acknowledge, as we did generally in the Introduction, that the voices of Samuel and of God are fictional words.[129] Much as we may share Samuel's passion for heeding God's voice, we must sometimes question if the *reported* voice of God is truly what God would say. If not, then faith itself would require that we *do* add or subtract from the reported words, in defiance of orthodox prohibitions (Deut 4:2; 12:32).

Now that Saul's fate is sealed, we can look back at how that happened. Saul's offenses do not in any way merit the severity of his punishment. In the end, "the story in chapter 15 is about Saul's sin in sparing the guilty Agag and God's subsequent refusal to spare the guilty Saul."[130] How do we explain God's rejection of him? We could speculate about God's own character, inner feelings, etc. But here again we must remember that the character of God is fictive, a creation of the biblical authors and editors. In fact, it would seem that Saul's fate is a result of his being in the wrong place at the wrong time—i.e., being Israel's *first* king. God's rejection of Saul reflects that deep anti-monarchical strain in Israel's sociology and theology, that position that sees in Saul the people's rejection of *God* (8:7). Saul bears the brunt of that in ways that clearly are unfair to him, whatever faults he may have. The unfairness for Saul will now become all the more clear when we track the rise of David. Indeed, Saul's jealousy over David will mirror God's jealousy over Saul as the king preferred over God (8:7). Gunn puts the contrast beautifully: "For David, Yahweh is 'Providence'; for Saul, Yahweh is 'Fate.'"[131]

The Man after God's Heart (16:1–13)

Samuel will never see Saul again (at least not alive),[132] and the narrator ends the Agag incident by reminding us that "the Lord was sorry that he had made Saul king over Israel." At this point the narrative picks up a collection of stories that scholars generally call "The Rise of David" that extends up to 2 Samuel 5. Interpreters disagree on the exact beginning and ending, but 16:1–13 could conclude a unit beginning with 9:1 (with the

---

129. See Alter, *Art*, 36–37, on "invented dialogue" in "the creation of fictional character."

130. Polzin, *Samuel*, 142.

131. Gunn, *Fate*, 116, and 128 on jealousy.

132. Unless Saul sees him in the incident in 19:18–24; the other exception is the conjuring of Samuel's ghost, see below at 28:3–25.

anointing of Saul and David as a frame), and 16:14 is a major turning point, as we shall see. If 2 Sam 5:10 (or v. 11) is the end, then David's rise is framed at the beginning by the turning of God's spirit to him and away from Saul, and at the end by David's perception that God has established his realm. Throughout the story, David succeeds because "God is with him" (16:18; 2 Sam 5:10). We shall see numerous times in which David's rise correlates with Saul's demise, but the narrative strains to show that David's actions are innocent, not only regarding Saul and his family, but other characters and situations as well. The list includes treason, desertion to the enemy, and regicide, just for starters. Thus some scholars characterize the story of David's rise as apologetic or even propagandistic. I use a contemporary colloquialism—"spin"—to describe the ways in which the story attempts to put David in the best light. However, there is enough "dirt" in the story for other scholars to claim that overall it *condemns* David![133] One has called David a "'bloodthirsty, oversexed bandit.'"[134] The difference between the two Davids (or two readings) simply reflects the complexity of David's character. As Birch puts it, "He is both pious and pragmatic, idealistic and self-serving, fearless and calculating."[135] As Rosenberg points out, the editors do not even explicitly represent David as pursuant of being king; "it is only the *reader's* hindsight (or that of one who knows the tradition) that makes David an aspirant to the throne."[136] Given this complexity, we cannot reduce the story of David to a political agenda. All of the characters are far too human in both their nobility and their degradation to serve as cardboard representatives of an ideology.[137]

The opening line of chap. 16 provides another link to the Agag incident when God asks Samuel why he continues to grieve over Saul. Why, indeed? On the surface, one would think that Samuel is gleeful rather than grieving, but we have seen before signs of Samuel's ambivalence toward the king. Initially, Samuel acceded to God's wishes, calling Saul the focus of "all Israel's desire" (9:20), anointing him as God's chosen savior of God's people (10:1), and publicly praising his distinction (10:24). But Saul's stubborn refusal to follow orders turned Samuel against him. Now God's elect has become God's reject. Samuel is stuck in grieving "on what might have been."[138] A more cynical reading would suggest that Samuel is grieving because he won't have Saul to kick around anymore![139] Much as he initially opposed the monarchy, he wanted to control the king according to his own interests. At any rate, now God echoes Samuel's own rejection of Saul (15:26; 16:1b), saying

133. Regarding 2 Samuel 11–20, Campbell and O'Brien, *Unfolding*, 296, note that "the rich ambiguity of the text throughout allows both admirers and belittlers of David to find plenty to their liking." Cf. also Fokkelman, *King David*, 417–18.

134. John L. McKenzie, quoted in Birch, *1 and 2 Samuel*, 1095 n. 113.

135. Birch, *1 and 2 Samuel*, 1095. Cf. Alter, *David Story*, xxi–xxii.

136. "1 and 2 Samuel," 130.

137. Alter, *David Story*, xxi–xxii, even recognizing that "the author of the David story was in all likelihood firmly committed to the legitimacy of the Davidic line."

138. Birch, *1 and 2 amuel*, 1098.

139. Polzin, *Samuel*, 154.

"I have seen a king among the sons" of Jesse (v. 1b, AT). Ultimately, *God* is in control of who is and who is not the king, thus subverting whatever power Samuel presumed to exercise. (The corollary of this subversion is that the *author* is ultimately in control!) Moreover, when Samuel returns to his hometown of Ramah after completing his mission (v. 13), he virtually disappears from the narrative except for a brief appearance in 19:18–19[140] and his ghostly apparition in chap. 28. He has dominated the narrative of 1 Samuel up to now, and his absence leaves a prophetic vacuum that will not really be filled until much later in Israel's history (Elijah and Elisha).

The story in 16:1–13 resembles that of Saul's selection (10:20–24) in that the most insignificant family member of Jesse the Bethlehemite is God's choice. God instructs Samuel to go to this family, from whom God has identified the new king. Samuel immediately worries that, if Saul hears of this, Saul will kill him, an anxiety that later proves to be well-founded, though David will be the target. God counters with the stratagem of offering a sacrifice, presumably instead of saying, "I've come to anoint a new king." The elders of Bethlehem tremble in fear of Samuel (maybe they have heard of what he did to Agag!),[141] but he assures them that he has come peaceably and they and Jesse's family prepare themselves ritually for the sacrifice.

Samuel looks over the sons of Jesse and naturally assumes that the eldest is God's anointed (it *is* a patriarchal culture). But God says not to consider Eliab's appearance or stature, because "I have rejected him," using the same word as for Saul! Not only does God not consider the "outward appearance," but "looks on the heart." Samuel's mistake reflects more than cultural bias, however; it is a final judgment against his failure as a true prophet, for he cannot see as God sees, twice mistaking "physical for regal stature."[142] So Jesse presents one son after another (he has seven), but none will do. When Samuel asks if is there is another, Jesse says only the youngest, "but he is keeping the sheep." It is reminiscent of Saul hiding among the baggage (10:22). Samuel summons him, and, indeed, "he was ruddy, and had beautiful eyes, and was handsome," and God says, "He's the one. Anoint him." Verses 7 and 12 are not contradictory, however, because the point of the former is size ("stature"), not good looks.[143] Samuel wanted the tall eldest son; God wants the short runt of the family. Nevertheless, here is the model for Michelangelo's statue. Perhaps God sees beneath the beauty as well (although we will have occasion to wonder what that might be). Samuel anoints him "in the presence of his brothers," and immediately "the spirit of the Lord came mightily upon David from that day forward," and Samuel makes his final exit.

---

140. This incident provides a doublet for the saying about Saul as a prophet (cf. 10:9–13). Samuel is presiding over a band of charismatic prophets, and Saul succumbs to their ecstasy (see below).

141. The same root is used in 14:15 (three times) to describe the "panic" in the Philistine camp.

142. Alter, *Art*, 158; cf. 149; Polzin, *Samuel*, 153–55, pointing out that the root for "see" occurs ten times in the story.

143. Fokkelman, *Crossing Fates*, 131, contrasting Saul's height (10:23).

Now we know who the other man of God's choosing is (13:14; 15:28), but there will be no public inauguration of David until 2 Samuel 2. Until then, only Samuel and perhaps David's family knows, although even that is left unclear.[144] Certainly there is no place in the unfolding narrative where any of these characters discloses what they have seen. Moreover, there will be numerous times when David insists that *Saul* is still God's anointed, even though this acknowledgment serves the story's Davidic leaning. The secrecy creates a mode of suspense as we follow the story, for often we will wonder if God's appointment will be foiled by human actions.

The Man under God's "Evil Spirit" (16:14-23)

> *Bill Moyers described [Lyndon] Johnson . . . as not only paranoid but deeply depressed . . . "He would just go within himself, just disappear—morose, self-pitying, angry . . . He was a tormented man." . . . He was erratic. One day he would be in a down mood and the next he would be quite upbeat. He could be in a deep depression, and then "24 hours later no one who had seen him this way would ever have suspected it."*[145]

The closing line of the anointing story connects to the opening line of the story of David's rise by the catchword "spirit." When the spirit comes mightily upon David, we may think of similar incidents with the judges and with Saul.[146] But v. 14 presents us with a radical departure from any previous patterns: "Now the spirit of Yahweh departed from Saul, and an evil spirit from Yahweh terrorized him" (AT). This spiritual movement is the turning point of the entire narrative that began in chap. 1. In a sense it is an explicitly theological statement of what has already happened at 16:1, where God instructed *Samuel* to turn from Saul to David. From here on,[147] there will be a progressive deterioration of Saul politically and personally, paralleled by a progressive rise of David. Saul's turmoil is clearly spiritual, or we might say psychological. He will often appear to be mentally imbalanced, but one may ask if, in fact, *God* is imbalanced! After all, this incursion of God's evil spirit presents a theological, rather than a psychological, explanation of Saul's subsequent behavior.

The biblical authors sometimes explain human behavior as caused by God, such as the understanding of a person's stubbornness or "hard heart," as with the Pharaoh of Egypt (e.g., Exod 4:21; 8:15),

---

144. Presumably the elders of Bethlehem also witness the event, but the narrator does not have Samuel say *why* he is anointing David—even to David!

145. Dallek, *Flawed Giant*, 282, 284. Moyers is talking in particular about 1965 and the effect of the Vietnam War on Johnson's moods.

146. The particular verb here that has the connotation "mightily" is used only with Samson among the judges, then with Saul (10:10; 11:6) and David (16:13). It is used also in 16:13 for the *evil* spirit from God.

147. An exception to this turn of the spirit is a second, parallel story about Saul's *prophetic* spirit possession in 19:23-24; cf. 10:10-16.

not to mention Eli's sons (2:25). An even closer metaphorical analogy is the "evil spirit" that God sends to foil Abimelech (Judg 9:23), or, later, Ahab (1 Kings 22).[148] In the end, the authors seemingly would rather risk impugning the morality of God than the power of God, so that, if God is in control, then "evil" events are attributed to God (cf. Isa 45:7). The concept is only somewhat more palatable if we translate the Hebrew word "evil" as "misfortune," "trouble," or "calamity." Even in contemporary piety, it is not uncommon to hear people explain a tragic occurrence (a car accident, tornado, or flood) by saying something like "God must have a plan." Theologically, at least two major issues are at stake: one, that of "theodicy," of seeking to understand and explain why bad things happen in God's world,[149] and two, of human freedom and destiny, the tension between God's sovereignty over history and human autonomy. How is Saul responsible for his actions if God's "evil spirit" is driving him? Does God take away the new heart originally given to Saul (10:9) when God withdraws the benign spirit? How can Saul love God with all his heart (12:24) if God is in *control* of his heart? What is the difference between such biblical characters, apparently doomed by God's rejection, and the figures in classical Greek literature, where the gods determine human fate?

These are enormously difficult questions to answer, and would quickly lead us into the fields of philosophy and systematic theology.[150] The authors are struggling to express their belief that God is indeed sovereign over history even as they portray characters who seem very clearly to have a will of their own. However, in this case (16:14), what happens is not a punishment for Saul's sin, whatever one might think of his various faults. We have already seen such punishment at work in response to the sin of Eli's sons (2:17, 27–36), and will see it numerous times again, most notably in the family turmoil of David (2 Samuel 12). But with Saul the arrival of God's "evil spirit" seems to be more like the flip side of "Providence" than punishment.[151]

We should not allow a false piety to prevent us from acknowledging when a picture of God is morally reprehensible (we have already done that with the concept of "holy war" as ethnic cleansing). Gunn addresses the issue directly in his study *The Fate of King Saul*, the title itself suggesting Gunn's view that fate (i.e., here the inimical will of God) determines Saul's demise far more than any faults

---

148. Niditch, *Judges*, 117, suggests a subtle combination for the "evil spirit" of God in Judg 9:23, but it fits here perhaps even better: "The notion of an evil spirit also captures the psychoanalytical aspect of moods that may sour and relationships that may self-destruct without overt cause or motivation. The deity is behind all events."

149. An eloquent example is the popular book by Kushner, *When Bad Things Happen to Good People*.

150. For a brief overview on Calvin's doctrine of providence related to the questions raised here see Stroup, *Calvin*, 31–33. He notes that Calvin's insistence on all events as governed by God, even those that are evil to us, can be "morally offensive" to many modern readers. On the other hand, our putting evil "outside of God's transforming and redeeming reach" raises its own questions.

151. To repeat a line from Gunn (*Fate*, 116): "For David, Yahweh is 'Providence'; for Saul, Yahweh is 'Fate.'"

on his part.¹⁵² The "evil spirit" from God evokes "the dark side of God" that we do not easily entertain.¹⁵³ Gunn's assessment is unsparing: "If we are to condemn Saul for his jealous persecution of David, how much more is Yahweh to be condemned for his jealous persecution of Saul!"¹⁵⁴

In assessing the effect of the "evil spirit" on Saul, one can appreciate the severity of the word for "terrify" in that it occurs most frequently in the book of Job, that quintessential revelation of human terror in the face of God's apparently inexplicable punishment. Job uses the word numerous times in describing God's wrath: "the arrows of the Almighty are in me; my spirit drinks their poison; the terrors of God are arrayed against me."¹⁵⁵ In 1 Sam 16:14, it sounds as if there are two divine spirits—one beneficent and the other malevolent, one abandoning Saul, the other entering.¹⁵⁶ We can see the development of such an understanding as it moves toward positing a separate power of evil, namely, "Satan" or the Devil.¹⁵⁷ Here there is no such move. The *characters* in the story simply repeat what the *narrator* has already said when they address Saul directly: "an evil spirit from God is terrifying you" (AT). If the writer responsible for v. 14 had v. 15 in his source, he has prefaced it with an authorial comment that affirms the truth of what the char-

---

152. Note also Fokkelman's title for his volume addressing 1 Samuel 13–31: *The Crossing Fates.*

153. Gunn, *Fate*, 129. Gunn also has a brief essay on providence in *King David*, 108–10, where he addresses the issue with regard to 2 Sam 11:27, 12:24, and 17:14, on which see the next chapter.

154. Gunn, *Fate*, 129; cf. also Fokkelman, *Crossing Fates*, 691, and Polzin, *Samuel*, 125, who refers to "the mysterious coexistence of divine omnipotence and human freedom," and asserts that *God* is "the one who ultimately sets up Saul" for rejection." The rejection is "impenetrable," and the selection, "full of mystery" (p. 158). Regarding 18:10, one wonders "if the evil spirit of God . . . is not just as much cause as effect of Saul's evil actions" (180). Birch, *1 and 2 Samuel*, 1091, responds that God's "dark side" simply reflects Saul's inadequacy, and that "Saul was not fated to fail." Brueggemann, *Samuel*, 59, seems to reject the concept of fate ("His destiny was not imposed upon him.") but also says "What he chose had in fact already been chosen for him." For Alter, *Art*, 33, a dialectic "between God's will, His providential guidance, and human freedom, the refractory nature of man," pervades biblical narrative in general (cf. 112–13; cf. 176). See also Gottwald, *Politics*, 251–252, who concludes his study with the observation that this tension runs throughout the narrative, even though Gottwald has avoided the "metadiscourse" that puts God in control, and he refers to Yehezkel Kaufmann's phrase "'the dual causality principle.'"

155. Job 6:4; cf. 7:14; 9:34; 13:21; and Ps 88:15, the only lament psalm without any shred of hope. Imagine an Evil Spirit alongside the familiar Holy Spirit and the implications of dualism become clear.

156. Here we may note the daring comment of Jobling, *I Samuel*, 297–98, where he observes the tendency in contemporary interpretation to favor "poly" over "mono," e.g., an appreciation for the plurality of meaning, which leads him to ask, "Is monotheism the world's fundamental problem? At least it seems high time to listen to the wisdom of polytheism." Polytheism, he argues, would help explain the inconsistencies in God's actions in chaps. 8–12, both rejecting and inaugurating kingship—"there is a conflict at the very heart of things" (299). Polytheism has the luxury of not needing to lay everything at one god's feet—both good and bad—but the theological and philosophical implications are mind-boggling..

157. In 2 Sam 24:1, an angry God incites David to take a census; the parallel account in 1 Chr 21:1 replaces God with Satan, who, of course, plays a prominent role in the prologue to Job (as "*the* satan," or prosecuting attorney of the heavenly court). Compare the "lying spirit" from God that frustrates king Ahab in 1 Kgs 22:19–23.

acters themselves are thinking. If the author of both the commentary and the dialog are the same, then the writer has employed the dialog to confirm the truth of his own opinion! Thus, if we the readers concur with the narrator's judgment, both we and the actors (here the servants) share the same perspective.[158] Such collusion can easily lead us to a prejudicial understanding of Saul.

Although we already know who David is, of course, the first story in which he plays an active role (16:15–23) introduces him as if he is new—"a son of Jesse the Bethlehemite." A courtier of Saul suggests that music can soothe Saul's savage beast, so Saul says "see for me someone who can play" (AT), making his selection conform to God's (16:1b). Another courtier recommends David, who certainly seems fit for a king: "skillful in playing, a man of valor, a warrior, prudent in speech, and a man of good presence; and the Lord is with him." We have not heard that last phrase since it was applied to Samuel (3:19), but we will hear it frequently,[159] affirming that David's progress derives from divine companionship. When David plays for Saul, "the evil spirit would depart from him." Because we have read the account of Saul's rejection and David's anointing, we the readers can see the irony here already. The evil spirit from God seems to be subject to human manipulation. The one who relieves Saul of his turmoil has already relieved him of his throne, albeit not *de facto*. Fokkelman puts it well: "While Saul and his court think they are welcoming a musician, we realize that the Saulide monarchy is dragging in a Trojan horse."[160] David has also won Saul's love (v. 21), but that will soon change.

The Giant Slayer (Chap. 17)

The next story—David and Goliath—is surely one of the most famous biblical tales, but probably few readers have noticed its composite nature, much less the political agenda that it serves. Once again, David and his family are introduced to the reader as if for the first time (vv. 12–14). David commutes between Saul's court and his family sheep (v. 15), yet at the end of the story neither Saul nor his military commander, Abner, knows who David is (Saul's prior love for him notwithstanding), one of the clearest examples of independent literary sources.[161] But the most arresting problem appears much later, when we learn that, in fact, it was one Elhanan who slew Goliath (2 Sam 21:19)! David would not

---

158. On the relationship between dialog and narration, the former being dominant, see Alter, *Art*, 65.

159. See 18:12, 14; 16:18; 17:37; 18:28–29; 2 Sam 5:10.

160. Fokkelman, *Crossing Fates*, 135.

161. There seem to be two sources beneath the present narrative. E.g., there are two beginnings, vv. 1–2 and 19; there are two fearful reactions, vv. 1 and 24; Goliath and David approach each other several times, vv. 40–41, 48. Note also that David's naiveté (v. 33) contradicts his reputation as a bold warrior in 16:18. Polzin, *Samuel*, 161–76, strenuously asserts the artful composite integrity of the story over against the traditional literary criticism based on repetitions. However, he seems to leave open the possibility that there is a "literary history" behind the present text, emphasizing that the story is "a carefully crafted construction" rather than a "heavy-handed" editorial hodgepodge (167; cf. 188). Cf. also Alter, *Art*, 148. Contrast Birch, *1 and 2 Samuel*, 1108, and Campbell, *From Joshua to Chronicles*, 135, among others.

be the last hero to attract legends originally attributed to others.[162] But the story is told with such drama and colorful detail that one scarcely notices the problems. As Alter has shown, in the present order of chs.16 and 17, we see two different aspects of the character of David, the former a more "'vertical' view which moves from God above to the world below" (i.e., the movement of the Spirit), and the latter, a "'horizontal'" view that is more "human-centered" and folkloristic. This dual perspective is another example of divine and human co-operation—"the spirit descending . . . [and] a young man ascending."[163]

As the youngest of Jesse's sons, David is a shepherd boy and a step-and-fetch-it, while his older brothers are in Saul's army. Saul is scarcely a bold General Patton here, however, for when the Philistine challenges them to a duel, "Saul and all Israel . . . were dismayed and greatly afraid" (v. 11). The story skillfully alternates scenes between the battlefront and David's gradual involvement as the family errand boy, which brings him to his brothers. He hears a report of Goliath's appearance, how "he has come up to defy Israel" (v. 25), introducing a key word in the story (the same Hebrew as "reproach"). The speaker adds that Saul "will greatly enrich the man who kills him, and will give him his daughter and make his family free in Israel," promises that we have not heard from Saul himself. This is the stuff of Romantic legend, but the implication of the reward is stunning, for marrying a king's daughter is an avenue to power, perhaps even the possibility of succeeding to the throne (see below at 18:17).[164]

There are inconsistencies in the text due to composition,[165] but the focus is on David's reaction to the report of Goliath: "What shall be done for the man who kills this Philistine, and takes away the reproach from Israel? For who is this uncircumcised Philistine that he should reproach the armies of the living God?" (v. 26, AT). In Hebrew narrative the first words of a character often are highly significant, and these are the first words from David. The import is twofold: David is motivated by both politics and piety, promoting himself and defending God's honor, a combination that we will see repeatedly.

David's bravado is reported to Saul, who summons him, and David immediately volunteers to fight with Goliath (*David's* heart will not fail, v. 32). Saul questions David's ability, given his military inexperience, but David replies that his experience in rescuing sheep from wild beasts will serve him well—and, that God, who rescued *him* from the beasts, will come to his aid. Apparently Saul and his army had no such trust! Here David displays a combination of self-reliance and reliance *on God* which again illus-

---

162. The reference to Elhanan may be considered more reliable historically simply because it is not likely that someone would invent it to contradict the Davidic legend.

163. Alter, *Art*, 152; cf. 166 on the Joseph narrative, again emphasizing the artistic result of redactional composition.

164. The promise of freedom probably refers to exemption from compulsory service to the king; cf. McCarter, *I Samuel*, 304.

165. The first part of David's question in v. 26 sounds as if he has not just heard what is said in v. 25; his encounter with his brother Eliab in vv. 28–30 does not fit well with v. 22.

trates a subtle theology of divine action in co-operation with human agency.

Saul accepts David's offer and sends him off with the blessing, "may the Lord be with you!"—which, of course, we already know to be the case. There is a humorous moment when David can't even walk when wearing Saul's heavy armor, which also highlights the simplicity of David's own weapons: a staff, stones, and a slingshot. Implicitly, David's zeal for God is his true armor, something that Saul lacks even when clothed in metal.[166] The author spares nothing in emphasizing the enormous size of the giant—almost ten feet tall with a spearhead of twenty-two pounds! (Today he would have ammunition belts across his chest and hold an AK-47 in one hand, a grenade launcher in the other). The unusually detailed description presents Goliath as "an obtusely mechanical conception of what constitutes power."[167] What Goliath sees is the handsome lad that we met in 16:12. He taunts David for his youthful and rather puny appearance, which prompts a lengthy speech by David that emphasizes the theological lesson of the story.[168] David comes "in the name of the Lord of hosts," whom Goliath has defied, swearing by his own gods. God will give Goliath into David's hand, "so that all the earth may know that there is a God in Israel," and Israel may acknowledge that it is God who wins the fight, not Israel's "sword and spear." Again, David's self-confidence is rooted in his trust in God as the Holy Warrior, and his ascription of the victory to God echoes the prior statements of Samuel (8:20; 12:12).[169] In other words, the speech casts David as having the makings of an authentic king who recognizes that *God* is the ultimate sovereign.

Everyone knows the ending: David kills Goliath with a single stone, then takes Goliath's sword and beheads him, at which the Philistines flee with Israel in pursuit. In a retrospective notice (vv. 55–56), we learn that Saul had asked whose son David was when he set out against Goliath, perhaps the first hint of an envy that will eventually consume him: is this "young man" the one who will replace *Saul's* son as successor (13:14; 15:28)?[170] Saul gets his answer when he summons David to court. There is confusion about what David does with the prize head,[171] but in the end he has it in hand when he meets Saul, supposedly for the first time. There is God's young new *nagid*—"king elect"—standing in front of the king

---

166. See v. 45; cf. "the whole armor of God," Eph 6:13.

167. Alter, *Art*, 81. The picture of a scrawny kid confronting a heavily armored giant conjures up the classic photograph of the youthful Chinese protestor standing in front of a tank in Tiananmen Square in 1989.

168. The speech seems to be inserted at the moment that the two meet (vv. 41, 48).

169. Cf. Exod 14:14, 30–31. The acknowledgment of God is prominent in the Exodus narrative (e.g., 9:14, 29); cf. also Josh 4:24.

170. Cf. Bodner, *I Samuel*, 189–90. The repeated question is an obvious signal of an account originally unaware of 16:14–23, although some interpreters deny the problem (e.g., Polzin, *Samuel*, 171–76, 187, unconvincingly, it seems to me).

171. In v. 54 David takes the head to Jerusalem, although that town did not become Israelite until after David became king. There is no comment about what he *does* with the head! He keeps the armor in his tent, but later we learn that Goliath's sword was deposited at the sanctuary at Nob (21:9).

whom he will replace, holding the head of the Philistine enemy whom the king was appointed to overcome, but feared instead. "I am the son of your servant, Jesse," he says, with all modesty.

Jonathan and David (Chaps. 18–20)

After David's killing of Goliath, Saul takes him into his court (this for the second time), and a deep friendship begins between David and Jonathan. Just as Saul loved David (16:21), so does Jonathan, only more so: "Jonathan loved him as his own soul" (v. 1 and 3; cf. 20:17). So Jonathan makes a covenant with David, something like our notion of "blood brothers." There are two ways that we can understand the love between David and Jonathan. As we have seen before, in a covenantal context, love and loyalty are synonymous expressions. In state treaties, "love" refers to allegiance, carrying political rather than emotional overtones.[172] The vassal is said to "love" the suzerain, expressing not a personal relationship but the political subordination of one party to another. The language of "love" can function in a similar but less political way within a deep friendship: "a friend loves at all times," says the proverb (Prov 17:17). Here love refers to fidelity and mutual support: "a faithful friend is a study shelter" (Sir 6:14). On the other hand, a number of scholars would argue that, in fact, the "love" between Jonathan and David is erotic.[173] A key text is the eulogy of David for Jonathan in 2 Sam 2:26, where he says, "your love to me was wonderful, passing the love of women." The language certainly might suggest a homosexual relationship, but the argument remains speculative and, needless to say, controversial.[174] In the end, it is clear that Jonathan and David enjoyed a deep, personal friendship in which they were committed to each other's safety and happiness, a loving relationship that involves more than political considerations and appears in the texts as far more intimate than any described for their relationships with others, including wives.

In an immediate political dimension of Jonathan's love, he gives David

---

172. Love as allegiance is the foundation of Israel's covenant with God as their suzerain (Deut 6:4-5), just as it is between human vassals and their suzerains. (cf. Josh 23:11). The word often translated "faithful love," "kindness," or "loyalty," is ḥesed, which is never used for romantic love; the word for both political loyalty and romantic love is [set aleph]ahab, making the distinction at times all the more difficult to discern. See 20:14 (ḥesed) and 20:17 ('ahab).

173. For a brief overview, see Schroer and Staubli, "Saul, David and Jonathan," 22–36, who say at the outset, "David and Jonathan shared a homoerotic and, more than likely, a homosexual relationship." So also Gunn, *Fate*, 93; Jobling, *I Samuel*, 161–65, who also argues that Saul's hostility toward Jonathan as well as David reflects the typical reaction of a father to his son's gayness. Moreover, Jonathan plays a role similar to that of the women in David's life, in that David is far more loved than loving. Cf. 19:1; 20:41. Contrast Bodner, *I Samuel*, 219; Fokkelman, *Vow and Desire*, 196-97. Birch, *1 and 2 Samuel*, does not rule it out but emphasizes the political meaning as well as the unimportance of marital love in ancient cultures (with which Michal might initially disagree [18:20] but later confirm [2 Sam 6:20–23]).

174. Clearly the "love" relationship represented in the treaties is not homosexual or even personal. Also, Saul loves David (16:20), as do Michal (18:20), and the people (18:16). King Hiram of Tyre will love David (1 Kgs 5:1 [NRSV "friend of"]; cf. 5:12). The interpretive issue does not seem ultimately resolvable, but we should not rule out the erotic simply because of prejudice.

his robe and armor, suggesting a divestiture of any claim to succeed his father, a most gracious gesture. Saul, for his part, appoints David as head of the army (presumably Jonathan's role), and everybody is happy—until David's renown as the giant-slayer makes him more popular than Saul, at which point Saul is *not* happy. Women greet the returning war hero with singing and dancing, chanting the lines "Saul has killed his thousands, and David his ten thousands." Saul seems almost childish in his jealousy; in fact, he misinterprets the meaning and significance of the little ditty, which has nothing to do with *contrasting* Saul's and David's prowess, much less their political clout.[175] But we see where his fear is leading: "what more can he have but the kingdom?" Since we know that his own son has just vested David with all but a crown, Saul's fear is not unfounded. Saul is "all too wrong" about the song, but "all too right, without knowing it," about David's threat.[176] But probably because of the process of composition, Saul never connects David with Samuel's announcement that God is seeking another as king. That is, we never read a line like "Saul said in his heart, 'This must be the man whom God has chosen instead of me.'" Rather, the animosity between the two develops naturally out of David's incredible success and Saul's deepening jealousy. "So," the narrator tells us, "Saul eyed David from that day on"—and it's what we would call the "evil eye."

An editor has juxtaposed Saul's envy with a scene in which the "evil spirit from God" again possesses Saul (18:10–16), anticipating a doublet with 19:8–10.[177] The language is ironic, in that the same word for "rushed upon" has appeared before with the judges, with Saul (10:10; 11:6) and with David (16:13)—but there it is not God's *evil* spirit. Similarly, the word for "raved" is the same as the word for "prophesied" at 10:10, but here the literal meaning of "ecstasy"—being "out of place"—means being "out of one's mind." God's benevolent spirit produced a charismatic prophet; the evil spirit has produced a raging madman—or perhaps we should say a man who is spiritually "bipolar." David's music no longer soothes the savage beast, and Saul tries to pin David to the wall with his spear. The sudden hostility toward the one who has provided spiritual relief indicates Saul's ambivalence: "David brings both cure and downfall, an untenable situation."[178] But David, like Dickens's "artful dodger," escapes harm. Verses 12–16 fit awkwardly,[179] but repeat God's abandonment of Saul in contrast to God's being with David. Saul sends David away, but again appoints him to lead the army. Everything David does is successful and everybody loves him—every politician's dream. Again, "love" in this context *is* political in that it expresses loyalty or allegiance more so than emotion, especially juxtaposed as it

175. The two lines are typical Hebrew poetry, in which an increasing factor is used to emphasize the point of the whole—i.e., that *both* Saul and David are heroes. Cf. Prov 30:15–16, 18–19; Amos 1:3, 6, 9, etc.

176. Fokkelman, *Crossing Fates,* 220.

177. The word "twice" at the end perhaps acknowledges the doublet; cf. "a second time" in v. 21 with Saul's second offer of a wife.

178. Fokkelman, *Crossing Fates,* 221.

179. V. 12 seems redundant with v. 10, and David's military appointment in v. 13 parallels v. 5.

is with David's military leadership. David in Saul's realm is much like his ancestor Joseph in Pharaoh's, a savvy, good looking guy who has the "right stuff" because God is at his side (Gen 39:2, 6, 23). No wonder Saul is "in fear of him" (AT).

In a further sign of his ambivalence, Saul now offers David his daughter, Merab, as a wife. There is no reference back to the promise of just this reward for killing Goliath, but David had heard of such a promise, and asked what would be done for Goliath's killer (17:25-26). David's success in all things comes in part from his knowing how to open the door when opportunity knocks. Thus there is a calculating part of David that is far more self-serving than his speeches (and the narrator's claims) would acknowledge. Alongside the passionate protestations "in the name of the Lord of hosts," David's question about what's in it for him makes one wonder if getting the king's daughter is his ulterior motive— politics blended with piety. Both Saul and David see "an opportunity" in the marriage, but for conflicting purposes.[180]

Again there is textual confusion, for suddenly Merab is given to another, and Saul offers David a second choice— Michal, who happens to love David (18:17-30). David proclaims his unworthiness to become the son-in-law of the king, saying, ironically, that he is "a man of no repute"! The giving and receiving of royal daughters was a means of gaining or granting political influence,[181] so Saul's gesture at first seems like a renunciation of his jealousy. Saul counters David's demurral, saying that he will not demand the usual monetary wedding present (in effect, the price of the bride in this patriarchal culture); instead he wants "a hundred foreskins of the Philistines" (who are rightly called the "uncircumcised," e.g., 10:26). Needless to say, Saul assumes that the Philistines are not eager to relinquish that body part, and therefore that surely *one* of them will be able to kill David in the process. Thus the marriage is only a crude trick, with Michal as a pawn, and Saul characteristically connects it to his personal vengeance against the Philistines (v. 25; cf. 14:24). But in no time David is back with his grisly bride price and Saul realizes that "the Lord was with David" (thereby implicating the Lord in the mutilation!), and that Michal is in love with him. Saul's fear deepens, "so Saul was David's enemy from that time forward," but David's fame only increases (vv. 29-30). With the marriage, Saul has risked putting David in a position of power in order to get him killed, and instead he gets a son-in-law that he hates and fears.

Saul now openly speaks to Jonathan and his servants about killing David, but Jonathan defends David's innocence, and warns Saul not to sin against someone who has not sinned against him—not to

---

180. Translating the phrases in vv. 20 and 26 about being pleased as "seeing an opportunity," with McCarter, *I Samuel*, 317-18; cf. Jobling, *I Samuel*, 151: it is ambition, not love that is David's motive.

181. Cf. 2 Sam 3:3; 1 Kgs 3:1. Clearly this practice was one example of the cultural misogyny under which women are mere chattel, or, at best, diplomatic pawns. See Hackett, "1 and 2 Samuel," 96-99. Later Saul will end the marriage (25:44), but David will get her back in a heartless move that devastates her current husband (2 Sam 3:12-16). The theological issue of such marriages will come to a head with Solomon and Ahab.

mention killing Goliath. Convinced, it would seem, by Jonathan's appeal, Saul swears that David will not die—"as the Lord lives." Yet immediately that "evil spirit" from God attacks Saul, and once again he is trying to pin David to the wall with his spear (19:1–10). Saul's invocation of the Lord seems only to have produced the Devil (as it were). David escapes to his house, but Saul sends a hit squad to kill him. In a humorous scene, David's wife Michal informs him of the threat, helps him escape out the window, then puts a religious image,[182] complete with clothing and a goat's hair wig, under the covers of David's bed. The disguise is not very flattering to David's hairdo but it works, and one can imagine Saul's surprise when the covers are removed and a mannequin is staring him in the face. For her part, Michal turns around and puts David in more danger when she lies and says that she helped David because he threatened her life (vv. 11–17).

Now yet another search for David by Saul turns comic. David escapes to the town where Samuel is living, and Saul sends messengers to seize him. Here Samuel seems to be the leader of a band of charismatic prophets just like the ones that had enveloped Saul in their frenzy after his anointing (10:10–11). But instead of Saul's messengers seizing David, they are seized by the Holy Spirit! In the three-fold pattern of a joke, Saul himself finally goes to the site and he too becomes possessed. In fact, he is so ecstatic that he flings off his clothes and lies around naked until the next morning, providing an alternate occasion for the proverb, "Is Saul also among the prophets?" (vv. 18–24). (One could imagine a different proverbial saying: "the emperor has no clothes.") Ironically, here the *good* spirit of God returns to Saul, but it prevents him from capturing the one who is truly blessed, an irony that a prophetic editor no doubt would have relished.

The story turns to the relationship between Jonathan and David. David asks what he has done to merit Saul's murderous pursuit and Jonathan assures him that he can protect him, as he has done before. David poses a test of Saul's intentions. The occasion is the feast of the full moon, though the literary complexity makes it a long time in rising.[183] Awkwardly, the narrator does not explain why David feels that he should be at the king's table when twice Saul has tried to skewer him, but, if he does not attend, the test will be to see how Saul reacts to his absence.[184] In the end, Saul is infuriated that David has snubbed him, and Jonathan informs David by means of a sign involving shooting arrows in a field.

---

182. NRSV translates *teraphim* with "idol." Often thought to represent a "household god," these objects more likely were connected with the veneration of family ancestors. See Miller, *Religion of Ancient Israel*, 72, citing the work of van der Toorn.

183. There are several temporal references that make for a confusing sequence (vv. 5, 12, 18, 24, 27); v. 11 is a puzzling interruption; v. 12 suggests that Jonathan will send news of the results, but in vv. 18–23 he himself does so with his bow and arrow trick; the trick seems unnecessary, however, in that David and Jonathan meet and talk after it.

184. Polzin, *Samuel*, 189–90 suggests that David engages in devious "subterfuge" manipulating the naïve Jonathan to provoke Saul, thereby showing Jonathan how much Saul hates David.

The emotional depth of this story appears in the conversations between Jonathan and David. "Love," "covenant," and "faithfulness" form the thread that binds them together. In David's initial appeal for Jonathan's help, he says, "deal faithfully with your servant, for you have brought your servant into a covenant of the Lord with you" (v. 8, AT). Here David addresses Jonathan deferentially ("your servant") and asks for his fidelity, grounded in the covenant they have agreed on before (18:3). Such fidelity (again, *ḥesed*) is the foundation of communal integrity, whether between individuals or within larger groups (notable precedents being Rahab and Ruth).[185] When Jonathan addresses David, he says "never cut off your fidelity from my house" (v. 15, AT). So Jonathan "made a covenant with the house of David." Here the personal and the political combine, since "house" can mean "dynasty." Then "Jonathan swore again to David by his love for him; for he loved him as he loved his own life."[186]

Needless to say, Saul is not happy about the relationship between his son and David (vv. 30–34). Indeed, when Jonathan defends David's absence from the feast, Saul flies into a rage, accusing Jonathan of shaming his family and jeopardizing the establishment of Jonathan's own sovereignty in the future.[187] So furious is Saul that he throws his spear at Jonathan, as he had done before to David, and Jonathan angrily leaves the house. There is another meeting between Jonathan and David, when Jonathan reports Saul's relentlessness. The two men kiss each other and weep together. Jonathan bids David farewell: "Go in peace," reiterating their covenant as watched over by God.

As poignant as the personal relationship is between Jonathan and David, the story serves a political agenda for David that will become more apparent later. At this point in the narrative, the characters would normally expect Jonathan eventually to succeed to Saul's throne, thus being the second king in the "house of Saul." But *we* already know that that is not to be, for God has forbidden it (13:13–14). Even so this story suggests that there was no rivalry, much less animosity, between the "house of Jonathan" and the "house of David." In fact, Saul may well have been correct that Jonathan was quite willing to cede his right to the throne to David. Moreover, when Jonathan says "May the Lord seek out the enemies of David," in effect he is condemning his own father, and legitimating the position of David. Later, the covenant between the two "houses" will play out in the fate of Jonathan's son, Ishbaal (2 Samuel 2–4), one of the "descendants" whom David is sworn to protect (v. 42), and David's innocence here (vv. 1, 32) will help to bolster his innocence there.[188] In effect, the narrator has protected David simply by not telling us much, if anything, about his inner thoughts, intentions, and feelings

---

185. Cf. Josh 2:12, "deal kindly"; Ruth 2:20, "kindness," 3:10, "loyalty." See also Mic 6:8.

186. AT, following the LXX; cf. McCarter, *I Samuel*, 337. Cf. 18:1, 3.

187. In v. 30 read "son of a rebellious servant girl," with McCarter, *I Samuel*, 343; the end of the verse means that Jonathan has brought shame to the womb that bore him.

188. Much the same will be true for another of Jonathan's sons, Mephibosheth.

(unlike what we learn about Saul's jealousy, anger, and hate, or Jonathan's selfless love and devotion, for example).[189] Whether he is a good man, or a man up to no good, often is impossible to tell.

A Pogrom on Priests (Chaps. 21–22)

David now goes to the town of Nob (21:1–9). The priest here is Ahimelech, the great-grandson of Eli, whose name evokes the man of God's oracle of doom from chap. 2. Unwittingly, David puts the wheels of fate in motion with an act as irresponsible as any Saul committed. Ahimelech welcomes him with anxious suspicion, asking why he is alone. David tells an outright lie in claiming that he is on a secret mission from Saul. Ahimelech, who apparently knows nothing of Saul's hatred for David (cf. 22:15), accepts the explanation.[190] David says that he needs food for his troops, who are waiting for him (here apparently in his role as Saul's military commander). Ahimelech has nothing but the "bread of the Presence," which would be something like a Christian priest saying that he had only consecrated Host on hand. He asks if David's troops have abstained from sex and are ritually pure, and David assures him that this is true. So Ahimelech gives David the sacred bread. All of this is overheard by one of Saul's servants, Doeg, who will soon disclose what has happened to Saul and fulfill the oracle on Eli's house. When David asks for a sword, Ahimelech gives him the one taken from Goliath, which is strangely stored "behind the ephod,"[191] the priestly vestment often used for divination. Perhaps it would have been wise for Ahimelech to make such a consultation before handing out food rations and a sword.

It is as if both David and Ahimelech intend to make the oracle of doom come true. Apparently, and ironically, David tells his lie in order to convince Ahimelech that he is not in danger, so that David can obtain the provisions he needs. But he *puts* Ahimelech in danger by persuading him to unknowingly cooperate with the man whom Saul considers a political subversive. In giving David both food and a weapon, Ahimelech is aiding and abetting the enemy. For his part, Ahimelech seems to have inherited the family gene of ritual impropriety. The soldiers' ritual state notwithstanding, the bread loaves are "most holy portions" of the offerings, reserved strictly for consumption by the priests (Lev:24:5–9). Thus Ahimelech's liturgical offense echoes that of his grandfathers, Eli's sons.

After a brief interruption,[192] we find David clearly on the run and hiding in a

---

189. Polzin, *Samuel*, 190–92, who suggests that David uses "duplicitous language" by asking Jonathan to lie about his absence from Saul's table, making us ask if his covenant with Jonathan will prove to be duplicitous as well.

190. For an alternative interpretation in which Ahimelech is consciously in collaboration with David, see Bodner, *I Samuel*, 225–26. Polzin, *Samuel*, 195, offers yet another, suspiciously subtle: David is "deceptively simple rather than simply deceptive" in that *God* the King has sent him on a mission.

191. In 17:54 David had put Goliath's armor in his tent.

192. Verses 10–15 seem disconnected chronologically and inconsistent with David's complex relationship with Achish much later (chaps. 27–31). Nonsensically, David flees to Gath, Goliath's hometown, and with Goliath's sword in hand! Not surprisingly the Philistines recognize

cave or stronghold (20:1–5).[193] Fearing retribution, his family joins him there, along with hundreds of people who are in distress, in debt, or otherwise malcontent, and David becomes their "captain." It has all the makings of a subversive faction, if not a kind of Robin Hood band. David then asks the king of Moab to provide protection to his family, which, in the context of the Former Prophets, means the safety of home in that David's great-grandmother was Ruth, the Moabite (Ruth 4:18–22).[194] David then, in effect, places himself in the hands of God (v. 3b), and, serendipitously, the prophet Gad appears out of nowhere to advise David to go into Judah. The combination of trust in God along with privileged knowledge from God will continually mark the story from here on. Saul, on the other hand, must operate on hearsay rather than what *God* says (v. 6).[195]

Saul, of course, is alarmed to hear of David and his band, but his anxiety is rapidly becoming paranoia. He accuses his fellow Benjamites of joining the conspiracy. He asks rhetorically if David can provide the privileges that Saul can—military appointments and gifts of real estate—reflecting precisely Samuel's warnings about the monarchy (8:15–18).[196] In fact, such gifts may well have been unjustly appropriated land that would leave the former owners destitute (Mic 2:1–2; 1 Kings 21), producing the kind of debtors that gathered around David. Although we have no details here, the situation suggests the possibility of economic deprivation and exploitation of the poor that we know from the later monarchy (e.g., Amos 2:6–8; 8:4–6; Isa 3:14–15).

Saul even includes Jonathan among the alleged conspirators, and complains that no one would tell him about Jonathan's dealings with David, at which point Doeg, Saul's chief of staff (and an Edomite) becomes a willing informant. He reports David's visit with Ahimelech, the gift of food and the sword, but fabricates something missing from the story—that Ahimelech "inquired of the Lord for him" (i.e., for David), presumably using the ephod. Saul summons all of the priests from Nob and accuses them of conspiracy with David. Ahimelech attempts a noble defense of himself and of David's loyalty to the king, protesting that he knew nothing of Saul's vendetta. But Saul will not listen, and orders his staff to kill all of the priests on the spot. Murdering a priest has a kind of intrinsic horror to it, and his servants refuse, but Doeg has no such compunctions, promptly killing eighty-five "who wore the linen ephod." It will not be the last of régimes that murders priests (and nuns), and Doeg completes the atrocity by slaughtering the entire population of

---

him, identifying him (ironically) as Israel's king, and quote the old ditty about David's victories. Fearful of king Achish (whom he will later appear to serve), David pretends to be insane. He is a man pretending to be mad fleeing from a madman.

193. Emending the word "cave" in accordance with vv. 4–5.

194. However, this assumes that the author knows of the genealogical conclusion to Ruth, which may well not be the case.

195. Cf. McCarter, *I Samuel*, 367; and Polzin, *Samuel*, 200–203.

196. The Philistine king Achish makes just such a land grant to David in 27:6.

Nob in a kind of "holy war" massacre.[197] Only one priest, Abiathar, escapes, thereby fulfilling another part of the oracle of doom (2:33). If David is a Robin Hood, Abiathar will become his Friar Tuck, adding an ecclesiastical contingent to David's band. Moreover, since Saul has annihilated all the other priests, he has left himself without "benefit of clergy," a situation that will ultimately drive him to despair (chap. 28).

Here we begin to see another remarkable character trait of David, not always in evidence: he is willing to recognize and admit mistakes (not just to say, in contemporary political parlance, "mistakes were made"). Here he takes responsibility, rightly so, for the massacre that has happened, all as a result of his duplicity with Ahimelech, and he takes Abiathar under his protective wing. Of course, the reader knows that what happened at Nob is a fulfillment of the oracle to Eli, even though the editor does not say, "this was to fulfill the oracle" (as elsewhere, e.g., 1 Kgs 2:27). Even so, we are left to ponder the way in which human actions—and *misdeeds*—and divine providence work together toward an end without either side being in complete control. No doubt the author of the oracle would not want to say that David's lie and Saul's massacre are the means that God chose to fulfill it, for then even God's hands would be stained with the blood of priests and innocent children, but the metaphor of the "hand of God" shaping events (see further below) risks just such a theological dilemma.

The Hand of David (Chaps. 23–24)

Following the Nob massacre, David puts his band to work in defending a town against the Philistines (23:1–14). The Philistines are harassing the inhabitants of Keilah by robbing their grain. David's men are wary of attacking the formidable Philistines, but David inquires of God and receives a favorable response. The priest Abiathar proves useful here in that he has brought an ephod with him, that being the apparent medium for God's communication, probably by means of the sacred dice (cf. 14:3; 21:9). The exchange of questions and answers seems almost comical to us if we take it literally,[198] but any military commander would do anything to have such an assurance of victory. David fights off the Philistines and thus "saves" the inhabitants of Keilah (v. 5, AT). David is pursuing Saul's mission (9:16) while Saul is pursuing David.

Hot on the trail, Saul prepares a siege of Keilah (23:6–14). When David hears of Saul's intention, he again consults the ephod, by which God confirms the news and says that, as David seems to suspect, the inhabitants of Keilah will surrender David. Apparently gratitude succumbs to fear. So David and his band escape again, this time into the wilderness. "Saul sought him every day, but the Lord

---

197. In the 1980s, Central American regimes, sometimes aided by United States policy, notoriously murdered priests and nuns who were alleged to be conspirators with leftist egalitarian movements. Gunn (*Fate*, 88) notes the almost identical wording of the massacre in 22:19 and 15:3.

198. See Alter, *Art*, 69–70, for the way in which dialogue is used to communicate what even the author assumed to be silent.

did not give him into his hand" (v. 14). In fact, that phrase "give into the hand" runs throughout this incident: ironically: God promises to give the Philistines into David's hand (v. 4); Saul thinks that God will give David into *his* hand (v. 7); but it is the ungrateful citizens of Keilah who would give David into Saul's hand; in the end God "did not give him into his hand." It is clear whose hand is involved in all the events. Moreover, David has the advantage of repeatedly knowing from God what will happen—because he asks—whereas Saul is completely left in the dark—because he does not ask, and erroneously assumes (v. 7). The darkness will engulf him in the end (chap. 28).

The hand motif now connects the next episode (23:15–29), in which Jonathan comes to David in his wilderness stronghold: "there he strengthened his hand through the Lord." Moreover, he encourages David, saying "the hand of my father Saul shall not find you" (cf. also v. 20). Now Jonathan has explicitly joined the opposition, and Saul's anxiety over Jonathan's succession to his throne is confirmed when Jonathan says to David, "you shall be king over Israel, and I shall be second to you," adding "my father Saul also knows that this is so." David and Jonathan make a covenant before God,[199] and the two part company again. The hide-and-seek between David and Saul resumes until Saul is forced to abandon his pursuit and do what he should be doing in the first place—fend off the Philistines (vv. 27–28).

The political implications of this incident are enormous. We know that God has rejected Saul as king as well as the possibility of a Saulide dynasty (13:13; 15:26). Now the latter is confirmed when the only candidate has, himself, abdicated the throne before ever occupying it. On his own volition, Jonathan has enacted the prophetic rejection of an unqualified hereditary monarchy. In addition, that potential heir has affirmed and approved David's authority to be the next king. David's rise to rule now has divine and royal approval; all that remains will be the acclamation of the people—and, of course, the death of Saul. The next incident provides David with the possibility of making that happen.

David's encounter with Saul in the cave at En-gedi (chap. 24) is one of two incidents in which David has the chance to kill Saul and refuses to do so (cf. chap. 26). This story has a humorous element that resembles the scatological story of Ehud and King Eglon of Moab (Judg 3:12–25). Still in pursuit of David, Saul enters a cave to relieve himself, specifically, to defecate (note the same phrase in Judg 3:24).[200] He does not know that David and his men are holed up deeper in the cave, and that David has literally caught Saul "with his pants down." David's men see a golden opportunity, the moment that God has promised to put Saul into David's hand (see below on this motif). We know of no such promise, although it resembles that of 23:4 where the Philistines are the prey.

---

199. Probably another sign of duplicate sources, as if they have not already made a covenant before (18:3; 20:8); however, here it could refer to the agreement on Jonathan's role when David becomes king.

200. Literally "cover one's feet," indicating that one used one's outer garment or robe as a kind of privacy screen. The detail is important because simply urinating would not put one in such a vulnerable position.

David sneaks up on Saul, but instead of killing him with his knife he cuts off part of Saul's robe. Engrossed in relieving himself, Saul does not even notice as David slinks away. Either David knows how to creep silently, or Saul is deaf.

After Saul leaves the cave, David goes to the entrance and delivers a lengthy speech (cf. 17:45–47), showing his respect by bowing to the ground and addressing Saul as "My lord, the king." He asks why Saul gives credence to the charges that David seeks to harm him, when God has just given Saul into his hand and yet David has spared Saul's life. "I will not raise my hand against my lord; for he is the Lord's anointed" (v. 10; cf. v. 6). (Neither here nor elsewhere does David ever acknowledge that he too is the Lord's anointed.) He then proclaims his innocence—"there is no wrong or treason in my hands. I have not sinned against you." Although he invokes God vengeance, he will not lay a hand on Saul. Saul recognizes David's voice and is overwhelmed with grief, calling David "son" as David had called him "father." He confesses that David is "more righteous" than he, and that Saul has continually repaid David's good with evil.[201] Then he acknowledges what Jonathan has already said: "you shall surely be king, and . . . the kingdom of Israel shall be established in your hand" (v. 20). He asks only that David not kill all of Saul's descendants, thus annihilating his family name, echoing the previous agreement between Jonathan and David (20:42).

Again the catchword "hand" from chap. 23 runs throughout the story.[202] God has given Saul into David's hands, but David will not lift up his hand against him; God will vindicate David from Saul's hand, and put the kingdom in the hands of David. The combination of God's invisible hand and Saul's concession speech validates David's position as the new king. Moreover, the language of both David and Saul is explicitly moral and juridical: wrong, treason, sin, judge, sentence, vindicate, good, evil, righteous. Here David's rise to rule is the providentially guided ascent by a man of unimpeachable integrity, just the kind of public image that a king would like to have.

David and Abigail (Chap. 25)

After a brief notice for the death of Samuel, yet another story will shield David from any accusations of wrongdoing (chap. 25). The story is about a man named Nabal and his wife Abigail. "Nabal" means "fool," suggesting an allegorical dimension to this story of "folly" (v. 25). But Nabal also is "surly and mean," and seems to be a stand-in for Saul, David's *real* enemy who seeks his life (v. 26, 29).[203] Apparently David and his band are providing protection in the field for Nabal's shepherds. The nature of the arrangement is unclear. No remuneration for this service is mentioned, but David sends messengers to Nabal, asking politely if Nabal will treat them to a fine dinner since they just happened

---

201. The Hebrew word for "good" appears four times in vv. 17–19 ("well," "safely").

202. The Hebrew word appears ten times in vv. 4, 6, 10–13, 15 ("against you" is "from your hand"), 18, and 20.

203. Gunn, *Fate*, 96–100; Polzin, *Samuel*, 205–13.

to have arrived on the occasion of a feast that accompanies sheepshearing (v. 11). But Nabal rudely rejects the messengers, saying that he doesn't know who David is (although he knows he is "the son of Jesse"!) and implying that he is a fugitive servant (v. 10). Why would Nabal pretend not to know David if David is working for him? Is David's protection, in fact, a kind of extortion? Nabal would rightly resent having to provide a lavish dinner for a gang of hoodlums whose "protection" was really restraint from their own plundering. On the other hand, why would Nabal's servant who explains to Abigail what is happening, not report such abusive behavior if it took place (v. 15–16)? Here, as elsewhere, we are left to puzzle over possible undercurrents of David's motives, significantly qualifying the glowing exculpation later in the story.[204]

David's response to Nabal's rebuff is to grab his sword and take four hundred men with him to crash the party. But Nabal's wife, Abigail, is as "clever" as he is mean, and beautiful to boot (v. 3). When she learns of David's approach and hears of her husband's rude behavior, she loads up her donkeys with enough food for a banquet and goes to meet David. Now we learn of David's full intentions; since Nabal has returned him evil for good, David will massacre the entire household, at least all the men—literally "everyone who pisses against a wall" (vv. 21–22, AT). The crude language (and spoken to a lady!) reflects male pride that does not deal well with insult. In fact, here David exhibits the drive for revenge that sometimes consumed Saul, and narrowly avoids the kind of massacre that Saul wreaked upon the town of Nob (v. 33, 39; 14:24; 18:25; cf. 25:33).[205] The story will attempt to clear David completely, but it cannot conceal a side of David's character that is frightening, prevented only by Abigail's shrewd diplomacy.

Abigail denounces her husband's behavior, and begs David not to be offended, then gives a speech worthy of those of David (vv. 26–31). She is convinced that God "has restrained you from bloodguilt and from taking vengeance." Abigail apparently is privy to David's status as "prince" that no one other than David could know, as if she was eavesdropping when God designated David to Samuel.[206] Clearly, her speech is designed not only to affirm that status but also to provide yet another vindication of David as a man of integrity in whom there is no guilt or guile. Moreover, she declares that "the Lord will certainly make my lord a sure house," because David is fighting God's battles. Here is the first hint that David will not only become king, but the founder of a long-lasting *dynasty*, exactly what

---

204. See Bodner, *I Samuel*, 260–62, for a summary of this interpretation. To Gunn, *Fate*, 96, the request looks remarkably like "a demand for pay-out in a protection racket." Fokkelman, *Crossing Fates*, 489, says, "Nabal has ignored the fact of the services which, although unasked, were nevertheless provided for the shepherds."

205. Later we will learn of bloodguilt "on Saul and on his house," due to an otherwise unknown incident (2 Sam 21:1). David, however, will commit his own atrocity in 26:8–12, but its immorality will go unnoticed by the narrator.

206. Chapter 16; cf. 13:14. In fact, the word "prince" is not even used in the anointing of David.

Saul was denied.²⁰⁷ Then she adds, "evil shall not be found in you so long as you live," putting David on a moral pedestal that no normal human could occupy, and certainly not David. He will remain in God's care, while his enemies will be rejected. David will have "no cause of grief, or pangs of conscience" once God has fulfilled the promises made to him, specifically appointing him "prince (*nagid*) over Israel." Once God has "dealt well" with David, Abigail asks that David "remember" *her* (v. 31). One suspects that her flattery throughout this speech, coupled with her death-wish over her husband (v. 26), reflects aspirations that *she* will be in that "sure house" as well, the probability of which is sealed by the end of the story.²⁰⁸

Given all of the royal language, it is ironic that Nabal's banquet is "like the feast of a king" (v. 36). It proves to be his last meal. Abigail waits until he has recovered from his drunkenness—though perhaps still hung over—to inform him of her actions, whereupon "his heart died within him; he became like a stone" (v. 37). Since the story ends with the death of Nabal and David's marriage to Abigail, one can easily imagine how suspicion would have been cast on David. The story attempts to negate any such accusation. David is innocent in the death of Nabal; in fact, *David's* own hand did not avenge the wrong (v. 33)— *God* is the one who conveniently struck Nabal (vv. 37–38, perhaps both literally and figuratively a "stroke"). Once again the line separating divine guidance from human actions is difficult to discern (and fraught with moral ambiguity), as when David says that Abigail has kept him from bloodguilt, then immediately that God "restrained" him from harming her, then that *her* actions determined the course of events (v. 34). However one interprets God's involvement, in the end one more foundation has been laid for the "sure house" of David.

Sparing the Anointed, Again (Chap. 26)

Now David's sparing Saul's life at the cave has its obvious doublet when the same thing happens in much the same way (chap. 26). The present story seems to pick up both the occasion and location of a previous betrayal by the Ziphites (23:19). The parallels with the En-gedi story are numerous: Saul given into David's hand; David encouraged to kill him; David's refusal to lay his hand on God's anointed; taking Saul's spear (instead of a piece of his robe); the confrontation and dialogue with Saul; Saul's repentance and acknowledgment of David's success. There is even the common detail of David comparing himself to a flea (24:14; 26:20). However, there are also some differences in theological expression. David accuses his opponents of driving him out of his participation "in the heritage of the Lord," i.e.,

---

207. The phrase appears in the oracle in 2:35 for the priestly line of Zadok, who will be closely associated with David and Solomon, and resembles the language of Nathan's oracle to David in 2 Sam 7:11; cf. 1 Kgs 11:38.

208. Abigail will not be the sole lady of the house, however. A wife exchange occurs in vv. 43–44, in which Saul takes away Michal and gives her to another, and David marries Ahinoam. Since the name "Ahinoam" occurs nowhere else than with Saul's wife, some speculate that David has appropriated her as part of his political agenda.

in the people of Israel and its land, even of telling him to "Go, serve other gods" (vv. 19-20). David will appear to do the former immediately in chap. 27, but as a ruse. As for divine involvement, here the narrator gives an explicit interpretation of the "deep sleep" that anesthetized Saul and his troops—it was "from the Lord."[209] So once again David comes off as not only innocent of any wrong-doing against Saul, but also the benefactor of God's providence and the one destined for success, as even Saul acknowledges. The difference between the two men also appears in the ironic significance of the spear: the weapon that Saul threw at David, David displays as the sign of his allegiance to Saul.

David, the Pseudo-Philistine (Chap. 27)

In the context of the previous doublet, David has good reason to doubt the sincerity of Saul's parting blessing. So, in apparent desperation, he decides that the only safe haven is to live among the Philistines (27:1—28:2). The previous anachronistic reference to this move to King Achish of Gath ended with David pretending to be a madman to allay any suspicions (21:10-15). Here the outcome is quite different. As he had hoped, Saul gives up his chase rather than try to penetrate into Philistine territory. David approaches King Achish as if he were one of his subjects and asks for a place in the countryside where he can settle, out of Achish's hair, as it were. Achish gives him a stronghold called Ziklag. No doubt David did not bring Goliath's sword to the negotiations (21:8-9)!

David now proceeds to deceive Achish into thinking that David is, in fact, a turncoat who is raiding Israel. Instead, David raids several other peoples who are unrelated to Israel.[210] In order to conceal his deceit, he massacres everyone—"leaving neither man nor woman alive"—so there will be no one to tell Achish the truth. Of course, he keeps the livestock as spoil, and the narrator adds the detail "and the clothing." Did they take it off the bodies, or just from people's closets? One wonders how anyone could wear second-hand clothing from a murder victim. It is not a pretty picture, especially of the one who, in several preceding incidents, refrained from incurring bloodguilt and, in effect, claimed the moral high ground of "righteousness." Yet here, as elsewhere, the narrator makes no judgmental statement, much less tell us that God is displeased. Saul lost his kingship because of a ritual faux pas with Samuel and for not slaughtering a king; David goes unscathed for an atrocity that rivals that of Nob. Indeed, the narrator tells us that "such was his practice all the time he lived in the country of the Philistines," which was sixteen months (vv. 12, 7). These were David's "killing fields" for a long time.[211] However, here

---

209. Note the same term in Gen 2:21 where God performs some surgery on the anesthetized Adam.

210. There is a relationship to the Kenites, v. 10, but here we should probably read "Kenizites," with the Greek text. The continuing presence of Amalekites contradicts 15:8.

211. The phrase was coined to describe the massacres by the Khmer Rouge in Cambodia in the 1970s. See other examples of such atrocities in the discussion of Joshua. Niditch, *War*, 129,

is an exemplary instance in which the simple inclusion of an incident is enough to condemn David, at least for the contemporary reader. Here "The story of David's rise to power is contrived as much against him as for him."[212]

Dark Night of the Soul (Chap. 28)

The book of 1 Samuel concludes with a battle between the Philistines and Israel. The narrator creates considerable tension regarding the role of David, for King Achish naturally assumes that David and his men will be fighting at his side (has he not been doing this, in effect, for sixteen months?), and says so to David. David's reply is wily in its ambiguity: "Very well, then you shall know what your servant can do." We wonder how David will get out of this mess, but before the final battle begins, the narrator takes us back to Saul, and his "dark night of the soul" (28:3–25).

The lament is the most common type of Psalm in the book of Psalms. Laments are often full of anguish, but all of the laments have some note of hope—except one, Psalm 88. It is unrelentingly wrenching:

> But I, O LORD, cry out to you;
>   in the morning my prayer
>   comes before you.
> O LORD, why do you cast me off?
> Why do you hide your face
>   from me?
> Wretched and close to death from
>   my youth up,
> Your wrath has swept over me;
>   your dread assaults destroy me.
> (vv. 13–16)

Saul could have penned this psalm, and there are few other biblical characters whose despair matches it, at least as witnessed in the texts (Job being a likely exception). Whatever one may think of Saul's failures—either those misjudgments that speak for themselves, or those sins condemned by characters like Samuel and by the narrator—it is difficult not to sympathize with him here, on the night before his death.

The narrator artfully weaves together the opening lines that set the scene: Samuel's death, Saul's expulsion of "mediums and wizards," the Israelites and Philistines poised for battle. Samuel's death, already reported in 25:1, is juxtaposed to the prohibition of mediums because they were competing sources of divination, using the term broadly to mean "divining the will of God." We have come to know Samuel as the dominating prophet who speaks God's word, but we have also seen other ways in which God reveals what will happen, especially the ephod and the sacred dice, Urim and Thummim.[213] Increasingly, such revelation came only to David. Now, when Saul is desperate, there is total silence.

Saul apparently sees the overwhelming military superiority of the Philistine force, and he is terrified. As others have done before, he seeks to discern God's will, and the author employs again the wordplay on his name, the English

---

includes this incident in the category of "the ideology of expediency."

212. Polzin, *Samuel*, 217. His focus, however, is not on the atrocity but on David's self-serving "duplicity."

213. Cf. 14:40–42; 23:6–12.

equivalent sounding something like "Saul sought."[214] But there is no answer, no matter by what legitimate means—dream, Urim, or prophet. So Saul asks his aides to find a medium, someone who could perform a séance. Ironically, Saul had supposedly expelled all such people from Israel, in accordance with biblical law.[215] That he was not totally successful is apparent from this story, but also from the time of the reforms of King Josiah, who had to do the same thing again. So Israel's first king will die after consulting a medium, whereas Israel's ideal king will die after abolishing them.[216]

Saul's aides seem to know all too readily of a medium at Endor, so Saul disguises himself and goes to her secretly by night. He asks her to conjure up a spirit, and she replies coyly that surely he knows how the king has prohibited such practices. Why is he trying to entrap her in performing an illegal act? Saul then swears an oath on the name of God that she will not be punished. Since only one person would have the authority to make such a promise truthfully, she may guess already who this strange visitor is. "Whom shall I bring up for you?" she asks. And Saul asks for Samuel.

Ironically, Saul breaks the Deuteronomic law by going to a medium, and in seeking Samuel he engages in the very activity that Samuel had before equated with rebellion (15:23)! Nevertheless, he keeps the intent of the law in that he does not *use* her as a medium for discerning the future, only to consult with a prophet, precisely the figure that God had said would be God's legitimate representative (Deut 18:9–19).[217] Of course, it is stretching the law to consult with a *dead* prophet, but Saul has no other recourse. Moreover, Samuel epitomized the Deuteronomic understanding of the function of a prophet as revealed by God to Moses: "I will put my words in the mouth of the prophet, who shall speak to them [the people] everything that I command. Anyone who does not heed the words that the prophet shall speak in my name, I myself will hold accountable." One might add, *even the king*, for precisely such disobedience to the prophet was the downfall of Saul. So here is Saul, abandoned by God, having to consult with the dead prophet who increasingly had no good word from God to give him, only condemnation. In a macabre way, the scene epitomizes the prophetic ideal: even in death, the prophet stands over the king.

There will be no final reprieve. Samuel comes up, and on seeing him, the medium cries out in distress, realizing now that this is, indeed, Saul himself who has deceived her. Perhaps her assumption is that Samuel would not allow him-

---

214. Also v. 16; the more technical term for such inquiring is used in v. 7.

215. Lev 19:31; Deut 18:9–14. Note also 1 Sam 15:23 and see Isa 8:19–20.

216. 2 Kgs 23:24–26 (cf. 2 Kgs 21:6). Moreover, Josiah consults with a legitimate *prophetess* (2 Kgs 22:13–20). The notice about Josiah abolishing the mediums leads immediately into the encomium that praises him as the faithful king, then immediately again into the reason for his untimely death.

217. Some scholars think that in an earlier version of the story, the spirit was anonymous (not Samuel), which would remove this qualification of Saul's offense. A prophetic editor has added vv. 11–12a and 17–18 so that Saul hears a lot more than a mere prediction of his death (McCarter, *I Samuel*, 421–23; somewhat similarly, Campbell, *Of Prophets and Kings*, 114, 118).

self to be conjured for anyone less than the king.[218] Saul immediately reassures her, and asks what she sees, since apparently Saul does not see Samuel himself. "I see a divine being coming up out of the ground," she says. When she describes him as "an old man . . . wrapped in a robe," Saul knows whose it is (the one he once ripped, 15:27!), and he bows his head in respect to his old nemesis.

Samuel, as we might expect, is not happy with Saul, whose conjuring has "disturbed" him in his rest.[219] Saul explains why he has conjured Samuel, his anxiety about the Philistines, God's abandonment of him, with no one to turn to but Samuel, "to tell me what I shall do" (v. 15, AT). The last phrase is ironic in that Samuel used precisely those words after anointing Saul: "wait until I come to you and tell you what you shall do" (10:8, AT). Saul did not wait, did not heed the prophet then, but asks now for Samuel's instruction. Samuel simply repeats Saul's acts of disobedience and God's word of judgment, now adding the identity of the one to whom Saul's kingdom will be given—David. The rest is all doom: God will give Israel into the hands of the Philistines, and Saul and his sons will join Samuel in death. The hand of the Lord, which so often had been in Israel's favor, now hands them over to their adversaries. The implication is that Israel as a corporate entity suffers the fate of Israel's king, whether for good or for ill, dependent on the king's obedience or disobedience to God's word through the prophet. This understanding of God's blessing or curse will hang over the narrative of the Former Prophets until the end.

Now the story focuses on Saul's reaction to Samuel's words. He is filled with fear and drained of strength, because he has not eaten "all day and all night." The medium—who remains nameless—provides the one, small touch of compassion that Saul so desperately needs. In some traditions, she is known as the "witch of Endor," reflecting a long history of misogyny against women who engaged in her profession. Yet the malevolent connotation of the term is anything but appropriate here. She is the only principal character in the story, both divine and human, who offers a shred of kindness. One might compare her gesture to that of the prostitute Rahab in Josh 2:12. Both women represent people whom Deuteronomic orthodoxy would expunge—a Canaanite whore and a "witch"—but both exhibit that elementally human "kindness" (ḥesed) that puts orthodoxy to shame.[220]

Suddenly, the medium takes charge and addresses Saul, who is lying prostrate on the ground. She says (paraphrasing), "I listened to you and did what you said, at the risk of my life. Now *you* listen to me." One can almost see her wagging her finger in Saul's face. "You need to eat," she says. "Eat, that you may have strength when you go on your way." She is the universal mother with a bowl of chicken soup. Saul, frozen in his fear and grief, refuses, but she, and his accompa-

218. The cause of her exclamation is much disputed. See the previous note; originally her reaction may have been to Saul's authoritative reassurance.

219. Cf. Job 3:17 ("troubling").

220. Jobling, *I Samuel*, 305, speculates that the medium is a Philistine, making her (as also female) "the most utterly Other" possible, as opposed to "the narrow ethnic identity that postexilic Israel is trying to take on."

nying servants, press him, and he agrees. The woman slaughters the "fatted calf" and makes some unleavened cakes, and Saul and his servants eat. The word for "slaughter" often means "sacrifice," so, in a sense, the medium is functioning as an ersatz priest, serving the one for whom sacrifice had been nothing but hurtful (10:8–14; 15).[221] Sometimes, eating is "a small good thing" at a time when nothing but bad things are happening.[222] For a moment, through the mercy of this woman, Saul has a companion in his grief—remembering that "companion" comes from the Latin words for "with bread." Through her hospitality, the meal thus takes on a sacramental quality, the only gesture that bears a redemptive dimension. The medium's dinner is the means for grace, reminding us of the *first* lady of the book, Hannah ("Grace"). Then Saul goes out into the night.

The Pseudo-Philistine's Dilemma (Chap. 29)

The focus now shifts back to the looming battle and to David's predicament of pretending to fight with the Philistines when his loyalty is really with Israel (chap. 29). The preceding stories have exonerated David of any wrongdoing against Saul and his heir-apparent, Jonathan. Now it is critical that David not appear to be a traitor, much less one who kills fellow Israelites. Fortuitously, the "lords of the Philistines" provide the perfect opportunity. "What are these Hebrews doing here?" they ask King Achish. Perhaps they remember that a band of Hebrews had once been on their side and deserted to Saul's forces (14:21), and they could easily switch sides again. Achish responds by identifying the Hebrews with David and his mercenary force, and defends David's loyalty. But the lords are adamant, insisting that David be sent behind the lines, and reciting the song about David's superior body count to that of Saul.

Now Achish summons David to tell him of his reluctant concession to his generals. Given what we know of David's duplicity before, the way in which Achish describes David is full of irony. "As the Lord lives, you have been honest," he says, totally oblivious to the way David had tricked him into thinking that David was raiding the Israelites (chap. 27). Moreover, Achish underscores his praise with an oath in the name of the Lord, the God of his enemy, rather than, say, Dagon (whose statue presumably has long been restored, chap. 5). Is Achish a convert, or simply being polite? In turn, David complains that he has done nothing to deserve Achish's decision to dismiss him, addressing him as "my lord the king," a continuing pretension to loyalty at the very moment that Achish is lauding his honesty. Then Achish replies: "I know that you are as blameless in my sight as an angel of God." Again, the word for God could refer to the God of Israel, or simply be translated "a divine angel." Achish's flattery rivals that of Abigail (25:29–31). Little does Achish know

---

221. So Hackett, "1 and 2 Samuel," 94b.

222. The phrase is the title of a short story by Raymond Carver in which a baker's provision of fresh rolls to a grieving couple helps them all transcend the grief and anger that have consumed them. The story is widely available in anthologies. See also Rubenstein, *Raymond Carver*. For another biblical story in which such hospitality is shown, see Gen 18:6–8.

that, if anything, David is a *fallen* angel in terms of his allegiance. Furthermore, *we* know that David earned his angelic status with Achish by committing the demonic massacre of innocent people.[223] Yet, for Achish, there can be no substance to any "evil report" about him.

To be sure, the narrator makes none of the ironic connections, leaving us to wonder if the unconditional praise of David that comes from Achish's mouth is the narrator's own assessment. Does he want us to remember David's lies and atrocities? Or does the importance of maintaining David's innocence against any charge of treason override any moral failings that David may exhibit? It will not be the last time that we are inclined to ask such questions.

David to the Rescue (Chap. 30)

When David returns to his base at Ziklag, he finds that some Amalekites have raided his camp, burned it down, and captured everyone who was there, including David's wives (chap. 29). Perhaps they were taking revenge for David's raids on them (27:8).[224] People are so distraught that some threaten David's life, no doubt blaming him for being away and leaving them defenseless, but, the narrator tells us, "David strengthened himself in the Lord his God." Part of that self-encouragement involves once again employing the ephod, with the help of Abiathar the priest. The very means of divination that was closed to Saul in his desperation is open to David, and predictably God assures David that he should pursue the Amalekites and that he will overtake and defeat them. Serendipitously, he comes upon a straggler abandoned by the Amalekites who leads David straight to their camp. David defeats them and, the narrator assures us, recovers *everything* that they had taken, both spoil and captives. In fact, when he returns to Ziklag, people say "This is David's spoil." The one whom some wanted to assassinate they now hail as the returning hero.

Finally, David must deal with the disgruntled soldiers who resent their comrades who did not join in the battle, but stayed behind because of exhaustion. The fighters want to exclude the others from enjoying any of the spoil, but David will have none of it. He dutifully acknowledges that the spoil is "what the Lord has given us," not what the soldiers have earned by their own efforts. Those who stay behind with the gear will share alike with those who fight in the battle, and the narrator tells us that David promulgated this decision as "a statute and an ordinance . . . to the present day."

Once again David proves to be the hero without fault, regaining all that was lost (including the wives) and, thereby, his reputation.[225] Moreover, his leadership skills include the wise resolution of internal disputes that otherwise could become fractious, and he formulates

---

223. Perhaps it was because of such a glaring incongruity that the LXX omitted the phrase.

224. This incident seems inconsistent with the claim in 15:8 that Saul had completely annihilated the Amalekites (except, of course, for king Agag), not to mention David's genocidal raids (27:8).

225. Polzin, *Samuel*, 221–23, holds a very different view: that chaps. 29–31 *blame* David for contributing to the defeat of Israel and the death of Saul because David did not join in the battle.

legislation exactly the way an effective judge would—or, for that matter, a king (cf. Psalm 72). If all of this sounds like the enhancement of David's royal rise, the end of the incident confirms the trajectory: David gives some of the spoil to "his friends, the elders of Judah, saying 'Here is a present [literally, a blessing] from the spoil of the enemies of the Lord'" (v. 26). After all, the people have declared it *David's* spoil, so it is his to distribute as he sees fit, and what better way to promote his aspirations than to reward his political base in the towns of Judah?[226]

With David completely cleared of any suspicion concerning his loyalty vis-à-vis the Philistines, his image of a rescuer rescued (after only a brief lapse), his skill as a military commander confirmed, his wisdom as a judge codified, and his benevolence to the community's traditional leadership manifest, we are ready for the death of Saul, assured that God's new anointed waits in the wings.

The Death of Saul and Jonathan (Chap. 31)

The story of Saul's death and the defeat of the Israelites by the Philistines consists of two scenes (chap. 30). Immediately the Israelites turn and run, and the Philistines surround Saul and three of his sons, killing Jonathan. Mortally wounded by arrows, Saul asks his armor bearer to kill him so that at least he will not undergo the shame of death at the hands of "these uncircumcised." His armor bearer refuses, terrified at the thought of committing regicide, so Saul commits suicide by falling on his sword, and the armor bearer follows suit. On learning of Saul's death, Israelites in the nearby towns abandon their homes and the Philistines become the occupying power.

In the second scene, the Philistines mutilate the bodies of Saul and his sons, stripping them and beheading them, and broadcasting "the good news to the houses of their idols and to the people." Dagon seems to be avenged (though unmentioned here), and the female deity, Astarte, receives Saul's armor in her temple. It is as if we are back at the low point of the ark narrative, with no hopeful outcome possible. But there is one poignant gesture of decency remaining. The Philistines hang the bodies of Saul and his sons on the wall of Beth-shan, a grisly display typical of military terrorism. But Saul still has his devotees, the inhabitants of Jabesh-Gilead, whom he had rescued from the eye-gouging of Nahash the Ammonite (10:27—11:15). A few brave men travel all night long to Beth-shan, take down the bodies, and return them to Jabesh, where they are cremated and their bones buried. In death, the one who was anointed to rescue the Israelites from the Philistines is rescued from the Philistines by Israelites.

---

226. The elders of Israel initiated Saul's kingship (8:4–5) and will be critical in anointing David as Saul's successor (2 Sam 3:17; 5:3). The Hebrew text prints the names of the beneficiaries as a list.

FIVE

2 Samuel

List of major characters:

Abner, cousin of Saul and general of his and later Ishbaal's army; killed Asahel, brother of Joab; murdered by Joab

Absalom, son of David who murders Amnon, mounts a revolt, and is killed by Joab's troops

Abishai, brother of Joab and Asahel, one of David's military leaders (a son of Zeruiah)

Ahithophel, advisor to David, then to Absalom; defeated by Hushai; probably father of Bathsheba

Amasa, cousin of Joab, head of Absalom's rebel army, then of David's, then replaced by Abishai, murdered by Joab

Amnon, son of David who rapes his half-sister, Tamar; murdered by Absalom

Asahel, brother of Abishai and Joab (one of sons of Zeruiah), killed by Abner

Barzillai, wealthy patron in Mahanaim who provided David and troops with food

Bathsheba, wife of Uriah with whom David committed adultery; mother of Solomon

Hushai, David's counselor, who frustrates the counsel of Ahithophel regarding Absalom's rebellion

Joab, brother of Abishai and Asahel (a son of Zeruiah), David's general, murders Abner, Amasa, and oversees killing of Absalom

Mephibosheth, lame son of Jonathan, supported by David (perhaps for monitoring)

Michal, daughter of Saul who loved David; given to David as wife; later given to another man; forcibly returned to David; spurns him and remains childless

Shimei, a Saul devotee, who curses David on his escape from Jerusalem

Uriah, husband of Bathsheba, murdered on David's orders

Zadok, priest along with Abiathar, supporter of David (will later supplant Abiathar)

Ziba, the servant of Mephibosheth, involved in David's escape and return to Jerusalem

In the Hebrew Bible, the textual division between 1 and 2 Samuel is apparent only in that suddenly we are at chapter 1 again. It was the Greek translation (the Septuagint) that made the first division, followed by Christian readings. Not until the fifteenth century did the Jewish canon follow suit. Moreover, the character Samuel is not even mentioned in 2 Samuel (even his ghost does not reappear, cf. 1 Samuel 28!). Developmentally, the material in 2 Samuel reaches both backwards and forwards, stitching together the so-called "rise of David" (1 Samuel 16—2 Samuel 5) and the so-called "succession narrative" of David (2 Samuel 9—1 Kings 2), although the latter title is highly misleading.[1] Another connection appears in chap. 6, where the movement of the ark to Jerusalem provides a conclusion to the ark story that began in 1 Samuel 4 (whether originally independent or not). Chapters 1–6 then set the scene for the climactic theological legitimation of the Davidic dynasty in the oracle of the prophet Nathan in chap. 7, to which there have already been hints.[2] Yet the editors have combined their sources so smoothly that most readers will not see an obvious seam where one source ends and another begins (and some scholars claim that they aren't there to begin with!).[3]

The canonical division of 1 and 2 Samuel also fits a pattern evident in preceding books in that it marks the death of a major character. Genesis ends with the death of Jacob and then his son, Joseph. Deuteronomy ends the death of Moses, concluding the story that began in Exodus 1. Even more closely, the books of Joshua, Judges, and 2 Samuel begin with the phrase "After the death of," followed by the respective character (Moses, Joshua, and Saul). First Samuel could not begin that way because there *is* no such character by the end of Judges, a vacuum central to the plot of 1–2 Samuel.

Honoring the Lord's Anointed (Chap. 1)

The first verse looks back to David's rescue of his family and others from the Amalekites, which concluded with David's political largesse in distributing some of his spoil to the Judean elders and various towns, including Hebron, soon to become David's political base (1 Samuel 28). David is in his stronghold in Ziklag, apparently unaware of the death of Saul and Jonathan and the defeat on Mt. Gilboa. A man claiming to be from Saul's forces arrives and informs David of the tragedy. Ironically, the man is an Amalekite, one of Israel's perennial enemies (and associated with Saul's failure, 1 Samuel 15)! Ostensibly he was an eye-witness to Saul's last moments, and he tells enough of the truth to convince David, but his story does not fit with what we know of Saul's death.[4] Instead,

---

1. As we shall see, the succession of Solomon is really only central to 1 Kings 1–2. Thus Fokkelman has used the simple title *King David* for 2 Samuel 9—1 Kings 2, suggesting (p. 427) that it is more descriptive than other scholarly constructs (following similar suggestions of Gunn).

2. There has been much dispute about the original relationship of ch. 6 to the "ark narrative" in 1 Samuel. For hints of the Nathan oracle, see 1 Sam 2:35; 25:30.

3. For example, Gunn, *King David*, 84, argues that the so-called "court history" begins with 2 Samuel 2–4 (and probably 5:1–3).

4. Cf. Fokkelman, *Crossing Fates*, 640–42.

he invents a scene in which he does what Saul's armor bearer was too terrified to do—accede to Saul's request to kill him—but David has no way of knowing that the Amalekite's story is false. Presumably, the Amalekite expects some reward for killing the man who wanted to kill David, but he is in for an unpleasant surprise. Rather than rejoicing, David and his attendants rip their clothes and fast, traditional gestures of mourning. David then interrogates the messenger, who again reveals his Amalekite identity. David then asks was he not "afraid to lift your hand to destroy the Lord's anointed?" The question closely resembles the language David used when he *refused* to do precisely that (1 Sam 24:6; 26:29). David then orders the man's immediate execution. The opening scene thus reinforces David's lack of animosity toward Saul and Jonathan, emphasizing that, on the contrary, he is overwhelmed with remorse. On the other hand, here is another situation (there will be more) in which David benefits from the death of Saul & Family for which he cannot be blamed. Indeed, the hapless Amalekite has brought Saul's crown, thus symbolically transferring his realm as well.

David now composes a lamentation over Saul and Jonathan. Traditionally, one of David's epithets is "the sweet Psalmist of Israel," which is why the book of Psalms is attributed to him. This lament alone could earn the reputation (as could 23:1-7). "How the mighty have fallen" provides a frame around the whole and around the last stanza (vv. 19, 25, 27). David anguishes over the possibility that the Philistines will gloat over their victory. He invokes nature to reflect his grief with a drought on the mountains and hills—a reversal of the fertility usually associated with royal figures (Ps 72:3, 6, 16), including David himself (2 Sam 23:4). He praises the military prowess of Saul and Jonathan, the closeness of their relationship, and their physical capabilities. He appeals to the women of Jerusalem to join in the lament, noting how Saul bestowed riches upon them. Finally, he expresses his poignant feelings about Jonathan, and how deeply they loved each other.[5] Some of the poem surprises us (Saul's wealth distribution), some is anachronistic (the women of Jerusalem), and some seems to contradict previous stories (e.g., Saul's alienation from Jonathan). Nevertheless, the honesty of the grief and the artistry of expression make it a beautiful eulogy.

The King of Judah versus the Son of Saul (Chaps. 2–4)

The story of David's rise in 1 Samuel made repeated efforts to demonstrate his innocence with respect to Saul, even after we knew that he would become Saul's replacement. Second Samuel 1 concludes that defense by showing David's grief over Saul and Jonathan, the final stage-setting for the public inauguration of David's monarchy in 2:1–4a. David's first action is to inquire of God what he should do. Such inquiry is a leitmotif in David's story, a willingness to place himself in God's hands, trusting in God's good will. Such reliance exhibits an acknowledgment of his vulnerability and of God's sustenance, a spiritual dimension to David's character that often will

---

5. On the nature of this love, see the discussion of 1 Samuel 18–19.

offset far less noble aspects, especially at critical junctures in the narrative (e.g., 15:24–26, 31; 16:9–12). The theological correlate is God's implicit guidance of the events that follow, sometimes (though rarely) stated explicitly by the narrator (e.g., 17:14). Thus David's political moves appear to be the movement of providence as well, a connection immediately apparent in the following verses that lead to David's public anointing.

Here David asks if he should move to "any of the cities of Judah." After all, he is still living in a stronghold given to him by the enemy who defeated Saul. "Yes," says, God; "Go to Hebron." So, with his two wives[6] and his men and their households, David proceeds to Hebron, which is the chief village in the territory of Judah. "Then the people of Judah came, and there they anointed David king over the house of Judah" (v. 4). David is now halfway to becoming the king of "all Israel," Judah being the southern half of the people (sometimes, and especially after 1 Kings 12, "Israel" will refer specifically to the Northern tribes, as can "Ephraim" and "Jacob"; sometimes "Israel" refers to all twelve, including Judah—which, of course, is the ideal).

The simple, reportorial style of v. 4, and the lack of any accompanying editorial comment, is stunning. David becomes king without the slightest reservation on the part of the characters or the narrator. After all the agonizing over the institution of the monarchy in 1 Samuel, it makes us wonder, what was all the fuss about? Of course, we already knew that God, through Samuel, had anointed David to be the next king. Even so, here the inauguration of *David's* monarchy seems to be completely without controversy. Monarchy is now assumed as the normal form of leadership, and it happens because God—like a savvy campaign advisor—knew just where David should go.

Now one more decision of David shows his political skill vis-à-vis Saul and Jonathan (2:4b–7). When David learns of the brave rescue of their corpses by the people of Jabesh-gilead (1 Sam 31:11–13), David sends a message of gratitude and praise for their "loyalty" (ḥesed) to Saul "your lord," invoking, in return, God's ḥesed for them, and promising that he too will reward them. He then encourages them to be valiant in the face of Saul's death, again referring to him as "your lord," concluding with the information that "the house of Judah has anointed me king over them." Since Jabesh-gilead symbolizes loyalty and respect for Saul, and represents, in a sense, the Northern tribes, the notice certainly hints that the valiant thing to do might be to join the inauguration movement.

Immediately, however, an alternative contender for Northern loyalty appears in the person of one of Saul's surviving sons, Ishbaal (2:8–11).[7] But his assumption of Saul's throne does not result from a populist action, much less divine guidance, as was the case with David. Rather, Saul's military commander, Abner, who apparently survived the debacle on Mt. Gilboa, "took" him and "made him

---

6. Abigail gets her wish, 2 Sam 25:31. It is also possible that Ahinoam was the wife of Saul (1 Sam 14:50); if so, that would be another political move.

7. In the Hebrew text the name is Ishbosheth, which means "man of shame," reflecting the narrator's view that the use of Baal in a name smells of heresy.

king," language that suggests Ishbaal's puppet position. His supposed realm includes several Northern groups and regions, concluding rather expansively with "over all Israel." (Soon, however, the Benjamites—Saul's tribe—will come to the fore [cf. vv. 25, 31].) The narrator then provides a regnal chronological formula, telling us that Ishbaal reigned two years, but that "the house of Judah followed David," who reigned seven and a half years in Hebron. We have to wonder by what authority Abner made Ishbaal king. There is some evidence that his father, Ner, was Saul's uncle, but even such a family connection does not convey the right to crown a king. Of course, Abner's assumption may simply be that, as Saul's only surviving son, Ishbaal succeeds to the throne by right of heredity, even though *we* know that Samuel had annulled precisely that dynastic succession (1 Sam 13:13–14). Although the narrator will soon use the term "house of Saul" (3:1), there was to be no such house left standing. Moreover, if Ishbaal's political base consists largely of Abner's support, it is shaky from the outset.

Abner's action clearly intends to counter the inauguration of David over Judah, and immediately representatives of the two factions meet in Gibeon—Abner and Ishbaal's supporters face off with Joab and David's supporters, Joab being *David's* military commander (vv. 12–32). Abner proposes a war game (the word for "contest" can refer to "play"), an ordeal the outcome of which is presumably determined by God.[8] Quickly, however, the game proves to be anything but playful, as the chosen sides promptly kill each other. In its wider significance, perhaps the game illustrates how suicidal tribal rivalries can be, especially between North and South, a competition that will undermine "all Israel" repeatedly (e.g., 20:1–2; 1 Kings 12).[9] Indeed, immediately the contest escalates into outright warfare, with Abner and "the men of Israel" losing badly. When Abner attempts to flee, Joab's brother, Asahel, pursues him. Abner warns him to stop, but Asahel is relentless, and Abner kills him with his spear.

Already the personal relationships of the characters affect their political loyalty and determine their actions, often with dire consequences (see Figure 1).

Joab, Abishai, and Asahel are the "sons of Zeruiah" (2:18), and cousins of David.[10] Abner, most likely Saul's cousin,[11] questioned how he could face Joab if Abner killed Joab's brother, Asahel (v. 22), but that didn't stop him from doing it. Now Joab and his other brother, Abishai, take after Abner (Abishai was the one who urged David to kill Saul, 1 Sam 26:8). When the Benjamites rally around Abner, he addresses Joab with an apparent overture of peace: "Is the sword to keep devouring forever?" Why, he asks, does Joab persist in pursuing his "kinsmen"? Surprisingly, Joab finds these rhetorical questions arresting, and

8. See McCarter, *II Samuel*, 98.

9. Indeed, fratricide dominates much of 2:1—4:1 and again connotes Israel/Judah strife. Abner's following question, "Is the sword to keep devouring forever?" (v. 26) will have an affirmative answer (cf. 12:10).

10. Zeruiah is either the sister or half-sister of David (1 Chr 2:12–16). It is unusual for the sons to be named by their mother.

11. There is some confusion about this; he could be Saul's uncle (cf. 1 Sam 9:1; 14:50; 1 Chr 9:36).

Figure 1: Families of Saul and David

Saul's children (those who are important characters):

sons:
Jonathan (father of Mephibosheth)
Ishbaal

daughters:
Michal
Merab

Saul's cousin:
Abner

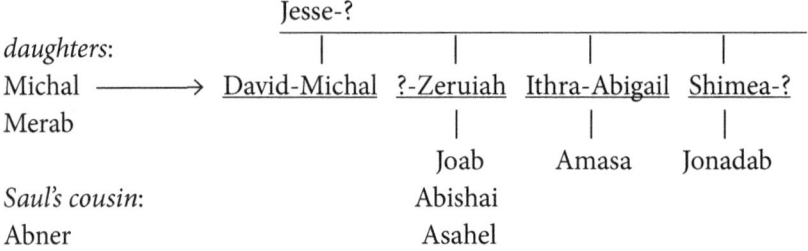

calls a halt to the battle. Unfortunately, the answer to Abner's rhetorical question will be yes.

The two sides return to their home turf, but immediately we see that the fraternal feelings cannot stifle personal vengeance or political rivalries. The narrator reports a long war between "the house of Saul and the house of David" (3:1), with the former growing weaker all the time. After a brief listing of David's numerous wives and offspring, the narrative focuses again on the role of Abner. Apparently not busy enough commanding the army, Abner is consolidating his power in the fledgling dynasty of Ishbaal. The narrator does not tell us *how* he does this, but Ishbaal accuses him of having sex with one of Saul's concubines named Rizpah.[12] Such an act was not merely sexual philandering; it was also an aggressive political move (the flip side of a monarch *giving* a daughter to another man, as with Michal and Merab).[13] Taking a woman from the royal harem, as it were, often preceded an attempted coup, another instance in which women were mere pawns for men's power struggles. Immediately after this incident, David will take his turn (as will *his* son Absalom, then Solomon's son, Adonijah).

Abner protests his innocence, reminding Ishbaal of his loyalty to Saul and his family and friends. He boasts that he could have given Ishbaal into David's hand, but did not—then proceeds to declare his desertion to David's side! What *God* has "sworn" to David, *Abner* will do, namely, "transfer the kingdom from the house of Saul, and set up the throne of David over Israel and over Judah" (3:10), yet another example of co-operation between God and humans. How Abner knows of this divine oath is a mystery,[14] but Abner is nothing if not confident in his own king-making capabilities, and Ishbaal is cowed.

---

12. Rizpah will reappear as a nobly tragic figure in ch. 21.

13. See above, n. 6, and the discussion of 1 Sam 18:17–29.

14. The only reference to God's swearing such an oath is in Ps 132:11, on which see below on ch. 6.

Now Abner sends messengers to negotiate with David, offering to broker Israel's allegiance to David in exchange for David's covenant with Abner. We do not know the conditions of that covenant, although it no doubt included amnesty for Abner and perhaps a prominent place in David's administration. Conceivably, Abner was jockeying for Joab's job, which would help explain Joab's actions later (chap. 4). We *do* know David's one condition, however—he will not even meet with Abner unless Abner brings with him David's former wife, Michal, Saul's daughter. We are back to woman-trading again, and David himself sends a message to Ishbaal demanding that he deliver Michal. David is even crass enough to mention how much he *paid* for her (in foreskins, no less; 1 Sam 18:20–29). Saul had given her to another man (1 Sam 25:44), and now there is a poignant scene in which he follows her on her way, weeping in his grief, until Abner, the escort, orders him to go back to his now empty home. David has callously shattered a deep personal relationship for political gain.

Now Abner follows through on his end of the deal. He appeals to "the elders of Israel," and then particularly to the Benjamites, Saul's tribe. According to Abner, the elders "have been seeking David as king" for a good while, something not explicit in the preceding narrative. But we know that "all Israel and Judah loved David" for his military leadership (1 Sam 18:16), a note that the elders will eventually repeat (5:2). Now is the time to act, says Abner, concluding that the act accords with God's promise to David: "Through my servant David I will save my people Israel from the hand of the Philistines" (3:18). Now for the first time David is identified as God's "servant," a title formerly applied to Moses and Joshua, and a key term later.[15] Additionally, Abner uses the same commissioning language that God had used for Saul (1 Sam 9:16), optimistically expanded to "all their enemies." Having made his stump speech for David, Abner then returns to him to report his success. David entertains Abner and his aides with a feast, after which Abner offers to seal the agreement by bringing "all Israel" to sign the treaty with him, "that you may reign over all that your heart desires" (3:21).

To protect David from any suspicion over what follows, the narrator emphasizes that David dismisses Abner "in peace" (v. 21, 22, 23). Why would he not since Abner apparently is the diplomat who can deliver the treaty David wants? But now the simmering animosity between Abner and Joab spills over. When Joab returns to Hebron from a lucrative raid, he learns of Abner's visit, although the treaty goes unmentioned. Joab is incensed, arguing with David that Abner has come as a spy, not a friend. Surprisingly, there is no response from David. But Joab sends a squad after Abner, hauls him back to Hebron, and personally stabs him to death. As both the narrator and David put it, the murder of Abner was revenge for "the blood of Asahel," and David declares himself

---

15. Here is another connection with Psalm 132 (the ark liturgy; v. 10); for Moses see Deut 34:5; Josh 1:2, 7; for Joshua, Josh 24:29; Judg 2:8. Key texts later are 7:5 and 1 Kgs 11:13, 32–38.

and his kingdom guiltless, thereby protecting his future dynasty.

David punishes Joab only by pronouncing a curse on him and *his* "house," a reticence that we will see again. David then orders Joab and everyone else to mourn Abner, and David himself participates in the burial. He even delivers a lament similar to that for Saul and Jonathan, but much more modest. The implied rebuke of Joab, however, is clear in that David says that Abner was murdered "as one falls before the wicked." Finally, David adds fasting to his gestures of grief, the result of which is a rise in his popularity rating: "*All the people* took notice of it, and it pleased them; just as everything the king did pleased *all the people*. So *all the people* and *all Israel* understood that the king had no part in the killing of Abner son of Ner" (3:36–37). The narrator's spin on the story, which he had already summarized in v. 30, could not be clearer, especially with the emphasis on "all *Israel*." Nevertheless, David adds one more eulogy for Abner as "a prince and a great man . . . *in Israel*." And in case even that is not enough, he confesses that he is "powerless" (literally "soft") in handling the violence of Joab and his brothers, anointed though he may be. All he can do is utter another curse: "The Lord pay back the one who does wickedly in accordance with his wickedness." David is already a governor who is sometimes powerless to govern those in his administration, a fault that will engulf his family, as well.

With the one who made him king dead, Ishbaal loses heart completely, along with "all Israel" (4:1). Still, he is the remaining hurdle for David's plan to unite North and South. After introducing two traitors, the narrator tells us parenthetically of a son of Jonathan named Mephibosheth (there's that "shame" again [*-bosheth*]) who is lame, information that we will need later (chap. 9). Resuming the story, the traitors enter Ishbaal's house while he's taking his noonday nap, stab him to death, and decapitate him, escaping with the head in hand.[16] Their hope is to curry favor with David for killing his political opponent, but, of course, they have made a huge mistake. When they present him with the head, claiming that "the Lord has avenged my lord the king this day," David decries the murder, "when wicked men have killed a righteous man on his bed," and rewards them with the blood vengeance their deed has earned. He hangs their bodies (*sans* feet and hands) by the pond at Hebron. Ishbaal's head is buried in the tomb of Abner, the one who had made him king. By declaring the murders "wicked," and the victim "righteous," David again shows himself to be completely innocent in this final elimination of a contender from the house of Saul (though the question of Mephibosheth remains).

The King of Israel and His Holy City (Chaps. 5–6)

Now the stage is finally set for David's acclamation as king of the united tribes, North and South (5:1–5). Representatives of all the Israelite tribes come to him at

---

16. Verses 4:6 and 4:7 are a doublet. The stomach seems to be the favored target in these stories (2:23; 3:27).

Hebron and illustrate the proverb that everyone loves a rich uncle—they claim him as their kinfolk. They then echo the previous statement of Abner: "For some time, while Saul was king over us, it was you who led out Israel and brought it in" (cf. 3:17 and 1 Sam 18:16). They also repeat a version of David's commissioning by God as "ruler" (*nagid*, "prince" or "king-elect"). Verse 3 completes the acclamation when the "elders of Israel" come to David "the king"; David makes a covenant with them "before the Lord, and they anointed David king over Israel." The narrator then provides a regnal formula for the time David was king at Hebron and (soon to be) in Jerusalem.

There are a number of interesting features to this brief, albeit momentous, account. There is an emphasis on the location in Hebron (three times in vv. 1–3). The quotation from God in v. 2b discloses the narrator's omniscience, not that of the tribes (who could not know of David's selection in 1 Sam 16:1–13)[17] thus presenting a theological interpretation of the political election by the tribal leaders. David now is not only God's "servant" but also the "shepherd" of Israel (an ancient metaphor for monarchy, cf. 7:7). The combination of vv. 2 and 3 suggests that the elders are the official representatives of "all the tribes of Israel," and the ones who formally "anoint" David as king (although the narrator already calls him "the king" when they come to him). The elders have thus taken on the anointing role of Samuel, who no doubt would have loved to be here (no prophet appears until Nathan in chap. 12). Finally, the official transaction raises a question that was not directly addressed in all the diatribes about the monarchy in 1 Samuel 8 and 12: if David makes a covenant (or treaty) with the people, how does that affect the people's covenant with God? In a sense, the diplomatic language of statecraft again poses the question that the editors *have* addressed, namely in what sense is God still Israel's "king" now that David is their king?

A king needs a capitol city and a palace, and David now procures both of those (he also needs a temple, on which see below). He conquers the fortress at Jerusalem, inhabited by the Jebusites, who had taunted David by saying that even the blind and lame could defeat him.[18] He exercises his royal prerogative in renaming the city after himself—Davidsburg, as it were (cf. the Russian tsar's Petersburg). David immediately wins a royal friend in King Hiram of Tyre, who builds David a palace of cedar trees (the cedars of Lebanon were renowned for producing excellent lumber; cf. 7:2). The narrator concludes each of these incidents with a theological statement of David's divine favor. After conquering Jerusalem, "David became greater and greater, for the Lord, the God of hosts, was with him" (5:10). After building his palace, "David then perceived that the Lord had established him king over

---

17. Cf. Abigail's speech in 1 Sam 25:30 and Abner's in 2 Sam 3:9, all anticipating the language of 2 Sam 7:8.

18. The NRSV of 5:8 depicts David as ordering the killing of disabled people! The text is notoriously complicated. Note McCarter's reading in the HarperCollins NRSV annotations (David orders that there be no survivors who are maimed, a slightly more palatable meaning!).

Israel, and that he had exalted his kingdom for the sake of his people Israel" (5:12).

Here would have been a perfect ending for the original story of David's rise to power, but the editors have trumped that conclusion with the next unit (5:13—8:18) that focuses on divine presence and promise. The section has a concentric structure with the arrival of the ark in Jerusalem and the dynastic oracle of the prophet Nathan at the center (chaps. 6–7), framed before and after by lists (5:13-16; 8:15-18) and military reports (5:17-25; 8:1-14). In effect, the arrangement leads up to David's defeat of the Philistines (at long last), then leads ahead to the expansion of David's empire. The matching pairs in the concentric structure, furthermore, involve a development from Israel's premonarchic situation to the monarchic status quo (from family list to bureaucratic roster, from defensive wars to imperialistic wars, from meandering ark to established temple [cf. below]).[19]

Hearing of David's accession to the throne, the Philistines apparently see a threat arising from their former presumed ally and they mount an offense (5:17-25). There may be some humorous irony in the name of the battlefield they choose: Rephaim, which can mean "ghosts"! David again seeks God's advice and receives assurance that he will defeat the Philistines, which he promptly does, confiscating the idols that the Philistines abandon. They try again, and God even suggests a particular military strategy, which proves successful.

There are a number of theological and political features to chap. 5 that resemble a literary and ideological pattern evident in the literature of other ancient Near Eastern monarchs (primarily royal annals).[20] The pattern proclaims the exaltation of a king by his deity, and can have its cosmic counterpart in the deity's own exaltation.[21] The king reports his military victories, often credited to the presence of his god, who forms the vanguard of the army, devastating the enemy (5:20, 24; cf. Judg 5:4). Armies often carried standards or emblems of their deities, much the way modern armies use flags, and, as we have already seen in 1 Samuel 4–6, the capture of such objects (the ark) may represent the victory of one's forces (or the abandonment of one's god). The military victories may lead to the founding of a city and the construction of a palace for the king and a temple for his god. The narrator explicitly uses language suggestive of this pattern in describing God's presence with David, and David's own reading of the events as evidence that "the Lord had established him king over Israel, and that he had exalted his kingdom." The completion of this pattern will occur immediately in chap. 6 with the triumphal return of the ark and the construction

---

19. Birch, *1 and 2 Samuel*, 1240, citing the work of James Flanagan. Cf. also Linafelt, *Ruth*, xxi–xxii, who sees a structural parallel in the book of Ruth. Fokkelman, *Throne and City*, 263-65, opposes this view.

20. See my study, *Divine Presence*, especially 214–18. We will return to the ideology when we come to ch. 7.

21. The pattern appears in various stories about the gods as well. One may see its outlines in Exodus 15 (from victory to the defeat of other peoples to God's enthronement in God's sanctuary).

of a tent sanctuary to house it. Although the language in chap. 5 is far less bombastic than the self-glorification in other kings' annals, the royal ideology is on its way to the lofty status exhibited in such passages as Ps 2:6—"I have set my king on Zion, my holy hill," in which God is the ruler of the universe and God's king in Jerusalem is above all earthly counterparts. Retrospectively, David's defeat of the Philistines and capture of their idols provides a dramatic closure to the earlier story of the Philistine victory and capture of the ark (1 Samuel 4–6). As Fokkelman puts it, "we learn of the gods only after the defeat of their worshippers has supplied proof of their impotence."[22]

David now completes the process of his royal accession by bringing the ark from where it had been left (here called Baale-judah; cf. 1 Sam 6:19—7:2). In locating his capitol in Jerusalem, David has chosen a city that straddles the boundary between South and North, unlike Hebron—a shrewd political gesture of inclusiveness to the northerners. Now he incorporates the ark which is both a military palladium and a liturgical representation of God's presence among God's people. Both city and ark are expressions of the ideal union of "all Israel."

The ark is carried on a new cart, befitting its holiness, and the liturgical procession is wildly celebratory, with people dancing "before the Lord" (i.e., before the ark) to the tune of all sorts of instruments. But suddenly the celebration comes to a halt when one of the participants, Uzzah, makes the mistake of grabbing the ark, presumably to prevent its tumbling from the cart. The ark's holiness makes it charged with numinous power, lethal to anyone unauthorized to handle it, and Uzzah dies instantly.[23] David is both angry and afraid, and rightly so. He names the place "Bursting Out Against Uzzah" (cf. the etymology in 5:20). His question—"How can the ark of the Lord come into my care?"—reminds us of the question at the end of the earlier ark story: "Who is able to stand before the Lord, this holy God?" (1 Sam 6:20). Indeed, the incident certainly puts a damper on the crescendo of exaltation up to this point, a reminder (as was the earlier ark story) that no one, not even a King David, can control the power of God.

But the delay does not last long. After the death of Uzzah, David had sent the ark to be under the care of one Obed-edom, and, after three months, it became apparent that the ark was a blessing, rather than a curse. So David tries again, thinking "I'll bring the blessing back to my own house!" and this time is successful.[24] David is so ecstatic that he dances in front of the ark virtually naked, a sight that is repulsive to his wife, Michal, although we do not know exactly why.[25] David completes the procession by installing the ark in a tent shrine that he has pitched for it, offering sacrific-

---

22. Fokkelman, *Throne and City*, 174.

23. See the discussion of 1 Sam 6:19. Cf. Exodus 19, where God has Moses warn the people not to even "touch the edge of the mountain" unbidden, lest they die (v. 12), and not to move forward "to look" (v. 21) or else God will "break out against them" (v. 24, using the same word as 2 Sam 6:8).

24. For the textual grounds on this reading see McCarter, *II Samuel*, 165–66.

25. Exum, *Plotted*, 60–61, rejects various suggestions and focuses on the political dimension (see below).

es, bestowing his blessing on the people, and then providing them with a feast, fit, as we say, for a king. Again, much of this resembles liturgical events known in other ancient Near Eastern cultures, events that help to legitimate David's new monarchy. Now Jerusalem already deserves its later name—the "Holy City."

Everybody goes home, including David, "to bless his household," but he receives a cold welcome from Michal, who ridicules him for his ostensibly indecent behavior, "uncovering himself" in front of servant girls, "as any vulgar fellow might shamelessly uncover himself." David defends his actions as spiritually appropriate to God's choosing him as king—choosing him instead of Saul, he points out. The narrator ends the incident enigmatically, informing us of Michal's childlessness "to the day of her death." We are left to wonder if the cause of that is her refusal to have sexual relations with the husband she once loved but now finds so repulsive, or David's corresponding rejection—or if it is a punishment from God, who does have a reputation of opening, and closing, wombs.[26] Perhaps the more critical point is that there will be no potential candidate for the throne who comes from both Saul's and David's lines (no son who is both Clinton and Bush, as it were). The narrator has emphasized this aspect by unnecessarily reminding us that Michal is "the daughter of Saul" (6:20, 22). After all, such a child (a son, of course) could claim both Saul's former throne and the dynasty of David (soon to be announced). If Michal's childlessness results from David's sexual repudiation, his abstinence is more political than personal.

In retrospect, the Michal incident functions as a parallel to the Uzzah incident in that both put a damper on David's transfer of the ark—God's wrathful outburst temporarily halts David's plan, denying his control of the ark; Michal's scornful outburst repels David's intended household blessing, denying his exploitation of her as a political pawn. It rained on David's parade two times.

Exaltation—Royal and Divine (Chap. 7)

Very little happens in this chapter in terms of action, but it is easily the most important passage in the Former Prophets to this point, and one might argue to the end. It assumes a sweeping historical perspective that takes in Israel's redemption from Egypt, Israel's covenant with God, the settlement in the land, and the period of the judges. The chapter consists almost entirely of speeches, like other pivotal passages (Joshua 23; 1 Samuel 12). We can summarize what does happen briefly: David says to the prophet Nathan (who appears out of nowhere) that he has a house and God does not. Nathan at first says do what you want, but then over night receives an oracle, the two parts of which take up over half of the chapter. David then goes into the tent sanctuary housing the ark and delivers a lengthy (and rather stilted) prayer of gratitude.[27] The

---

26. As is often the case, the narrative here does not answer such questions; cf. Alter, *Art*, 125.

27. Weinfeld, *Deuteronomic School*, includes this prayer in the genre of the "prophetic oration" typical of the Deuteronomic school (cf. 1 Kgs 8:22–53 [a long prayer indeed!]; 2 Kgs 19:15–19).

narrator makes few comments (vv. 1–2a, 4a, 17–18a), merely introducing the speeches.

The key word throughout the chapter is "house," occurring fifteen times. As in English, the word can denote a royal dynasty or a building, and in Hebrew "house" can refer more specifically to a temple—a "house of God." The multiple meanings provide the wordplay that forms the basis for a theology of the Davidic empire. This text has its companions in Psalms 89 and 132. No other king in Israel's history receives such attention (indeed, no other is mentioned by name in the Psalms, all of which, of course, are ascribed to David), suggesting the critical significance of Nathan's oracle.

David says that he is dwelling in a house, while the "ark of God" dwells in a tent, referring back to 5:11 and 6:17. Nathan infers, no doubt rightly, that David wants to build a house for the ark. His initial encouragement, however, immediately proves to be misguided when he receives a "vision" from God (vv. 4, 17). As we have noted before, the construction of a palace and a temple were the primary visible expressions of a king's victories and sovereignty, and important in establishing the king's political legitimacy.[28] Thus the failure of David to build a temple represents a serious inadequacy. Whatever historical reasons may explain the author's portrayal of God's denial,[29] the present text employs the significance of temple as house in the explanation. God's initial question is "will *you* build me a house for my dwelling?" (AT). The syntax suggests an emphasis on who will be the builder, rather than the act of construction itself. The following lines, however, suggest that the very notion of a house for God (or the ark) is out of the question. "I have not dwelt in a house," says God, "but *I* have been moving about in a tent or tabernacle ever since bringing Israel out of Egypt" (AT).[30] The syntax emphases the second pronoun "I," and the verb is iterative—i.e., suggesting constant motion (also v. 7). God has always been on the move, utterly mobile. God has never asked any previous leaders of Israel for a house, much less one of cedar—i.e., an upscale house, a mansion (cf. 5:11).[31]

We know of a "tent or tabernacle" from numerous other sources. Exodus 25–31 presents God's elaborate instructions for building a sanctuary "so that I

---

28. Miller, *Religion*, 91–92, compares Ugaritic mythology, suggesting that the tent reflects traditions associated with the god El, along with notions of divine assembly and covenant, whereas a temple is associated with Baal's victory and enthronement, itself legitimating the human king of Ugarit. Thus the temple in 1 Kings 8 will be a kind of compromise: a temple but with the ark of the *covenant* inside.

29. Meyers, "David as Temple Builder," argues that, in fact, David's inability to build the temple was connected with the plague that coincided with his census (a story in 2 Samuel 24). The census would have facilitated the employment of forced labor in the construction (cf. 2 Sam 20:24), an unpopular social institution. The coincidence of the plague, interpreted within the story itself as sinful (24:10), would also easily have been "seen as a dramatic message from Yahweh that David should desist from the project that required the levy . . ." (372).

30. The use of the word "house" for the Shiloh sanctuary in 1 Samuel 1 and 3 is either anachronistic or ignored by the author, who is of the "one-God, one-place" party.

31. Polzin, *David*, 76–77, observes that the contrast between mobility and stability extends to David who is no longer a shepherd but a prince (from pasture to house, as it were).

may encamp among them" (25:8 AT). A complementary tradition knows of Moses' "tent of meeting" (Exod 33:7-11). Indeed, the overall climax of the Exodus story is not the liberation from Egypt (chs.1-15) or even the revelation of the law (chs.19-24) but the erection of this tent shrine and the moment when God comes down, represented by a cloud covering the tent of meeting and God's glory filling the tabernacle (chaps. 25-31; 35-40).[32] It is the *movement* of this cloud that guides Israel out of Egypt and through the wilderness to Canaan (Num 9:15-23), sometimes associated with the movement of the ark (Num 10:33-36; cf. 1 Samuel 6).

A tent is not normally fixed to a certain place. It is an inherently moveable dwelling, the best example of which is a tent used for the sport of backpacking (to speak personally). One arrives at a camping site, sets up the tent, spends the night, then the next morning takes the tent down and moves to another site, precisely the movement described in Num 10:11-28. Moreover, the word "tabernacle" (*mishkan*) derives from the verb root *shakan*, which means "to pitch a tent, to encamp," a meaning obscured by translating it as "to dwell."[33] The latter seems the same as the translation for another word, *yashav*, but this word usually has the connotation of *sedentary* living.[34] The oracle in our text says that God is not sedentary by nature. To use colloquial language, God is no "couch potato."

This metaphoric field of camping is rich with theological implications. Coupled with the metaphor of the cloud, the imagery vividly describes God's presence among the people even as it *obscures* that presence visually. Similarly, the verb "encamp" intrinsically implies the action of *decamping*, or "breaking camp," and therefore the possibility that God will *leave* Israel, given the right conditions. Both the visual and the iterative metaphors protect God's transcendence and prevent the possibility of "putting God in a box" (a problem that we saw in the ark narrative in 1 Samuel). The metaphors also provide a graphic means of describing God's absence and God's inscrutability, hence the title of a classic mystical writing, *The Cloud of Unknowing*.[35] The Deuteronomists coined their own way of emphasizing the transcendence of God by talking about God's *name* dwelling in the sanctuary, rather than God's self, a kind of ontological slight-of-hand. Such condescension is precisely what God allows when the two parts of the oracle

---

32. Note how tent and tabernacle, cloud and glory, complement each other here (Exod 40:34). The cloud phenomenon began with the departure from Egypt (13:21-22; 14:19-20) and includes the appearance of God on Mt. Sinai (19:9; 24:12-18). The tabernacle becomes a portable Mt. Sinai. There is a clear allusion to Exod 40:34 in the dedication of the temple under Solomon (1 Kgs 8:10-13), on which see below.

33. The distinction applies more to God's dwelling than Israel's (see the next note also). In v. 10 *shakan* means "to dwell" (NRSV "live"), and permanence is implied.

34. Cross, *Canaanite Myth*, 245-47, explores the distinction, arguing that it "is maintained systematically and consciously" only in later material and is not present here in 7:5-6. Nevertheless, it is "clear that Yahweh was understood to prefer his traditional tent." Note Ps 68:16 where the two words are used in parallel.

35. Here we touch on the apophatic tradition, in which God is ineffable, on which see Lane, *Solace*, ch. 4, especially "The Cloud-Covered Mountain as Apophatic Metaphor," 101-4.

come together in v. 13: "he [Solomon] shall build a house for my name" (cf. Deut 12:5, 11, 21), a prediction that is fulfilled in 1 Kings 8.[36]

In sum, the first part of the oracle says: *You* will not build me a house (temple), for I do not need or want one, being essentially mobile. The obvious question arises: why does God go on to permit *Solomon* to build a temple? But first let's look at the second part of the oracle (vv. 8–12), signaled by "now therefore."

The second part pursues the word play on "house": *You* will not build me a house (temple); *I* will build *you* a house (dynasty). God reviews God's commissioning of David, the shepherd boy, to be "prince over my people Israel" (1 Sam 16:11; 13:14). God has always been with David, defeating his enemies, and God will "give you rest from all your enemies." God's people will therefore live in security. Then comes the dynastic promise: God will "raise up" David's offspring" and "establish his kingdom." "He shall build a house for my name, and I will establish the throne of his kingdom forever." The constellation of "raise up" (or "confirm"), "establish," and "forever," occurs repeatedly to the end of the chapter. The dynastic language here ties in with that used in the oracle about the house of Eli being replaced by the "sure house" of Zadok at the beginning of 1 Samuel (2:35). Once that replacement is complete (1 Kgs 2:27, 35), the ideal priest and king will be in place. David's dynasty will be "the establishment," indeed.

Now the details: God will be a father to the king, and the king, a son to God. This paternal/filial relationship was typical of other ancient notions of monarchy, and appears in even more grandiose terms in Ps 2:7 and 89:26. Moreover, God will punish the king "when he commits iniquity," "with blows inflicted by human beings" as God's agents, but, God says, "My loyalty will not turn away from him, as I turned it away from Saul, whom I turned away from before you" (AT). Here again is that charged word *ḥesed*, often translated by "steadfast love," and meaning loyalty, allegiance, faithfulness, or commitment. And here the stark difference between Saul and David, already manifest in many ways, is summarized in its strongest terms—with all its unfairness. Saul *might* have founded a dynasty (1 Sam 13:13), but God annulled it. Until now, the dynastic nature of David's monarchy was, at best, implied; here it is stated in no uncertain terms. David's will not be annulled, under *any* conditions—disciplined, yes, but never destroyed. "Your house and your kingdom shall be made sure forever before me; your throne shall be established forever."

There is no really satisfactory answer to the question of why David and not Saul.[37] As we have already seen in 1 Samuel, the reasons for Saul's rejection seemed almost contrived rather than substantial, both instances involving

---

36. Including another possibility that God will be "boxed in." The key lines there are "The Lord has said that he would dwell in thick darkness. I have built you an exalted house, a place for you to dwell in forever" (vv. 12–13). See the discussion on 1 Kings 8.

37. Birch, *1 and 2 Samuel*, 1091, follows Fretheim in arguing that God had learned from the experiment with Saul that a conditional kingship did not work.

alleged disobedience to the authority of the prophet Samuel—and a rather *authoritarian* prophet at that. God did not reject Saul, for example, because he massacred the priests at Nob, but because he failed to slaughter King Agag at the right time. Similarly, God had David anointed and now has confirmed his dynastic succession despite numerous examples of David's moral faults: lying, marauding, extorting, and—above all—his own massacring of innocent men, women, and children (1 Sam 27:8–12). In the end God was against Saul (remember that "evil spirit") and *for* David, who will later presume to say "the spirit of the Lord speaks through me" (2 Sam 23:2). God's "for" and "against" have no rational or moral explanation. Moreover, the dynastic promise explicitly rules out annulment, even when the king "commits iniquity" (v. 14). Psalm 89 refers to this promise as God's "covenant" with David, and reiterates its unconditional nature in even stronger terms: the Davidic kings may break the law, disobey ordinances, violate statutes, and not keep God's commandments, and for this God will punish them, but God will never withdraw God's *ḥesed* or "violate" the covenant (vv. 30–34). Samuel must be rolling over in the grave to which he returned after confirming just the opposite to Saul (1 Samuel 28).

Nathan's oracle presents as radical a change for God as it is for human leadership. God is compromising God's mobility—with all the risks for God's transcendence—just as God is compromising in appointing an *eternal dynastic* monarchy—with all the risks for God's sovereignty and for justice in Israelite society (cf. 1 Sam 8:11–18). Nevertheless, there is a reward for these risks, and it is the flip side of the monarchical coin that we examined at 1 Samuel 8, the potential *benefits* of dynastic stability not just for David and his house, but also for all Israel. A permanent institution of government can, in fact, be a good thing, as we outlined in discussing 1 Samuel 8. A *standing* army can provide military security more efficiently than a spontaneous militia; a *centralized* administration can do things collectively that local communities cannot accomplish on their own, including the execution of justice; an *eternal* promise from God can provide far more assurance than serendipitous movements of the Spirit.[38]

God's unilateral and unconditional covenant with David and David's successors seems to stand in stark opposition to the Deuteronomic covenant theology that has informed the Former Prophets up to this point. We need only remember how the book of Joshua began with God's stern admonishment for him to "act in accordance with all the law that my servant Moses commanded you" (1:7), turning neither to the right nor the left, and Joshua's own admonition of the same point in his farewell address, warning that if the people disobeyed God, God would destroy them, and they would perish from the land (Josh 23:16). Indeed, the Mosaic covenant is bilateral and conditional: depending on the people's pledge of allegiance and on

---

38. Even Polzin, *David*, 78, who constantly condemns the monarchy as Israel's fatal error, can say regarding "royal house and divine temple ... that the building up of both will have a stabilizing effect upon the nation," providing "permanence and continuity."

their obedience to the commandments, promising rewards (blessings) for obedience, and punishment (curses) for disobedience, and the consequences are ultimate—"life and death" (Deut 30:19). In short, the ultimate punishment is *capital* punishment.

Yet most scholars agree that much of Nathan's oracle comes from the Deuteronomic editors. Much as they held to the covenant theology of their constitutional document (Deuteronomy), nevertheless they had to come to terms with the unconditional Davidic covenant, just as they had to come to terms with the origin of the monarchy itself. The Deuteronomic (or Sinaitic) covenant often mirrors international treaties of the ancient Near East (see Excursus 1); the Davidic covenant resembles another type of document in which a king grants land and/or dynasty as reciprocation for the service of a subordinate vassal. In one such treaty, the grantor says to the grantee: "After you, your son and grandson will possess it, nobody will take it away from them. If one of your descendants sins . . . , the king will prosecute him at his court . . . . But nobody will take away from the descendant of Ulmi-Teshup *either his house or his land* in order to give it to a descendant of someone else."[39] The Deuteronomists, in effect, blended the two covenant traditions (Sinaitic and Davidic). They accomplished that in numerous ways, such as including the "law of the king" in Deuteronomy itself (17:14–20), where the king receives the same kind of admonishment as did Joshua, "*so that* he *and his descendants* may reign long over his kingdom in Israel" (though not forever!). In the end, the editors faced several historical facts: Saul's monarchy failed and he was killed; David's monarchy flourished (despite David's faults) and, even at the bitter end of the Former Prophets, a Davidic king remained (however humiliated). Their task was to explain these facts given the stories at hand, in the context of the Mosaic and Davidic covenants.

Why, then, does God allow Solomon to build the temple and not David? The answer turns on the complicated literary history of this chapter. McCarter suggests a three-stage development in which portions originating in the Solomonic court were reinterpreted, finally within the Deuteronomic perspective.[40] Originally, God responded favorably to David's suggestion of a house, reciprocating with God's provision of a house (dynasty) to David. But David was not able to fulfill his wish because he was preoccupied with securing the "rest" from Israel's enemies that God had promised (7:11; cf. especially 1 Kgs 5:3). In the second stage, God criticizes David's request on the grounds of freedom of mobility (vv. 5–7). Only God is capable of building a house, making David's suggestion presumptuous, "an act of royal supererogation."[41] Here God's promise of a dynasty comes as a kind of defiance of David's presumption. In the third stage, Solomon became the authorized builder of the temple, a fulfillment of God's ancient promise to Moses (Deut

---

39. Weinfeld, *Deuteronomic School*, 79 (his italics; proper name transliterated here). See also McCarter, *II Samuel*, 207–8.

40. McCarter, *II Samuel*, 224–31.
41. Ibid., 225.

12:5). David was not at the right place *at the right time*; Solomon was both.

For the Deuteronomists, 2 Samuel 7 is a watershed in Israel's history and a crucial mid-point in the Former Prophets. The provision of rest from enemies, of a central place of worship, and of a stable government that eliminates the danger of anarchy (Judges 17–21), follows a trajectory from God's promises to Moses to Nathan's oracle to David.[42] Thus all of Deuteronomy, Joshua, and Judges lead up to this point, and, as we shall soon see, it will often look like the *high* point in all that follows.

In all of this—the rejection of Saul and favoring of David, the construction of a temple, the warning against national destruction over against the promise of an eternal dynasty—ultimately at stake is no less than the judgment and the grace of God. Israel's history, in fact, is full of characters like David who in some way received God's blessing *despite* their moral failures, a prime example being the eponymous ancestor Jacob, the scoundrel whose new name—Israel—gave the people their identity.[43] Moreover, the Deuteronomic understanding of Israel's election was rooted not in any national merit but in the sheer love of God: "it was not because you were more numerous than any other people that the Lord set his heart on you and chose you . . . ; it was because the Lord loved you" (Deut 7:7–8a; cf. 9:1–5). God loved you because God loved you. That is a succinct expression of grace, and, if we read on in v. 8, Moses says "*and* kept the oath that he swore to your ancestors," i.e., the ancestors in Genesis. That oath has striking similarities to the promise to David: unconditional, unilateral, and eternal,[44] yet just before this passage Moses had warned that God "will destroy you quickly" for disobedience. So the Deuteronomic view of Israel's election incorporates *both* types of covenant theology: conditional and unconditional, unilateral and multilateral, finite and eternal, within an uneasy tension, which will seem to come almost to the breaking point by the end. Can God's "*steadfast* love" be downcast instead?[45]

The tension between God's judgment and God's grace or mercy is hardly limited to our current discussion. All generations of the faithful, especially in Western religious traditions, have had to struggle with it, on both a personal level and a political level. The danger in unconditional love is a "cheap grace" that God bestows without any human

---

42. Cf. ibid., 217–18.

43. Jacob receives God's blessing immediately after deceiving his father and cheating his brother out of the family birthright (Genesis 27–28). Both Jewish and Christian tradition continued this emphasis on grace. A Rabbinic Midrash on Exod 33:19 tells of a treasure beyond merit on which those who *have* no merits can rely, because God says "I will show mercy on whom I will show mercy." St. Paul says "while we were enemies we were reconciled to God" (Rom 5:10). As Alter, *Art*, 117, observes, "there is often a tension, sometimes perhaps even an absolute contradiction, between election and moral character."

44. See Gen 13:15. Abraham had his faults, as well (cf. Gen 12:10–20; 16:1–7).

45. Other texts will seem to take the conditional beyond punishment with the possibility of an annulment such as is ruled out in 2 Sam 7:15–16. Cf. Ps 132:12 and Ps 89:38–51, the latter turning upside down the promises in 89:1–37! We will see the promise of dynasty whittled down as we move into 2 Kings, but whether it is ever annulled within the Former Prophets is highly debatable (see below on 2 Kgs 2:2–4).

responsibility (a type of parental love that we call "permissive"). The danger in an unbending judgment is a moralistic God who is a kind of heavenly accountant with no compassion or forgiveness for disobedience (to continue the analogy, the type of discipline meted out by tyrannical parents). Somewhere in between there is a balance ("tough love"). Although Nathan's oracle emphasizes the unconditional and eternal aspects of the covenant with David, the "toughness" is there. Moreover, like the dynastic promise, the punishing sword will be "forever" as well, and it will not take long in coming. As Polzin deftly puts it, "God's permanent love reveals itself as a two-edged sword."[46] Yet the promise to David is that, as radical as the punishment might be, destruction will never become annihilation—literally, a reduction to nothingness. The importance of this promise for subsequent tradition cannot be underestimated. Thus Brueggemann can say that it is "the most crucial theological statement in the Old Testament."[47]

Finally, the political implications of 2 Samuel 7 are no less important than the theological, and, in fact, the two dimensions are inseparable. The movement toward the exaltation of both God and David that we have already seen in chaps. 5–6 comes to fruition here (and, again, in Psalms 2, 89 and 132). The exaltation of the Davidic king appears most clearly in the filial adoption formula: "I will be a father to him, and he shall be a son to me" (7:14). Ps 2:7 adds the metaphor of procreation, and Ps 89:26–27 employs sibling hierarchy in designating the king as "the firstborn, the highest of the kings of the earth." The political correlation of the king's filial exaltation is his victory over enemies—in effect, his universal reign reflects God's universal dominion, and vice versa.[48] Another feature of exaltation is incomparability, again both divine and human. In his thanksgiving, David says "you are great, O Lord God; for there is no one like you, and there is no God besides you," then he says "who is like your people, like Israel?" (8:22–23). Similarly, Ps 89:6, 17 lauds God's incomparability "among the heavenly beings," coupled with Israel's king ("horn") as "exalted."[49] Thus the imperial theology rooted in David's monarchy concentrates enormous power in the king, a power all the more awesome in that the king himself becomes a quasi-divine figure. One immediate result of this royal self-consciousness is David's exalted ego, plainly manifest in his prayer, which combines theological flattery with personal self-aggrandizement. In effect, David moves from gratitude to glorification to grabbing, virtually ordering God to "do what you have promised" and implying that the magnification of *God's* name is now conditional on God's making a great name

---

46. Polzin, *David*, 80–81, also pointing out the similarity to Eli's priestly dynasty (1 Sam 3:13–14). Polzin seems to go too far, however, in suggesting that "God may choose to keep a house in existence *forever* in order that its punishment may be kept in force *forever*" (80, his italics; cf. 127). This sounds like a worthy precedent for hell.

47. Brueggemann, *First and Second Samuel*, 259.

48. Pss 2:8–11; 89:22–23; 132:18.

49. Cf. 2 Sam 2:10b: "exalt the horn of his anointed" (AT).

for David (v. 25, 9). Clearly the possibility exists to realize Lord Acton's famous proverb: "Power tends to corrupt; absolute power corrupts absolutely."[50]

Imperial Enlargement and Largesse (Chaps. 8–10)

> *If Rome was ambivalent about empire, so, too, was America. While the founders worried about creating a too-powerful executive, later artists represented George Washington in imperial, on occasion even godly, garb. By the 19th century, our democratic rhetoric had been coupled with imperial ambitions, as America, like Rome, expanded over large territories.*[51]

The arrangement and chronology of the next three chapters is confusing, and perhaps confused.[52] As noted above, chap. 8 concludes a concentric unit beginning at 5:13. Chapter 9 is the traditional beginning of the "Succession Narrative" that ends in 1 Kgs 2:46, although that title is hardly descriptive. The events in chap. 10 may precede chap. 8 chronologically. In 8:3–4 David defeats King Hadadezer, yet he reappears in 10:16. The same applies to the Ammonites (8:12; 10:6), and to at least some group of Arameans. Moreover, 8:11–14 looks like a summary and conclusion of David's various wars. On the other hand, there are reasons why the canonical order makes sense. One could argue that Hadadezer survives to fight another day, in part because, inexplicably, David refrains from disabling *all* of his chariot horses (8:4).[53] In terms of literary connections, the motif of God's presence with David links 8:6, 14 with 7:9. Also, chap. 10 begins with the same theme as chap. 9—David showing *ḥesed* ("kindness," "loyalty").[54] Similarly, in 10:7 David withdraws from the fighting and stays home, sending Joab and his troops to do the work, foreshadowing the situation reiterated at 11:1. Ultimately, the chronology does not seem crucial to an interpretation of the three chapters.

Together chaps. 8 and 10 describe the expansion of David's realm beyond the unified state of Israel (consisting of North and South) to a full-fledged em-

---

50. Politically, we can compare the unconditional Davidic promise with popular slogans of the 1960's and '70s, "My country, right or wrong," and "love it or leave it," slogans leveled against those critics of American foreign policy in particular (Viet Nam), many of whom rightly saw themselves as acting out of the prophetic tradition of ancient Israel. Similarly, the heretical sound of "God curse America" suggests that God will never do such a thing. See the Introduction and Summary and Conclusion, as well as my study, *Deuteronomy*, 151–53, "Blessing and Curse in America."

51. Klein, "'Ancient Rome & America' in Juxtaposition," W9. One of the artistic depictions of Washington had him wearing horns, probably following portrayals of the king as a "horn" in such texts as 1 Sam 2:10 (NRSV "power").

52. Campbell, *Joshua to Chronicles*, 155, treats chaps. 9–10 as an appendix to the surrounding material.

53. The NRSV of 8:3 ("struck down") might imply killing, but the word does not necessarily mean that (cf. vv. 1–3, 9, translated as "attacked" or "defeated"). The word comes close to our idiom of a military strike.

54. Hanun's bad manners are nothing compared to his eye-gouging father, Nahash, Saul's old enemy. See McCarter, *II Samuel*, 270, and the possible connection with Nahash's son in 17:27.

pire consisting of vassal states. The geographical span is impressive, including the Philistines on the West and all of the major peoples on the East bank of the Jordan, extending north into Syria—no less than five nations. In fact, if David is the subject of the monument restoration in v. 3, he has extended his domain far to the East (the river Euphrates). The Philistines, who dominated all of 1 Samuel, are dismissed as almost incidental in 8:1 (they were virtually eliminated in chap. 5), the rest focusing on the East bank contingents, summarized in v. 12. In some ways, this chapter resembles the annals of Assyrian kings, recounting their imperial aggression (usually in first-personal bombast). Three times David "strikes" military targets (vv. 1–3, AT), defeating his enemies. The conquered rulers bring "tribute" to him, and David seizes the spoils of war—gold, silver, and bronze, along with various weapons. These he "dedicates" (or "consecrates") to God. Some rulers wisely see what's coming and voluntarily acknowledge David's sovereignty, whereby David apparently appropriates vassals formerly loyal to Hadadezer (8:9–10; 10:19). David posts "garrisons" in some of the occupied territories to maintain control.

Chapter 8 in particular seems to fulfill God's promise in 7:11 of eradicating David's enemies, with the narrator twice emphasizing God's protection: "the Lord saved David wherever he went" (vv. 6, 14, AT). Similarly, David "won a name for himself" (8:13), just as God had promised (7:9). Once again, God's support of David entails the horrors of warfare, in particular the terrorist tactic of the arbitrary execution of prisoners (v. 2).[55] In short, chaps. 8 and 10 add to the exaltation of David that we have already traced. Having formed a united monarchy of Judah and Israel, established a capitol, and paraded the sacred ark into the city, David has made significant progress in realizing God's promise of secure territory (7:10), even though there are more enemies to come (already 11:1). Moreover, the narrator describes David not only as a conquering hero, but also as the model administrator of "justice and equity to all his people" (8:15), precisely the role that the ideal king is supposed to play.

Chapters 8 and 10 surround the story of Mephibosheth, Saul's grandson, perhaps suggesting that there is a threat at home potentially equal to that abroad. Chronologically, chap. 9 may belong *after* 21:1–14, where all the remaining sons of Saul are executed *except* Mephibosheth (cf. v. 1 here). Alternatively, chap. 9 could originally have connected with the end of chap. 4 and the death of Saul's son Ishbaal (as well as those in 1 Samuel 31).[56] David might well suspect that Mephibosheth could follow the example of his brother, who was a rival king over several tribes before his assassination. Despite God's nullification of a Saulide dynasty (1 Samuel 13), any surviving male could pose a threat to David's burgeoning empire. If David's

---

55. Cf. Niditch, *War*, 130–31. Rosenberg, "1 and 2 Samuel," 131, notes the irony that David had once sent his parents into the protective care of the Moabites, 1 Sam 22:6!

56. So Gunn, *King David*, 68, followed by Birch, *1 and 2 Samuel*, 1276. Campbell and O'Brien, *Unfolding*, 294a, see three independent traditions on Mephibosheth (adding 19:28). Polzin, *David*, 100, sees ch. 21 as a flashback.

motivation in finding (and controlling) any such survivor is political, he emphatically poses it as a fulfillment to his agreement with Jonathan, that he would never terminate his "faithful love" (ḥesed) to Jonathan's successors (1 Sam 20:15). Three times David repeats his intention to "show kindness (ḥesed) to Jonathan," which is also called "the kindness of God" (vv. 1, 3, 7). When one of Saul's aides, Ziba, informs David that there is, in fact, a son of Jonathan named Mehibosheth, and that he is lame, David has him brought to court. Lest we forget, the narrator emphasizes his family line: "Mephibosheth son of Jonathan son of Saul" (v. 6). Mephibosheth promptly bows down before David and declares himself David's servant. David tells him not to be afraid (he may well be trembling at this point), repeats his pledge of "kindness" to Jonathan, and even promises to restore to Mephibosheth "all the land of your grandfather Saul" (v. 7). The produce of the land will provide for Ziba and Mephibosheth's other servants, but Mephibosheth himself will always eat at David's table, a point made three times, once by David, the others by the narrator (vv. 10, 11, 13). The story contains one ironic phrase, in that Mephibosheth's description of himself as "a dead dog" (v. 8) is precisely the phrase that David had used facetiously of himself in mocking Saul's hostility toward him (1 Sam 24:14). So, on the one hand, the survivor of David's former royal enemy grovels before him like a dog, and a lame one at that; on the other hand, David has acted nobly and faithfully in showing "kindness" to Mephibosheth and welcoming him to "eat continually" at the royal table. Ironically, the image foreshadows how the Former Prophets will end, with *David's* heir, Jehoichin, eating continually at the table of the king of Babylon (2 Kgs 25:29).

The Messianic Murderer (Chaps. 11–12)

> *"I did not have sexual relations with that woman, Ms. Lewinski."*
> —President Bill Clinton
>
> *"What I find interesting is the story of David, and the way in which he fell mightily—fell in very, very significant ways, but then picked up the pieces and built from there."* [57]
> —Mark Sanford, governor of South Carolina, regarding an extramarital affair
>
> *Doonesbury cartoon probably referring to Sanford et al., Aug. 7, 2009: An adulterous senator has come to an address in Washington, D.C. where an "elite conclave" counsels his ilk: "As Senator X lays out his problem. 'What to do about my soulmate's husband?' The family deliberates, evoking their heroes . . . A list that unfortunately includes Hitler and Mao. 'Maybe we should whack him.'" [says one participant]*

The plot of this story is quite simple: David commits adultery, and when the woman becomes pregnant, he has the cuckolded husband murdered, and takes his wife as his own. It is simply astound-

---

57. *Winston Salem Journal*, 27 June 2009, A5.

ing that this story is part of the "court history" of David. More specifically, it is astounding that the editors *included* such a story, and that no one covered up the story sufficiently to prevent its publication.[58] Presumably, no legal action was required under a "freedom of information act." The editors have simply hung up the story on the clothesline that contains so much other dirty linen from Israel's past. Indeed, some of the stories in Judges make this one seem relatively mild. But this story is about David, Israel's ideal king, the one after God's own heart (1 Sam 13:14), the one whose numerous faults largely went unnoticed in 1 Samuel. Never once did a narrator there say that something David did "was evil in the eyes of God" (v. 27b, AT)—even massacre (1 Sam 27:9). But here he is the anointed adulterer, the Messianic murderer.

The story of David, Bathsheba, and Uriah is a gem of Hebrew narrative art.[59] Reported actions are terse (at least one month is telescoped into half a verse—v. 5a); reported speech defines the characters in vivid language that is unintentionally self-deprecatory. The story divides into five parts: an introduction (v. 1); David's adultery with Bathsheba (vv. 2–5); David's attempt to cover up his adultery using Uriah (vv. 6–13); David's collusion with his general, Joab, in the death of Uriah (vv. 14–25); and the conclusion, in which Bathsheba becomes David's wife (vv. 26–27a), and the narrator renders God's displeasure (v. 27b).

The word "send" dominates the story, occurring thirteen times (and frames the following confrontation with Nathan in 12:1, 25). In fact, much of the story consists in the sending and receiving of messages (and messengers)—i.e., "reports" (four times).[60] David is the primary subject of the verb "send" (seven times), but all of the major characters do their sending—except for Uriah, which reflects his role as *object* of the verb and victim. David's constant "sending" reflects his dictatorial power and shields him from the actions. The pregnant Bathsheba apparently cannot personally go to him to announce her condition—she sends; he does not communicate in person with Joab—he sends a letter and Joab sends a messenger; above all, he does not have to witness Uriah's death, much less get his hands bloody. David is like the contemporary CEO of a major corporation—totally inaccessible to anyone who has a complaint. But David's "Teflon" shield will not remain slippery, for the first words of chap. 12 are "the *Lord sent* Nathan" the prophet.

The setting of the story refers back to the Ammonite war when David sent Joab and the army to fight, and stayed home in Jerusalem.[61] "Staying" (NRSV "remain") is another key word (cf. vv. 11–12), here playing on the other meaning of "enthronement." "At the turning of the year, at the time of messengers going out, David sent Joab . . . and David

---

58. Notoriously, the book of Chronicles omits this story.

59. Among many studies, that of Steinberg, *Poetics*, ch. 6, provides a rich analysis particularly of the narrator's reticence and the gaps in the story that produce exquisite ambiguity, on which also see Alter, *Art*, 75–76.

60. For Polzin, *David*, ch. 5, "Messengers" is the unifying theme in all of 11:1—12:31.

61. In 10:17, however, David himself leads the battle.

was staying in Jerusalem" (v. 1).[62] Two temporal clauses lead to David's first sending, but David himself is staying. Throughout the story, David sends and stays. *This* king is not going to war, giant-killer and "man of valor" though he may be (1 Sam 16:18); indeed, the next verse finds him lounging on his roof (the recreational equivalent of our deck or patio), just having finished his afternoon nap.

David looks down at his next-door neighbor's home and sees a beautiful woman taking a bath. Clearly, she was bathing outside, but the extent of her exposure is unknown, much less her thoughts and feelings. David sends someone to find out who she is, which, of course, is defined by the males to whom she "belongs": "Bathsheba, daughter of Eliam, the wife of Uriah the Hittite."[63] "And David sent messengers and took her, and she came to him, and he slept with her (and she was purifying herself from her menstrual impurity), and she returned to her house" (v. 4, AT). The sentence is a model of prose brevity—virtually all verbs, no adjectives. There is widespread disagreement about Bathsheba's role, ranging from a temptress to a victim of rape. The text is ambiguous. For example, it says that David "took her," but also that "she came to him" (v. 4; instead of "he brought her").[64] The NRSV translation "to get her" hides the aggressive character of David's action; in fact, such "taking" was precisely the kind of grasping that the prophet Samuel had warned against (1 Sam 8:10–18; cf. 2 Sam 5:13). A male authority figure automatically has power over anyone, especially women in a patriarchal culture—how much more the king! Such exploitation can easily qualify as rape. On the other hand, her coming to him could imply consensual sex, and we never hear any kind of protest similar to that of Tamar (13:12–13). But Bathsheba is never allowed to speak. In the entire story, the narrator allows her only two words (in Hebrew)—"I am pregnant." Her *name* never is the subject of a verb, only "the woman" or "the wife of Uriah" (vv. 5, 26). From the beginning, her identity is restricted to her social role as daughter, wife or sexual object (if not victim).

The parenthetical phrase referring to Bathsheba's ritual purification means that her menstrual period was over, and therefore that her husband, Uriah (who *did* go out to war), cannot be the father.[65] However, her compliance with ritual rules—with "sanctifying herself" (v. 4, AT)—is juxtaposed with "he slept with her," thus highlighting David's

---

62. Here I follow the MT instead of the LXX ("kings" and "messengers" are quite similar in Hebrew, and "to battle" has no precedent in the MT). So also Fokkelman, *King David*, 50–51 ("envoys"), who notes the connections with the dispatching of agents in 10:2, 4 as well as in ch. 11.

63. "Hittite" simply designates Uriah's geographical ancestry; he is a full Israelite.

64. See Klein, "Bathsheba Revealed," 48–49;

Exum, *Plotted*, 21; Birch, *1 and 2 Samuel*, 1284b–85, 1288–89. Birch offers an extensive and enlightening discussion of interpretations that attempt to "soften the impact of the story." Campbell, *Joshua to Chronicles*, 160, says: "The Hebrew gives no indication of consent whatsoever."

65. While both men and women were required to bathe after having sexual intercourse, and women were required to bathe at the end of their menstrual period (Lev 15:18–19), the significance here involves paternity. Some see the bathing and the cleansing as the same act, e.g., Exum, *Plotted*, 26.

breach of moral law, indeed, one of the Ten Commandments (Deut 5:18). Her announcement prompts more sending by David, in this case, an order to Joab to send Uriah home for a furlough. David assumes that any man who has been away fighting a war will no doubt want to enjoy having sex with his wife when he is home. That will solve David's problem. Uriah must have thought it strange that an ordinary soldier on leave would have an audience with the king, but David's motive is clear. When he tells Uriah to go home and "wash your feet," he probably gives a scurrilous wink, for the phrase usually means just what it says, but "feet" is also a euphemism for penis. Just to be sure, when Uriah "goes out" a present from David "goes out" after him (v. 8, AT). But David has underestimated Uriah. He does not go home and sleep with his wife; he sleeps at David's door, apparently in the servants' quarters!

When David hears of Uriah's refusal, he summons him again for questioning. Uriah's response is pure irony: "the ark and Israel and Judah" are "staying" at the front [66] (while David is "staying" in Jerusalem), and all the other soldiers, even Joab, are "camping in the open field," no doubt eating rations, so how can he go home to wine, dine, and sleep with his wife ("sleep" occurs six times in the story)? We know from elsewhere that Uriah was one of David's elite troops (2 Sam 23:39).[67] Here he is the perfect soldier, scrupulously adhering to the military code of honor that condemns any sexual activity of combatants as taboo, and therefore a threat to God's presence with the troops.[68] Uriah emphasizes his conviction by swearing an oath based on the life of David, the one about to take *Uriah's* life. David tries one more tactic. He tells Uriah to stay another day, and on the next day David treats him to a dinner, plying him with enough wine to get him drunk. Still Uriah refuses to go home to sleep with his wife; instead "he went out to sleep on his bed" (literally, "place of sleeping") at David's door.

The third scene shifts to the battlefront and more of David's sending. Verses 14–15 surely present one of the most outrageous examples of executive tyranny engaged in a totally callous and ruthless act of evil. David sends a letter to Joab "by the hand of Uriah" ordering Uriah's death. Joab is to place Uriah at the front, then have everyone pull back, leaving him alone as a target. The man is

---

66. "Booths" is possible, and intended to parallel "camping," but the place Succoth is more likely.

67. Possibly along with Bathsheba's father, if he is the Eliam in 2 Sam 23:34, which would compound David's treachery even further.

68. Deut 20:9–14. More precisely, the passage says "when you go out (as) a camp against your enemy" (AT), and refers to nocturnal emissions as defiling. From the latter we infer that sexual intercourse would also be defiling, something that before David had carefully prevented among his warriors (1 Sam 21:5). One could argue that a strict, literalistic reading of the ordinance would allow for a soldier *at home from* the war to engage in sex. If that is the case, Uriah's abstinence is all the more conscientious. Although the connection is loose, there is further irony in that other military regulations provide an exemption from military service for a man who has not "taken" his wife, lest he die in battle and another "take" her (Deut 20:7, RSV). Sternberg, *Poetics,* 201–9, raises the possibility that Uriah knows of his wife's infidelity, and the pregnancy, and that his refusal to go home is a silent defiance of the king (and not an ostensible honoring of a military code). Again ambiguity leaves us only speculation.

carrying a contract on his own life and Joab is the hit man (although his hands too will remain unbloodied). Here is the ultimate instance of David's sending and staying—murder by memo. Perhaps realizing that David's scheme will be too obvious, Joab alters the strategy, such that numerous soldiers also die (less suspicious that way).[69] Now it is Joab's turn to send. He dispatches a messenger with the news, and, of course, he has to cover up *his* refusal to follow David's exact strategy, so he instructs him to conclude his casualty report with a footnote about Uriah being among the dead, thus assuaging the king's anger at the body count. An intriguing line in his imagined response from David alludes to the death of Abimelech when the woman threw a millstone on his head (Judg 9:50–55). One wonders if the allusion is an unconscious perception of danger that David is bringing on himself, or an ominous sign from the narrator. As Sternberg artfully presents the analogy: "Warrior King Laid Low by Woman"![70]

The messenger reports to David as instructed, but elaborating rather artfully on the battle scene. He does not wait for David's anticipated anger, however, but proceeds forthwith to the critical point: "your servant Uriah the Hittite is dead also." David's response is far from angry; it equals in cold cruelty his previous dispatch: "Do not let this matter be evil in your eyes, for like this and like that, the sword devours" (v. 25, AT). Soon his words will come home to haunt him.

In the conclusion, "the wife of Uriah" laments for her husband for the appropriate amount of time, after which David sends one last time: "he sent and gathered her to his house and she became his wife, and she bore for him a son" (v. 27a, AT). The use of the word "gather" (NRSV "brought") is strange. Gathering is something one does with crops, fire wood, popular assemblies, or troops, among other things, but not one's bride, a final indication of David's utilitarian attitude toward this woman.

Then comes the narrator's concluding line: "but the matter that David had done *was* evil in the eyes of the Lord" (v. 27b, AT). To David and, presumably, to Joab, the whole incident was not evil, contrary to virtually any standard of morality other than "might makes right." It is no less appalling that this immorality appears in the king who, we were told, "administered justice and equity to all his people" (8:15). Yet he has broken at least three of the Ten Commandments: he has coveted his neighbor's wife, committed adultery, and murdered (Deut 5:17–18, 20). Now it is time for God's sending.

God sends the prophet Nathan to David, and his message is quite different from the euphoric oracle in chap. 7. If anything, it is an illustration of the warning that God will punish the king "with a rod such as mortals use, with blows inflicted by human beings" (7:14, there referring to David's successor). But before Nathan pronounces a new oracle here, and without any introductory remarks, he tells a parable. Stories are "captivating." They draw in the listeners or readers so that they become part of the plot and identify with one

---

69. Sternberg, *Poetics*, 213–14. For feminist readings, see Bal, *Lethal Love*, 10–36.

70. Sternberg, *Poetics*, 221.

or more characters. The story becomes their story (in fact, this process of narrative identity formation stands behind the authority of Scripture itself). We seem to be instinctively sympathetic especially with the underdog in a story, and, conversely, critical of those who take advantage or even harm the underdog. Just so, Nathan's parable captivates David.

It is a simple story of a rich man who is too greedy to take one of his own lambs to provide dinner for a guest, and, instead, takes the lamb of a poor man—indeed, his *only* lamb, and one that is really more "like a daughter" than potential food or even a pet. When David hears the story, he immediately identifies with the poor man, condemns the raw injustice of the rich man's action, and renders a verdict: "the man who has done this is a hellion" (v. 5, AT).[71] David's reaction shows that the story has touched his sense of integrity. However much he has sinned, his "good side" is still intact.[72] Not only has the story captivated David; it also has served as an unwitting self-incrimination. Nathan responds with two words (in Hebrew): "you are the man." Then comes the oracle, preceded by the prophetic messenger formula ("Thus says the Lord").

We have already seen confrontations between a prophet and a king in the stories of Samuel and Saul, whatever we may have thought about the fairness of Samuel's criticism. In a sense, the confrontation between Nathan and David is more exemplary because there is no doubt about David's guilt or the seriousness of his offenses. There will be more such confrontations to come in the Former Prophets, and they are prominent in some of the writing prophets as well.[73] Here is the source for the well-known phrase—"speaking truth to power." Nathan begins with a summary of God's gracious acts on behalf of David, specifically God's protection of him from Saul, giving him Saul's "house" (i.e., what should have been *Saul's* dynasty), and even giving Saul's wives "into your bosom." The last we know nothing of, but it connects with the same phrase in v. 3, and it is possible to read "daughters of Israel and of Judah" instead of "the house of," thus deepening the analogy with the parable (rich man:many lambs // David:many women).[74] After all, we have already heard of David's sizeable harem (5:13)!

Nathan then moves to indictment, first theologically, then morally.[75] David has "despised the word of the Lord to do what is evil in his sight," contrary to David's words to Joab (11:25). He has taken Uriah's wife and murdered him. David's taking stands over against God's

---

73. Isaiah 7–8; Jeremiah 22; Amos 7:10–17.

74. As noted before, it is possible that David took Saul's wife, Ahinoam (1 Sam 14:50). Moreover, we could read v. 8 as entirely referring to women: "I gave you the daughter of your master (Michal; Merab) and the wives of your master into your bosom, and I gave you the daughters of Israel and Judah."

75. The oracle takes the literary form of a "covenant lawsuit;" cf. Hosea 1; Micah 6.

71. Literally "son of death," following McCarter, *II Samuel*, 299 ("a fiend of hell"), who points out that a death sentence would make the punishment of financial reparation in v. 6 impossible!

72. Fokkelman, *King David*, 79. After all, if David was an unconscionable tyrant, he might have responded by saying, "So what? Might makes right."

giving (v. 8; see above on 11:4). The hands that had opened to receive God's gift now are closed in a reckless grasp for power and control.[76] Now comes the verdict ("now therefore," v. 10)—*quid pro quo*. Just as the sword of the Ammonites killed Uriah, so the sword "will never depart" from David's house—"forever." It is a grim and radical qualification of the "forever" dynasty—"forever" punished. Nathan's prophecy resembles the proverbial saying of Jesus that those who live by the sword will die by the sword (Matt 29:52). David's own proverb that the sword devours willy-nilly (v. 25) has already underscored his use of violence in the *abuse* of power. Indeed, much of 2 Samuel illustrates how violence breeds its own vengeance (of course, one could extend this observation to much of Joshua through Judges!). Violence is at the root of much "evil" (or "trouble," "calamity"), so Nathan continues: just as David did "evil," so God will "raise up evil" against him (v. 11, AT; cf. 11:28; 12:9); just as David took Uriah's wife, so God will take David's wives and give them to another man, even from within David's own household, who will "sleep" with them publicly, in contrast to David's sleeping with Bathsheba in secret. The oracle is referring not to public sex acts but to sex acts that are known to the public—as we shall see, specifically his own son Absalom (16:21-22)—and "the sword" will soon find its victims within David's family (ch. 13). More widely, the sword will continually divide Judah from Israel, providing an affirmative answer to Abner's previous question to Joab (2:26). Thus, like the oracle that loomed over the opening of 1 Samuel (2:27-36), Nathan's is a "prophecy after the fact," i.e., a retrospective interpretation of the events that are about to happen. Objectively, there is no obvious direct consequence of David's immoral acts evident in the acts of his family that follow. However, psychologically, one could argue that David's permissive parenting, coupled with children who lack *self*-control as well, led to the family disasters that unfold. David's sexual immorality also provided a poor role model for his sons, especially if we assume that they knew of the Bathsheba affair. But Nathan's perspective, of course, is theological: these events are set in motion by God, who is the ultimate agent behind the sword, the sex, and the evil. Once again, the human characters will seem to act on their own, yet the author of the oracle sees them as fulfilling the will of God ("*I* will raise up trouble;" "*I* will take your wives ... and give them"). Again we can cite the two proverbs-in-tension: "The perverse get what their ways deserve"; "will [God] not repay all according to their deeds?" (Prov 14:14; 24:12).

David responds with an admission of guilt: "I have sinned against the Lord."[77] According to law, both he and Bathsheba would be executed by stoning (Lev 20:10; Deut 22:22)[78]—but that is not what happens, needless to say. Instead, Nathan responds to the con-

---

76. Birch, *1 and 2 Samuel*, 1229, 1293, citing Gunn.

77. David's confession is the setting for the classic Psalm of repentance, Psalm 51.

78. Even if Bathsheba is raped, she would be executed because she did not cry out for help (Deut 22:23-25)!

fession with a kind of pardon: "the Lord has transferred your sin; you shall not die."[79] But in the same breath he repeats David's sin against God and says that David's *child* born to Bathsheba will die. Again, Nathan is not simply predicting what will happen; he is announcing what God will *do*, and in the next line that becomes clear: "The Lord struck the child that Uriah's wife bore to David, and it became very ill" (v. 15b).[80] Here the narrator affirms the truth of Nathan's judgment. David throws himself into an anguished petition for the life of the child, but to no avail. So distraught is he before the death, his servants fear that he might harm himself after the death, but, to their surprise, David abandons the customs of grief, bathes, splashes on some cologne, and changes clothes. When questioned, he says that his anguish was in the hope that God might be "gracious" to him, and when that failed, there was no point in continuing his vigil: "now he is dead; why should I fast?"

The aftermath of David's adultery and murder graphically illustrates once again how God favors him over Saul, but also how dire the consequences of disobedience can be, nevertheless. Like Saul, David has despised the word of God (cf. 1 Sam 15:26), and, indeed, his sins are far greater than those for which Saul was condemned. Like Saul (1 Sam 15:24-26), David confesses his sin, but David himself is pardoned, whereas Saul was not. Nevertheless, the "trouble" that will come upon David, immediately with his dead child, and thereafter with the rest of his family, will sometimes make him *wish* that he were dead (18:33). That God kills the *son* instead of the sinner, is a punishment that we find troubling, to say the least. In fact, later in Israel's history a prophet will announce God's prohibition of precisely this kind of retribution (Ezekiel 18). This problem is simply another aspect of the issue of divine causation that we looked at above. Whatever we may think of that, it is clear that pardoning sin does not mean there are no consequences; here and elsewhere it means that the guilty party will not *die* as a consequence, but the death of a child is surely the most devastating loss that a parent can undergo, and David would not be the last to wish for his own death instead. It is true that David and Bathsheba have a new son, Solomon, whose name is based on the root for "Shalom." But bereaved parents will attest to the agony of a grief so deep that no "replacement" can assuage. Still, the birth of Solomon is the first instance in which God's promise of progeny despite punishment is manifest (7:14-16), and looks forward to the protagonist of 1 Kings 1–11. Nathan's confrontation began with God's sending him, and now concludes with God's sending him again, but with a very different message regarding David's and Bathsheba's new son: "the Lord loved him."[81] We may see the "spin" for *Solomon's* story beginning here; on the other hand, Solomon is the child of adultery and would have been an insignificant character if his father's cover-up had succeeded.

---

79. McCarter's translation, *II Samuel*, 293. The literal meaning is "cause to pass over." Cf. Zech 3:4 ("taken your guilt away").

80. "Strike" here is the same word used for the death of Nabal in 1 Sam 15:38.

81. The alternate name Jedidiah appears only here.

Now we return to the Ammonite war, the progress of which was interrupted by David's affair (vv. 26–31). General Joab conquers the royal city, prudently suggesting that David come and deliver the *coup de grâce* so that David will get the credit. As part of the spoil, David returns home with the golden, bejeweled crown that had adorned the head of the statue of the Ammonite god, Milcom. David drafts the Ammonites into various kinds of manual labor, and returns to Jerusalem. The narrator makes nothing of it, but the king comes home wearing a divine diadem.

Here we may pause to look back and look ahead. In the present, canonical text, the story of David's rise to power stretches from 1 Samuel 16 to 2 Samuel 7, from the shepherd boy who is the runt of his family to the king who unites all the tribes of Israel and founds a dynasty that God promises to last forever. The story as a whole often reveals an apologetic purpose, attempting to show David in the best light possible despite circumstances and actions that, in themselves, might be questionable, if not condemnable. Above all, David succeeds because God is continually with him, making the story at once one of human political skill and providential guidance. As if in fulfillment of God's promise of "rest," chaps. 8–10 show David nearing the peak of his military successes and political power, pausing to relate the Bathsheba incident and Nathan's rebuke, and resuming with the final conquest of the Ammonites and the golden crown (10:6–14; 11:1; 12:26–31). But what a pause that is! The "house" that God promised to David in chap. 7 will become the "house" out of which God raises up trouble, and in which the sword will never cease to rage. Thus, just as Nathan's dynastic oracle in chap. 7 represents the apex of David's rise to power, chaps. 11–12 represent the brink of David's descent into trial and tribulation (chaps. 13–20). One commentator has rightly characterized the rise as "David under the blessing," and the descent as "David under the curse."[82] The narrator has marked the turning point with the trenchant comment in 11:27b: "the thing that David did was evil in the sight of Yahweh" (AT). In some ways, that turn is almost as severe as its counterpart in 1 Samuel 16:13–14, where the "evil spirit" from God turns against Saul, just after the (good) spirit of the Lord had infused David. Of course, God has promised *not* to abandon David as God had abandoned Saul (7:15), but in what follows David will often seem to be Godforsaken indeed.

The Vulgar Valentine: The Rape of Tamar (Chap. 13)

One of the great ironies about the character of David is that the shrewd politician, mighty warrior, and especially the adulterer and murderer, can be *too* "nice." At least when it comes to family dynamics, David shows a stunning lack of parental judgment that deserves the label "permissiveness," creating a model of family dysfunction worthy of, say, a Tennessee Williams play. David is one of those historical figures whose public persona of success and prestige is radically different from his private life, full

---

82. Carlson, *David, the Chosen King*.

of failure and shame.⁸³ The Bathsheba incident simply opened a window into the private life that now spills out uncontrollably. Much of what follows will confirm the judgment of one pastoral theologian: "Probably in no other context of human life does our sinfulness show as clearly as it does in the family."⁸⁴

David's household situation makes the contemporary difficulties of "blended families" seem utterly simple, in that he must manage eight wives and (eventually) eighteen children (See Figure 2).

Figure 2: David's children

David's children (+mother's name):

sons (oldest to youngest):
    Amnon (Ahinoam)
    Chileab* (Abigail)
    Absalom (Maacah)
    Adonijah (Haggith)
    Shephatiah* (Abitai)
    Ithream* (Eglah)
    Solomon (Bathsheba)
       *not acting characters

daughter:
    Tamar (Maacah)

The rape of Tamar by her half-brother, Amnon, and his murder by the vengeful half-brother, Absalom, immediately exhibits the family dysfunction. Already Nathan's warning proves true: there is trouble within David's house, and the sword will never depart from it (12:10–11). This is a story of honor and shame in which the one shamed is the most honorable, and a story of love and hate in which love is distorted into lust or into parental pampering and hate brings desolation and death. It is also yet another story in which men abuse and humiliate a woman. Thus the story of Tamar reflects that of Bathsheba, but here Tamar (a royal princess) will end in despair, unlike Bathsheba, who becomes the queen (and later, the Queen Mother).

The plot of chap. 13 takes place over a five year period. Both the narration and the dialogue emphasize the family relationships with deliberate redundancy (son, brother, sister). Absalom has a beautiful sister named Tamar. Their half-brother, Amnon, loves her (NRSV "fell in love" is overly romantic). In fact, "It was so distressful for Amnon that he became ill" (v. 2, AT). He is literally "love-sick" over her. We soon learn what this means: a sick form of love. He wants to have sex with her, but sees no way "to do anything to her" since she is a virgin. In such a culture, a woman's virginity was absolutely crucial to maintain her honor and marital eligibility (and therefore the honor of her family). A new wife who was found *not* to be a virgin was subject to death by communal stoning (Deut 22:13–21).⁸⁵ The narrator's description

---

83. As the poet W. H. Auden puts it, "Private faces in public places / Are kinder and nicer / Than public faces / In private places." Quoted by Rubin, "Matron for a Nation," W6.

84. Anderson, *Family*, 97.

85. It is appalling to read the legislation on this (cf. the situation of a woman accused of adultery by her husband in Num 5:11–31). If the accusing husband is wrong, he must pay a fine—to the woman's *father*—and the husband may not divorce her, despite what her wishes might be. If he is right, the men of the town will stone her at her parents' front door. Proof is by "evidence of virginity," i.e., a cloth with the woman's vaginal blood stains from her wedding night, apparently carefully secured by the woman and deposited with

of Amnon's frustration already suggests that for him Tamar is simply a sex object that he could *do* something *to*.

But Amnon has a friend, Jonadab, who is "crafty," and he has a solution to the problem. Amnon should *pretend* to be sick,[86] and when David comes to inquire of his condition, have Tamar sent to him to prepare some special "cakes" for him. Then he can pull her into bed and "do to her" exactly what he wants (although Jonadab does not say so explicitly). The ruse is simply a way to get Tamar into Amnon's bedroom (instead of, say, a servant); it does not make any sense in terms of a possible excuse for his behavior, unless, of course, he would claim that the sex was consensual. As for the menu, the request for "cakes" (v. 6) plays on the word root *lbb,* which means "heart" (five times in vv. 6, 8, 10), and the related verb apparently is a derivative that means to bake "heart-shaped cakes."[87] It is as if, in his attempt to "do to" Tamar what he wants, Amnon is asking for Valentine cookies, but he is driven by a vulgar appetite.

The ploy works. David falls for it, not knowing that summoning Tamar will subject her to the same sexual exploitation of which he was guilty with Bathsheba, and by his son against his daughter, no less—*incestuous* rape. Tamar dutifully prepares the Valentine cookies, apparently in Amnon's own kitchen and "in his sight," and presents them to him. But Amnon needs to be alone with her, of course, so he dismisses his servants, and asks Tamar to bring the food into his bedroom. Then he seizes her and says what he wants "to do to her": "Come, lie with me, my sister." "No, my brother," she says, "do not dishonor me, for one does not do this in Israel; do not do this obscene thing" (v. 12, AT). The last phrase has its exact parallel in the story of the rape of the Levite's concubine in Judg 19:23–24 and the rape of Dinah in Gen 34:7.[88] Ironically, such obscenity is also charged against a bride who is *not* a virgin (Deut 22:21).

Part of Tamar's plea further illustrates her status as an object of exchange: she says that her father will "not withhold me from you," if Amnon will but ask. Her suggestion implies that David would be quite willing to ignore the illegitimacy of marriage between half-siblings (Lev 20:17; Deut 27:22).[89] In any event, Amnon would not listen, "and he was stronger than her, and assaulted her, and laid her" (v. 14, AT). The Hebrew of the last two words uses the grammati-

---

her family for just such an occasion. The condemnation of the woman charges her with the same "disgraceful act" that Tamar invokes (v. 12, "anything so disgraceful," AT).

86. The word is the same as in v. 2, but there "made himself ill" (NRSV) is misleading, in that the *pretence* only begins here.

87. The verb also can refer to sensual "encouraging" (Song 4:9; cf. English etymology). See Hackett, "1 and 2 Samuel," 99–100. McCarter, *II Samuel,* 314, reads "hearty dumplings" instead of "cakes."

88. NRSV "do not do this vile thing." The Judges story also uses the same words for "abuse," "obscene thing," and "seize." There the rapists had wanted the male visitor, and declined the offer of the householder's virgin daughter! The word "dishonor" is used here in the same sense as in Deut 21:14 (there of a captive woman). In 13:14 it refers more to the assault than the result.

89. McCarter, *II Samuel,* 323–24 concludes that the prohibition extends to half-siblings, so "the sacrilege in the present text is incest." Birch, *1 and 2 Samuel,* 1304, sees the question of incest as unsettled.

cal direct object marker rather than the usual preposition "with," again emphasizing how she is a mere "sex object" rather than a subject in her own right (hence my use of the vulgar "laid"). The narrator then describes Amnon's post coital feelings in a way that further reveals his utilitarian depravity: "Then Amnon hated her with such great hatred that the hatred with which he hated her was greater than the love with which he loved her" (v. 15a, AT). This is a fairly rare authorial probing of a character's inner feelings, exhibiting remarkable psychological insight. Clearly we should translate the word "love" here as "lust," except that it would not contrast as well with the word "hate." Rape obviously is not compatible with love; it is not even really so much an erotic act as it is an act of power and violence. Furthermore, as Hackett observes, rapists often become enraged after the act because they see their own weakness in their victims.[90] Finally, he dismisses her with cold fury in only two words: "Up! Out!" (AT).

Tamar's response again reflects the cruelty of a patriarchal culture. She says that Amnon's sending her away is worse than the act of rape itself. The reason for this has to do with the way in which she is now not only a rape victim but also no longer marriageable, part of the "shame" that she must bear (v. 12). As we saw above, if she were to marry, and her husband realized that she was not a virgin, she would be executed. In fact, another statute requires that a man who has raped an unengaged virgin must marry her, and is not allowed ever to divorce her (Deut 22:28–31). His only penalty is a monetary fine paid to the woman's father; thus the woman's victimization includes having to be married to her rapist![91] Amnon summons a servant and issues a cold order: "Send that one away and lock the door" (v. 17, AT). Tamar the victim does not even get a personal preposition, much less her name.[92]

Now Absalom enters into the story. Tamar displays her shame and grief in the traditional customs of tearing her clothing (here, a robe distinctive of virgin princesses) and putting ashes on her head. When Absalom sees this, he immediately asks "Has Amnon your brother been with you?" Clearly he implies unwanted sexual advances, and one wonders why he suspects this without hesitation. He then orders her to be resigned to her plight in a way that again typifies rape victims, especially within a family: "Keep quiet; after all, he's your brother; don't worry about it" (my paraphrase). Apparently his advice is intended to be comforting, but it also reveals an inability truly to understand the depth of despair in a rape victim. In fact, the last we hear of Tamar is in the next line: she becomes a recluse in Absalom's house, "a desolate woman."

When David learns what has happened, he is angry, "but he would not punish his son Amnon, because he

90. Hackett, "1 and 2 Samuel," 100.

91. This law does not refer to siblings, but it is interesting that David does not apply it to Absalom (see below), although, again, Tamar would not relish marriage with the rapist who hates her.

92. Once again we can compare the words of President Bill Clinton in his public declaration of innocence: "I did not have sexual relations with that woman, Ms. Lewinski," although at least he calls her a woman and uses her name.

loved him, for he was his firstborn" (v. 21).[93] The administrative leniency that David exhibited with Joab (3:26–39) now extends to his family. The cultural privileges of the firstborn (e.g., property inheritance and, in royal circles, succession to the throne), here extends to amnesty from immoral and criminal acts. Clearly, David is no practitioner of parental "tough love" and his favoritism for the sexual abuser precludes any justice for the abused. The rapist gets off scot-free while the victim's life is ruined forever. Such parental bias typically exacerbates sibling rivalries, and so it is with Absalom, who seethes in silent anger against Amnon. Again, a twisted "love" has produced hate (v. 22).

Absalom is unwilling to follow his advice of resignation to Tamar. For some reason he waits two years for revenge, but then plots with his servants to murder Amnon (vv. 23–29). The occasion is a sheepshearing party, to which Absalom invites "all the king's sons" and David himself, but David declines (he doesn't want to be a burden!). Absalom prepares "a feast like a king's feast," then orders his servants to watch for "when Amnon's heart is merry with wine," and, on signal, to kill him, which they promptly do. Much of this sounds very similar to the story of Nabal (Abigail's "Fool" of a husband) in 1 Sam 25:7, 11, 36, although there the host is the one who dies. Perhaps there is an allusion to Nabal's death in that the "obscene thing" that Amnon does is literally "foolishness" (v. 12, AT). As Proverbs says, "the iniquities of the wicked ensnare them ... and because of their great folly they are lost" (5:22–23).

Apparently the rest of David's sons fear that they will be lost as well, if Amnon's murder is only the beginning of a political bloodbath, so they immediately mount up on their mules and flee. Scarcely have they left when their fear becomes a rumor—"that Absalom had killed all the king's sons" (v. 30). Now David is the one to tear his clothes in grief until Jonadab reappears, last seen prompting Amnon's folly. Jonadab assures David that, in fact, it is only Amnon who was murdered, and that Absalom had been planning the deed ever since Tamar's rape. The formerly "crafty" friend now proves callous. That Absalom's simmering rage is news to David suggests again how out of touch he is as a parent. But, says Jonadab, the king should "not take it to heart"—the same advice that Absalom gave Tamar (vv. 33, 20). One wonders if, in fact, Jonadab (who apparently was *not* at the party) was the one to spread the rumor as a devious way of dampening David's reaction to Amnon's death—after all, only one out of so many, what a relief! Scarcely have the words left his mouth when all the king's sons ride up on their mules and *everyone* weeps over Amnon (except, no doubt, Tamar). There is some redundancy and confusion in the closing verses (37–39).[94]

---

93. The last part of the verse is missing in the Hebrew text but in the Greek and Qumran manuscripts, a glaring instance of textual error with significant interpretive consequences. Cf. also v. 27 regarding Absalom's feast.

94. Absalom's flight appears three times in vv. 34–38. Verse 39 requires textual emendation. I am following McCarter here (*II Samuel*, 329, 335), whose reading is based primarily on the Qumran text. One can read v. 39 just the opposite, however: "David longed intensely to march out

David mourns Amnon "day after day." Meanwhile, Absalom flees to his maternal grandfather in Geshur. By the end of three years, David is "consoled over the death of Amnon," the fraternal rapist, and his hostile feelings for Absalom are spent. Time seems to heal the wounds, but trouble is still brewing, and the sword is still thirsty.

The Return of the Prodigal (Chap. 14)

Joab sees David's yearning for Absalom, and now devises a scheme for Absalom's return. The narrator does not tell us Joab's motivation. It could be his concern that David is too preoccupied with his family troubles to perform his royal tasks adequately. If we follow the analogy of the story that Joab invents, he is even more concerned that Absalom will lose his standing as first in line to succeed David to the throne.[95] But whence such concern over Absalom? Joab will soon have reason to doubt the wisdom of his scheme. In fact, wisdom (and the lack thereof) is a prominent feature of this incident.

Instead of approaching David directly, Joab solicits a "wise woman" to relay his message. Apparently her wisdom consists not so much in judgment as in an artful skill at weaving a story against Absalom" (Fokkelman, *King David*, 126, following K. Jongeling). Thus Joab's trick in ch. 14 either persuades David to take the next step, having resolved his hostility, or to do just that—and welcome Absalom home. As McCarter points out, if David is already yearning for Absalom, why would Joab need to invent his little parable?

convincingly, as well as a combination of boldness and tactfulness in addressing the king. We hear only the beginning of Joab's own invention, and then her version when she comes before David. Presumably she is appealing to David in his royal role as the arbiter of justice.[96]

"Save me," she begs (v. 4, AT), then launches into her tale of woe. She is a widow, one of whose sons has killed the other, and the family is seeking the life of the murderer in accordance with the custom of blood vengeance (Deut 19:11–13; Num 35:16–21). But if her second son dies, she will be left with no children, and her deceased husband will have no son to carry on his name.[97] Yet the family insists, even if they must "destroy the heir as well" (v. 7).[98] She is also not above flattery, praising David as "like the angel of God, discerning good and evil" (v. 17).[99] David tells the woman to go home, and he will "give orders concerning you." But before she leaves she vows to take on herself any guilt that might otherwise accrue to David and his throne (after all, she's asking him to break the law; see below). Again David reassures her of his protection, and again she persists, asking David to swear on the Bible (as it were), and he does so.

---

95. Although he would be behind David's second son, Chileab, we hear nothing of the latter other than his birth order (3:3).

96. Cf. 8:15; Ps 72:1–2, 12–14; 1 Kgs 3:16–28.

97. For the importance of this, see Deut 25:5–10, and our previous reading of Ruth 4.

98. Probably vv. 15–17 belong after v. 7, thus McCarter, *II Samuel*, 335–36; Birch, *1 and 2 Samuel*, 1313.

99. The association between wisdom, divinity, and discerning between good and evil appears in Gen 2:17; 3:5–6, 22. Cf. 1 Kgs 3:9. Cf. also v. 17; Ps 8:5 attributes angelic-like status to all human beings.

But the woman is not finished. In fact, only now does she get to the *real* story behind her tale. She asks permission to speak openly, and when David grants it, she draws a direct analogy between her tale and what has happened with Absalom. "Why then have you planned such a thing against the people of God?" she asks. Then she accuses David of convicting himself, inasmuch as he has not brought the banished Absalom home. David has jumped to defend her son, the fratricide, but refuses to be reconciled to Absalom, *his* family's fratricide. At this point, the woman's story functions much as did Nathan's parable in chap. 12; she could easily say "you are the man."

It is not clear how David has acted "against the people of God."[100] Somehow banishing Absalom puts the realm at risk. Possibly, she is referring to this when she says "the people have made me afraid." Of course, analogies tend to break down at some point, and hers does in that David still has *many* sons, not just one. At this point David suspects Joab's involvement, and when the woman confirms that, she again praises David: "my lord has wisdom like the wisdom of the angel of God to know all things that are on the earth." The wise woman presumes to know a wise man when she sees one, and her flattery approaches divinization (perhaps David is wearing that captured deity's crown [12:30]). But we recall that the last person to make such an angelic analogy was dead wrong (Achish, 1 Sam 29:9). We have to wonder just how wise David has been so far in his parenting skills (not to mention philandering skills). Moreover, the wisdom of reconciling to Absalom without any negative repercussions for his crime is not obvious (and will prove less so quite soon). Ironically, in his familial devotion to Absalom, David is undermining the "family values" that undergird the justice of blood vengeance (whatever we may think of that system). Furthermore, the wise woman's parable makes the case for compassion, but her wisdom does not extend to knowledge of Absalom's volatile personality. As McCarter puts it, "The result of this subordination of the need of the society . . . to the interests of an individual will be a swift unraveling of the social fabric."[101] Nevertheless, David speaks to Joab and grants Absalom's return, which delights Joab to no end since it seems to confirm his favored status as David's chief aide. Little does he know what forces he has set in motion, and what will be required of him to stop them. Soon Absalom is back in Jerusalem, but still ostracized from David's own house.

At this point the narrator describes Absalom's physical beauty, without a freckle from head to toe (like father, like son—1 Sam 16:12). The crown of his attractiveness is a thick head of hair, weigh-

---

100. McCarter, *II Samuel*, 358 suggests a parallel with the parable. Just as David ruled that the family should welcome back the son, so the people should welcome back Absalom, but they cannot do that if he is in exile. More simply, it may be that Absalom is a popular Prince Charming, as he proves to be in the next chapter.

101. *II Samuel*, 351. As he points out (following a suggestion of Conroy), in retrospect, this story will have a mirror image in that of the "wise woman" of Abel in ch. 20, where the interests of society take precedence over that of an individual (the rebel Sheba).

ing no less than six pounds at its annual cutting. Perhaps the length of time explains not only the length of hair but the depth of Absalom's vanity. Though incidental here, this anatomical feature will figure prominently in Absalom's fate, and it will *not* be beautiful (18:9). We also learn of Absalom's own family, including a daughter named for none other than his desolate sister, Tamar. She inherits the family genes: "she too was a beautiful woman."

Two years pass with no meeting of father and son, and Absalom grows impatient. He tries to have Joab serve as mediator, and when Joab is unresponsive, Absalom has his servants set fire to Joab's field, and that *does* get Joab's attention. Perhaps at this point *Joab* is questioning the wisdom of Absalom's return. Absalom says that he might as well still be in exile, and he wants to meet with David no matter what happens: "if there is guilt in me, let him kill me." But the father who would not punish one son for rape will also not punish the other for murder. Absalom comes to court, prostrating himself in front of his father, and David welcomes the prodigal home with a kiss (cf. Luke 15:20!). He doesn't even slap his hand.

The Unrepentant Prodigal (Chap. 15)

I have sometimes wished that Jesus had told a sequel to the parable of the prodigal son in which the son reverted to his old ways or worse: perhaps it could be the Parable of the Recidivist Son. Would his father welcome him home the *second* time? No sooner has David kissed Absalom, welcoming him home, than Absalom turns around and plans a revolution, and it is four years in the making. His tactics include adopting the trappings of royalty, claiming the legal high ground, populist campaigning, and a public rally. First Absalom acquires a chariot and fifty men to run in front of it, doing what Samuel warned the king would do (1 Sam 8:11). It's something like a contemporary motorcade complete with a limousine (flags waving) led by a phalanx of motorcycle cops. Now he "looks Presidential," to pursue the analogy. More significantly, he claims that he would make a better "judge" than his father in administering justice. Early every morning Absalom parks himself at the city gate, in effect the courtroom where justice was arbitrated.[102] Here people would bring their law suits for a decision by a judge, who would ultimately be under the authority of the king. Absalom imposes himself, asking everyone where they are from, and declaring their "claims are good and right," but "there is no one deputed by the king to hear you." "If only *I* were judge in the land!" he exclaims. One could question his impartiality, however, because if every legal claim is "good and right," it sounds like Absalom is more interested in gaining supporters than determining justice (in fact, we could translate the last word in v. 4 as "I would *declare* him right;" contrast Deut 25:1). That impression deepens when we see Absalom glad-handing everyone, declining their genuflections as royal subjects, even as he is plotting to be the king. He doesn't just kiss babies—

---

102. Ruth 4:1–6; 1 Sam 4:12–18; 2 Sam 19:8; Amos 5:10–15.

he kisses everyone! So, the narrator tells us, "Absalom stole the hearts of the people of Israel."

Clearly Absalom is playing the populist for his own advantage, but is his criticism of the judicial system groundless? Why would he gain a following if what he says about the courts is not true? Were there, in fact, numerous cases in which people felt that their just claims were denied, or not even heard? Did many people not "get their day in court"? In the preceding story, the wise woman gains access not only to a judge but to the king himself, but that is because Joab solicited her help. How would the family in the story feel about David's decision? And if such was David's inclination, how would he rule on other cases? Has the monarchy weakened the previous system of justice? Did David quickly fall into the "ways of the king" criticized in 1 Sam 8:10–18? Absalom would not be the first or last politician to seize on a legitimate issue and turn it into his self-promotional cause. However, the narrator does not answer any of these questions.

Whatever the grounds for Absalom's claims, his intention is obviously seditious, making us wonder in retrospect if his murder of Amnon—then the first in line to the throne—was more than personal revenge. After four years of campaigning, Absalom asks David's permission and blessing for a pilgrimage to the family home at Hebron. He needs to fulfill a vow that he made in Geshur that he would worship the Lord in Hebron if God would bring him back to Jerusalem (v. 8; cf. Gen 28:20–22). Whether or not Absalom has invented this vow on the spot, in intent he is violating the commandment against making wrongful use of God's name (Deut 5:11)—if he's lying, it's a double violation. In the context of what we know from Nathan's judgment oracle in Chap. 12, there is also irony as well; literally his vow is to "serve" God (and Hebron is missing from the MT), which is precisely what his revolt will do, albeit unconsciously.[103] He is headed for the place where David was first proclaimed king of Judah (2:4), so one wonders why David is not suspicious. But, ironically, David sends him off "in Shalom" (v. 9, AT).[104]

Absalom immediately sends "secret messengers [the word also can mean "spies"] throughout all the tribes of Israel," encouraging them to shout "Absalom has become king at Hebron!" when they hear the sound of the trumpet. The logistics of this ploy are unclear, along with the presence of two hundred guests who know nothing of the plot (v. 11).[105] But "sounding the trumpet" can signify the inauguration of a new king, obviously its purpose here.[106] Absalom then adds two key figures to his conspiracy. One is David's advisor, Ahithophel, who probably is the grandfather of Bathsheba, and

103. Halpern, *First Historians*, 233, in the context of his larger discussion on causation (see below).

104. The word resonates with the second part of Absalom's name, as well as the word for "pay" in v. 7.

105. Obviously there is no trumpet loud enough to be heard throughout all Israel! Cf. 1 Sam 13:3, Saul's conscription. Fokkelman, *King David*, 173, suggests a kind of trumpet relay from one city to another. Do Absalom's guests become immediate converts, joining the growing conspiracy in v. 12?

106. At the anointing of a king: 1 Kgs 1:34, 39; 2 Kgs 9:13; 11:14. Note also the association with sacrifices (v. 12, cf. 1 Sam 11:14–15).

may have his own ax to grind.¹⁰⁷ The other, we learn later (17:25), is Amasa, Joab's nephew, who heads Absalom's army.

The King in Flight (15:13—17:29)

> *The true hero is flawed. The true test of a champion is not whether he can triumph, but whether he can overcome obstacles—preferably of his own making—in order to triumph. A hero without a flaw is of no interest to an audience or to the universe, which, after all, is based on conflict and opposition, the irresistible force meeting the unmovable object.*¹⁰⁸

Absalom's revolution gains numerous followers, and David hears of the defecting "hearts" in the same words that the narrator had used (vv. 14, 6). David's personal security force numbers well over six hundred men (v. 18), so Absalom's contingent must be daunting for David to respond immediately with an order to abandon Jerusalem, lest there be no escape.¹⁰⁹ (The curious detail about David leaving behind "ten concubines" to "look after the house" sounds almost comical, but probably was inserted to prepare us for Absalom's exploitation of them in 16:20–23.)¹¹⁰ David exhibits dignity in retreat, however, for he explains his reaction not only as self-protection but also as protection of the inhabitants of Jerusalem (v. 14b). Without him there, Absalom's forces are not likely to attack the city.

The narrative now introduces a series of character vignettes involved in David's retreat (Ittai, Abiathar and Zadok, Hushai, Ziba, and Shimei; 15:19—16:14, marked by italics below). In various ways, these incidents further illustrate David's integrity, faith, and strategic intelligence. The narrator marks the stages geographically moving Eastward—leaving the city behind, crossing the Wadi Kidron, ascending the Mount of Olives, reaching the summit, over the other side, to Bahurim, to the Jordan River valley, crossing the Jordan (17:22), and finally coming to Mahanaim (17:24). More broadly, the retreat itinerary then has a mirror image in David's *recrossing* the Jordan and *returning* to Jerusalem in 19:9—20:2. Since the latter ends with yet another failed revolt, all of chaps. 15–20 have a circular structure.¹¹¹

In David's retreat, he moves from his fortress in the highlands to the lowest place in the world, the "thickets of the Jordan," the opposite of a "safe land" (Jer 12:5); he moves from the city to the "wilderness" (15:28; 16:2), a place "utterly desolate, a veritably impenetrable jungle, inhabited by wild beasts."¹¹² Symbolically, he is moving from security to vulnerabil-

---

107. On the connection see 11:3; 23:34.

108. Stein, *Racing in the Rain*, 135–36.

109. In 18:7 twenty thousand of Absalom's troops are killed. Again, such numbers are often inflated.

110. Editorial activity is suggested by the repeated departure (vv. 16a, 17a).

111. The turning point is Absalom's death and David's grief. Also appearing in reverse order are Shimei, Ziba, and Mephibosheth, and David's hapless concubines.

112. Cohen, "Jordan," in *IDB* 2:976a. Even "the forest of Ephraim" will devour more of Absalom's troops than warfare (18:8).

ity, from pride to humiliation, from royal status to refugee status. Crossing over the Jordan puts him outside the boundary of the land of promise (a kind of reversal of Israel's story in Joshua 3–5), and the root for "cross (over)" appears numerous times.[113] The prodigal Absalom had escaped beyond the Jordan, then returned to Jerusalem; the prodigal's father must now reverse that journey in escaping his son. The boundaries crossed are not only geographical; they are also familial, political, and spiritual. David's journey is a "rite of passage"; in effect, it is his *via dolorosa*.[114]

David abandons the city, followed by all of his entourage, stopping "after the last house" (presumably on the periphery), while all security forces pass by.[115] David encourages one of his security force leaders, Ittai the Gittite, to return to Jerusalem, along with his family. Apparently he is a foreigner who only recently joined David's forces, and David does not want to uproot him again so soon. But Ittai will have none of it; he will go wherever David goes, "whether for death or for life" (a devotion akin to that of Ruth for Naomi, Ruth 1:8–17). Ittai's loyalty will result in his being in charge of one third of David's forces (18:2). The narrator concludes this episode, saying "the whole country wept aloud" as all the army who accompanied David passed by (v. 23).

We can no more take this literally than we could Absalom's acclamation from "all the tribes of Israel" at the sound of the trumpet. Moreover, there is a tension between what seemed to be a mass movement toward Absalom and David's universal support.

David orders the priests, Abiathar and Zadok, to take the ark back to Jerusalem. Probably they have brought the ark because of its association with God's presence in warfare (cf. 1 Samuel 4).[116] But David does not make the same mistake that led to the loss of the ark before. On the contrary, rather than holding on to the ark as a "security blanket," David finds his security in the one who is enthroned above it. "If I find favor in the eyes of the Lord," he says, "God will bring me back," and he will see the ark again in its place. But if not, he says, "let God do to me what seems good to God" (v. 26, AT). There is a humility in David's hope for God's bringing him back that contrasts with the devious manipulation of such a wish with Absalom (v. 8). There is also irony in that Abiathar is the descendant of those priests who did *not* trust in God more than they trusted in the ark. Characteristically, David's deep trust in God does not exclude shrewd efforts of his own: the priests are also to be his spies.

David and company ascend the Mount of Olives, all of them weeping, covering their heads, and walking barefoot. The gestures are those of mourn-

---

113. Three times in 17:16 and 19:18 alone.

114. See the discussion of Joshua 3–5 on rite of passage.

115. Here and elsewhere in this section, NRSV "the people" probably means "the army" (so McCarter, *II Samuel*, 360–61), which is clear in 18:1 (literally "the people who were with him").

116. There is a curious similarity between the movement of the ark here in crossing the Wadi Kidron (a stream bed) and in Josh 3:17, where the priests stand with the ark until the people cross over the Jordan.

ing, shame, and defeat (cf. Jer 14:3–4; Isaiah 20), suggesting the picture of a penitential pilgrimage, or even the departure of exiles. Despite David's concern for Jerusalem and for loyal aides, despite his trust in God instead of the ark, his retreat is an ignominious and painful admission of weakness. Yet again, his honest recognition and public display of this weakness gives him a dignity that ennobles his grief.

In the midst of David's retreat, he learns that Ahithophel has joined the conspiracy, and David prays to God to "turn the counsel of Ahithophel into foolishness," perhaps playing on the meaning of Ahithophel's name, "brother of folly." When David comes to the summit of the Mount, the narrator tells us two things: this is "where God was worshiped," and "Hushai the Archite came to meet him," dressed in the signs of mourning (v. 32). The juxtaposition is an immediate answer to David's prayer, and another of those serendipitous moments in which both God and human beings seem to be inextricably at work. It also illustrates the modern saying, "praise God and pass the ammunition." Hushai, like Ittai, wants to accompany David, but David has a better idea. Hushai will return to Jerusalem and pretend to defect to Absalom, becoming David's undercover spy. So, David says, "you will defeat for me the counsel of Ahithophel" (v. 34), just what David asked *God* to do! Hushai will work along with Zadok, Abiathar, and their sons to relay information to David. The duality of agents (God and Hushai) has a matching pair at the end of the incident: Hushai and Absalom enter Jerusalem at the same moment.

David has now "passed a little beyond the summit" when Ziba, the major domo for Saul's grandson Mephibosheth, appears (see chap. 9) with donkeys for the king's household to ride, and others laden with enough bread and fruit to feed all of the escaping entourage, even a skin of wine "for those to drink who faint in the wilderness." It's like manna from heaven. David asks him "where is your master's son?" (referring to Jonathan). Ziba replies that Mephibosheth "is staying in Jerusalem" (16:3, AT). One could translate "he is enthroned in Jerusalem," and the next words confirm that meaning, for Ziba quotes Mephibosheth as saying "Today the house of Israel will give me back my grandfather's kingdom." Is Ziba's report true, or has he fabricated it? If true, then Mephibosheth is a threat that has already appeared once in the person of Ishbaal (2:8–11), and David could have *two* revolts to contend with. Later (19:24–30) Mephibosheth will challenge Ziba's accusation, but for now David accepts it and immediately makes a royal bequest: "All that belonged to Mephibosheth is now yours," and Ziba bows in gratitude.

David now arrives at Bahurim and undergoes the most humiliating experience of his journey. Shimei, "a man of the family of the house of Saul," comes out fuming and cursing David and his entourage, throwing stones at all of them as if they were condemned criminals:[117] "Go away, go away, you man of blood, you worthless man" (16:7, AT). He

---

117. One could translate "he stoned David and all the servants," since the same phrase is used for capital punishment (e.g., Josh 7:25; Deut 13:11; 17:5).

then upbraids David, saying God "has avenged on you all the blood of the house of Saul, in whose place you have reigned" (AT), and has given the realm over to Absalom. "Look at you," he says, "immersed in your evil, for you are a man of blood" (AT).

It is difficult to say which is more astounding—the brazenness of Shimei or the restraint of David. When Abishai (one of those hothead sons of Zeruiah) says that no such "dead dog" should be allowed to curse the king, and offers to relieve Shimei of his head, David instead rebukes Abishai (cf. 3:39). David then gives a remarkable interpretation of Shimei's verbal abuse. If David's own son is seeking to kill him, surely it is not surprising that this *Benjamite* is throwing stones (referring to Shimei's familial ties to Saul). To this David adds a theological explanation: "let him curse; for the Lord has bidden him." Shimei speaks as a prophet! Verse 7 even begins with "thus says Shimei" (AT), which echoes "thus says the Lord." Indeed, it sounds as if he was privy to Nathan's rebuke of David in 12:10–11. "The Lord has given the kingdom into the hand of your son Absalom," he says, and "disaster has overtaken you," echoing the "disaster" that Nathan had predicted (12:11, AT). Shimei also frames his speech with the phrase "man of blood," reflecting Nathan's prediction that the sword would never depart from David's house (12:10). However, Shimei is not referring to the blood of Uriah; he is referring to "all the blood of the house of Saul, in whose place you have reigned" (16:8, AT). This charge *reverses* Nathan's previous affirmations of God's election of David over Saul (7:8, 15; 12:7–8). In fact, much of the propaganda of the story of David's rise was directed against precisely this charge that David had unjustly usurped Saul's throne and collaborated in his death. It is all the more surprising, therefore, that David does not welcome Abishai's offer to silence Shimei by beheading him. Not only does David affirm Shimei's cursing and stone-throwing as divinely inspired, he also seems to receive the blows (both verbal and physical) as a kind of penance: "It may be that the Lord will look on my distress, and the Lord will repay me with good for this cursing of me today." This hope for redemption thus continues the penitential dimension of David's flight. Shimei continues to hound him, running alongside, cursing, "throwing stones and flinging dust at him." No wonder *David and his entourage arrive worn out at the Jordan*, where they are refreshed (16:14).[118]

David is now at the place at which he had told the priests he would await word from them, "at the fords of the wilderness," i.e., on the west bank of the Jordan River (16:28). The narrative now pauses in tracing David's retreat, shifting scenes to Jerusalem and Absalom's deliberations with the two advisors, Ahithophel and Hushai. As planned, Hushai has appeared before Absalom and in effect declared his allegiance to him. Absalom sarcastically asks if this is his loyalty to David, and why did Hushai not go with him. Hushai's response artfully says one

---

118. The word for "weary" is the same for "faint" in v. 2. Apparently the food and wine have run out! The word for "refresh" literally means "re-soul" or "re-animate."

thing literally but quite another figuratively. His initial greeting, "Long live the king!" presumably addresses Absalom but really refers to David. The same applies to his avowal to remain with "the one whom the Lord and his people and all the Israelites have chosen." No doubt Absalom thinks of himself, but Hushai means David, especially the crucial inclusion of *God's* election. Nowhere has even Absalom made such a claim—indeed, his speeches have been devoid of any theological dimension, except for the ruse about his vow (16:8). We know that there is only *one* person whom God has chosen. Nevertheless, Hushai concludes with a straightforward commitment to Absalom.

Absalom now turns to Ahithophel and asks for his advice. Ahithophel makes two recommendations. The first is that Absalom proceed forthwith to the king's harem and have sexual intercourse with those concubines who were left behind, and to do this publicly, in a tent set up on the roof. The move is as subversive politically as it is abusive personally—in effect, a claim to David's realm (cf. 3:7; 12:8). The act is also a fulfillment of Nathan's oracle of punishment in 12:11. *There* the agency of the incident is attributed to God (12:11–12); here it is the advice of Ahithophel (cf. below on Hushai). How ironic then when the narrator says that Ahithophel's counsel was highly esteemed, "as if one consulted the oracle [word] of God" (v. 23). As far as we know, *Ahithophel* has not made such a consultation, but, unknowingly, he has repeated God's word uttered by the *prophet*, thereby also making Absalom the agent of the "evil" God will raise up (12:11). God has not chosen Absalom to be king, but Ahithophel's advice appoints Absalom as the rod of God's anger (Isa 10:5).

Absalom wastes no time in carrying out Ahithophel's first suggestion. The second shifts from a symbolic subversion of the king to assassinating the king. Ahithophel suggests a strategy that confirms his reputation. Surprisingly, he volunteers to lead a strike force of twelve thousand men immediately ("tonight"), overtake David and his entourage, throw them into a panic, and when everyone flees, "strike down only the king" (v. 2). Ahithophel will then return to Jerusalem, bringing all of David's followers with him, "as a bride comes home to her husband," and everyone will be happy ("at peace"). Absalom and the elders of Israel are pleased with the advice.

But Absalom now summons Hushai, tells him Ahithophel's plan, and asks for his opinion. Hushai respectfully disagrees with the renowned advisor. Instead of finding a weak David, they will find the legendary warrior who is "enraged, like a bear robbed of her cubs." Moreover, David is too shrewd to spend the night bivouacking with the troops, but will find a separate hiding place, making it difficult to take him out all alone. That means that a battle is inevitable, and when some of Absalom's forces fall, the others will "melt with fear." So, says Hushai, Absalom should hold off on pursuing David until he can amass a much larger army, "like the sand by the sea for multitude," and then Absalom himself should lead the attack. Then they (Hushai includes himself) will kill both David and those with him. Even if

David retreats to a city, then "all Israel will bring ropes" and drag the whole town into the valley.

Absalom and his followers find Hushai's suggestion better than Ahithophel's. Perhaps they are persuaded by the hyperbolic metaphors. They could well be intimidated by the picture of David as an enraged mother bear, his mighty warriors slaughtering Absalom's troops, who (like Israel's traditional enemies) melt in fear.[119] They also do not see the irony in Hushai's metaphors. The rebels will be like the sand of the seashore in number, but elsewhere the image is used for the enemies whom Israel has defeated.[120] The rebels will fall on David "as the dew falls on the ground," but one could take that metaphor to suggest gentleness![121] The rebels will kill everyone with David, but that would be a massacre certain to evoke precisely the opposite of Ahithophel's plan. Finally, dragging an entire city away with ropes is a ludicrous image appealing to Herculean bravado. The entire plan, of course, is to allow David time to escape beyond the Jordan River, and Absalom falls for it.

Again a single verse juxtaposes divine and human co-operation—Hushai's counsel and God's ordering of the events: "'the counsel of Hushai is better'. . . and Yahweh ordered the good counsel of Ahithophel to be disdained, so that Yahweh might bring evil to Absalom" (v. 14, AT). The NRSV "*for* the Lord had ordained" simply interprets the all-purpose "and," but here "and" suggests more clearly that, in the view of the narrator, the events are a *conjunction* of human and divine purpose. Such explicit commentary by the narrator is surprisingly rare. We have already seen examples of similar involvement by God in the stories of Samson and of Eli & Sons (Judg 14; 1 Sam 2:25). Here is a refined theology of history. God guides the events of the story providentially, but not in a way that one could describe as "divine intervention." God doesn't appear in a theophany (e.g., Josh 5:13-15), speak through an oracle (2:1), or a prophet (chap. 12). God doesn't send thunderbolts (1 Sam 7:10), strike the enemy (5:24), send anyone into a panic (Judg 4:14), or even into a "deep sleep" (1 Sam 26:12).[122] One could remove the narrator's brief reference to God and nothing in the surrounding story would need to be changed. It would seem that human wisdom (Hushai's) determines the course of events. God does not operate unilaterally, and the characters *seem* to operate independently, but somehow human actions and divine intent are mutual. The characters (including God) *co*-operate, suggesting a subtle understanding of action and agent. Hushai

---

119. Exod 15:15; Josh 2:11; 5:1.

120. Josh 11:4; Judg 7:12; 1 Sam 13:5.

121. Cf. the words in "Morning Has Broken": "Sweet the rain's new fall, Sunlit from heaven, Like the first dewfall, On the first grass." Cf. also Deut 32:2; Ps 133:3 (about people living together harmoniously!); Prov 19:12 (contrasted to a king's anger).

122. An exception in close proximity to 12:24b is 12:15, where God strikes dead the first child of David and Bathsheba. This is the only time within chaps. 9-20 that God is said to act directly, but even here the author may have "complementary causation" in mind in terms of illness (cf. Halpern, *First Historians*, 245, and 1 Kgs 14:1-16). More generally, see his discussion on the miraculous (246-54), and the detailed list of divine actions in Figure 19 (254-63).

does not consult with God, but Hushai's words are in tune with God's word, not the highly esteemed Ahithophel's (16:23). One could almost describe such narration as "secular," but only in comparison to such direct interventions as mentioned above. In many ways, therefore, the story here resembles the book of Ruth, where, as we have seen, God does not act in any observable way to advance the plot of the story. As a result, the "world" of the story bears a remarkable resemblance to our own.[123]

In some ways, the next section in the story of David's escape (17:15–29) seems inconsistent with Absalom's decision to follow Hushai's plan. Presumably, Absalom was to take his time in mustering a huge military force, but Hushai sends word via his priestly collaborators that David must immediately cross the Jordan, lest he be "swallowed up" by Absalom's forces. The syntax of v. 17 ("used to go") suggests ongoing spy activity, but apparently the entire escape story takes place within less than twenty-four hours.[124] Similarly, here a "servant-girl" brings word from Zadok to relay to Jonathan and Ahimaaz, who "could not risk being seen entering the city" (Jerusalem), which fits with Absalom's pursuit of them, but in 15:27–28 the priests are in Jerusalem, apparently feigning neutrality. The priestly brothers tell David to "cross the water quickly," because Ahithophel has counseled immediate pursuit. On the other hand, David arrives at Mahanaim just as Absalom is crossing the Jordan, suggesting a sizeable lead of some twenty miles. Presumably, the haste is to give David as much lead as possible.

In any event, David makes his escape, aided, in part, by the collusion of a woman in Bahurim whose protection of the priestly spies reminds us of Rahab in Joshua 2. Another scene shift takes us back to Jerusalem, and the despondent Ahithophel, the esteemed counselor, who, on learning of his failure, hangs himself.[125] Another shift, and David arrives at Mahanaim, we hear of Amasa's appointment as Absalom's chief-of-staff,

---

123. There has been much discussion of the key texts (another will be at 1 Kgs 12:15). For a brief overview, see Gunn, *King David*, 108–10 ("Providence"). We have touched on the notion of co-operation before regarding Hannah, Saul, and David. My reading is very similar to Halpern, *First Historians*, 232–35, who uses the phrase "complementary causation" (232). In fact, he points out numerous examples throughout the Former Prophets. Historical events are the "products of divine and of human motivation" (232). "Divine and human intention converge from different directions" (233). "Human interests are the agencies of [God's] activity, manipulated in reaction to Israelites' behavior" (233). For a broader application, see Fretheim, *God and World*, 22–26. Birch, *1 and 2 Samuel*, 1366, refers to "the unique combination of divine providence with human personality, through which God has chosen to work." Cf. also Alter, *Art*, 126, 154. Gottwald, *Politics*, 251–52 talks of "the paradox of freedom and determinism" and refers to a phrase of Yehezkel Kaufmann that sounds a lot like that of Halpern: "'the dual causality principle.'" Fokkelman, *King David*, 193, uses the phrase "synergism of Providence and human action" (cf. 187, 191, 205). Calvin and others employed the categories of primary and secondary (or "intermediary") causes, on which see Stroup, *Calvin*, 30–33. Cf. also Linafelt, *Ruth*, xvi–xvii.

124. Presumably we are to think of several exchanges of messages during the process, as in 15:31.

125. Fokkelman, *King David*, 230, points out that Ahithophel dies with dignity, not desperation: he first settles his legal affairs, and after death receives burial "in the tomb of his father" (17:23).

and the rebel forces are "encamped in the land of Gilead." Again back to Mahanaim, where David and his entourage are greeted by three men who provide them with a virtual feast at the end of their long journey, recognizing that "The troops had been hungry and weary and thirsty in the wilderness" (v. 29, AT).[126] Connections between two of these benefactors and Saul's grandson, Mephibosheth, suggest that David is in favor with at least some of his former rival's constituents.[127]

Mahanaim becomes David's base of operations (ch.18). Formerly, it had been Ishbaal's base (2:8), and its history goes back to Jacob, who, on his way home from exile, had encountered angels here at the "camp of God," prayed to God to protect him from his revengeful brother, Esau, and spent a harrowing night nearby wrestling with God (Genesis 32). One wonders if we are to think of the exiled David having this story in mind as he awaits the outcome of even worse family trouble.

---

126. There is no tense in the Hebrew, and, since David has emerged from the wilderness, not still in it, it makes sense to translate in past tense. On the three men see 9:4–5; 10:1–2; 1 Sam 10:27; 2 Sam 19:33; 1 Kgs 2:7.

127. Machir had housed Mephibosheth at one point (9:4), and Barzillai's home is in Gilead, the location of Mephibosheth's fledgling kingdom—he was "king over Gilead, etc." (2:9)—with its capitol in Mahanaim, where Barzillai will continue to send his support for David from his home in Rogelim (19:32).

"O My Son Absalom!" (18:1—19:8)

> *In cities, mutinies; in countries, discord; in palaces, treason; and the bond cracked 'twixt son and father. This villain of mine comes under the prediction; there's son against father: the King falls from bias of nature; there's father against child.*[128]

David musters his troops and divides the leadership three ways, with Joab and brother Abishai, along with Ittai, being in command. But David wants to be the commander-in-chief—to "go out with you." After all, this is how David rose to power and popularity in the first place (1 Sam 18:6–9, 13–16). His troops will have none of it, arguing that, if the rebels spot David, they will go after him alone. Interestingly, the warning echoes the foiled plan of Ahithophel (17:2–3), and, in reverse, that of Hushai (i.e., perhaps to make *Absalom* the target, 17:11). Ironically, it will be Absalom who is caught alone and helpless. Instead, David's troops say, David should remain in the safety of the city and help them from there. David agrees, and stands "at the side of the gate" as the troops march out to battle. As a result, David is not involved in what happens to Absalom, and thus cannot be blamed by Absalom's supporters (a situation similar to his excusal from the battle of Gilboa, 1 Samuel 29). The scene of David standing by the gate reminds us of David's retreat from

---

128. William Shakespeare, *King Lear*, I.ii. 108–10.

Jerusalem, when he stood by as the troops passed in front of him (15:17–18, AT), but now he is on the offensive. Moreover, there is an ironic connection to Absalom's first attempt at subversion, when he "stood at the side of the way of the gate" (15:2, AT). Soon the "gateway" will lead to Absalom's defeat, and then to David's restoration (19:8). As the troops march out, however, David does not give an encouraging speech to the troops worthy of a General Eisenhower before D-Day. Instead, in the hearing of all, he issues an order to his three generals: "Deal gently for my sake with the young man Absalom." Here they are, all about to face the possibility of death because of Absalom's revolt, and David orders them to protect him! It's a tall order, indeed, and will not be heeded, whether or not the generals salute and say, "Yes, Sir."

The narrator tells us that David's forces engage *Israel* in battle "in the forest of *Ephraim*,"[129] and that "the army of *Israel* was defeated there by the servants of David" (v. 6–7, AT). This threefold reference to Israel/Ephraim points to the likelihood of renewed opposition to David from those Northern elements who were more closely associated with Saul, over against Judah, David's home base. David will need to deal with such divisions after the revolt is over. At any rate, there is "a great slaughter" of the rebels, a phrase similar to that in Ahithophel's plan (17:9) and reminiscent of Israel's defeat in the ark story (1 Sam 4:17). Ironically, more of the forces of Ephraim are "devoured" by the *Forest of Ephraim* than by the sword (v. 8, AT)! Contemporary soldiers who have had to fight in jungles would recognize the danger.

Absalom's fate is no better, and there is nothing gentle about it. Riding on his mule (the royal mount of the times) he goes under an oak tree and his head catches in the limbs while his mule continues on. Usually interpreters connect this with the previous reference to Absalom's exceedingly long hair, and his exceeding vanity (14:25–26), though the text simply says his head is caught. There he hangs, an easy target, "between heaven and earth" which is neither here nor there—it is nowhere, just as his revolt is soon to be. But when one of David's soldiers happens upon him, he does not seize the opportunity to kill the rebel king. He tells Joab about it, and Joab asks why he did not do so, saying that he would have won, say, a hundred dollars. The soldier replies that he would not kill the king's son for a *thousand* dollars, for he had heard David order Joab and the others to "protect" Absalom. The soldier also rather boldly accuses Joab of hypocrisy in that Joab would not defend him if he *did* kill Absalom. Joab does not want to "waste time" quibbling. By now he has reached the hapless Absalom, and he takes three sticks and strikes them against Absalom's chest.[130]

---

129. This is the only reference to such a forest, and the geographical designation is odd since the territory of Ephraim is on the west side of the Jordan. Some text traditions read "Mahanaim," no doubt to correct the problem. But the author may be more interested in politics than geography! See further below.

130. Not the "darts" of NRSV. See McCarter, *II Samuel*, 406–7. Alter (*David Story*, 306) also reads "sticks" but "thrust them into Absalom's heart." Cf. the same verb and preposition for

A platoon of armor-bearers then surround him and inflict the *coup de grace*, but otherwise there is nothing gracious about Absalom's death. Cunningly, Joab has made himself an accomplice in Absalom's death, but not the sole agent (just as no one on a firing squad knows whose bullet was the lethal one).

There is something inescapably poignant in the picture of Absalom hanging "between heaven and earth," totally helpless and mercilessly killed. It is reminiscent of World War II photographs of the bodies of paratroopers, hanging in the trees where their chutes entangled them, easy targets for enemy rifles. Despite Absalom's murderous vengeance, political pretensions, and filial rebellion—despite even his apparent willingness to kill his own father—his pitiful end may evoke the readers' sympathy (it certainly will do that for David!). In the same vein, Joab's ruthless treatment seems unnecessarily brutal. It is not the first time that Joab has used violence to protect what he sees as the best interests of David (not to mention his own personal vengeance, 2:24–27), and it will not be the last. Ironically, in the end he has had to kill the favored prodigal whose return he had orchestrated before. But here is the caveat: we can easily imagine David welcoming Absalom home once again, if not with a kiss, and we can also wonder if the recidivist son would yet again return to his ways, provide the spark for rebels, and seek the life of the father who loves him so.

There will be no royal burial for this prodigal prince. Joab calls back his troops, at least preventing *their* slaughtering of Israel to continue, a gesture that is no doubt more for politics than pity, and another resemblance to *Ahithophel's* advice (17:2–3). They fling Absalom's body into "a great pit in the forest" (presumably still "of Ephraim"), and cover the spot with "a very great heap of stones," the resting place for other troublemakers and villains (Achan; King of Ai).[131] But Absalom does not die without a tombstone, as it were. He had already erected for himself a monument to perpetuate his name, which, in fact, the narrator tells us still exists and indeed fulfils his wish—"Absalom's Monument." Still, there is irony: the monument of this would-be king is in the "King's Valley,"[132] but his body is devoured by the Forest of Ephraim.

The narrator now gives us a disproportionately long scene describing how David hears of Absalom's death, producing an artful suspense (18:19–32).[133] It is as if the author wants to delay as long as possible the painful moment when the news is finally reported, and the length of

---

Jael's tent peg, Judg 4:21. Fokkelman, *King David*, 247–48, also reads three sticks; Joab uses them to dislodge Absalom from the tree, whereupon the soldiers kill him. (He suggests that the three sticks represent the three troop divisions, 18:2.) The main point is that Joab's actions alone do not kill Absalom, and David's deathbed order of execution (1 Kgs 2:5–6) refers to Joab's killing of Abner and Amasa (see below), but not to Absalom.

131. Josh 7:26, including, as here, the etiology of a place name; Josh 8:29.

132. Otherwise only in Gen 14:17; Absalom (or the narrator) has forgotten that he does, in fact, have three sons (14:27), unless we are to interpret his action as completed before a son was born, or that they have predeceased him.

133. "The News of Defeat" is a literary form appearing also in the report to Eli (1 Sam 4:12–17). See Gunn, *King David*, 55–56.

the scene will reflect the depth of David's grief. Ahimaaz, one of the priestly spies, offers to run to David with the news that God has "delivered him from the power of his enemies." The whole scene is about a "news" report, and the root word appears ten times (three in v. 20 alone; NRSV "[good] tidings"). Virtually everywhere else, the word denotes *good* news (the Greek equivalent is *euangelion*, which gave us "evangel"). But Joab knows that the news will *not* be good news to David, because Ahimaaz omitted the little matter of Absalom's death. So Joab tells Ahimaaz that he will not be the messenger, and dispatches a Cushite instead. When Ahimaaz persists, Joab points out that "you [will] have no reward for the tidings," perhaps to protect Ahimaaz from the fate of previous messengers to David. Indeed, just before executing the murderers of Ishbaal, David recounts for them what he did to the messenger who "thought he was bringing good news" about the death of Saul, only to meet his own death as "the reward I gave him for his news" (4:10).[134] Nevertheless, "come what may," Ahimaaz says, "I will run," so Joab says, "Run."

The scene now shifts to David, who is "sitting between the two gates" of the city of Mahanaim, the very place at which he reviewed his departing troops and ordered them to protect Absalom (18:4–5). Clearly he and everyone else is waiting for news from the front, for a sentinel is posted on the roof, and he will provide the first glimpse of a messenger (something like a sailor on the mast looking for land). Suddenly the sentinel sees in the distance a solitary figure running toward the city, and informs David, who not surprisingly says, "If he is alone, there are tidings in his mouth." The Cushite continues to draw nearer, when the sentinel sees another runner behind him. "A man running alone," announces the sentinel again, this time to the gatekeeper. One wonders if the indirect reporting reflects the sentinel's puzzlement at his own words—the man is *not* alone. Why are there two messengers?[135] David says, "He also is bringing tidings," even though he is not alone. Then the sentinel thinks he can identify one of the runners, whose stride is "like the running of Ahimaaz son of Zadok." Apparently, Ahimaaz was the cross-country champion, now in the lead ("first one"). David's reading becomes more assured: "He is a good man, and comes with good tidings."[136]

Indeed, one would think so, for the moment Ahimaaz reaches David he shouts "All is well!"—literally, "Shalom."[137] Ahimaaz then bows to the ground and amplifies his message that God "has delivered up the men who raised their hand against my lord the king." But David's first concern is for only *one* of those men, as it was when the troops departed: "Is it well with the young man, Absalom?" Literally, "Shalom to the young

---

134. The word for "reward" is based on the root for "news," and occurs only in these two stories in this sense.

135. The second occurrence of the word "another" in v. 26 is not in the Hebrew.

136. The word for "news" can be translated "good news/tidings," but here the separate word for "good" is used two times.

137. "All is well" is suitable, but hides the connection with "Absalom" (see below). For a similar situation (including a runner) see 1 Kgs 5:21–22, where "Is everything all right?" and "Yes" both are merely the word *shalom* (the former with a question mark).

man, to Ab-shalom?" Here the meaning of Absalom's name becomes most significant—"Father of Shalom," i.e., of "peace" or "wholeness" or "wellness." Originally, it was apparently "My father is peace" (Abi-shalom).[138] The irony is obvious: "My-father-is-peace" has brought nothing but trouble. But at this point Ahimaaz's eagerness to be the messenger apparently succumbs to cowardice in delivering *all* of the message. "Oh," he says, "I heard a big commotion around Joab and his men but don't know what it was about" (v. 29, my paraphrase). Even if this were partly true, of course, Joab has *told* him what it was about, so Ahimaaz clearly does not want to be the bearer of *bad* news. David tells him to stand aside, and turns to the Cushite, who has finally arrived, for a second opinion.

The Cushite's message begins favorably also: "Good tidings for my lord the king!" But when he adds that God has "delivered you today from the power of *all* those who rose against you" (v. 31, AT), David asks the same question about Absalom, and the Cushite answers obliquely but definitively: "May the enemies of my lord the king, and all who rise up to do you harm, be like that young man." To say that David "was deeply moved" (NRSV) is to put it mildly: he convulses, he shakes violently, he trembles (the word is used for earthquakes and terror). He climbs the stairway up to a room over the gate, weeping all the way and lamenting: "O my son Absalom, my son, my son Absalom! Would I had died instead of you, O Absalom, my son, my son!"

One thing that should never be said to someone in the shock of grief is, "You shouldn't feel that way." Feelings are the outward expressions of what we might call one's "autonomic spiritual system." In some ways it is as difficult to stop them as it is to stop breathing. David's rebel son has just been stabbed to death, his body unceremoniously buried on the battlefield. If David held out hope for the redemption of this prodigal, that hope is dashed forever. Moreover, David has now lost three sons to death and a daughter to the shamed oblivion of singleness. The daughter was raped by one of the sons, and he in turn murdered by the brother. The two sons each stood first in line to the throne. David has every reason to tremble in grief, all the more so in that he knows all of this "trouble" to be according to the will of God, a punishment for his sin (12:11). As Birch aptly says, "There is no more poignant portrayal of human grief and desolation in all of Scripture than in this single verse."[139]

But David as parent has all along been part of the problem, directly affecting the role of David as king. David became king because of his military skills and courage, and his shrewd political assertiveness, but David as parent has been nothing but passive and accommodating. Now David's grief over Absalom threatens the very future of his monarchy. After all, he has wept in public, wishing that he had died instead of Absalom—that is, the king whose advisors and troops

---

138. See McCarter, *II Samuel*, 101, on the change; cf. names like "Abi-melech," "My father is king," etc. Thus two sons have the root for "shalom" in their names (i.e., Solomon, 12:24).

139. Birch, *1 and 2 Samuel*, 1339.

have risked *their* lives to defeat his rebel son now wishes that the rebel had won and he had lost. The narrator uncovers the danger of this attitude in describing the mood of the returning troops. There is no ticker-tape parade. They have heard of David's grieving, and Joab has received a report of it. "So the victory that day was turned into mourning for all the troops" (19:2). It is the equivalent of turning a wedding into a funeral. Worse, David's grief for the death of his enemy makes his own troops feel ashamed: "they stole into the city that day as soldiers steal in who are ashamed when they flee in battle." And again here the narrator repeats David's lament, now "in a *loud* voice": "A my son Absalom, O Absalom, my son, my son!"

Joab has had enough. He is not the kind of man that one would describe as "sensitive"—and he *does* think that David shouldn't feel that way—but he has a keen sense for political situations. We also have to respect his courage in confronting the king, since Joab is the one who hurled three projectiles against Absalom's chest and supervised his execution. Nevertheless, he reads the mood of the troops correctly, and sees the political danger. He comes to David and, without any polite greeting, much less bowing down, he tells David what David needs to hear, something that political advisors often refrain from doing. He says, you have shamed the very officers who saved your life today, and the lives of all your family members (including those concubines), "for love of those who hate you and for hatred of those who love you." In fact, Joab says, if all of his troops were dead and Absalom were alive, it would be "all right" to David (v. 6, AT). Then Joab *tells* the king what to do: "Now get up, get out there, and speak heart-to-heart with your servants, or else, by God, not a single one of them will be here tomorrow, and this trouble will be greater than all the troubles you have seen in your life" (v. 7, AT). Joab is not one to mince words, even with the king, and, of course, he is right, and fortunately David can see that and has the humility to accept it and the wisdom to do what he is told. David gets up and returns to his seat in the city gate, and the troops hear of it, and come to him. The narrator does not report any speech; apparently the gesture is enough. In fact, the city gate has figured prominently in the story of the battle and its denouement, marking the onset of fighting (18:4), the messengers' reports (18:24, 26), David's reaction and the alienation of his troops (18:33), and finally his return and reintegration as their king (19:8). The movement is something like abdicating and then reclaiming his throne.

The Return of the King (19:9–43)

With David reconciled to his troops, it is now time for him to return to Jerusalem, a process as drawn out as was his retreat. However, David cannot simply get up and go. Apparently the political situation requires an *invitation* from his former constituents. After all, Absalom's revolt was a civil war, exasperating the old tensions between the North and the South. Thus vv. 9–15 address first the Israelites (as in Northern tribes), and then the "elders of Judah" in the

South. Despite some ambiguous references, "the Israelites" are identified as Absalom's supporters, and they have fled to their homes. Now "all the people were disputing through all the tribes of Israel" regarding David's return. He is, after all, the conqueror of the Philistines who has "delivered" them, who fled because of Absalom. This is the first we have heard of an anointing of Absalom, but the intention must have been to rival David's status. Now, the people ask, "why do you say nothing about bringing him back?" Who the "you" is here is not clear, and the question remains rhetorical.

Apparently David hears of the controversy, and the implied invitation, because he now sends a message through his priestly cohorts in Jerusalem to the "elders of Judah," asking why they didn't beat the Israelites to the punch. After all, David and they are kinfolk. So, for that matter, is Amasa, the rebel military leader (17:25), whom David now appoints as his own commander, explicitly "in place of Joab." It would be something like Abraham Lincoln (in his last remaining week) appointing Robert E. Lee as commander of the Union Army, and booting out General Grant. Clearly, the staff change is for David's political advantage, as becomes immediately evident when Amasa convinces "all the people of Judah as one" to invite the king back to Jerusalem. Again, Amasa's power base suggests that Absalom enjoyed considerable support in Judah. No doubt David also has personal reasons for firing the man who helped kill his son. Joab is left to simmer, but not for long.

Knowing he will be welcomed home, David now leaves Mahanaim and returns to the Jordan River, "and Judah came to Gilgal to meet the king and to bring him over the Jordan" (v. 15). Gilgal, of course, is associated especially with Saul's monarchy (1 Sam 11:14–15), so David seems to be making yet another symbolic gesture appealing to the Northern tribes. The rest of David's return journey occurs in slow motion, similar to the stages of his escape; not until 20:2 will he actually arrive in Jerusalem. The stages are marked by the appearance of four individuals who figured in David's escape—Shimei, Ziba, Mephibosheth, and Barzillai (19:16–40).

We last saw Shimei as he was cursing David, flinging dust and stones, calling David a murderer and a scoundrel, stained with "the blood of the house of Saul" (16:7–8). David had declined Abishai's offer to remove Shimei's head, and now Shimei comes to David, hoping to keep it a little longer. A Benjamite, he has "hurried to come down with the people of Judah to meet King David," and brought a thousand fellow Benjamites. Close at his heels is Ziba and his household, "the servant of the house of Saul," who is also in a rush to greet David. Ziba and company take charge of helping David and his household across the river, "to do whatever seemed good to David" (v. 18, AT; the narrative returns to him later). But the narrative time seems to pause with David poised on the East Bank, for he is still "about to cross" in v. 18b, and again in v. 31, and does not cross until v. 39.[140] The pause may be a way to resolve the most recent encounters between David the Southern king

---

140. Verse 18 is textually confused, but uses the root for "cross" three times.

and representatives of the Benjamite base of Saul, before David returns to the West Bank, reflecting again the tribal rivalries seen in vv. 9–15.[141]

Shimei, at least, seems adroit at exploiting David's need not to alienate any further his Northern constituents. He pleads for David to forgive his sin in cursing him, but also points out that he is "the first of all the house of Joseph" to welcome David, and, of course, he has come down with the people of Judah, and there are a thousand of his tribal compatriots standing there, as well. What is David to do? Abishai has his usual answer: off with his head! After all, Shimei has "cursed the Lord's anointed." But it will not help David's need for Northern support if he executes one of their own before their eyes, much as he may want to for personal retribution. So his answer to Abishai is as much an appeal to the Benjamites and other Northerners: "Shall anyone be put to death in Israel this day? For do I not know that I am this day king over Israel?" After all, David has just come from the civil war in which thousands of Israelites were killed; killing another would only exacerbate tensions.[142] The second line acknowledges that his political base has to include the North if he truly *is* "king of Israel" and not just "king of Judah." (It's like what newly elected Presidents often say to the opposing camp: I want to be *your* President also.) Then David turns to Shimei and swears to him, "You shall not die." Later we will realize that he had his fingers crossed behind his back (1 Kgs 2:8–9).

Now an even more direct connection with the former monarchy of Saul appears when none other than Saul's lame grandson, Mephibosheth, joins those eager to greet the returning king (19:24–30).[143] He has not exactly decked himself out for the occasion: he hasn't bathed, trimmed his beard, or changed clothes since the day David left Jerusalem (perhaps to demonstrate how needy he is without his servants). David asks why he did not accompany him in his retreat, saying nothing of his encounter with Ziba, much less Ziba's claim that Mephibosheth had exulted in Absalom's initial success as an indication that Israel would "give me back my grandfather's kingdom" (16:3). Mephibosheth seems to be aware of Ziba's accusation, however. Surely he would have noted Ziba's absence, along with all the donkeys, bread, raisins, fruits, and wine missing from the larder (16:1). Mephibosheth has rushed to meet David in order to defend himself, and he tells a different story: he had asked Ziba to saddle a donkey for him to ride and accompany David (Mephibosheth being unable to walk), but Ziba (presumably the servant of whom he speaks) had deceived him. Perhaps Mephibosheth saw Ziba saddling those donkeys thinking his order

---

141. Unlike the others, Barzillai would represent supporters of David in Gilead, an area associated with Saul's popularity (the hero of Jabesh-Gilead) and Mephibosheth's former capitol (2:9).

142. Unless the figure twenty thousand refers to both sides, that is the number of Israelite casualties in 18:7. Note that Saul exercised similarly wise judgment in 1 Sam 11:12–13.

143. Verses 24b and 30b out of context seem to suggest that David has already returned to Jerusalem (and "from" in v. 25a must be supplied).

was being followed, only to see Ziba disappear with them and all their burdens. At any rate, Mephibosheth concludes his appeal with flattery: let David do what he thinks best, since he is "like the angel of God," an analogy that David by now may find a bit trite (cf. 1 Sam 29:9; 2 Sam 14:17). Whereas Saul's family might have been "doomed to death," David gave him a place at his table, so what right does he have to ask for more? The answer to this rhetorical question could be—he has *every* right to his ancestral inheritance, unless the *king* has appropriated every right to govern it (cf. again 1 Sam 8:14). But that is precisely what David assumes when he answers that he is tired of dealing with Mephibosheth's household affairs and then announces his decision: "you and Ziba shall divide the land." This resolution radically alters David's previous decree in which he gave Mephibosheth *all* of Saul's property and appointed Ziba as major domo, but not joint owner (9:9). But the decision also reneges on his transferring "all that belonged to Mephibosheth" to Ziba (16:4). Apparently David still wants to honor his pledge to protect Jonathan's family (1 Sam 20:14–17), but also feels gratitude to Ziba for all that bread, fruit, and wine. Perhaps he also still buys Ziba's story. Mephibosheth responds with another rhetorical flourish: "let him take it all, since my lord the king has arrived home safely." Mephibosheth seems not to be motivated by greed, and if, in fact, Ziba was lying, *his* half of the estate is the product of extortion and David the victim of deceit.[144] In that case, "The one who is physically lame is morally and psychologically the only one who emerges from these entanglements inviolate."[145]

Barzillai makes the final cameo appearance in joining the welcoming party, but not, like Hushai and Mephibosheth, with his hand out (19:31–43). On the contrary, he was the one who supplied David and his troops with much needed food and drink when they arrived at Mahanaim worn out after their escape (17:27–29), and while bivouacked there as well. Now he has accompanied David to the Jordan to say farewell.[146] David invites him to Jerusalem so that David can now return the favor, but Barzillai declines, reciting a litany of old age infirmities. He would only be a burden, he says; better to stay in his home for the remainder of his days. Instead, he proposes that Chimham take his place in the largesse of the king. Presumably Chimham is a son (cf. 1 Kgs 2:6), and perhaps more in need of help since his name means "Faint"! David agrees, blesses Barzillai, and—finally—crosses the Jordan, following his troops, and proceeds to Gilgal, escorted now by "all the troops of Judah, and also half the troops of Israel."[147]

The moment David steps foot in Gilgal, however, he faces controversy once again involving the tensions be-

---

144. Fokkelman, *King David*, 32–39, argues that Ziba *is* lying and that David's decision is reprehensible. On the other hand, if David still finds Ziba's story credible, his decision is *generous* to Mephibosheth, as it has been to Shimei.

145. Ibid., 39.

146. Textual problems create considerable ambiguity as to whether or not Barzillai actually crosses the Jordan. McCarter's translation, for example, assumes that he does not, altering vv. 31b, 36a, and 39 (*II Samuel*, 413–14).

147. Here, as often above, reading NRSV "people" as "troops, army."

tween North and South, and *he* is the bone of contention. As we saw at the outset of David's retreat, the word for "cross (over)" has occurred numerous times, sometimes meaning simply "pass on, proceed," but particularly referring to crossing the Jordan, either in retreat or in return.[148] The river is a boundary or threshold that is more than geographic, as if crossing the Jordan eastbound signifies the loss of David's sovereignty, and crossing it westbound signifies his restoration. Everyone wants to be the first to welcome David home, no doubt assuming that royal favors will result, with Shimei and Mephibosheth already vying for the lead. Now at Gilgal the Northerners address their complaint to David, demanding to know why the Southerners (from Judah)[149] have "stolen you away," i.e., brought the king across the Jordan—as if he was a prize or trophy. Or perhaps the metaphor would be "stealing the show." The Judeans answer the question before David can, arguing that they come first because they are kin to David, i.e., he too is a Judean. They also claim that they have not "eaten at the king's expense," nor has he given them any favors. The Northerners respond to the qualitative argument of kinship with a quantitative argument of numbers: there are ten Northern tribes and only one Southern, so the Northerners own "ten shares in the king," as if he is a piece of property. They also play the "me first" card—they were the first to even *speak* about bringing back "*our* king." But, the narrator tells us, the Judeans speak more forcefully than the Northerners and seemingly win the shouting match. David, however, has said nothing.

Rebellion, déjà vu (20:1–22)

David's silence does nothing to resolve the tribal hostility, suggesting that his wisdom is *not* like the angel of God (19:27 etc.). From ch.13 on David has been of a divided mind over his sons Amnon and Absalom, frozen in indecision, in contrast to his decisiveness before chap. 11. Now his schizoid mind contributes to the schism between Israel and Judah.[150] The chapter division somewhat obscures the immediacy of what happens next: "right there, it so happened, was a man, a scoundrel, and his name was Sheba" (20:1, AT). The Hebrew word order places "and there" (my "right there") first to emphasize that what happens is temporally instantaneous, spatially at the Gilgal sanctuary, and socially within the fractious meeting of competing tribes. Moreover, Sheba is a Benjamite—the ghost of Saul, as it were, and yet *not* a son of Saul, thereby demonstrating that contenders to David's throne are not limited to that family. David's silence is filled by the blast of a trumpet sounding another call to rebel arms—and he hasn't even arrived in Jerusalem!

Sheba adds a poetic couplet to his music: "We have no portion in David, / no share in the son of Jesse!" How quickly things can change. Only a moment before the Israelites had claimed that they

---

148. For example, six times in vv. 39–41 alone (including NRSV "went on" and "brought").

149. Literally the phrases are "people/army of Judah," "people/army of Israel" (v. 40), and "men of Judah," "men of Israel" ("man" being used distributively, this pair occurring three times in vv. 41–43, and in 20:2, 4).

150. Fokkelman, *King David*, 316.

owned *ten* shares of David, but David's refusal to correct the perception of an exclusive claim on him by the Judeans has alienated them once again. Sheba's language suggests disinheritance. Now "all the men of Israel" (AT) who had been so eager to be at the head of David's welcoming party abandon him instead and follow Sheba's order: "Everyone to your tents, O Israel!" The author, quite likely, is aware that this same call for desertion will mark an even more serious revolt under David's grandson, Rehoboam, who seems unable to learn from history (1 Kgs 12:16).

The huge crowd assembled at Gilgal suddenly dissolves as all the Northerners shake the dust from their feet and head home, whereupon the Judeans close ranks around David, who *finally* comes "from the Jordan to Jerusalem." The long journey is over, but the homecoming is bitter—indeed, it seems that politically David is right back where he started. His inability to supervise his family led to Absalom's revolt; his inability to supervise his Judean constituents has contributed to Sheba's revolt. The revolt will not last long, but the incident illustrates the long-standing tension between North and South, a tinder box just waiting for the spark of revolution, which a fire-brand like Sheba is all too willing to ignite.

David's first action on returning home is to ostracize the concubines that he had left to keep house in his absence, the women whom Absalom had promptly used as sexual flags for his revolt. His reasons may be partly moral (the semblance of incest),[151] partly punitive, but surely also egotistical—male pride. Absalom usurped his sexual harem as well as his throne. The incident is full of irony, nonetheless. "David came into his house" but "did not come into" his concubines, whom he "placed in a house of keeping," whereas before he had left them to "keep house" (AT). In refusing to have sex with them, he makes them "living widows" (AT), which in turn suggests that he is the dead husband (if not also the impotent king). Their forced abstention "until the day of their death" resembles that of his wife Michal, who "had no child to the day of her death" (6:23), and his daughter, Tamar—dishonored, desolate, and sequestered—whose rape set in motion all of David's troubles (13:20).[152] It is a miserable homecoming indeed.

Next David attends to Sheba's revolt, ordering his chief of staff, Amasa, to muster the troops and report to him in three days. Amasa seems to dillydally, raising David's concern that Sheba will have time to establish a base of operations. So David replaces Amasa with Abishai (Joab's brother), and orders him to take David's servants and pursue the rebel, and Joab and David's special forces join in the pursuit. Apparently, Amasa catches up and pulls in front of them.[153] He has already been promoted over Joab, and perhaps now is attempting to take over from Abishai. At first, Joab appears to greet Amasa genially. As he approaches him, Joab's sword slips out of its sheathe and falls to the ground. He asks the customary "how are you?" (literally

---

151. Cf. Amos 2:7; Lev 18:15; 20:11–12.

152. On Michal, see Alter, *David Story*, 322.

153. There is considerable grammatical ambiguity in 20:7–8, making it difficult to discern exactly what happens.

"how is your peace?"), adding the affectionate "my brother," and, with his right hand pulls Amasa's face to him by the beard as if to give him a kiss, but it is the "kiss of death." Using his left hand, Joab either quickly grabs the fallen sword or pulls a hidden dagger from his coat and stabs Amasa in the stomach. Joab seems to have mastered the lethal abdominal thrust which he used to dispatch Abner (3:27). Perhaps he also knows the story of Ehud from Judges, who assassinated the Edomite king Eglon using the same left-handed tactic (Judg 3:21–22). The stories vie in gruesomeness. In dying, Eglon loses control of his bowels; Amasa loses his bowls completely. The narrator tells us laconically that Joab did not need a second thrust.

Without the slightest hesitation, Joab and Abishai resume their pursuit of Sheba. One of Joab's soldiers exploits the situation to bolster loyalty, saying "Whoever favors Joab, and whoever is for David, let him follow Joab," but, just as rubbernecking creates traffic jams, so the soldiers' macabre fascination with Amasa's corpse, wallowing in guts and gore, halts their progress. So the soldier hauls the corpse into a field and throws a coat over it, and the rubbernecks move on.

Sheba has, indeed, gained a considerable lead, fleeing "through all the tribes of Israel" far to his home turf in the North, and, just as David feared, he has holed up in a city fortress, joined by his fellow Bichrites. It proves not to be a safe spot after all, however. While Joab's troops are in the process of battering down the wall, a "wise woman" asks to talk with Joab, who says "I'm listening."

Appealing to the local tradition of settling disputes, the woman says that she is "one of those who are peaceable and faithful in Israel," apparently including the rest of the city's inhabitants (without the Bichrites). Why then would Joab destroy such a city when he is really after only one man? When she refers to the city as "a mother in Israel" and "the heritage of the Lord," she cinches the argument. Implicitly, she and the rest of the city do not agree with Sheba that they "have no heritage in the son of Jesse" (20:1, AT).

Now that destroying the city is equated with civil matricide, Joab says that it is the last thing he will do. Though the woman seems already aware of it, Joab identifies Sheba as the rebel and offers to withdraw from the siege if the good citizens will hand him over. The woman promptly agrees, offering in turn to provide Joab with Sheba's head. She takes her "wise plan" to her fellow citizens who immediately concur, cut off Sheba's head, and throw it over the wall. Joab blows the trumpet to recall his troops, who scatter "to their tents," an ironic conclusion to the now headless rebel's trumpet call to Israel to go "to their tents" in revolt (20:22 [AT] and 20:1).

The "wise woman" of Abel in the story presents a counterpart to the wise woman of Tekoa in ch.14, who persuaded David to bring Absalom back from exile.[154] There the interests of individuals (reconciliation with Absalom) trumps the interests of society (justice for a murder victim), to the peril of the nation; here, the interests of a society (the

---

154. McCarter, *II Samuel*, 351, 431, following Conroy, *Absalom!*

town of Abel, and by extension David's realm) trump the interests of an individual (the life of Sheba). With Absalom, David's refusal to cut off his son "from the heritage of God" puts that heritage in jeopardy (14:16); with Sheba, cutting off the rebel *preserves* the "heritage of God" (20:19).

In its brutality, the Sheba incident reminds us of the stories in Judges. Here we have disembowelment and decapitation. The brutality focuses on Joab, whose violence has already consumed Abner, Amasa, and Absalom. The former two were connected to David's attempts to placate the Northern tribes and former constituents of Saul, and Joab's murder of them cannot have helped David's agenda. Joab had accused Abner of spying for Mephibosheth, but that charge was groundless, and Joab's motive seemed to be more from personal vengeance over Abner's killing his brother. Joab's motive in murdering Amasa is patently jealousy, although Amasa did exhibit some inadequacies as chief of staff (20:5). When the reckoning comes (as it will in 1 Kings 2), it will be for the murder of these two generals, not for the death of Absalom, who, after all, was more like Sheba than David ever wanted to admit.

Standing back and looking at the whole of chaps. 13–20, we can see how the entire narrative illustrates Nathan's oracle of judgment in chap. 12—God has raised up trouble (or "evil," "calamity") from David's house, and the sword has not departed from it. After Nathan's euphoric dynastic oracle (chap. 7) and the military successes of David's early reign (chaps. 8–10), when "the Lord gave victory to David wherever he went" (8:14), everything is downhill beginning with David's adultery with Bathsheba: rape led to fratricide, led to filial alienation, led to filial rebellion (which could have led to both regicide and patricide), led to political revolt, led to civil war, led to the death of Absalom. Even with victory in the civil war, the rest of the story has few highlights (Barzillai being one) and is full of violence, grief, and political factions, and David doesn't even step foot back into Jerusalem before there is another revolt. As many scholars argue, with good reason, originally the story probably moved directly from the death of Sheba to David's final days (1 Kgs 1:1—2:10).[155] Even with the intervening material, however, the overall picture is the same: most of David's reign was *full* of "trouble." If a single vignette summarizes David's life post-Bathsheba, it could be that of Shimei, spitting out his curses and flinging dust and stones at the king in a vindictive rage, screaming "disaster [or "evil," "calamity"] has overtaken you" (16:8). The king who seemed to be under God's blessing up to chap. 11, subsequently seemed more to be under God's curse. And yet the David whom we see especially in chaps. 15–19 is a nobler figure (and certainly a more human one) that the one who precedes. His nobility comes not from his royalty, but in his response to suffering, humiliation, and death. The man's piety is deepened by those experiences, revealing an attitude of faith and trust in God's

---

155. Chapters 21–24 are almost universally recognized to be an eclectic insertion, although by no means without significance or careful shaping, as we shall see. Even in place, chaps. 21–24 are framed with stories in which David must deal with a famine and with plague!

guidance that is far more profound than the earlier consultations for political and military strategy (e.g., 2:1; 5:19). For all of the unfairness to Saul that we have acknowledged, we must also recognize that Saul never exhibited such trust. We never saw him place himself in God's hands the way that David did in the midst of his trouble (especially 16:11–12). Perhaps that is what God saw in David's heart from the outset (1 Sam 13:14; 16:7).

Nevertheless, God's commitment to David and his dynasty embroils *God* in far less noble ways than one might want. When the narrator tells us of God's will to "bring ruin (or "trouble," "evil," "calamity") on *Absalom*" (17:14b) the narrator signals that God will not allow *David's* trouble to destroy his reign. Shimei is wrong when he asserts that God "has given the kingdom into the hand of your son Absalom" (16:8). In that sense, the story of David's miseries also illustrates Nathan's *dynastic* oracle when it says that, come what may, God will not withdraw God's "steadfast love" from David and his house (7:15). That love must operate in the midst of immorality, strife, and violence, however, including the possibilities that either Amnon or Absalom *could have* become the successor to David, the one who continued his dynasty, were it not for their own failures and God's opposition (coupled with Absalom's revenge and Hushai's cleverness). But we cannot say that God did not want a rapist or a murderer to be king, because David is at least the latter if not also the former. God has raised up "evil" against David by Absalom, but in the end God wills to bring "evil" against Absalom *for* David. The "rod of God's anger" is broken for the sake of keeping the promise of God's "steadfast love." The Messianic murderer endures through the disgraced grace of God.[156]

Interlude (Chaps. 21–24)

The editor has assembled an odd collection of materials to form a kind of interlude before taking us to the end of David's life and the struggle for his succession in 1 Kings 1. In chaps. 21–24 the apparently independent units are held together in a chiastic structure (i.e., ABC:CBA):

> famine from God, expiation, relief
> > David's warriors: giant slayers
> > > David's poem: song of thanksgiving
> > > David's poem: last words
> > David's warriors: the elite
> plague from God, expiation, relief[157]

Especially in the framing stories, the portrayal of God is far from savory. In the first, God sends a famine to punish Israel for blood guilt incurred by Saul, resulting in a massacre of Saul's remaining sons. In the second, God incites David to administer a census, then punishes him for doing so, sending a plague that kills seventy thousand people. The assumption of corporate punishment that engulfs a people because of the sin

---

156. Brueggemann, *Samuel*, 350, puts it well: "David lives in a world of blood, power, violence, and force . . . [and] it is in, with, and under such reality that God keeps promises."

157. McCarter (*II Samuel*, 443) suggests that originally chap. 9 (Mephibosheth) was a conclusion of the famine story in ch. 21 and moved by an editor subsequent to the Deuteronomistic edition.

of a royal figure illustrates a common ancient Near Eastern world view.[158] In the end, as we have already noted, this assumption will govern the fate of both Israel and Judah.

Revenge on the House of Saul (21:1–14)

In the opening story, a three-year famine prompts David to seek an oracle from God (how, we are not told), and God tells him that the famine is a result of "blood-guilt on Saul and on his house, because he put the Gibeonites to death" (v. 1).[159] We know nothing of this incident otherwise. Had Saul acted as charged, he would have been in breach of the covenant that Joshua made with the Gibeonites, "guaranteeing their lives by a treaty" (Josh 9:15), even though they were Canaanites (and rather artful thespians to boot), as the narrator tells us here in v. 2. In contrast to David, who does ask for God's guidance here, Joshua and the Israelites were fooled by the Gibeonites because they "did not ask direction from the Lord" (Josh 9:4). Before realizing who they really were, they swore to them that they would let them live; then they *had* to let them live, "so that wrath may not come upon us" (Josh 9:20), which is precisely what the famine in our story represents.

That Saul "put the Gibeonites to death" and "tried to wipe them out" sounds like complete annihilation (v. 2; cf. v. 5), but obviously there are still some Gibeonites around. According to the Joshua story, the Gibeonites became virtual slaves, "hewers of wood and drawers of water for the congregation and for the altar of the Lord" (Josh 9:27). Here is another interesting connection to the plague story in chap. 24: it ends with David purchasing land and constructing an altar, presumably on the spot that the later temple will be built. Moreover, the owner of the land is, like the Gibeonites, not an Israelite but a native Canaanite (i.e., a Jebusite, one of the original inhabitants of Jerusalem). At any rate, David consults with the Gibeonites and asks how he can "make expiation" for Saul's crime, so that God's wrath will be replaced by the Gibeonites' blessing (v. 3). They reply that they don't want financial reparation, nor is it up to them "to put anyone to death in Israel." But when David presses them, they ask *him* to authorize killing seven of Saul's sons, although the Gibeonites will do the dirty work. They will "impale them before the Lord at Gibeon on the mountain of the Lord" (v. 6). And David says, "I will hand them over" (literally "I will give," perhaps better "I yield"). It is a gruesome irony that the Gibeonites—who, in fact, were part of the Amorites, Israel's perennial enemy, and whose very existence in the land of Israel goes back to Israel's honoring a promise to protect them, which promise they gained by deceit—would exact blood vengeance on the innocent sons of the former king of Israel!

---

158. As Wyatt puts it (*Religious Texts*, 232, n. 55), "Famine threatens all his subjects when the king is punished for his sins. His impending death presages universal death." He is discussing a king figure in Ugaritic epic, but also refers to the curse in Deut 28:1–6, 15–19.

159. For famine as divine punishment cf. Amos 4:6; 1 Kgs 8:37; 2 Kgs 8:1; of course famine can result from drought as punishment also (Deut 28:22–24; 1 Kgs 17:1).

It is disturbing enough that God has initiated all of this with the revelation to David, and before that, sending the famine. It is even more repugnant that the Gibeonites will impale[160] their victims "before the Lord." Presumably this refers to a sanctuary of some sort, most likely a "high place" dedicated to "Yahweh-at-Gibeon" (AT).[161] No doubt the Gibeonites would say that the famine is God's punishment for Saul's "bloodguilt," resulting from the breach of an oath sworn in God's name, which thereby "takes the Lord's name in vain" (Deut 5:11), so the sacrificial victims whose death will expiate the guilt and restore God's blessing must be appropriately exhibited to God in some form of ritual.

David does honor the oath that he swore to Jonathan to preserve Jonathan's descendants (1 Sam 24:21–22), by sparing Mephibosheth (21:7), although here was an opportune time to get rid of someone whose loyalty was at least questionable (16:3 *versus* 19:26).[162] But, after all, the Gibeonites have asked for *Saul's* sons, and those are the ones that David hands over. Apparently David has forgotten how moved he was to protect a *fictional* man from blood vengeance (chap. 14). From David's point of view, however, handing over Saul's sons in order to remove the famine from "the heritage of the Lord" (v. 3) is not all that different from the citizens of Abel handing over Sheba for the sake of "the heritage of the Lord" (20:19). In some ways, the situation is similar to that of Achan in the book of Joshua, whose offense against God threatened the entire community, and whose execution (along with his family) eradicated the danger (Joshua 7). On the other hand, if the Barzillai of v. 8 is the same as the man who so generously provisioned David and his troops, then David is handing over his benefactor's five grandsons to death![163]

The grisly expiatory ritual proceeds, and the impaled corpses hang "on the mountain before the Lord." It is at the time when the barley harvest would normally occur, perhaps anticipating the rain that will confirm the efficacy of the ritual (v. 14). But the mother of two of the victims, Rizpah, will not abandon them even in death (she was Saul's concubine allegedly involved with Abner, 3:6–8). She takes sackcloth, the traditional fabric for mourning, and spreads it out on

---

160. The exact meaning of the word is unclear; impaling involved thrusting a sharp pole up through the abdomen, on which the victim's corpse would hang (the Assyrians used this to terrorize besieged cities). See McCarter, *II Samuel*, 442. Birch, *1 and 2 Samuel*, 1358 lists no less than five possible translations.

161. That is, to the manifestation of God associated with this particular sacred place (cf. Gen 31:13; 2 Sam 15:8), mentioned in 1 Kgs 3:4. Thus McCarter (*II Samuel*, 436) reads "to Yahweh-in-Gibeon on the mountain of Yahweh." High places (later, most often condemned by the Deuteronomists) include the site of Samuel's sacrifice in 1 Sam 9:12 (NRSV "shrine"). For such ritual execution before the deity, see Lloyd, "Anat and the 'Double' Massacre," 158. On local divine manifestations, see Miller, *Religion*, 77–79.

162. The Mephibosheth in v. 8 is a son of Saul, not Jonathan's, and we should read "Mippibaal" instead (McCarter, *II Samuel*, 439).

163. See 17:27–29; 19:31–39. Here and at 1 Sam 18:19 Saul's son-in-law, Adriel, is identified as a Maholathite, which was a part of the Gileadites. McCarter (*II Samuel*, 442) thinks it "quite possible" that the two Barzillais are the same. David rewards the *sons* of Barzillai in 1 Kgs 1:7. It is also intriguing that Merab (reading with the LXX and NRSV in v. 8) is the daughter whom Saul at first offered to and then withdrew from David (1 Sam 18:17–27).

a rock to make a space for her grieving, and she fights off the usual predators of exposed corpses—birds and wild animals. When David hears what she has done, he goes to Jabesh-gilead, where the bones of Saul and Jonathan are buried, disinters them and brings them back to the tomb of Saul's father, Kish, in the land of Benjamin. There he also buries the bones of the seven sons of Saul, providing some dignity for them similar to that given by the men of Jabesh-gilead to Saul, whose body also was exposed (1 Sam 31:12–13). "After that, God heeded supplications for the land" (v. 14).

This is one of those stories, like many in Joshua and Judges, that we find extremely disturbing. What devotees of God think that God wants to see them do to those deemed out of favor with God is unceasingly appalling (and not limited to ancient history). Again, we are confronting understandings of corporate guilt, punishment, and expiation that are radically different from our own, one of those religious beliefs that is internally logical but reprehensible *theo*logically.[164] For us, the story does nothing to commend the figure of God, who is the ultimate offended one, and whose punishment against the offender involves such ungodly violence against those who have committed no offense. To turn the connotation around, here it is the understanding of *God* that is offensive. But that is to read the story from a contemporary perspective, rather than that of an ancient audience. For them the troublesome question was not how David and even God could condone and even demand such an atrocity, for the logic of blood guilt was a given. Rather, the story addresses the question, *why* did David order the execution of Saul's remaining sons, an act that obviously removed any further contenders for Saul's throne? Was this a ruthless political move? The answer in the story is that, *given* the commonly accepted theology involved in blood guilt, David really had no choice; he saved Israel from famine: indeed, the act of expiation was demanded by God. That David spared Mephibosheth—now the sole surviving rival—and treated the remains of the victims with dignity only adds to David's merit. Thus the plot of the story is not resolved with the executions but with the gracious actions of Rizpah and David.[165] In the end, the story functions the way many already have in "spinning" David's actions vis-à-vis Saul and his family. As McCarter puts it, "David did not act out of malicious self-interest . . . [but] as a benefactor of the house of Saul!"[166] Of course, for David, the whole matter was a serendipitous opportunity in which doing the will of God just happened to coincide with doing what was best for David.

---

164. For many contemporary readers, the execution itself would require expiation!

165. See Fokkelman, *Throne and City*, 189–290.

166. McCarter, *II Samuel*, 445. Brueggemann, *Samuel*, 336–338, has a very different reading: the charge against Saul is "a piece of Davidic fabrication" enabling David to eliminate potential rivals, part of the wider perspective of chaps. 21–24 that "protest against a picture of David that is too affirmative and uncritical." For a similar view, see Gunn and Fewell, *Narrative*, 122.

David's Fellow Giant Fighters (21:15–22)

This brief section recounts the exploits of David and his soldiers against the Philistines, not acknowledging the claim earlier that David had subdued them (8:1, 12). The clause "again there was war against the Philistines" occurs four times for the four battles summarized in v. 22. Traditionally the four enemy combatants are called "giants." In fact, the most famous of them, Goliath, here is killed by Elhanan (vv. 19–21), suggesting that David later stole the show, as it were.[167] The phrase translated "descendants of the giants," however, may well mean something more like "the crusaders of Rapha," referring to an elite military group devoted to the god named Rapha.[168] Nevertheless, these crusaders are clearly formidable opponents, given the descriptions of their high-powered weapons and oversized bodies (especially the one with twenty-four toes and fingers!). Still, they are all defeated by David's warriors—but *not* by David. In fact, one reason for including at least vv. 15–17 here might be the implication that David is past his prime as a giant-slayer. It is remarkable that the one whose defeat of Goliath is told in such detail before now is too "weary" to fight at all (v. 15). Someone must do the fighting for him (Abishai, always willing and eager). Indeed, David's troops issue *him* an order: "you shall not go out with us to battle any longer, so that you do not quench the lamp of Israel" (v. 17). David's military leadership—so vital to his previous career—is over. He will no longer "go out and come in" before Israel (1 Sam 18:16, AT).[169]

The Poet Laureate of Israel (22:1—23:7)

David lives in tradition as the "sweet psalmist of Israel,"[170] an example of which we have already seen in his eulogy over Saul and Jonathan (1:17–27). A large portion of the biblical book of Psalms is attributed to him (similarly, Proverbs is attributed to Solomon). Apparently David was skilled not only in playing the lyre (1 Sam 16:17–23), but in singing his own lyrics to the tunes. The poem here has an almost exact parallel in Psalm 18, and v. 1 here appears in slightly different wording as the superscription to the Psalm. There are numerous superscriptions connecting a psalm with an event in the life of David, suggesting that he *wrote* the psalm as a reflection on that experience. There are psalms for "when he fled from Absalom" (Psalm 3), "when Doeg the Edomite came to Saul" and ratted on David (Psalm 52), and notably

---

167. I.e., Elhanan is probably the one originally associated with Goliath; it is unlikely that someone would invent that connection if David was always the giant slayer. The giant's taunting in v. 21 is another detail that connects with the story in 1 Samuel 17, where it occurs repeatedly (NRSV "defy" or "reproach").

168. So McCarter, *II Samuel*, 449–50, who uses the term "votaries"; *The Jewish Study Bible* has "descendant of the Rapha"; Alter (*David Story*, 333) uses "offspring of the titan." "Mercenaries" might also work, but I suggest "crusader" because it carries the connotation of a religious motivation rather than monetary.

169. In the structurally corresponding passage, 23:9–24, David accompanies his soldiers in various exploits but we do not hear of him leading them in battle.

170. One possible translation of the final phrase in 23:1 (NRSV "the Strong One of Israel").

"when the prophet Nathan came to him after he had gone in to Bathsheba" (Psalm 51; see below). If all such superscriptions are valid, he spent a lot of time throughout his life writing poetry. No doubt he would have disagreed with Plato's suggestion that poets be banned from the Republic.

Our poem is a *te deum*, i.e., a hymn of praise to God, usually sung liturgically, as indeed this poem may have been. The opening lines, in which a variety of metaphors describe God's security (vv. 2b-3), would make an appropriate counterpart to a more contemporary hymn like Luther's magisterial "A Mighty Fortress Is Our God." The introduction in v. 1 situates it at the time when God's promises to David to defeat "all his enemies" are fulfilled (cf. 7:9, 11), those enemies including Saul. Indeed, one could easily read the preceding narrative about David as a collection of deliverance stories, with the poem placed here in the narrative as it draws near to David's old age and death. Paired with the song of Hannah in 1 Samuel 2, the two victory songs frame the entire story, focusing on the ways in which God, incomparable among other deities, has brought some low and raised up others on high (1 Sam 7:2; 2:7b).[171] Canonically, the placement of the hymn also resembles that of the last words of Jacob (Genesis 49, also a poem), Moses (Deuteronomy 32, another poem, but the whole book is Moses' farewell discourse), and Joshua (Joshua 23–24).

The introduction certainly summarizes the substance of the poem, in which David repeatedly praises God for deliverance (e.g., vv. 3, 4, 17–18, etc.). David describes his trouble and God's deliverance in cosmic language: "the cords of Sheol entangled me, / the snares of death confronted me." David has certainly had enough trouble in chaps. 12–20 alone to warrant such an "underworldly" description. To put it more bluntly, his life has been hell. Out of this distress he cries to God, and God hears him "from his temple" in heaven. The result is a magnificent example of a numinous theophany, or divine appearance, in which God is manifested in the classic ancient metaphor of an earth-shaking thunderstorm.[172] Indeed, God seems to *be* such a storm, as the meteorological phenomena are identified with anthropomorphic descriptions: his voice is thunder, his arrows are lightning, and the wind is God's breath (cf. Psalm 29). In some ways, the imagery fuses with that of a ferocious dragon, with smoke coming out its nose and fire from its mouth. Elsewhere, Israel used the same language to describe historical events, the Exodus in particular, but also God's creation of the world. Fortunately for David, the terrifying, overwhelming God of the storm is on his side, and against his enemies, for God reaches down and pulls him "out of

---

171. On the framing, see Fokkelman, *Throne and City*, 354, and Birch, *1 and 2 Samuel*, 980 and n. 27, 1365, the latter following especially the insights of Polzin, *Samuel*, 33–34, who provides an extensive list of the parallels.

172. Within the Former Prophets, cf. Judg 5:4–5; 1 Sam 7:10. Cf. also Psalm 29; 77:16-8; 68:7-8. The storm-god imagery figures prominently in the confrontations with Baal worship in 1 Kings 17–19.

mighty waters," delivering him from his "strong enemy" (v. 17).

In the middle section of the poem, however, the reader runs into a description of David that is difficult to swallow. Verses 21–25 are framed by the assertion that David *deserved* God's deliverance as a reward for his righteousness and "cleanness." He has kept God's ways, not acted wickedly, followed all God's ordinances and statutes, indeed he has been blameless before God, and kept himself from "guilt." David is a veritable Mr. Goody-Two-Shoes. No doubt, Uriah would protest this claim, as would the victims of the massacres in 1 Sam 27:8–12, and Shimei would see no connection here to the "man of blood" whom he curses (16:5–8). Indeed, David's own children might well question it, given David's favoritism and lack of discipline that contributed to the problems with Absalom. But here we are probably seeing the awkwardness of ascribing a poem to David that he most likely did *not* write (note v. 51b). At least it is difficult to reconcile the poet here who proudly displays "the cleanness of my hands" (v. 21) with the penitent poet of Psalm 51 (the "post-Bathsheba" poem), who asks God to "wash me thoroughly from my iniquity," and who yearns for "a clean heart" (vv. 2, 10). However, David *has* exhibited a complex combination ranging from deep piety to ruthless evil! At any rate, the poem here shows a remarkable insight into the relationship between theology (e.g., God as awesome storm) and spirituality (the poet's inner strength), as when he uses the same word to describe both "the brightness" of God's theophany (v. 13) and the way God "brightens" his inner darkness (v. 29, AT).

The last section of the poem focuses on God's support for David's prowess in warfare and advancement in politics, resulting in the exaltation of both God and David (cf. above on 5:10–11). It is still a *te deum*, but there is a lot more about David here as well.[173] At times the claims seem bombastic, lauding David as "the head of the nations," which seems like an exaggeration of David's regional hegemony (8:12–13). But again, we should not expect an exact correlation between the poem and the narrative that precedes. Rather, the *te deum* fits within a royal theology certainly developed after David's own reign, evidenced in numerous other Psalms (especially Psalms 2; 72; 89:1–37). The political exaltation of David over the nations corresponds with the exaltation of the God of Israel over all other gods (v. 32), another theological development that appears more fully elsewhere, especially in the exilic section of Isaiah.[174] Here are the seeds of later monotheism as well as universal Messianism, rooted in God's promise to David in chap. 7 that is summarized here in v. 51: "[God] is a tower of salvation for his king, / and shows steadfast love to his anointed, / to David and

---

173. The self-glorification here resembles that often seen in the annals of Assyrian kings. On the theme of exaltation, see my study, *Divine Presence*. Polzin, *David*, 204, aptly says: "God has transformed him into a miniature of himself—a quasi-god in royal garb," but tempered by the humbling in v. 28 (207).

174. I.e., "Second Isaiah," chaps. 40–55. Note the close parallel between v. 32 here and Isa 44:8b: "Is there any god besides me? / There is no other rock; I know not one." Cf. also Isa 43:11; 45:5, 18, 21.

his descendants forever." In such a way, later generations could read the story of David as a sign of God's promise to *them* as well.

The editors have paired David's *te deum* with his "last words," although they are not the last literally (23:1–7). The opening phrase, "now these are the words" (AT) closely resemble the introduction to the book of Deuteronomy ("these are the words"), inviting a comparison between David and Moses. In Deuteronomic tradition, Moses is the prophet par excellence (Deut 34:10–12), and in his final words David assumes the role and authority of a prophet as well—the prophet-king. As we shall see, there are also parallels between David's last words and the farewell poem of Moses in Deuteronomy 32.

Although spoken in the third person, David's poem begins with the rest of v. 1: "The oracle of David." The same literary form appears in the closest parallel to v. 1b, the oracles of Balaam, a colorful foreign diviner whom an enemy of Israel hired to curse Israel, but who ended up blessing Israel instead (Numbers 22–24). In two of his oracles, Balaam also claims to be the medium for the words of God, ironically for a foreigner, and much to his employer's dismay (cf. Num 24:3–4, 15–16). Otherwise, the expression "oracle of" most often has God as the subject, which already suggests something of the authority David is assuming. Here David's oracular status is coupled with his exaltation, a theme that we have observed before, including at the end of chap. 22. The oracle identifies David with four expressions. He is the "son of Jesse," designating his ordinary family roots, but he is also someone extraordinary: "the hero whom God has exalted, the anointed of the God of Jacob, the favorite son of the Fortress of Israel" (AT).[175]

Now David issues his oracle, which begins with yet another claim to divine inspiration: "The spirit of the Lord speaks through me, / his word is upon my tongue." We knew from the stories of David's election that God's Spirit was with him, as with other previous leaders, including Saul), empowering him in his actions, but here the divine inspiration is *verbal*—David, like prophets in general, is the medium for God's word. "God's word is upon my tongue" (v. 2b, cf. Jer 1:9; Ezek 3:1–3). Here again David's last words resemble the opening lines of Moses' valedictory poem, where he summons heaven and earth to hear the words that he speaks (Deut 32:1). Similarly, David then says that *God* has spoken, and uses the metaphor of "the Rock of Israel," just as Moses calls God "The Rock" (Deut 32:4).

---

175. Numerous translations of the final phrase are possible and none is absolutely certain. The first and third words are clear—"pleasant one" (the root for the name Naomi) and "Israel." The second word is the troublemaker. The MT has "songs of." The NRSV emends to "Strong One." David could be the subject or object of "pleasant one," e.g., the favorite singer or the favorite subject of the songs. I follow those who see the second word as referring to God, in parallel with the preceding phrases which end with a divine epithet. My "Fortress" resembles the NRSV and McCarter's "Stronghold" (McCarter, *II Samuel*, 476), often paired with rock, as below, frequently in ch. 22, and elsewhere. "Favorite son" mimics an American expression for a political or hometown notable (albeit androcentric; there could be a "favorite daughter").

The message from God appears in vv. 3b-4: "One who rules over people justly, is like the light of morning when the sun is rising, a morning without clouds, shining from rain-soaked grass from the ground" (AT). The image evokes the experience of waking up after a night of rain to see brilliant sunshine, sparkling on the wet grass (cf. the hymn "Morning Has Broken"). Sunlight and water, two gifts of creation essential to life, appear together. In a climate in which rain was seasonal, wet grass signifies far more than a nice suburban lawn—it signifies fertility and blessing, the very power of life itself. In the ancient Near East (and arguably everywhere and always) a political figurehead like the king often represented this power, indeed, was the primary *channel* of this power from the creator. Psalm 72, a prayer for the king, exemplifies this understanding of royal mediation: "May he be like rain that falls on the mown grass, like showers that water the earth" (v. 6). Here also is the essential connection to fertility—"May there be abundance of grain in the land"—and the sociological extension of fertility—"may people blossom in the cities like the grass of the field" (v. 16). Again, similar language appears in the "Song of Moses," here connected to the fruitfulness of words: "May my teaching drop like the rain, / my speech condense like the dew; / like gentle rain on grass, / like showers on new growth" (v. 2).[176]

As David's poem makes clear, this fructifying power inheres to the king *if* the king promotes justice. That is why Psalm 72 begins with the invocation, "Give the king your justice, O God." In fact, "prosperity for the people" is contingent on providing "deliverance to the needy" (vv. 3–4; cf. 12–14). David pairs ruling justly with "ruling in the fear of God," fear meaning not so much fright as awe and reverence, which, in ancient Israel, is also the beginning of wisdom (Prov 1:7). Despite our theological difficulties with the story of the Gibeonite's revenge in chap. 21, the presupposition operating there is that God has imposed a drought *instead of* sending rain because of the injustice done to the Gibeonites. If we also recoil from a direct cause-and-effect connection between injustice and natural (i.e., meteorological) phenomena, ancient Israel (and the ancient world in general) had no such compunction. As we have noted before, this connection pervades the prophetic understanding of covenant theology (especially blessing and curse).[177] That theology provides a check on any notion that the king *automatically* channels blessing. At the end of the *books* of Kings, it will be all too apparent that such a notion is disastrously wrong.

The next section of David's poem asks rhetorically if, in fact, his dynasty ("house") is not "like this with God." That is, David's dynasty *is* a channel of blessing like rain on the grass, and the assurance is rooted in God's promise to David recounted in the story of Nathan's oracle in chap. 7: "For he has made with me an everlasting covenant, ordered in

---

176. Cf. Isa 55:10–11 and note the connection with the Davidic covenant, now "democratized," in v. 3.

177. For examples, see Hos 4:1–3; Amos 4:6–12. Drought plays a major role in the stories of Elisha and Elijah later on.

all things and secure" (v. 5). The promise in chap. 7 does not use the phrase "everlasting covenant" (or even simply the word "covenant"), although the substance is there in the ubiquitous use of the word "forever." The phrase most often refers to God's covenant with the ancestors mediated through Abraham and Sarah (Gen 9:16; 17:7, 13, 19; Ps 105:10).[178] The blessing of God's covenant ties in with the botanical language of the grass in v. 4: God will "make to sprout" all David's help (the root means "to save") and desire (AT). God's covenant with David's dynasty is like rain on the ground that makes seeds germinate and plants grow.[179]

On the other hand, David's assurance may also rest on his administration of justice if the final section of the poem refers to rulers who are *unjust* (vv. 6–7).[180] The word translated by "the godless" in the NRSV is an abstract noun (roughly *Beliyaʿal*) that could mean "godlessness." It is used in 22:5 parallel to Sheol ("perdition"). Perhaps more significantly, the expression "offspring of Beliyaʿal" ("worthless fellows," "perverse lot") appears frequently in previous stories referring to rascals in general (Judg 19:22; 20:13), including Nabal (1 Sam 25:17, 25); political malcontents (1 Sam 10:27; 30:22), including Sheba (2 Sam 20:1); and also to the offspring of political leaders (Eli's sons, 1 Sam 2:12). The foul-mouthed Shimei accuses David of being a "man of Beliyaʿal" ("Scoundrel," 16:7).

Whether unjust subjects of the king or an unjust king, the figure in v. 6 clearly stands in opposition to the order and security established by God's covenant with David. If it is an unjust king, the metaphor of the worthless thorn bush, untouchable and suitable only for burning, also contrasts with the well-watered grass of v. 4. Moreover, the metaphor resembles that used in the parable of Jotham, where the "bramble" accepts the nomination as king, in contrast to the olive tree, the fig tree, and the vine, which, instead, prefer to continue producing their oil, delicious fruit, and wine. Here the bramble may well be the *source* of a destructive fire in society (Judg 9:8–15).

In some ways David's last words represent the ideal monarchy from the prophetic perspective. If the king is raised up and anointed by God and rules justly, the king can be the source of perennial blessing for the people. But implicit is the possibility that the king might be the opposite—an unjust ruler who brings destruction. Whereas the negative possibility seemed most prominent in the narrative of the rise of the monarchy (1 Samuel 8 and 12), here the positive stands out. On the other hand, the "evil" that sets in subsequent to David's murder of Uriah sometimes makes Shimei's characterization of David as *Beliyaʿal* seem quite fitting! In that context, the poem here takes on an irony

---

178. Many scholars think that the formulation of the Abrahamic covenant is based on the Davidic. Note the approximation of the phrase in Ps 89:28 (and, as we have seen, its apparent failure in 89:39!). Cf. again Isa 55:3 where the covenant is identified with David but now made with the people.

179. The language is prominent in the exilic Isaiah. See my study "Stars, Sprouts, and Streams."

180. These verses are quite ambiguous, possibly referring instead to *subjects* of the king who are disreputable.

similar to that in the preceding *te deum* when it touts David's "blameless" probity (22:24-25). Also, we wonder if the prophets may have worried about a king who claimed the authority that they presumed to exercise—to know and speak the word of God. Perhaps it would not be such a good idea for the king to be "among the prophets" (unless he is simply an ecstatic one, 1 Sam 10:12).[181] David has already performed priestly functions, and the royal theology rooted in Jerusalem would bestow an eternal priesthood on the king to match the eternal covenant (cf. Psalm 110). So the king who is a priest is here also a prophet. More often than not, the prophets felt compelled to speak God's word *against* the king (e.g., Samuel against Saul, Nathan against even David). What if the king claimed his own legitimacy in saying "thus says the Lord"? The prophets wielded enormous power, as we have already seen with Samuel and Nathan. To combine that power derived from divine inspiration with the political power of the throne would be to produce a potentially overwhelming (and overweening) force, one quite capable of theocratic tyranny.[182]

David's Elite Fighters (23:9-39)

The first part of this section (through v. 23) resembles the structurally matched section in 21:15-18 in that various exploits of David and his warriors are reported. Most likely all of these happened prior to current narrative time (e.g., v. 13 and 1 Sam 22:1). Here, however, the collector arranges the material to focus on "the Three"—David's top ranked warriors—and "the Thirty"—the next rank down, of which only two men are featured. The rest of the section is a list of other members of the Thirty (numbered erroneously in v. 39). The names of some of the characters in this section cannot help but evoke chuckles from the modern reader, especially the two sons of Dodo. Each of the brief vignettes in vv. 8-23 could provide the kernel for a much expanded story like that of David and Goliath in 1 Samuel 17. The best candidate would be the incident in which Benaiah, armed only with a staff, fights with a "handsome" Egyptian, armed with a spear—and uses the Egyptian's own spear to kill him, much as David used Goliath's sword (after stunning him with his slingshot). Where the Egyptian came from we do not know (we would expect a Philistine). There is an ironic twist at the end of this list (rewarding the persistent reader), where Uriah the Hittite receives a posthumous notation. Why save his name for last? Coming here at the end of numerous stories of David's warriors, Uriah is the warrior who fought for David but whom David murdered. If nothing else,

---

181. Though not referring to this text, Polzin, *Samuel*, 186, suggests that Samuel promoted and Saul practiced the "illicit commingling [of prophecy] with kingship" that was part of the ruin of both (cf. 1 Sam 10:5-13; 18:10; 19:18-24).

182. Birch, *1 and 2 Samuel*, 1073, rightly compares the founders of the United States who "did not wish kings to control religious rituals and practices." One can see a modern example of this in the ruling Ayatollah Ali Khamanei of Iran, who is both the religious Supreme Leader and the supreme political power, transcending that of President Ahmadinejad. At this writing (2010), constituents of the political challenger are questioning the authority of the Ayatollah,

and another Ayatollah (Rafsanjani) has come to their defense.

he reminds us of the David who is *not* the honored commander-in-chief, nor the ideal prophet-king, nor blameless before God, nor just to his subjects.

A Plague on the House of David (Chap. 24)

The book concludes with the strange story of a plague, matching the drought story of 21:1–14. There the reason for God's wrath was clear—blood guilt on the house of Saul. Here there is no explanation. The opening clause resembles the way some stories in Judges began, with God provoked against Israel (cf. Judg 3:7–8), but here, instead of sending him as a deliverer, God initially uses David as the *means* for God's punishment. In fact, God orders David to conduct a census, and, when the census is finished, punishes him for doing so! It is as if that evil spirit from God that tortured Saul has now turned against David as well (1 Sam 16:14). God's anger is simply capricious.[183] In the parallel account in Chronicles, the editors simply could not tolerate this split in the divine personality, so they substituted "Satan" in place of God (1 Chr 21:1), thereby helping to pave the path to dualism.

What is so wrong about conducting a census? Why does Joab protest? Although initially the census is to cover the whole people, later it seems to be limited to men old enough to bear arms (v. 9). The census is part of Israel's "Selective Service," determining the strength of the army, which is one of those improbable

> Why should this [plague] be either a test of faith sent by God, or the evil working of the Devil in the world? One of these beliefs we embraced, the other we scorned as superstition. But perhaps each was false, equally. Perhaps the Plague was neither of God nor the Devil, but simply a thing in Nature, as the stone on which we stub a toe.[184]

figures—a total of 1.3 million men. We can understand the problem in two ways. One concerns the ritual purity required of the troops.[185] Before entering into service, soldiers were supposed to contribute a monetary offering "to make atonement" "so that no plague may come upon them for being registered" (Exod 30:11–16; also a great fund-raiser for the sanctuary!). One who is numbered among the "host" of Israel, which is also God's "host," cannot be in a state of defilement.[186] In our story, there is no indication that such a ritual was followed, leaving those canvassed vulnerable to God's punishment, which will

---

183. Attempts to explain, much less excuse, the divine behavior here would soften an inexplicable divine sadism, however much we may not want to draw that conclusion.

184. Brooks, *Year of Wonders*, 215.

185. Such purity was involved with David's troops in 1 Sam 21:5; Uriah in 11:11; cf. Deut 23:9–14. See McCarter, *II Samuel*, 512–14.

186. Note the list of army "hosts" of those "counted" in Numbers 2 (AT, NRSV "company" and "enrolled;" the latter word is that used in 2 Sam 24:2 for "take a census"). The tribal "hosts" also appear in Numbers 10, listed at the moment of the departure of the people from Sinai (vv. 11–28). These hosts are the human contingent in the combined army of God that includes heavenly forces, referred to in Num 10:36, and notably in David's challenge to Goliath: "I come to you in the name of the Lord of hosts, the God of the armies of Israel" (1 Sam 17:45; cf. Josh 5:14).

also extend to the people as a whole. Presumably this was Joab's fear, which soon proves to be well founded. An alternative is more sociological: the census is the administrative means not only for a military draft but also for taxation, both forms of governmental control that depart from the pre-monarchical community, indeed, "ways of the king" that appear in Samuel's anti-monarchy speech in 1 Sam 8:10–17. Joab's objection reflects Samuel's position.[187] It also seems possible that these two understandings are not mutually incompatible.[188]

As soon as David receives the census figures, he is "stricken to the heart because he had numbered the people" (v. 10). Perhaps he has realized his error too late, but the narrator does not inform us of David's rationale. He confesses his sin to God and asks for pardon. In the morning he gets his answer, but through his "seer," "the prophet Gad" (apparently one of David's religious counselors). God offers him a choice of three punishments—a sort of "choose your poison"—three years of famine on the land, three months fleeing from his enemies, or three day's of "pestilence." David chooses the last, arguing that he would rather fall into the merciful hands of God than his enemies, although in this story one wonders about the difference between the two (perhaps he also has had enough of famine [chap. 21] and flight [chaps. 15–17]).[189] David phrases his answer in pious words, but he conveniently skips over option two that would minimize public harm but put him personally in danger.[190] As a result, God promptly sends a plague on the entire people (emphasized by "from Dan to Beer-sheba"), wiping out seventy thousand people in three days, a fast-moving epidemic indeed.[191]

God calls an end to the plague just as God's grim agent stretches out his hand toward Jerusalem "to destroy it" (cf. Exod 12:23). "The Lord relented concerning the evil," another of those situations reporting God's change of mind (Exod 32:14; 1 Sam 15:10). At that moment the angel is standing "by the threshing floor of Araunah the Jebusite." David again confesses his sin and begs God to punish him and not the people (v. 17).[192] Gad, who seems to read the king's mind as well as know God's will, promptly shows up and provides an act of penance. If David will "erect an altar to the Lord on the threshing floor of Araunah," the plague will end (v. 18). Araunah appears quite willing to give up his property—even for free—if it will end the plague, but David insists on purchasing the property and the materials for a sacrifice, lest his gesture seem shabby. With fifty shekels of silver in hand, Araunah hands over the property, David constructs the altar, and God ends the plague, there-

---

187. Gunn and Fewell, *Narrative*, 126; Birch, *1 and 2 Samuel*, 1380; Brueggemann, *Samuel*, 352 ("an act of bureaucratic terrorism"!).

188. Alter, *David Story*, sees a combination, plus a universal dislike for being numbered at all (cf. our expression regarding bureaucratic impersonality, "a name and not just a number").

189. However, famine would also be from God (ch. 21), so David's reasoning seems faulty.

190. Gunn and Fewell, *Narrative*, 126.

191. As often, surely an exaggerated figure. A large city at the time would probably have had a population of only two thousand; cf. McNutt, *Reconstructing*, 152.

192. This verse suggests a different version of the story from v. 16. It appeared that the plague ended in v. 16, but v. 25 may suggest that it continued to rage *outside* Jerusalem.

by reconstituting David's reputation as a savior. Threshing floors were often places charged with a numinous power, probably connected to the fertility of crops, and thus to God's blessing, and this place will become the location for that temple that God forbade David himself to build (7:13). Thus the story ends as a kind legend about how David *did* found the *site* of the temple that Solomon would construct (cf. Bethel, Gen 28:11–22).

How should we read this collection in chaps. 21–24 regarding David? There is room for considerable ambiguity.[193] Does the administrator of forced labor in David's so-called cabinet (20:24) suggest royal exploitation, if not oppression, or is that simply a given with monarchy? Does he manipulate (or even invent) a situation that provides the opportunity to eradicate Saul's survivors, or does he save his people from drought? Is his *te deum* hypocritical—a cynical *te davidum*? Does he abrogate to himself prophetic powers, or accurately describe God's using him as a medium for revelation? Does he rule in justice or, in fact, is he "godless"? Does the information about Elhanan disclose David's slaying Goliath as a fake? Is David's abhorrence of blood ironic (23:17)? Does the placement of Uriah's name function to remind us of David's chief crime? Does his grasp for administrative control cause the death of seventy-thousand, or does he save his people from uncontrolled divine fury?

Most likely, the editor has taken the lists, poems, and stories that contain potentially damaging implications regarding David and spun them to produce a positive image, a process familiar from many of the stories in 1 Samuel 16 up to this point. Chapters 21–24 have interrupted the original narrative that led from Sheba's revolt in chap. 20 to the death of David and the struggle of his would-be successors in 1 Kings 1–2. But looking forward, the Gibeonite story finally removes the possibility of any of Saul's contenders to the throne, and David's altar lends his prestige to the future temple site. In both stories, David is absolved from blame. He didn't cause the famine (or demand the executions), and he didn't cause the plague. In fact, *God* is behind both (or, again, for the Chronicler on the census, David could say "the Devil made me do it"). Moreover, the two central poems in which David gives thanks for God's deliverance and proclaims himself the oracular medium for divine blessing are framed by stories in which David delivers Israel from potential destruction and restores God's blessing, either through the Gibeonites (21:3) or by founding the sacred space from which blessing will flow (cf. Pss 24:5; 84:4–5). Thus David is not the "king who had brought grief to the people" but "a king who had saved them from grief."[194] With this final apologetic spin on David, the way is now open for the rise of Solomon.

---

193. See Gunn and Fewell, *Narrative*, 121–28.

194. McCarter, *II Samuel*, 518.

SIX

1 Kings

List of major characters:

Abiathar, Priest under David, sole survivor of house of Eli, competitor of Zadok; banished by Solomon

Adonijah, eldest son of David; replaced by Solomon, then executed

Ahab, king of Israel, married to Jezebel, opposed by the prophet Elijah

Benaiah, head of David's private mercenaries, Solomon's hatchet man

Ben-hadad, name of numerous kings of Aram (Syria)

Elijah, prophet in time of Ahab

Elisha, prophet who succeeded Elijah

Gehazi, servant of Elisha

Jehu, fanatical reformer who eliminated the house of Ahab (not to be confused with the brief appearance of the prophet Jehu in 1 Kgs 16:7)

Jeroboam I, first king of northern Israel, blamed for fall of the North

Jezebel, wife of Ahab, king of Israel, opponent of the prophet Elijah

Joab, commander of David's army

Josiah, ideal king of Judah, implemented Deuteronomic reformation

Naboth, vineyard owner framed and executed by Ahab and Jezebel

Nathan, prophet at court

Rehoboam, son of Solomon and his successor

Solomon, son of David and Bathsheba, third king of Judah and Israel

Zadok, priest under David and Solomon who founded priestly line competing with Levitical line, represented by Abiathar

The books of Kings can hold their own for fantastic stories: a king who burns himself to death; an ax head that floats on water; a mother who cooks and eats her own child; and a queen who becomes dog food. There is a prophet who can make a king's hand shrivel (and unshrivel), and another who can raise the dead, and who, to evoke Superman, is faster than a speeding chariot, is a survivalist who can live forty days in the wilderness without food or water, and who departs this mortal life like a rocket. The books often refer to other historical records which, unfortunately, we do not have: e.g., "Book of the Acts of Solomon," "Book of the Annals of the Kings of Israel" and "of Judah." There are also numerous stories that fit in the category of "prophetic legends." Indeed, often the narrative is as much about prophets as it is about kings, easily earning the title "Former Prophets," if it has not already been deserved from 1 and 2 Samuel. The reigns of some kings receive only a short passage; those of others relatively large blocks of material.[1] As with previous books, the intention of the writers and editors is not only to provide an historical narrative, but also and even more so, a theological commentary on that narrative. Thus we will often find sizeable gaps in the historical information about a particular ruler's reign, even if that ruler had an international reputation (e.g., Omri). The method of presentation is not strictly chronological; rather, the narrative moves from one king to another (e.g., A to B), sometimes including material about another king (B) who lived simultaneously with the other (A)—i.e., one in Judah, the other in Israel. Then the narrative will focus on the next king's reign (B), even if already partially presented under king A. Thus there are overlapping "panels" which move back and forth chronologically, instead of straight forward.[2] Needless to say, the method can create considerable confusion, which is compounded by the problem that some kings have the same name (and in North and South!). Overall, the editors have marked the reigns of each king with a summary introduction and conclusion, basically telling us if they were good kings or bad kings—the good kings being the ones who tried to correct the religious unorthodoxy of their predecessors. The chief, indeed, almost exclusive, concern in those evaluations is sacerdotal—the worship of Yahweh alone, at the proper place, in the proper manner, conducted by the proper personnel.

Clearing the Deck (Chaps. 1–2)

There are good reasons for seeing 1 Kings 1–2 as the conclusion to the stories of David in 1 and 2 Samuel, especially since here he finally dies. In retrospect his "last words" in 2 Sam 23:1–7 will prove to be premature after we hear his deathbed words. Because Solomon's rise parallels David's dying, many scholars see these chapters more specifically as the conclusion to a "succession narrative" that traces Solomon's ascendance to the throne, beginning in 2 Samuel 9. However, only in 1 Kings 1–2 does the question about David's successor really come to the foreground, even though Solomon is clearly the subject of such passages as Nathan's oracle concerning the building of the temple in 2 Sam 7:13.

Whether in the present context or another (e.g., connecting to 2 Samuel 20), the opening scene seems to have jumped over David's later years to his final days (vv. 1–4).[3] Suddenly he is an

---

1. Solomon, 1 Kings 1–11; Jeroboam, 1 Kings 12–14; Ahab (and Elijah), 1 Kgs 16:29—33:40; Elisha (and various kings) 2 Kings 2–9; 13; Hezekiah, 2 Kings 18–20; Josiah, 2 Kings 22–23.

2. See Nelson, *First and Second Kings*, 8–9, who uses the computer analogy of "windows" from which one moves back and forth.

3. Verses 1–4 could be an editorial insertion, elaborating on v. 15, which now seems redun-

old man, wrapped in a blanket, who still cannot get warm. His servants apparently are concerned with more than his body temperature, however, for their suggestion of finding "a young virgin" to heat up his bed clearly implies an attempt to raise his libido as well. As we have seen (e.g., 2 Sam 23:2–4), the figure of the king was associated with fecundity. He was a channel for divine blessing that would fructify people, crops, and the land in general. In other cultures, the king acted out this role liturgically in rituals involving sexual intercourse. There is no such activity here, but David's waning sexuality calls into question his potency, a remarkable sign of aging in the man who had seven wives and ten concubines. Now even the presence of the beautiful Abishag in his bed is not enough to revive him, however, for "the king did not know her sexually" (v. 4). The king is impotent.

Immediately the significance of potency shifts from the sexual to the political, from the one who is impotent to those who seek to take his place as potentate.[4] David's oldest surviving son, Adonijah, is the first contender, and the narrator wastes no time in giving us his opinion: Adonijah is an arrogant upstart who "exalts" himself in the same way as his deceased half-brother, Absalom.

Their political aspirations seem to have been orchestrated by the same campaign manager: a chariot procession with fifty runners in front, a handsome appearance, conspirators among David's inner circle, and a barbeque dinner with "all his brothers, the king's sons, and all the royal officials of Judah," as guests (cf. 2 Sam 14:25; 15:1–12). If the location is historical fact, it nonetheless sounds sinister: Snaking Rock and Spy Spring (Zoheleth, En-rogel, v. 9, AT)![5] The dinner is supposed to be a kind of inaugural banquet, and later we hear that the guests are saying "Long live King Adonijah!" (v. 25).[6] Adonijah's supporters include Joab, the former head of David's military, and Abiathar, the priest and sole-survivor of the massacre at Nob (1 Sam 22:20). Abithar and Zadok had supported David in his struggle with Absalom (2 Sam 15:26–29; 17:15). But Adonijah does not favor Zadok with an invitation, nor the prophet Nathan, nor Benaiah (chief of David's personal bodyguard), much less David's one other son, Solomon. The narrator also tells us that Adonijah "was born next after Absalom," thus emphasizing Adonijah's understandable expectation that he will be the successor. And he reveals one other similarity between Absalom (and other siblings) and Adonijah—David "had never at any time displeased him

---

dant. Verse 5 would make a good beginning on its own.

4. In the Ugaritic epic of Kirta, his son challenges his authority to rule on grounds of juridical negligence but also physical infirmity that implies sexual impotence: "Like a bedfellow is illness, / (your) concubine is disease!" See Wyatt, *Religious Texts*, 239. Greenstein, "Kirta," 41, uses somewhat less suggestive language: "consort" (literally "sister") and "company."

5. Conversely, the spring Gihon ("Gusher") is the location for the inauguration of Solomon (vv. 33, 38).

6. Note the context of sacrifices with the establishment of Saul's monarchy, 1 Sam 10:8; 11:15. It is possible, though, that Bathsheba and Nathan have exaggerated the situation—there is no report *by the narrator* of Adonijah's kingship in vv. 9–10.

by asking, 'Why have you done thus and so?'" (v. 6). David seems never to have learned the lesson about permissive parenting (cf. 2 Sam 13:21, 39; 19:1–8), but it will be Adonijah who pays the price.

Despite Nathan's absence from Adonijah's party, he has heard about it, and that Adonijah had become king, and he promptly goes to Bathsheba and informs her, adding that the one who was incapable of "knowing" Abishag now does not know what Adonijah is up to (cf. also v. 18). On the other hand, Adonijah does not know what is happening back in David's bedroom, and will not know until it is too late (v. 41). The author has arranged the scenes in such a way that Adonijah is partying all the while oblivious to the events that will bring his reign to an end before it has really begun. Nathan assumes the role of privy counselor to the queen, warning her that both her life and Solomon's are at risk. The danger of a coup d'état among the king's sons has its precedent (2 Sam 13:30). Nathan instructs Bathsheba to go to David and remind him of his previous oath affirming that Solomon "would be king" after him (v. 13, AT). We know nothing of this, but David confirms it in v. 30. Then she is to inform David of Adonijah's move, and while she is still speaking, Nathan will come in and back her up. Bathsheba complies, but adds her own words: "all Israel" is waiting for David to name his successor, suggesting that his decline is public knowledge, and if David does not take charge she and Solomon will be "counted as offenders."

Judging from this scene alone, Bathsheba enjoys a favored status with David, as does Nathan, even though the last we heard from him was his rebuke of David *because of* Bathsheba (2 Samuel 12). Nathan follows his scenario, posing slightly different versions of the question—has David designated Adonijah as successor without letting his servants know? Nathan asks if David *does* know what is going on and has not let *him* know. David responds by summoning Bathsheba again (presumably each person leaves when the other arrives, cf. v. 32), and reaffirming his promise of Solomon's succession, adding "so will I do this day" (v. 31). Both Bathsheba and Nathan have been bowing and scraping before the king (vv. 16, 23; the same language is used for obeisance to God), and Bathsheba adds one more bow and the obligatory wish, "May my lord King David live forever," something which clearly is not in the cards.

Now David issues orders to Zadok, Nathan, and Benaiah, putting his decision into motion. They are to gather David's various officials, set Solomon on David's mule (the mount of royalty), proceed to the Gihon spring of Jerusalem, "anoint him king over Israel," blow the trumpet, and proclaim "Long live King Solomon!" In fact, David authorizes Solomon as his immediate successor even before his own death, having him sit on his own throne, "king in my place," "for," David says, "*I* have appointed him to be ruler (*nagid*) over Israel and over Judah" (v. 35).[7] In other words, Solomon is at once "crown prince" and king (something like the monarch of England abdicating to the Prince of

---

7. Following the LXX with the emphatic "I." The MT has "him," emphasizing the object.

Wales). The statement contains a remarkable combination of developments in the institution of the monarchy. Compare the initiation of the monarchy when God said to Samuel, "you shall anoint [Saul] to be ruler (*nagid*) over my people Israel" (1 Sam 9:16; cf. 10:1); or compare the transition to David, when God said "I have seen among [Jesse's] sons a king for me" (1 Sam 16:1, AT). There the selection is God's to make, mediated through the prophet. Of course, with Saul, there was no question of a competitor because he was the first king. Still, both the donkey story and the lottery story emphasized God's control over the process. Even the text that might reflect an originally independent tradition in which Saul was crowned by the people now appears as a "renewal" of God's previous selection (1 Sam 11:14–15). The same applies to David. Although "the people of Judah anointed David king" (2 Sam 2:4), as did subsequently "all the elders of Israel," the preceding narrative has already established David as God's choice, as acknowledged by those elders (2 Sam 5:2–3). Also different here is the participation not only of Nathan the prophet but also Zadok the priest and Benaiah the captain of the royal guard, representing three spheres of power, with Benaiah no doubt in full military dress.

In effect, David has issued an executive order on his own (the word "appointed" could be "commanded" as well), thus subverting both the assumption of primogeniture and God's initiative. If Bathsheba is correct, "all Israel" *expected* David to make such an order (v. 20). Of course, *God* had already subverted primogeniture by bypassing Jonathan. But in this story, we have not heard a single word from God, even to Nathan, who here seems to be more a lobbyist for Solomon. As if realizing the vacuum, Benaiah responds to David's orders with the wish that they will prove to be *God's* will also: "May it be so! May Yahweh, the God of my lord the king, make it so" (v. 36, AT).[8] It's as if Benaiah is saying, "Let's hope God goes along with this!" He then also invokes God's being "with Solomon" as God was so frequently "with David," and concludes expansively with the hope that God will "make his throne greater than the throne of my lord King David." On the other hand, the narrator gives no indication that what has happened is *against* God's will, and the negative assessment of Adonijah at the outset suggests the narrator's own approval. We know nothing of Solomon's merits for the position, however, other than being the son of Bathsheba and the favorite of his supporters. Presumably, the notice at Solomon's birth still holds true: "the Lord loved him" (2 Sam 12:24). The question will be whether that love is adequately requited.

The three agents proceed with their charge, with Zadok doing the actual anointing (vv. 38–40). The "horn of oil" comes "from the tent," the sanctuary erected by David to shelter the ark (2 Sam 6:17). Whether or not this is the same horn used by Samuel, its presence along with the sacred ark clearly implies

---

8. This translation, like the NRSV, follows numerous alternative textual traditions. "May it be /make it so" translates the Hebrew cognate for our word "amen."

divine sanction to the ritual (even if God has not spoken). The inaugural parade back to the palace then strikes up the band, producing an earthshaking noise, and the scene shifts back to Adonijah's rival inaugural party (vv. 41–48). They have scarcely finished their feast when they hear all the commotion, and Joab notices above all the shrill blast of the trumpet. His puzzlement soon finds its answer when Abiathar's son, Jonathan, arrives, *not* with the "good news" expected of a good man (v. 42)[9]—"Solomon now sits on the royal throne" (v. 46). Not only that, but everyone is shaking David's hand and expressing their hope that Solomon will be even more famous than his father, and David has offered a prayer of thanks to God for granting one of his offspring succession to his throne, whereby David seems to confirm the wish previously expressed by Benaiah. As David has ordered, so God has done (v. 48).

At the very moment that Abiathar was celebrating his inauguration, another was taking place that would nullify his own. Never has a party broken up so suddenly, or with such fear—everyone goes home, and Adonijah himself flees for his life. Apparently he runs to the tent from which Zadok took the anointing oil, or at least to the sacrificial altar associated with it. There fugitives would find asylum if they held on to the horns that decorated the altar's corners.[10] Adonijah must resort to these horns because his brother benefited from the *anointing* horn. He refuses to let go until Solomon swears not to execute him, which Solomon does on the condition of Adonijah's honesty, and then sends him home.

Chapter 2 opens with the aging David on his deathbed, issuing a series of orders to Solomon. There are two parts—a pious encouragement in the faith and a settling of scores. The Christian use of the word "testament" in "Old / New Testament" derives from this tradition of a deathbed testimony delivered at key times of transition.[11] The encouragement (vv. 2b-4) also sounds very much like that addressed to Joshua by God in Josh 1:7-9. David charges Solomon to be courageous and to follow everything that is in "the law of Moses," referring to the book of Deuteronomy (cf. Deut 17:14–20). Obedience to God's rules will result in God's establishing *Solomon's* rule. Here David repeats the dynastic promise first delivered to him by Nathan, but with a notable change: in 2 Sam 7:11–12 the promise is unconditional, qualified only by the threat of punishment, but not termination. Here the promise is conditional. Solomon is to keep all of God's rules "*so that*" he may prosper and "*so that*" God "will establish his word" to David (AT). In other words, God's confirmation of that word will come *as a result of* Solomon's obedience. David then repeats the "word" of promise: "*If* your heirs . . . walk before me in faithfulness with all their heart and with all their soul, there shall not fail you a successor on the throne of Israel." The promise will continue if the kings

---

9. Note the similarity to the announcement of Absalom's death in 2 Sam 18:27.

10. Presumably Exod 27:1-2; 21:12-14 suggest the custom involved here.

11. E.g., Jacob, Genesis 49–50; Moses, Deuteronomy; Joshua in Joshua 23–24.

adhere to the Great Commandment of Deut 6:4–5. On the other hand, the condition concerns the *extent* of the *realm*, not the *extension* of the *dynasty*. That is, "the throne of Israel"—the unified people of North and South—is at stake, not the continuation of the dynasty itself.[12] That unity will not last much longer than Solomon himself (cf. chap. 12); the dynasty's future will remain a question to the end of Kings. Only two kings will fully live up to David's charge (Hezekiah and Josiah, 2 Kgs 18:5; 22:2; 23:25), and the latter's rule will be tragically short.

In the second part of the deathbed speech David turns to recompense and rewards (vv. 5–9), "a will and testament worthy of a Mafia chieftain," as Robert Alter so aptly puts it.[13] The recompense first involves Joab's murder of David's two military leaders, Abner and Amasa, actions that were done to *David* as well as them. David describes Joab as covered in blood not from battle but from murders done in peacetime. He advises Solomon to act "according to your wisdom," but defines what that should be—not to let Joab live to old age. On the other hand, Solomon is to reward the sons of Barzillai for their father's act of mercy and generosity in supporting David in his flight from Absalom. Then requital comes again, this time against Shimei, the Benjamite who *cursed* David in his flight from Absalom. Although Shimei had subsequently asked David's forgiveness, and received a pardon, Solomon was under no such restraint, and David again suggests what Solomon's wisdom should conclude: "you must bring his gray head down with blood to Sheol." The narrator then reports David's death and burial, leaving one to wonder what it would be like to die with the last words on one's lips words of bitterness and revenge.[14]

There is a notice about the length of David's reign, and then yet another confirmation of Solomon's succession: "So Solomon sat on the throne of his father David; and his kingdom was firmly established." A new era has begun.

Adonijah's next move is incredibly stupid (2:13–25). Solomon had promised to spare him as long as he did not act out of line, but Adonijah now goes to Bathsheba and asks her to ask Solomon to give him David's bedroom companion, the beautiful Abishag as a wife. Although she was not described as a concubine, she most likely now belongs to Solomon, making Adonijah's request seem like a gesture of political defiance, if not outright subversion. We have seen the same issue before, most notably with Ishbaal and Abner.[15] Taking the king's concubine is tantamount to an attempt at taking the king's throne. In making his request, Adonijah reiterates his claim, alleging that "all Israel expected me to reign" (v. 15), contrary to what Bathsheba had previously said, that "all Israel" was waiting for David to *decide* who should reign (1:20). Nevertheless,

---

12. So Halpern, *First Historians*, 161, 163, referring also to 8:25–26 and 9:4–9.

13. Alter, *David Story*, xiv.

14. David's wish is something like saying "may he go to hell," in that Sheol (a kind of shadowy underworld) "very often has to do with punishment." See Levenson, *Resurrection*, 73. Thus David's absolutely last word is "Sheol," perhaps a risky valediction!

15. 2 Sam 3:6–8; cf. with Absalom, 2 Sam 16:21–22.

Adonijah acknowledges the "turn" of events that established Solomon on the throne, even that "it was his from the Lord," a divine confirmation that we have yet to see.

Bathsheba does go to Solomon, who bows *to her* and has the Queen Mother enthroned at his right hand. She then conveys Adonijah's request as if it were her own, and at first Solomon says of course he will grant anything she asks. But his reply to the request shows how subversive it seems to him: "ask for him the kingdom as well! For he is my elder brother." Indeed, he says, why not add Abiathar and Joab as well, not, of course, as husbands to Abishag but as accomplices to Adonijah's attempted coup. Instead, he vows to take Adonijah's life, and his vow claims divine sanction of his position (which, again, we have not heard): God "has established me and placed me on the throne of my father David, and . . . made me a house as he promised" (v. 24). The language again recalls Nathan's oracle of 2 Samuel 7:11: "the Lord will make you a house," referring to David's offspring. Then in the same breath Solomon dispatches Benaiah who promptly puts Adonijah to death.

Now Solomon turns to the priestly conspirator, Abiathar, and banishes him to Anathoth, saying that he will not execute him since he has "carried the ark of the Lord God before my father David." The narrator interprets Abiathar's exile as "fulfilling the word of the Lord that he had spoken concerning the house of Eli in Shiloh," referring to 1 Sam 2:27–36, where Abiathar is the one who will be left to weep, and Zadok is the one who will have his own priestly house to serve the house of the anointed.

Now it is Joab's turn. Hearing of Adonijah's death, he too flees to the "tent of the Lord" and grabs the horns of the altar, but it will be no sanctuary for him as well. When Benaiah (by now, clearly Solomon's hatchet man), approaches him, Joab insists that he would rather die in the tent rather than elsewhere.[16] Benaiah returns to tell Solomon, who orders him to kill Joab where he is nonetheless. If Joab is inside the tent, he is executed in front of the holy ark; if he is outside, his blood on the altar replaces that of the sacrificial animal. In issuing his order, Solomon affirms that Joab's blood will remove the guilt on David's house for the blood Joab has spilled, thus fulfilling David's dying wish. Indeed, Solomon's defense of David's righteousness is effusive (if not also *self*-righteous), concluding with the conviction that his dynasty will enjoy "peace from the Lord forevermore." Having banished Abiathar and executed Joab, Solomon is now free to confirm Benaiah in the position he had under David, chief of his personal bodyguard, and Zadok as priest (v. 35; cf. 2 Sam 8:17). This continuation of David's administration reiterates the extent to which the monarchy has displaced the old militia, as well as co-opted the sacerdotal institution. The relationship with the latter will become even cozier when the king builds his temple.

---

16. The situation is confusing in that the altar would not be inside the tent (since it is a sacrificial altar requiring fire), yet Benaiah orders Joab to "come out."

Finally, there is Shimei (2:36–46). Solomon does not follow David's orders but grants him conditional asylum in Jerusalem, provided that he will not leave the city limits. But after three years, Shimei makes the mistake of traveling to the town of Gath in pursuit of escaped slaves, and on his return Solomon summons him, reminding him of the condition (which Shimei himself had declared to be "fair"). Shimei has not only broken Solomon's "commandment" but also his "oath to the Lord," and Solomon cannot help but remind him also of "all the evil" that he did to David in cursing him. Solomon then concludes with another florid glorification of himself and David, claiming that the curse has been reversed: "But King Solomon shall be blessed, and the throne of David shall be established before the Lord forever." Benaiah, Solomon's grim reaper, has more work to do.

"So," we hear once again, "the kingdom was established in the hand of Solomon" (v. 46b; cf. v. 12).

The events in chs.1–2 thus legitimate Solomon's claim to the throne in a number of ways. The narrator characterizes his opponent as an arrogant, deceitful, rebel, much like Absalom. David himself authorizes the succession of Solomon, as the people expect him to do (according to Bathsheba). Solomon's supporters include the formidable figures of the Queen Mother, the prophet Nathan, priest Zadok, and royal guardsman Benaiah. Solomon's execution of Adonijah is presented not as a matter of revenge or mere political expedience but the proper punishment for one who has made a subversive move. The exile of the priest Abiathar is far better than the death he deserves. Similarly, the execution of Joab is demanded to remove blood guilt, and that of Shimei only after he has broken an agreement that he himself described as "fair." As with various acts of his father, Solomon cannot help the fact that all of these events are also in his interest politically.

Solomon's Exceptional Wisdom, Except . . . (3:1–28)

David is remembered as the "Sweet Psalmist of Israel," and many of the Psalms are associated with him; Solomon is remembered as a wise man, and the books of Proverbs, Ecclesiastes, and the Song of Solomon are ascribed to him.[17] David has already alluded to Solomon's wisdom, even though still telling him what he should do (2:6, 9). The story of the two harlots in 3:16–28 is probably the most popular one about Solomon, as "David and Goliath" is about his father. The story provides an instant illustration of the wisdom that Solomon will ask for and receive from God in 3:3–15. But the narrator introduces both passages with reference to two issues that will call Solomon's wisdom into question. One, Solomon's first official act is to arrange a marriage with a foreign woman, a daughter of the Pharaoh of Egypt. Such marital arrangements were common in ancient Near Eastern realms, functioning not to fulfill romance, much less the wishes of the bride, but to seal a political

---

17. Prov 1:1; Eccles 1:1; cf. 1 Kgs 4:32. The ascription especially of Ecclesiastes is suspicious in that it presents a radically different type of wisdom from that of Proverbs, namely, skepticism.

liaison of mutual benefit to the groom and the father-in-law. (On a lesser scale, a similar arrangement may characterize the marriage of David to Merab, 1 Sam 18:17.) The marriage here signifies Solomon's remarkable prestige in that Egypt was a superpower—Solomon is marrying up! But the problem inherent to such marriages, from the perspective of Deuteronomic theology, was the tendency for the Israelite king to cater to his wife's need to practice her own religious faith, worshipping her own god or gods, a slippery slope leading to his apostasy if not also that of his people. We have seen this issue before, and it will come to center stage later (chap. 11). In a worst-case scenario, Solomon's first act not only seals a marriage but also Israel's doom—not a wise move!

The second problem concerns worship at the "high places" (vv. 2–4). The high places were venerable holy sites frequented by figures as orthodox as Samuel.[18] They never appear in Joshua or Judges, but suddenly become an issue here in the reign of Solomon, and subsequently with Jeroboam in the North (cf. especially below on 13:1–2). Although such worship was common and accepted earlier, the Deuteronomist condemns it, again on the basis of the book of the law of Moses. One way to control ritual is to centralize it under a single authority, which is what the ordinance on sacrifice accomplishes—only the single place that God chooses to put God's name is authorized (Deut 12:13–14, 21). That will mean that all sacrifices are to be performed at the temple in Jerusalem (also thereby providing a monopoly for the temple priesthood). The problem with high places is not that they are associated with apostasy (worshipping other gods) but that they violate the law of centralization. However, one could argue that the law is also intended to *prevent* apostasy by placing all worship under the thumb of the Jerusalem priesthood.

As with other orthodox criteria, we can see two sides to the issue. On the one hand, centralization seems authoritarian, exclusive, and rigid, if not fanatical. Orthodoxy ("right dogma") is always open to the danger of self-righteousness, the smugness of "being right," as well as an intransigence that refuses to accept change (hence the amusing definition of "dogma" as "the living faith of the dead that has become the dead faith of the living"). On the other hand, centralization provides what we might call theological "quality control." Just as there were as many Baal's as there were local shrines venerating him, so there was the potential for numerous Yahweh shrines, and therefore the possibility of numerous *understandings* of Yahweh, and therefore numerous Yahweh's. We have noted before the references to "Yahweh-of-Place-Name."[19] Was the Yahweh of Hebron the same as the Yahweh of Gibeon? Thus one way to read the Shema (Deut 6:4) is "Yahweh our God is *one* Yahweh." Moreover, in addition to quantity, as it were, there is quality. We can see what could happen at local shrines in the story of Micah and the images in Judges 17 (even though there is no editorial condemnation there).

---

18. 1 Sam 9:12–26; 10:5 (NRSV "shrine").

19. Reading 2 Sam 15:7 as "Yahweh-in-Hebron"; "Yahweh-at-Gibeon," 2 Sam 21:6; cf. Gen 31:13, perhaps "El-Bethel."

Of course, as the narrator notes, Solomon has not yet built the temple, so both he and the people continue to use the high places. Indeed, God is about to show up at the high place also! Nevertheless, like foreign wives, the high places will become a major problem, which is why the narrator has to explain and excuse Solomon's presence at Gibeon that follows as an exception that proves the rule. Thus the Hebrew word *raq*, "except that, only, nevertheless," appears at the beginning of v. 2 and the middle of v. 3. In v. 3 it introduces Solomon's use of the high places as the exception from his otherwise obedient love of God, again to which David had encouraged him and provided the model (v. 3a). The narrator is signaling that the problem identified frequently in the narrative that follows begins here.[20] Failure to remove the high places will mark the negative Deuteronomic assessments of the southern kings;[21] the kings who *do* destroy the high places (Hezekiah, Josiah) will serve as the positive role models. A king can do *everything* right, and be under the tutelage of a priest, and *still* be criticized for not removing the high places (Jehoash, 2 Kgs 12:2–3). As we have observed before, the orthodoxy of a later time is imposed retrospectively to judge the characters.[22] As the next two stories will tell, Solomon is an exceptionally wise man, but with exceptions. The effect is to frame the stories in a way that undermines any unqualified exaltation of the king.

> *The Pilgrims and Puritans of New England fled to America in part to escape what they saw as rigid requirements of the established church (proper vestments, compulsory tithes, hierarchical authority, ordination regulations, required weekly church attendance in a designated building—even the removal of hats by men in worship). But when they became established in America they began to see the problems of decentralized worship. When agricultural needs required abandoning a central parish community, changes loomed. "For William Bradford, dispersal was new, and threatening. Many men and women soon lived much too far away to come to the meetinghouse on Sunday. This in itself might undermine the religious mission of the Pilgrims . . . Bradford made plain his fears that the loss of solidarity endangered the very purpose of New England."[23]*

---

20. See 1 Kgs 15:14; 22:43; 2 Kgs 12:3; 14:4; 15:4, 35. The criticism regarding the high places in these royal evaluations is only one of numerous criteria used by the Deuteronomic Historians.

21. Such accusations against northern kings occur only with Jeroboam I (1 Kgs 12:31–32) and a general one at the end of Israel's story (2 Kgs 17:9, 11, 29, 32).

22. See Excursus 4. On the high places and other sacerdotal phenomena, see Halpern, *First Historians*, 224–28.

23. Bunker, *Making Haste from Babylon*, 403. Cf. again Deuteronomy 12, the ordinance on centralization of worship, especially vv. 13–14. Ecclesiastically the spectrum of church authority has played out in numerous ways, in particular in terms of church polity—with the hierarchical, "episcopal," churches on one side (the pope being the supreme example) and the "free," "congregational," churches on the other

The opening story (vv. 4–15) has Solomon at the "principal high place" at Gibeon, where he is reputed to have offered no less than a thousand burnt offerings. God appears to him "in a dream by night." We have not seen such a direct statement of a divine appearance (theophany) since the reported revelations to Samuel in 1 Sam 3:21.[24] God's appearance is also God's first involvement in chaps. 1–3, and the first time that God speaks and, in effect, affirms Solomon's succession to the throne. What God *says* is also a politician's dream: "Ask what I should give you." It takes Solomon a while to get to the request, which is preceded by a verbose recounting of God's "steadfast love" (*hesed*) to David, who, he says, "walked before you in faithfulness, in righteousness, and in uprightness of heart." Solomon also acknowledges that *he* is God's gift to David "to sit on his throne today." At v. 7 Solomon shifts to a humble attitude (a rarity, so far), expressing his unworthiness in terms of childlike naiveté. The phrase "go out or come it" can be a reference to military or political leadership (e.g., 1 Sam 18:13). He contrasts his diffidence with the greatness of the people whom God has chosen, expressed in language reminiscent of the promise of multitudinous offspring made by God to the ancestors in Genesis (v. 8).[25] Finally, he comes to his request: "Give your servant therefore a listening heart to judge your people, able to discern between good and evil; for who can judge this your great people?" (AT). A "listening heart" is open to both God and human subjects, and may echo the language of the Shema ("hear") in Deut 6:4–5 (cf. also Isa 50:4–5). In a word, Solomon has asked for wisdom, a trait defined by the moral discernment he describes (cf. Gen 2:9; 3:4–6).

The narrator now interrupts to tell us how pleased God is with this request, then reports God's reply. Like Solomon's speech, God's is couched suspiciously in the language of the Deuteronomist. God praises Solomon for not asking for longevity, wealth, or "for the life of your enemies" (i.e., their *death*!), but "the understanding to discern what is right" (literally "to hear justice"). (Of course, Solomon has already rid himself of key enemies, but the story makes no such allusion.) As a reward, God gives him not only wisdom unlike that of any king before or after, but also "riches and honor" equally incomparable. Finally, God offers to lengthen his life "if you will walk in my ways, keeping my statutes and my commandments, as your father David walked." Solomon returns to Jerusalem and stands in front of the ark, and he offers sacrifices there *instead of* the high place, a wise move in the eyes of the orthodox.

---

side (e.g., the "Freewill Baptists"). See also the quotation from Bunker's book in the discussion of Josiah's reform.

24. Using two different words, "appear" being the same as in 1 Kgs 3:5. The reference in Samuel is apparently to continued appearances, though we do not hear of these elsewhere. The statement concludes the nocturnal appearance to the young Samuel in 3:1–18, especially v. 10. Before Samuel there were similar appearances of a divine messenger with Joshua (Josh 5:13–15), Gideon (Judg 6:12), and Samson's parents (Judg 13:3). The dream setting most closely resembles stories in Genesis (e.g., 20:3; 31:24; 28:13; 47:7).

25. Gen 12:2; 13:16; 15:5; 16:10; 22:17; 32:12; see below on 4:20–22.

Both Solomon's and God's speeches have used the language of covenant obedience that marked David's deathbed encouragement to Solomon. Most remarkable is the way all three speeches imply or state outright that David himself provides the model of perfect fidelity to God. This may come as a surprise to the reader who knows full well of David's numerous shortcomings, especially his adultery with Bathsheba and murder of Uriah, and some even worse that were reported without commentary (e.g., the massacre in 1 Sam 27:8–12). This idealization of David will play a key role in the books of Kings, providing the reason why, despite numerous kings who were *not* faithful or obedient, God nevertheless allowed the Davidic dynasty to continue and did not destroy Israel quickly, as Deuteronomy warns (but the adverbial qualification "quickly" is also significant, as the end of the narrative will show). What is different here from the unconditional promise in the Nathan oracle of 2 Samuel 7 is the synergistic relationship between God's mercy and David's integrity: *God's* fidelity to David is "*because*" David exhibited "uprightness of heart" toward *God* (3:6)—that is, a reward for good behavior.[26] We will return to the Davidic model when we come to the evaluative summaries that mark the transitions from one king to another.[27]

Solomon's gift of wisdom is immediately put to the test. Two prostitutes appeal to him to settle a "custody dispute." They are roommates who gave birth at the same time, but one baby died and the other lived. Both women claim that the live baby is hers. Since there are no witnesses (not to mention DNA tests) there would seem to be no way to discern which woman is telling the truth, but Solomon instantly solves the problem by suggesting the gruesome solution of slicing the baby in half with a sword and giving a half to each claimant. The liar thinks this is a reasonable solution, but the true mother immediately begs Solomon to let the baby live and give it to the other woman. Royal wisdom uncovers maternal love, which reveals the truth, and Solomon awards custody to the truthful woman. Then "all Israel heard of the judgment that the king had rendered [literally 'judged']; and they stood in awe of the king, because they perceived that the wisdom of God was in him, to execute justice [or 'judgment']." At the outset of his reign, Solomon appears as the ideal son of the ideal king, to whom God has given justice as well as wisdom (cf. Psalm 72; 2 Sam 23:3–4). But adjudicating social, political, and economic issues will prove far more difficult than resolving a custody suit.

Imperial Majesty (Chaps. 4–10)

The title of a classic scholarly article, "Temple Building, a Task for Gods and Kings," aptly describes the next few chapters.[28] As we have seen before with regard to 2 Samuel 6–7, in the ancient Near East the erection of a temple was often the first project a king would un-

---

26. "Because" translates *ke ʾasher*, literally "according as" or "since."

27. One such summary (1 Kgs 15:5) does acknowledge the Bathsheba/Uriah incident as an exception, as we shall see.

28. Kapelrud, "Temple Building."

dertake (Gods did the same in myth).[29] The building served a dual function: one, it established the king's political authority and celebrated any victory that led to his rule, and two, the temple was dedicated in gratitude to the deity who was the patron of the king. In 2 Samuel 7, of course, Nathan's oracle frustrated David's intent to build a temple, postponing it for his successor. David had already built a palace, and Solomon will add his own (7:1–14), but the focus of 5:1—9:9 will be the temple, constituting a disproportionate amount of reporting compared to the rest of the books of Kings. Leading up to that, the narrator tells us of Solomon's administration, the opulence of his lifestyle, and more about his wisdom. Overall, numerous references retrospectively to the exodus from Egypt suggest that the temple, in fact, represents the fulfillment of God's promise to be present with Israel as a people from the beginning; on the other hand, numerous warnings of the consequences of covenant disobedience suggest that God's presence is conditional and can be withdrawn. Thus, in its larger literary context, the story of the temple building stretches back to the book of Exodus—when there was a "tabernacle" and no temple—but also forward to the end of the books of Kings, when Solomon's temple will be no more.

Solomon's administrative staff roster (4:1–6) ends with a notice that will have far-reaching consequences: "Abda was in charge of the forced labor." David had already instituted such a draft (2 Sam 20:24), but we heard no more of it. We will hear a great deal more about Solomon's in 5:13–18 and later, when this unpopular form of taxation will spark a revolution in the reign of his son, Rehoboam (chap. 12). Other political issues appear in the administrative districts listed in 4:7–19. This subdivision of Israel apparently cut across traditional tribal boundaries, in effect, forcing a "federal" system on the people. In addition, it may be that Judah, the home of David and Solomon, is exempt from taxes on goods.[30] If that is the case, it obviously would revive the old resentment between the northern tribes and Judah that had already threatened to tear apart David's reign, and thus *not* be a wise move.

There is, however, no hint of political trouble in the following report of the prosperity of both king and people (4:20–28). In fulfillment of the old promises to Israel's ancestors, they are now "as numerous as the sand by the sea," echoing Solomon's previous comment (3:8). They are also well fed and happy. Indeed, the narrator uses utopian expressions: everyone "under their vines and fig trees" (i.e., safe and secure, cf. Mic 4:4), with "peace on all sides." Solomon's sovereignty extends from the Euphrates River in the east to the border of Egypt in the west—a substantial realm meriting the name of empire, and again meeting ear-

---

29. Examples of the latter include the Mesopotamian myth *Enuma elish*, with Marduk's victory and establishment of Babylon, and, in Ugaritic mythology, the construction of a house for Baal after the defeat of Yam and Mot. A similar mythic pattern appears in Exodus 15 with God's victory and the establishment of God's "abode" and "sanctuary" (v. 17).

30. Sweeney, *I & II Kings*, 88–89.

lier expectations.[31] The subject peoples pay tribute to Solomon, that is, they pay an imperial tax that supplements the domestic tax on his own people's goods. All of the taxes are necessary to pay for the enormous opulence of Solomon's court and officials, not the least of which is the food required to feed them (4:22–28). Transposed into English units, the royal board *per day* included 1,260 bushels of grain, thirty cattle (both grain- and grass-fed), and 100 sheep, along with wild game in profusion (adding up cattle alone, almost eleven thousand head per year!). Then there had to be enough grain and straw to maintain no less than forty thousand horses (v. 26, or is it only twelve thousand [10:26]?). The material prosperity and international sovereignty already fulfill God's promise at Gibeon of "riches and honor" (3:13). The next report returns to Solomon's wisdom (4:29–34), which, like Israel's population, is "as vast as the sand on the seashore." The string of comparisons and superlatives presents Solomon as virtually the wisest man ever to live, a prolific author of proverbs and songs, renowned throughout the world.

Chapter 5 now turns to the temple construction, for which Solomon contracts with King Hiram of Tyre, who had built David's palace, using the highly prized cedar timber of Lebanon (2 Sam 5:11). Here is the first of several references back to Nathan's oracle in 2 Samuel 7. Solomon explains David's inability to build a temple by his preoccupation with war, whereas Solomon now enjoys that "rest on every side" that God had promised (5:4; cf. 2 Sam 7:11). So Solomon is ready to fulfill God's other promise that David's son would build a house for God's name. Hiram is quite willing to strike a deal, offering to provide the timber in exchange for his *own* royal board—including no less than two hundred eighty thousand bushels of grain per year (and the construction will take seven years, 6:37–38). Combined with Solomon's own needs, the per diem total for grain alone came to twelve hundred and sixty bushels. The narrator once again reminds us that "the Lord gave Solomon wisdom," and concludes with the negotiation of the treaty between the two kings (5:12).

Temple building, of course, requires considerable work, and now we hear once again about the forced labor (5:13–18). All told, Solomon's work force numbers about a quarter million! Even if the figures are exaggerated, clearly the temple construction is consuming enormous economic and social resources. For the work in Lebanon alone, ten thousand men are on shifts of one month there, two on furlough at home, likely producing considerable disruption and hardship for their families. One wonders who was left to produce all that grain for the court. Again, the narrator does not acknowledge the negative connotations of forced labor here, but the policy fits with Samuel's diatribe against the monarchy in 1 Sam 8:11–18. It is also ironic that Israel celebrated the liberation of their ancestors from forced labor to the Pharaoh in Egypt for *his* building projects (e.g., Exod 1:11), and Deuteronomic legislation prescribed forced labor for

---

31. E.g., Gen 15:18–19; 32:12; Deut 1:7–8.

those native inhabitants who surrendered to Israel.[32]

If the date introducing chap. 6 is not intended to be ironic, the narrator is oblivious to the symbolic implications of forced labor: Solomon began to build the temple "in the four hundred eightieth year after the Israelites came out of the land of Egypt." The reference seems to serve another purpose, and that is to connect the temple with what we might call a divine trajectory—the movement of God's presence from Egypt to Mt. Sinai (or Horeb) to Mt. Zion (8:1). The account of the construction of the temple is interrupted two times—for a brief divine speech to Solomon (6:11–13), and for an account of the palace construction (7:1–12), which took six years longer. We will return to the trajectory and the speech when we come to chap. 8.

We needn't focus on the details of the temple architecture or its furnishings.[33] Basically, the floor plan consisted of three spaces, each of increasing holiness: the vestibule, the sanctuary, and the inner sanctuary. The latter two are also called the "holy place" and the "most holy place." Comparable church architecture would be narthex, nave, and apse. The ark of the covenant resided within the "most holy place,"[34] protected by two over-arching cherubim, fearsome creatures far more like gargoyles than Valentine cherubs. The enthronement of God above the ark now moves to the innermost room as God's throne room, the place where God resides. God's victory over cosmic forces is represented by the gigantic "molten sea"—a tank some seven and a half feet high and forty five feet in diameter, holding over eleven thousand gallons of water. In ancient myths, the sea represents the powers of chaos that God conquered in creating the world, thus establishing God's sovereignty.[35] The two massive pillars (6:21) invoke God's blessing by "establishing power." In short, the temple is the royal residence of God.

Deuteronomic theology represents a later and different understanding of the temple as the shrine of Israel's covenant with God. The ark's holiness derives primarily from its function as a container of the covenant document (Ten Commandments), not from its numinous quality as God's throne, a point emphasized by the narrator in 1 Kings 8:9 (cf. Deut 10:1–5). "The presence of the ark and the inscribed law within it is in some sense the presence of Yahweh with

---

32. Deut 20:11; cf. Josh 16:10; Judg 1:28. In 9:20–22 a distinction appears between those native peoples who were not exterminated and are now slaves, and Israelites, who are not slaves but soldiers and officials. Thus the Israelite forced labor is a form of taxation and not slavery (which is permanent). Sweeney, *I & II Kings*, 145, suggests also that only Israelites (not "foreigners") were allowed to work on the temple; see Campbell and O'Brien, *Unfolding*, 344a.

33. See the diagram in the HarperCollins edition of the NRSV (524–25) or similar diagrams in other versions. For what follows here, see Smith, *Memoirs*, 15–16, where he summarizes several recent studies on the temple.

34. An architectural feature followed by contemporary Jewish "temples," with the Torah scroll in a cabinet called the ark at the front of the sanctuary.

35. See Ps 74:12–15; 77:16–18; 89:9–10; 93:3–4; 97:1–5; Isa 51:9–11. The same cosmic struggle appears in myths from Babylonia and Canaan; see further below on 1 Kings 19 and the Baal myths.

the people."[36] Thus the temple functions something like "Independence Hall" in Philadelphia, where the original copy of the Declaration of Independence is enshrined.[37] The emphasis is highly significant in that God's *presence* in the temple is not assured by the presence of the ark but by the king's (and people's) obedience to the covenant document *within* the ark. The distinction is directly related to the notion that God's *name* dwells in the temple, but not God's self (see below). David had intended to build a temple for the ark (2 Sam 7:2); Solomon has built a temple for God's name.[38] Once the ark has entered the temple, we will not hear of it again.

One word appears throughout the account more than any other—gold. The ark and cherubim are covered in gold, and there is a golden altar, table, lampstands, and all sorts of liturgical utensils—all gold. Even the floors and walls are covered in gold (6:19–22, 28–32; 7:48–50). The narrator is at pains to emphasize the opulence of the temple (not to mention the palace, e.g., 7:9–12), an opulence that matches that of the royal board. Indeed, Solomon "overlaid the whole *house* with gold, in order that the whole house might be perfect" (6:22). This opulent description may well reflect a later retrospective view of the temple as symbolic of Israel's "golden age."[39] The golden altar seems lavishly expensive and artificial compared to the ancient altar made not even with stones but earth (Exod 20:24)! It is difficult to reconcile this notion of perfection with the alleged author of Prov 3:14 (wisdom is "better than gold") or Eccles 2:8–11 (the accumulation of "gold and the treasure of kings" proves to be "vanity"). Could Solomon utter the testimony of the Psalmist, who says "Truly I love your commandments more than gold" (119:127)? This question lurks behind the heart of the dedication account in chap. 8.

The conditionality of God's presence is the issue that dominates much of the dedication ceremony and the long-winded prayer of Solomon. As suggested above, there are two "processions" at work here: one, a liturgical one in which the ark is brought from its humble tent shrine into the magnificent temple, and, two, a theological one in which God's presence has completed its long journey from Egypt to Sinai to Zion. Of course, the two are connected in that the ark itself represents God's presence. We have seen the liturgical procession before, when David brought the ark from its temporary housing into his new city of Jerusalem (2 Samuel 6), a ritual resembling similar temple dedications by other ancient Near Eastern kings. The two ark processionals share common features: "bringing up the ark" (2 Sam 6:2, 12/1 Kgs 8:1); copious animal sacrifices (6:13/8:5); setting the ark "in its place"

---

36. Miller, *Religion of Ancient Israel*, 158–59.

37. One might pursue the analogy in contrasting the National Cathedral in Washington DC.

38. On this and other differences from 2 Samuel 7 here, see Campbell and O'Brien, *Unfolding*, 352.

39. Smith, *Memoirs*, 17, points out that some of the expressions about gold are examples here of Akkadian loanwords dating from the eighth to the sixth centuries BCE.

(6:17/8:6); royal blessing on the people (6:18/8:14); a sacrificial feast for the people (6:18–19a/8:62–65); dismissal of the people (6:19b/8:66). But the ritual procession of the ark is only the liturgical expression of the theological "procession," if we may call it that. That movement began with God's appearance to Moses, commissioning him to liberate his people and bring them to worship God "on this mountain" (i.e., Sinai/Horeb; Exod 3:12). That task was completed when God, in a "pillar of cloud," led Israel out of Egypt (Exod 13:21–22), then descended in a cloud to meet the people on that mountain (Exod 19:9). Having covenanted with them, God then summoned Moses into the cloud on the mountain (Exod 24:15–16) and ordered the construction of a sanctuary, where God would "dwell among them" (Exod 25:9), a promise fulfilled at the end of the book when the tabernacle is completed: "Then the cloud covered the tent of meeting, and the glory of the Lord filled the tabernacle. Moses was not able to enter the tent of meeting because the cloud settled upon it, and the glory of the Lord filled the tabernacle"(Exod 40:34). Exodus then concludes with a notice that the cloud eventually led Israel "at each stage of their journey" through the wilderness to the land of Canaan (cf. Num 9:15–23; 10:11). The climactic moment at the tabernacle dedication in Exodus closely resembles that in 1 Kings 8:10–11: "And when the priests came out of the holy place, a cloud filled the house of the Lord, so that the priests could not stand to minister because of the cloud; for the glory of the Lord filled the house of the Lord."

The descent of the cloud to the temple represents the conclusion of a magnificent divine journey in which God's presence has moved from one mountain to another, from Sinai to Zion, a journey, of course, that was also Israel's journey. Although God's presence may have been associated with a sanctuary before (e.g., Shiloh, 1 Samuel 3), we have heard virtually nothing about the "tent of meeting" in the Former Prophets outside of 2 Samuel 6, and certainly not about the dramatic advent of God's glory into a temple. Thus, in its present canonical context, the advent of God's glory constitutes the conclusion of the story of Israel as a people that runs from the book of Exodus through all the intervening books to 1 Kings 8. From this perspective, everything between Exodus 40 and 1 Kings 8 is preparation, and the dedication of the temple becomes the moment in sacred time located at the center of sacred space that orients Israel's history as a sacred people.[40]

In a sense, 1 Kings 8 thus represents a *liturgical* counterpart to 2 Samuel 7. In the latter, we saw how the Mosaic covenant tradition combined uncomfortably but inevitably with the Davidic covenant tradition, with their respective hallmarks of conditionality and un-conditionality. Here the transition from the Mosaic "tent of meeting" to the Solomonic temple exhibits the same kind of theological tension, most eloquently expressed in the poetic lines that introduce Solomon's

---

40. On the latter, see Exod 19:6; Deut 7:6, 14:2, etc. This event may be foreshadowed in Gen 14:17–20 where Abram is blessed by the priest of God Most High (El Elyon) at Salem, another name for Jerusalem (see Ps 76:2).

verbose prayer of dedication: "Then Solomon said, 'Yahweh has said that he would encamp in thick darkness. I have built you an exalted house, a place for you to dwell in forever'" (8:12–13, AT).

The language of divine presence that includes "cloud," "glory," and "thick darkness," derives from the common ancient Near Eastern depictions of God as a storm deity, something that we have noted before.[41] Although cloud and glory often appear in parallel, the cloud functions to hide God's glory, which itself is a metaphor for what we might call God's being (to use an ontological term; the Hebrew word means "heaviness, substance, splendor, honor," etc.). The advent of the cloud and glory signify God's presence without allowing God to be seen. "Thick darkness" involves the same imagery, in that it refers to the dark clouds associated with a thunder storm. Such language sets a precedent for ways of understanding God's presence that extend into the New Testament and beyond, illustrated by such mystical classics as *The Cloud of Unknowing* (cf. Mark 9:7; 13:26; Acts 1:9). Ultimately God cannot be known by seeing, only by hearing, which is why Deuteronomy has an extensive elaboration of God's appearance in giving the Ten Commandments, with God "shrouded in clouds," when Israel "saw no form; there was only a voice" (4:11–12). It is not mere coincidence that Judaism's fundamental statement of faith is called the "Shema," transliterating the first word in "Hear, O Israel, the Lord is your God" (Deut 6:4). "Hear," not "look," is the central commandment.[42]

The preceding commentary applies quite well to 1 Kgs 8:12, and is necessary in order to realize how problematic the next verse is: "I have built you an exalted house, a place for you to dwell in forever." Significantly, Solomon shifts from the third to the second person, addressing God more intimately, and thus assuming that God is present more than distant. The pronominal change points to the question about God's transcendence and immanence that we noted in discussing 2 Sam 7:4–7. The issue turns on the difference between the two verbs, "encamp" and "dwell." The former refers to a form of being present that is inherently mobile; the latter, a presence that is implicitly permanent. "Encamp" is the Hebrew word *shakan*, and provides the root for "tabernacle"—*mishkan*. "Dwell" is the word *yashav* and used most frequently to refer to living in a house, i.e., a fixed residence. Thus Solomon's claim seems to contradict what he quotes God as saying. God may have expressed a desire to remain hidden and mobile, he says, but *I* have built you a house to dwell in nonetheless. This points to the reason *why* God tells David that God has never wanted to dwell in a house before, but has "always been moving about in a tent or tabernacle" (2 Sam 7:6). Thus

---

41. See Excursus 4. Note how Ps 97:1–2 connects the language of "thick darkness" with God's universal sovereignty.

42. This aniconic tradition has its own potential problem in that one can make words (including words reportedly said by God) into "idols" just as easily as one can with, say, a statue. More broadly, excluding visual modes of divine self-revelation also excludes art as a medium. Looking is equally a way of "attending to" manifestations of the divine, especially in nature, even given the Deuteronomic prohibitions (e.g., Deut 4:15–20).

the reversal of this divine preference in allowing David's son to build a temple seemed inexplicable and required considerable editorial energy. Here we see the danger involved in that reversal. Imagine the absurdity of trying to capture a thunderstorm and containing it within a building and you have some handle on Solomon's claim about God. Solomon seems to say that he has shut God in a house and locked the door.

The other key word in Solomon's claim, of course, is "forever," raising again the issue of un-conditionality in 2 Sam 7:13: "He shall build a house for my name, and I will establish the throne of his kingdom forever" (cf. vv. 16, 24–25, 29). If God dwells in the temple forever, then presumably Solomon's throne will continue forever as well—in fact, *yashav* can refer to enthronement. The rest of Solomon's prayer, however, repeatedly rejects such a notion, in that Solomon's voice here is often the voice of the Deuteronomist. This voice already has sounded a warning in the midst of the building report (6:11–13), when God's word comes to Solomon saying, *if* you will "keep all my commandments," *then* "I will *encamp* among the children of Israel, and will not forsake my people Israel" (AT). Here God's promise to Moses regarding the wilderness tabernacle (Exod 25:8) appears again, but with all the conditionality of the Mosaic covenant tradition. God's presence in the temple is not permanent; God remains mobile, and, in the face of breach of covenant, God will leave.

The prose prayers beginning in 8:14 repeatedly use another key term, namely God's name. Already in 2 Sam 7:13 God allows Solomon to "build a house for my name." This formula is the Deuteronomist's theological compromise: God's name is present in the temple, but not God's self. God's name thus, in effect, supplants the other, more "corporeal," notions of God's presence in the Priestly image of God's "glory," especially when we note that the "glory" is *visible* because of the enveloping "cloud."[43] Combine "name" and "encamp" and the result is a dual emphasis on God's transcendence that profoundly qualifies God's immanence (e.g., Deut 12:5, 11). Whereas in the poetic line, v. 13, Solomon says "I have built *you* an exalted house," in the subsequent blessing on the people he uses the name formula no less than four times in eight verses (8:14–21). The blessing in 8:14–16 reiterates once again the substance of the Nathan oracle, with the promises of a Davidic dynasty and a temple, concluding with another reference to the ark as the container of the covenant God made with Israel when God "brought them out of the land of Egypt." In 8:22–26 Solomon then petitions God to confirm the promises, again with the critical "if" clause.

A major shift then appears in the series of petitions beginning at 8:27. The danger of enclosing God implied in v. 13 is directly contradicted: "But will God indeed dwell (*yashav*) on earth? Even heaven and the highest heaven cannot

---

43. Weinfeld, *Deuteronomic School*, 201, part of an entire chapter on "The Concept of God and the Divine Abode" in Deuteronomic theology. Note again the homily in Deuteronomy 4 on Israel's receiving the Ten Commandments at Mount Horeb, and its emphasis: "You heard the sound of words but saw no form" (v. 12). See also Smith, *Early History*, 142–44.

contain you, much less this house that I have built!" (cf. Deut 10:14). Though one may pray *toward* the temple, God is not there. Solomon asks that *God* will look toward the house where God's name is, and hear the prayer: "O hear *in heaven* your dwelling place." Heaven—not the temple—is the place where one may properly talk of God "dwelling" using the word *yashav*. The temple may serve as a geographical orientation for prayer (something like the way Mecca does for Muslims), but heaven is where prayer is received. This emphasis ("hear in heaven") occurs seven times in vv. 31–53 (cf. Deut 26:15).

The prayers in vv. 27–53 mark another shift in that most are intercessory or penitential, asking God to "hear and forgive" (v. 30, AT). Solomon asks God to forgive sin associated with offenses against one's neighbor, defeat in battle, drought, famine, and—above all—captivity and exile (the latter, vv. 34, 46). In fact, while one reference to exile asks God to "bring them again to the land that you gave their ancestors" (v. 34), the more extended reference to exile in vv. 46–53 seems resigned to an indeterminate captivity. Here repentance may lead to forgiveness, but the consequence of that is not return to the homeland; it is compassionate treatment by their captors (v. 50).[44] Even there Israel can still hope to be God's special people "separated from among all the peoples of the earth."[45]

As is the case elsewhere, it is difficult to pinpoint the situation of the narrator vis-à-vis the Babylonian exile that concludes the books of Kings. It is quite possible that the narrator knows full well the fate of northern Israel, defeated and led into captivity by the Assyrians in 721 BCE, but is writing before the demise of Judah, in effect saying, "this will happen to us also if we do not obey." In fact, there are several parenthetical comments here and later that indicate the continuing existence of the dynasty and temple at the time of writing (8:8; 9:21; 10:12). Similarly, even the prayer that assumes a setting of continuing captivity is still addressed toward Jerusalem and the temple (8:48). The clearest indication of an exilic setting will appear when *God* appears one more time to Solomon (see below on 9:1–9).[46]

Solomon concludes his speech with another blessing on the people, delivered in priestly fashion, and a sacrificial feast (8:56–66). Again he refers to the "rest" that God has given the people, according to God's promise long ago to Moses (Deut 12:10–11), and, of course, subsequently to David. The claim that God has fulfilled *all* God's promises is precisely the claim that Joshua had made in Josh 23:1, 14. These connections provide further evidence of the Deuteronomist's penchant for dramatic speeches delivered on momentous occasions. The

---

44. In these verses there is a wordplay on the similar-sounding roots *shuv* and *shava* ("turn/return/repent" and "take captive") Cf. Deut 30:1–10, where the wordplay on "repent" does hope for a return to the land. On indeterminate captivity, cf. Jer 29:1–23.

45. Cf. Exod 19:3–4; Lev 20:24; Deut 10:15.

46. Sweeney, *I & II Kings*, 109, 113, 130, argues that the warning in 6:11–14 derives from a preexilic editor who saw Solomon as obedient. Halpern, *First Historians*, 168–71, argues against an exilic setting for the author.

blessing concludes by extolling God's uniqueness, using monotheistic language that will become prominent during and after the exile (Deut 4:35, 39; Isaiah 45, six times), and with a final appeal for obedience couched in language typical of royal evaluations to follow (v. 61; cf. 11:4; 15:3, 14). The dedication ceremony then ends with a gargantuan sacrifice (120,000 sheep alone!), no doubt necessary to feed everyone at the "festival," and then the people depart for their "tents,"[47] "joyful and in good spirits because of all the goodness that the Lord had shown to his servant David and to his people Israel." "Israel is poised to realize the ideal of a united people with a wise and just king, living in peace and prosperity, worshiping the one God at the one shrine in Jerusalem."[48]

But God has the last word with regard to the temple dedication, delivered in the form of another "appearance" like that at Gibeon (9:1–9; cf. 3:5–15), and it puts a damper on all the hoopla. On the one hand, God has heard Solomon's prayers and has "consecrated this house that you have built, and put my name there forever"—even adding that God's eyes and heart "will be there for all time." But immediately the "forever" is qualified by the condition of covenant obedience on the part of Solomon and his successors. With yet another reference to the Nathan oracle of 2 Samuel 7, the throne will be established forever *if* they follow the example of David's integrity (idealized again). If they do not, but "go and serve other gods," God will "cut Israel off from the land" and cast out of sight the very temple that Solomon has just built. The golden house that Solomon wanted to be "perfect" (6:22) will remain so only if Solomon's heart is "perfect" (9:4, AT). Otherwise, the house of gold will become a "heap of ruins."[49] Rather than signifying God's uniqueness among the peoples of the earth (8:60), Israel will signify God's judgment, becoming an object of mockery and derision to those who see the devastation (9:7–9), in effect, the evidence of God's curse rather than God's blessing (cf. Deut 29:22–29). Thus the very founding of the temple, a moment that represents the majesty of the Davidic-Solomonic empire, already foreshadows that time when there will be no empire or temple (2 Kgs 25:9), even though here that time appears hypothetical. The "if" of the catastrophe corresponds to the "if" of the covenant.

Chapter 9 concludes with assorted reports of Solomon's further dealings with King Hiram (9:10–14, 26–28), more information about the forced labor, notices about the house for Pharaoh's daughter, and a superfluous reference to the completion of the temple. Notably,

---

47. The "festival" may refer to the "feast of booths," which celebrated Israel's wilderness journey when they lived in tents (cf. v. 2; Lev 23:33–43). The dispersal resembles that in 2 Sam 6:19, but there people return to their houses.

48. Campbell and O'Brien, *Unfolding*, 342.

49. The MT says: "will become high," using a word that can be a divine name (Elyon, "most high") or an expression of exaltation, which might make sense ironically. Sweeney, *I & II Kings*, 139–40, sees vv. 8–9 as most likely referring to the destruction of the temple, but not conclusively. He even suggests that the expression in v. 7 ("cast out," Sweeney's "expel") does not necessarily imply destruction. For Campbell and O'Brien, *Unfolding*, 360b, destruction is clearly envisaged. Halpern, *First Historians*, 157, does not see the exile addressed here.

the gift of twenty cities in Galilee to Hiram again shortchanges the north, not to mention in effect the relinquishing of some of the "Canaanite" land that God had given to Israel! But all of this seems pedestrian compared to the story of the Queen of Sheba in chap. 10.

As if we did not already know enough about Solomon's riches and wisdom, an exotic queen from another land arrives to remind us. The Queen of Sheba, probably from Arabia, comes to find out if all the stories about Solomon are true. Accompanied by "a very great retinue" which flaunts her own wealth, she poses questions or riddles for Solomon to answer, which he does with ease. The Queen looks over the court, with all the magnificence that was reported earlier, and promptly loses her skepticism, declaring that the story she had heard was true, and, if anything, an inadequate picture. Waxing religious, she pronounces happy all of Solomon's wives and subjects, blessed by God who has "delighted" in Solomon and loved Israel. She then lavishes more riches on Solomon, which he obviously does not need, and he returns the favor, at which point she heads home.

Here, as before, the narrator seems dazzled by Solomon's reputation, and "gold" again appears frequently, along with an ivory throne, and thousands of horses and chariots. Solomon seems to have the "Midas touch," to anticipate a much later king. All of his silverware is *not* silverware—it is gold. *Silver* is grossly inferior—"as common in Jerusalem as stones." Thus God's promise of "riches and honor" incomparable to any other monarch has come true (3:13): "King Solomon excelled all the kings of the earth in riches and in wisdom" (10:23). But, to refer to yet another famous king, "something is rotten in the state of Denmark."[50]

Imperial Adversaries, Human and Divine (Chap. 11)

The English colloquialism "hype" probably comes from the word "hyperbole," meaning exaggeration, extravagant claims, and the preceding chapters have been full of hype about Solomon. He is the wisest and wealthiest of kings. Only by occasionally reading between the lines could one see Solomon's weaknesses. Marrying a foreign wife was one (according to Deuteronomic criteria). The imposition of forced labor was another. Two others that do not necessarily *seem* to be questionable are the acquisition of numerous horses and all that gold, but both are explicitly prohibited by the "law of the king" in Deut 17:14–20. More specifically, the law prohibits the king from acquiring "silver and gold . . . in great quantity," and there is Solomon sitting on his golden throne (10:18). The law also prohibits sending people *to Egypt* to acquire horses, since God has forbidden Israel from ever returning to the land from which God had liberated them. It would be like doing business with the enemy. Yet that is precisely where Solomon has obtained his horses, and chariots to boot (10:28). Ironically, then, Solomon may be riding around in a later model of the chariot that Pharaoh drove in pursuing Israel's

---

50. Shakespeare, *Hamlet*, act I, scene 4, line 90.

ancestors (Exod 14:6–7), and, as we have already noted, Solomon's forced labor recalls the slavery imposed by the Pharaoh as well. Thus the repeated references to Israel being "brought out of Egypt" may attract a connotation unintended by the original narrator (especially 8:21, 51, 53; cf. 8:9; 6:1). Solomon's golden Jerusalem may seem more like the Pharaoh's "iron-smelter" (8:51).[51]

Nowhere in chaps. 5–9 does the narrator condemn Solomon's marriage, forced labor, horses, or wealth, much less refer to them as breaking the "law of the king."[52] Indeed, much of the acquisitions appear to be part of the narrator's celebration of Solomon's imperial majesty. After all, it was *God* who provided not only Solomon's wisdom but his "riches and honor" as well (3:12–13). Thus the voice of the narrator through much of this material seems to be singing a different tune from the voice of the Deuteronomist who speaks in Deuteronomy 17. Where we *have* heard the latter (or one sympathetic to it) has been in the repeated warnings about the consequences of disobedience to the covenant with God, and now those warnings come into effect in chap. 11.

The report about Solomon's marriage to the daughter of Pharaoh in 3:1 appeared without any commentary. In fact, there too the narrator might have seen such an alliance, common among ancient Near Eastern royal families, as flattering—Solomon has married into aristocracy! Now, however, the danger inherent to such a marriage comes to the fore. The Egyptian princess is not alone—Solomon "loved *many* foreign women," "seven hundred princesses and three hundred concubines," which must set some kind of record. But the picture is not of a Playboy; rather, it is a king whose political aspirations lead him to make as many alliances as possible. Presumably, these marriages were political in nature, and the nations listed were already subsumed into David's empire. As Gottwald notes, "High-level diplomatic marriages, entailing the recognition and practice of foreign cults alongside the official state cult, were a staple of ancient Near Eastern politics."[53] When a king gave his daughter in marriage to another, it was functionally the equivalent of a contemporary nation providing an embassy in a foreign country. This was simply one way states sealed their treaty relationships. The narrator, however, ignores the political dimension, equating the marriages with disobedience to the Deuteronomic prohibition of intermarriage with native populations: "Make no covenant with them [or] . . . intermarry with them, giving your daughters to their sons or taking their daughters for your sons, for that would turn away your children from following me, to serve other gods. Then the anger of the Lord would be kindled against you, and he would destroy you quickly" (Deut 7:3–4).[54] Although

---

51. Cf. Sweeney, *I & II Kings*, 146–47.

52. Conceivably, the "law of the king" is later than the original narrator of 1 Kings 6–10 (most scholars think that the law was a *reaction* to Solomon's excesses). It is striking that even in chap. 11 the narrator refers to the prohibition of intermarriage in Deuteronomy 7 but makes no reference to the prohibition in 17:17 of acquiring many wives. On the other hand, the royal prohibition does not mention "foreign" wives.

53. Gottwald, *Politics*, 181.

54. This is precisely what the editorial frame-

the Deuteronomist does not specify it here, the problem with covenants (or "treaties") in general (including "vassal treaties") was that the documents would invoke the gods of each party, easily implying *recognition* of the "other gods."[55] But here the focus is explicitly on *marriage* covenants, i.e., alliances between royal families to establish cordial diplomatic relations. Thus the intermarriage prohibition is not really concerned so much with *all* Israelites—the boy and girl next door, as it were—but with royal families.[56] The core problem with intermarriage is not ethnic purity but theological orthodoxy.[57]

To the Deuteronomist, Solomon's political diplomacy masked his theological duplicity. Paraphrasing the Deuteronomic text he charges that Solomon's "wives turned away his heart after other gods, and his heart was not true to the Lord his God, as was the heart of his father David" (11:4).[58] Again we hear echoes of the Shema, "you shall love the Lord your God with all your heart" (Deut 6:5). One of Solomon's wives is an Ammonite, and Solomon worships Milcom, "the abomination of the Ammonites" (the nomenclature makes the author's opinion quite clear). Another is a Sidonian, and Solomon worships Astarte, the Sidonian goddess (and a most popular one). So it goes—potentially a pantheon of seven hundred deities! Since Solomon builds a "high place" for each of his wives to use in worshiping their gods, there must be one around every corner of Jerusalem. The problem of such marriages will reach crisis proportions when we come to the infamous couple Ahab and Jezebel. As we saw, Solomon was excused from worshiping at the high place at Gibeon because he had not yet built the temple, but now it is a different matter. The high places here represent two separate theological problems for the Deuteronomist: they violate the prohibition of *any* places for sacrifices other than the temple, and they are (to the Deuteronomist) associated with the worship of other gods (e.g., Baal), a direct result of intermarrying with Canaanites. Later, the ideal King Josiah will destroy the chapels for foreign gods that Solomon built (2 Kgs 23:13).

Now the quid pro quo of the covenant warning comes into play. Since Solomon's "heart had turned away from the Lord," the Lord will turn away from him, and from the promises God has made: "I will surely tear the kingdom from you and give it to your servant" (11:11). If a "servant" and not a son is to succeed

---

work of Judges charged (Judg 3:5–6), which we saw to be highly inflated (cf. Josh 23:12 ; Judg 14:2–3; Ruth 1:4).

55. Gottwald, *Politics*, 225: "Treaties between states regularly call upon the gods of all parties to sanction compliance with the treaty terms." Of course, the Deuteronomist ignores the problem that the making of such treaties was often the only way to prevent being destroyed by a suzerain instead of paying tribute, a problem that comes into play later with the Assyrian empire. See Excursus 7.

56. Cf. Miller, *Religion of Ancient Israel*, 89: "the 'paganizing' of Yahwism in the state religion was less a pervasive Israelite phenomenon than it was a feature of the politics of the royal court."

57. Interfaith marriages are still not without tensions in our own time (Hanukkah candles or a Christmas tree or both?), although, of course, far more accepted by most people.

58. This statement also ignores *David's* marriage to foreign women, e.g., Maacah, a Geshurite, 2 Sam 3:3.

Solomon, at first one might think that this means the dynasty will come to an abrupt end, but that is not the case. No sooner has the punishment been pronounced than it is qualified, invoking what will become a kind of Deuteronomic mantra—"for the sake of your father David." First, the punishment will not come in Solomon's lifetime, but in that of his son. No doubt the son (Rehoboam) will not consider this fair, but the author is already giving a theological explanation of why the kingdom is torn from him and not his father. Since there will be ample political mistakes by Rehoboam himself that lead to the split (12:12-19), we see how paramount is the sin of apostasy and its consequences for the Deuteronomist in the books of Kings. The Deuteronomist overlooks David's sins (adultery, murder) and idealizes his theological orthodoxy; on the other hand, the Deuteronomist overlooks Solomon's accomplishments (an era of peace and prosperity) and demonizes his sin of heterodoxy, subordinating any other (e.g., the social injustice involved in forced labor; see below on chap. 12). In a sense, the effect is to make theology absolute and ethics relatively subordinate, the love of God predominant and the love of neighbor relatively unimportant. The resulting theological problem of theodicy (justifying God's ways) will only intensify later.[59]

The second qualification is that "the *entire* kingdom" will not be torn away, for God will reserve one tribe for Rehoboam, which, of course, is the southern tribe of Judah, David's home base. Again, the qualification is "for the sake of my servant David and for the sake of Jerusalem, which I have chosen" (11:13). Here we see how closely knit are palace and temple in the fabric of divine election—God's anointed and the place for God's name, David and Jerusalem. Here Nathan's oracle remains in force: if David's son "commits iniquity," God will "punish him with blows inflicted by human beings," but God's love will remain, as will David's house and kingdom (2 Sam 7:14-16). The *dynastic* promise remains unconditional. Neither here nor anywhere else does God make it conditional on obedience, thus leaving open the possibility of its being "forever."[60] As mentioned numerous times, this is a possibility to which we shall return at the end of Kings. But, as we have also seen before, the punishment can be severe indeed, in this case, the dissolution of the kingdom *as* "all Israel," including both North and South. Solomon is only the first generation in the dynasty, and already the ideal of a unified people of God collapses. Looking ahead to the prophetic oracle that concludes the chapter, God confirms that the punishment will not be "forever" (v. 39), but

---

59. For a similar generational delay in punishment, cf. with Ahab, 1 Kgs 21:29. The most disturbing example will be how God's wrath is not assuaged even by the sterling righteousness of king Josiah (2 Kgs 23:26-30). Indeed, in the case of Josiah, the punishment for the heterodoxy of one king will trump even the reward for the orthodoxy of another! Later, Ezekiel will condemn such retribution, quoting the proverb "the fathers have eaten sour grapes and the children's teeth are set on edge" (Ezek 18:2). See further below on 12:15.

60. Cf. Halpern, *First Historians*, 162–67; Sweeney, *I & II Kings*, 160–61; Nelson, *First and Second Kings*, 76. See below on the "lamp" in 11:36.

what will suffice to prompt the end of punishment?

Chapter 11 exhibits a typical editorial pattern in that the opening commentary and divine speech (vv. 1–13) serve to explain the cause of historical incidents (vv. 14–25) that otherwise might seem isolated and only the result of human motivations. The punishment at least *starts* in Solomon's lifetime, and thus conflicts with the previous utopian description in 4:24–25. It does not take long for the "blows inflicted by human beings" to strike, although it isn't clear exactly what those blows entail (11:14–25).[61] The narrator tells us that God raises up adversaries in Edom and Damascus (Aram). Both seem to be former enemies of David who have returned for revenge, now that David and his fierce general Joab are dead.[62] Hadad the Edomite had fled to Egypt and found asylum with the Pharaoh, in whose court Hadad's son was raised "among the children of Pharaoh" (11:20).[63] Ironically, the adoption motif reminds us of none other than Moses, and since Solomon is the opposing power, it puts him in the role of Pharaoh himself, adding to the associations we have already noted with building projects and slave labor.[64] Similarly ironic is the career of Rezon, which bears a striking resemblance to that of David. At any rate, the Edomite and Aramaen pieces of David's empire are now in trouble.

Far more significant than the adversity of Edom and Aram is an internal revolt that the narrator sees as the means by which God tears the kingdom from Solomon (11:26–40). In effect, this passage repeats what we already know from the previous divine speech, but the agent is the prophet Ahijah and we learn that Solomon's servant in question is Jeroboam. The sequence from divine speech to prophetic speech confirms that the prophet is, indeed, speaking for God. Similarly, the narrator explicitly sanctions Jeroboam's rebellion by initially reporting it and then immediately explaining it with the story of Ahijah's oracle (11:26–27a). Jeroboam is from Ephraim and a capable young man whom Solomon places in charge of the forced labor over the "house of Joseph." Perhaps Solomon thinks that a fellow northerner will be more acceptable to his laborers, but he will find that Jeroboam is on *their* side.

Ahijah and Samuel both are prophets connected to Shiloh. The scene in which Ahijah encounters Jeroboam and delivers his message has a striking resemblance to the scene in which Samuel encountered Saul, only in reverse: Jeroboam is the beneficiary of the encounter, Saul was the victim (1 Sam 15:27–28). Saul accidentally tore off a piece of Samuel's robe, and Samuel declared the damage to be a sign of what God was about to do to Saul's kingdom, giving it to "a neighbor of yours." Ahijah, all decked out in a "new overcoat" (AT) which he has chosen for the occasion, appears out

---

61. Nelson, *First and Second Kings*, 70, points out that the incidents began some time ago. The narrator "is distorting time" chronologically to enhance narrative time ideologically.

62. For Edom see 2 Sam 8:13–14; on Aram, 2 Sam 8:3–8; 10:15–19.

63. One assumes that this was *not* the same pharaoh whose daughter became Solomon's wife.

64. Cf. Sweeney, *I & II Kings*, 157, 159, who sees a much stronger correlation.

of nowhere while Jeroboam is traveling on the road all alone. No doubt Jeroboam is dumbfounded when this stranger approaches him and suddenly tears off his overcoat and rips it into pieces, inviting Jeroboam to take ten for himself. Immediately Ahijah explains his bizarre action with a prophetic messenger introduction: "thus says the Lord." God is about to tear the kingdom from Solomon and give ten tribes to Jeroboam, leaving one[65] "for the sake of my servant David and for the sake of Jerusalem." Ahijah repeats the message with added indictments about Solomon's apostasy.[66] For his part, David, whose positive evaluation is invoked eight times in the chapter, now also becomes the "fief" (NRSV "lamp") that God will maintain in Jerusalem "always."[67] Ahijah concludes the commissioning by announcing that God has selected Jeroboam to become "king over Israel," meaning, of course, the northern tribes, adding the same covenant conditions that applied to David and Solomon. If Jeroboam is obedient, God will "build an enduring house" for him, like that of David, again recalling the "sure" house of the Nathan oracle (2 Sam 7:16).[68] But, again, how "enduring" the house will be depends on how faithful Jeroboam is. In contrast, God then underscores the perpetuity of the Davidic dynasty by promising a limit on the punishment inflicted against David's descendants—"but not forever" (11:39). This limitation will soon appear all the more gracious when we learn the fate of the northern realm which Jeroboam will found (see below on 14:15-16). But Judah's history itself will involve many times when someone might well ask, "but for how *long*?" (cf. Pss 74:9–11; 79:5–7; 89:46, all exilic).

Not surprisingly (although a bit awkwardly), the narrator tells us that Solomon understandably sought to kill Jeroboam, although we do not know how Solomon could know of the revolt which, at this point, is only waiting in the wings. Jeroboam flees to Egypt and refuge with King Shishak (presumably not Solomon's father-in-law), as did Hadad before him. Solomon's marriage alliance now seems overdue for divorce.

Just as 1 Samuel 8 functioned to influence the way we read the stories of the rise of Saul, so 1 Kings 11 functions to influence the way we read the next story of the division of North and South (i.e., "Israel" or "all Israel" and Judah +

---

65. The math does not work, of course. Presumably the author is thinking of Judah and Benjamin as one tribe, or discounting Levi, which has no territory.

66. The MT has a plural subject at the beginning of v. 33 ("they"), perhaps another editorial attempt to place the blame on the people as well as Solomon (cf. Campbell and O'Brien, *Unfolding*, 371–72). Solomon's diminished role perhaps is implied by calling him a "chieftain" (11:34, AT [NRSV "ruler"]), a word usually referring to tribal leaders (e.g., Josh 22:14; Numbers 7 [twelve times]). However, another possibility is a later use of this term for a future Davidic successor (Ezek 34:24).

67. I am following the meaning of the translation "yoke," a metaphor for "dominion." See Sweeney, *I & II Kings*, 158; Nelson, *First and Second Kings*, 76; Campbell and O'Brien, *Unfolding*, 370. Halpern, *First Historians*, 157, has introduced the variant "fief." Lovely as the "eternal flame" metaphor may be, "fief" carries the appropriate political connotation.

68. The phrase also closely resembles that in the oracle to the young Samuel regarding the priestly dynasty of Zadok (1 Sam 2:35), and in Abigail's reference to David (1 Sam 25:28).

Benjamin; 12:1–20). Lest there be any mistake, the incident is framed at the end with another prophetic pronouncement (12:21–24).

A House Divided (12:1—16:28)

On the grounds of 12:1–20 alone, we would conclude that the breach between north and south resulted from political and economic issues having nothing to do with religion. Rehoboam smoothly succeeds to Solomon's throne, but sovereignty over Judah does not automatically result in sovereignty over the northern tribes. Rehoboam must travel to the northern city of Shechem where "all Israel" has come "to make him king." David sealed his rule with such a two-stage process (2 Sam 2:1–4; 5:1–3). Solomon apparently did not need northern approval, which perhaps suggests that a problem has developed during his reign. We saw the problem coming back in chap. 4 when Solomon divided the tribes into somewhat artificial administrative districts and imposed forced labor apparently only on the northern tribes. The narrator alerts us to a potential rift immediately by reporting the return of Jeroboam from Egypt, and already he seems to be in a leadership position with "the assembly of Israel."[69] Now the people express their dissatisfaction directly to Rehoboam, asking him to "lighten the hard service of your father . . . and we will serve you." The word "serve" here plays on the meanings of labor and political allegiance. Their burden was not only the forced labor but also disproportionate taxes (4:7–19) and loss of land (9:11). Their request seems reasonable enough, and made without any threat (Jeroboam notwithstanding).

Rehoboam asks for three days to think things over, then consults with "the older men" who attend him. They suggest a magnanimous response, using the key word "serve": "If you will be a servant to this people today and serve them, and speak good words to them when you answer them, then they will be your servants forever" (v. 7). Their advice assumes a remarkably profound understanding of the role of the king as one who is a servant to the people as much as they are servants to him. Such royal service is what it means for the king to administrator justice, to "defend the cause of the poor of the people, give deliverance to the needy, and crush the oppressor" (Ps 72:4). But Rehoboam immediately dismisses their advice and turns to "the kids who grew up with him" (AT), and their advice is as childish and arrogant as the elders' was mature and humble.[70] They first suggest that Rehoboam establish his machismo by saying, "My little thing is thicker than my father's waist" (v. 10, AT), probably a phallic image.[71] Then he should follow up with another image verging on sadism: "My father laid on you a heavy yoke; I will add to your yoke. My father disciplined you with whips, but I will discipline you with

---

69. For different versions of Jeroboam's role in the MT and LXX, see Sweeney, *I & II Kings*, 167–70.

70. Sweeney (ibid., 170) notes that the word for "young men" (NRSV) really means "children" or "boys."

71. The word "little thing" occurs only here. It may refer to his "little finger" or "penis." See Sweeney, *I & II Kings*, 170 ("little thingie") and Nelson, *First and Second Kings*, 79.

scorpions" (v. 11). Rehoboam's reply to the people's request is stinging indeed!

Before reporting the people's response, the narrator inserts another of those comments that interpret what is happening as a result of the will of God: "So the king did not listen to the people, because it was a turn of affairs brought about by the Lord that he might fulfill his word, which the Lord had spoken by Ahijah the Shilonite to Jeroboam son of Nebat" (12:15). The key word for "turn of affairs" occurs only here (the verb means "turn," "turn around"). In effect, this statement summarizes the view of the narrator already expressed in the oracle to Solomon in 11:11, as well as in the immediately preceding oracle of Ahijah. God has decreed directly and indirectly through the prophet that Solomon will lose most of his kingdom under the reign of Rehoboam, and now God has "confirmed his word" (AT). The commentator does not wait until *after* reporting the revolt in v. 16, so it is specifically Rehoboam's refusal to "*listen* to the people" that is attributed to *God's* will. It is as if God has stopped up the king's ears, and now the king will suffer the consequences. The charge against Rehoboam is stunning in that it constitutes a complete reversal of Solomon's previous request for wisdom in governing: "Give your servant therefore a listening heart to govern your people" (3:9). Now God seems to have withdrawn the gift from his son.[72] The division of North and South—an enormous event in Israelite history—is not primarily due to the human characters and their decisions but to God's will, and that will is the means of God's judgment, and that judgment is directed against the religious sin of apostasy, not of Rehoboam, but of his father. Here again is the Deuteronomic theology of history that informs the entire Former Prophets.[73]

We have seen a very similar commentary in a very similar situation in the story of David. When Absalom sought advice about pursuing David, he chose the counsel of David's spy, Hushai, instead of Ahithophel, a foolish decision that played right into David's hands. There the narrator said "for the Lord had ordained to defeat the good counsel of Ahithophel, so that the Lord might bring calamity on Absalom" (2 Sam 17:14, AT). The clear implication is that Absalom's listening—or at least his judgment—is determined by God's will, which is to bring "calamity" on Absalom, whom God has raised up as "calamity"

---

72. Note the similarity with Eli's sons, who "would not listen" to his warnings because of God's will (1 Sam 2:25). As suggested regarding 1 Sam 16:14 and 2 Sam 17:14 (see also below), the theological issue of human freedom versus divine will appears sharply in the plague stories of Exodus and the stubbornness of the pharaoh. For one example, note the key words in Exod 9:12: "But the Lord hardened the *heart* of Pharaoh, and he would not *listen* to them, just as the Lord had *spoken* to Moses." See Isa 6:9. Sweeney, *I & II Kings*, 171, says of 12:15, that God is "a trickster who works to undermine the human protagonists," and that "Rehoboam has done nothing to justify divine punishment." The northerners might want to disagree with the latter assertion, protesting what Nelson, *First and Second Kings*, 82, calls the "oppressive totalitarianism" of Rehoboam (but Nelson also sees the theological explanation of the revolt as dominating the account).

73. Halpern, *First Historians*, 228–35, has a thorough discussion of the issue under the rubric "Myopia and Selection in DtrH." The Deuteronomist generally reduces "a welter of concrete motives to that of piety" (229).

for *David* because of Bathsheba (2 Sam 12:11). Since the word for "calamity" often is translated as "evil," one can see the theological problem (already discussed at 2 Samuel 17). In short, the narrator of 1 Kings 12 has given us two ways of understanding the reasons for the division of north and south: a socio-economic reason (forced labor) and a theological reason (God's will). Moreover, the two reasons are not even related—that is, God's judgment here is not connected to the social injustice of the forced labor, or even to Rehoboam's fault, but to Solomon's devotion to other gods.[74] For the narrator, the latter is determinative. Nevertheless, and to the narrator's credit as an historian, we have no trouble seeing how the course of events could be explained *without* the theological commentary.[75] In short, we have another remarkable example of what we have called "co-operation" between the human and the divine. Still, the Deuteronomist clearly believes that God's will is the determining factor—that is, the co-operation is not truly multilateral or balanced, but tips in favor of God's intentions.

Now the narrator reports the moment of civil revolt when the people cry out (12:16): "What share do we have in David? We have no inheritance in the son of Jesse. To your tents, O Israel! Look now to your own house, O David." The outcry closely resembles that sounded by a former rebel, Sheba, against David (2 Sam 10:1, AT): "We have no share in David, no inheritance in the son of Jesse. Everyone to your tents, O Israel!" In response, Rehoboam sends his chief supervisor of forced labor to regain control, and the northerners promptly stone him to death, at which point Rehoboam flees to Jerusalem. "So," the narrator concludes, "Israel has been in rebellion against the house of David to this day" (12:19).[76] But Ahijah's prophecy is only half fulfilled. The other half authorized Jeroboam to become king over Israel, and that is what happens now, at the initiative of "the assembly" (20:20).[77] Now the "house of David" is reduced to the tribe of Judah once again. When Rehoboam begins to muster his troops to attack the rebels,

---

74. We will explore this point more fully later. Although the "Latter Prophets" (i.e., those with named books) certainly condemn corrupted forms of worship, their focus often is on social injustice, especially the oppression of the poor by the rich (e.g., Amos 2:6–8; 5:10–15; 6:4–8; 8:4–6). The Chronicler presents a completely different story: Solomon never sins, and Rehoboam is the sole cause of the division (cf. Halpern, *First Historians*, 154).

75. To Campbell and O'Brien, *Unfolding*, 373, "12:15 reconciles the two views." Cf. Halpern, *First Historians*, 232: here the historian "distinguishes mundane causation [taxation] from divine interference [divine punishment of Solomon] . . . Yhwh determined the outcome, but other considerations moved the human actors." Cf. Brueggemann, *1 & 2 Kings*, 158, 278–80, 312; he warns against the extremes of "fideism," in which God determines everything, and "cynicism," in which human actions are "void of meaning" (194). Despite the controlling factor of God's will, the human characters are held responsible for their actions, as in the case of Baasha (see below on 16:7), whose "house" is condemned to be punished "like the house of Jeroboam" because Baasha "destroyed" Jeroboam's house, an act that executed God's will!

76. This contemporizing comment suggests a version of the story that predates the fall of the north in 721 BCE.

77. There is some inconsistency in that 12:20 seems unaware of 12:2–3. Here again one can see a political action effected by the assembly as fulfilling what God had already ordained.

another "man of God," Shemaiah, steps out of nowhere and conveys "the word of God" to "the king *of Judah*" (AT), not to "fight against your kindred the people of Israel." "This thing is from me," says God, "So they heeded the word of the Lord and went home again, according to the word of the Lord" (12:21-24).

This brief incident underscores the historical perspective outlined above, as well as a feature of the narrative that complements it: history, in the narrator's view, ultimately is an unfolding of "the word of the Lord" as conveyed by a prophet, especially with regard to the king. Thus the critical role played by Samuel as God's prophet in the stories about Saul and David continues in figures such as Ahijah, Shemaiah, and at times an otherwise unnamed "man of God."[78] They too, in effect, are "king-makers and king-breakers," and their words hold enormous authority because they claim to be *God's* words, and, here at least, are so acknowledged by the characters. If it is true that God's will determines the course of history, for the narrator the corollary is that the prophets are the agents of that will, and thus figures whose power rivals that of the kings themselves. One such figure has just made Jeroboam king, another has protected him, yet another will break him. Jeroboam is the rod of God's anger against Solomon, but he will soon be at the other end of the stick.

The narrator now will follow the reign of Jeroboam until his death, then switch back twenty-two years to complete the story of Rehoboam's reign (12:21-31). This pattern will continue throughout Kings, rather than tracing the respective histories of northern and southern kings simultaneously. Thus the chronology will often move back in time as well as forward.

Jeroboam's first recorded actions are intended to discourage Israelites from maintaining their loyalty to the Davidic dynasty (12:25-33). He fears that Israelites will want to go to the temple in Jerusalem to offer sacrifices, which will tempt them to "turn again to their master, King Rehoboam." The means Jeroboam employs are not so much political as sacerdotal. In effect, he creates an alternative to the religious system of Judah. He rebuilds two historical cities, Shechem and Penuel, the former serving as his residence.[79] To the modern reader, there would seem to be nothing wrong with creating places for worship, a priesthood, and a new annual festival alternative to those in Jerusalem. In fact, Bethel, the very name of which means "House of God," could certainly compete with Jerusalem for a place on the historical register, boasting an altar built by Abraham and a shrine by Jacob.[80] Indeed, Jeroboam is simply

---

78. Note the "man of God" who delivers the determinative oracle in 1 Sam 2:27. Samuel also is called a "man of God" in 1 Sam 9:6-8. See below on chap. 13. Such a figure will appear repeatedly in much of Kings.

79. Jeroboam seems to be *rebuilding* the two towns: Shechem had a long and checkered history as a city of both religious and political significance—the place where Joshua gathered all Israel in covenant (Joshua 24), but also the scene of Abimelech's infamous royal pretensions, and the site of a temple dedicated to the Canaanite god Baal-berith ("Lord of the covenant;" Judg 9:1-6); Penuel traces its origin back to the story of Jacob's wrestling match with God (Gen 32:30-31).

80. Gen 12:8; 28:12-22; 35:1. Wyatt, *Mythic Mind*, 80-82, 88, argues that Jeroboam's innovation was actually a reformation, returning to the worship of El in an attempt to reject the wor-

establishing his rule and power with sanctuary building in the same age-old way that David and Solomon pursued. His "innovations were not intended to reject allegiance to Yahweh but rather to elude political entrapment,"[81] i.e., allegiance to Rehoboam. But the narrator presents Jeroboam's motive as solely political and *anti-temple*—i.e., anti the *Jerusalem* temple. The narrator hides Solomon's political motives in "the façade of piety," but emphasizes Jeroboam's political motives to portray his *impiety*.[82]

On the other hand, Jeroboam opens himself to suspicion with the production of not one but two golden calves. To the contemporary reader, the very phrase "golden calf" connotes idolatry, made famous by the story in Exodus in which Aaron creates a golden calf, thereby evoking God's wrath (Exodus 32). Indeed, he used virtually the same words as Jeroboam: "These are your gods, O Israel, who brought you up from the land of Egypt" (Exod 32:4). From a critical perspective, it is difficult to determine which story has influenced the other,[83] but in any case with Jeroboam it was an act easily confused with idolatry,

if not so intended. It is quite likely that the calves were created to be pedestals above which God was thought to be invisibly enthroned, much as God was "enthroned on the cherubim" of the ark (cf. Exod 25:22; 1 Sam 4:4; Ps 80:1). If so, the calves were *not* idols to be worshipped in themselves, but symbols intended to point to the reality of God. Nevertheless, by addressing the calves as "your gods," Jeroboam seems in danger of reducing God to the statues, something strictly prohibited in the Ten Commandments and emphasized in Deuteronomic theology (Deut 5:8–10; 4:15–19). Similarly, the plural address suggests that there is more than *one* god. Further, the author labels the use of these images as "sin" because "the people went before" them (12:30, AT), that is, stood facing them in worship (thus NRSV "went to *worship* before"). Thus the use of the images seems to violate the first Commandment, "you have no other gods *before me*" (Deut 5:7). As if these dangers were not enough, the iconography of the calf would be similar to that of the bull, an image connoting divine fertility and power widespread throughout the ancient Near East. Although the imagery is used for the God of Israel,[84] it was easy

---

ship of Yahweh—the latter being an imposition during the Davidic-Solomonic monarchy. He sees the original of 12:28 as "El is your god, Israel, who brought you up out of the land of Egypt." One could add to Wyatt's argument in noting Jeroboam's choice of Penuel and Bethel as worship centers (both containing the divine name *El*, as does "Israel"). See Excursus 4.

81. Gottwald, *Politics*, 82.

82. Halpern, *First Historians*, 229. Campbell and O'Brien, *Unfolding*, 375, see vv. 26–27, 28b as the Deuteronomist's negative version of the otherwise neutral report (vv. 25, 28a, 29).

83. The plural "gods" fits better with Jeroboam's two calves, suggesting priority to the Jeroboam account.

84. Cf. "the bull of Jacob" (NRSV "mighty one"), Gen 49:24; Isa 49:26; Ps 132:2, 5. Wyatt, *Mythic Mind*, 80–83, along with others, argues that El was originally the deity who brought the Israelites out of Egypt, noting Num 23:22 and 24:8 (where "God" is the name *El*, and translating "wild bull" for "wild ox"); cf. also Ps 106:21. He sees the "calf" as a "parody" of the bull image imposed by a later editor (85), a polemic similar to that in Hos 8:5–6. Some scholars see Yahweh represented as a bull image in the depiction associated with "Yahweh and his ʾasherah" (see Excursus 4). Coogan, "Canaanite Origins," 119, describes Yahweh as portrayed with "bovine

to associate it with *other* gods, particularly "Bull El" of Canaanite religion.

The other major problem with the calf images is that they are intended to discourage the people from going to the temple in Jerusalem to offer their sacrifices, thereby defying the Deuteronomic insistence that the temple was the central and *only* place for such worship (Deut 12:5–14). It is debatable when this regulation was instituted, quite likely later than the time of Jeroboam, which may be why the narrator does not explicitly refer to it.[85] But certainly any editor influenced by the reforms of the later kings Hezekiah and Josiah would make the connection. That Jeroboam constructs houses on the "high places" in the land in addition to the calf shrines in Bethel and Dan simply compounds the offense. Similarly, the establishment of a priesthood outside the official Levitical line would be considered unorthodox (Deut 18:1–8). The creation of an alternate liturgical date for the Feast of Tabernacles added a change in sacred time as well as space. In short, through his efforts to establish independent religious institutions in Israel, Jeroboam has "made the people to sin," an act that the narrator will repeatedly remind us of, and which will eventually spell Israel's doom. It's time for the appearance of another "man of God."

The King with the Shriveled Hand (13:1–10)

Chapter 13 introduces the first of numerous prophetic legends that the editors incorporated into the Former Prophets, the most prominent being those about Elijah and Elisha. In all of these stories, the prophetic figure is identified as a "man of God," as here. Presumably these legends were generated in small communities of prophets that scholars sometimes call "guilds."[86] The legends are marked by bizarre actions, supernatural miracles, and portentous signs, not to mention fascinating characters. Sometimes the stories have little to do with the surrounding narrative, but often the legends incorporate the kings of Judah and Israel and continue the prophetic involvement in political events that we have seen beginning with Samuel. Although similar to the other legends in many ways, the story in 1 Kgs 13:1–10 seems more like a kind of editorial imitation of one in that it provides the basis for a prophecy-fulfillment sequence that will be concluded in the account of Josiah's reform, some three hundred years after the fact (and a century after the *fall* of the northern kingdom). Thus the editorial function of the legend here is a parade example of the Josianic Deuteronomic historian at work.

---

ears" and probably even a tail in the picture accompanying the Kuntillet inscription regarding Yahweh's ʾasherah. Cf. McCarter, "Aspects of the Religion," 147: "depicted with some of the features of a bull." Others, however, dispute that the depiction is of Yahweh at all.

85. In fact, the abuses of Jeroboam and others may well be why the later Deuteronomists thought it necessary to insist on a central place of worship in Jerusalem. Nelson, *First and Second Kings*, 81, suggests that the narrator is "insisting on obedience to liturgical principles of a later age," but that the criticism is justified by subsequent experience.

86. See further below on 18:4.

The story takes place at the altar that Jeroboam has installed at Bethel. Jeroboam is standing by the altar, preparing to offer incense, presumably for the first time. Suddenly a "man of God" appears. He has come from Judah "by the word of the Lord," and he proceeds to address not Jeroboam but the altar itself. He says, "a son shall be born to the house of David, Josiah by name," and then predicts what he will do: sacrifice on the altar "the priests of the high places" whom Jeroboam has appointed (i.e., their descendants), and burn human bones on the altar, thus defiling it. The prediction has its exact fulfillment in the reforms of Josiah (2 Kgs 23:15–20), which must assume that the altar that is about to be destroyed was rebuilt.[87] We are barely into the first reign of northern Israel and already we have its end in sight. We also have an indication of the rivalry and hostility that the prophets (and Deuteronomic editors) will hold for those whom they consider heterodox, sometimes with bloody consequences. Thus the incident does not concern directly the downfall of the northern kingdom politically (though that is implied); rather, the focus is on destroying the illicit *religious* institutions. The explicit reference to Josiah's reforms suggests that the denunciation of the high places as heterodox here in the legend is an anachronistic importation from that later time (cf. above on Solomon's high places, 11:7–8).

Having finished his prediction, the man of God then gives a sign which will prove the legitimacy of his agency and message:[88] "the altar shall be torn down, and the ashes that are on it shall be poured out." At this moment, Jeroboam stretches out his hand, pointing at the prophet, and orders, "Seize him!", but instantly his hand shrinks and is paralyzed, frozen in the futile gesture of royal command. At the same moment, the altar is torn down and the ashes scattered; the narrator does not say how, but we may imagine a kind of spontaneous collapse and a sudden wind that carries away the ashes, something worthy of a Harry Potter film. Jeroboam is just as suddenly humbled, and asks the prophet to intercede for him to God, a function that prophets sometimes played (cf. 1 Sam 7:8; 12:19–23). The man of God complies, at which Jeroboam's hand is restored—but not the altar. Jeroboam is so grateful that he invites the prophet to lunch and promises a gift for him, but the prophet declines, citing his divine instructions to neither eat nor drink there, and to return to his home by a different route from which he came.

The Prophet and the Lion (13:11–32)

The story of the man of God is not finished, however, for another incident occurs which has nothing to do with the political situation or religious institutions but everything to do with the prophetic understanding of "the word of the Lord" (13:11–32). There is another man of God in Bethel, "an old prophet," who hears from his sons (or his disciples)[89]

---

87. I.e., the altar reappears for Josiah's own demolition (2 Kgs 23:15)!

88. Cf. Exodus 4; Judg 6:17; 1 Sam 2:34, etc.

89. The language of father/son can be official rather than personal in a prophetic guild. Cf. 1 Kgs 2:12 where Elisha, the disciple of Elijah, addresses the latter as "father."

about the incident with Jeroboam and the altar. He catches up with the man of God on his way home, and invites him to his house for lunch. The man of God repeats what "the word of the Lord" had said to him, prohibiting his eating or drinking in Bethel. But the old prophet claims to have a more recent "word of the Lord" delivered by an angel, instructing the prophet to offer his hospitality. The narrator informs us that the old man "was deceiving him," but gives no hint of a motivation. His behavior becomes all the more inexplicable, for when the man of God complies and is enjoying his lunch, the old prophet suddenly receives a *genuine* "word of the Lord" which condemns the man of God for not *obeying* "the word of the Lord." The old man also announces the consequent punishment: the man of God's "body will not go to the tomb of your ancestors" (v. 22). He might have added, your body won't even make it home, for when the man of God resumes his journey, now riding a donkey provided for him, a lion attacks and kills him.[90] The surreal nature of the incident is highlighted when the lion stays on one side of the corpse, and the donkey on the other, two unlikely sentinels (something like Isaiah's lion and calf, Isa 11:6). Passersby see this bizarre spectacle and report it in Bethel, and when the old prophet hears the news, he correctly concludes that the corpse belongs to none other than the hapless man of God. One might expect an anguished *mea culpa* from him, but instead he confirms the verdict: the man of God "disobeyed the word of the Lord" (v. 26), not admitting that he himself had reported a *false* word from the Lord. The prophet rides his own donkey to the place where the corpse lies, finding that "the lion had not eaten the body or attacked the donkey." Things have gotten "curiouser and curiouser," just like Alice's experience in Wonderland. The prophet retrieves the corpse, takes it to his home, mourns for his "brother," and buries him in his own tomb, thus fulfilling the word from the Lord. He instructs his sons to bury his own body alongside the bones of the man of God when he dies, "for," he avers, "the word which he proclaimed by the word of the Lord will surely come true concerning the altar which is in Bethel, and against all the houses of the high places which are in the cities of Samaria" (13:32, AT).

The connection with the altar story seems like an artificial editorial addition, a suspicion strengthened by the reference to "Samaria," the first in the books of Kings. The reference is anachronistic in that Samaria was not so named until King Omri purchased the site in the 9th century and made it the northern capital city (1 Kgs 16:24). The conclusion in 13:33–34 also seems to refer back to Jeroboam and the altar incident ("after this event"), since his persistence in appointing priests is related to that and not the death of the man of God. The final verse will become the standard Deuteronomic formula for Jeroboam's failure and its consequences: "This matter became sin to the house of Jeroboam, so as to cut it off and destroy it from the face of the earth" (13:34; cf.

---

90. Note the same fate of another prophet who refuses to obey the word of God as commanded by his colleague, 1 Kgs 20:35–36, perhaps compounded by his refusing to be part of the symbolic judgment against Ahab that follows.

Deut 6:15). The denouement of the dynasty will not be long in coming—Jeroboam's son will be the last.

Though the two stories in chap. 13 are tied together at the end, the second is really not about politics or even religious institutions, but about the prophets who claim to know the "word of the Lord." How can one be sure if a prophet is telling the truth or not? That is, how is one to determine who is a true prophet and who is a false one? In the story, the man of God makes a fatal error in trusting a fellow prophet's word, instead of sticking to the word that he has received directly. We do not know why the old prophet would lie, or, for that matter, why God would apparently send a true word through him *after* he lied. In Deuteronomy, the section on prophets condemns one who "presumes to speak in my name a word that I have not commanded the prophet to speak," warning that "that prophet shall die" (Deut 18:20), but the old prophet of Bethel does not die. Nevertheless, the genuine word of God is not open to interpretation by the recipient or alteration by another, and it is unsparing to anyone who deviates from it, whether king or prophet, even the prophet who has *delivered* the word of God to the king. Despite the enormous authority that the prophets hold, they do not control the word of God any more than David could control the numinous power of the ark (2 Sam 6:6–11) or Solomon's temple could control the glorious presence of God (1 Kgs 8:27).

Death to the House of Jeroboam (14:1—16:23)

Until the end of chap. 13, the focus was on the destruction of Jeroboam's illicit altar and related religious institutions. The last verse then turned to the sin of the "house of Jeroboam" and its future destruction, which is the main focus of another prophetic story in ch. 14. This tale is poignant in that it involves the illness and death of Jeroboam's child, Abijah. In order to obtain a prognosis on his son, Jeroboam orders his wife to disguise herself and go to the prophet Ahijah in Shiloh, bearing gifts. Perhaps he hopes that this prophet who had mediated God's appointment of him as king will at least tell them what will happen to the child, if not mediate a blessing for healing. He assumes a role for the prophet that is more like the man of God as "seer" (cf. 1 Sam 9:6–10), and, indeed, Ahijah proves to be clairvoyant indeed—he can "see clearly" even though he is blind (14:4). His vision, of course, comes from God, who reveals what is about to happen before the queen arrives at his door. Much to her surprise, he knows who she is and she needn't say a word (and doesn't for the entire story). Ahijah immediately identifies her and tells her that he has "heavy tidings." In an earlier version of the story, it may be that the prophet simply informed her that the child would die, but in the present text, she first has to listen to a rather lengthy condemnation of her husband's misdeeds. The divine message begins by recounting God's election of Jeroboam to be king over northern Israel, torn from the "house of David," then turns to the judgment that he has not been "like my servant David," again conjuring the idealized model of covenant obedience. Jeroboam has "done evil above all those who were before you," presumably Solomon (there being no precedent in the North), making for himself gods and molten images, provoking God to anger by turning his back on God. Now comes the consequence: "therefore, I will bring evil upon the house of Jeroboam," namely, the death of all males. The language is earthy: every one who urinates on the wall will be consumed just as dung is burned up. And the language is grisly: anyone in his family who dies in the city will be eaten by dogs, and anyone who dies in the countryside will be eaten by birds.[91] Scatological behavior will result in scatological punishment, without even the dignity of burial. Once again a prophetic king maker has turned into a king breaker.

Now Ahijah returns to the subject of the sick child. The moment the queen enters the city, the child will die, leaving us to imagine the horror she must feel with each step toward home. The only saving grace for the child—innocent as he is, after all—is that all Israel will mourn for him and his body *will* be buried, "because," says the prophet, "in him there is found something good to the Lord, the God of Israel, in the house of Jeroboam" (14:13, AT). The child's death, therefore, does not seem to be part of the punishment of Jeroboam (contrast the death of David and Bathsheba's first son, 2 Sam 12:14); the prophet has simply foretold what will happen—the child dies before the punishment comes. In the view of the storyteller, the child does not suffer because of the father's sin; the child *avoids* suffering because of his own unique goodness. Then the prophet jumps back to the political: God will "raise up for himself a king over Israel" who will execute the judgment just announced.

Another editorial comment interrupts the narrative in 14:15–16, postponing the sad arrival of the queen. Here the judgment extends far beyond Jeroboam and his family to include all of Israel as a nation. God will uproot Israel "out of this good land that he gave to their ancestors, and scatter them beyond the Euphrates." Before the story of Israel's first king is finished, the narrator tells us how *Israel's* story will finish—in exile. The responsibility for this disaster is shared by both king and people.[92] "*They* have made *their* sacred poles, provoking the Lord to anger." On the other hand, v. 16 places the blame on Jeroboam: "because of the sins of Jeroboam, which he sinned and which he caused Israel to sin" (AT), providing the formula that will appear repeatedly in subsequent royal evaluations. Again the narrator is explaining the reason for the way Israel's story ends, and there is an enormous shift from all previous warnings. Here the fate of the nation is sealed; it is not posed as a *possibility* depending on whether or not the king and people are faithful (if . . . then), even if the author

---

91. This macabre phrase will appear numerous times regarding other dynasties. There is, however, no report of the fulfillment of this prediction in the demise of Jeroboam's family in 15:27–30. The language is another example of similarities to the vassal treaties of Esarhaddon; see Weinfeld, *Deuteronomic School*, 131–34.

92. On this shift, see Campbell and O'Brien, *Unfolding*, 357b.

is *writing* from exile (e.g., 9:6–7). The end is posed as already determined (because . . . therefore), without offering a reason for why God *postpones* the punishment for two hundred years (there is no idealized David to take credit). The author's theological concern for nailing down the cause of Israel's downfall here at the beginning overrides any narrative concern for the development of plot, much less suspense. The author is more concerned with presenting an editorial rather than reporting a story. No doubt a southern bias appears here in the voice of the prophet, insisting that the northern kingdom was doomed from the start, and to the author, *rightly so*. Thus this passage together with 2 Kings 17:7–18 frames the entire history of northern Israel. The effect here, in 14:15–16, is as if Charles Dickens's *A Christmas Carol* ended with the death of Tiny Tim and Scrooge himself—i.e., as if the answer that Scrooge poses to the Ghost—"Are these the shadows of things that Will be, or are they shadows of the things that May be, only"—is answered by "things that *will* be." Thus the biblical audience who *is* in exile might well ask Scrooge's next question: "Why show me this, if I am past all hope?"[93] This is a question about the Former Prophets as a whole that we will have to address at the end.

With the inserted diatribe completed, the story then returns to the arrival of the queen, whose footsteps to the threshold of her home track the death of her child, and a final reminder that the incident is "according to the word of the Lord." The narrator concludes with a summary of "the rest of the acts of Jeroboam," but, as will be true of others to come, the summary is quite abbreviated. We hear only vaguely "how he warred and how he reigned." If we want more details, we are referred to the Book of the Annals of the Kings (which, alas, we do not have). Otherwise, the narrator has told us all that is deemed significant theologically, which is to say a reduction of twenty-two years of reign to the construction of heretical religious institutions. Jeroboam's son Nadab succeeds him, presumably not knowing the doom that awaits him.

With the death of Jeroboam, the narrator returns to conclude the seventeen-year reign of Rehoboam in Judah (14:21–31), reminding us that Jerusalem is the place chosen for God's name, and (on the other hand) that Rehoboam's mother was one of those foreign women—Naamah the Ammonite (a second reminder comes in v. 31, lest we forget). Verse 21 begins the usual regnal summary (age at succession, length of reign), which normally continues with an evaluation of the king. However, the following verses do not mention any fault of Rehoboam; rather, the judgment is against the *people* of Judah, leaving Rehoboam without any explicit editorial evaluation at all. "Judah did what was evil in the sight of the Lord . . . more than all their ancestors," which is saying a lot if we remember the book of Judges. In fact, the opening line here sounds very much

---

93. Dickens, *A Christmas Carol*, 82. Halpern, *First Historians*, 227, makes a similar point about the destruction of Judah despite Josiah's piety and *because of* Manasseh's sin: "by tracing the exile to Manasseh, [the exilic Deuteronomistic historian] deprived these reigns [the last four] of all suspense: Josiah *could not* reverse Yhwh's judgment, and his reform, so pregnant with fervid hope, was utterly trivial" (italics original).

like the repeated references to Israel's cyclical wrongdoing there (e.g., Judg 2:11; 3:7, 12, etc.). The misdeeds include building high places and making pillars and sacred poles (Asherim, again), as well as prostitution connected in some way with the temple. The NRSV is misleading in translating the single word *qadesh* for "male temple prostitutes," but the root of the word has to do with "holiness," strangely enough. The issue is complicated, but sexual promiscuity *as religious ritual* is not likely in view.[94] In any case, for the author the combination of misdeeds constitutes "all the abominations of the nations that the Lord drove out before the people of Israel" (14:24; cf. Lev 18:24–30), an action of purification that vv. 15–16 have already predicted for northern Israel. It is as if the people of Judah have conspired to see how many of God's orders issued in Deut 7:5 they can reverse ("break down their altars, smash their pillars, hew down their sacred poles").

By juxtaposition (14:25–28), the narrator now implies that punishment for Judah is immediate when King Shishak of Egypt raids Jerusalem, stripping the temple and palace of their treasures, including those golden shields of Solomon. All the glitter did not last that long, nor the benefits of Solomon's marriage alliance through Pharaoh's daughter. The vulnerability of both palace and temple foreshadow the way in which *Judah's* end will come as well. The author then reports of continual war between Judah and Israel (conflicting with the implication of 12:21–25).

Whereas the summary notice on Rehoboam omitted any evaluation of him and focused on the people instead, Rehoboam's son Abijam receives the first full example of the formula. Here we may pause a moment to look at the form and function of these regnal summaries that mark the progress of the narrative to the end of Kings. The summaries appear in two parts, an introduction to the king's reign at his succession and a conclusion at his death (e.g., 15:1–5 and vv. 7–8). The introduction presents the editor's religious evaluation; the conclusion presents incidental facts. Like the surrounding stories, the introductory formulas reflect a process of ongoing editorial interpretations and additions. There are formulas for both northern and southern kings, sharing numerous character-

---

94. The usual word for prostitution is *zanah*. Some scholars have assumed that prostitutes (both male and female) associated with the temple or with worship meant that there was a "fertility cult" in operation (e.g., Nelson, *First and Second Kings*, 101). Texts like Hos 4:13–14 seem to support such a reading. However, other scholars have challenged the assumption, arguing that prostitution connected to worship involves (1) poor people who resorted to prostitution in order to pay votive gifts to the temple (banned in Deut 23:17–18), (2) prostitutes who were in effect used by the temple for income (hence 2 Kgs 23:7), or (3) simply the kind of sexual promiscuity that accompanies religious gatherings (cf. Hos 4:18, "sexual orgies"). However objectionable these might be, they are a far cry from sex as part of the ritual. Nineteenth-century camp meetings in America might suggest an analogy for the third, when sexual promiscuity was common enough to coin the saying that "more souls were made than saved"! Pardee, *Ritual and Cult*, 234, 239–40, argues that the use of the same term in the Ugaritic texts offers no support for the notion of cult prostitutes or a "fertility cult," and that imposing such an interpretation on the biblical texts is "at least tendentious." See van der Toorn, "Cultic Prostitution," 512–13; Goodfriend, "Prostitution," 505–10; Yee, "Hosea," 208–9; Miller, *Religion of Ancient Israel*, 205–6.

istics. Put simply, there are some kings who "do right," and some who "do evil." There are reforming kings who excel all others, especially Hezekiah and Josiah; there are evil kings who constitute the villains (Jeroboam, Ahab, Manasseh). By and large, virtually all of the northern kings are condemned for following the precedent set by "the sins of Jeroboam," left unspecified but presumably reflecting his innovations reported in 12:25–33. As we have observed, the substance of the formula already appears in 14:16. The southern kings are judged positively if they follow in the way of David, negatively if they do otherwise, but the former, despite their merits (and except Hezekiah), are all criticized for not removing the high places. Thus the summaries focus exclusively on sacerdotal matters, i.e., forms of worship, even though the stories of the kings may contain blatant offenses of other kinds (most infamously, Ahab). Matters that are merely political, economic, or social, at best get an aside. Significantly, for quite a few kings, the characteristic of a leader that is politically uppermost—power—is explicitly relegated to such footnotes.[95] The editor is more concerned over piety than power. Clearly, those who provided these summaries firmly believed that the sacerdotal practices of the kings determined the course of history for both Judah and Israel. Correlating those practices with the fate of individual kings, however, would prove to be far more difficult than any theoretical formula could explain. Sometimes virtually all the narrator tells us about a king is contained in the summary, or at least the only explicit theological evaluation appears there. Abijam provides a good example (15:1–8): "He committed all the sins that his father did before him," although the narrator has not reported them (again, Judah's offenses appear instead). Unlike David, "his heart was not true to the Lord his God," but, as promised, God "gave him a fief in Jerusalem" (AT),[96] i.e., "his son after him" (cf. 11:36; here is the sole caveat regarding "the matter of Uriah the Hittite"). Otherwise, we learn of the continuing war with Israel, and that's it for Abijam.

Abijam's son Asa is the first reforming king in Judah (15:9–15), and he has a long reign of forty-one years. He removes the so-called "prostitutes" associated with the temple (see above on 14:24) and idols attributed apparently to Abijam and Rehoboam, plus removing the Queen Mother and her Asherah, which he burns with fire, in good Deuteronomic fashion.[97] But, true to form, this good king does not remove the high places; *nevertheless,* his heart is "true to the Lord all his days."

King Asa's piety does not protect him from trouble, nonetheless (15:16–22). In the seemingly unending war between North and South, King Baasha seeks to cut off access to Jerusalem by building a fortress nearby. Asa, whose piety had included the acquisition of silver and gold votive gifts (15:15), now must use them for his defense budget. Apparently not confident in his own

---

95. Beginning with Asa, 15:23; cf. 16:5, 27: 22:45; 2 K 10:34; 13:8, 12; 14:15, 28; 20:20.

96. NRSV "lamp." See above n. 67.

97. There is some confusion about the kinship with Maacah (cf. 15:2). On the burning, cf. Deut 7:5.

forces, he offers a "present" (or "bribe") to secure the help of King Ben-hadad of Aram (northeast of Israel [modern Syria]), who already has a treaty with Israel. Ben-hadad promptly takes the silver and breaks his treaty, attacking the cities of Israel and conquering several of them (including Dan, the location of one of Jeroboam's golden calves [12:29]), whereupon Baasha backs off. It will not be the last time that international alliances will factor in the ongoing hostility between Judah and Israel.

Following the summary of Asa, we turn to Israel and Nadab, the son of Jeroboam (15:25–32). We already know his fate from the gruesome prophecy of Ahijah (14:10–11), but since he walks in the way of Jeroboam, he seems to earn it on his own. Baasha enters again (still premature of his formal introduction, v. 33), and immediately kills Nadab, takes his throne, and proceeds to murder "all the house of Jeroboam," with the narrator reminding us again that this fate is "according to the word of the Lord" spoken through the prophet (whose name coincidentally is the same as Baasha's father), "because of the sins of Jeroboam." All we have learned about Nadab is that he was evil and assassinated (15:25–27). The narrator refers us, as usual, to the rest of his acts, having given us absolutely none. With Nadab's reign concluded, we turn to the reign of Baasha, apart from his connections to the previous kings of Judah (15:33—16:7).

It seems that wherever there is a miscreant king, a "man of God" or prophet can materialize out of nowhere, and now suddenly such a character named Jehu appears, "the word of the Lord" having come to him. The introduction has already numbered Baasha among the followers of Jeroboam's sin. Now the prophet pronounces the corresponding judgment on his dynasty, which sounds very much like that meted out to Jeroboam himself (14:7, 10–11), including corpses that become dog food.[98] Baasha himself, however, goes to his grave in one piece. An editor has tacked on redundantly another brief summary of the judgment oracle, singling out the "work of his hands" (idols?) as well as Baasha's "being *like* the house of Jeroboam, and also because he *destroyed*" the house of Jeroboam (16:7). Here a prophet condemns the very destruction that is "according to the word of the Lord" mediated through *another* prophet in 15:29! By now a pattern of assassinations is observable that marks a major difference between Judah and Israel. Assassinations will occur in both realms, but in Israel they will extend to the king's entire family because the perpetrators intend to found their own dynasty, whereas in Judah, the purpose of the assassinations is "not to usurp the Davidic line but only to seat a different Davidic ruler."[99] Thus the theological guarantee of the permanence of David's throne finds a political counterpart in the relative stability of Judah's dynastic continuance.

---

98. See 14:11. This macabre judgment seems to be inspired by the story of Ahab and Jezebel. Only there does the prediction come true (1 Kgs 22:38; 2 Kgs 9:33–37).

99. Gottwald, *Politics*, 77; cf. McNutt, *Reconstructing*, 172. Rosenberg, "1 and 2 Samuel," 129, suggests that David himself set the precedent for such respect for the dynasty he would found in his refusal to assassinate Saul, God's "anointed."

Excursus 4: "According to the Word of the Lord"

Here we may pause again to observe another editorial pattern generally called "prophecy and fulfillment," the way things happen "according to the word of the Lord" (15:29). At this point, the phenomenon is hardly new to the Former Prophets. Various characters have acted in accordance with God's word. Israelite soldiers discriminated about the booty of war "according to the word of the Lord" delivered through Joshua (Josh 8:27). God advised Joshua himself, of course, to act "in accordance with all the law" of Moses, which is God's word (Josh 1:7). God's self-revelation to Samuel was through "the word of the Lord" (1 Sam 3:21), and others used the ephod or sacred "dice" to discern God's word (1 Sam 30:7; 1 Sam 14:41). Saul's experience after his commissioning was an immediate fulfillment of Samuel's predictive "signs" (1 Sam 10:1–13). The most succinct example of acting by the word is in 2 Sam 2:1: "David inquired of the Lord, 'Shall I go up into any of the cities of Judah?' The Lord said to him, 'Go up.'" Here word and act are immediate. But we have seen examples of how the narrator connects prophecy and fulfillment that are separated by a much longer time, the most illustrative being the oracle of the "man of God" in 1 Sam 2:27–36. The man uses the typical prophetic message introduction ("thus says the Lord"), and predicts events that are not only relatively immediate (the fall of the priestly house of Eli), but also that do not happen for many years (the domination of the priesthood by Zadok, 1 Kgs 2:35). This "man of God" sets the precedent for his colleagues who begin to pop up in 1 Kgs 12:22 (Shemaiah), and will do so frequently. Again, the fulfillment of the prophet's word can be immediate, as in the "sign" of the destroyed altar in 13:1–5, or the death of the child (13:12–13, 17–18), or the fulfillment can be long-range, as in *Josiah's* desecration of the altar three hundred years later (13:2). Soon we shall see an event "according to the word of the Lord" stretching all the way back to Joshua (16:34 and Josh 6:26). The editors have used the phrase repeatedly in the books of Kings. Obviously it is another example of the deep influence of the prophets that we have observed beginning with the character of Samuel.

In Kings, the phrase functions in a way similar to those occasional editorial commentaries like the one in 1 Kgs 12:15 ("a turn of affairs brought about by the Lord"), presenting many of the same theological questions. The "according-to" phrase expresses the author's conviction that history really does correspond to the will of God, even though the characters seem to act independently—and often we might add, immorally—and they are held responsible for their actions. The result can be irony bordering on absurdity, as in the case of Baasha. His massacre of the house of Jeroboam happens "according to the word of the Lord" pronounced by the prophet Ahijah (15:29; 14:10–11), but subsequently another prophet (Jehu [not to be confused with the later king]) *condemns* Baasha for the massacre (16:7), so he too is murdered and his family massacred, "according to the word of the Lord" (16:12). The word of the Lord that willed the destruction of the house of Jeroboam has now condemned the agent of that striking for doing so! God has broken the rod of God's anger. The narrator does not tell us why Baasha "conspired" against Nadab, or why Zimri "conspired" against Elah (15:27; 16:9). We can only guess about the political or economic or social causes of such coups d'état. The author's concern instead is to insist on the sovereignty of God over history.[100] We should not be surprised by now; after all, the narrator was even willing to assign an "evil spirit" to God in order to explain the bizarre behavior of King Saul (1 Sam 16:14).

The oracle against the house of Baasha soon comes true in that his son Elah reigns only two years before being assassinated by an upstart military leader named Zimri. Apparently Elah was too drunk to know what hit him (16:8–10). Zimri promptly assassinates all the males of "the house of Baasha," including "his friends," and the narrator reiterates the fulfillment of "the word of the Lord" delivered by the prophet Jehu. Here again we know that Jeroboam's sins are ultimately behind the judgment, but the narrator explicitly includes Baasha and Elah among the sinners as well, specifically referring to the use of "idols" (v. 13).

Zimri will not enjoy his power for long—he reigns for only seven days (16:15–20). His coup hardly has universal support, however, for "all Israel" appears again as an actor, and makes Omri "king over Israel" instead of Zimri. Omri and his troops abandon the siege of the Philistine city begun by Nadab (15:27; 16:15), and besiege Israel's capital city, Tirzah, instead. Facing apparently overwhelming opposition, Zimri commits suicide by immolating himself along with the royal residence. The narrator concludes the story by explaining Zimri's fate as "because of the sins that he committed" (16:19), making us wonder what else other than regicide he had time to do in seven days! However, Zimri's revolt leads to a civil war within "all Israel," with half following Omri and half an otherwise unknown figure named Tibni, but the narrator gives us no details, saying without explanation "so Tibni died, and Omri became king." Thus the first three kings after Jeroboam were all assassinated over a span of little more than twenty-five years, and the fourth *would have been* assassinated had he not killed himself first.

Outside of Israel, Omri became known as a powerful and prosperous king, so much so that the Assyrians called his realm "the land of Omri" long after his reign was over. The difference between this reputation and the account of the Deuteronomic editors is another striking example of their focus on religious matters, for here Omri receives only a brief notice after the report of his successful victory in the civil war: he built the new capital city of Samaria, having purchased the land (16:24).[101] Other than that, the summary adds him to the list of the imitators of Jeroboam's sins. Readers of the Former Prophets will probably remember him best as the father of his infamous son, Ahab. Typically, the narrator also ignores events in the reign of Ahab that a historian would insist on including, above all, the battle of Qarqar in 853, when Ahab led a coalition of forces against the Assyrian king Shalmaneser III. The Assyrian Empire

---

100. Cf. Weinfeld, *Deuteronomic School*, 21–22: "Every event of religio-national significance must occur as a result of the word of God which foreordained that event and to which historical reality must exactly conform."

101. Formerly, Samaria appears as a region (13:32), probably anachronistically.

arose under Shalmaneser I in the 14th century, but did not begin to affect seriously Palestinian countries until about the time of Ahab. The Assyrians will play a major role in the story later on, but for now they remain in the shadows.

The Troubler of Israel (Chaps. 17–22)

We have already seen numerous conflicts between prophets and kings beginning with Samuel and Saul, then Nathan and David, then a "man of God" and Jeroboam, and Jehu and Baasha. The stories in chs.17–22 intertwine the characters of Elijah and Ahab and other prophets. Elijah is introduced abruptly in 17:1 as if we know him, perhaps because he became such a well-known figure in subsequent tradition (including later Judaism and Christianity). Surely Elijah is one of the most colorful figures among all the prophets (and that's with rather stiff competition). He can run as fast as a chariot, disappear into thin air, call down fire from heaven, create drought, and make rain—not to mention raise the dead. For his part, Ahab comes off as a pale wimp, and it is Jezebel who ought to wear the crown.

Many of the stories in these chapters (and in those involving Elijah's successor, Elisha, in 2 Kings), represent the literary genre of "prophetic legends," like the anecdotes about the "man of God" and the old prophet in chs.13–14. Some of the stories portray the prophets as miracle workers involved in the lives of ordinary people, and probably had nothing to do with Ahab or other kings originally, but the editorial context always comes back to the national political stage. Thus the legends are woven together with more historical accounts of international relations and military campaigns, as well as domestic issues. Overall, the function of these stories is to highlight the authority of the prophets as the agents of the God of Israel, and to affirm God's sovereignty over and above all contenders, especially the Canaanite god Baal.

The narrator introduces Ahab in 16:29–34 with a unique distinction: he "did evil in the sight of the Lord more than all who were before him" (16:30), a charge paraphrased again in v. 33. Ahab's offense is a more flagrant example of Solomon's—succumbing to the influence of a foreign wife. Ahab married Jezebel, a woman whose name eventually entered the English language with the meaning of "an evil and scheming woman." However one might question such a stereotype, for the narrator there *is* no question. Jezebel is "the daughter of King Ethbaal of the Sidonians." Sidon is a coastal city of Phoenician background some twenty-five miles north of Tyre, and the king's name clearly reveals who the main deity was—Ethbaal, meaning "Baal is with him." The narrator immediately tells us that Ahab not only worshipped Baal but also built a temple and altar in his name. To round things off, he also made a "sacred pole," i.e., an Asherah. As we saw with Solomon, such marital benefits for the foreign wife were simply part of common ancient Near Eastern diplomacy. As Gottwald puts it, "Ahab's building of a Baal temple in Samaria is the implementation of an interstate treaty protocol that accords his Tyrian wife the diplomatic privilege of a place to practice her cult away from her homeland. This gesture does not signal a jettisoning of the Yahweh cult."[102] Needless to say, the narrator does not see it that way. Ahab's acts "provoked the anger of the Lord" (16:33), as the following narrative will show.

The narrator concludes the introduction of Ahab with an apparently irrelevant event: the rebuilding of the ancient city of Jericho by a man from Bethel (16:34). However, two dimensions of this event serve the narrator's overall interest. First, it is seen as a fulfillment of prophecy connected to a saying by Joshua after destroying the city (Josh 6:26),[103] and, second, the builder who laid the foundation did so at an enormous cost—the sacrifice of his firstborn child, the most abhorrent practice attributed to Canaanite religion.[104] Here the custom involves a builder who would honor the deity and invoke the deity's blessing by sacrificing his firstborn, which must have made for a macabre dedication ceremony—the cornerstone was also a tombstone. Here the child's name may well be ironic: Abiram can mean "My father is exalted" or "My father is arrogant." Thus the narrator has introduced Ahab as guilty of apostasy worse than any of his predecessors, associated by literary juxtaposition with child sacrifice, an object of Josiah's reforms (2 Kgs 23:10), and concluded with the phrase that signifies the fundamental conviction of the prophets—that ultimately history is shaped "according to the word of the Lord." That word is on its way to Elijah the Tishbite.

The narrator has tied together the first series of stories about Elijah and Ahab with the theme of life and death expressed through the motifs of drought/rain and hunger/food. All of these associations are at the heart of the competition between the God of Israel and Baal. Previously in the Former Prophets there have been rather vague references to Baal or "the baals."[105] The plural refers to numerous manifestations of Baal at various sacred places.[106] Israel's history included a similar phenomenon with the god El, assimilated without problems.[107] As we have seen with regard to Judges, "in premonarchic Israel, Baal worship was con-

---

102. Gottwald, *Politics*, 82. (The word "cult" here does not have the modern connotation of a wildly unorthodox or fanatical religious group, although one can argue that both Jezebel *and Elijah* exhibit such traits!)

103. The narrator is assuming that the Joshua text refers to child sacrifice, which is not evident. Later stories will be set at Jericho with no indication of a problem (e.g., 2 Kgs 2:15-17).

104. Deut 12:31; 18:9-10, where the child is burned to death (see below on 2 Kgs 16:3). The sacrifice of the firstborn plays a large role in Israelite literature, e.g., Genesis 22 and Exodus 13:11-16 (in the latter, and probably implied in the former, the sacrifice of firstborns is prohibited and replaced by redemption with an animal substitute). For an example of child sacrifice by the Moabite king Mesha in the context of warfare, see 2 Kgs 3:27.

105. E.g., Judg 2:11-13; 6:25-32; 1 Sam 7:4. See Excursus 4.

106. E.g., the Baal of Peor, Num 25:3; Baal-berith ("of the covenant"), Judg 8:33; Baal-perazim, 2 Sam 5:20.

107. E.g., El Elyon ("Most High"), Gen 14:18; El Shadday ("Almighty," but more likely "of the Mountain," El Bethel (literally "God of House of God," Gen 35:7). Yahwistic examples would include "Yahweh-in-Hebron (2 Sam 15:7) and "Yahweh-in-Gibeon" (2 Sam 21:6). In some ways the belief is similar to that in the various manifestations of the Virgin Mary, e.g., Our Lady of Guadalupe, etc. Some scholars see an attempt to downplay or even eliminate the role of El in some traditions (e.g., Wyatt, *Mythic Mind*, chaps. 1 and 7; see also below).

sidered a legitimate practice," although the Deuteronomic editors condemn it.[108] To them, Baal and Yahweh were completely incompatible, partly because they competed, as it were, in providing fertility. As we have noted before, both were storm deities who brought the annual rains which made agriculture—and therefore life itself—possible.[110] In this sense *both* were "fertility gods."[111] What was it, then, that made Baal so special? Why worship Baal rather than (or in addition to) the God of Israel? The answer has to do with which deity would have seemed to be the better rainmaker.

Excursus 5: The Clash of Storm Deities

Ancient people were far more dependent on seasonal rain than people in the contemporary developed world.[109] While they could store grain temporarily, so that a single year's crop might well last into the next year, several years of drought in a row could spell disaster. Certainly there was no grocery store with its canned or frozen goods providing virtually every imaginable food year round. In our well-fed affluence it is easy to ridicule ancient people and their preference for a storm deity like Baal whose rain made life possible, or a fertility goddess like Asherah whose procreative power might be available to people's deepest needs for survival. All over the ancient Near East, archaeologists have unearthed little clay figurines of females with exaggerated breasts, and we dismiss them as examples of "primitive" thought. Indeed, we may also be embarrassed by biblical texts that extol God's blessing "of the breasts and of the womb" (Gen 49:25).[112] But in disparaging such religious beliefs, we risk the inability to appreciate the desperation that one might feel in the face of famine, and how that desperation would lead one to worship any and *every* deity who held some promise of blessing. Why risk worshipping only one deity when several offered the hope of well-being? If both Yahweh and Baal

108. Smith, *Memoirs*, 25.

109. However, drought in undeveloped countries periodically mirrors the problem, and climate change is bringing the problem much closer to home in developed countries as well. Our difficulty in understanding someone drawn to a rain god is directly connected to our personal detachment from farming and growing livestock, a detachment that has perilous environmental consequences for how we live on the earth. See Hiebert, *Yahwist's Landscape*, 146–49; Davis, *Scripture, Culture, and Agriculture*, 52; Mann, *God of Dirt*, 51–54.

110. See below and Excursus 4. A good example of the storm imagery is in Ps 18:8–15. The god Hadad of Aram was also a storm deity.

111. Cf. Miller, "Aspects," 59: Ugaritic mythology "cannot be reduced to a description of it as reflection of a basically fertility religion any more than one can do that with Israelite religion (where drought was of equal concern and the deity viewed as dispenser of fertility, rain, and the like)."

112. Smith, *Memoirs*, 261, and *Early History*, 52, suggests that the figure in the background here is, in fact, the goddess Asherah, as the consort of El ("Breasts-and-Womb" can be her name); so also Freedman, "Religion of Early Israel," 325. However, Tigay, "Israelite Religion," 193, n. 116, argues plausibly that such figurines are as likely *human* females and "represent what women in particular most wanted," namely, fertility and children. Note how Hosea turns upside down the fertility language of womb and breasts (9:14).

provide rain, why not worship Baal as well and hedge one's bets? Moreover, the two deities may well not have appeared to be equal competitors. Baal would have seemed to be the *expert* of the two in this regard, because the myths about Baal focused on his connection with nature's cycles and the onset of the rainy season. As the myth of Baal says, "Baal will begin the rainy season, / the season of wadis in flood; / and he will sound his voice in the clouds, / flash his lightning to the earth."[113] The dry season corresponded to Baal's defeat and death by the god whose name *means* "Death" (Mot), who swallows up Baal along with his rainstorm; the rainy season corresponded to Baal's return to life, and the counter-defeat of Death (though not finally!): "alive is Valiant Baal, / for the Prince, Lord of the earth, exists!"[114] Although the Baal myth obviously is the background for the divine competition in the Elijah stories, an even closer parallel appears in the epic texts in the form of drought as punishment for human sin, to which we will return below.

Although Yahweh is also portrayed as a storm deity, it is certainly not as a dying and rising one, and may reflect a different meteorological background.[115] But even more importantly, the biblical texts focus on the Exodus story of God's liberating Israel from slavery and claiming them as God's covenant people. Often the imagery of God as a storm deity served to illustrate this story set in historical time rather than a story set in seasonal time: "The clouds poured out water, your lightnings lit up the world, your way was through the sea, you led your people by the hand of Moses."[116] It would certainly be true for God to say "I am the Lord your God, who provides you with rain." Indeed, Deuteronomy extols God's rain-making capability, contrasting Canaan, with its need for seasonal

---

113. Translation from Coogan, *Stories*, 101 (a wadi is like an arroyo, see below). For somewhat different translations see Wyatt, *Religious Texts*, 101; Smith, "Baal Cycle," 129.

114. Wyatt, *Religious Texts*, 137. Cf. Coogan, *Stories*, 113. However, this does not mean that we should reduce the Baal stories to a seasonal pattern, nor the deities to "nature gods," as if they had no transcendent significance beyond the meteorological. See Wyatt, *Religious Texts*, 101, 388, and especially 109, n. 155. In Psalm 29, for example, God's voice is very closely identified with a thunderstorm ("voice" and "thunder" being the same word). In a sense, this picture of God is rejected or at least qualified in the subsequent story about Elijah (1 Kgs 19:11–12), on which see below.

115. An intriguing factor in this divine competition of storm gods may have made Yahweh the loser. Smith, *Origins*, 146, surmises that Yahweh's background in the arid southern region around Edom ("possibly in northwestern Saudi Arabia," p. 140) suggests "a warrior-and-precipitation-producing god associated with mostly *inland desert* sites with *less rainfall*" than the coastal home of Baal (my italics).

116. Ps 77:17–20, abbreviated. For the narrative texts see the "pillar of cloud and fire" of Exod 13:21; 14:19–20; the cloud and related imagery in 19:9, 16; 20:18; cloud combined with "the glory of the Lord," 24:15–17. We discussed the cloud/glory phenomenon with regard to the temple in 1 Kgs 8:10–13 and Exod 40:34–38. For the wilderness journey, see Num 9:15–23. Outside the narrative texts but still about the Exodus, see Ps 68:7–8. The mythic language about the storm deity as warrior also overlaps with the allusions to God's defeat of chaos (sometimes as a monster) at creation, in ways similar to other ancient Near Eastern myths, e.g., Pss 74:12–15; 77:16–8; 89:9–10; 93:3–4; 97:1–5. The cosmogonic mythic language also appears in Exod 15:8–10 with the Pharaoh as the enemy, a fusion of myth and history. In Ugaritic myth, Sea (Yam) is the cosmic enemy; in Exod 15:8–9 sea (Hebrew *Yam*) is the *weapon* of Yahweh against the historical enemy of the Pharaoh. Similarly, Yam's other name is "Judge River," and Israel's crossing the Jordan River incorporates that mythic dimension as well in Ps 114:3. One of the classic studies of this subject is that of Cross, *Canaanite Myth*, especially 112–44.

rains, to Egypt, where irrigation from the Nile was always possible. God "will give the rain for your land in its season, the early rain and the later rain, and you will gather in your grain, your wine, and your oil" (Deut 11:14). But God the rainmaker here is inextricably linked to the preceding passage which recounts the Exodus story of God the liberator (11:1–7); and God's continuing maintenance of the rain depends on Israel's not "serving other gods" (11:16–17)—i.e., obedience to God the *law* giver.[117] In fact, God almost always uses some version of self-identification invoking the Exodus: "I am Yahweh your God, who brought you out of the land of Egypt." We never see that formula with the words ". . . who brings you the rain."[118] Similarly, the annual agricultural festivals at an early date combined celebration of Yahweh's gift of rain and therefore harvests with a celebration of Yahweh's liberation of the Hebrews from Egyptian slavery (Exod 23:14; Deut 16:9–12).[119] Even assuming that the people of Elijah's day would identify with those liberated some four hundred years previous,[120] in a drought they more likely would identify with those who needed rain.[121] When looking at Israel's God one might well see a storm deity who preferred to use the weapons of thunder, lightning, and rain to defeat Israel's historical enemies like the Pharaoh,[122] while (as creator) also

---

117. See also Lev 26:3–5, 14, 20; Hos 2:8; on God's *withholding* rain, see the covenant curse, Deut 28:22, and Amos 4:7; Jer 3:3. Some Ugaritic texts clearly illustrate the common view that the gods could and would withhold rain as punishment for sin (e.g., Anat punishes the hero figure Aqhat for impertinence; Athirat punishes Keret for breaking a vow, see below), but we do not see the provision of rain conditioned by communal obedience to law and justice, and certainly not in terms of worshipping only one god. The Baal cycle focuses on rain and drought as part of the cosmic order (and disorder), an intra-divine conflict that is out of human control and not directly influenced by human behavior. Conversely, despite the above similarities, drought is *never* understood as reflecting Yahweh's death or non-being. On the other hand, assuming an automatic connection between human fault and drought has it own theological problems!

118. The closest parallel to "who brought you out of Egypt" would be Ps 147:8, "who prepares rain for the earth" (AT), but the grammar is different and the Psalm is probably post-exilic. Psalm 104 is a hymn of praise to God as creator, but, curiously, the aquatic emphasis is on springs and streams, with only one brief allusion to rain ("from your lofty abode making the mountains drink," v. 13 [AT]).

119. See Miller, *Religion*, 81–84; however, this does *not* mean that nature is rendered unimportant, contrary to many biblical scholars; see Hiebert, *Yahwist's Landscape*, 136–39.

120. More broadly, one's identity as liberated slave required inculcating the exodus story within each generation, a process of re-enactment epitomized in the Passover seder (Exod 13:26). Thus the Passover *haggadah* criticizes the participant who suggests that the exodus only happened long ago. What is involved is a rich, profound understanding of *memory*. If the statement in 2 Kgs 23:22 is true that no Passover had been celebrated since the days of the judges, then the identity of Yahweh as liberator would possibly be less prominent.

121. See Jer 2:4–8, though drought is not mentioned. To the extent that Deuteronomic theologians emphasized God's liberator image and downplayed God's creator image—especially *qua* rainmaker—they were shooting themselves in the foot by providing all the more reason for a farmer to turn to Baal, the rain specialist. Gottwald, *Politics*, 171, argues that Yahwism was more appealing than Baalism because Yahweh combined all three crucial functions—"fertilizer of fields," "enforcer of communal justice," and "leader of the armies," whereas Baal and others provided only one or two. My argument here is that, in time of drought, one might well opt for the weather specialist.

122. In addition to fighting the Pharaoh (e.g., Exodus 13–14), God also employs storm weaponry against other enemies of Israel (Judg 5:4–5, 20–21; 1 Sam 2:10; 7:10; 2 Sam 5:20; 22:7–20).

providing rain for agriculture.[123] When looking at Baal, one might see a storm deity who used thunder, lightning, and rain exclusively to do what a storm deity was *supposed* to do—counteract the *cosmic* enemies of sterility, drought, and death—and thus to provide the grain, wine, and oil (the essential agricultural products).[124] In the stories that we have of Baal, we do not see him engaged in historical events at all, or, at best, only in vague allusions[125] (unlike other ancient Near Eastern deities).[126] Better to choose the weather specialist, or at least add him to one's list of deities deserving of worship.[127] This competition is the

---

123. For a full theology, we would have to explore God's creation *in addition to* God's "acts in history." For a long time, the latter preoccupied scholars, leaving an unfortunate vacuum or, worse, implying that any theology of nature was suspect. Thus Israelite religion was idealized as historical (German scholars gave us the word *Heilsgeschichte*, "salvation history"), whereas Canaanite religion was denigrated (if not demonized) with terms like "pagan," "nature religion" and "fertility cult." For one helpful corrective, see Hiebert, *Yahwist's Landscape*. The "God who acts in history" has its own problems, not the least of which is the claim of geographical territory as a God-given right, allowing for the extermination of competitors (as we have seen in the book of Joshua).

124. These three often appear together, as in the description of drought in the Ugaritic tale of Keret: "Exhausted was the bread in their granaries; / exhausted was the wine from their wineskins; / exhausted was the oil from [their] v[ats]," Wyatt, *Religious Texts*, 231–32 (Text 1.16 iii 14–16). See Hos 2:8–9, 22, where the divine competition is the issue. Furthermore, the god Dagon (of the ark story in 1 Samuel 5) is the father of Baal in some Ugaritic texts, and his name probably is equivalent to the Hebrew word for "grain."

125. Of course Yahweh's role as creator is also cosmic; here we are talking about a question of balance. The role of the gods at Ugarit in historical events is not at all clear. Anat fights against "town," "people," and "men," but even here we have "a broad cosmological scenic representation" (Wyatt, *Religious Texts*, 73 n. 17), or the story may reflect the ritual execution of prisoners of war as practiced by Ugaritic kings (Lloyd, "Anat and the 'Double Massacre,'" 161). Similarly, Baal "seized sixty-six cities, / seventy-seven towns," which might mirror a human king's actions (ibid., 108 n. 150), but even so is a far cry from the innumerable instances of Yahweh's interventions in human affairs. Some scholars see these stories as reflecting political issues with the Ugaritic kings, including a use of the stories to legitimate a particular dynasty, but such a reading is speculation based on possible implications (Smith, "Baal Cycle," 84–85; Wyatt, *Religious Texts*, 177, 221). So far, we have not seen anything in these texts even approaching the way biblical stories involving God serve the purpose of promoting a king like David, or terminating a king like Ahab. Jezebel's father may be Ithbaal ("Baal is with him") but we never see a text about him (or any Ugaritic king) like 2 Sam 5:10: "David became greater and greater, for the Lord, the God of hosts, was with him."

126. In the "Moabite Stone," which refers to events behind 2 Kings 3, the Moabite king Mesha claims that the Moabite god Chemosh acted precisely as Yahweh does (indeed, he refers to Yahweh): he (Chemosh) "saved me from all the kings and caused me to triumph over all my adversaries." Chemosh orders Mesha, "Go, take Nebo from Israel!" and he annihilates the population (the "ban," or *ḥerem*, as in the Joshua stories). "Chemosh drove out [the king of Israel] before me" (Albright, "Moabite Stone," 320). The storm imagery for Yahweh as a divine warrior also has much in common with Mesopotamian gods and goddesses, e.g., Inanna, Marduk, Ninurta, etc. See my study *Divine Presence*, especially chap. 1.

127. Cf. Dever, "Contribution of Archaeology," 231: "fertility motifs naturally predominated in a marginal-zone society and economy that depended on precarious rainfall agriculture," and 244 n. 56: "if a religion is to be evaluated by its ability to relate the individual symbolically to the *actual* conditions of existence—its integrative power—then we may judge Canaanite religion to have been perhaps more profound, more 'authentic,' than the rather austere Yahwism of their period; and apparently many Israelites agreed." In this context note how radical is the statement in Hab 3:17: "Though the fig tree does not blossom," and there is no fruit, no olives, nor field crops, nor meat from the stall, "yet I will rejoice in the Lord."

problem that stands behind the initial stories about Elijah, one that also often preoccupies the *Latter* Prophets, especially one like Hosea (e.g., Hos 2:1–13).[128] Especially from the Deuteronomistic perspective, the primary question is always political in the sense of acknowledging divine sovereignty—to which god does one pledge absolute allegiance?[130]

In chs.17–19 the character of Baal comes to center stage but (to pursue the metaphor) only because the other characters *refer to* him in their speeches (and the narrator in his reporting)—otherwise, Baal is decidedly *off* stage, an absence that Elijah will mock in chap. 18. The mockery begins more subtly in 17:1. Elijah appears without further introduction and speaks to Ahab: "As the Lord the God of Israel lives, before whom I stand, there shall be neither dew nor rain these years, except by my word." The God of Israel is the true "fertility deity," and is represented by the prophet. Indeed, the situation resembles one in the Ugaritic epic of Aqhat: "Seven years Baal is absent, / Eight, the Rider of Clouds: // No dew, no downpour, . . . / No welcome voice of Baal."[129] In some ways the parallel is even closer than in the Baal myth (the battle with Death/Mot) in that here drought results from the imposition of a curse as punishment for sin by the human character Aqhat. Aqhat has broken a vow to the goddess Anat; Ahab has broken the covenant with Yahweh, bringing on the resultant curse.[131] Thus the drought in both stories is an *ad hoc* crisis, not a seasonal pattern (i.e., not simply the time in between seasonal rains). God can turn off and turn on the rain (17:1; 18:1), irrespective of the time of year (cf. Gen 7:11–12; 8:2). In the biblical story, the drought will last three years (18:1), and serves not only as punishment but also as a test, the latter becoming clear in chap. 18. There is no response from Ahab, and he remains peripheral throughout chs.17–19. Instead, we jump to three legends that reveal the wonder-working power of Elijah.

Two of the first three stories, as well as the one beginning at 18:1, open with "the word of the Lord" telling Elijah where to go (17:2, 8), and two of the first three stories conclude with a reference to "the word of the Lord." In the first story (17:2–7), the word directs Elijah to a place east of the Jordan River. God tells him to "drink from the wadi," and that

---

128. Indeed, Wyatt, *Mythic Mind*, 72, cites G. Oestborn's comment that "the relation between Yahweh and Baal is 'the main problem of the history of the Old Testament religion.'"

129. Parker, *Ugaritic Narrative Poetry*, 69 (col. I:42–46); similarly Wyatt, *Religious Texts*, 296 (1.19 I:40–46). Note how David uses the same language in his lament over Saul and Jonathan, 2 Sam 1:21, suggesting that the mountains mourn their death by having "no dew or rain" upon them. As with the figure of Aqhat here, the same effect follows upon the death of Baal, and the royal figure of Keret. As Wyatt puts it (*Religious Texts*, 232 n. 55), "Famine threatens all his subjects when the king is punished for his sins. His impending death presages universal death." He also refers to the curse in Deut 28:1–6, 15–19. A seven-year famine appears in the Joseph story (Genesis 41) and in another prophetic legend in 2 Kgs 8:1–6.

130. Certainly political struggle and sovereignty are important in the Baal mythic cycle as well, but the politics is only among the gods.

131. Deut 28:22; cf. 2 Samuel 21; 1 Kgs 8:35; Amos 4:7.

God has "commanded the ravens to feed" him as well. A wadi is a streamed that may or may not have water running in it, depending on the season and the amount of rain (cf. the arroyos of the American Southwest).[132] Thus, in the midst of a drought, Elijah's drinking from the wadi is the first miraculous element in the story, accompanied, of course, by the raven delivery service. Verses 5–6 repeat vv. 3–4 almost woodenly (only adding meat to the menu), demonstrating that the prophet does, indeed, act "according to the word of the Lord." But soon the wadi also dries up, "because there was no rain in the land." The drought is in full effect. So the "word of the Lord" tells Elijah to go back across the land of Israel and up the coast to Zarephath, some twelve miles south of the port city of Sidon—deep in "Baal country," as we might say, and, in fact, Jezebel's home turf (16:31; 17:8–16). Now God has "commanded a widow" to feed him instead of the ravens. Sure enough, Elijah runs into a widow who is out gathering firewood. When he orders her to give him some water and some bread, she replies that she has only enough flour and oil at home to make one last meal, and then she and her son will die. Her situation is that of people in the Ugaritic epic of Keret, when Baal's rains have stopped: "Exhausted was the bread in their granaries; / exhausted was the wine from their wineskins; / exhausted was the oil from [their] v]ats.'"[133] Elijah encourages her not to be afraid, to first do what he has asked, and then prepare her own meal. Then he delivers a prophetic message: "For thus says the Lord the God of Israel: The jar of meal will not be emptied and the jug of oil will not fail until the day that the Lord sends rain on the earth." The woman does as she is told, and indeed Elijah's prediction proves true, "according to the word of the Lord." Elijah's protection of the impoverished widow provides the justice due her according to Israel's covenant tradition (e.g., Deut 24:17, 19, 20, 21; 26:12–13).

Elijah has prevented the death of the woman and her child from starvation, but the third story (17:17–24) is initiated when the child becomes deathly ill: "there was no breath in him." The woman ("the mistress of the house")[134] now turns on Elijah and accuses him of coming to bring death to her son as a punishment for her sin. Elijah takes the child in his arms and goes to his room on the second floor, laying him on his bed. Then he prays, asking God if God has "brought calamity [or 'evil'] even upon the widow" and her son.[135] Then Elijah performs some kind of magic therapy

---

132. For those unused to such terrain, it is amazing to walk up a perfectly dry stream bed, then notice some dampness that very gradually becomes wetness, and then finally see running water.

133. Wyatt, *Religious Texts*, 231–32 (1.16 iii 14–16). The brackets indicate reconstructed text from damaged tablets.

134. To paraphrase in English, "the baalette of the house," since "baal" means "lord, master, husband." It is possible that this unnecessary information evokes the god in question.

135. The text does not identify the woman as Canaanite or Israelite, but more likely she is the former (her reference to Yahweh is not inconsistent with that, see Rahab in Josh 2:8–11). The "even" then might suggest the question of why God's punishment against Ahab would extend to her.

by stretching himself out on top of the child three times, accompanied by another prayer: "O Lord my God, let this child's life come into him again," and God does precisely that. Elijah brings the child back downstairs and hands him over to his mother, saying, "See, your son is alive." Then the woman (and the author) acknowledges Elijah's prophetic authority: "I know that you are a man of God, and that the word of the Lord in your mouth is truth."

Elijah has now demonstrated that he has miraculous power, or perhaps better that he is the authorized mediator of God's power, including the power to provide food in the midst of famine and even to bring the dead back to life. Thus he embodies the very divine power that Baal supposedly exhibits. Moreover, Elijah is a "true" prophet, and this status is crucial as we move into the next story, one of the most dramatic in the Hebrew Bible—Elijah's confrontation with the prophets of Baal at Mt. Carmel (18:1–46). It is also one of the most horrifying stories of sectarian bloodshed. Elijah is not interested in facilitating "inter-faith dialogue."

We are now into the third year of the drought, and "the word of the Lord" sends Elijah back to Ahab, saying "I will send rain on the earth." But God does not tell Elijah to say that to Ahab, so Elijah has a critical piece of information hidden from the king. In fact, Elijah's journey is interrupted by a report on the severity of the famine and Ahab's attempt to deal with it. Ahab summons his chief of staff, Obadiah, and a flashback immediately interrupts *that* scene to tell us two important facts: Obadiah "revered the Lord greatly," and Jezebel "was killing off the prophets of the Lord" (18:4). Jezebel's devotion to Baal has become religious persecution of devotees of Yahweh. She isn't interested in interfaith dialogue either, and this is the first instance in the Former Prophets of violence against Israelites *because of* their religious faith. Obadiah, however, is undaunted, and he has subverted her pogrom by hiding a hundred prophets of God in caves, as well as providing them with "bread and water" (just as God had done for Elijah). These refugees were members of a prophetic community (or "guild"), vaguely resembling later monastic communities, headed by one or more prophets, who were sometimes called "father."[136] If the figure of one hundred is accurate, there were quite a few (especially if concentrated in the North); but the opposing prophets numbered nine hundred and fifty, and they dined at Jezebel's table (18:19). Now Ahab, unaware of Obadiah's opposition to Jezebel, orders him to search for grass to "to keep the horses and mules alive"— there is no mention of food for the people! The two of them divide up the land for the search (improbable work for the king himself, it would seem).

136. Second Kings 2:12. On the community (literally "the sons of the prophets"), cf. 1 Kgs 20:35, 41. Note also 19:18–24 and the ambiguous use of the term "father" in 10:12. This community is probably not yet involved with the prophets who appear in 1 Sam 10:5–6,10–13. See Wilson, *Prophecy and Society*, 140–41; Miller, *Religion*, 179–80. Some scholars see these northern prophetic circles as the origin of at least one of the major components of the Deuteronomistic history, as well as part of Deuteronomy itself. Presumably they brought such works to Judah after the fall of Samaria in 721 BCE.

Obadiah is on his way when he runs into Elijah, whom Obadiah recognizes, suggesting the notoriety that Elijah must have enjoyed (or even that Elijah is the "father" of the commune). Obadiah bows in reverence and asks rhetorically, "Is it you, my lord Elijah?" and Elijah says "It is I," then sends him to Ahab to inform him of Elijah's availability. Obadiah's response illustrates the fear instilled by Jezebel, suggesting that "handing him over" to Ahab would be like sentencing him to death for his sins. That is, Ahab would realize that Obadiah must be one of Elijah's supporters, and kill him on the spot. Obadiah then reports how Ahab has sent his intelligence agents to all the surrounding nations, searching for Elijah, and making them swear an oath that he was not to be found. Besides, he argues, if he conveys Elijah's message to the king, Elijah might not be there to defend him, because "the spirit of the Lord will carry you I know not where" (18:12). Obadiah is referring to Elijah's reputation for supernatural disappearances (most dramatically illustrated by his ascension into heaven at death, 2 Kgs 2:11).[137] But Elijah assures Obadiah that he will, in fact, show up, so Obadiah arranges for a meeting between king and prophet.

The meeting is a classic example of the proverb about "truth speaking to power" (cf. Amos 7:10–17; Jeremiah 7). Ahab's words on seeing Elijah at first are the same as Obadiah's in the same situation: "Is it you?", but what follows is an ironic reversal of Obadiah's greeting. Instead of bowing and addressing Elijah as "my lord," Ahab addresses him as "you troubler of Israel." The accusation is typical of corrupt political authorities who try to invalidate the cause of protestors by labeling them as "troublemakers" ("outside agitator" has been another). Elijah's response turns the tables: "I have not troubled Israel; but you have, and your father's house, because you have forsaken the commandments of the Lord and followed the Baals."[138] Without waiting for a response, Elijah tells Ahab to "have all Israel assemble for me at Mount Carmel," along with the prophets of Baal and Asherah, nine hundred fifty in all.

Ahab does as he is told, and Elijah's first words are a condemnation of the *people's* theological indecision, "limping with two different opinions." "If Yahweh is God," he says, "follow him; but if Baal, then follow him." The people stand mute, perhaps wondering if there isn't a third choice—following *both*. Elijah says that only he is left among the prophets of Yahweh, as if he has not heard what Obadiah said before.[139] He then proposes an elaborate sacrificial test to see who is the true god. The Baal prophets will prepare one bull to be burned, and Elijah an-

---

137. This is one similarity with the phenomena associated with shamans in other cultures.

138. A close parallel to the phrase is in 1 Chr 2:7 referring to Achan as "the troubler of Israel" (using an alternate spelling), recalling the story of "trouble valley" in Joshua 7. Jonathan accuses Saul of troubling the land in his rash order involving fasting, 1 Sam 14:29. Jer 23:33–40 employs a pun on the word "burden" that has the same effect.

139. Strangely, there is no mention of the prophets of Yahweh here or later in the story. Perhaps they were afraid to come out! Elijah will make the same complaint in 19:10. The reference in 19:18 is not necessarily to prophets, but at least fellow Yahwists. In 18:22 he refers only to the prophets of Baal, not Asherah.

other. They will call on the name of their respective deities, and "the god who answers by fire is indeed God."[140] The people think this is a good plan, and Elijah graciously invites the Baal prophets to go first. They prepare the sacrifice and call on "the name of Baal from morning until noon": "O Baal, answer us!" "But there was no voice, no answer." Now they are the ones who are limping,[141] apparently referring to some ritual dance around the altar. At noon, Elijah mocks them. Cry louder, he says. Maybe Baal is preoccupied, or using the potty, or has wandered off, or is on a trip, or maybe he's just sound asleep.[142] So the Baal prophets cry louder, and resort to self-laceration, "until the blood gushed out over them," a mourning custom also associated with the mythical death of Baal.[143] They rave on and on, but still there is "no voice, no answer, and no response." In effect, they are crying "Where is Baal?" echoing a line from the myth of Baal, uttered because of drought—"Where is the Prince, Lord of the Earth?" And since "Prince" is the word *Zebul*, they are also calling out Jezebel's name, *iy zebul*—"Where is Zebul?"[144]

Now it's Elijah's turn. He has the people gather round him, then he repairs "the altar of the Lord that had been thrown down" (18:30). Literally, he "heals" the altar, an unusual use of the word that comes close to personification.[145] Here we also realize that someone—the Baal prophets and Jezebel?—has torn down the altar of Yahweh, whereas the altar of Baal is still standing (18:26).[146] To this extent, the choice between deities had already been made. Elijah now uses twelve stones in the repair, representing the twelve tribes of "the sons of Jacob, to whom the word of the Lord came, saying, 'Israel shall be your name'" (18:31). The allusion is to the story of Jacob's wrestling match with God (Gen 32:22–32), when God gives him the new name of "Israel." Thus the narrator has again evoked "the word of the Lord," tying it to Northern Israel's very identity as a people. In effect, by "healing" the altar, Elijah also is healing their spiritual brokenness by bringing them back to the worship of Yahweh instead of Baal. Hence, he builds "an altar *in the name of* Yahweh" (v. 32, AT).

But Elijah wants to make the test more challenging, so he digs a trench around the altar, then has the people drench the firewood with water three times until the trench is full. Perhaps using that much water in a drought raises

---

140. The subject of "call" in v. 24 is still the people (v. 22), but it is the prophets who call in v. 26.

141. The root of the word for "limp" here and in v. 21 is elsewhere used for lameness (e.g., 2 Sam 4:4).

142. "Using the potty" is a version of an ancient reading for "turned aside."

143. See Wyatt, *Religious Texts*, 308 and n. 255. Cf. Hos 7:14.

144. "Prince" is one of Baal's alternate titles. See Coogan, *Stories*, 84, and for the text, also Wyatt, *Religious Texts*, 138; Smith, "Baal Cycle," 159. The title is deliberately corrupted in the name Baal-zebub, "Lord of the Flies" (!), 2 Kgs 1:2 (cf.

with Ish-bosheth, "Man of Shame," instead of Ish-baal, "Man of Baal," 2 Sam 2:8). Note the original spelling in Matt 10:25.

145. The word almost always refers to the healing of illness or personal injury. A close parallel is Jeremiah's metaphor of Israel as a broken pot, Jer 19:10, but even here the real referent is the people, not a pot.

146. Assuming that v. 26 refers to an existing, not an *ad hoc*, construction.

the stakes in the test even higher! Elijah then prays, addressing Yahweh as "God of Abraham, Isaac, and Israel," replacing the usual "Jacob" with "Israel," again emphasizing the North:[147] "let it be known this day that you are God in Israel, that I am your servant, and that I have done all these things by your words" (v. 36, AT). Thus the test not only determines who is truly God, but also who is truly God's servant acting on divine authority (cf. with Moses, Exod 14:31). While v. 36 might seem to limit Yahweh's sovereignty ("God in Israel"), v. 37 specifies the divine identity more personally and universally: "that you, Yahweh, are God" (AT).[148]

In the 1980's there were several massive blackouts in places like New York City due to power failure, prompting numerous cartoons depicting the moment just before the lights went out. One of the cartoons showed a revival preacher presiding over an enormous tent meeting, and he was saying, "Give us a sign, O Lord!" The moment in our story is like that, and on Elijah's word, "the fire of the Lord" descends from heaven, burning up not only the sacrifice and the firewood, but also melting the stones and sand of the altar itself and vaporizing the water in the trench. At this, all of the people fall on their faces and shout an affirmation of faith that would warm the heart of any revival preacher: "Yahweh indeed is God; Yahweh indeed is God!" (v. 39, AT). The contest is over. Baal the expert rainmaker is all dried up. Yahweh, who brought Israel out of Egypt, also is the creator of heaven and earth, who brings (or withholds) the rain.[149] God's fire from heaven has turned back the hearts of the people (v. 37b); their return (the equivalent of repentance) opens the way for God to restore the rain, a lesson that one would hope to sink in.

But now the story turns bloody, for Elijah orders the people to seize the prophets of Baal, brings them to the Wadi Kishon, and kills them (the word is often used for sacrifice). With four hundred and fifty corpses, one can imagine their blood running down the wadi instead of water. For contemporary readers, the scene surely puts a damper on the celebration of Elijah's victory. What for a moment had become a humorous tale, poking fun at the pagan prophets, suddenly turns deadly serious, ending in a massacre. The author sees the violence as retaliation of that started by Jezebel, and her murder of the prophets of Yahweh. Whatever events stand behind the text, they are probably far more complicated. As we shall see more fully

---

147. I.e., the usual threesome is Abraham, Isaac, and Jacob. Another exception is in Exod 32:13.

148. Here is a case when it is important to remember that "the Lord" is a reverent avoidance of using the divine name, thought to be Yahweh, but the statement "Yahweh is God" is more clear as a theological *claim* than the apparently tautological "the Lord is God," especially in the context of the contest with Baal.

149. It is nevertheless interesting that the author does not make this point more explicitly. That is, allegiance remains the chief concern, as in Joshua's valedictory challenge: "choose this day whom you will serve" (Josh 24:15); the nature of God (as redeemer or creator) seems secondary. Similarly, the universal implications of God as creator are not evident, as they are when we come to the exilic author called Second Isaiah (e.g., Isa 40:12–31). See my study, "Stars, Sprouts, and Streams."

later, Jezebel may well have had reasons to suspect the Yahweh prophets of political subversion, and being the daughter of a Canaanite king, felt no compunction in putting a stop to it.[150] The author, of course, will not see things from her perspective; restoring the purity of Israel's faith required a radical action. Assuming that many, if not all, of the Baal prophets were not foreigners but Israelite converts, according to covenant theology they were traitors deserving of capital punishment. Deuteronomy is quite clear on this (Deut 13:1–5). Prophets who entice the people to serve other gods "shall be put to death for having spoken treason against Yahweh your God—who [note again, not 'brought you rain,' but] brought you out of the land of Egypt and redeemed you from the house of slavery." In fact the "test" of faith is not who can accurately predict omens, but which deity a prophet follows. Executing false prophets is deemed the only way to "purge the evil from your midst." Ultimately, the law of corporate guilt operates in order to prevent the corruption from spreading to the entire people (an ideology that we first saw with Achan in Joshua). However much we may recoil at the resulting massacre of the prophets, to the author the logic of covenant theology was inescapable, and lethal if circumvented.

Serendipitously, on the day that I wrote the preceding paragraph—two days before the beginning of Hanukkah—columnist David Brooks wrote an intriguing op-ed about the origins of that Jewish holiday. Much of what he says applies remarkably well to Elijah's triumph over the prophets of Baal. In 167 BCE the Jewish zealots were the Maccabees, who revolted against the anti-Jewish religious persecution of Hellenistic rulers and reinstated their purist, uncompromising understanding of Jewish religion. Arguably, Elijah and the prophets he represents were predecessors of the Maccabees. As Brooks writes about the latter, "They had no interest in religious liberty within the Jewish community and believed that religion was a collective regimen, not an individual choice." In other words, religious pluralism was of no interest to them; indeed, "assimilation" was tantamount to abomination, and the Maccabees proved as brutal in defending their faith as the Hellenists were in attacking it. As Brooks suggests, popular versions of the Hanukkah story romanticize it as bravery fighting an evil empire, and it is true that "The Maccabees heroically preserved the Jewish faith. But there is no honest way to tell their story as a self-congratulatory morality tale. The lesson of Hanukkah is that even the struggles that saved a people are dappled with tragic irony, complexity and unattractive choices."[151]

150. Cogan, *I Kings*, 447, and Camp, "1 and 2 Kings," 110, suggest that Jezebel may well have been motivated in her opposition to the prophets by the realistic fear of their meddling and *their* opposition to Baal. Camp also cites Rofe in his conclusion that the figure of Jezebel "is the work of a postexilic author-editor, whose shifting of the blame to the foreign woman forms part of that era's polemic on the dangers of intermarriage." Gottwald, *Politics*, 222, argues that the picture of Ahab and Jezebel as promoting exclusive worship of Baal and of Elijah as "fanatically insistent on the exclusive worship of Yahweh at the state level" is probably overdrawn.

151. *The Winston-Salem Journal*, 16 Dec 2009, A23. The progress to which Brooks refers is Hellenism itself, to which one might compare

We are still waiting for the rain, promised at 18:1, and now it comes (18:41–46). Elijah suddenly is back with Ahab, and tells him to eat and drink, "for there is a sound of rushing rain." Eating and drinking by Elijah and the widow in chap. 17 offset the drought; now with Ahab they signal the end of the drought. Elijah proceeds to the top of Mount Carmel, apparently accompanied by Ahab and one of Elijah's servants.[152] From there one could look west over the Mediterranean, where storms would arise. Elijah orders the servant to look toward the sea and report what he sees. At first there is nothing, but then "a little cloud no bigger than a person's hand." That is enough for Elijah, who knows the rain is coming, and he orders the servant to alert Ahab of the deluge about to happen, lest he be stuck in his chariot. Soon "the heavens grew black with clouds and wind; there was a heavy rain," and Ahab rides off to his home in Jezreel, but by no means leaving Elijah in the dust—the prophet can run as fast as a speeding chariot, and arrives back at Jezreel ahead of the king! The two apparently part without a royal word of thanks for the rain. We are about to learn that Jezebel is not pleased either.

A Burned Out Prophet Like Moses (Chap. 19)

Like a petulant child who has been bullied, Ahab might have said to Elijah, "I'm going to tell," for that's exactly what he does—he reports to Jezebel "all that Elijah had done," including dispensing with her house prophets. It seems that Ahab defers to his wife for action, as we will see again later, and Jezebel is as assertive as Ahab is diffident. She immediately sends a messenger to Elijah with a death threat, invoking "the gods" in her favor, and suddenly Elijah, who seemed fearless before Ahab, is terrified of Jezebel. The one who was able to resurrect the life of the dead now flees for his life lest he die (v. 3).

The story of Elijah's flight takes the form of a spiritual pilgrimage back to the place that represents Israel's origin as a covenant people—Horeb, "the mount of God" (v. 8; alternatively Sinai). Horeb was the place where Moses received his commission to be the leader of the Exodus from Egypt, and to which he returned with the people to mediate God's covenant with them (Exod 3:1, 12; 19:1–3). In retracing the way of Moses, Elijah embodies the *promise* of Moses that God would provide "a prophet like me from among your own people" (Deut 18:15).[153] Of course, Elijah's actions in defending the faith have already placed him in that tradition, but his journey makes contact with the story of Moses in ways that accentuate the analogy.

---

aspects of ancient Canaanite culture. See also McBride, "Essence of Orthodoxy," 134, 149, for an appreciation of Deuteronomic orthodoxy as "sublime" despite its "savage results" and "occasionally horrifying aspects."

152. It is not clear what "go up" means in vv. 41–42. Elijah goes up to the top of Carmel, as does his servant, and Elijah has the servant tell Ahab to "go down" in v. 44, but why is that necessary if Ahab is standing there as well? There seem to be different literary sources here (note that rain is audible in v. 41 but the clouds are still far off in v. 44).

153. This text stands in tension with the concluding words of the book, which claim that "there has never been a prophet like Moses" (34:10), although the difference may be the quantity of "signs and wonders" performed.

Like Moses after killing an Egyptian (Exod 2:15), Elijah flees south to Beersheba, leaves his servant there, and proceeds further south into the wilderness, and after a long day he collapses at the base of a tree, asking "that he might die." He has had enough. "Take away my life," he prays, putting God in the uncomfortable position to which Jezebel aspired. It is as if the great victory at Carmel never happened, for Elijah is depressed, hopeless, even suicidal.[154] Perhaps we could call it "prophetic burnout." He falls asleep, but suddenly he is rudely awakened. An angel is "punching" him, saying, "Get up! Eat!" (v. 5, AT).[155] Moses had encountered an angel also, but was not so rudely treated (Exod 3:2). Elijah looks around him and there at his head is a hotcake and water. The one previously fed by ravens is now fed by an angel. He eats and drinks, then lies down again, no doubt hoping to get some sleep. But the angel punches him again, saying, "Get up. Eat, or the way will be too difficult for you" (AT). The food is bread for the journey, and it is apparently high in calories because Elijah travels for forty days and nights on it (adding stamina to speed among his athletic strengths, 18:46).

Elijah's long journey ends when he comes "to Horeb the mount of God" where he enters "the cave" (AT). The definite article perhaps suggests that he is at the "cleft of the rock" where God had placed Moses to protect him when God's glory "passed by" (Exod 33:21–22; 34:5–6), as God will "pass by" Elijah (see below). Now "the word of the Lord" comes to Elijah, asking what on earth he is doing there. Elijah answers rather plaintively, reporting how "zealous" he has been on God's behalf, in contrast to "the Israelites [who] have forsaken your covenant, thrown down your altars, and killed your prophets" (19:10). Here there is no mention of Jezebel; instead, Elijah blames his fellow Israelites for the religious persecution. "I alone am left," he says, "and they are seeking my life, to take it away." God orders him to "go out and stand on the mountain before the Lord."[156]

> Then behold, Yahweh was passing by
> and a mighty, powerful wind was breaking apart the mountains
>   and shattering the rocks before Yahweh—Yahweh was not in the wind;
> and after the wind, an earthquake—
> Yahweh was not in the earthquake;
> and after the earthquake, fire—
> Yahweh was not in the fire;
> and after the fire, a sound of sheer silence (AT).[157]

154. See Campbell and O'Brien, *Unfolding*, 396, for reasons to see chap. 19 as an independent tradition.

155. The word for "touch" in the NRSV often means "hit, punch, strike." The angel is not gentle!

156. There is considerable ambiguity here. One can read with the NRSV "for the Lord is about to pass by," or more likely see that phrase as belonging with the following phenomena (also in participial form), as I have done. God summons Elijah out of the cave, whereas God had put Moses *in* a crevice to protect him, and Elijah does not emerge until v. 13. Perhaps God may pass by immediately subsequent to God's order to "go out," while Elijah is still inside the cave, listening, and he comes to the mouth of the cave only when all the phenomena are over and he hears the silence.

157. There are as many translations of this phrase as there are translators, but clearly it is "the quiet after the storm," to turn a proverbial saying. The troublesome word is the adjective *daqqah*, which elsewhere means "powdery," Exod 32:20, "thin" or "flaky" (manna, which is also "as fine as frost," Ex 16:14), or "dusty" (Isa

Before we listen to the "voice" that follows, we may note the significance of the silence that precedes, "a silence more profound and mysterious than the absence of noise."[158] Here again there is an analogy with Moses at Horeb, but also a difference. In the Exodus traditions, God's "glory" will pass by Elijah, or God pronounces "the name, Yahweh," then passes by him (33:22; 34:5–6). The "glory," as we have seen, is part of the imagery of the storm deity throughout the Horeb (Sinai) story, and all of the phenomena that pass by Elijah are part of the same imagery—wind, earthquake, fire.[159] But God is not *in* the wind or earthquake or fire, they "go *before* Yahweh," and that is the point.[160] Again, the competition with Baal is probably in view. Although God has demonstrated control over the rain, and thus bested the storm deity at his ostensible expertise, God is not *identified* with or reduced to the phenomena of the storm. Perhaps most telling here is the sound of silence. In both Canaanite and Hebrew texts, "thunder" is the storm deity's "voice"—indeed, the word is the same, *qol*.[161] When God and Moses converse at Horeb, God does so "in thunder" (Exod 19:19). One entire poem is a hymn to the "voice/thunder" of God in a storm (Psalm 29): "the God of glory thunders" (v. 3), *revealing* the glory of God. Indeed, some scholars think that this hymn was originally addressed to Baal.[162] God's thunder is reverberating on the sea, splitting trees, whirling and writhing, making the ground shake, and flaming with fire. So when the "sound" that comes *after* the storm phenomena at Elijah's cave is the "sound of sheer silence," it is a way of saying that God's manifestation is not in any way contained by such imagery. Thus God has not only trumped Baal the rain expert at his own game, but "stolen his thunder" as well (to coin a phrase). Before there was no "voice" of Baal be-

---

29:5). The word for silence is used in a passage in Job 4:12–16 where Eliphaz is describing a nightmare, rife with the language of a numinous encounter, including goose bumps; the silence immediately precedes the speaking of a voice on behalf of God, just as here. Although the metaphor in 1 Kgs 19:12 is auditory, an interesting spatial parallel might be the Celtic notion of "thin places" where one is likely to encounter the spiritual world (an example from the Hebrew Bible would be Jacob's dream encounter, Gen 28:10–22, especially v. 17).

158. The phrase is from James's novel, *The Private Patient*, 4.

159. See the discussion of 1 Kgs 8:10–12 above. The "glory" is often parallel to "cloud" or "thick darkness." See Exod 19:9, 16–20; 20:18–21; 24:15–18. For all three of the motifs together, see Ps 18:7–14. The "earthquake" most likely refers to the way the ground seems to shake when there is an enormous burst of thunder, e.g., "when Addu [an Akkadian deity] bellows, the mountains tremble," Mann, *Divine Presence*, 37, from Tukulti-Ninurta Epic. Cf. with Baal: "At his h[oly] voice the earth quaked . . . the hills of the ear[th] tottered," Wyatt, *Religious Texts*, 109.

160. The motif of a divine vanguard that goes before the deity, especially in battle, is widespread in the ancient Near East, and, by definition, it precedes the deity rather than *being* the deity, although at times it would be difficult to separate the two. Here the author emphasizes the distinction. Cf. my *Divine Presence*, chap. 1.

161. For Baal, note "Baal sounded his holy voice, / Baal thundered from his lips . . . / the earth's high places shook," Coogan, *Stories*, 105 (ellipsis his); for other translations, cf. Cross, *Canaanite Myth*, 149; Smith, "Baal Cycle," 136–37 (col. VII:27–35).

162. See Cross, *Canaanite Myth*, 151–156. Note that "the heavens" and the "firmament" "tell" / "report" the "glory [*khavod*] of God [El]" in Ps 19:1. "The fire of God" (as in 18:38) is also closely connected with God's nature (cf. Ps. 29:7).

cause Baal was absent (18:26, 29); here God is present but not in the "voice." For the author, "the word of the Lord," which has driven the narrative of chs.17–19, is primarily that word mediated through the prophet to guide the events of history, which is exactly what follows in vv. 15–18. On the other hand, if this story is a repudiation of Baal as rainmaker and storm deity, it therefore stands in tension with the Israelite traditions that portray Yahweh in exactly those terms. It is simplistic and, in fact, wrong to say that Yahweh is a "god of history" and that Baal is a "nature god." While we do not see Baal involved in historical events as Yahweh is, they are *both* "nature gods" in that both provide life-giving water (see Excursus 5). It is one thing to say that Yahweh, not Baal, is the true rainmaker and it is Yahweh's voice, not Baal's, that one hears in thunder; it is quite another to suggest that neither rain nor the awesome power of a thunderstorm reveal anything essential (i.e., ontological) about the nature of God, as, again, Psalm 29 affirms. At risk is an appreciation for God as the creator and sustainer of nature that is inseparable from and as important as our appreciation for God as actor and redeemer in history.[163]

However important the silence may be, it is not the way God communicates here; rather, it draws attention to the oral communication that follows. The "sound" (*qol*) of silence leads to the "voice" (*qol*) that speaks. The effect of the silence is like that of saying "Shhh!" in a room of people, and having them immediately become silent and anticipatory—what does this person have to say that is so urgent? The next interchange between Elijah and God shows just how God is involved in Israel's history: "then there came a voice (*qol*) to him that said, 'What are you doing here, Elijah?'"[164] When God addresses Elijah again with the same question, Elijah gives the same answer. God says for him to return to the way he has come, which could refer to both his geographical journey and his social role. God commissions him to go to "the wilderness of Damascus," and there to "anoint Hazael as king over Aram," then back to Israel, where he is to "anoint Jehu" as king. Before Elijah can protest that he has, indeed, had enough, God also tells him to "anoint Elisha . . . as prophet in your place." The former two will be rods of God's anger against Ahab, with Jehu killing any who escapes from Hazael, but God will "leave seven thousand in Israel, all the knees that have not bowed

---

163. See Hiebert, *Yahwist's Landscape*, 72–74: rain is "a manifestation of God's activity in the world," and "nature and history alike assume the sacred status that contact with the divine bestows." Note also the quotations on 129–130 stating traditional scholars' distinction between history and nature, and his discussion of history and myth in the storm/sea conflict on 132–136. Contemporary poets are often attentive to spiritual experiences in nature. For poems addressing the numinous dimension of storms and the ocean, see my study of the poetry of Mary Oliver, *God of Dirt*, chap. 4.

164. In a sense, the redaction of the Exodus story in Exod 19–20 makes a similar point, as Childs has noted (*Exodus*, 372–373). By placing the Ten Commandments in between the storm phenomena (i.e., before 20:18–21), the people are reacting not just to the thunderous voice in the theophany but also to the words of God in the law. The Deuteronomic name theology does something similar with the theophanic language of God's presence in the temple.

to Baal, and every mouth that has not kissed him."

God's commission speech is remarkable in a number of ways. For the first time, the word "anoint" is used for a foreign ruler, demonstrating that God's sovereignty extends beyond the nations of Judah and Israel. God is not just a "patron deity" of a single people; God's will stands behind international events, and God can elect whomever God chooses as leaders of other governments.[165] Second, God charges Elijah with the same task as God had done with Samuel, ordering the anointing of one king of Israel even before the other is gone. In the ensuing stories, prophets will become even more deeply involved in political events. Third, Elijah is *not* alone, as he fears, for there are seven thousand faithful in Israel; moreover, God authorizes the anointing of a replacement for Elijah in the person of Elisha, extending the anointment to prophets as well as kings. Elijah will still have work to do, including one more confrontation regarding Ahab and Jezebel (chap. 21), but at least he can see his retirement in sight.

Elijah seems eager to retire, for he finds his replacement first. Elisha is busy plowing his fields, probably with some field hands, since there are twelve teams of oxen at work. Elijah passes in front of him and throws his overcoat over him, hence our expression, "passing on the mantle."[166] It is the equivalent of anointing him. At first Elisha abandons his oxen and runs after Elijah, but he asks for a momentary deferral of his duties until he can kiss his parents goodbye. Elijah will have none of this sentiment, however, for there is work to do! So he tells Elisha to go back home, but when Elisha does so, he slaughters all the oxen (twenty-four, no less!), cooks the meat, and gives it "to the people," whoever they are. We must assume that he did not take time to kiss his parents, who no doubt were also not happy to have their oxen on the menu. Of course, the story suggests how all-consuming the call to prophetic work could be, how a "follower" or "servant" of a figure like Elijah at times was required to abandon everything—including livelihood—to become a disciple.[167]

A Breach-of-Treaty Treaty (Chap. 20)

Chapter 20 describes Ahab's war with the Arameans and the deep involvement of two anonymous prophets. As far back as David's time, the Arameans were perennial enemies of both Judah and Israel—or friends, if the price was right.[168] Previously Asa of Judah had

---

165. Cf. Amos 9:7 where Yahweh not only "brought up" Israel but also the Philistines and the Arameans! In the Exile, Second Isaiah will emphasize this with Cyrus, the Persian king, as God's "anointed" (Isa 45:1).

166. The "passing in front of" also provides a catchword connection with "pass by" in 19:11, as does "kiss" in vv. 20 and 18.

167. If Elisha was already a member of the prophetic guild, then the appointment is to be the "father" of the group after Elijah. Obviously there are parallels here with the way in which Jesus gathers disciples, e.g., Mark 1:16-20 ("immediately"), and Matt 10:34-39. Elisha's role as "servant" to Elijah resembles the relationship between Joshua and Moses (Exod 33:11).

168. In fact, Deut 26:5 records a tradition in which Israel's ancestors (Abram and/or Jacob) were Arameans. In 2 Sam 8:5-8 David defeats them; in 1 Kgs 11:23-25 they are an adversary of Solomon. There is considerable debate about the

expended all his treasures to purchase their aid in fighting off Israel (15:16–22), and thereby break the treaty that the Arameans had with Israel at the time. Now King Ben-hadad and a coalition of other kings is attacking Samaria, and he sends a message to Ahab demanding that he hand over all of his silver and gold, as well as "fairest wives and children." Ahab immediately caves in, replying that "I am yours, and all that I have." Perhaps emboldened by Ahab's meekness, Ben-hadad ups the ante, threatening to send his agents through every house in Israel, taking whatever they want. At this point, Ahab consults with "the elders of the land," who seem to be made of sterner stuff and advise him to stand firm. Ahab did not report how the new threat involves the households of his servants as well (presumably including the elders), and he sends a mixed message back to Ben-hadad: Ahab will comply with the first demand, but not the second. Ben-hadad replies with an oath invoking the gods (20:10, cf. with Jezebel, 19:2), employing a metaphor suggesting the enormous number of his forces over against Ahab's. As if to better Ben-hadad's rhetorical skill, Ahab replies with a proverb: "One who puts on armor should not brag like one who takes it off." Now Ben-hadad has had enough (and enough to drink as well!), and orders the soldiers to take their positions in the siege of Samaria (20:12).

In the next scene (20:13–22) "a certain prophet" suddenly materializes and approaches Ahab with a "thus-says-the-Lord" message: God will hand the massive Aramean army over to him, by which Ahab will "know that I am Yahweh" (20:13, AT). The latter phrase appears prominently in the Exodus narrative to demonstrate God's power over against the Pharaoh (e.g., 6:7; climactically in 14:4, 18). Here the intent is to bring Ahab to an acknowledgment of Yahweh's sovereignty, which so far seems to be lacking (see below also on v. 28). In fact, Ahab responds with a skeptical question: "By whom?" No doubt he is surprised (as are we readers) that God's message is one of support rather than condemnation, weal instead of woe. God's reply is "By the young men who serve the district governors."[169] Ahab then asks who will start the fighting, and the answer is "You." The narrator tells us that the young men number only two hundred thirty-two, whereas Ben-hadad's troops are a "great multitude" (20:15, 13). We have seen such disproportionate numbers before, notably in Gideon's highly selective draft of three hundred out of thirty-two thousand (Judg 7:2–8)! The point is the same: God is powerful enough to conquer any of Israel's enemies so that large troops are unnecessary. Ahab does not seem confident in being outnumbered, however, and musters "all the people of Israel, seven thousand."

By now Ben-hadad and associates are thoroughly drunk at their tailgate party (20:16), no doubt affecting their military judgment. The Israelite young men issue forth from the city

---

history behind the story in 1 Kings 20, including whether Ahab is the original king in question.

169. Sweeney, *Kings*, 242, reads "provincial commanders," "the squires of the established warriors." This term and "commanders" in 20:24 appear in mostly late documents (exilic or postexilic).

(apparently without the additional seven thousand),[170] whereupon Ben-hadad foolishly orders that they be taken alive, whether they are hostile or not. Suddenly the whole Israelite force is engaged, however, each man killing his designated target, and the Arameans retreat in defeat. The narrator reports the delayed entry of Ahab (20:21) and attributes the victory to him, but one has to wonder if this is what God had in mind in telling Ahab that *he* would initiate the fighting. Now the prophet reappears and advises Ahab that the battle may be won but the war is far from over: Aram will come again in the spring.

The third scene (20:23–30) shows the narrator's omniscient point-of-view when he reports the conversations that take place within the Aramean command center, where Ben-hadad's advisors are engaged in a little theological speculation. Their argument is that Israel has succeeded because "their gods are gods of the hills," so if the Arameans shift the battle to the low-lying plain, they will win. The assumption suggests that *their* gods are gods of the plains, where they will be more powerful (one of those gods being the one for whom the king is named—Hadad, another storm deity).[171] A further assumption is that the power of each god is limited to a particular geographical territory, or even topographical feature. The test of divine power vis-à-vis terrain thus reminds us of that between Baal and Yahweh over the control of rain. Needless to say, the assumption is a set-up for the narrator's demonstration of its falsehood. The Aramean advisors then suggest a military strategy of replacing the various kings with "commanders" and mustering an army equal in size to that which was defeated. To all this Ben-hadad agrees.

As the prophet had predicted, Ben-hadad mounts his next offense in the spring near the town of Aphek. The narrator emphasizes the relative size of the two opposing forces by describing the Israelites as "like two little flocks of goats," whereas the Arameans fill the country (20:27). Now yet another "man of God" appears before Ahab with a "thus-says-the-Lord" and informs him of the Aramean conversation to which we were privy. God clearly resents being identified as "a god of the hills" and not "a god of the valleys," and now "will give all this great multitude" into the hand of Ahab, who once again (and *finally*, one would hope) will "know that I am Yahweh" (20:28, AT). After a stand-off of seven days, the forces engage and, of course, the Israelites slaughter the Arameans—one hundred thousand in a single day. The rest flee into the ostensible protection of Aphek's walls, only to have the wall fall and kill twenty-seven thousand more. Yahweh is apparently a god of towns as well as hills and plains (witness the former Jericho).

Ben-hadad somehow manages to escape the collapsing wall and hides in a closet.[172] One expects that he will soon

---

170. There is some ambiguity with v. 19, where "the army followed them," and in v. 21 Ahab's foray seems anticlimactic. Perhaps the young men go out first alone as a ruse, then, after Ben-hadad's forces attack, the army joins them (cf. a similar situation in Josh 8:3–7).

171. The "Ben" is the word for "son of."

172. Literally "a room in a room," elsewhere translated "inner chamber" (1 Kgs 22:25; 2 Kgs 9:2).

meet his end by the hand of Ahab, but Ben-hadad's servants have yet another scheme, and this one saves his head. Somehow they think that there are numerous "kings of the house of Israel," and, more importantly, that they are "merciful." They suggest that they disguise themselves as mourners, then go to Ahab and appeal to him to spare Ben-hadad's life. Whether or not Ahab is swayed by the disguise, he expresses surprise that Ben-hadad is still alive, and promptly says, "he is my brother," using the standard word to express a treaty alliance. No doubt the messengers are as surprised as we are and rightly see Ahab's words as the sign they were looking for, nodding their heads vigorously and saying, "Yes, Ben-hadad is your brother." When Ben-hadad himself appears, Ahab invites him into his chariot for a tête-à-tête and the two kings agree to a treaty by which they will not only stop fighting but allow each other economic trading privileges (and Ahab will regain some territory). Ben-hadad returns home and everyone is happy—except the real Victor of the war.

The final scene (20:35–43) begins with what at first seems an irrelevant incident involving two of the "company of prophets." "At the command of the Lord," one asks the other to hit him and his colleague refuses, whereupon the first imposes a punishment for disobedience of death by lion (apparently the prophetic executioner of choice, 13:20–24). The point of this bizarre incident immediately appears when the first prophet finds a colleague willing to punch him in the head, for the wounded prophet uses his injury to trap Ahab in a self-convicting parable, much the way Nathan caught David with his little lamb story (2 Samuel 12). The prophet wraps a bandage around his head, covering his eyes, enough to disguise his identity but not enough to hide his bruises, pretending to be a war casualty. When Ahab passes by, the prophet (as soldier) addresses him with a concocted story about his irresponsibility in allowing a captive enemy soldier to escape, saying that he was warned by his superior of the consequences of failure: "your life shall be given for his life." Ahab responds to the story by telling the prophet that he has just convicted and sentenced himself, whereupon the prophet dramatically tears the bandage from his face. Ahab immediately recognizes him as one of the prophets, and now hears the word of judgment: "Thus says the Lord, 'Because you have let the man go whom I had devoted to destruction, therefore your life shall be for his life, and your people for his people."

Taken together, the series of stories in chap. 20 bears a striking resemblance to two others, the confrontation between Samuel and Saul in 1 Samuel 15, and one to come, when the prophet Isaiah will announce to King Hezekiah God's salvation of Jerusalem from the Assyrians (2 Kings 19). As for the latter, until near the end of chap. 20 the prophets have surprisingly appeared as defenders of the king on behalf of God. There is no hint of the hostility of Ahab's wife, much less of the mutual massacres referred to in chap. 18. Such prophetic support suggests a complexity in the prophet/king relationship that we have not seen before (prophets *can* be agreeable!).[173] On the other hand, in the former parallel, the prophet Samuel condemned King Saul for failing to execute Agag, according to the rules of the "ban" (*herem*). Here the prophet condemns King Ahab for the same thing ("devoted to destruction," *heremi*, literally "my banned man"). To make matters worse, Ahab has also broken the covenant rules which prohibit showing mercy to such an enemy or making treaties with them (Deut 7:2). His treaty with Ben-hadad is a breach of treaty with God. While the kings' treaty may seem like a desirable way to end a war, in the prophetic view, as we have seen, such entanglement is dangerous in that the treaty documents may invoke the gods of both sides, thus implying tacit recognition of "other gods." Here with Ahab (as with other kings), the treaty also seems like a foolhardy move on Ahab's part, given the poor record of Aram in keeping its side of such bargains! The result, the prophet says, will be an ironic reversal: Ahab and his people will die in place of Ben-hadad and his, another example of corporate punishment in covenant theology. Although the anticipation is less straightforward here than before (e.g., 14:15–16), it is another confirmation of Israel's end. So Ahab returns home, "resentful and sullen" (20:43), precisely the attitude (21:4) that will immediately involve him in a domestic issue more damning than any international folly.

---

173. See Wilson, *Prophecy and Society*, 88, for a summary of the distinction between "peripheral intermediaries" (those tending toward anti-establishment views), and "central intermediaries" (those tending toward establishment support).

Naboth's Vineyard (Chap. 21)

> Alas for those who devise wickedness
> and evil deeds on their beds!
> When the morning dawns, they perform it,
> because it is in their power.
> They covet fields, and seize them;
> houses, and take them away;
> they oppress householder and house,
> people and their inheritance.
> Therefore thus says the Lord:
> Now, I am devising against this family an evil
> from which you cannot remove your necks;
> and you shall not walk haughtily,
> for it will be an evil time.
>
> Mic 2:1–3 (c. 720 BCE)

If one had to choose a single incident from all of the Former Prophets to illustrate the dangers inherent to monarchy, to marrying foreigners, and, implicitly, to forgetting the God of Israel and following Baal, this story would qualify. The editors have often used speeches or explicit commentary to warn of these dangers.[174] Here the story works its own powerful critique (until a brief, and rather limp, editorial at the end). This is a classic story about the arrogance of power and the way in which religious heterodoxy leads to social injustice. Here the prophet is the voice of conscience and integrity, speaking for the victim who is silenced by a ruthless régime. Here we see how forsaking the God "who brought you out of the land of Egypt, out of the house of bondage," leads to abandoning the covenant between God and

---

174. E.g., Deut 7:1–6; Josh 23:12–13; 1 Sam 8:11–18; 1 Kgs 11:1–8.

people, and the rule of law that binds the community together, creating a just and peaceable society. It is a failure of memory that destroys the ethos of the people (cf. Deut 24:17–22). If there is a defense for the Deuteronomic orthodoxy that often seems authoritarian, xenophobic, and fanatical, it is in this story. However much we might read Jezebel's zeal for Baal as the legitimate practice of her own religion, and her conflict with the Yahweh prophets as politically defensive, her action here is unconscionable.

The narrator tells the story in classic Hebrew narrative style, employing much repetition. The redundancy is not wooden, however, but points to a central question of values, with the categorization of Naboth's vineyard a prime example—his refusal to relinquish it appears four times. Naboth has a vineyard adjacent to Ahab's summer palace in the lush valley of Jezreel. Ahab wants the vineyard so he can plant a vegetable garden.[175] He asks Naboth if he will exchange it for another garden, or sell it for "its value in money." The request is more like an order—"give me your vineyard"—but the deeper problem concerns how one values land. For Ahab, it is simply a commodity that can be exchanged for one of equal value, or sold for money. For Naboth, the land is "my ancestral inheritance," and he accompanies his refusal with an oath invoking God (something like our "by God," if used reverently). He also uses the word "give" rather than "sell." One's land is as much "heritage" as "inheritance." Israelites normally would own a piece of land for generations; in fact, in some legislation, such ownership is ultimately inalienable, so that, even if sold, after a period of years it reverts to the original owner.[176] All of the land of Israel is the *people's* inheritance from God, who is the supreme landlord, and all Israelites are tenants, not owners in the strict sense.[177] Thus there is a deep religious significance to one's land. Although one *may* sell it (e.g., to prevent destitution), it is actually priceless. When Ahab says to Naboth, "name your price," he demonstrates a completely different way of valuing land.

The next scene (21:4–7) presents a withering picture of Ahab as a petulant child. He goes home "resentful and sullen" and straight to bed, with his face turned toward the wall, and refuses to come out for dinner. Jezebel comes to him and asks why he is "so depressed that you will not eat." Ahab whines to her what has happened, this time placing the offer of money first and misquoting Naboth by omitting the crucial word "inheritance." Jezebel's response joins company with Lady Macbeth when she says to *her* husband, "You do unbend your noble strength to think / So brainsickly of things . . . / Infirm of purpose!"[178] Such

---

175. Literally "a green garden." The adjective applies to both trees and plants (Exod 10:15), but here seems to refer specifically to vegetables (cf. Deut 11:10).

176. This is in the year of Jubilee, Lev 25:10, 25–28. Note also that, in donating land to the temple, land that one has purchased is in a different category from land that is one's inheritance (Lev 27:22).

177. Lev 25:23; a particularly early version of this is in Deut 32:8–9, one of the texts in which Elyon is the chief god, who distributes nations and their territories to the other deities, including Yahweh.

178. *Macbeth* II, ii, 62, 69.

infirmity is certainly not one of Jezebel's character traits. When Ahab pouts, she will pounce. "*You* now run the government over Israel," she says (AT). "Get up, eat some food, be happy; *I* will give you the vineyard of Naboth the Jezreelite" (AT). In Hebrew the emphatic position of "I" replaces the emphatic position of "you" in the first sentence. It is clear who gives the orders in the royal palace, providing some irony to her insistence that Ahab rules. Jezebel will give to Ahab what Naboth refused to give. As a Sidonian and daughter of a king named for Baal (16:31), Jezebel has no knowledge of Israel's religious understanding of land.[179] She also apparently has no use for the notion that the king was the defender of justice, not the perpetrator of *injustice*—a tradition certainly known among her own people.[180] She clearly understands "government" (or "kingship") to entail absolute power, something we have already seen in her pogrom against the prophets. Might makes right, and the king enjoys the right of *pre*eminent domain.

Jezebel takes charge (21:8–16), writing letters "in Ahab's name" and sealed with his seal, ordering the death of Naboth. She sends them "to the elders and the nobles who lived with Naboth in his city."[181] Here is another subversion of traditional communal values, whether out of fear of Jezebel or (worse) a disregard for the rule of law equal to hers. Her plot is all the more sinister in that it exploits religious custom: she calls for a fast, a ritual normally reserved for times of crisis, often penitential in nature and supplicating God's compassion.[182] She also debases a gesture of social honor with a shameful purpose, having Naboth seated at "the head of the assembly," only to have him falsely denounced by "two scoundrels" seated with him. They accuse him of blasphemy and sedition: "You have cursed God and the king." The offense is punishable by death, imposed by stoning, a sentence carried out immediately with Naboth.[183] The noble

---

179. See the discussion of this in Davis, *Scripture, Culture, and Agriculture*, chap. 6. Some scholars argue that the prohibition of intermarriages that we have discussed reflects the post-exilic Jewish community's concern over foreign wives obtaining ancestral land from Jewish families, so prohibition protects *Jewish* wives from being disinherited (and thus cannot be dismissed as misogynistic). See Eskenazi, "Ezra-Nehemiah," 123–24. Could Jezebel have been a major impetus for this also, since she appropriates the land of Naboth?

180. The king as the "shepherd" of his people and the defender of the weak and oppressed is a commonplace in the ancient Near East and hardly limited to Israel. In the Ugaritic stories Kirta's son accuses him of irresponsibility, saying "You've let your hand fall to vice. // You don't pursue the widow's case, / You don't take up the wretched's claim. // You don't expel the poor's oppressor. // You don't feed the orphan who faces you, / Nor the widow who stands at your back." See Parker, "Aqhat," 41–42. Similarly, the king figure of Daniel "Takes care of the case of the widow, / Defends the need of the orphan" (58).

181. The "sending" here and in v. 14 reminds us of the actions in the story of David and Bathsheba, as, of course, does the abuse of power.

182. E.g., Jer 36:9; 2 Chr 20:3; Ezra 8:21; in Isa 58:6 the proper fast is "to loose the bonds of injustice"! For the prophetic critique, see also Jer 14:12; 36:4–8.

183. Exod 22:28: "You shall not revile God, or curse a leader of your people." Cf. Lev 24:15–16, which specifies the means of execution as stoning. Blasphemy is so horrendous that the author employs a euphemism meaning the opposite ("to bless") so as not to even write the offensive words.

crowd is a lynch mob. Again the narrator repeats all of Jezebel's orders in reporting their execution, and the executioners report back to the queen. Jezebel immediately gives orders to Ahab again: "Get up, take possession of the vineyard of Naboth the Jezreelite, which he refused to give you for money, for Naboth is not alive, but dead" (AT), thereby repeating the commercial categorization of land. Ahab does as he is told (was he still in bed?), thereby accepting not only the vineyard but also culpability for how it became his.

The transition to the next scene consists of a synchronous movement of king and prophet. Just as Ahab "goes down" to the vineyard, "the word of the Lord" tells Elijah to "go down" and meet him there (21:17–24). God gives Elijah two messages to relay to Ahab, the first asking rhetorically if he has "murdered, and also taken possession" (AT), and the other a grisly prediction that dogs will lick up his blood where they licked up the blood of Naboth. But Ahab speaks first, and his reaction to seeing Elijah reminds us of their first reported encounter ("You troubler of Israel," 18:17): "Have you found me, O my enemy?" "I have found you," Elijah answers, and they are both talking about something more than Ahab's spatial location. Elijah does not repeat the rhetorical question God has given him, but makes his own indictment: "I have found you. Because you have sold yourself to do what is evil in the sight of Yahweh, I [Yahweh] will bring evil [calamity] upon you" (21:20–21, AT). The accusation is appropriate to Ahab's commercial language about the vineyard. Ahab has "sold out" to greed and violence, and in the process "sold his soul" to Baal (if not to the Devil), and the judgment is a typical quid-pro-quo—evil for evil, calamity for corruption. The rest of the judgment predicts the end of Ahab's dynasty ("house") as well as the disposition of Jezebel's corpse, what we might call the "dog food" motif, by now familiar from Jeroboam and Baasha.[184]

An editor has added a brief commentary in 21:25–26, apparently as a kind of moral summary of the story. It repeats the description of Ahab's uniquely profound evil-doing (16:30), but in picking up a key word from the story—"sold himself"—it allows the story to inform the meaning of "evil."[185] It also emphasizes Jezebel's incitement, thereby reiterating the Deuteronomic disapproval of intermarriage with non-Israelites. In v. 26, however, the focus shifts to the priestly concern of idolatry—Ahab's abominable "going after idols," comparing him to the native Amorites whom God had expelled for the same abominations (cf. Deut 7:1–6; Lev 18:24–25). If the "evil" of v. 25 embraces the preceding story, the focus in v. 16 seems astonish-

---

184. For Jeroboam see (14:10–11), for Baasha (16:3–4). Most likely the motif is original to the Ahab/Jezebel story and imported into the others; cf. also Jer 7:33. The prediction about Ahab's blood soon comes true, albeit in Samaria (22:38), and that of his dynasty in 2 Kings 10 (without mention of dog food); Jezebel's fate is reported in gruesome detail in 2 Kgs 9:35–37.

185. The verb form for "sell *oneself*" is rare, and is used with "evil" only in this story and, in editorial comments, only here in v. 25 and the similar commentary of 2 Kgs 17:17. Possibly related to this are the narrative formulas in Judges where the consequence of Israel's doing evil is God's "selling" them into the hand of their enemies (2:14; 3:8; 4:22; 10:7).

ingly narrow, even oblivious to the story, raising once again the question of theological myopia, in which adherence to sacerdotal matters trumps adherence to matters of social justice. Idolatry is not part of the story and would seem to pale in significance compared to murder. On the other hand, it may well be that the editor's concern is precisely to emphasize how serious idolatry is by tying it to the evil in the story. That is, idolatry, especially coupled with worshiping other gods, *leads to* all other breaches of covenant. Still, it is surprising that the editor does not take the opportunity to spell out just how extensive those breaches are.

In fact, what the king and queen have done constitutes a systemic violation of Israel's covenant ethos. Of course, as a devotee of Baal, Jezebel would not identify with that ethos, which is precisely the problem, especially from the perspective of Deuteronomic theology. In this one incident alone, she and Ahab have broken at least half of the Ten Commandments (Deut 5:6–21): they have coveted, used God's name in vain, borne false witness, stolen, and, of course, murdered. In doing so they have violated the neighbor mentioned five times in Deut 5:20–21—and Naboth is *literally* their neighbor. Add what we know otherwise—for Ahab, following another god and making an idol (16:32-33)—and the count comes to seven out of ten. Expand the spirit of the commandment regarding the Sabbath to include the ostensibly sacred time of a fast, and we have eight, leaving only honoring parents and adultery. In terms of irony, the most damnable offense is the blasphemy in falsely accusing *Naboth* of blasphemy ("wrongful use of the name" of God, Deut 5:11). That part is compounded by the single adherence to the letter of the law: they have used two witnesses, required for capital sentences (Deut 17:6), albeit "scoundrels." Even without editorial commentary, the story is enough to condemn the characters without quoting the law (or, to use Jewish terms, the *haggadah* [narrative] includes within it the *halakah* [way of life]). If one does not commit one's loyalty to the God who brought Israel out of Egypt, one can live as if exempt from the words that God spoke to Israel at Sinai/Horeb. If one has not been borne to God "on eagle's wings," one need not obey God or keep God's covenant; if one's identity is not shaped and governed by the narrative of God's redemption, the way one lives is not subject to the "now, therefore" that demands responsibilities appropriate to that redemption (cf. Exod 19:4–5). In short, theology drives morality, and, to the Deuteronomists, a false theology drives immorality.[186] Here again a problem inherent to Baal worship might be at work: just as the Baal myths do not portray Baal as engaged in historical, political events like God's involvement in the Exodus, so they do not portray Baal as issuing a code of law for the human community that prohibits coveting, blasphemy, and murder, nor, more broadly, exploitation and oppres-

---

186. Of course, this is not to suggest that only an Israelite would see immorality in coveting a vineyard and murdering its owner in order to possess it. See above, n. 180. But it is to suggest that Israel's understanding of monarchy was inherently covenantal, with all of the implications for a just society that the covenant entails.

sion of the powerless.[187] The myth does not *remind* people of an historical *memory* that grounds moral behavior (Deut 24:21–22). To the extent that Ahab has become a Baal devotee—even if simply because he is "infirm of purpose" before his wife—he has lost that memory and thus the moral world that it requires.

Ahab's response is remarkably humble. In the traditional gestures of repentance he rips his clothes, dons sack cloth, and fasts (a *genuine* fast of repentance, compared to the fake one!). He becomes "docile" (AT), quite a contrast to his angry, sullen attitude from before. In response, "the word of the Lord" comes to Elijah, pointing out how "humbled" Ahab has become, as a result of which God "will not bring the disaster [or 'evil'] in his days," but in the days of his son and "on his house." It is quite a reprieve for one whose evil-doing surpassed all others (v. 25), enough to make us suspect that an editor has composed vv. 27–29 simply to explain the delay of the "disaster." But once again, the father has eaten sour grapes and the son's teeth will be set on edge.[188]

A True-or-False Test (Chap. 22)

> *My Dear Fellow Clergymen:*
> *While confined here in the Birmingham city jail . . . I think I should indicate why I am here . . . I am in Birmingham because injustice is here. Just as the prophets of the eighth century B.C. left their villages and carried their "thus saith the Lord" far beyond the boundaries of their home towns . . . , so I am compelled to carry the gospel of freedom beyond my own home town.*
> —Martin Luther King, Jr.[189]

In chap. 18 we saw a contest between the prophets of Baal and Elijah, the prophet of Yahweh—four hundred fifty against one (not counting Asherah's prophets, 18:19). In chap. 22 a quite different contest occurs, for the contestants all claim to be prophets of Yahweh.[190] The contest thus raises a question that is as difficult to answer as "who is God?"—namely, "who is the true prophet and who is the false?" Some two hundred and fifty years later, the prophet Jeremiah will have to deal with the same problem.[191] Here four hundred prophets of Yahweh say one thing, and only one—Micaiah—says another. How is one to determine

---

187. At least such texts have not appeared so far in the excavations that produced the mythic tales. Ancient Mesopotamian texts, on the other hand, reveal considerable similarities to portions of biblical law, including the divine sanction (e.g., the famous "Code of Hammurabi").

188. Ezek 18:2. See above on Rehoboam (11:12).

189. "Letter from Birmingham Jail," in *Why We Can't Wait*, 76–77. The letter is addressed to a group of clergy who questioned the appropriateness of King's involvement in civil rights demonstrations.

190. This story may be independent of chap. 18, where all but one hundred of the prophets of Yahweh had been killed, and now there are four hundred!

191. Jer 23:9–40 and chap. 28. See below.

who is right? It is all too easy for us to identify with Micaiah as soon as we learn that Ahab doesn't like him, but if we look more objectively at the problem from the king's perspective, we might understand the difficult position he is in. The issue concerns a declaration of war, and therefore national security, and the decision will lead either to victory or defeat, life or death. If four hundred advisors say one thing, and only one says the opposite, what ruler would follow the advice of the loner?

Three years after concluding the peace treaty with Aram, Ahab decides to break it in an attempt to regain the town of Ramoth-gilead. Since Judah has a mutual-defense treaty with Israel, Ahab asks King Jehoshaphat for his assistance. Perhaps as a sign of disapproval, the narrator consistently refers to Jehoshaphat by name, but to Ahab only by "the king of Israel"—except in reporting the oracle against him in v. 20. Jehoshaphat initially expresses his solidarity with Ahab, but also suggests that Ahab solicit "the word of the Lord," a precaution before battle that we have seen previously (e.g., 1 Sam 23:2). Ahab assembles the prophets who are apparently court advisors and asks them if he should make war or not? What unfolds is a classic confrontation between prophets functioning in different roles—central and peripheral.[192] Central prophets work within the court to aid and support it; peripheral prophets work from outside, often to undermine if not even subvert the king's authority. Sometimes the same prophet can play *both* roles. Here, every one of them says the same thing: "Go up; for the Lord will give it into the hand of the king" (22:6)—just the kind of Q and A that David once experienced (2 Sam 2:1). But Jehoshaphat, for some reason, asks if there isn't another prophet of Yahweh available. Perhaps the unanimous agreement of four hundred prophets on such a momentous decision seems suspiciously optimistic and over-confident. Ahab replies that yes, there is another, but he "never prophesies anything favorable about me, but only disaster."[193] Jehoshaphat replies, "don't *say* such a thing," as if Ahab's complaint is a failure in "positive thinking." The two kings are enthroned near the city gate (something like the county court house), arrayed in their finery, and all of the prophets are "prophesying before them," i.e., reveling in ecstasy (but, one would hope, not naked—cf. 1 Sam 19:18–24). One of them named Zedekiah ("son of Canaan"! [AT]) engages in an act that seems like voodoo but, in fact, is within the repertoire of legitimate prophecy: he adorns his head with iron horns, and, using the prophetic messenger formula, says "thus says the Lord: With these you shall gore the Arameans until they are destroyed."[194] All the other prophets chant their encouragement as well—the king will "triumph."

Meanwhile, Ahab's messenger has found Michaiah and clued him in on

---

192. See Miller, *Religion*, 180–81; Wilson, *Prophecy and Society*, 88, 202–6.

193. In *The Iliad*, 4, (Book I, lines 101–105), Agamemnon raises the same complaint against the seer, Calchas: "you never yet prophesied smooth things concerning me, but have ever loved to foretell that which was evil."

194. Jeremiah dons a yoke to demonstrate Judah's captivity, and the false prophet, Hananiah, breaks it (Jer 28:10).

what has happened, suggesting that he might find it wise to agree with the other prophets. Michaiah says he'll say what God *tells* him to say, but when he arrives before Ahab he trots out the same encouragement as the other prophets. One can imagine him smirking as he does this, and Ahab is not fooled. "How many times must I make you swear to tell me nothing but the truth in the name of the Lord?" he asks, even though he has already indicated his displeasure in *hearing* the truth. Michaiah complies. "I saw all Israel scattered on the mountains," he says, "like sheep that have no shepherd." And he heard God say, "let each one go home in peace." Hearing this, Ahab turns to Jehoshaphat and says, "what did I tell you? All he prophesies is disaster" (AT). As if anticipating the demand for some proof of his claim from Jehoshaphat, Michaiah elaborates on what he has seen and heard, thereby revealing the heart of prophetic authority: he has "stood in the council of the Lord," to use a phrase from Jeremiah (Jer 23:18). The heavenly council consists of God and "all the host of heaven," to use Michaiah's phrase. In its earliest forms, the council was, in effect, a pantheon of deities (Deut 32:8; Ps 29:1; 89:5–7; see Excursus 3). Later, the deities clearly lost their equivalent status (Psalm 82; Deut 33:27)[195] and became "children of God," spirits, "messengers" ("angels") with names, and the nameless Host. Ultimately, the prophets based their authority to speak for God in their status as human attendants to the heavenly council: they spoke what they had heard and seen. As in Micaiah's case, their access to the council could be through a vision (Isa 6:1–13; 40:1–11; Ezekiel 1);[196] more frequently, the prophet simply receives the revelation of God's word.

In the scene before us, Micaiah is reporting his vision at the very moment that all the other prophets are "prophesying" before the kings. The implication here, at least, is that the true prophet is not necessarily the one who displays the most dramatic "charismatic" behavior, but the one whose words authentically represent *God's* words. Anyone, actually, can preface a statement with the phrase "thus says the Lord," making it difficult to determine true from false prophecy on that phrase alone.[197] Indeed, Micaiah's vision shows just how deceptive such a claim might be, for, in fact, the four hundred prophets are saying precisely what a "lying spirit" from God's council has *told* them to say. More pointedly, the prophets are mere puppets, for the "lying spirit" is "in the *mouth* of all his [Ahab's] prophets" (22:22). In a sense, they could rightly claim that *their* message is from the divine council as well! Their prophecy is deceptive because God has designed it to deceive. In some ways, the "lying spirit" from God reminds us of the "evil spirit" from God that so badgered King Saul (1 Sam 16:14), with all of the theological problems it raises.[198] On the other hand,

---

195. At one point, the most notorious member of the council, of course, was Satan, but at the earliest stage he was not the full-blown devil, only "*the satan*," meaning something like the "Attorney General" (cf. Job 1–2).

196. Sometimes expressed by a special word for "vision," *ḥaza*.

197. Cf. the story of the two prophets in 1 Kings 13.

198. Brueggemann, *Kings*, 280, insists that we not allow our "standards of morality" to dis-

at least Ahab *knows* what God is doing, because God's true messenger has told him: I am telling the truth, which includes the fact that they are telling a lie because God has *made* them lie in order to deceive you and cause your downfall. Through Micaiah, God, as it were, has "shown his hand," indeed has shown that "the deck is stacked;" it is up to Ahab to decide how he will play the rest of the card game.

Elijah's charges directly challenge the religious establishment (much as Martin Luther King, in the letter quoted above, challenged the "white church and its leadership" as "archdefender[s] of the status quo").[199] Zedekiah, the prophet sporting the horns, does not make Ahab's decision any easier. He slaps Micaiah in the face and challenges his story, asking sarcastically "Which way did the spirit of the Lord pass from me to speak to you?" Micaiah replies, "you will find out on the day you go hide in a closet" (my paraphrase), no doubt referring to the disaster that is coming. At this point Ahab has had enough, and he orders that Micaiah be thrown into prison (he will certainly not be the last prophet who finds himself there).[200] Micaiah's reply to Zedekiah points to the acid test for true versus false prophecy, namely, accuracy: the prophecy is true if it *comes* true. This is Deuteronomy's solution to the problem (18:22), one which Micaiah employs as well (cf. Jer 28:9). When Ahab concludes his sentencing with the words "until I come back in peace" (22:27, AT), Micaiah says that if that happens, then God has not spoken through him after all. The problem with the accuracy criterion, of course, is that by the time the prophecy comes true it will be too late!

The narrator tells us nothing about the two kings' deliberations, only that immediately they set out for war, apparently persuaded by the lie. Ahab does not exactly distinguish himself on the field of battle. He suggests that Jehoshaphat wear his royal garb while Ahab disguises himself as a regular soldier. Why Jehoshaphat would agree to such stupidity we do not know, but the result is not what Ahab intended. The King of Aram has ordered his soldiers to bear down on Ahab when they see him, which they proceed to do when they see Jehoshaphat in his regalia. But when he cries out, they somehow realize they have the wrong man and back off. On the other hand, a random arrow finds it way into a chink in Ahab's armor and mortally wounds him (it is not hard to guess who the narrator thinks to be the *real* bowman).[201] Carried off the field of battle, he sits propped up in his chariot, watching the defeat of his forces as he bleeds to death. When Israelite and Judean forces learn of his death, they all retreat, every man to his city.

---

miss the text's claim about God's "willful inscrutability" which works to "overthrow excessive human ambition."

199. King, "Letter from Birmingham Jail," 89, 92.

200. Hence the quotation at the beginning of this section. The list includes Jeremiah (Jer 37:11–16), John the Baptist (Luke 3:20), Jesus (Mark 15:6–9), Paul (e.g., Col 4:3), and, of course, innumerable figures (of all religious faiths), famous and unknown, down to the present.

201. Thus Brueggemann, *Kings*, 280: "This account dares a connection between *divine resolve* and a *chance arrow*" (italics his). "Such is the scandal of faith where 'God acts in history.'"

The oracle from the heavenly council has come true: each one has gone home in peace without their leader (v. 17).[202] And Micaiah's prophecy is proved true: Ahab will *not* return home in peace (v. 28). Finally, the prophecy of Elijah comes true (in part) when dogs lick up Ahab's blood as it drips from his chariot, "according to the word of the Lord that he had spoken" (v. 38).[203] (The narrator does not see fit to tell us if, in fact, Micaiah was released from prison despite Ahab's failure to return "in peace"!) The narrator then concludes Ahab's story with a summary evaluation, noting all of Ahab's accomplishments in architectural constructions, but, thanks to the Deuteronomist, the "ivory house" will not be his most lasting monument.

The book of 1 Kings ends rather lamely after the dramatic stories about Ahab, Elijah, and Micaiah (22:41–53). Typically, the narrator jumps back to the beginning of the reign of Jehoshaphat of Judah, telling us that he did "what was right in the sight of the Lord" by following the example of his father Asa. Even though he failed to remove the high places and prohibit the people from worshipping there, he did complete the removal of offensive temple personnel.[204] In terms of his "secular" affairs, we hear that he made peace with Israel, and "how he waged war," but without mention of the preceding story of military disaster. He refused to cooperate in a joint commercial venture with Ahaziah, Ahab's son, to which the narrator then turns. Ahaziah is judged to be evil, following the way of his mother and father, as well as Jeroboam's sinful precedent, and the book ends with God's anger provoked once again.

---

202. Strangely there is no mention of Jehoshaphat after his escape. Similarly, the oracle referred only to Israel and Ahab.

203. See 21:19. This happens in Samaria, not Jezreel, and the prostitutes' blood bath is a surprise. We assume that the author did not see enough discrepancy here to render the prediction *untrue*!

204. Verse 46. The NRSV has "male temple prostitutes," on which see the discussion above of 14:24 and n. 94 above.

SEVEN

2 Kings

GIVEN THE CONFUSING DUPLICATION of names, intermarriage, and assorted murders, a brief genealogy of the House of Omri (father of Ahab) may help the reader:

Figure 3: House of Omri

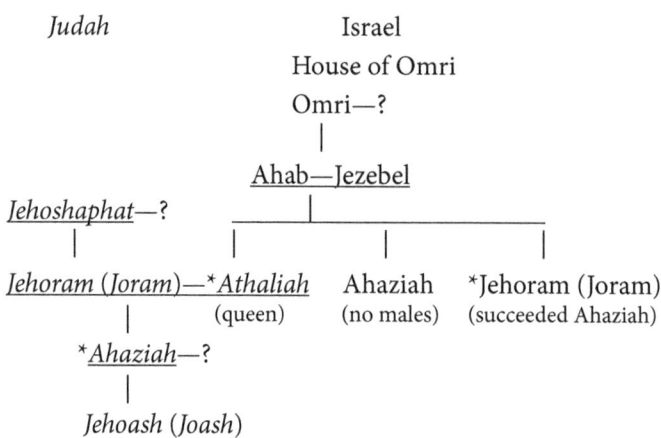

*assassinated in Jehu's purge

against Israel," but waits until 3:4–27 to give us the details. Probably the editorial move is similar to that in 1 Kgs 11:26, where the initial report of Jeroboam's revolt leads into a retrospective theolog-

Swatting the "Lord of the Fly" (Chap. 1)

The books of Kings were originally a continuous document. Perhaps those who divided it into two saw fit to do so after the death of Ahab. After noting his death, the narrator tells us that "Moab rebelled

ical reason for it. Here the behavior of Ahab's son Ahaziah may provide further reasons for Moab's revolt, in addition to Ahab's own faults, although the narrator does not say so explicitly. Otherwise, the story in chap. 1 stands on its own as another prophetic legend that extols the wonder-working power of Elijah just as it serves to condemn the king for apostasy to Baal (like father, like son).

The story has the three-part form of a folktale, with the typical repetitions. Ahaziah has fallen through the second floor roof and incurred a serious injury. He sends messengers to find out his prognosis, but instead of seeking Yahweh's word, he turns to "Baal-zebub, the god of Ekron." The name is a deliberate corruption of the title "Baal Zebul," "Prince Baal," into "Baal of Fly."[1] The God of Israel, being omniscient, knows what is happening and sends God's own messenger (or "angel"—the words are the same), to Elijah, instructing him to intercept the messengers and send them back to Ahaziah with *Yahweh's* reply to his question. The physical prognosis is negative because the *spiritual* diagnosis is positive—positive in the medical sense of confirming the presence of a lethal disease. Ahaziah has a case of terminal infidelity, and he will never get up off his sick-bed.

The messengers dutifully return to Ahaziah and report Elijah's message. When Ahaziah hears the description of the man who sent them—"a hairy man, with a leather belt around his waist"—he immediately recognizes him: "It is Elijah, the Tishbite." Undaunted by the prophet's irascible reputation, Ahaziah now sends a platoon of fifty soldiers to escort Elijah back to him. Elijah is "sitting on the top of a hill" (a posture assumed by the stereotypical sage in many contemporary cartoons). The platoon commander conveys the king's message for Elijah to come down, addressing him as "O man of God." Elijah replies that if he really is a man of God, fire will come down from heaven and roast the commander and his platoon, which is exactly what happens. After all, Elijah is something of a pyrotechnical wizard (cf. 18:38), and no one to mess with!

The same sequence happens a second time with the same result, but when the third platoon arrives, the commander wisely assumes a deferential attitude. He must have heard a report of the fate of his predecessors, and he humbly falls on his knees and begs Elijah to be merciful. Now the angel intervenes again and assures Elijah that it is safe to accompany this commander back to the king, and upon arriving Elijah repeats God's prognosis. No sooner have the words left Elijah's mouth than the narrator tells us, laconically, "so he died according to the word of the Lord that Elijah had spoken." The "Lord of the Fly" never even got a chance to offer a second opinion.

"Swing Low, Sweet Chariot": A Double Assumption (2:1–18)

Another three-part prophetic legend now describes Elijah's departure as well as his replacement by Elisha—the former an "assumption" in the sense of an ascent into heaven, the latter an "assumption" in the sense of a transfer of office. The narrator alerts us to God's imminent taking up of Elijah, but delays the climactic moment with an anecdote about the parting of the two prophetic figures. Three times Elijah tells Elisha to stay where he is while Elijah proceeds to a place to which

---

1. As noted previously, "Zebul" is part of Jezebel's name. Note the "zebul" spelling in Matt 10:25. Later the figure as Lord of the Flies will fuse with the Devil.

God is sending him, and Elisha refuses to abandon him. They move from Bethel to Jericho to the Jordan River. Each time they are met by a "company of prophets" who ask Elisha if he is not aware that God is about to "take your master away from you?" Elisha says that yes, he knows, and tells them to be quiet.² When they come to the Jordan, Elijah removes his mantle and rolls it up, apparently into the shape of a tube, and then strikes the river with it, at which point the water divides in two and he and Elisha cross over on dry ground. It's a handy trick to have when there is no bridge. The crossing obviously resembles that of the Israelites when they were fleeing from Pharaoh (Exod 14:21), and thereby portrays Elijah as a wonder-worker like Moses (who used his staff for the same purpose), as well as echoing the crossing of the dammed-up Jordan for Joshua (Josh 3:13–16; 4:6–7). Elijah is the "prophet like Moses" one more time.

Once over the river, Elijah asks Elisha what favor he would ask of him before he is "taken from you," and Elisha asks for "a double share of your spirit."³ Elijah says that his wish will be granted as long as Elisha sees his ascension, and suddenly a "chariot of fire and horses of fire" materializes and a "whirlwind" whisks Elijah up into heaven.⁴ Elisha does, indeed, witness this moment and cries out, "Father, father! The chariots of Israel and its horsemen," referring to the heavenly hosts. Then Elijah disappears from sight and Elisha tears his clothes in mourning over his lost mentor.

Now that Elijah's assumption into heaven is over it is time for Elisha's assumption of his prophetic office, and he picks up the mantle of Elijah that fell off before his ascent. He returns to the Jordan and strikes the water with the mantle, uttering an invocation: "Where is Yahweh, the God of Elijah?" (AT). Instantly the water parts again, and Elisha crosses over, not only wearing Elijah's mantle but also clearly empowered to perform the same wonders. When he returns to Jericho, the company of prophets sees him coming and apparently his status as Elijah's successor is written all over his face: "The spirit of Elijah rests on Elisha," they all proclaim. Not having seen Elijah's ascension, they suggest that they send out a search party to find Elijah, in case God has spirited him away and thrown him down on some mountain or into some valley.⁵ Elisha assures them that the search is futile, but they press him, he relents, and sure enough, Elijah is gone for good.

Elisha's reputation as a wonder-worker gains more momentum in the next two incidents (2:19–22 and 2:23–25). The people of Jericho point out that, despite the favorable location of the town, the water supply is bad, "and the land is unfruitful."⁶ Elisha orders them

---

2. It may be that both Elijah and the other prophets are worried about Elisha's being in danger at the moment when God comes for Elijah, either from the accompanying phenomena (fire) or being taken along for the ride.

3. Cf. Num 11:17, 25, about shared power of prophesying; also 1 Sam 10:6; 19:20.

4. Such a chariot appears in another vision to Elisha in 2 Kgs 6:17, and note the title "father" in 6:21.

5. There is some confusion here in that earlier the company of prophets in each place seemed to know that God was about to "take up" Elijah away from Elisha. Here the Jericho contingent does not seem to be aware that the departure was permanent.

6. Presumably the story assumes the rebuild-

to bring a new bowl with some salt in it, throws the salt into the spring and—with a "thus-says-the-Lord"—voilà, the water is potable (literally "healed," cf. 1 Kgs 18:30). "Now," he says, "neither death nor unfruitfulness will come out of it again" (AT), and the narrator affirms that the spring is still potable "to this day." It seems counter-intuitive to us that salt water would be drinkable, but the idea may have to do with salt's preservative capacity.[7] The story is not interested in chemistry, however, but in again showing Elisha's powers, and here he, like Elijah, performs a miracle that is reminiscent of Moses' purifying water in the wilderness (Exod 16:22-25a). It is also possible that preventing "death and unfruitfulness" from emerging from the well has a mythical dimension in that Death (Mot) is a chthonic deity prominent in Ugaritic literature—just as Elijah mediated Yahweh's power over Baal, Elisha mediates Yahweh's power over Mot.

The basic meaning of the word "unfruitful" in vv. 19 and 21 is "to be bereaved of children," which almost lends some irony (probably unintended) to the next episode. Elisha is on his way to Bethel when a group of boys accost him, shooing him away with the taunt "baldhead" (apparently one of Elijah's traits that Elisha does *not* share is hairiness). Elisha utters a curse on the boys "in the name of the Lord," whereupon two bears emerge from the woods and maul forty-two of the boys (although apparently not killing them).[8] Then Elisha continues on his way to Mount Carmel and finally to Samaria. This wonder makes *us* wonder if Elisha has a problem with "anger management," but it again illustrates the power that he exercises as God's prophet.

A Failure of God's Word

The prophetic legends of chaps. 1–2 now lead into another story of prophetic involvement in international political affairs (chap. 3), the revolt of King Mesha of Moab, already intimated at 1:2. Readers interested in historical accuracy and objective reporting will find this story most frustrating because we also have a rare extra-biblical document apparently written about the time of the event, and it is exceedingly difficult to reconcile the two. The latter is the famous "Moabite Stone," also called the "Mesha Inscription," as it appears to be an account of the Moabite revolt told from the perspective of Mesha himself.[9] The inscription provides fascinating similarities to a number of biblical motifs, to which we have already alluded. As reported, the incident easily could appear in the book of Judges with some simple reversing of the divine names. Mesha concedes that Moab had suffered oppression by Omri and Ahab because Mesha's god, Kemosh (or Chemosh), was "angry with his country." But then Kemosh raised up Mesha and, the king

---

ing of Jericho in 1 Kgs 16:34. Even so, one wonders how the town could have survived to this point without potable water!

7. Salt thrown on enemy soil ruins it (Judg 9:45). On the other hand, salt may have some purifying capacity in ritual (Ezek 43:24).

8. The meaning of the word is "cleave, break apart," but it can be used for a tearing wound (Ezek 29:7). This is probably not a good text for a "Children's Sermon."

9. For the text see *ANET*, 320; see Dearman, *Mesha Inscription*, for the text and extensive discussion.

claims, "delivered me from all the kings," and "drove him (the king of Israel) out from before me." Kemosh ordered him, "Go seize Nebo from Israel," which he did, putting it to the ban (ḥerem), killing everyone in the city; then he hauled off "th[e ves]sels of Yahweh and dragged them before Kemosh."[10] Mesha then busied himself with some urban redevelopment, including the construction of a "high place" in honor of Kemosh, using the slave labor of captured Israelites. The story sounds very much like that of the Philistine capture and display of the ark in Joshua 5, the use of enslaved enemies (e.g., Joshua 9; Judg 1:28–35), and the framework for many of the Judges "deliverer" stories (recall the pattern in Judg 2:11–16). It is almost as if the biblical editor of Judges had read Mesha's inscription and plagiarized the schema. Thus the basic theology here is that which undergirds the entire Former Prophets—oppression signifies divine punishment, not divine defeat; victory signifies renewed divine favor. Here also is the earliest extra-biblical reference to Yahweh, and it easily could be from the perspective of those into whose hand Yahweh "sold" Israel (e.g., Judg 3:12; 1 Sam 12:9).

Correlating the Mesha Inscription with the historical details of the story in 2 Kings 3, however, is fraught with problems. The chronology with the Israelite kings is confusing and probably irresolvable; the Mesha inscription may have fused a series of revolts into one; in fact, the two texts may report different incidents. In the biblical story, both Israel and Judah, along with their vassal, Edom, attack Mesha and initially they are victorious, until Mesha employs a desperate tactic—he goes to the top of the wall and sacrifices his firstborn son in full view of his besiegers, who immediately break off the siege and return home. Above all, comparing the two texts illustrates how different they are in terms of historiography. The biblical account incorporates a prophetic legend involving Elisha such that the two are virtually inseparable. In fact, the main thrust of the biblical account seems to be yet another glorification of the prophet's uncanny power—until Mesha's sacrilege overpowers everyone.

The biblical story begins with the standard editorial introduction (3:1–3): Jehoram, Ahab's son, "did what was evil in the sight of the Lord" (although not as outrageously as his parents), following in the sin of Jeroboam. Then the narrator returns to the Moabite revolt, describing Mesha as a "sheep breeder" who must pay tribute to Israel in the form of hundreds of thousands of skins. When he rebels, Jehoram calls on his other two vassals, Jehoshaphat of Judah and the king of Edom, to join in the counterinsurgency. After a week's march, their forces run out of water, and Jehoram despairs, complaining that "the Lord has summoned us, three kings, only to be handed over to Moab," a rather pessimistic interpretation of the events. As in a similar situation before, Jehoshaphat suggests consulting with God through a prophet (1 Kgs 22:4–5), and it turns

---

10. Following the translation of Jackson, "Language," 97–98. The brackets indicate broken text making an exact reading difficult. A previous line also reports the capture and display of some object, Jackson's translation being "the altar hearth of its DWD" (l.12).

out that Elisha is suddenly present.[11] Jehoshaphat confirms that "the word of the Lord is with him," perhaps remembering the accuracy of Micaiah in the previous incident. At first, Elisha rebuffs the kings' approach, sardonically suggesting to Jehoram that he go to "your father's prophets or to your mother's" (3:13).[12] Jehoram repeats his conviction that Yahweh is behind their ostensibly doomed mission, and Elisha replies that, were it not for God's benevolent regard for Jehoshaphat of Judah he wouldn't even *glance* at Jehoram (the merit of David is at work for Jehoshaphat). Then he calls for a musician (perhaps there is a fife and drum corps) and the music transports him into an ecstatic trance ("the power of the Lord came on him," 3:15), from which he delivers God's message. Although they will see "neither wind nor rain," God will fill up the arroyo to the brim, and that's just for starters, for God "will also hand Moab over to you," thus dispelling Jehoram's fear of the opposite. The coalition will conquer every city and devastate the countryside.[13] The next morning "the country was filled with water."

Now all the Moabites are in arms, and when they see all the water (as if there is a flood), it looks "as red as blood," perhaps because of the red soil in the region.[14] The Moabites jump to the conclusion that the coalition of kings must have got into a dispute and killed one another, filling the countryside with blood! When they move to despoil the enemy, the Israelites surprise them with a counter-attack, and the Moabites retreat. Israel ruins the land, as instructed, then besieges the one town where the walls are intact, the last redoubt of Mesha. Mesha mounts a futile counter-offensive against the Edomite flank, then flees back to the city. In desperation, he goes up to the top of the wall, in view of the besieging forces, and sacrifices his firstborn son. The narrator says that Israel "withdrew from him and returned to their own land" because "great wrath came upon" them, without saying *whose* wrath.[15]

Even without considering the Mesha Inscription, the biblical story has a strange conclusion. Elisha's prophetic power in providing water is effective at first (indeed, beyond his expectation!), and seems to be part of Moab's defeat (even if not intentionally so), but finally the prophet is no match for the Moabite king's horrific gesture. Jehoram's fear that God had handed them over to Moab was countered by God's promise to hand Moab over to them, only to be proved wrong at the end, an unparalleled failure of God's word. In fact, *if* the "wrath" at the end is a vague reference to the Moabite god's, Yahweh's

---

11. Why he would be accompanying the troops is a mystery; in v. 12 the kings "go down" to him, suggesting a different location. In many of the following stories, however, Elisha is often virtually a member of the royal court.

12. It is not clear if these are so-called prophets of Yahweh as in ch. 22, or prophets of Baal, but all of the latter supposedly were killed in 1 Kgs 18:40.

13. Against the rules of warfare in Deut 20:19–20. There is a curious parallel between the Israelites' stopping up springs and Mesha's constructing reservoirs for springs in the Inscription (lines 23–25).

14. The water is coming from the adjacent country of Edom, which means "red."

15. Sweeney, *I &II Kings*, 284, suggests the meaning of "they became angry," but anger seems a strange motivation for retreat. Campbell and O'Brien, *Unfolding*, 415, see the wrath as Yahweh's.

failure would seem all the more astonishing. On the other hand, if Yahweh is in complete control, then "God seems to have been on both sides, or neither."[16] Yet again, the failure may be Israel's, not God's, a failure of nerve in face of the enemy (even given Mesha's horrific act) that elsewhere God has warned against (e.g., Deut 20:1-4), but it is puzzling why the narrator does not make that point explicit.[17] With the Inscription in view, the two accounts are similar in that they both report a defeat for Israel, but the means to the defeat are quite different. Even if the final "wrath" is a hint at Kemosh, the biblical author—who elsewhere disparages the deity[18]—certainly does not make an explicit attribution of victory to him. Given the extent of Israel's destruction of Moab, Mesha's victory is a Pyrrhic one, at best.

Striking Oil (4:1-7)

We now return to four prophetic legends that have no direct political bearing but, in the context of the ongoing challenge of Baalism, may continue the critique of the preceding Elijah stories. Here again the God of Israel is the deity who provides food for life and defeats death—what Baal is supposed to do. In the first story, a widowed wife of one of the company of prophets appeals to Elisha when a creditor is threatening to take away her children in payment for her debts—one way to handle bankruptcy. The law allowed such an action in which the children would become indentured servants to the creditor for six years, then released. Needless to say, the policy left much to be desired—a severe version of "workfare," easily exploited by the wealthy.[19] Even when everyone acts legally, an economic *system* can be oppressive.

> *Interview with Isabelle Allende, about her historical novel on Haiti,* The Island Beneath the Sea:[20]
>
> *Jeffrey Brown: This theme of slavery is very much alive today as well.*
>
> *Allende: There is slavery in the country and there is slavery everywhere, including in the United States . . . not sex slaves in trafficking in Southeast Asia. I'm talking about whole villages that live in debt bondage. For example, a million people in Pakistan that live like slaves. They don't call it slavery but it's the same thing, children that are sold. In Haiti today there are 300,000 children that are domestic slaves, because they are given by the families or sold by the families because they cannot feed them, and these children, five, six years old, do all the domestic work, treated terribly.*

---

16. Nelson, *Kings*, 170, who also confirms the possibility "that a power hostile to Yahweh was victorious here" (168). So also Brueggemann, *Kings*, 315, 317.

17. Compare the tradition of Israel's failure to take possession of the land when it was given to them (Numbers 13-14; Deut 1:20-21, 26-33). Here the people, like Jehoram, claim that God has handed them over *to their enemies*. Sweeney, *I & II Kings*, 284, attributes the failure to Israel (see previous note).

18. E.g., 1 Kgs 11:7, 33; 2 Kgs 23:13.

19. See Mic 2:1-5, the passage quoted with regard to Naboth's vineyard. On the sociological background, see McNutt, *Reconstructing*, 159-160. The Deuteronomic revision of earlier legislation on debt servitude is in Deuteronomy 15.

20. PBS Newshour, 24 May 2010.

Elisha asks the woman what assets she has, and she says nothing but a jar of oil. He tells her to go to her neighbors and borrow all the empty vessels she can find, then start pouring oil from her one jar into the vessels. She does as he says, and fills all the vessels. When she reports the successful venture, Elisha advises her to sell some of the oil and pay off her debts, and use the rest to live on. Clearly this resembles the story of Elijah's providing meal and oil for the widow in 1 Kgs 17:8–16. Elisha not only mediates God's life-giving provision of oil (basic to a Palestinian diet), but also protects a widow and redeems her children from potential servitude.[21] As with Elijah, Elisha's protection of the impoverished widow provides the justice due her according to Israel's covenant tradition.[22]

A Boy for Bed and Breakfast (4:8–37)

In the second story, Elisha has a well-to-do patron who provides bed and breakfast. (Neither the woman nor the other family members are named, but she is called the "Shunammite woman," indicating her home.) When Elisha becomes a frequent visitor, the woman constructs a special furnished room for him on her second floor. When she proposes the renovation to her husband, she refers to Elisha as "a holy man of God," but she does not say that she expects a reward for her beneficence. Then one day Elisha, who is traveling with a servant named Gehazi, tells him to summon the woman.[23] He tells Gehazi to ask the woman what favor she would like for Elisha to give her in exchange for her hospitality. Perhaps she would like for Elisha to put a good word in for her with the king, or one of the military top brass. (Here the prophet portrays himself as in the loop with the king.) The woman says simply "I live among my own people," suggesting modestly that she needs no such reward. Elisha asks Gehazi what he thinks he can do for her, and Gehazi points out that the couple has no children and her husband is old. Elisha summons the woman again and tells her in nine months (as it were) she will be holding a baby in her arms. Stunned and overwhelmed, the woman begs Elisha not to make false promises, but in the next sentence the narrator tells us that she does, indeed, bear a son, "as Elisha had declared to her." Elisha's wonder-working now extends to infertile couples, again exhibiting God's control over life, but his treatment of the woman is both condescending and patronizing—he did not even ask her if she *wanted* a child.[24]

All goes well until the child has become a young boy, when one day while out in the field with his father he is struck by a painful headache. His father takes him home, puts him in his mother's lap, and within hours the boy

---

21. Grain, wine, and oil are the three basic ingredients of the Palestinian diet and often appear together in biblical and Ugaritic texts (see Deut 11:14 and n. 124 in the previous chapter).

22. Protection of widows was a widespread ethical norm in the ancient Near East, e.g., Deut 24:17–21; 26:12–13.

23. There is some confusion in that she "stood before him" in v. 12, then is summoned again in v. 15.

24. The story assumes a high valuation of motherhood, as with Hannah in 1 Samuel 1. The promise of a child to a barren couple is a type-scene (e.g., Gen 18:1–15 [especially v. 10]), here with remarkable complications!

is dead. The woman takes the dead boy up to Elisha's room and lays him on Elisha's bed. Then she orders a donkey to be saddled and she rushes off to find Elisha. When Elisha sees her coming, he dispatches Gehazi to intervene, and she tells Gahazi that everyone in the family is well. But when she comes face to face with the prophet, she falls to the ground, clasps his feet, and tells the truth. Gehazi tries to pull the woman away, but Elisha discourages him, noting the woman's severe distress and saying that "the Lord has hidden it from me and has not told me." The *prophet* is not omniscient, even if God is. Elisha promptly orders Gehazi to take Elisha's staff, go with the woman, and place the staff on the face of the child. But the mother will have none of this. She wants the prophet himself, not a substitute, and she insists that she will not leave without Elisha, who then follows her home.

Gehazi gets to the house first, goes upstairs, and performs the trick that Elisha had suggested, to no avail. "There was no sound or sign of life." Apparently the magic is not in the stick, so the mother was right after all! Elisha goes upstairs and closes the door. He prays to God, then engages in a complicated ritual of body-to-body contacts (one even sounds like CPR!). The boy's body becomes warm. Elisha walks around the room, bends over the child, and the boy sneezes seven times, and opens his eyes. Elisha summons the mother and says, "Take your son." She falls at his feet again, then takes her son, and leaves (but the two will meet again in 2 Kgs 8:1–6). This story resembles that of Elijah in 1 Kgs 17:17–24 and both illustrate God's power over death. Unfortunately, when God gave him the gift of healing, God did not give him a warm bedside manner, and he comes across as insensitive to the woman who deserves his personal attention in lieu of Gehazi's delegated responses (e.g., 4:13, 26, 29). Even though she is Elisha's patron, she is simply "the Shunammite woman." Were it not for this mother's care for her son and her assertiveness with the prophet, the child would have remained dead.

Death in the Pot (4:38–41)

After the raising of the dead, the next episode may seem relatively mundane, but it again involves the subject of providing food in the midst of famine and overcoming the power of death. Elisha is presiding over the "company of prophets," and he orders his servant to prepare a stew for their dinner. The appointed cook goes out to the field to gather some kind of wild herbs and gourds (the exact meaning unclear) which he adds to the stew. When the prophets taste it, their evaluation is far less than complimentary, however. They cry out, "O man of God, there is death in the pot!" It isn't clear if their reaction is to the taste or to some kind of immediate gastric distress (one wonders if the cook got the wrong kind of mushrooms). Whatever the problem, the stew is inedible, so Elisha resorts to one of his magic tricks, throws some flour in the pot, and says *bon appétit* (cf. 2:19–22). "There was nothing bad in the pot" (AT).

A Multiplication Miracle (4:42–44)

The final episode in the series also has to do with food, although there is no mention of famine. Someone brings some bread and fresh grain to the circle of prophets, something like the old American custom of laypeople bringing their garden vegetables to the country preacher. Elisha orders that the food be distributed, but one of the prophets points out that there are a hundred of them, and not nearly enough food. Elisha repeats his order, adding a "thus-says-the-Lord" and the assurance that there will even be leftovers, which is exactly what happens, "according to the word of the Lord." The two formulas appear only here in the sequence of four stories, perhaps as a way of summarizing the prophetic reading of what has happened. Otherwise, the stories function on their own to demonstrate the prophet's powers and to legitimate Elisha's succession to Elijah's role.

A Prophet to the Nations (5:1–19)

Here is a healing story that demonstrates the versatility of Elisha's power and the universality of Yahweh's dominion. Naaman, the "commander of the army of the king of Aram," has a serious skin disease for which "leprosy" was the generic diagnosis. Naaman's wife has an Israelite slave girl captured on one of the many military encounters between the two realms. She suggests that Naaman seek out the help of "the prophet who is in Samaria," who will cure him. Elisha has quite a reputation as a healer. The king of Aram holds Naaman in high esteem "because by him the Lord had given victory [or 'salvation'] to Aram." So here it is already clear that God not only controls the outcome of battles but also sometimes hands *Israel* over to enemies—something we have known since the failed first attack on the city of Ai (Joshua 7). Of course, there is a more recent example, that being Aram's defeat of Ahab and Jehoshaphat that resulted in Ahab's death (22:19–26). Naaman reports the slave girl's suggestion and the king readily agrees, offering to send a diplomatic letter to the king of Israel with a recommendation. Warring with each other does not prevent some humanitarian gestures. Naaman proceeds to the king of Israel, bearing considerable silver, gold, and fine clothes as a potential reward for Elisha. When the king reads the letter, however, he mistakenly thinks that the king of Aram is asking *him* to perform the healing: "Am I God, to give life or death?" he wails. He immediately suspects some kind of bellicose motive.

When Elisha "the man of God" hears what has happened he sends a message to the king of Israel suggesting that he send Naaman to him, "that he may acknowledge that there is a prophet in Israel" (5:8, AT). The point is not informational but—ultimately—theological.[25] Acknowledgment means recognition of authority—Elisha's *prophetic* authority. So Naaman proceeds to Elisha's house and Elisha relays a message to him through a servant (cf. 4:12–13, etc.). Naaman doesn't even get a chance to talk to the prophet or ask for his help, he has only to go to the Jordan

---

25. Cf. the similar formula throughout the plague narratives of Exodus (e.g., Exod 5:2; 6:7).

River and wash seven times and he will be healed. But Naaman does not like this plan of treatment. He was expecting to speak to Elisha himself—after all, he is "a great man," backed up by "horses and chariots" (vv. 1, 9, cf. Ps 20:7!). He also had assumed that Elisha would perform some sort of hocus pocus and "call on the name of Yahweh his God" (AT). If washing in a river was all he needed to do, he could have stayed home and bathed in his own, which would be like the Mississippi compared to the Jordan. So he turns on his heels and leaves "in a rage." But one of his servants suggests that he take a more reasonable approach. If Elisha had told him to do something really difficult, would he not have done it? So why not do this simple thing, and be healed? Naaman sees the wisdom in this, and goes to the Jordan River, dips himself in it seven times, "according to the word of the man of God," and he is healed—"his flesh was restored like the flesh of a young boy, and he was clean" (5:14). "Clean" here does not mean free from dirt but ritually pure, free of defilement. Indeed, in the Levitical regulations, a "leprous" person was quarantined until cured (cf. 7:3). Thus Elisha's healing of the man's disease shows him not only to be a prophet, but also a priest, whose authority it was to supervise such a cure.[26]

Naaman's cure has also made him a convert, as it were. He returns to Elisha and proclaims his belief: "Now I acknowledge that there is no God in all the earth except in Israel" (5:15, AT). Before, God's domain was not limited to the hills but included the valleys (1 Kgs 20:28); here that domain is world-wide. Moreover, the statement seems to go beyond a political affirmation—that the God of Israel is supreme above all other gods—and moves to a monotheistic claim—that the God of Israel is the *only* god. Such a claim picked up considerable momentum in the Exile and afterwards, making this text an obvious candidate for some editorial embellishment, needless to say.[27] Naaman's interpretation of his own confession seems to reverse his claim, however, for he asks to dig up "two mule-loads of earth"—Israelite soil—to take home with him. "A little while ago he despised Israel's river, now he wants the soil of Yahweh's homeland."[28] Since he vows never to offer a sacrifice to any god other than Yahweh, he needs some of Yahweh's home turf to build an altar, a notion that seems inconsistent with the previous confession that Yahweh's sovereignty extends over "all the earth." He also asks for God's forgiveness when, as part of his official duties, he *does* bow down to other gods—namely, Rimmon,

---

26. See Lev 13:1–17; ch. 14; note the elaborate ritual in 14:6. On the quarantine see 13:45–46 (the wilderness setting of an encampment is assumed). Bathing of body and clothes is also involved, and various procedures are done seven times (although that is a traditional unit of time measurement). The declaration "he was clean" is precisely that of the priest, Lev 13:6; 14:10.

27. Similarly, it is one thing to say, "you shall not worship other gods," but quite another to say, "there *are* no other gods." Even the first commandment is a version of the former (Deut 5:7). We have looked at other examples before in discussing early Israelite "polytheism" and the divine council (e.g., Exod 15:11; Deut 32:8–9; Ps 82:1). For exilic texts, see especially Isaiah 45. See Excursus 3.

28. Nelson, *Kings*, 179.

the god of Aram. All of this Elisha grants with the benediction, "Go in peace."

When Naaman made his confession of faith, he also offered Elisha a present, presumably the riches he had brought with him for the purpose. Elisha swore an oath, strenuously declining the offer, but his servant, Gehazi, has no such scruples. He swears the same oath ("as the Lord lives") in deciding to get something out of Naaman—"that Aramean," he says disparagingly. Elisha offered healing to this foreigner; Gehazi sees him only as someone to exploit. When Gehazi catches up with him, Naaman asks if everyone is alright, and Gehazi says yes, but that some other prophets have arrived and are in need of assistance. All he needs is "a talent of silver [about seventy-five pounds] and two changes of clothing." Naaman is so grateful for his healing that he gives Gehazi *two* talents of silver and servants to carry the loot. Gehazi has them hide it away and heads back to Elisha, who asks him where he's been. "Oh, nowhere in particular," he answers (AT), but Elisha knows the truth. Indeed, he is something of a shaman (as well as prophet and priest) in that he (literally, his heart) was present when Gehazi struck his deal with Naaman. After disclosing that, he asks rhetorically if it is appropriate to accept such rewards. To do so turns a gracious act into a commercial venture; it also undoes the subversion of who is truly a "great man" (i.e., Elisha as helper, Naaman as the helpless). Then he pronounces a curse on Gehazi, a kind of *quid pro quo*—Gehazi will be afflicted with the very disease from which Naaman was cured, as will his descendants, "forever." So Gehazi leaves, "leprous, as white as snow." It's not a story his descendants will enjoy telling.[29]

The Floating Ax Head (6:1–7)

This little story again illustrates Elisha's miraculous powers. The company of prophets proposes moving to more comfortable quarters by the Jordan River where they will construct a wooden shelter, and Elisha agrees. In the process of felling trees, however, one of the prophets accidentally drops his ax into the river and it sinks to the bottom. He issues a distress call to Elisha, emphasizing that the loss is all the greater since he had borrowed the ax and will be subject to payment for it. Elisha goes to the spot where the ax sunk, cuts off a fresh stick, and throws it in the water.[30] Instantly the ax floats to the surface, and the workman retrieves it. Elisha the Magnificent has done it again!

Chariots of Fire (6:8—7:20)

The two stories in this section take us from the sublime to the horrific. There is much humor in the telling, but also the grim reality of human desperation and subhuman depravity. It is almost as if the editor wanted to show the radically different sides of the human condition simply by juxtaposing two stories that seem to contradict each other (joined at 6:24). Both stories involve the king of Aram, Israel's perennial enemy and/or friend, depending on the circumstances (cf. 1

---

29. Gehazi soon reappears in another story about the Shunammite woman, with no reference to the "leprosy" (8:1–6).

30. Cf. the new bowl in 2:20 and the act of throwing there and at 4:41.

Kings 20), although it is not likely that the king is the same in each incident, much less that the incidents actually occurred in the sequence presented here.[31] The first story begins in the Aramean camp with the king briefing his military officers on the location of their next attack. Then suddenly we are in the king of Israel's court, where Elisha sends word informing the king precisely what the Arameans are planning, and the king warns the targeted town, allowing them to prepare in such a way that it is obvious to the Aramean king that there is an informant in his ranks. When he demands to know who it is, one of his officers tells him that it is not one of them but none other than Elisha, "the prophet in Israel, who tells the king of Israel the words that you speak in your bedchamber" (6:12). There is no need for the intelligence people to bug the king's court when they have Elisha and his extra-sensory perception, another indication of the prophet's shamanic characteristics already displayed to Gehazi's dismay (5:26). The Aramean king immediately orders the capture of Elisha, and he sends a disproportionately large hit squad to find him—horses, chariots, and "a great army."

Now the scene shifts to Elisha's location in the town of Dothan.[32] One of his servants wakes up in the morning, looks outside, and there surrounding them is this massive army, armed to the teeth. "Alas, master!" he cries, as did his colleague of the ax head (vv. 6, 15), "What shall we do?" Elisha responds with the words typical of an announcement of salvation—"Do not be afraid"[33]—adding the reason, "there are more with us than there are with them." It is the gift of a prophet to be able to see what others cannot, so Elisha prays to God to open the man's eyes so that he may see, and when God does that, the man sees the truth behind Elisha's assurance: "the mountain was full of horses and chariots of fire all around Elisha." There are more with Elisha than there are with the king of Aram—all the Host of Heaven (cf. Ps 27:3; 68:17).

Now the Arameans make their move, and Elisha prays again, asking God to strike them with blindness. Clearly this has become a story about who can see and who cannot. God grants Elisha's request, and instantly the enemy troops are struck blind. Now Elisha approaches the Arameans who, of course, cannot see him so they cannot know who he is (assuming that they could have recognized him otherwise). Elisha pretends to be someone else. "You're going the wrong way," he says "You've got the wrong town. Follow me and I will lead you to the man you're looking for" (6:19, AT). So all the horses and chariots and the "great army" form a line, no doubt with each soldier holding the hand of the one in front of him (and the one in the *very* front holding *Elisha's* hand!), and they play follow the leader, the leader being the very man whom they're *looking* for (cf. "go and *see* where he is," v. 13, AT). The military march has become something like a comical circus parade.

---

31. For one thing, there were numerous kings named Ben-hadad, often making it impossible to determine which one is involved.

32. In v. 17 he seems to be on a mountain, however, perhaps corresponding to Elijah's hilltop location in 1:9.

33. Cf. Gen 15:1; Deut 1:21; Josh 8:1; Isa 7:4, etc.

Elisha leads them right into the city of Samaria, a kind of reversal of the Trojan horse story. Elisha prays again, asking God to open the Arameans eyes "so that they may see," and when God does that they see that now *they* are surrounded by their enemy. When the king of Israel "sees" his enemy surrounded, he turns to Elisha, addressing him with the honorific title "Father," and asks, "Shall I kill them? Shall I kill them?" The repetition perhaps suggests that the king asks the question with an almost childish eagerness. Then Elisha has another surprise up his sleeve. "No!" he says. Since it wasn't the king's forces that captured the enemy, instead of killing them he should *welcome* them with a banquet, then let them go (cf. Ps 23:5!). So the king prepares "a great feast," and after they eat and drink, they head home "to their master." One would love to hear how *they* tell the story. Of course, the ending is also ironic in that Elisha is still free to listen in on the king's bedroom conversations!

Would that all the biblical stories could be like this one, a kind of farce full of humor, poking fun at the enemy without demonizing them, almost like a scene out of *Gulliver's Travels*, or that wonderful incident in World War I where the enemies dropped their guns and played soccer on Christmas Day. Here is a nonviolent resolution to conflict in which God protects the potential victims, disables the aggressors, and the enemy is treated to a banquet and sent home, never again to instigate aggression. But the world more often is not like that, as the next story reminds us.

No sooner has the narrator told us that "the Arameans no longer came raiding into the land of Israel" than they do so, besieging the very city where they had been wined and dined! Clearly we are dealing with originally independent stories (6:24—7:20). This one will plumb the depths of evil like none other, which is saying a lot compared to what we've seen before. The description of the siege is utterly realistic given what we know from other sources. The narrator does not tell us how long the siege has been in effect, but it is long enough that all food supplies are depleted and there is a devastating famine. Food is so scarce that the price is outrageous just for a donkey's head, and cooked over burning bird dung to boot. In this setting the king of Israel appears at the city wall when a woman accosts him with a plea for help. "Let the Lord help you," he says rather cynically, admitting that there was nothing he himself could do, king or not, for the storehouses are empty. But then the king seems to realize that the woman is not asking for food, but something else. "What is your complaint?" he asks, and the woman tells him something far worse than he had imagined.

Another woman has suggested that the two of them kill their children and eat them, with the woman who is speaking to the king going first. And that is what she did: "we boiled my son and ate him" (6:29, AT).[34] But then the other woman hid her own child, refusing to keep her side of the bargain. We read of such cannibalism under siege from other texts, so there is no reason to think that such a

34. Gruesome as it may be to specify the manner of cooking, the word usually means "boil" and, in Exod 12:9, it is contrasted with roasting by fire. But specifying the manner seems to make the horror all the more palpable.

scene is unrealistic.³⁵ This was part of the horrendous facts of warfare (one should say "*is*," not "was"). Perhaps even more shocking is the implication that the first woman is complaining about the injustice done to her by the other! The king is shocked as well, and tears his clothing in the traditional custom expressing distress or grief—indeed, he was already wearing sackcloth, no doubt in dismay over their predicament. But his other reaction is to find someone to blame, that being Elisha, and he swears that he will behead the prophet that very day.³⁶ (That will not help the woman, but she now drops out of the story.) Perhaps the king assumes that the prophet has had something to do with the famine (as did Elijah in 1 Kings 18), but there is no indication of that in the story. In the previous story, the king of Aram was after Elisha; here it is the king of Israel who wants his head.

It will not surprise us by now that Elisha knows of the king's intention before the royal messenger even arrives at his door. Elisha is presiding over the elders (perhaps there for a crisis consultation), and he tells them to lock the door before the messenger of "the murderer" arrives. Then suddenly the king himself shows up and makes an accusation that reminds us of Ahab's charge against Elijah: "This trouble is from the Lord" (cf. 1Kgs 18:17). Then he adds his pessimism: "Why should I hope in the Lord any longer?" But Elisha pulls another surprise. Instead of launching into a judgment speech about how the king deserves what is happening, he announces that a reversal of the famine is imminent. The very next *day*, they will be selling the finest flour and grain in the Samarian market for a pittance. At this, the captain of the guard who is accompanying the king scoffs: "Even if the Lord were to make windows in the sky, could such a thing happen?" That is logically true, of course; rain the next day would not magically produce bread. But then, he has forgotten that he is *talking* to a magician, that is, the prophet through whom God works wonders. Elisha replies confidently: "You shall see it with your own eyes, but you shall not eat from it."

Now suddenly the story takes a turn that at first seems totally off track (cf. 1 Kgs 20:35–37). Four "lepers" (again, the term is ambiguous) who are outside the city gate (because they are quarantined), are talking about the options open to them and conclude that it is a "rock-and-hard-place" situation: if they stay where they are, the Arameans will see them as the enemy and kill them, but if they go into the city, they will die of famine.³⁷ They choose something in between: they will defect to the Arameans who might accept them as turncoats, and

---

35. See the graphic description in the covenant curses of Deut 28:53–57; cf. also Lev 26:29; Lam 2:20; 4:10; Ezek 5:10. Cannibalism under siege appears in the curses of other ancient Near Eastern treaties and in historical annals: "Famine broke out among them, and they ate the flesh of their children to satisfy their hunger," from the annals of Ashurbanipal, c. 650 BCE, quoted by Weinfeld, *Deuteronomic School*, 127.

36. Yet another sign of the independence of the two stories; Elisha was the savior in the previous one!

37. The implication is that food is still available outside the city; they also assume that they will be *admitted* to the city, which is questionable, given their taboo status, a problem that presumably would apply to the Arameans' receiving them as well.

at least they won't die of starvation. So they head out for the Aramean camp, no doubt waving a white flag, only to find the camp abandoned. The narrator tells us why: "For the Lord had caused the Aramean army to hear the sound of chariots, and of horses, the sound of a great army," a horde of mercenaries hired by Israel, the Arameans suppose, and they have fled for their lives. Of course, *we* know the source of that sound—it is the chariots of fire that the Arameans cannot see.[38] They have had an "audition"—rather than a vision—and they are terrified. The horses and chariots and great army of Aram (6:14) yield to the invisible but very noisy army of the Host of Heaven. So frightened are they that they leave all their equipment and supplies behind, including silver, gold, and—best of all—food. Illogically, they even abandon their horses! The "lepers" enjoy a great feast, then carry away as much loot as they can, making two trips.

But then the "lepers" have second thoughts, partly out of concern for others and partly out of concern for themselves. If they fail to report this wonderful news to the king, and later it is found out, they will be condemned, so they return to the city gate and shout their news up to the gatekeeper, who relays it to the king (after this, the "lepers" disappear from the story). Paranoia seems to pervade the royal court, and the king immediately suspects a trick leading to an ambush (cf. 5:7). But a servant suggests that they send out some scouts to investigate, mounted on the few horses that have survived the famine.[39] The scouts confirm the story, finding the Arameans' escape path littered with even more discarded equipment. So the Samarians flock out to the Aramean camp and despoil the ones who were intent on despoiling them. The siege is over, but the narrator cannot help but drive home the fulfillment of Elisha's prediction to the king's commander in inordinate detail (7:16b-20). The king has assigned the hapless man to monitor the city gate, and the crowd—perhaps in their stampede to get to the loot—tramples him to death, again, "according to the word of the Lord" (v. 16). And Elisha still has his head.

Taken together the two stories reveal a deep ambivalence which perhaps is best expressed by the metaphor of the chariots of fire. Those chariots encircled Elisha and protected him from the Arameans, then they *surrounded* the Arameans and drove them away, but there were no chariots of fire to rescue the baby from being murdered and cannibalized by his own mother. The narrators present us with fantastic stories of miraculous deliverances and magical performances, but they do not whitewash the gruesome realities of history that make these tales "horror stories" as well as "hero stories."

The Shunammite Woman, Reprise (8:1–6)

The narrative now returns to the Shunammite woman of 4:8–37, without

---

38. Note the similarity to other divine interventions, such as God's thunderous voice that panics the Philistines in 1 Sam 7:10, or the loud war cry in Josh 6:5, 20.

39. There is confusion in the text due to a duplication. Why are five horses mentioned and only two men (v. 14)? One wonders if we are to assume that the horses had been eaten, again, not unrealistic in time of siege.

explaining why the two stories are separated. She is simply "the woman whose son he had restored to life." Elisha warns her to take her household and move temporarily to some other place because God has declared a seven-year famine, for reasons unknown. In fact, the main point of the story has nothing to do with famine but with Elisha's influence in helping the woman when she returns after the seven years are over. She has acted "according to the word of the man of God," but when she returns she apparently discovers that someone has appropriated her house and field (the circumstances remain vague). She goes to "cry out" to the king for help (8:3, AT). As we saw with Naboth, an Israelite's land was considered to be inalienable unless extreme circumstances required its sale, which has not happened here. It is interesting that the woman in this story functions as the head of the household, including apparently ownership of the property.

The narrator suddenly shifts scenes to the court, just as the woman is on her way, and shows us Elisha's servant Gehazi entertaining the king, who is asking him to recount "the great things that Elisha has done." There is no evidence of Gehazi's "leprosy" here, much less the king's desire for Elisha's head, and Gehazi seems to be on friendly terms with the king. He is just telling the king the story about the Shunammite's son when the woman appears and makes her plea. Grammatically, everything seems to be happening at the same time, and Gehazi needs only gesture to the woman (with son in tow) and say, "Here is the woman I was telling you about" (AT). The king questions her and she apparently tells him her problem, whereupon the king immediately appoints an official to take care of it, restoring her property as well as the "revenue of the fields from the day that she left the land until now." In the previous story about her, Elisha had offered to speak on her behalf to the king, and she had declined. She hasn't asked for it here either, but she has dutifully followed his advice and is rewarded by his influence, albeit indirectly. Here Elisha is almost like the powerful and well-connected congressional representative—just dropping his name is enough to get things done for his constituents.

Prophecy and Assassination (8:7–15)

This story provides the fulfillment of the commission that God had given Elijah at Horeb to appoint Hazael king of Aram (1 Kgs 19:15). The narrator does not seem bothered by the discrepancy of the prophet in question, and Elisha does not "anoint" Hazael as prescribed. One can easily describe his involvement as conspiratorial, however. He has gone to Damascus "while King Ben-hadad of Aram was ill."[40] One wonders if Elisha knows of the illness and even intends to take advantage of it to complete his mission. Ben-hadad obviously has no suspicion, for he sends Hazael to Elisha to get a prognosis (much like Ahaziah with Elijah, 1:2). We have heard nothing about Hazael since Elijah's commis-

---

40. Again, it is difficult to say which Ben-hadad is involved, but certainly not the one who wanted to kill Elisha or who besieged Samaria; more likely it would be the king whose commander, Naaman, was healed by Elisha. Even Hazael will have a son named Ben-hadad (13:3).

sioning. Hazael pays a visit to Elisha, bearing lavish gifts (which this time Elisha does not seem to refuse, cf. 6:26). When Hazael asks for the kings' prognosis, Elisha tells him to say, "You shall certainly recover," but, Elisha says to Hazael that Ben-hadad will die, a prognosis from none other than God. Then we have an enigmatic sentence: "He fixed his gaze and stared at him, until he was ashamed." Most likely Elisha is the one staring and Hazael is the one who looks "ashamed."[41] Perhaps a better translation would be "embarrassed." The scene may involve one of those meaningful looks that a person can make that says a lot without words, here "if you get my drift." Maybe Elisha raised an eyebrow or even winked. Clearly he knows that Ben-hadad is about to die and Hazael take his place. Then suddenly Elisha breaks into tears, and when Hazael asks why, Elisha says because he knows what horrible things Hazael will do to his own people, Israel, atrocities including "dash in pieces their little ones, and rip up their pregnant women." There will be no such atrocity reported of Hazael (see below, 10:32; 13:7). Nevertheless, as with the murder and cannibalism in 6:28–29, Elisha's fear is a realistic depiction of the inhuman brutality of war, evidenced elsewhere (e.g., 15:16; Amos 1:13; Hos 13:16). Hazael protests his inability to do such a thing (though apparently not his reluctance!), and Elisha informs him of what we already know—God has made him king over Aram. Again, the narrator is cryptic. Hazael returns to report to Ben-hadad and tells him exactly what Elisha had said, but the next day he uses the sick king's bed-cover to smother him to death. "And," the narrator says laconically, "Hazael succeeded him."

By now, prophetic involvement in the change of regimes is old hat, beginning with Samuel and Saul. From the prophetic perspective, the kings who supplanted those who were condemned were acting as God's agents, rather wittingly or not. At first such "king makers and breakers" seemed to be the messengers relaying God's decisions, although sometimes Samuel seemed to have his own intentions as well. One could even see Samuel's anointing of David as an incitement to revolt, but it is unimaginable that we could suspect him of suggesting to David that he *kill* Saul. If our reading of the conversation between Elisha and Hazael is correct, the role of the "kingmaker" has taken another step in that Elisha is not only announcing Hazael's imminent rule, he is also implying that he should kill Ben-hadad to make that happen. Elisha comes close to being God's "hit man," or at least he orders the "contract." Given Elisha's involvement here, one can see why Jezebel would have looked on the prophets of Yahweh with suspicion! Moreover, we can say that Elisha has taken *two* steps in that his king-making extends beyond Israel and Judah to another nation. Thus *God's* sovereignty extends to that nation as well, and implicitly others. That other nations (or enemies) served God's punitive will has been clear from the story of Achan in Joshua 7, but the appointment of specific rulers is new (as antic-

---

41. Alternatively, the "shame" is Elisha's over his role in causing the disaster that makes him weep in 11b.

ipated, of course, in 1 Kgs 19:26–40). Presumably, Ben-hadad's death serves God's purposes, although so far nothing has been said about *why* Ben-hadad had to go (unlike with the kings of Judah and Israel). Given the ominous prediction of what Hazael will do to Israel, that purpose has more to do with using Hazael as the "rod of God's anger" rather than punishing Ben-hadad's sins.[42] It is really the House of Omri at which the rod is directed.

The formal introduction of Jehoram (Joram) of Judah (8:16–24) condemns him for following the notorious example of his in-laws, Ahab and Jezebel, who had married off their daughter Athalia to him (another of those treaty agreements). So Joram is the first king of Judah to have "walked in the way of the kings of *Israel*" (v. 18). Here the problem of marriage to a foreigner for the purpose of political alliance extends to the second generation as well. The notice is interesting in that it illustrates how effective is the guarantee of David's dynasty, here so much so that it can outweigh the "evil" from Israel that has infected *Judah*. Thus "the Lord would not destroy Judah" (8:19). On the other hand, the narrator does report that Edom revolted successfully against Judah, thus taking away another piece of the former Davidic empire. Then the narrator moves on to Jehoram's son, Ahaziah, who also "walked in the way of the house of Ahab," i.e., his grandparents, Ahab and Jezebel, have now corrupted both kingdoms and two generations of kings.

Jehu's Bloody Coup (Chaps. 9–10)

With Elisha in place as Elijah's successor and Hazael on the throne of Aram, there is yet one more part of God's commissioning of Elijah remaining—the anointing of Jehu as king over Israel (1 Kgs 19:16). This will be no peaceful transfer of office. Jehu's revolt will result in *two* regicides—Joram of Israel and Ahaziah of Judah. Joram's fate was sealed with his *parents'* sins, of course, and the unfairness of this seems all the worse given his relatively good report card from the Deuteronomist (3:2–3). Although he "did what was evil," yet "not like his father and mother, for he removed the pillar of Baal that his father had made." In this regard, Joram was a *reformer*, resembling none other than the one who will assassinate him—Jehu. And, in the end, *both* of them are condemned for following "the sins of Jeroboam" (10:29). (For the relationships of the royal families involved in the following, see again Figure 3.)

Remarkably, the entire account of Jehu's reign of twenty-eight years is reduced to his fanatical obliteration of the Omride dynasty and his religious "reform," at most spanning a few days. Otherwise, the narrator refers us as usual to the "Book of the Annals of the Kings of Israel" (10:34–36). Similarly, the figure of Elisha the prophet dominates the instigation of the revolt (9:1–13), suggesting that God's will drives the events, as previously expressed to Elijah, but then Elisha disappears from

---

42. The offense is not likely to be against a deity who is not his own. Amos 1:3—2:3 condemns the regimes of other nations for what we would call humanitarian offenses. Oracles against other nations are prominent in the other writing prophets.

the narrative.⁴³ In fact, it is likely that the revolt resulted from a military coup reacting to the apparent inability of Joram to protect Israel from the Arameans. From a straight historical perspective, the revolt probably was due to the politics of national security; from the narrator's perspective, national security was jeopardized by matters of "theology and justice."⁴⁴ The justice issue, of course, stems from the murder of Naboth, to which there are numerous allusions in 9:1—10:17. The theological part is the focus of the aftermath of the revolt and Jehu's ostensible annihilation of the Baal devotees in 10:18–36. As television news reporters sometimes say, "some of these scenes may be disturbing; viewer discretion is advised."

The story begins with Elisha commissioning a disciple to carry out Elijah's original commission of anointing Jehu as king, a task that we must assume Elijah transferred to him. Otherwise, we have not seen the language of anointing since that of Solomon in 1 Kings 1, and the situation is reminiscent of Samuel's anointing of both Saul and David (1 Sam 9:16; 16:1). Elisha instructs the messenger to find Jehu where he is stationed at Ramoth-gilead, take him aside, pour the oil on his head, and pronounce the inaugural words: "Thus says the Lord: I anoint you king over Israel." Then he is to make a quick exit. Apparently Jehu and other senior military officers are at the front in the continuing battles with Aram (cf. 1 Kgs 22:1–40), and the messenger bursts into their strategic planning meeting, saying that he has a message for the commander. Since they are all "commanders," Jehu asks which one, and the messenger names him, then the two go into an inner room and the messenger does as he has been told, but says quite a bit more. The messenger delivers a rather lengthy explanation of *why* Jehu is to assassinate Joram *because of* the offenses of Ahab and Jezebel, specifically shedding "the blood of my servants the prophets, and the blood of all the servants of the Lord." The message spells out the termination of the Omride dynasty, comparing it to that of Baasha and Ahijah, in terms synonymous with preceding predictions going back to Jeroboam, concluding with the "dog food" motif.⁴⁵ Then the messenger disappears as quickly as he came.

When Jehu returns to his fellow officers, they naturally want to know why such a "madman" has come, apparently referring to Elisha's unsightly appearance (imagine the long hair and disheveled clothing of the stereotypical "hippie"). Jehu at first deflects their question, but they shrewdly figure out that he is hiding something, and when pressed he repeats the inaugural declaration, at which

---

43. Cf. Campbell and O'Brien, *Unfolding*, 27, who see the Jehu story as the conclusion of their "Prophetic Record" document.

44. The phrase is Sweeney's, *I & II Kings*, 323, who suggests that Elisha may have had little to do with Jehu. Compare again the account of the division of the kingdom under Rehoboam, 1 Kings 12. The revolt would make sense without 9:1–13 and possibly v. 15 ("thus" in v. 14 is simply "and" in Hebrew, and can start a new story) and there are a number of idiosyncrasies that suggest an account before later editorial flourishes (e.g., 9:22, "whoredoms and sorceries"; the circumstance of 9:25b; and "for the blood of his children" in 9:26).

45. Jeroboam, 1 Kgs 14:10–11; Baasha, 1 Kgs 16:4; Ahab, 1 Kgs 21:21–24. The complex of images probably is original to the Jehu story.

point all of his fellow officers spread their cloaks for him (something like "putting out the red carpet"), blow the trumpet, and proclaim "Jehu is king" (cf. 2 Sam 15:10; 20:1). Apparently the top brass is ready for a coup and eagerly join in the "conspiracy."[46] Jehu warns against any new leaks, then mounts his chariot, musters a platoon, and speeds off to Jezreel, where King Joram is licking his wounds and King Ahaziah (his nephew) is visiting. The narrator describes Jehu's approach to Jezreel in another of those deliberately drawn-out scenes with multiple repetitions that heightens the dramatic tension as we wait for the ax to fall.[47] The sentinel in Jezreel sees the platoon approaching in the distance and Joram sends out a messenger to ask "Is it peace?" meaning "Is everything alright?" or simply "How are you?" (the basic expression for "hello"). The polite welcome shows no suspicion, but of course it is ironic to us, knowing that Jehu is hell-bent on deposing the king. Jehu rebuffs the messenger, ordering him to fall in line behind, and when the sentinel sees what has happened he reports to Joram, who sends out a second messenger, with the same result. But now the sentinel apparently can see Jehu driving his chariot at the front of the platoon, and he tells the king, "It looks like the driving of Jehu son of Nimshi; for he drives like a maniac" (9:20).[48] Apparently Jehu has had his share of speeding tickets, but more tellingly the word for "maniac" is the same root as the word for "madman" that describes Elisha (9:11). The two men are certainly akin in their fanatical zeal.

Joram now decides to drive out and welcome Jehu himself, accompanied by King Ahaziah. In a moment of grim serendipity, they all come together "at the property of Naboth the Jezreelite." Joram repeats his question, "Is it peace, Jehu?" but Jehu's reply is anything but peaceful: "What peace can there be, so long as the many whoredoms and sorceries of your mother Jezebel continue?" By "whoredoms" Jehu is not referring to any sexual improprieties of Jezebel but using a metaphor of harlotry to condemn her worshipping of Baal.[49] Surprisingly, this is the only use of such a term in the Former Prophets outside of the editorial commentaries in the book of Judges.[50] It is surprising because prophets like Hosea and Ezekiel seem almost fixated on the metaphor which they use to describe Israel's unfaithfulness to God and adultery with Baal or other deities.[51]

---

46. The word "conspired" in 9:14 is used in Amos 7:10 by a royalist priest to condemn the prophecy of Amos as treasonous. Note that 9:14 may be the original beginning of the account, and v. 15 repeats what we already know from 8:28–29.

47. Cf. 2 Sam 18:24–32.

48. Jehu's name came down through history in the expression "drive like a Jehu," whereas "murder like a Jehu" might be more appropriate.

49. Hence coupling it with "sorceries," which occurs far less frequently (e.g., Deut 18:10).

50. Programmatically in Judg 2:17, specifically in Judg 8:27 for Gideon's idolatrous "ephod," then generally again in 8:33. If course, the scandalous nature of the language of prostitution makes the story of Rahab in Joshua 2 all the more ironic (cf. also Judg 11:1; 16:1).

51. E.g., Hos 1:2; 2:6; 4:12, etc.; Ezek 16:15–17; 23:33–36, etc. Unfortunately, the language of prostitution, employed with Israel as "wife" to Yahweh as "husband," easily lends itself to all sorts of misogyny, if not even the physical abuse

Since the word *baal* means "lord" or "husband" (and can be used for Yahweh in that sense), infidelity easily evokes the marital language of adultery.[52] Add to adultery any suggestion of a material benefit resulting from it, i.e., some form of "payment," and adultery becomes "prostitution" (NRSV's "whoredom").[53] Contemporary English employs the word in a similar way to describe "selling oneself" to an unworthy cause. Here Jehu's accusation is really more concerned with *Ahab's* prostituting himself to Baal, even though he names Jezebel, and rather unfairly, one has to note, in that for *her* worshipping *Yahweh* would be "prostituting" herself![54]

With Jehu's less than friendly greeting, Joram finally realizes what is happening, turns his chariot around and shouts a warning to Ahaziah—"Treason!" But it is too late. Jehu draws his bow "with all his strength" and shoots an arrow straight through Joram's shoulder blades and into his heart. Jehu then orders that Joram's body be thrown on "the plot of ground belonging to Naboth the Jezreelite." As defense of his regicide, he reminds the soldier with him of something heretofore unknown to us: that the two of them had been with Ahab when Elijah confronted him at Naboth's vineyard, and had overheard the judgment pronounced against him and his dynasty, that God would "recompense" Naboth's murder (9:25–26, AT).[55] The root of the word is *shalom—this* is the answer to Joram's question about "peace," but certainly not the one he was expecting. Once again the outcome has been "in accordance with the word of the Lord" (9:26). As Nelson puts it, "God is restoring shalom, strangely enough, by the murderous violence of political revolution."[56]

But Jehu is not finished. The original judgment against Ahab applied explicitly only to his male descendants (1 Kgs 21:21), but Jehu extends it to include Ahab's daughter Athaliah and here, her son Ahaziah. Jehu pursues him and orders him shot, and the wounded king manages to live long enough to flee to Megiddo, where he dies. At least he has the dignity in death to be buried "with his ancestors in the city of David" (9:28). Such will not be the case with Jezebel, of course, as we have known all along. When Jehu arrives at Jezreel, Jezebel—a queen to the last—puts on her makeup and dons a fancy hat (at it were), look-

---

of women. Passages like Hos 2:6, 10–13 take on a blood-chilling connotation when read with abusive husbands in mind.

52. See Excursus 3.

53. E.g., grain, wine, oil, the three basic provisions of any god worthy of divinity—Hos 2:5.

54. In this sense, the demonizing of Jezebel simply ignores any possibility of devotion to Baal or any other deity as legitimate even for non-Israelites. For other ways in which Jezebel may be seen more positively, see the citations of Brueggemann, *Kings*, 203.

55. In 1 Kgs 21:19, however, the prediction about the blood was only about Ahab, not his descendants (that came in vv. 22–24). The particular verb form occurs only here. The reference to "the blood of his [Naboth's] children" might imply other murders to secure his land, but there is no indication of this elsewhere.

56. Nelson, *Kings*, 202, citing Olyan. Cf. Brueggemann, *Kings*, 403: "If not misperception, then the theological problem is even more acute: for the linkage, if truly perceived, draws Yahweh shamelessly close to violence."

ing down out of the window.[57] She asks the same question as did Joram—"Is it peace?" but clearly, unlike her son, she is not fooled, adding "Zimri, murderer of your master," referring to the upstart (and probably commoner) who had also "conspired" against King Asa of Judah and wiped out the house of Baasha (1 Kgs 16:9–13). Jezebel may also be suggesting that, like Zimri, Jehu's reign will only be seven days (1Kgs 16:15)! But those are her last words, and ironically so in that they are spoken by one murderer to another. Jehu looks up at the window and shouts, "Who is on my side?" Several people look out, no doubt wanting to be on the *right* side, and immediately do what Jehu orders, throwing Jezebel out the window to plunge to her death. There her blood "spattered on the wall and on the horses, which trampled on her." Jehu then demonstrates just how cold *his* blood can be by walking nonchalantly into the palace and having lunch, on his way ordering that the "cursed woman" be buried since, after all, she is "a king's daughter" and deserving of such a dignity. But she will not have that either, for all that is left of her body is "the skull and the feet and the palms of her hands." The dogs got there in the end, and of course the narrator reminds us one final time that "This is the word of the Lord which he spoke by his servant Elijah the Tishbite" (9:36). There is something new, however, that makes Jezebel's end as scatological (literally) as it is gruesome—the dogs will defecate on the field of Naboth, thereby depositing her in it (v. 37). The dog food has become dog dung.

But Jehu is still not finished with Ahab's family, for Ahab "had seventy sons in Samaria" (10:1). Apparently these sons are still children, or at least under age as potential successors, for they are supervised by "guardians" ("trustees" might be a better translation). In a cruel twist of irony, Jehu seems to mimic Jezebel's methods in sending letters to the officials of Samaria, presumably soliciting their support of the royal sons, suggesting that the guardians select "the best qualified" and make him king. The suggestion is really a test of the guardians' loyalty, however, and their response is similar to that of Jezebel's courtiers who threw her out the window: terrified, understandably, at Jehu's wrath, they agree that they are powerless to oppose him. "So the steward of the palace, and the governor of the city, along with the elders and the guardians," send a reply assuring Jehu that they have no intention of appointing a king, and that he should do "whatever you think right" (10:5). Jehu's response is to fill in the *carte blanche* with the darkest of orders: they are to behead all seventy sons (a standard round number) and bring their heads to Jehu the next day. The boys—all seventy, the narrator emphases—are under the care of the "leaders of the city, who were charged with their upbringing," but when they read Jehu's letter they summarily decapitate the boys and put their heads in baskets and send them to Jehu—"seventy persons," the narrator emphasizes yet again. Jehu orders that the heads be divided into two piles and stacked up on either side of the city gate to remain overnight. The gruesome spectacle was

---

57. The motif appears elsewhere in numerous texts (e.g., Judg 5:28) as well as artifacts from archeological sites.

a common tactic of imperial terrorists, making Jehu more like an Assyrian overlord than God's anointed!⁵⁸

The next day Jehu apparently assembles the people of Jezreel and assures them that they are "innocent," noting that it was he who "conspired" against his "master and killed him." But then he asks, "who struck down all these?" The implication seems to be that, since the officials of the city and the "trustees" of the children were all complicit, then the *whole town* is *not* innocent after all. Yet Jehu goes on to say that the real agent in all of this was God: "the Lord has done what he said through his servant Elijah." "The word of the Lord" has been fulfilled, with nothing left out (10:9–10). These are Jehu's words, of course, and not the narrator's own commentary, but we will hear a similar confirmation from the mouth of God as well (see below).

Still Jehu is not finished: he "killed all who were left of the house of Ahab in Jezreel, all his leaders, close friends, and priests,⁵⁹ until he left him no survivor" (10:11). Then he heads out for Samaria, and on the way encounters "kin of Ahaziah" who are on their way to "visit the royal princes and the sons of the queen mother," which of course was the wrong thing to say to Jehu, who immediately has them "slaughtered"—"forty-two in all," the narrator points out; "he spared none of them." Next Jehu comes upon a man named "Jehonadab son of Rechab," the latter the founder of a group called the Rechabites who made even Jehu seem like a benign reformer.⁶⁰ Jehonadab avows that he is a true supporter of Jehu, so Jehu invites him into his chariot, from which he can see his "zeal for the Lord." When he arrives at Samaria, he annihilates "all who were left to Ahab," "according to the word of the Lord that he spoke to Elijah" (10:17).

One would think that *finally* Jehu's pogrom is finished, but not so, for there are still all those worshippers of Baal (10:18–31). What happens now will outdo even Elijah's slaughter of the priests of Baal in 1 Kings 18. Cynically, Jehu assembles all the people and pretends that he will worship Baal even more devoutly than did Ahab. Inexplicably, word of his rampage does not seem to have made the Baalites suspicious, but then again *they* do not know what we know, that Jehu's coup was instigated by the prophet Elisha in service to the word of Yahweh, not Baal. So when Jehu declares that he is sponsoring a great revival service for Baal, and that all of the prophets, priests, and devotees of Baal had better show up (or else), they all crowd into the temple of Baal. In fact, Jehu's altar call goes "throughout all Israel," so it is standing room only. The narrator, of course, has clued us in that Jehu is acting "with cunning in order to destroy the worshipers of Baal," and that is precisely what he proceeds to do. Accompanied by his zealous buddy, Jehonadab, Jehu addresses the assembly with a final warning: any devotee of Yahweh should leave. One

---

58. Cf. the annals of the Assyrian king Shalmaneser III regarding one conquered town: "I slew with the sword 300 of their warriors. Pillars of skulls I erec[ted in front of the town]," *ANET*, 277b.

59. Presumably the priests of Baal, even though Joram had "removed the pillar of Baal" (3:2).

60. See Jeremiah 35.

wonders if some poor Yahwist stayed where he was out of sheer terror since Jehu had already said that anyone who was missing would die! Then Jehu commences the service by offering "sacrifices and burnt offerings." At the moment that Jehu has finished with the sacrifice, his thugs rush into the temple and slaughter everyone (eighty are stationed outside the door lest anyone escape).

"Thus Jehu wiped out Baal from Israel," says the narrator. What Elijah began with the *priests* of Baal, Jehu has supposedly completed with all the *worshippers* of Baal. Then the narrator presents one of the most troubling of commentaries on the carnage (10:29-31). First there is the irony: "Only, Jehu did not turn aside from the sins of Jeroboam . . . the golden calves that were in Bethel and in Dan" (10:29, AT).[61] The blood has not even congealed before we find out that ultimately the massacre was in vain! Jehu the reformer is no better than Jeroboam the reprobate, and the narrator emphasizes the association of the two by referring explicitly to the "golden calves," the first (and almost last) reference to these "idols" since their construction in 1 Kgs 12:28.[62] Jehu removed the "pillar" associated with Baal but left the "calves" associated (illicitly) with Yahweh, which leads to the second point: Yahweh explicitly applauds what Jehu has done. "The Lord said to Jehu, 'Because you have done well in carrying out what I consider right, and in accordance with all that was in my heart have dealt with the house of Ahab, your sons of the fourth generation shall sit on the throne of Israel.'" This is an astonishing statement in which God not only approves of Jehu's bloody massacre but *rewards* him for it with a lengthy dynasty.[63] There is something particularly chilling in the use of the phrase "all that was in my heart," suggesting that the totality of God's emotions, thinking, and will were expressed by Jehu's relentless violence. Then irony appears again with another *criticism* of Jehu from the narrator: "Jehu was not careful to follow the law of the Lord the God of Israel with all his heart," ending with another reference to the "sins of Jeroboam." Thus the language so deeply expressive of the Deuteronomic theologians' ideal—"with all your heart" (Deut 6:5)—is used to condemn the king whose murderous zeal has *warmed* the heart of God. It may be that the framing criticisms of vv. 29 and 31 are intended to dull the approval in v. 30, but they leave a lot to be desired. If there is a caveat to our reading of Jehu's fanaticism, it can only lie in the problem intrinsic to covenant theology that we have observed beginning as early as the execution of the entire family of Achan (Josh 7:24-26). The purging is extreme because the alternative is even more so, nothing short of the destruction of the entire people that would result from the divine curse that sanctions the covenant (Deut 28:15-68). For those who believed deeply in Yahweh as covenant suzerain of Israel, and the

---

61. The exception ("only") regarding Jehu's zeal resembles that regarding Solomon's wisdom in 1 Kgs 3:2-3 (see there).

62. The Deuteronomist will make one more reference to the calves in his summary commentary on the fall of the northern kingdom in 2 Kgs 17:16.

63. The fourth and last will be Zechariah, who lasts only six months (15:8-12).

consequences of shifting allegiance to "other gods," the eradication of apostasy was driven by the desire "to secure for the state the endangered blessing of Yahweh."[64] Ultimately, then, any critical assessment of radical reformers such as Jehu will have to examine the radical requirements of the covenant theology that motivated them.

> *A few weeks ago in the [Egyptian] coastal city of Marsa Matrouh, an enraged mob of some 3,000 angry Muslims gathered after Friday prayers. After the mosque's imam exhorted them to cleanse the city of its infidel Christians, called Copts, they went on a rampage. The toll was heavy: 18 homes, 23 shops and 16 cars were completely destroyed, while 400 Copts barricaded themselves in their church for 10 hours until the frenzy died out . . . [Previously,] passengers in a drive-by car fired at random into Christians leaving a Coptic Christmas service on Jan. 6. The massacre killed seven and left 26 seriously wounded.*[65]

Athaliah: Judah's "Bloody Mary" (Chap. 11)

Jehu's assassination of both Joram and Ahaziah has left a political vacuum in Judah, for Ahaziah's son eligible to succeed him by birthright is only an infant. Ahaziah's mother Athaliah quickly moves to fill the vacuum, very much her mother's daughter! While she has considerable power as Queen-Mother,[66] she would have more as Queen. Her first move is the "destroy all the royal family" (literally "all the seed of the realm"),[67] thereby threatening the life of her own grandson. But Ahaziah has a sister who is just as plucky as Athaliah, and takes the infant boy, Joash, and steals him away to a bedroom, along with his nurse. At some point she transfers the boy to a room in the temple, where he remains for six years while Athaliah reigns, the first and only queen in Israel or Judah. The story suggests the fragility of the Davidic dynasty at this point, and thus the fragility of God's promises involving it. The situation is not unlike that in the Exodus story when the mother and sister of the infant Moses save him from Pharaoh's persecution. Ironically here, the survival of Joash, the great-grandson of Ahab and Jezebel, will mean that the Davidic dynasty will always have the Omride dynasty in its family tree (see again Figure 3).

When the child turns seven, it is a priest, Jehoida, who takes the role previously played by prophets, orchestrating a coup against the queen. There were a number of reasons to do so, her attempt to annihilate the Davidic line being primary, but also because she is

---

64. Gottwald, *Politics*, 226.
65. Zaki, "Egypt's Persecuted Christians," A15.
66. Cf. Bathsheba in 1 Kings 1–2; also 15:13. See also Sweeney, *Kings*, 344, for the political dimensions of Athaliah's Phoenician connections.
67. The NRSV "set about to destroy" is misleading, in that the Hebrew says she "destroyed." Similarly, the phrase in v. 2 literally should read "the children who were being put to death." There is no indication later that Athaliah realizes that Joash has escaped, until the coup begins — perhaps it was easy to be off by one in the body count!

a Northerner, and daughter of Ahab and Jezebel (and therefore a Baal worshipper). The temple priesthood and the royal court were mutually nourishing politically and economically as well (see below on chap. 12), so Jehoiada is protecting his own livelihood. His plot shows how powerful the priesthood could be. First he summons the palace guards, reveals to them that Joash is alive and well, and puts them under oath to join the coup. Jehoiada employs an intricate use of the guard to "surround the king" with a protective ring, armed with weapons originally belonging to David, no less. The heir to the throne of David is defended by the shield of David. Once the guards have secured the entire perimeter of the temple and the outer courtyard, Jehoida brings out the boy, places the crown on his head, and presents him with the "insignia" (v. 12, AT),[68] whereupon everyone else proclaims him king, claps their hands, and shouts "Long live the king!"

The installation seems to be a kind of ad hoc inauguration ceremony that involves the people (who apparently have been summoned, v. 13), in addition to Jehoida and the palace guard. When Athaliah hears all the commotion, she rushes out of the palace to the temple, where she sees "the king standing by the pillar, according to custom," with all the military brass, the fife and drum corps, and "the people of the land" celebrating and blasting away on the trumpets. Of course, Athaliah is not inclined to join in the celebrating, and, instead, engages in another custom—rending her clothes in the sign of distress—and cries, "Treason! Treason!" (her brother's cry, 9:23). But there is nothing she can do, with the top brass supporting Jehoida and the young king, and Jehoida unhesitatingly orders that she be removed from the temple (it *is* sacred ground, after all), taken outside, and killed (and at the stable door, not the front door, of the palace!).

Jehoida's next move is to solidify the young king's political authority by making a covenant (*berit*) "between the Lord and the king and people, that they should be the Lord's people; also between the king and the people" (11:17). The covenant is two-fold, first binding king and people to God, and second binding king and people. The very foundation of the covenant between God and people is contained in the words, "I will be your God, and you shall be my people."[69] Whether such a formal renewal of the covenant was part of every accession to the throne we cannot know (Josiah orchestrates a similar ceremony later, 23:3). Here the act is similar to David's covenant with the elders of Israel, following upon his anointing

---

68. What the "insignia" (Hebrew *'edut*, NRSV "covenant") is remains puzzling. The word usually refers to the "covenant" document that Moses deposited in the ark (hence "the ark of the covenant," Exod 25:16, 21, 22). It is tempting to connect this "covenant" with the copy of the law that the priests are supposed to present to the new king, according to Deut 17:18 (cf. Nelson, *Kings*, 209), but that text may well be later and it refers to "the *torah*." Also, literally, Jehoida "placed *on* him the crown *and* the *'edut*," suggesting that the *'edut* is some form of vestment (perhaps like the priestly *ephod*), hence my "insignia." Another possibility is to emend the text to read "armlet," a word used along with "crown" in 1 Sam 1:10; cf. Weinfeld, *Deuteronomy*, 86, n. 3. No direct connection is drawn with the "covenant" (*berit*) in v. 17.

69. See Exod 6:7; 19:5-6; cf. 2 Sam 7:7-11; the relationship is dissolved then restored in Hos 1:9-10, 2:23.

by Judah.[70] Although Joash, of course, succeeds to the throne by birthright, the people play a crucial role, as in both cases with David; here they are "the people of the land," a group that will continually support the Davidic dynasty.[71] Indeed, their participation is mentioned three times (11:14, 18, 19), indicating that the coup is not only instigated by the priestly authorities and the military, but has a significant popular base as well (cf. 1 Kgs 12:20). Interestingly, it is also "the people of the land" who take the lead in proceeding from the inauguration to a religious reformation. The purge of Baal worship in Samaria by Jehu now finds its parallel in Jerusalem. The people go from the house of God to "the house of Baal" and tear it down, shattering "his altars and his images," and killing "the priest of Baal." Then Jehoida directs an inaugural parade for Judah's new monarch, leading to the palace, where the boy king takes his seat "on the throne of the kings." All rejoice, and all is quiet, now that Athaliah has been killed. The narrator concludes with a brief notice that Jehoash "was seven years old when he began to reign," but the rule has really been a theocracy led by the priest, Jehoiada.

Temple Repair to Royal Ruin (Chap. 12)

With the account of the reign of Jehoash (=Joash) of Judah, once again the sacerdotal myopia of the narrator frustrates any interest in historical detail. Jehoash has a long reign of forty years and yet all that we will know about him will be his frustration in repairing the temple and a capitulation to Hazael of Aram—and his assassination. Otherwise the standard evaluation says that he "did what was right in the sight of the Lord all his days," because he was "instructed" by the priest, Jehoiada, "*except that* the high places were not taken down" (v. 3, AT), and the people continued to worship at them. Even a good king has lapses.

In reporting Jehoash's repair project, the narrator doesn't tell us how old the boy king has become, but apparently old enough to act more or less on his own, even vis-à-vis Jehoiada (v. 7). He orders that all the money collected in the offering plate (as it were) be used in repairing the temple, which evidently has grown rather shabby in roughly one hundred years. It soon becomes clear that the temple priests are not eager to comply, figuring that to do so will deduct from their own profits—they being dependent on the offerings for their livelihood. So nothing happens for some unspecified time, but the king finds out and demands to know why the priests are not following his orders. The priests do not get to state their views, but they agree to compromise, the substance of which becomes clear only at the end of the incident (12:16): they will no longer accept any money from their "donors" but they will continue to receive "the money from the guilt offerings and the money from the sin offerings" for their own (one might think they need to make a guilt offering themselves!). In exchange, they

---

70. Israel: 2 Sam 5:3 (cf. 2 Sam 23:5; Ps 89:3); Judah: 2 Sam 2:4.

71. Nelson, *Kings*, 210, follows others who identify this group with "the rural gentry who stood solidly behind Yahweh and the Davidic dynasty in opposition to the nobility of Jerusalem." Cf. their role in 2 Kgs 21:24 and 23:30.

will not have to use the "offering" money for the repair budget. To insure compliance with the agreement, Jehoiada (who seems to be the high priest) constructs a collection box and stations it at the door of the temple, carefully supervised by the gatekeepers. The latter, being honest men (v. 15), distribute the funds to the various construction workers involved in the repairs. The narrator also points out emphatically that *none* of the repair money was used to make expensive liturgical equipment—a golden bowl or silver trumpet, for example (v. 13)—and everyone is happy in the end.

Clearly the interest of the narrator is to praise the king for repairing the temple, the building and institution that is the physical representation of Deuteronomic theology, the place where Yahweh's name resides, and shrine of the "ark of the covenant"—not to mention being the monumental symbol of the Davidic empire. Even if the king failed to get rid of the high places, maintaining the upkeep of the temple was the most important way in which he "did what was right" (v. 2). Combined with the destruction of the temple of Baal and execution of its priest, even though that happened under Jehoiada's direction, his reign overall makes him one of the great reformers, with a job evaluation second only to the later kings Hezekiah and Josiah.

If the repair of the temple burnishes its monumental gleam, however, the juxtaposition of the next incident dulls it. The perennial hostility of Aram resumes with King Hazael laying siege to Jerusalem, continuing his role as the rod of God's anger (1 Kgs 19:15–17; 2 Kgs 8:12). He has already "trimmed off" parts of Israel (10:32–33), and now has turned to Judah. His purpose, as is always the case in such attacks, is to extend his political domination and to collect booty, and Hazael will seem like a mouse compared to later imperial warlords from Assyria and Babylonia. Apparently Jehoash doesn't even wait for the siege to begin before he capitulates, denuding the temple of "all the votive gifts" donated by his royal predecessors, as well as his own, "all the gold that was found in the treasuries," and handing it over to Hazael, who promptly withdraws. In hindsight, it is fortunate that Jehoash did *not* manufacture more golden vessels for the temple, for they would have ended up in the hands of Hazael. So, in the end, the king who has restored the temple to its grandeur must submit his realm to degradation, a turn of events that the narrator records without comment. The "house of the Lord" is lifted up, but the "house of David" is brought low.

Perhaps Jehoash's capitulation did not sit well with some in his realm, which might explain the assassination that ends his life. Later, the dilemma of how to respond to such a siege will present agonizing choices to the kings of Israel and Judah, no doubt partly because of opposing factions (see Excursus 7). Again the narrator frustrates our historical interest in causes, simply reporting that two of Jehoash's servants kill him. Apparently the purpose is not to usurp the throne for themselves, however, for Jehoash's son, Amaziah, succeeds him (and will not wait long in avenging his father). Notably, Jehoash's superior piety in doing "what was right" in God's eyes does not save him, foreshadowing the fate of the ideal king, Josiah. In the end, he too falls to the curse on the house of Omri pronounced by Elijah (although the narrator does not draw the connection), even though Jehoash has reigned over the house of David.

Jehu's Successors, the Death of Elisha, and the Resurrection of the Dead (Chap. 13)

Here the narrator jumbles kings' names and events in a bewildering chronology. Whether intentionally or not, the jumble reflects the turbulent events that run through chap. 15. Two brief accounts of the reigns in Israel of Jehoahaz and Jehoash (alias Joash), son and grandson of Jehu, present very little historical information, each concluding, as usual, with their deaths. But then the narrator returns to the reign of Jehoash to relate his legendary experience at Elisha's deathbed, then returns ever so briefly to Jehoahaz, then back to Jehoash. Added to this confusion is the alternation between the royal names of Jehoash and Joash, as well as the fact that both Judah and Israel have a king by that name, as well as by the name of Ahaziah! See Figures 3 and 4.

Figure 4: House of Jehu (followed House of Omri)

> Jehu
>
> Jehoahaz
>
> Joash
>
> Jeroboam II
>
> Zechariah

The account of Jehoahaz's reign (13:1–9) reads like a typical story from Judges with the sin-anger-oppression-cry-deliverance-recidivism pattern, and we are not even told who the "savior" is.[72] About all Jehoahaz does here is to pray to God for help, and God, who has handed Judah over to Aram, acts as if the "oppression" is a surprise, and heeds the prayer. But, for the second time, the narrator tells us that Jehoahaz followed in the sin of Jeroboam, and even after deliverance he allows the *'asherah* ("sacred pole") to remain standing in Samaria, presumably in the sanctuary. Just how desperate his prayer must have been is suggested by the extent to which Aram has decimated his armed forces, leaving him with little defense. One suspects that behind the "salvation" may lie a bit of tribute paid to Aram, as with Hazael, but, before we know it, Jehoahaz is sleeping with his fathers. Nevertheless, the narrator will return to the subject of Hazael's harassment in 13:22–23.

Jehoash, Jehu's grandson, at first seems to win the award for least-information: three verses and nothing but a summary evaluation (13:10–13). All he has to show for his sixteen years in office is that he too followed Jeroboam's sin, fought mightily against Judah (a rare reference to that ongoing squabble), and died. But then the narrator returns to a scene in his life when he was present at

---

72. Cf. Judg 2:18; 4:3; 6:9; 10:12, all using the same word for "oppress." Sweeney, *I & II Kings*, 355, 364, suggests that salvation comes under Jeroboam (14:27). Hallo and Simpson, *Ancient Near East*, 129, suggest that the savior is Adadnirari III, with whom Joash made an alliance. Nelson, *Kings*, 217, leaves it open, noting that God is ultimately the agent in any case.

the death of Elisha, who has a few more tricks up his sleeve before departing this world. Elisha, of course, was a fervent supporter of Jehu and his bloody coup, and now he continues that support with Jehu's grandson. No doubt in gratitude for Elisha's support of his family, Joash goes to Elisha on his deathbed and weeps over him, uttering the same exclamation that Elisha had spoken when he saw Elijah taken up into heaven (13:14; 2:12). Perhaps it reflects the affection and respect he feels for Elisha that Joash addresses him as "My father," as if Joash were one of the company of prophets. Then he invokes "the chariots of Israel and its horsemen!" perhaps in the hope that Elisha will somehow make those "chariots of fire" appear one more time, especially since Hazael has destroyed most of the *army's* chariots. Elisha seems to have something similar in mind. He orders Joash to assist in one of his magic tricks in which Joash shoots an arrow from the window "eastward," the direction of Aram. Elisha proclaims the missile to be "the Lord's arrow of victory" which will make "an end" of the Arameans. Then he tells Joash to strike the ground with the remaining arrows, which Joash does three times. Elisha now is angry, saying that he should have struck five or six times so that he would make "an end" of Aram, but now Joash's victory will only be three-fold. No doubt Joash thinks that Elisha has just *promised* an end, and wonders why Elisha didn't tell him the requisite number of strokes to begin with, but it is too late, and Elisha dies. Or so it would seem, but there is something of his spirit that lives on even after he is buried. In a rush to evade a band of Moabite marauders, people who are about to bury the body of another dead man throw it into Elisha's grave instead (the logistics of this being unclear), and when his corpse touches Elisha's bones, the man comes to life and stands on his feet. Even after death the power of the prophet can raise the dead.

The narrator now returns to Hazael's "oppression" of Israel under Jehoahaz (13:22, AT). Contrary to the impression left by God's sending a "savior," here Hazael continues to make trouble "all the days of Jehoahaz." On the other hand, the narrator presents an assurance of God's grace and compassion for Israel grounded in the "covenant with Abraham, Isaac, and Jacob" (13:23; cf. Gen 17:7).[73] In effect, that ancestral covenant here functions for Israel just as does the Davidic covenant with Judah, promising that God will not "destroy" Israel or "banish them from his presence." The allusion and assurance are unique to the books of Kings, and no sooner has the narrator stated it than he seems to take it away with the little phrase "until now." Presumably the narrator is writing from a time after the destruction of Israel that takes place in chap. 17, a "grace period" of only some sixty years—a rather severe restriction on the meaning of "everlasting," but one that is not new to the Former Prophets (e.g., the house of Eli, 1 Sam 2:30). Indeed, the import of that little phrase

---

73. The permanence of the covenant promise is most clear in the later, Priestly author's formulation, using the term "everlasting covenant," a description also of the Noachic covenant in Gen 9:16 and used by David of his own in 2 Sam 23:5.

will burden the very end of the Former Prophets with the burning question of *all* Israel's future. But the narrator turns immediately to the fulfillment of Elisha's prediction of Jehoash's threefold success against the Arameans, suggesting by juxtaposition that God's compassion at least extends into the immediate future.

A Breach in the Wall of Jerusalem (14:1–22)

The narrative now returns to Judah and the reign of Amaziah, the son of the assassinated king Joash. As soon as he has things in control, he kills the assassins to avenge his father's death, but then makes a remarkably gracious gesture—he does not kill the *children* of the assassins. We are so used to dynastic bloodbaths, not to mention *God's* inflicting the punishment deserved by a parent on his children instead, that Amaziah's abstention seems all the more surprising. Moreover, the narrator explains Amaziah's action by quoting a verse from Deuteronomy: "the parents shall not be put to death for the children, or the children be put to death for the parents, but all shall be put to death for their own sins" (Deut 24:16). This is the only reference to this verse in the entire Former Prophets, a prohibition ordered by God (through Moses) that even *God* seems to forget innumerable times. The reason for the discrepancy, of course, is the author's intent on finally attributing everything to God's control of history. The narrator seems to interpret numerous events with a different text in mind, namely the Second Commandment, where God warns of "punishing children for the iniquity of parents, to the third and fourth generation" (Deut 5:9), ignoring the apparent rescission later in the book.[74] God as historical agent trumps God as juridical amender. The narrator is endlessly bent on pointing out Israel's infractions of Deuteronomic law, but obviously unwilling to make the same criticism of God, who *gave* the law. Thus the death of the first child of David and Bathsheba, Rehoboam's loss of the kingdom of Israel, the death of Jeroboam's descendants, even the deferral of punishment against the arch villain Ahab on to his children, all go without any acknowledgment that the "word of God" at work in such injustices contradicts the *words* of God in the law.

Amaziah is no pacifist, however, for the next incident reports his military defeat of the Edomites and slaughter of ten thousand soldiers, thereby regaining some territory that had been lost some fifty years before under Jehoram (2 Kgs 8:20–22).[75] Then, apparently emboldened by his success, he sends a message to Jehoash of Israel suggesting a face-to-face encounter. Judah has often been subservient to Israel, if not Israel's vassal, and Amaziah's suggestion seems to be a challenge to this relationship. Jehoash responds with a little fable reminiscent of the more famous one

74. The same revision appears in Deut 7:10. In fact, *The Jewish Study Bible* translates there: God "*instantly* requites with destruction those who reject Him—never slow with those who reject Him, but requiting them *instantly*" (emphasis added). Ezekiel 18 gives a more extended discussion of the issue; cf. also Jer 31:29–30.

75. Thus the revolt of Edom "to this day" in 8:22 is outdated.

by Jotham (Judg 9:7–15), warning that he will trounce Amaziah if they meet, which is exactly what happens, thanks to Amaziah's stubbornness. Not only does Jehoash capture Amaziah, but he tears down a large section of the wall of Jerusalem, loots the temple and palace treasuries, and leaves Amaziah in Jerusalem only in exchange for hostages. Perhaps Amaziah's ignominious defeat is the reason for *his* assassination (as with his father), and he is succeeded by his sixteen-year-old son, Azariah (also called Uzziah).

Overall, the story in chaps. 13–14 presents a remarkable ambiguity that belies the Deuteronomic editor's ideology. The Israelite King Jehoash whose evil resembles that of Jeroboam (13:11) ends up the winner, and the Judean King Amaziah who "does right" as David and follows the "law of Moses" ends up the loser.[76] In fact, Jehoash's defeat of Judah, destruction of part of the wall of Jerusalem, looting "the house of the Lord," and deporting some of its citizens, all foreshadow what will happen to Judah in the end. Here Israel desecrates the place in Judah that God has chosen.[77]

Forty-one Years of Prosperity in a Flash (14:23–29)

The account of Jeroboam II is another that gives us very little historical information for a reign that saw many accomplishments, and some failures, depending on who you ask. Jeroboam reigned from 786 to 745 BCE, forty-one years. Aside from the usual condemnation for *deserving* the name Jeroboam the Second (i.e., following Jeroboam the First's sin), the narrator tells us of his military and political successes, extending the border of Israel, including the recovery of Damascus and the city of Hamath (vv. 25, 28). In fact, since he dominated Judah as well, "he was the first and only monarch ever to restore control over the entire extent of the empire once controlled by David and Solomon."[78] Here the narrator identifies that expansion as "according to the word of the Lord" (v. 25). There is also an unusual comment about God's responding to the distress of Israel by sending Jeroboam as a savior, the fulfillment of God's answer to Jehoahaz's plea in 13:4–5, somewhat in the manner of the Judges stories. The narrator then adds that "the Lord had not said that he would blot out the name of Israel from under heaven," contradicting the prediction in 14:15–16 (the latter perhaps from a later editor). It is as if the editor here is not aware of the devastation of Israel soon to come in chap. 17.

Also odd is the reference to the prophet Jonah (presumably the subject of the book named for him), identified as the source of the oracle predicting Israel's expansion. Part of the oddity of that reference is the *absence* of references to the major writing prophets, i.e., the "Latter Prophets," within the

---

76. Cf. Nelson, *Kings*, 219.

77. Cf. Campbell and O'Brien, *Unfolding*, 436, who also point out that looting the temple vessels (as opposed to the treasury) happens only here and with Nebuchadnezzar of Babylon.

78. Sweeney, *I & II Kings*, 368.

Former Prophets, one of the intriguing puzzles about its historiography (and in the Hebrew Bible Jonah is part of the Writings, not the Prophets). Although there is a classic confrontation between Amos and the priest of Bethel, Amaziah, in which Amaziah accuses Amos of political conspiracy against Jeroboam (Amos 7:10–17), we hear nothing of that here, nor any of Amos's various oracles. In fact, the account here seems to praise Jeroboam as the savior sent by God, seeming to side with the priest over the prophet. The reign of Jeroboam was a period of enormous prosperity and political stability for some, but crushing poverty for others, an economic injustice that the writing prophets roundly condemn, but we could not know that from the account here. Similarly, Hosea, another major prophet who worked in (northern) Israel is absent. Later on, Jeremiah, a figure of enormous significance in the religious history of Judah, is missing, as is Ezekiel, whose career spanned the end of Judah and the exile. We also hear nothing from Micah, another prophet who worked in Judah. The only major prophet who appears will be Isaiah, who plays a prominent role in the reign of Hezekiah (2 Kings 19–20), yet even so there is no reference to his role in the Syro-Ephraimite war (Isaiah 7; see below on 2 Kgs 15:29—16:20). Aside from Isaiah, the historical vacuum produces a narrative that is something like a history of the American South from 1955 to 1965 that never mentions a prophetic figure like Martin Luther King Jr.

Enemies Within and Without (Chap. 15)

The narrative now moves quickly with very brief accounts of seven kings, five of them from Israel, these five revealing again the chronic political instability of the North. In four of the five, there is a "conspiracy" and assassination, and two of the reigns are for only six months or even one month. The narrator steps to the fore occasionally with a theological comment, telling us that Azariah of Judah, who "did what was right," nevertheless was struck with "leprosy" by God (inexplicably), and reigned fifty-two years, apparently in quarantine, while his son ran the show (15:1–7); that Zechariah of Israel was assassinated in fulfillment of God's promise to Jehu, that is, he had the misfortune of being the fourth and therefore last member of the dynasty (15:8–12); and that God sent two enemies against Judah (15:37). One other notable fact is Menahem of Israel's act of barbarous genocide: "He ripped open all the pregnant women" in one town (15:16).

But the most significant entry in this chapter is that of King Pul of Assyria (15:19). We have not heard of Assyria before due to the author's customary focus on things religious, but the Assyrian presence has directly affected Israel and Judah for about a century before the time of Menahem. Eventually the Assyrians will destroy Samaria and devastate the land of Judah, only to yield later to the Babylonians, who will come and finish the job.

Excursus 6: The Assyrian Menace

Geographically, ancient Palestine was a corridor for imperial advances from end to end—Egypt from the south, Assyria and then Babylonia from the north (and later the Persians, then the Greeks, then the Romans, etc.). Early in Israel's history, Egyptian power held sway—hence Solomon's marriage to an Egyptian princess. But beginning in the 9th century, the Assyrians (ancient Iraq) began to expand their empire to the west, sped on by "a military machine of unequaled efficiency."[79] The cruelty and ferocity of the Assyrian *blitzkrieg* was deliberately honed to terrorize local populations into surrender: slaughtering thousands of soldiers, impaling captured prisoners on stakes outside the city walls, piling heads in front of city gates, burning entire cities to the ground, deporting captives into exile. Fortunately, we have evidence of the Assyrian movements because they left lengthy, detailed (and bombastic) annals, some of which refer to Israelite kings.[80] In 853 Ahab joined an anti-Assyrian coalition that included his erstwhile enemy, the Arameans, in the battle of Qarqar, a successful attempt to turn back the Assyrian onslaught of Shalmaneser III (although the latter claimed victory). The temporary peace treaty between Ahab and Ben-hadad (1 Kings 20), followed by renewed hostilities (chap. 22; 2 Kings 6:24), fits in this sequence of events. The success at Qarqar did not last long, however, and within ten years Shalmaneser was back with a vengeance, conquering much of the area north of Israel, and bragging about the submission of others: "I received the tribute of the inhabitants of Tyre, Sidon, and of Jehu, son of Omri."[81] Fearless as he was as a so-called reformer, Jehu was cowed before the Assyrians, and became their vassal. His grandson, Joash, also paid off the Assyrians.[82] A period of decline in Assyria due to internal political weakness allowed the Arameans once again to harass Israel and Judah (2 Kgs 12:17–18), but Adad-Nirari III renewed Assyrian power and attacked the Arameans. Once again, however, Assyrian power waned, allowing roughly fifty years in which both Israel and Judah could regain some control during the reigns of Jeroboam II (Israel) and Azariah and Jotham (Judah), but the pendulum soon swung again with the rise of Tiglath-Pileser III. He is the "King Pul" of 2 Kgs 15:19 (his full name appears in v. 29), whom Menahem paid for protection (or rather, the taxpayers did—v. 20). Within two years, Menahem's son Pekahiah succumbed to a conspiracy led by Pekah, probably spurred on by an anti-Assyrian faction. Pekah lasted twenty years, during which Tiglath-Pileser rampaged through the surrounding area, extending his conquest into "Gilead, and Galilee, all the land of Naphtali" (15:29). Finally, a pro-Assyrian faction led by Hoshea assassinated Pekah, although Tiglath-Pileser brags that he placed Hoshea on the

---

79. Hallo and Simpson, *Ancient Near East*, 125. Cf. Isa 5:26–30.

80. See *ANET*, 256–300. As Gottwald, *Politics*, 90, notes, "If we had only the biblical accounts to go by, we would have no idea of the major role played by Assyria in Syro-Palestinian politics during the dynasties of Omri and Jehu."

81. *ANET*, 280b, erroneously giving an ironic name for the *exterminator* of the house of Omri!

82. Hallo and Simpson, *Ancient Near East*, 130; Sweeney, *Kings*, 358.

throne as a puppet.[83] Eventually Hoshea would preside over Israel's destruction.

In short, much of Israelite and Judean history after 850 BCE reverberated to the vicissitudes of Assyrian aggression, as well as the jockeying for power among the various surrounding nations like Aram, Ammon, Moab, etc., sometimes acting in concert against Assyria, sometimes fighting among themselves, at other times aligning with Assyria to protect themselves from each other. Assyria increasingly employed terrorism to increase both its political power and its wealth. The price on subject states was enormous. Resistance or rebellion against Assyria brought immeasurable suffering in terms of both military and civilian casualties; compliance brought the burden of that strangely euphemistic word "tribute," which was basically money extorted on the basis of fear. Menahem paid the equivalent of roughly *seventy-five thousand pounds* of silver, exacted by a tax on Israelite citizens (at least one pound per person).[84] Add such tribute from a single city to that from others and one can imagine the enormous wealth that filled the coffers of imperial Assyria, and also appreciate why anti-Assyrian factions would sprout up. Here in chap. 15 the swing of the political pendulum is dizzying. Shallum's coup against Zechariah (15:10) was probably anti-Assyrian (and pro-Aramean); Menahem's coup against Shallum (15:14) was probably pro-Assyrian; and the assassination of Menahem's son Pekahiah by Pekah was anti-Assyria (15:25).[85] Pekah's anti-Assyrian and pro-Aramean policy (fomenting the Syro-Ephraimite War, see below), led to Israel's destruction.

One imperialistic tactic invented by the Assyrians would have far-reaching consequences: the deportation of citizens to Assyria, sometimes combined with the importation of Assyrians or other peoples into the native land. We see the first report of such a deportation in 15:29, and, of course, ultimately both Israel and Judah will suffer this fate. Thus, beginning at least in the mid-9th century, the threats of exile in the covenant traditions of Israel are utterly realistic portrayals of how a suzerain would deal with insubordinate vassals, i.e., how Yahweh would deal with Israel, which Deuteronomic theology saw as the same thing.[86]

There was a significant difference between those conquered territories that Assyria annexed as provinces, with Assyrian rulers installed, and those that were allowed the slightly more independent status of vassal, with their own native rulers. In the former, the Assyrians tended to dictate religious practices, but "residents of vassal states were free of any religious obligations toward their Assyrian master."[87] The difference becomes important in determining the source of both Israel and Judah's apostasy in the ensuing chapters of Kings. Since neither state was annexed up to their respective destructions, it means that whatever allegedly illegitimate worship practices are reported cannot be attributed to coercion by the Assyrians.

---

83. *ANET*, 284.

84. The tax is on all the "men of wealth" (15:20, AT).

85. Sweeney, *I & II Kings*, 371–72.

86. The dating to 850 BCE is one reason why some scholars would insist that the treaty model in Israel's covenant—especially the blessings and curses—could not have been composed before that.

87. Cogan, *Imperialism and Religion*, 49.

Ahaz and Assyria (Chap. 16)

Like Jehoram, Ahaz's job evaluation condemns him for walking "in the way of the kings of *Israel*" (cf. 8:18). The narrator then presents a cluster of offenses that seem to crop up with especially disobedient kings or the entire people: child sacrifice (making a child "pass through fire"); "abominable practices" of the Canaanites, "whom the Lord drove out before the people of Israel;" sacrificing at the high places, and "under every green tree." We have seen much of this list with Judah (1 Kgs 14:22–24, associated with Rehoboam), will see it again with reference to Israel's demise (17:8, 10, 17), and with the arch-villain Manasseh (21:2–6), whom one editor blames for Judah's demise (21:10–15). This is the first time we have seen a reference to child sacrifice in Israel or Judah, which was peculiar to worship of the god Molech, and no doubt the most heinous of practices attributed to the native peoples.[88] The phrase "under every green tree" also appears in the prophet Jeremiah's condemnation of Israel, and is probably associated with Asherah (often represented by the stylized tree or "sacred pole") and especially with the metaphor of adultery or prostitution for covenant infidelity (cf. Jer 2:20; 3:6, 13). As one commentator says of Jeremiah, "graphic images of apostasy include an insatiable whore, an ox that breaks its yoke, a vine that bears strange fruit, a stain that will not wash off, and the lust of a young camel and a wild ass in heat."[89] Compared to this, the Deuteronomic editor seems quite restrained.

The narrator now turns to the event known as the Syro-Ephraimite War, 735–732 BCE. The name comes from the two nations who together are attacking Judah—Syria (Aram), and Ephraim (i.e., Israel, using the alternate tribal name). Their purpose was to coerce Judah into joining a rebellion against Assyria. Instead, Ahaz seeks Assyria's help in repelling Israel and Syria. We have a different perspective on the same event in the book of Isaiah, who, by now, is a prophet closely connected to the king (Isa 7:1—8:15). Strangely, the narrator makes no reference to Isaiah at all, even though later he will play a critical role during the reign of Hezekiah (ch. 18). Since our purpose is primarily to follow the thread of the narrative of 2 Kings, we will not compare the two accounts at length. We must note two important differences, however. First, in the book of Isaiah, the prophet conveys God's assurance that Judah has nothing to worry about, that the king needs only to wait quietly for God's salvation. Ahaz is reluctant to follow this advice, but Isaiah does not tell us what Ahaz does. Second, Isaiah predicts that God will save Judah from Aram and Israel by using "the king of Assyria," who will come and destroy them. Again, nothing is said about any contact between Ahaz and Assyria, and the outcome of the predictions also is not reported.

In 2 Kings, Ahaz plays a much more active role. He clearly is intimidated by Syria and Israel (and rightly so)

---

88. See 2 Kgs 23:10; Lev 20:2–5; Deut 12:31; 18:10. The practice was in the valley of Hinnom just below the temple. The prior example was that of the Moabite king (3:27).

89. Perdue, "Jeremiah," 1116 n. for 2:20–28.

because he immediately sends a message to Tiglath-Pileser, the Assyrian king, submitting to his sovereignty and asking for his help: "I am your servant and your son. Come up and save me" (16:7, AT). In other words, Ahaz has become Tiglath-Pileser's vassal,[90] and sends the customary "tribute" of silver and gold from the temple and "the treasures of the king's house."[91] Tiglath-Pileser wastes no time in responding, promptly attacking Damascus and carrying its people off to exile, not to mention killing their king, Rezin. Strangely, the narrator does not report any such attack against Israel, but their time will soon come. In fact, Ahaz may well have made the right move politically, and it is not unprecedented to seek Assyrian help, as we have just seen with Menahem (15:19–20; cf. Asa, 1 Kgs 15:16–21).[92] Hezekiah will do the same thing, before turning into a rebel (18:13–14). Here there is no overt criticism from the narrator of Ahaz's decision to submit to Assyria, certainly nothing like that in Isaiah, where trusting in Tiglath-Pileser means *distrusting* God (see Excursus 7 below).

After Assyria has done its work, Ahaz goes to the conquered territory of Damascus "to meet King Tiglath-Pileser," no doubt to thank him. The narrator does not report anything further about their meeting, only that Ahaz happens to see "the altar that was at Damascus," and is so taken with it that he decides to have a copy of it made for him in Jerusalem, a task dutifully completed by the priest Uriah. Upon his return, Ahaz offers sacrifices on it as a kind of dedication, then he moves the existing "bronze altar that was before the Lord" to another location. He orders the priest now to use the new "great altar" for the regular sacrifices, saying that Ahaz will use "the bronze altar" only "to inquire by." Ahaz then strips the bronze from two of the temple furnishings—the frames of the basin stands and the oxen that held up the "sea" (1 Kgs 7:23–37), moving the latter to a more modest "pediment of stone."[93] He also removes some other parts of the temple structure and the palace. "He did this," the narrator says, "because of the king of Assyria" (16:18). The reference is not to a sacerdotal imposition by the Assyrians,[94] but to a demand for even more tribute than the silver and gold that Ahaz has already offered, as if Tiglath-Pileser is an Olympic champion who wants all *three* medals! Surprisingly, the narrator does not criticize the Aramean altar despite its original association with "other gods." But Ahaz is not presented as an apostate, rather he comes off as an inno-

---

90. NRSV "servant," but rightly translated as "vassal" at 17:3. Regarding Hoshea, see below. Ahaz's appeal as vassal to his protective suzerain resembles that of the Gibeonites to Joshua: "come up and help me" (Josh 10:4).

91. One would think there was nothing left given all the previous looting. See 1 Kgs 14:26; 15:10; 2 Kgs 14:14.

92. Ahaz's submission to Assyria results in precisely what Isaiah had predicted—Assyria's conquest of Judah's enemies—only not the way Isaiah intended. Sweeney, *I & II Kings*, 380, suggests that Isaiah's advice "must have seemed ludicrous" to the king.

93. The stands apparently were replaced since they appear in Jer 27:19.

94. Cogan, *Imperialism and Religion*, 113; cf. Nelson, *Kings*, 224–25; others see an Assyrian requirement here. Sweeney, *I & II Kings*, 384 sees no imposition but still suggests that the altar was "a symbol of Judah's subservience to Assyria."

vator with a great idea for the latest in altar styles. If there is an implicit complaint here, it is in the humility required in denuding the temple for that bronze "medal," but the price to pay was far less than it would have been had Ahaz chosen the wrong side.[96]

Excursus 7: The Vassal's Dilemma

Ahaz's vassalage provides an opportunity to focus on the dilemma that faced virtually all rulers in the ancient Near East but which took on peculiar theological dimensions due to Israel's covenant with God. At issue is a more particular aspect of the general covenant theology that we sketched in a preliminary fashion in Excursus 1. Israel is Yahweh's vassal and must pledge allegiance only to Yahweh, by whom Israel will then be protected from enemies, but, if Israel rebels, Yahweh will punish them. Moreover, as suggested most clearly by the ritual coronation of Jehoash of Judah in 2 Kgs 11:17, there apparently were dual covenant relationships, one between God and the king and people, and the other between the king and people separately, perhaps represented by "the people of the land." Thus the king and people swear fealty to God as God's vassal, and the people swear fealty to the king. This ritual has clear similarities to royal coronation ceremonies in ancient Near Eastern texts.[95] Just as political treaties forbid the vassal from making separate treaties with other kings, so Israel's covenant polity forbids making covenants with "other gods." But the theological problem is inherent to all treaties between Israel and nations as well, and for two reasons: one, a treaty written by an Assyrian king would invoke Assyrian gods to sanction it (with blessings and curses, cf. Deuteronomy 28–29). Thus "Swearing to serve the king was at the same time acknowledging the rule of the Assyrian god."[97] Two, pledging allegiance to the Assyrian king himself would obviously call into question the absoluteness of the Israelite king's allegiance to Yahweh.[98] We can see the problem in Ahaz's appeal to Tiglath-Pileser: "I am your servant and your son." Similarly, the NRSV translates "servant" with "vassal" in 17:3 regarding Hoshea's relationship to Assyria. But the language of servant and son also typifies the relationship between the Israelite king and Yahweh, especially in the Davidic court theology. We first saw this relationship in the Nathan oracle of 2 Sam 7:14, where God says "I will be a father to him, and he shall be a son to me." In an apparent coronation ceremony, God says to "his anointed," "You are my son; today I have begotten you" (Ps 2:2, 7). In Ps 89:26–27 the king says to God "You are my Father," and God designates him "the firstborn" (cf. vv. 3–4; 2 Sam 23:5). So Ahaz's submission to Tiglath-Pileser poses a fundamental question: whose son is he, really? Which "father" will he obey? The problem is only compounded when Ahaz says, "save me" (16:7, AT).

The inescapable tension between fealty to God and fealty to the Assyrian

---

95. Weinfeld, *Deuteronomic School*, 85–90.

96. Nelson, *Kings*, 225–27, provides a lengthy list of reasons why the new altar is treated positively by the narrator, noting that it apparently is the same one that is *not* destroyed by Hezekiah or Josiah (18:22; 23:9).

97. Cogan, *Imperialism and Religion*, 45.

98. In a sense, this was part of the problem with the monarchy to begin with (e.g., Judg 8:23; 1 Sam 10:19; 12:12).

king produced agonizing dilemmas for the kings of both Israel and Judah. Inherently, Israel's covenant with Yahweh seemed to require an "isolationist" foreign policy; practically, the enormous political power and military machines of empires seemed to require something far more defensive. Given the ruthless aggression of the Assyrians (as well as the Egyptians, and then the Babylonians), sometimes submitting to vassalage was the only alternative to certain defeat and devastation, but submission also brought with it the enormous economic drain of resources as tribute. It was damned if you do and damned if you don't. There was also the problem of being caught in the middle between vying imperial powers, often Egypt to the South and Assyria to the north, each of whom sought to seduce vassals from the other. On whom should the king rely? Or there were regional conspiracies of vassals plotting rebellion—should the king join them? Or, as in the case of Ahaz, a king's weakness might lead him to conclude that only submitting to the Assyrians would save him from smaller, regional, enemies, including his own tribal relations (Israel). On the domestic front, the king would have to contend with pro- and anti-Assyrian factions which sometimes fomented assassinations.

As if the problems of *Realpolitik* were not enough, the king would also have to deal with prophets, who often condemned alliances with other nations as not only strategically foolish but also as *religious* apostasy, given the covenant theology sketched above—making the dilemma also that of *God's* damnation (curse) or its opposite (blessing). Thus Hosea (750–722 BCE), located in the North, condemns Israel's foreign entanglements as the equivalent of "straying" from and "rebelling" against Yahweh. Israel is like a silly dove flitting back and forth between Egypt and Assyria (Hos 7:8–13). Hosea likens Israel's foreign relations to adultery with "lovers." It is even worse than prostitution in that Israel (the prostitute) pays the *customer* (Hos 8:8–10), adding another ironic dimension to the word "tribute"![99] Roughly about the same time, Isaiah (located in the South) makes similar denunciations (30:1–7; 31:1–3), and, more than a century later—and early in his career—Jeremiah will join the prophetic chorus (Jer 2:18–19). Furthermore, one can hear various prophets recommending diametrically opposing foreign policies at various times. Thus Isaiah insists that Ahaz and Hezekiah not give in to the Assyrians or other enemies; on the other hand, later in his career, Jeremiah insists that the Judean king *surrender* to the Babylonians who are attacking Judah *on behalf of Yahweh*. Indeed, Jeremiah will even refer to the Babylonian king Nebuchadnezzar as Yahweh's "servant" and tell the Judean king Zedekiah that *he* must *serve* Nebuchadnezzar (27:6, 11). Now pledging allegiance to the foreign king is *not* apostasy but, in fact, the way of obedience to God! Becoming (or remaining) a vassal to Babylon is consistent with being Yahweh's vassal. It is no wonder that Jeremiah will be accused of deserting to the enemy and imprisoned, barely escaping execution (Jeremiah 37). (He will not be the last prophet to be accused of treason!) To add even further to the dilemma, the king at times confronted diametrically opposite advice from prophets, all of whom claimed to speak for Yahweh (e.g., Jeremiah 28, already Micaiah in 1 Kings 22). Thus the prophetic recommendations for national security run the gamut from nationalist isolationism to humiliating capitulation.

---

99. Cf. Wolff, *Hosea*, 143.

The Fall of Israel: "The End has Come" (Chap. 17)

The narrator recounts the final defeat of Samaria and Israel in six verses, then gives us seventeen verses of theological explanation—a few facts and a long sermon—which should come as no surprise to the reader by now (17:1–6, 7–23). Then the narrator tells us whom the king of Assyria brought to settle in Samaria, and of their heterodox practices, coupled with another homily (17:24–34a, 34b-41). The two sections each end with the phrase "to this day" (vv. 23, 41).

When Shalmaneser of Assyria besieges Samaria, Hoshea capitulates and becomes his vassal, paying the usual tribute. But soon Shalmaneser finds "treachery" in Hoshea. The word is the same as "conspiracy," which we have seen many times involving domestic politics, coups, and assassinations. Indeed, it was through "conspiracy" that Hoshea assassinated Pekah and claimed the throne (15:30). Now Hoshea has conspired with King So of Egypt, and *stopped* his payments of tribute to Shalmaneser. King So seems to be of no help, however, when Shalmaneser seizes and imprisons Hoshea, then invades all of Israel, besieging Samaria again. The city holds out for three years, but in the end Shalmaneser conquers it and carries off the Israelites to exile in Assyria. From prediction to fulfillment it took some twenty-five years, but the oracle of the prophet Amos has come true: "the end has come" (Amos 8:2).

Of course, we have known what the end would be ever since the prophet Abijah, some two hundred years before, had announced Israel's doom, "because of the sins of Jeroboam, which he sinned and which he caused Israel to sin" (1 Kgs 14:16, AT). But the editor who spoke there (or one from the same tradition) now cannot resist delivering the longest piece of commentary in the entire Former Prophets. There are three sections reflecting levels of redaction. The first focuses on the people's sins (vv. 7–18), the second shifts to Judah and seems to presume its fall (vv. 19–20), and the third shifts the focus back to Jeroboam, the old bugaboo (vv. 21–23). The litany of offenses does not include anything new, although the language at times is distinctive.[100] The first section embraces Israel's history from the Exodus to the present, and condemns Israel as a people, with only a brief allusion to their kings (v. 8b). The emphasis is on how Israel behaved as did the "nations" who inhabited Canaan before Israel's settlement (vv. 8, 11, 15): Israel "walked in the customs of the nations" (v. 8) *instead of* the "customs" of Yahweh's covenant (v. 15, AT). "Therefore," just as Yahweh "drove out" the nations from before them, God has "removed *them* out of his sight" (vv. 8, 18). The narrator emphasizes the analogy by using the word for exile ("carry away"): just as God "carried away" the Canaanite nations (v. 11), so God has "carried away" Israel (v. 6). Wanting to "be like the nations" has worked out rather differently than Israel originally intended (1 Sam 8:5)! Similarly, just

---

100. As noted above, a similar cluster of motifs appears in 1 Kgs 14:22–24 and 21:2–5. Campbell and O'Brien, *Unfolding*, 442, point out that some of the alleged offenses of Israel here previously were applied only to Judah (e.g., pillars and *'asherim* on the high places; child sacrifice; divination).

as the Israelites were "like the nations," so they were like their ancestors, who are mentioned three times (vv. 13–15). Just as God gave their ancestors "commandments and customs in accordance with all the law," which their ancestors disobeyed, so God sent "every prophet and seer" to warn them to "repent," but they refused to listen to them. Now none is left "but the tribe of Judah alone" (v. 18).

Not so fast, says the editor of vv. 19–20: "Judah also did not keep the commandments of the Lord their God but walked in the customs that *Israel* had introduced." Here it seems that Israel is to blame for Judah's sins, reminding us in particular of how a previous editor blamed Ahab and Jezebel for just such an infection (8:18). Israel walked in the customs of the nations and Judah walked in the customs of Israel. Thus "the Lord rejected *all* the descendants of Israel . . . and banished them from his sight."[101] If "all Israel" refers to both North and South, the editor is clearly writing at a time *after* the fall of Judah. If it refers only to the Northern kingdom, then the editor is warning Judah, probably at the time of Josiah, that it may suffer the same fate as Israel.[102]

Now another insertion makes sure that Jeroboam receives adequate blame for the fall of Israel (vv. 21–23). He drove Israel from God and "made them commit great sin," which they willingly continued after him. Then the section concludes with another reference to God's removing Israel out of sight, as predicted by the prophets: "So Israel was exiled from their own land to Assyria until this day." If the narrator is writing *before* Judah's fall, then the preceding sermon is a warning for *them* to "repent." The editor now has proof that all the preceding warnings about Israel's destruction were true. If the sermon is after the fall of Judah (like vv. 19–20), then it is a justification of God's punishment.

With the first homily finished, the narrator resumes the story of what happened to the *land* of Israel demographically, with "Samaria" now representing the whole area (17:24–41). Here the focus is not on the people of Israel in exile, but the various peoples whom the Assyrians "carried away" from *their* homes to take Israel's place, a frequent policy for defeated nations. At first they do not worship Yahweh, which one would not expect, but apparently Yahweh is not pleased by this neglect, and sends hungry lions among them.[103] The people complain to the king of Assyria, arguing that the lions are a punishment from Yahweh for the people's misbehavior, which itself is due to their ignorance of "the law of the god of the land." They request that the king send one of the Israelite priests back to Samaria to teach the law to the occupying peoples, and the king sends a priest to Bethel, where he teaches the people "how they should worship Yahweh" (v. 28, AT). If the priest follows the example set by the heterodox appointees of Jeroboam I (1 Kgs 12:31), there will be

---

101. The reference to "plunderers" resembles the editorial framework in Judg 2:14, 16.

102. Campbell and O'Brien, *Unfolding*, argue for the former; Sweeney, *I & II Kings*, 391–92 argues for the warning; Nelson, *Kings*, 231, reflects both readings.

103. Lions seem to be God's animal of choice for such punishment; cf. 1 Kgs 13:24; 20:36; more generally, wild beasts are associated with Israel's original settlement, e.g., Exod 23:29; Deut 7:22.

no improvement. In fact, all is not well, for the narrator is concerned that the occupying peoples continue to practice their former religions, installing idols in all the towns, and one group even sacrificing their children. Nevertheless, "they also worshiped the Lord," appointing "all sorts of people" from among themselves as priests to sacrifice at the high places. "So they worshiped the Lord but also served their own gods," "to this day" (vv. 33–34). Even though the subject is these foreign peoples, the narrator nevertheless launches into another homily which seems to contradict what was just said: "they *do not* worship the Lord," or obey the law, which Yahweh "commanded the children of Jacob, whom he named Israel." Presumably the point here is that one cannot *truly* worship Yahweh and other gods at the same time, which is the point of the concluding sermonic remarks. The foreign peoples are judged by the same standards as was Israel: "to this day their children and their children's children continue to do as their ancestors did."[104]

As Campbell and O'Brien suggest, one can read the passage in 17:7–41 as the record of alternating voices arguing with each other over the issue of inclusiveness over exclusivity.[105] The opening section (vv. 7–23) presents the standard Deuteronomic line of disaster resulting from worshiping other gods; vv. 24–33 "subvert this view by pointing to a more inclusive theology, the successful worship of both YHWH and their national gods by the relocated people"—hence no more lions; then vv. 34–40 counter with a reaffirmation of orthodoxy; and finally v. 41 speaks one more time for the inclusive line of vv. 24–33.[106]

Hezekiah: Reformation and Redemption (Chaps. 18–20)

The next three chapters report the religious reformation accomplished by Hezekiah and the astonishing deliverance of Judah from the Assyrian king Sennacherib, but end with another prediction of Judah's fall. Reconstructing the historical events behind the encounter with Sennacherib is notoriously complicated, and, of course, not our purpose here. There are numerous allusions to the events in the book of Isaiah (e.g., chaps. 28–33), along with a considerable portion from the narrative found here (Isaiah 36–39).[107] However, the Isaiah account does not have 18:14–16, which means that the Kings account presents *two* separate trips of Sennacherib against Jerusalem, whereas in Isaiah it is only one. Whatever the historical facts are, the return of Sennacherib's agents here in v. 17 does not make sense, given Hezekiah's submission and payment of tribute in vv. 14–16.[108] As a result, the entire account

---

104. Here is a precedent for the much later stigmatizing of Samaritans that will elicit a parable from Jesus of Nazareth (Luke 10:25–37).

105. *Unfolding*, 445–46.

106. There is at least one problem with this otherwise ingenious reading: it is difficult to see how any author could deem child sacrifice as a sign of "successful" syncretism (v. 31)! Possibly vv. 25–28 were originally independent of the context (v. 29 literally does not have "but" or "still").

107. Sweeney, *I & II Kings*, 397, 410–11, argues that the Isaiah text comes from that in 2 Kings.

108. Here the question of literary sources and differing accounts comes into play. Sweeney, *I & II Kings*, 411–12, argues against multiple sources,

of Hezekiah would be positive in chaps. 18–20 except for 18:14–16 (submission) and 20:12–19 (showing off). Generally, the book of Isaiah portrays Jerusalem's experience throughout as a humiliating punishment from God, even though Assyria (God's rod of anger) does not escape divine judgment either. Also, Isaiah was a prophet in the Davidic tradition for whom Jerusalem was God's holy city, but Isaiah was also quite willing to describe it as a "whore," full of murderers, rebels, and thieves (Isa 1:21–22).

In 2 Kings, Hezekiah is the first great reformer (with precedents in Jehoash, 11:17—12:16, and Asa, 1 Kgs 14:11–13), doing "what was right in the sight of the Lord just as his ancestor David had done." Specifically, "he removed the high places, broke down the pillars, and cut down the sacred pole [Asherah]." He even removed "the bronze serpent that Moses" (of all people) had made, since "the people of Israel had made offerings to it."[109] Hezekiah's job evaluation is unparalleled: "He trusted in the Lord the God of Israel; so that there was no one like him among all the kings of Judah after him, or among those who were before him"

(18:5). He "clung" to God and obeyed the commandments, and Yahweh was with him wherever he went, making him successful, and thus a king in the image of Joshua (or the reverse).[110] Coupled with his piety, there is also Hezekiah's foreign policy: "He rebelled against the king of Assyria and would not serve him." In important ways, then, Hezekiah represents the Deuteronomic ideal of a king up to this point—one who *serves* God and no other—and, as we shall see, one whose fidelity *is* spectacularly successful in at least one moment.[111] According to the chronology here, Hezekiah had reigned for seven years when Samaria fell to Shalmaneser, and the narrator gives us a brief summary of what we have read in chap. 17 (18:9–11). The effect of this reminder is to set up Hezekiah as the antithesis to Ahaz, God's reward for trust over against God's punishment for disobedience. In the end we will have to ask whether the reward outweighs the price paid.

Shortly after the fall of Samaria, Hezekiah shifted his loyalty to Egypt (18:21) whose Pharaoh was always applying pressure from the south. Isaiah condemns such an "alliance" taken on without consultation of Yahweh (Isa

---

suggesting that v. 17 demonstrates the injustice of Sennacherib's actions despite Hezekiah's submission, showing the Assyrian as despicable and arrogant. Cf. also Nelson, *Kings*, 237, who compares Sennacherib to Stalin. That interpretation could have a parallel in 1 Kgs 20:1–6 where Ahab's acquiescence to Ben-hadad's demands only produces *more* demands.

109. For some reason the narrator has overlooked this object that seems to come dangerously close to idolatry. The etiology of the object, perhaps resembling the caduceus of medicine, is in Num 21:4–9, where it is used for healing by sympathetic magic. Some scholars think that the story was composed precisely to explain Hezekiah's action.

110. Note especially the connection with obedience and "success" in Josh 1:7–8. Some scholars argue that the figure of Joshua, in fact, is modeled after Hezekiah and, even more so, Josiah. On the phrase "after him," see the next note.

111. It is for these reasons that some scholars argue for a Hezekian edition of the Deuteronomistic history, i.e., one concluding with Hezekiah's reform and miraculous deliverance from Sennacherib—a high note indeed! Still, the exclusion of kings "after him" in v. 5b would have to be a later addition, but prior to Josiah, who was the reformer par excellence.

30:1–5), and, indeed, soon thereafter Sennacherib resumed Assyria's aggression, including a devastating campaign against "all the fortified cities of Judah" (2 Kgs 18:13). Isaiah is probably referring to this when he says "your country lies desolate," and describes Jerusalem's lonely isolation as "like a booth in a vineyard" (Isa 1:7–8). Sennacherib describes it as "like a bird in a cage."[112] In the account here, Hezekiah's rebelliousness comes to a sudden and humiliating conclusion at this point, confessing to Sennacherib that "I have done wrong"(or "sinned") and offering to pay whatever it costs to avoid destruction (18:14). The price is high indeed: the equivalent of some twenty thousand pounds of silver and over two thousand pounds of gold! Hezekiah loots the temple and palace treasuries, in effect reducing Solomon's house of gold to wood.

Presumably Sennacherib departs with his booty in hand, but in v. 17 suddenly his agents are back "with a great army," demanding a conference with Hezekiah. Hezekiah sends his own agents to negotiate outside the city wall. Sennacherib's chief negotiator is his major-domo, the Rabshakeh (Sennacherib's Chief of Staff), who gives them a message for their king, the substance of which suggests that Hezekiah is still in revolt, contrary to vv. 14–16. Hezekiah should not lean on Egypt for support, "a broken reed of a staff," nor should he rely on Yahweh, whose "high places and altars" Hezekiah has removed, nor should he rely on his own strength, which is pitiful. The word "rely" (or "confidence") occurs four times in vv. 19–22 (cf. 19:10).

"Trust" would be another translation, and, of course, it points to a major theological theme of the confrontation with Sennacherib, connecting back to the introductory emphasis on Hezekiah's trust (18:5). Here, Hezekiah at first trusts in Pharaoh, then reverses his stance and submits to Sennacherib, then reverses again and rebels (presenting a more complicated portrayal than in Isaiah).[113]

Now the Rabshakeh clinches his argument by claiming that rebellion against Assyria is, in fact, rebellion against Yahweh, for it is none other than Yahweh who said to the Assyrians, "Go up against this land, and destroy it" (v. 25). On the one hand, the Rabshakeh does not understand how Hezekiah's reform is in obedience to Yahweh (whom the Rabshakeh assumes Hezekiah has offended); on the other hand, he speaks like a Deuteronomic theologian in arguing that *his* mission is *God's* mission. We have heard God's warnings over and over again, and, when all is said and done with Hezekiah, we will hear it again (20:17–18). The prophecy of Isaiah is full of such assertions. Indeed, that is why we have repeatedly been us-

---

112. *ANET*, 288.

113. In Isaiah, Hezekiah at first seems much more willing to trust in his own resources, defenses, and foreign alliances before placing himself in the hands of God. In addition to 30:1–5 mentioned above, see 22:8b-11, where Isaiah criticizes Hezekiah's repair of the city fortifications, and even the tunnel that he constructed for water supply (see below on 2 Kgs 20:20). By omitting the submission incident (2 Kgs 18:14–16), the Isaian account emphasizes that, when he finally *does* heed God's word from the prophet, all is well. As Sweeney notes, *Kings*, 411, "The result is a virtual whitewash of his character in the Isaiah version."

ing the phrase "the rod of God's anger" (Isa 10:5) long before now.[114]

Apparently many citizens of Jerusalem have gathered on top of the city wall in an attempt to eavesdrop on the negotiations, and Hezekiah's agents do not want them to hear the Rabshakeh's threats, much less his disturbing theology. So they ask him to speak in Aramaic, a dialect quite similar to Hebrew, but different enough that the average person would not understand it. But the Rabshakeh does just the opposite, now shouting directly to the spectators, using the standard messenger formula—"Hear the word of the great king, the king of Assyria! Thus says the king." "Do not let Hezekiah deceive you," he says. Hezekiah cannot deliver them, nor will Yahweh. If the people want to live, they must surrender and come out of the city. They will be allowed to live in security ("eat from your own vine and your own fig tree")[115] for a while, until the Assyrians take them away—but even then, says the Rabshakeh, they will live in "a land like your own"—a land of grain and wine, of bread and vineyards, of olive oil and honey, describing it in a way that clearly resembles the picture in Deut 8:7–9, as if the Rabshakeh is a student of Moses. He is certainly a master of spin, making exile sound like living in the Promised Land! Then he returns to the subject of deliverance, arguing that no god has delivered any other people from the hand of the Assyrians, and he provides a list of recent examples, ending with Samaria. "Who among all the gods of the countries have delivered their countries out of my hand, that the Lord should deliver Jerusalem out of my hand?" (18:35).

Neither the Rabshakeh nor the narrator seems to be concerned with the inconsistency of this argument with respect to the previous claim that Yahweh has *handed over* Jerusalem to the Assyrians (v. 25). Nevertheless, the people on the wall are dumbfounded and, under orders from Hezekiah, they make no response. The messengers return and report to Hezekiah, who, on hearing the message, tears his clothes and covers himself in the garb of mourning. Then he sends his aides to the prophet Isaiah, expressing his distress. "It may be," he says, "that the Lord your God heard all the words of the Rabshakeh," words which "mock the living God," and that God will rebuke them. Then he asks Isaiah to pray for "the remnant that is left," referring to Jerusalem, isolated and alone as it is.[116] Hezekiah assumes that the prophet enjoys a special intimacy with God ("*your* God") that will make him an effective mediator, a function that prophets do perform. His words also sound very much like those of David when he reacted to Goliath's challenge to Israel, "mocking the armies

---

114. "Against a godless nation I send him, and against the people of my wrath I command him," 10:6; the rest of the poem through v. 19 condemns Assyria's arrogance ("as if a rod should raise the one who lifts it up") and pronounces God's judgment; cf. 14:12–27. The same theme appears below in 1 Kgs 19:25–28. Assyria is often identified as the "enemy from the north," Isa 5:26–30, a terrifying description of the Assyrian war machine.

115. Cf. 1 Kgs 4:25; Micah 4:4. For the opposite, cf. Hos 2:12; Jer 5:17; 8:13. The Rabshakeh's suggestion here will later be that of Jeremiah (see Jer 21:8–10).

116. Later the "remnant" will play a large role in the prophecy of Isaiah (e.g., 6:13; 10:20–27; 11:11, 16). See below on 19:30–31.

of the living God" (1 Sam 17:26, AT), except that Hezekiah is *not* playing the role of the deliverer, just as the Rabshakeh has said. Isaiah sends back a most reassuring message, beginning with the standard encouragement of an oracle of salvation—"Do not be afraid" (v. 6).[117] Hezekiah need not worry about the words that have "mocked" Yahweh (v. 6, AT). God will "put a spirit" in the king "so that he shall hear a rumor and return to his own land; I will make it happen by a sword in his land" (18:7, AT).

The narrator does not report a reply from Hezekiah to the Rabshakeh, although the following scene suggests that Hezekiah rejected him, for he returns to Assyria to find Sennacherib preoccupied with a revolt by Libnah as well as a threat from Ethiopia (Egypt). Then the Rabshakeh is suddenly back at Jerusalem repeating a summary of his previous arguments (vv. 10–13).[118] Again the narrator records no reply from Hezekiah here, or for the rest of the story, but the plot assumes that Sennacherib maintains his siege. On receiving the Rabshakeh's message, Hezekiah heads for the temple and displays the document before God, then delivers an eloquent prayer, one which sounds suspiciously like other such prayers delivered by Israel's leaders steeped in the language of Deuteronomy (2 Sam 7:18–29; 1 Kgs 8:22–53).[119] Rather than appeal to Yahweh as the redeemer of Israel's history, Hezekiah addresses Yahweh as the creator of heaven and earth, and thus the sovereign of the universe.[120] Hezekiah repeats Sennacherib's reproach—"to mock the living God" (v. 16). He acknowledges Sennacherib's power to destroy other nations, but argues that their gods cannot protect them because "they were no gods but the work of human hands—wood and stone."[121] Instead, when Yahweh saves Jerusalem, Yahweh's unique divinity will be demonstrated to all the world. Hezekiah's prayer, of course, expresses his trust in Yahweh's power to deliver them, a complete turn-around from his prior submission. His defiance also contrasts to the meekness of his predecessor, Ahaz, who *did* "serve" the Assyrian king (16:7) and who, according to Isaiah, did *not* trust in the prophet's promise of delivery.[122]

---

117. See Deut 1:21; 3:22; Josh 1:9; Judg 6:23; cf. Isa 7:5 for the oracle to Ahaz.

118. It might seem that vv. 8–9 fulfill immediately the prediction in v. 7, but this proves to be anticlimactic to 19:36–37. Also, the connection between vv. 8–9 and 10–13 is ambiguous. Much of the historical confusion about the story concerns the uncertainty of how many times Sennacherib's forces attacked Jerusalem, as well as how many negotiations actually took place. The speech by the Rabshakeh in 19:10–13 represents a continuation of the previous negotiation, but a separate campaign might be involved, or vv. 10–13 might be a duplicate version of 18:19–35, since the same argument is presented here: Hezekiah should *not* rely on Yahweh to deliver Jerusalem.

119. Cf. also Jer 32:16–24; Nehemiah 9 and Daniel 9. See Weinfeld, *Deuteronomic School*, 32–45, on the genre of "The Liturgical Oration."

120. The emphasis on Yahweh as creator will be the basis for answering the question, How can Yahweh still be Israel's redeemer after Jerusalem is destroyed? See Isaiah 40 and related texts.

121. The latter phrase is also Deuteronomic and probably exilic. Cf. Deut 4:28; 28:36, 64 (both referring to exile); 29:17. Rather than destruction, normal Assyrian practice was to remove statues of gods to signify the abandonment of the conquered people's gods. See Cogan, *Imperialism and Religion*, chap. 2.

122. The central line in Isaiah's oracle there is "If you do not stand firm in faith, you shall not stand at all" (Isa 7:9), but Ahaz is so distrusting that he will not accept Isaiah's offer to ask for any

Apparently God has transferred the prayer to Isaiah, who is *God's* messenger. In fact, beginning with Ahaz's initial capitulation in 18:13, much of the episode involves the delegation of messengers between two powers, that of Sennacherib, and that of God, a motif that is repeated in the oracle (19:23), and concludes with the heavenly "messenger" of destruction (19:35). The exchange of messages points to the central question: whose authority to say "thus says" is reliable? Who is *really* the "great king"? Although the message in the oracle is for the benefit of Hezekiah, it is directed at Sennacherib. One of the central themes in the theology of Isaiah is the holiness of Yahweh, especially in contrast to the hubris of human beings.[123] Yahweh is "the Holy One of Israel" (19:22) and will not tolerate the arrogance of kings who brag of their power and military conquests. Thus the oracle repeats the key word "mock" (vv. 22–23) in introducing Sennacherib's boasts, which include his military power, his far-flung empire, his extraction of prized cedars from Lebanon, and his digging of wells. His words conclude with a claim to have "dried up with the sole of my foot all the streams of Egypt," a metaphor that evokes *Yahweh's* feats of drying up waters in saving Israel.[124] Thus Sennacherib's megalomania extends to pretensions of the divine.

The next part of the poem turns to Yahweh's sovereignty over history. Again, Sennacherib, like virtually all other potentates, is the rod of God's anger, and, as Isaiah says elsewhere, it is absurd for the rod to tell the hand that holds it what to do, or pretend that it has acted on its own (Isa 10:15–16). All that Sennacherib has done Yahweh had "planned from days of old," including the conquest of peoples, which Yahweh compares to plants that are "blighted" before they can mature. Then the oracle turns to judgment. Yahweh has Sennacherib's number, as it were, and because of his arrogance Yahweh will make him abandon his siege and return to his homeland, like an animal pulled by a hook in its nose. Here Yahweh's ultimate control over events that we have seen repeatedly extends back to the distant past, if not the beginning of time. What previously seemed like ad hoc decisions of God related to specific occasions here literally take the shape of a *plan*, literally "I did it long ago, I shaped it from days of old" (19:25, AT). Here all of *history* seems to be an outworking of what God intended from the outset, an elaboration of the prophetic understanding of God's effective "word," setting a precedent for much more elaborate concepts like "predestination."[125]

Isaiah's message now seems to address Hezekiah (19:29–34), offering a sign, often part of a prophetic oracle (e.g.,

---

sign he wants as confirmation (7:10–12). Again, the contrast with Ahaz is diminished by Hezekiah's initial submission in 2 Kgs 18:14–16. For Hezekiah, the key line would be in Isa 30:15: "in trust shall be your strength."

123. Cf. Isa 6:1–5; 2:10–17; 5:15–16; for Assyrian kings, see 10:5–19; 14:12–27.

124. Josh 2:10; 4:23; Isa 19:6; 42:15; 44:27.

125. On the "plan," cf. Isa 14:24–27, which could easily fit with the mysterious death of Sennacherib's army in our story (19:35), as could Isa 10:16. See also Isa 22:11, which may refer to the irrigation project of 2 Kgs 20:20; also Isa 25:1 and 41:1–24, which also concerns a proof of divinity; 44:6–8.

20:8; Isa 7:11). The promise picks up the horticultural language of v. 26—within three years the decimated land of Judah will again be ready for cultivation (and provide food of its own in between).[126] The metaphor then applies to the notion of a "remnant of the house of Judah," which will "take root downward, and bear fruit upward." In a rather ambiguous phrase, Isaiah says that the remnant "shall go out" of Jerusalem, all of this accomplished by "the zeal of the Lord of hosts." The question is—where will the remnant go, to exile, or to freedom?

Then the oracle again turns to Sennacherib. Isaiah promises that he will not come into Jerusalem, or even shoot a single arrow. He will return to his home, says Yahweh, "For I will defend this city to save it, for my own sake and for the sake of my servant David" (19:34). The fulfillment of the prophecy follows immediately in a direct intervention of God, here in the persona of an angel (the final "messenger," to use its literal translation). It is the "angel of death," who devastates the Assyrian army overnight.[127] Then Sennacherib returns to Nineveh, where he is assassinated by two of his own sons, who then flee, leaving the throne for the next bombastic emperor, Esar-haddon.

Isaiah is clearly a prophet thoroughly rooted in the tradition of Yahweh's promise of a Davidic monarchy reigning secure from Jerusalem or Zion, where Yahweh "dwells" (Isa 8:18). Historians offer differing reasons to explain the mysterious death of the Assyrian army and Sennacherib's withdrawal to Ninevah. Most likely, Sennacherib needed his troops to defend Assyria from the growing menace of Babylon, and could not wait for the siege to do its work. His annals confirm the destruction and mass deportations recorded in 2 Kgs 18:13, as well as demanding and receiving enormous tribute from Jerusalem. The narrator and Isaiah, of course, clearly see the event as a miraculous intervention of God. Historically, "Both sides could then claim success"—Sennacherib for his triumph and booty, and the biblical sources for Yahweh's protection of Jerusalem.[128] For the Deuteronomic theologians, the event demonstrated the rewards for those who trusted in God and refused to serve any other "king," even though subsequent events will seem to *disprove* such a connection (Josiah, see below). This is one reason why the reign of Hezekiah would have been a favorable time for the conclusion of one version of the Former Prophets. The promise of God to maintain the Davidic dynasty and to dwell on Zion "forever" inherently opened up the possibility of hope for a future despite the apparent reversals of historical events. The prophecy of Isaiah, more than any other voice, elaborated on that promise, developing it into a vision of the future that we can call "eschatological."[129] Yet,

---

126. The situation resembles that of the Sabbath for the land; cf. Lev 25:1–7.

127. Note that the slaughter in v. 35 is not anticipated in vv. 32–34 or 19:7.

128. Sweeney, *Kings*, 413. He also notes the other historical similarities between biblical and Assyrian texts, including the patricide of Sennacherib and succession of Esar-haddon (412).

129. Cf. Isa 2:2–4; 9:2–7; 11:9, and frequently in Second Isaiah (e.g., Isa 40:9; 46:13; 51:3, 11, 16). The continuation of the future promise appears in the Christian use of the Isaiah passages for Advent, and in the Jewish hope expressed at the end of the Passover Seder: "next year in Je-

for all his utopian imagery, Isaiah also could speak of divine judgment against the city that came very close to destruction (hence, again, the significance of a "remnant"). The "daughter of Zion" that here proudly scorns the Assyrians (19:21) elsewhere Isaiah condemns for her "haughty" flaunting of Yahweh (Isa 3:16–17). Zion may survive, but the city will first have to go through the refiner's fire (1:7–9, 21–31). In fact, despite Hezekiah's miraculous escape, the brief notice in 2 Kgs 18:13 already suggests how limited it was, for Sennacherib has already captured "all the fortified cities of Judah." In his annals, Sennacherib claims to have taken 200,000 prisoners into exile, a figure that may well not be wildly exaggerated.[130] Looking ahead, it will not be long before the refiner's fire engulfs Jerusalem as well.

The account of Hezekiah's reign now turns to two other incidents, both set *prior to* the preceding story,[131] one involving his health (20:1–11) and the other involving the health of the nation (20:12–19). Both incidents involve the postponement of calamity, and if the first demonstrates Hezekiah's continuing trust in God, the latter demonstrates his cynicism.

Hezekiah has become mortally ill, and Isaiah (ever the clairvoyant) comes to him with an oracle confirming his imminent death. Hezekiah responds with a prayer to God for healing, based on the merits of his sterling behavior, and he weeps bitterly. Immediately his humility and trust in God are rewarded by another oracle received by Isaiah before he has even left the palace. The God of his "ancestor David" will heal him, the "prince" of God's people, and he will have fifteen more years to live. Isaiah, who apparently is also knowledgeable about herbal remedies, then prescribes a potion to cure the boil, presumably the source or a symptom of his illness.[132] When Hezekiah asks for a sign to confirm the oracle, Isaiah offers a choice between turning the clock back or forward (as it were), and Hezekiah shrewdly chooses the option that he thinks the more difficult—backward movement.[133] Isaiah appeals to God and the miracle is done.

The second incident begins with a courtesy visit of messengers from the king of Babylon, supposedly motivated by his concern over Hezekiah's illness. The actual historical setting does not fit with the narrative sequence here.[134] Most readers will realize, of course, that Babylon will be the place where the Judeans will spend their exile, so the story takes on a kind of "Trojan horse" dimension. The narrator does not disclose Hezekiah's motivation (is it pride?), but he not only welcomes the emissaries, he takes them on a tour of all the treasures of his realm, unknowingly allowing the future enemy to case the joint. But Isaiah

---

rusalem." See the Summary and Conclusion for more on this.

130. Cogan, *Imperialism and Religion*, 102.

131. Note 20:6b and the contradiction between 20:13 and 18:15–16—by now Hezekiah has nothing to show off!

132. Cf. the situation with Ahaziah and Elisha, with a far less favorable outcome (2 Kings 1).

133. The miracle is even more impressive than Joshua's having the sun stand still (Josh 10:12–13).

134. Sweeney, *Kings*, 423, suggests the real historical setting was a conspiracy between Judah and Babylon in revolt against Assyria, perhaps in 705 BCE.

knows, as we would expect by now, and when he questions Hezekiah, and hears who the visitors are, and what they have seen, he delivers his final oracle to the king: all the treasures that Hezekiah has displayed will become booty for the king of Babylon, and some of his sons will be among the exiles, reduced to the role of eunuchs in the Babylonian court. Then Hezekiah responds with a surprising evaluation of the oracle as "good," accompanied by a thought (not spoken) that displays an astonishing cynicism: "Why not, if there will be peace and security in *my* days?" One could argue that Hezekiah is the prototype of all those political leaders for whom short-term prosperity is paid for by the next generation. The king who did what was right "just as his ancestor David had done" does not seem concerned over the potential end of Davidic *descendants*.[135]

The narrator now concludes the reign of Hezekiah by telling us of the king's most remarkable accomplishment in providing for national defense: "he made the pool and the conduit and brought water into the city" (19:20). The "conduit" is a long tunnel chiseled through solid rock that brought water from the Gihon spring outside the city wall, thus providing a reliable supply during times of siege.[136] One who was *not* impressed was Isaiah, who saw the defensive move as a lack of trust in God. The tunnel represented human planning that failed to consult God's plan, using the same language as the oracle above (Isa 22:11).[137] Isaiah was not one to use the proverb, "praise God and pass the ammunition." That the tunnel construction receives one third of a verse and the miraculous deliverance some thirty six verses illustrates the criteria of historical value typical of the Deuteronomic movement. Isaiah's insistence on defying Sennacherib turned Hezekiah into something of a hero and confirmed the Deuteronomic ideal of divine reward for human obedience, but in the end, with Judah devastated and depopulated, one has to wonder if the price was worth it. Had Hezekiah continued in his subservience to Sennacherib, paying his annual tax, it would have saved his people from enormous suffering. One can quote the proverb, "live free or die." But was saving face worth losing "all the fortified cities of Judah"?

Manasseh, the Harbinger of Doom (Chap. 21)

With Manasseh the narrator has unleashed the full force of Deuteronomic outrage. *Everything* reported is evil. The extremity of evaluation corresponds to the extremity of Manasseh's mark on Judah's history, at least according to the voice that speaks the prophetic word of judgment in vv. 12–14. Leading up to that, the narrator presents the most extensive list of offenses for any king, even Jeroboam. Manasseh seems to have instituted a kind of "counter-reformation," undoing all the efforts of his father. He rebuilds high places, reinstalls altars for Baal as well as the "host of heaven," plac-

---

135. If, as is often the case, the word "eunuch" means that his sons will be castrated, the implications for the David dynasty are obvious.

136. I say "is" because the tunnel still exists (I walked through it in 1965, knee-deep in water).

137. Literally "you [plural] did not regard the one who does it, and the one who shaped it long ago you did not see." Cf. 2 Kgs 19:25.

es an Asherah in the temple, consults with all sorts of illicit spiritual mediums, and, worst of all, engages in child sacrifice. After pronouncing the judgment, the narrator also will add that "Manasseh shed very much innocent blood," without telling us more.[138] Presumably, this is a rare inclusion of social injustice in the editorial condemnations that otherwise focus exclusively on sacerdotal matters, as we have often seen. In the diatribe against the North in chap. 17, the narrator compared the people's offenses to those nations whom God drove out of Canaan; here the narrator takes it one step further, saying that Manasseh not only followed such "abominable practices" but did things "*more wicked than all* the Amorites did" (vv. 2, 11). Thus what Jeroboam is to Israel's fall—causing Israel to sin—so Manasseh is to Judah's fall—causing Judah to sin (v. 11). The verdict follows immediately after repeating the conditional presence of God's name in the temple and Israel's occupation of the land—"forever . . . if only . . . ." (vv. 7-8).

The outcome of all this evil is God's decision to "wipe out" Jerusalem "as one wipes out a dish, wiping it and turning it upside down" (v. 13, AT). Jerusalem will suffer the same fate as Samaria and the house of Ahab. The magnitude of the decree appears in the acknowledgment that Judah is "the remnant of my heritage," like a little square of fabric remaining out of the beautiful quilt that God had made, and yet God has decided to throw it away (v. 14). The finality of the decision is like that pronounced on Israel long before its end, because of Jeroboam's sins (1 Kgs 13:15-16). One of the ironies here is that Manasseh had a long and apparently happy reign of sixty years, "the longest enjoyed by any king of Judah or of Israel."[139] The discrepancy between the longevity of his reign and the largeness of his evil produces an enormous challenge to the Deutueronomic doctrine of reward and punishment, virtually the flip side of Hezekiah's example. In effect, the solution to the problem will be to say that Masasseh's evil was disproportionate to any good that any other king could do—including Josiah—as we shall soon see (23:26-27).

After the death of Manasseh, the narrator gives us a brief account of the reign of his son, Amon, who was just as evil as his father, and who lasted only two years before being assassinated, probably due to internal squabbles over ties to Assyria. In turn, "the people of the land" kill the assassins and make Amon's son Josiah king, a role similar to their support for King Jehoash before (2 Kgs 11:13-20).

King Josiah at Last, Alas (Chaps. 22-23)

This is the story that the entire Former Prophets has been eagerly anticipating, and, at one point, specifically predicting (1 Kgs 13:2), for Josiah is the darling of the Deuteronomists, the great reformer, the ideal king: "He did what was right in the sight of the Lord, and walked in all the way of his father David; he did not turn aside to the right or to the left" (22:2). Only Josiah walked such a straight line,

---

138. Cf. Jer 7:6; 22:3, 17; Mic 3:9-11.

139. Gottwald, *Politics*, 69.

in accordance with the "law of the king" in Deut 17:18–20.[140] Most likely, Josiah is the apex and conclusion of the first major edition of the Deuteronomistic history.[141] On the other hand, this is the story that another editor, probably from the Exile, has dreaded, for it relates the premature death of Josiah, a tragedy that seems to shake the foundations of Deuteronomic theology. To the former editor, the story of Josiah is the fulfillment of a dream; to the other editor, it is the actualization of a nightmare. To the former, the story is the earnest of God's blessing; to the other, the sign of God's curse. In the present text, the result will be similar to the overall story of Hezekiah, which told of miraculous deliverance only to end with morbid doom.

The story of Josiah includes a report about his temple renovations, the discovery of the "book of the law" in the temple, the prophecy of Huldah regarding the book's warnings, the religious reformation, and finally the report of Josiah's death. Josiah's "reformation" was not exclusively religious, but involved both domestic and foreign politics.[142] Josiah's covenant with God (23:3) may represent a repudiation of his treaty submission to Assyria,[143] as may his fatal confrontation with Pharaoh Neco (23:29) but the text says little in the way of historical explanation (23:29, see below). The interest is in the *theological* explanation. Similarly, the result of the centralization of worship in Jerusalem is to create unemployment of local priests, affecting their livelihood, but there is only a brief allusion to such economics (23:9).[144] Josiah's policies may well have intended a political renaissance of the Davidic empire with a reunited Israel and Judah, but in the text the focus is on the people's covenant unity with God (23:1–3).[145] One has to read between the lines to see those factors extraneous to the narrator's exclusively sacerdotal focus.

Josiah is only eight years old when "the people of the land" execute his father's assassins and place him on the throne. We learn nothing of the first period of his reign, when senior advisors must have run the show, probably including at least some of those mentioned in the ensuing narrative—Shaphan, the secretary, and his son Ahikam; Hilkiah, the high priest; and others (cf. 22:12). When Josiah is twenty-six years old, he orders a disbursement of funds to the

---

140. Cf. Sweeney, *I & II Kings*, 441, who points out that the latter phrase is peculiar to Deuteronomy and applied only to Joshua (Josh 1:7; 23:6), who is a kind of alter ego of Josiah.

141. Or the second edition, if a Hezekian one preceded it, as many think.

142. On the political dimensions to the reform, see Cogan, *Imperialism and Religion*, 113; Weinfeld, *Deuteronomic School*, 85, 100; Gottwald, *Politics*, 83; Miller, *Religion*, 79. Some scholars argue that the religious reforms themselves were expressions of national independence from Assyria; others see the reforms more as reactions to Canaanite influences unassociated with Assyrian policies.

143. See Weinfeld, *Deuteronomic School*, 100, and the previous note.

144. Such changes involved political struggles between priestly groups whose rivalries go back at least to the time of David. For a brief summary of the issues, see Miller, *Religion*, 171–74.

145. Josiah's incursions into the territory of Samaria (23:19), at the time an Assyrian province, suggest that he was taking advantage of the Assyrian's preoccupation with the Babylonians. Similarly, the desecration of the sanctuary at Bethel, associated with the founding of the Northern kingdom, also paves the way for a reunification, a kind of reversion of Jeroboam's intent (1 Kgs 12:25–29).

workers who apparently are already engaged in temple repairs, similar to that undertaken by King Jehoash and the priest Jehoiada two hundred years before (chap. 12).[146] It is in the process of these repairs that Hilkiah discovers the "book of the law" and gives it to Shaphan to read. Shaphan then reports to the king on the progress of the repairs, and also reads the book to Josiah (which would take quite a long time if it were the present book!).

Most scholars think that this book refers to at least some version of the canonical book of Deuteronomy. Considerable debate still exists about just how much of the book would have been involved, when it would have been composed, and by whom. One way to determine the contents is simply to compare the reforms reported in 2 Kings 23 with their counterparts in Deuteronomy. Moreover, the "book" in question certainly contained frightening words of divine judgment warning of "disaster" (or "calamity," "evil"), most likely at least some of the curses from Deuteronomy 28, as well as other warnings of destruction as punishment for disobedience (e.g., Deut 7:4). As for the "discovery" itself, again the narrator supplies no details for historians.[147]

Josiah's immediate reaction is the customary display of mourning and distress—he tears his clothes—an appropriate response in that the book informs him of "the wrath of the Lord that is kindled against us" because of his ancestors' refusal "to do according to all that is written concerning us" (22:13). The gap in time between then and now could be enormous—some six hundred years.[148] But Josiah's perception that the book concerns "us" and not just the ancestors is exactly what the authors of the book had in mind when they had Moses say, "The Lord our God made a covenant with us at Horeb. Not with our ancestors did the Lord make this covenant but with us, who are all of us here alive today" (Deut 5:2–3). The contemporaneity of the book is also evident later in the narrator's references to it as "*this* covenant" or "*this* book," as if it is at hand on the narrator's desk (23:3; cf. Josh 1:8).

Josiah sends his aides for a consultation with the prophetess Huldah, who does not have good news. God will indeed bring the disaster on Jerusalem just as the book says, because the people have abandoned Yahweh and "made offerings to other gods." She does have *relatively* good news for Josiah, however: because of his penitential response to the book,

---

146. The language of 2 Kgs 22:4–7 closely resembles 12:4–16.

147. Opinions range from the implied surprise of Hilkiah just happening to find a scroll tucked away, covered with dust, to a kind of "pious fraud" in which the authors of the book "planted" it in a spot where they knew it *would* be found, fully intending that it would instigate the very actions that Josiah, in fact, implemented (all the more likely if, in fact, the authors were the tutors who had indoctrinated the king from his childhood). In noting the parallels between the reform and the legislation, one must keep in mind the possibility that some of the latter were composed explicitly for the former (i.e., the composing and the reforming went hand-in-hand).

148. The brevity of American history, at least, makes it almost impossible to construct an analogy, since we can scarcely conceive of a period of some six hundred years during which Americans went about their business completely ungoverned by the Constitution. One might instead compare what British history would have been like had the Magna Carta disappeared until the time of King George III.

he will not live to see the disaster, but will be "gathered to your grave in peace" (22:20). Thus the reprieve for Josiah is similar to that of Hezekiah, who would not live to see the city fall to Babylon (20:16–19), and, ironically, even more like that pronounced on Ahab, the ideological polar opposite of Josiah, whose repentance prompted a divine postponement of "disaster" until "his son's days" (1 Kgs 21:27–29).

As in previous cases, the pronouncement of fate may rob the reader of any suspense, but it does not seem to prevent the characters from acting their role.[149] Oblivious to the futility of his actions, Josiah nonetheless immediately initiates his reformation (chap. 23).[150] His first move is to renew the covenant between God and people that stands at the heart of Deuteronomic theology (vv. 1–3). The word "all" occurs repeatedly here: all the elders and all the people of Judah, all inhabitants of Jerusalem, priests and prophets, and all the people assemble, and Josiah reads all the words of the "the book of the covenant," promising to keep the commandments "with all his heart and all his soul," and "all the people" join in the covenant with him. In this covenant renewal, Josiah is going by the book, for there Moses orders "all Israel" to "appear before the Lord" at the place that God will choose, and for the elders and Levitical priests to read the Torah "before all Israel in their hearing" (Deut 31:9–13; cf. Josh 8:30–35; chap. 24). For the author, "all Israel" is finally together again, one in spirit, unified in commitment to the one God in the one place that God has chosen.[151]

Next Josiah orders the prohibition of all heterodox forms of worship and the destruction of various iconic representations associated with such worship (23:4–14). As we have noted at numerous points before, some of the "reforms" in fact may represent *new* forms of orthodoxy. That is, the Deuteronomists here are proclaiming various forms of worship heterodox even though before many people would have seen them as compatible with the worship of Yahweh, the use of an '*asherah* or "sacred pole" being one example. We also know that at least some sanctuaries escaped the purge described here.[152] The list of objects or practices deemed illegitimate is extensive: "the vessels made for Baal, for Asherah, and for all the host of heaven," "the image of Asherah" that was in the temple, the "pillars" and "sacred poles," and, of course, the various "high places," specifically those originally constructed by Solomon (v. 13). One heterodox practice we first hear about only as it is being eliminated—a sun cult (v. 11). The Wadi Kidron outside the city becomes the dumping ground, or the place for incineration. Other places Josiah "defiles," i.e., makes ritually impure and unusable, such as Topheth, associated with the ritual of child sacrifice (v. 10). Josiah also makes radical personnel changes. He eliminates "the idolatrous priests," i.e., those illegitimately appointed by the

---

149. Cf. Eli, 1 Sam 2:27–36; Saul, 1 Samuel 15; Jeroboam I, 1 Kgs 14:7–16.

150. We will return to the implications of Josiah's fidelity in the Summary and Conclusion.

151. Cf. Nehemiah 8 for a similar ceremony after the Exile. For the ceremony "by the pillar," see 2 Kgs 11:14.

152. The sanctuary at Arad had a "pillar" in its inner sanctum still standing when uncovered.

kings of Judah, who sacrificed to various alien deities (v. 5). As for the priests *of Yahweh* who were in the surrounding towns of Judah, Josiah evicts them and defiles the high places that they had used (vv. 8–9).[153] He destroys the houses of illicit temple attendants, and the seamstresses who make clothes for images of Asherah (v. 7).[154] All of these changes, of course, accomplish the centralization of worship in the Jerusalem temple under the authority of the high priest, as called for in Deut 12:5; 16:5–6, 11, 15–16. All other places, practices, and practitioners are expunged.

Josiah then moves his reform from Jerusalem to the Northern town of Bethel[155] and "all the shrines of the high places that were in the towns of Samaria" (22:15–20), and now the reformation takes on the dimensions of an "Inquisition." The incident represents a fulfillment of the prediction of the prophet in the story about Jeroboam I in 1 Kings 13, both the destruction of Jeroboam's altar and the fate of the prophet who subsequently disobeyed his divine orders (thanks to *another* prophet), sending him into the jaws of a lion. Accordingly, when Josiah disinters the bones from the tombs, using them to defile the altar, he leaves the bones of the two prophets to rest together in peace. Then the reform turns violent: "He slaughtered on the altars all the priests of the high places who were there, and burned human bones on them" (23:20).[156] No doubt Elijah was applauding from heaven (cf. 1 Kgs 18:40). With this bloody work done, Josiah returns to Jerusalem. He has now added one more item to his check list from Deuteronomy—he has broken down the altars, smashed the pillars, chopped down the sacred poles, and burned the idols with fire—and the idolatrous priests to boot (Deut 7:5). By destroying the high places created by Solomon and Bethel created by Jeroboam I, Josiah in effect is restoring Judah to its original sacerdotal orthodoxy.

> *Those who value pluralism must read the preceding account with increasing horror, and certainly no one wants to condone violence. But a perennial tension underlies Josiah's reform—the pros and cons of centralized religious authority, carefully regulated and enforced, over against the pros and cons of completely autonomous religious communities, with their freedom of conscience and expression. (The tension parallels that in terms of political government, e.g., monarchical over against tribal.) History is full of examples. In 1583, English Puritans (also called Separatists, and forerunners of those who came to America), resisted pressure from Queen Elizabeth to conform to Anglican ways. The conflict came to a head when some Puritans vandalized a*

---

153. There is some ambiguity about these priests who, in v. 9, seem to remain in their home towns. Deut 18:6–8 would allow them to make sacrifices in Jerusalem.

154. For "attendants" the NRSV reads "temple prostitutes," on which see n. 94 in chap. 6.

155. The connection with the previous reference to carrying ashes to Bethel is unclear (23:4).

156. Contact with human bones renders the places impure because of the association with death.

> church by writing graffiti equating Queen Elizabeth with Queen Jezebel! Elizabeth had several Puritan ministers convicted of nonconformity, banned the books written by Separatists, and, when two Separatists distributed copies anyway, she had the two men hanged and the books burned. Elizabeth's agent, Richard Bancroft, was a highly educated clergyman, later Archbishop of Canterbury. He was "not merely the compliant tool of despotism," but was convinced that the Separatist movement held grave dangers for disorder in the Church. "If every congregation went its own way, the schism that followed would cause an endless process of division. Christianity would fracture into countless squabbling sects. Bancroft forecast, accurately, an English civil war between denominations."[157]

Josiah concludes his reforms with a renewal of the Passover ritual, the celebration of Israel's redemption from Egyptian slavery, "as prescribed in this book of the covenant" (23:21–23; Deut 16:1–8). The narrator claims that this is the first Passover observance since the days of the judges; no other king had celebrated it. Since the Passover was the ritual that stood at the heart of Israel's identity as God's liberated and covenanted people, this was a fitting capstone to a reform that was also a renewal of national pride. For Americans, it would be something like renewing the celebration of Thanksgiving and Independence Day combined, after hundreds of years of neglect. With an additional reference to the removal of various heterodox media for revelation, the narrator then concludes the reform account by referring back to Hilkiah's discovery of the book that started it all, assuring us that Josiah "established the words of the law that were written in the book" (23:24). Then the narrator presents his summation, one quite similar to that on Hezekiah (18:5): "Before him there was no king like him, who turned to the Lord with all his heart, with all his soul, and with all his might, according to all the law of Moses; nor did any like him arise after him" (23:25). Josiah embodies the greatest commandment, Deut 6:5: "You shall love the Lord your God with all your heart, and with all your soul, and with all your might."

It would be difficult to exaggerate the force of the word for "still" in v. 26. Here the word functions as an "emphatic adversative," i.e., a giant expression of deep contradiction between what precedes and what follows. Josiah is the model king who loves Yahweh with all his heart; but that love is not reciprocated. Josiah turned neither to the right or left, but in the end it does not seem that Yahweh is "with him," much less that he "prospered" (cf. Hezekiah, 18:7; Joshua, Josh 1:7). Yahweh will not turn from the consuming wrath kindled especially by King Manasseh. Thus Yahweh announces (to no one in particular): "I will remove Judah also out of my sight, as I have removed Israel," echoing the words from 17:23. The inviolability of Jerusalem so evident in the

---

157. Bunker, *Making Haste From Babylon*, 92. See also the quotation from this book in the discussion of 1 Kings 8 and centralization of worship in the Jerusalem temple, and n. 23 there.

repelling of Sennacherib is over. There God said "I will defend this city to save it" (19:34; cf. 20:6). Here God says "I will reject this city that I have chosen, Jerusalem, and the house of which I said, My name shall be there" (23:27). It is as if the trajectory that led from Mt. Horeb to Zion, that movement of the "Glory of God" that led to the temple (1 Kings 8), is reversed.[158] The very focal point of the reformation, anticipated in Deuteronomy, i.e., the centering of the people in the name of God at the place that God would choose, goes out of focus, for the implication clearly is that God's name will *not* be there. What God has chosen, God can reject. The deepest irony is not simply the death of Josiah but also the failure of the very reforms that the Deuteronomic editors had envisioned ever since Solomon: finally a king has followed their wishes, but the entire endeavor will come to naught. Nevertheless, what we might expect to accompany the rejection of Jerusalem is not here: the explicit rejection of the Davidic dynasty. It was *for the sake of* David that God had sworn to protect Jerusalem (19:34; 20:6). What is to become of the "fief" that God had promised always to rule?[159] "The nation and people around the globe fell into a state of grief and anguish. The loss of someone who was so vibrant, so brimming with hope for the future of his presidency, his country, the world made his death inexplicable. "In Washington grief was agony," a White House aide later wrote. "It was all so grotesque and so incredible."[160]

The editor who composed the "adversative" lines of 23:26-27 clearly intended them to explain *why* Josiah would *not* die "in peace" (22:20), much less be blessed for all his reforming acts.[161] Why had God not "exalted his kingdom" the way God had done for David (2 Sam 5:12)? The answer is that God was more concerned to punish Manasseh than to reward Josiah.[162] Thus the insertion prepares us for the report of Josiah's premature death in 23:28-30. Once again, the report of such a momentous event is frustratingly terse. Presumably Pharaoh Neco is advancing north to join forces with the Assyrians in their defense against the

---

158. Indeed, this reversal of the "Glory of God" predominates the opening chapters of Ezekiel.

159. NRSV "lamp." See 1 Kgs 11:36; 15:4; 2 Kgs 8:19.

160. Dallek, *Flawed Giant*, 48, on the assassination of President Kennedy.

161. For Sweeney, *I & II Kings*, 446, the incompatibility suggests that Huldah's prophecy is "an element of an original oracle." On the other hand, Campbell and O'Brien, *Unfolding*, 459a, observe that the death is done by God ("I will gather you to your ancestors") and the burial "in peace" is done by the people (22:20). Presumably Campbell and O'Brien mean the latter as something like the way people say "now she is at peace" of someone who has died, particularly due to an unusually painful disease. Thus Josiah's premature death could be "a reward for his reforming attempts" (459b). Nevertheless, they see here "the deconstruction of the dtr [Deuteronomic] theology of reward and punishment." Nelson, *Kings*, 257 suggests that the phrase "in peace" is only understandable over against the devastation that Josiah will not see.

162. The Chronicler offers a radically different interpretation, namely that Josiah did not "listen to the word of Neco from the mouth of God," ordering Neco to undertake his mission (2 Chr 35:22), a point to which we shall return in the Summary and Conclusion. Similarly, the Chronicler has explained Manasseh's long reign with a story of his repentance, 2 Chr 33:10-13. Thus the reward/punishment scheme is intact!

Figure 5: House of Josiah

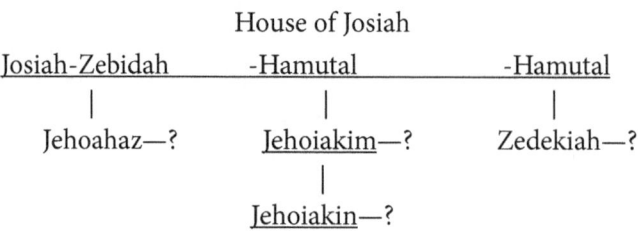

(Jehoiakin's great-grandson is Zerubbabel)

rising power of Babylonia, the ancient realm to the southeast of Nineveh. Josiah has taken an anti-Assyrian position, and may be in formal league with Babylon as well (cf. 20:12–13, despite the irony). Whatever the circumstances, Neco kills Josiah and once again the "people of the land" act to continue the Davidic line by anointing his son, Jehoahaz.

Beginning with Josiah, but especially with the last few kings, there is much more information about events in the book of Jeremiah than we will find here. Since it is not our purpose to reconstruct the history behind the text of the Former Prophets, however, we will limit our use of such material to brief allusions. Little over twenty years remain between Josiah's death and the final destruction of Jerusalem, and the editors have crammed all of that into the two remaining chapters. All of the remaining kings are condemned as evil. The first, Jehoahaz, does not last long. Within three months the Pharaoh replaces him with his brother, Eliakim and takes Jehoahaz to Egypt, where he dies. Neco renames Eliakim Jehoiakim.[163] Neco then imposes a penalty against Jerusalem of roughly seventy-five pounds of gold and seventy-five hundred of silver, and Jehoiakim turns around and imposes a tax on the people of the land to pay the bill.

"The End has Come," Again (Chaps. 24–25)

From here on out, the Babylonians replace both the Assyrians and the Egyptians as the dominant empire (24:1, 7), but Egypt continues to lure Jerusalem into alliance. The collapse of Jerusalem comes in two stages, marked by two rebellions against the Babylonians and two deportations of the citizens of the city. At first, Jehoiakim apparently is able to resist continued control by the Egyptians and allies himself with King Nebuchadnezzar, but within three years he has rebelled against him as well. The narrator describes attacks against Jerusalem by several regional nations (probably agents of the Babylonians), noting that God has "sent" them as punishment, just as the prophets had warned. Jeremiah was one of them. His "temple sermon" warned of exactly what the editor has predicted in 23:27—God was quite capable of destroying the temple

---

163. Replacing the generic name for God with the nickname for Yahweh. It is surprising that he does not make a complete change since both names basically mean "May God raise up," or "establish."

(Jer 7:1–15).[164] Jehoiakim remained unshaken, however; indeed when Jeremiah's scribe read Jeremiah's words to the king, he calmly shredded the document with his penknife and burned it (Jeremiah 36), a classic illustration of denial that contrasts sharply with his father, who shredded his clothes on hearing the Torah.[165] Rather than referring to such an incident, however, our narrator repeats the substance of the judgment against *Manasseh*, and concludes the reign of Jehoiakim (24:3–7).[166]

Jehoiakim's son, Jehoiachin rules for only three months, and when Nebuchadnezzar besieges Jerusalem, Jehoiachin surrenders and is taken captive, along with his mother, servants, and various officials (24:12).[167] Nebuchadnezzar also loots the temple, just as Isaiah had said would happen (20:16–18), and carries into captivity the king and virtually all officials and people of substance, leaving only the very poor (the word for "captivity" or "exile" occurs three times in vv. 13–16). He installs Jehoiachin's paternal uncle as king (see Figure 5), and names him Zedekiah (the name means "Yahweh is just"!), but Jehoiachin will make one final appearance.

The narrator introduces Zedekiah's reign with the usual condemnation, but here spreads the responsibility for Jerusalem's fall to the entire city and people (24:20). We know far more about this period from the book of Jeremiah. A coalition of neighboring states, encouraged by Egypt, conspires to revolt against Babylon and encourages Zedekiah to join them (as does the pro-Egyptian faction in Jerusalem). The agony of such a decision reaches its zenith here, heightened in part by the conflicting advice of Jeremiah and another prophet, Hananiah (see Excursus 7). Jeremiah recommends *not* joining the revolt but remaining loyal to the Babylonians, and even wears a yoke in public to dramatize the submission. Nebuchadnezzar, in fact, is God's "servant" whom Israel must now serve: "serve the king of Babylon and live" (Jer 27:17). Hananiah ridicules submission and recommends sedition. He joins the drama by *breaking* the yoke that Jeremiah wore, and prophesies the defeat of the Babylonians. Zedekiah opts for Hananiah's advice and soon is besieged by Nebuchadnezzar. Zedekiah hopes that God might "perform a wonderful deed for us" and make Nebuchadnezzar withdraw—after all, God has done this before, with Isaiah cheering on (much like Hananiah now!). Jeremiah says that, instead, God is fighting against him; only those who surrender will live (Jer 21:1–10; 38:17). In effect, then, Jeremiah argues against resistance and in favor of surrender to the enemy, especially since the enemy is God's servant! Surrender is the only way

---

164. Jeremiah also employs the "name theology" of the Deuteronomist here, and refers to Shiloh as a precedent for God's destruction of a sanctuary.

165. See 22:11 and Jer 22:11–19 (Shallum is Jehoiakim).

166. He probably died in Jerusalem. Second Chronicles 36:6 reports ambiguously that Nebuchadnezzar captured him and shackled him "to take him to Babylon," but it is not clear if that happened. Cf. Jeremiah's withering comments regarding Jehoikim's ignoble death and lack of burial (Jer 22:18–19).

167. There is some literary ambiguity here in that vv. 10 and 11 seem to be doublets; v. 12 and vv. 14–15 have some repetition, but the former refers to surrender, the latter to exile.

to save the city from being burned to the ground (Jer 38:17). He even writes a letter to those already in exile encouraging them to be resigned to their current situation (Jer 29:1–23).[168] It is no wonder that Hananiah and others accuse Jeremiah of treason and have him imprisoned, threatening his life.[169]

Jeremiah's warnings prove to be all too accurate. Nebuchadnezzar besieges the city to the point of starvation, and in desperation Zedekiah and his soldiers flee by night. The attempted escape is futile, however, because the Babylonian troops easily pursue and capture him, bringing him before Nebuchadnezzar. There is no mercy. Nebuchadnezzar orders the slaughter of Zedekiah's sons, making him watch, and then making it the last thing he sees by blinding him. Zedekiah then is shackled and taken to Babylon. Zedekiah's blind bondage resembles that of Samson, but Zedekiah will have no similar revenge (Judg 16:21–31). Ironically, the last king of Israel leaves the land of Israel from the same place ("the plains of Jericho") that Joshua had led the conquest of the land.[170]

So far Nebuchadnezzar has only dealt with the people of Jerusalem, especially the royalty and high society; now he will deal with the city itself, and especially the temple (25:8–21). The destruction is cataclysmic in Israel's history, which is probably one reason why the narrator suddenly has become a meticulous reporter in terms of temporal sequence, naming each stage by day, month, and year (25:1, 3, 8, 25, and finally v. 27). We almost expect to see the *hour* that things happen.[171] A month after the deportation Nebuchadnezzar's captain arrives and burns the temple, the palace, "and all the houses of Jerusalem." He tears down the city wall, then carries away whatever people were left and any "who had defected to the king of Babylon," again leaving only "some of the poorest people of the land."

The Babylonians (or "Chaldeans") carry much of the contents of the temple to Babylon, especially anything made of bronze, silver, or gold. The narrator even pauses to describe the bronze pillars in considerable detail (25:16–17). The description of the dismantling of the temple is like watching a film of its original construction under Solomon in reverse. The chief priest and his associates, along with various officials, and some sixty others, suffer the fate of Zedekiah's sons: the captain takes them to Nebuchadnezzar at his encampment at Riblah, and he orders their execution. Then the narrator concludes with the

---

168. Jeremiah prophesied not only doom but also hope, as in this letter where he speaks of God's plan for Israel's future. He also bought a piece of land in Israel, something like buying stocks in the midst of the Great Depression.

169. Zedekiah came to his rescue, but not with a great deal of courage. After Jerusalem fell, Nebuchadnezzar protected Jeremiah, but eventually dissidents fleeing to Egypt took him there, probably against his will, where he disappeared from history.

170. Cf. Sweeney, *Kings*, 467, noting also the connections with Josh 6:26 and 1 Kgs 16:34.

171. The temporal language resembles itinerary notices, especially in the Priestly material of the wilderness period (e.g., Exod 16:2; 19:1 and the departure from Horeb, Num 10:11). An even closer analogy would be the temporal references by which Ezekiel marks the departure of God's Glory from the temple (Ezek 1:1; 8:1).

cryptic notice, "So Judah went into exile out of its land" (25:21).[172]

Nebuchadnezzar appoints as governor Gedaliah, the grandson of Shaphan, who we know from the time of Josiah (22:3). Apparently a contingent of military leaders and their troops have escaped the disaster, for they come to see Gedaliah at the town of Mizpah. Gedaliah encourages them not to fear the Chaldeans, but to "live in the land, serve the king of Babylon, and it shall be well with you" (25:24). At least one person had been listening to Jeremiah's sermons. But Gedaliah is no more popular than the prophet, and he is assassinated by a member of the royal family, who then flee to Egypt. Indeed, in one of those exaggerated demographic comments, the narrator says that "all the people" go to Egypt, thus reversing the entire course of Israel's history as a nation.[173] They have fled in fear away from the homeland that God had promised they would never leave again (21:8); indeed, they have returned to the place where the book of Genesis *ends*—"in Egypt"—seemingly joining Joseph in his coffin (Gen 50:26). Indeed, since the rest of the people are in Babylon, the "land of the Chaldeans," Israel is split into pre-Abrahamic and pre-Exodus parts (cf. Gen 11:31—12:1). In terms of American history, it would be like returning to "pre-Columbian" time.[174]

The narrator now turns to a moment thirty-seven years later and the setting of King Jehoichin in exile, when the new king of Babylon has released him from prison:

> he spoke kindly to him, and gave him a seat above the other seats of the kings who were with him in Babylon. So Jehoiachin put aside his prison clothes. Every day of his life he dined regularly in the king's presence. For his allowance, a regular allowance was given him by the king, a portion every day, as long as he lived.

In the Summary and Conclusion of this book, we will look at how we might interpret this ending—is it one of hope, or one of despair? Is Jehoiachin's position promising or simply pathetic? Is he the end of the Davidic dynasty? The report of his deportation mentioned his mother and servants, but nothing about sons. What has happened to Zedekiah? His sons are all dead. Shall we assume that he has died also? The vague reference to Ishmael, literally "from the seed of the kingdom" (25:25), does not tell us anything more about him and, in any event, he too has fled to Egypt. Perhaps it is mere coincidence that he bears the name of the rejected son of Abraham who married an Egyptian (Gen 16:8–21).

Has the end come, indeed?

---

172. It is possible that this is the last line in one edition of the Deuteronomistic history, with the rest as additions (vv. 22–26 and 27–30).

173. Cf. Nelson, *Kings*, 263–64; Campbell and O'Brien, *Unfolding*, 466b.

174. As will see in the Summary and Conclusion, the author of vv. 22–26 may be a proponent of the "myth of the empty land," in which only those exiled to Babylon are *true* Israelites (or better now, Jews). Quite possibly, Palestine was no more empty at this point than America would have been had all the European colonists withdrawn!

Summary and Conclusion

"By the waters of Babylon"

On January 22, 2010, shortly after the devastating earthquake in Haiti, many celebrities from the film, music, and television industries presented a television benefit concert. The program consisted of musical performances and brief appeals for donations, along with film clips of the disaster and many uplifting stories of rescues. Some of the musical pieces were well known songs that took on a special meaning in context: "We Shall Overcome," "Sometimes I Feel Like a Motherless Child," "Bridge over Troubled Water." The last group of musicians was Haitian, and they began their set with another song, perhaps less familiar: "Rivers of Babylon": "By the rivers of Babylon, there we sat down / And there we wept when we remember Zion."[1] The folksong is based on Psalm 137, a lament reflecting the sorrow of the exiles in Babylon.[2] Here is an example of how an ancient story of a particular people at a particular time can become a story for all peoples and for all time. It is what makes a text "Scripture" and not just an historical document. Here was a group of singers and musicians, ultimately of African descent, many of them the offspring of former slaves, singing an ancient song composed by the descendants of former slaves in Africa (Egypt) who, though defeated and in exile, yet could "sing the Lord's song." The irony is even deeper for the ancient Israelites of the Former Prophets, whose larger story began on the eastern banks of the Jordan River and ended on the banks of the rivers of Babylon. That story sought to show how captivity was a punishment for the sin of abandoning the very Lord whose song they were singing. Yet, for the Haitians, captivity and exile could function as a metaphor for people who had no reason to identify with the sin in order to sing the song.[3] In fact, the

---

1. For one version, see Blood-Patterson, *Rise Up Singing*, 63.

2. The psalm contains some of the most bitter and hateful words of Scripture, invoking God's wrath against Israel's enemies, and applauding avengers who would dash their babies against the rock—an unmitigated venting of powerlessness, rage, and despair. However much we may recoil from such language, we must recognize the realism behind it. See below.

3. It would be interesting to know if any Haitians believed the earthquake to be a divine pun-

singers could be the *victims* of the sin of others (especially slavery), or the victims of a natural disaster (the earthquake), and still find in the story of ancient Israel a basis for interpreting their own story in the midst of calamity. The singing of that story—even as it refers to weeping, indeed, *because* it expresses *grief*—became a song of hope.

The Haitian identification with ancient Israel's story of captivity is hardly unique. Just as English Pilgrims crossing the Atlantic to America saw themselves as a "new Israel" crossing the Red Sea, so they also could identify with exiles who yearned to "make haste out of Babylon."[4] Every year during Advent many Christians sing the hymn, "O Come, O Come, Emmanuel, and ransom captive Israel, that mourns in lonely exile here." Every *day* there is someone who could sing the opening line of "The Haven of Rest": "My soul in sad exile was out on life's sea, so burdened with sin and distress." It is largely because of ancient Israel's wrestling with the theological and spiritual implications of their Babylonian exile that the very word "exile" came to signify far more than the political phenomenon of military defeat and deportation—devastating as that was and is. "Exile" became a symbol of alienation, but also of hope in the midst of despair. Thus the late theologian, preacher, and social activist, William Sloane Coffin, could say, "So where then in America does God dwell today? I would say that God dwells with those in America who feel geographically at home and spiritually in exile."[5] Coffin was probably reflecting his experience in various social movements—above all, opposition to the Vietnam War—experience that placed him among the dissenting prophets of his time. Thus, the way the Former Prophets ends, ironically, became the fertile ground for countless subsequent readers of the story: not in success but in failure; not in victory, but in defeat; not in arrogance, but in humiliation—and yet, not in despair, but, ultimately, in hope.

But, of course, all that is true only because the end of the Former Prophets did not spell the end of Israel. On the contrary, the end proved to be a new beginning of Israel in many ways, some of which we will explore in the following pages. But at the outset we need to recognize the simple yet astonishing fact that Israel still exists, not just in the *land* of Israel as a sovereign nation, but also as a community, the Jews, who are spread around the world, and who, of course, gave birth to another religious community, the Christians. In a famous exchange, King Louis XIV of France once asked the philosopher, Blaise Pascal, to give him a proof of the existence of God, and Pascal said, "Why, the Jews, your Majesty, the Jews." We might at least call Israel's endurance proof of the "Merneptah fallacy," a refutation of the claim of that thirteenth-century-BCE Pharaoh, in the

---

ishment, as such a natural disaster clearly is in biblical religion, e.g., Amos 4:6–10 and possibly 1:1. In the Former Prophets, drought often plays such a role.

4. The title of the book by Nick Bunker from which I have quoted a number of times. He is quoting from a document from 1629.

5. Coffin, *Credo*, 85. Some would label the clergy on the other side as "false prophets," comparing them to Jeremiah's opponent Hananiah (those who proclaimed peace when there was no peace, Jer 6:14), or Amos's (priestly) opponent, Amaziah.

earliest recorded evidence of Israel's historical existence, when he boasted, "Israel is laid waste, his seed is not."[6] It was not the last such claim to be proved wrong—including some with ancient Israel as the victor—but it is surely the most glaring.[7] Although I quoted the prophet Amos in entitling the last chapter above—"the end has come"—even this message of divine judgment proved to be equivocal.

If it is indisputable that Israel did not end when the Former Prophets ends, how we should understand the ending of that *narrative* is just the opposite—*highly* disputable. King Jehoichin is released from prison and dining at the table of the King of Babylon, looking much like the rather pathetic figure of Mephibosheth, as some have pointed out.[8] If the latter represents the end of the Saulide dynasty, does Jehoiachin indicate the end of the Davidic? What has happened to the promise of an "eternal" throne for David (2 Sam 7:13–17)? Similarly, what are we to make of the destruction of Jerusalem and the temple on Mt. Zion, where God's name was supposed to dwell forever (1 Kgs 9:3; 2 Kgs 21:7)? God had threatened to "wipe Jerusalem as one wipes a dish" (2 Kgs 21:13), but has God broken the dish as well? In short, the ending of the Former Prophets can be read in diametrically opposite ways. On the one hand, a Davidic king survives and seems to be treated with respect by his captors—a sign of hope. On the other hand, there is no indication here that the Davidic *dynasty* will survive after Jehoichin is gone—a sign of resignation, if not despair. The editor has given us a report without commentary. Brueggemann puts it wryly: the ending "does not speak clearly about either termination or possibility, a fact made clear by the remarkably energetic scholarly dispute on the passage."[9]

Looking beyond the Former Prophets, for a moment, we can see that *historically* the Davidic line eventually disintegrates, something like a "fade-out" in a film or sound recording. Of course, Jehoichin was not the only Davidic ruler in exile—he apparently had Uncle Zedekiah for company. But there is no mention of Zedekiah at the end of the Former Prophets, nor do we hear anything of his fate.[10] We do learn from the book of Chronicles that Jehoiachin's grandson, Zerubbabel, survived the exile and returned to Palestine, and that the Persian emperor appointed him as a district governor. But he will prove to be a disappointment to those who might have thought him to be the new David, and we do not know anything about his

---

6. *ANET*, 378. He includes others in his list of victories, most recognizably Canaan, Ashkelon, and Gezer. See n. 39 in chap. 1.

7. Thus, centuries later, Mesha would make the same claim: "Israel utterly perished forever"; Jackson, "Mesha Inscription," 97. We have noted numerous examples of supposed annihilation, only to find the town alive and well later: Jabesh-gilead (Judg 21:10–11; 1 Samuel 11); the Amalekites (1 Sam 15:8; 27:9; 30:1). Of course, Hitler's attempt to exterminate the Jews makes Merneptah's boast seem almost trivial. See below.

8. Polzin, *David*, 103–4; Gunn and Fewell, *Narrative*, 168–69; Birch, *1 and 2 Samuel*, 1276.

9. Brueggemann, *Kings*, 579. Jeremiah prophesied that "none of his offspring shall succeed in sitting on the throne of David, and ruling again in Judah" (22:24–30).

10. Ezek 34:23 may refer to both Jehoiachin and Zedekiah as concurrent Davidic descendants and the future appointment of only one "shepherd," here also using the old term "prince."

death, nor learn of any descendant who might claim to be a political successor. In short, retrospective from a later time, we know that Jehoiachin is, in effect, "the demise of the house of David as the ruling monarchy of Israel/Judah in Jerusalem."[11] But the narrative at the end of the Former Prophets does not make such a death pronouncement, which is surprising in itself since the narrator previously had declared Jehoiachin to be among those kings who "did what was evil" (24:9). When we look at Jehoichin here in the Babylonian king's dining room, we see that at least there is the *possibility* that the Davidic line will continue. The narrator has not chosen to repeat God's promise of *always* leaving a "lamp" for David,[12] but he hasn't said that the lamp is completely snuffed out either. In the end, God has not broken the promise of an eternal dynasty with David, even if the condition of punishing offenses is in the extreme (again, 2 Sam 7:13–16).[13] In fact, as we shall see more fully below, the Davidic *ideal* would blossom under the rubric of the "Messiah," i.e., the Anointed, as did the figure of Zion.

The reader may well be surprised that no Deuteronomic editor has given us a lengthy sermon at the end, much like that at the fall of northern Israel (2 Kings 17). But it is not as if we have not been warned of the outcome, or informed of the reasons. Overall, the Former Prophets is a theodicy. The term was coined by the eighteenth-century philosopher Leibnitz, based on the Greek words for God (*theos*) and "order, justice" (*dike*). Essentially, a theodicy attempts to justify God's governance of the world in the face of the existence of evil. In short, it attempts to show how God is good despite how bad everything else is. The Former Prophets is a theodicy in that it attempts to show how God is good despite all the evil that has consumed Israel. God was justified in punishing Israel because Israel repeatedly disobeyed God's commandments. The disaster that has overwhelmed Israel is Israel's fault.

Before we look at the problems with such a theodicy—and they are considerable—let us recognize the strengths. The Former Prophets is remarkably honest in *acknowledging* Israel's faults. Although there are certainly moments of national pride, especially regarding the expansion of the Davidic empire, even those celebrations are juxtaposed to passages that expose the shortcomings of both the people and their leaders. Thus David's rise to power leads into the *abuse* of that power in David's adultery with Bathsheba and the murder of

---

11. Sweeney, *I & II Kings*, 464–65.

12. 1 Kgs 11:36; 15:4; 2 Kgs 8:19, reverting to the traditional translation for rhetorical purposes (otherwise, "fief"). Cf. Halpern, *First Historians*, 59: the exilic Deuteronomist "need only have adopted the strategy of 1 Samuel 2:27–36 and rejected an eternal covenant to avoid all contradiction; yet he did not."

13. A monarch may still be vested with authority even when in exile, as numerous modern rulers have demonstrated. Thus Halpern, *First Historians*, 158 (cf. 219), insists that the end of 2 Kings is hopeful, and that there is never any previous indication that God's unconditional dynastic promise to David is broken, even though punishment includes the loss of the Northern tribes (1 Kgs 11:11–13) and the fall of Jerusalem. Thus, he argues, the exilic Deuteronomist still held to the doctrine of the unconditional covenant. Halpern's view stands in stark opposition to Polzin's negative view of the monarchy.

Uriah, actions that the narrator explicitly condemns as "evil" in the eyes of God (2 Sam 11:27b). Moreover, the expansion of his empire entailed the violence of warfare against neighboring nations, including such details as the calculated execution of prisoners of war (2 Sam 8:2), and the administration of that empire required the conscription of forced labor among his own people, a practice that would eventually lead to the secession of the North (2 Sam 20:24; 1 Kings 12). But David is simply one piece of clothing in a multitudinous display of dirty linen, strung out on almost every page of the narrative, from Joshua to the end of Kings, with the book of Judges, perhaps, winning the prize for the most horrific. And then, of course, the story ends in defeat and failure. Throughout, there are no "good guys" who are uniformly "good," none whom we can lift up as unimpeachable.[14] The characters inhabit the real world where mixed motivations make it difficult if not impossible to discern when a character is acting out of a genuine concern for the common good (not to mention according to Gods' will) or out of craven self-interest. Nowhere is such ambiguity more apparent than in the figure of the Lord's "Anointed," the Messiah, who as David is both Messianic murderer and the one close to God's heart. This moral ambiguity of the characters often provides a biblical illustration of the basic argument of a theologian like Reinhold Niebuhr, who warned against the facile and dangerously false distinction between the "children of light" and the "children of darkness."[15]

Arguably, composing and preserving such a history is ancient Israel's greatest gift to the discipline of historiography, especially *theological* historiography. Both ancient and contemporary history clearly show that the greatest danger is not the nation that sees itself as subject to God's judgment against hubris and injustice, and at times even suffering for that, but rather the nation that sees itself as a completely autonomous power, answerable to no higher authority, for it acknowledges none, responsible for no one's welfare other than its own (or only the elite within it). The greatest failure is the refusal or inability to *acknowledge* failure. Historiography is not only the domain of professional historians or theologians, but the burden that falls to all people who want to understand *truly* their own history within the framework of their religious beliefs. One wonders if Americans in general (i.e., *North* Americans) are capable of such historiography (and they are certainly not unique in this inadequacy). As I suggested in the Introduction, ancient Israel's historians did not hesitate to say "God curse Israel" as well as "God bless Israel," but we never hear an American

14. Historically, at least, we would have to include even Josiah in this, in that some of his religious reform, and much of the Deuteronomistic history written by his proponents, was clearly motivated by political self-interest.

15. See his book, *The Children of Light*. Niebuhr bases his thought in the simple observation that "the same man who is ostensibly devoted to the 'common good' may have desires and ambitions, hopes and fears, which set him at variance with his neighbor" (11). Similarly, the central point of Niebuhr's book *The Irony of American History* "is that our virtues and our vices are inextricably joined" (Elie, "Man for All Reasons," 88b). Cf. Tran, *Vietnam War*, 8: "the suggestion that responsibility demands heroism often produces atrocity in the guise of heroism."

version of the former. To anticipate a key word in our discussion below, one can argue, for example, that Americans by and large have refused to "remember" the Vietnam disaster in a way that honestly acknowledges our culpability.[16] Current events reveal deeper amnesia. As Paul Elie points out, Reinhold Niebuhr saw that America has to struggle with how to distinguish between "the courageous and the foolish uses of . . . power."[17] Elie argues that, in fact, we have failed to remember how the biblical story of Israel informed our own history from the outset: "[Biblical] history acts as a restraint on national pride, not a stimulant to it, for it is not merely history, but in some sense *our* history, a story that cannot but be a cautionary tale, for it tells us who we are and what we are prone to do." And then comes Elie's dismal assessment of where we are (in October, 2007): "The war in Iraq, and the debates about the war, suggest that this history is now lost to us."[18]

For Israel, of course, the nation pledged allegiance to a "higher power," and the model for that polity was primarily the treaty relationship between the suzerain and the vassal (see Excursus 1). As a theodicy, the Former Prophets presupposes that model, paradigmatically expressed in the book of Deuteronomy. Yahweh is the Lord of the covenant, who has imposed stipulations on Israel as Yahweh's "servant," and will reward obedience with blessing, but punish disobedience with curse. At the same time, the Former Prophets presupposes a theology common to the ancient Near East, attested in the Moabite Stone, as we have seen (2 Kings 3). Human defeat does not signify defeat of one's god; rather, it signifies *abandonment* by one's god because of the nation's offenses ("sins"), and abandonment may be represented by the abduction of the god's emblem. Indeed, a nation's god may be the ultimate *agent* behind the defeat of that nation. I have often referred to Isaiah's metaphor of Assyria as the "rod of God's anger" as an example of this theology (Isa 10:5). The ark story in 1 Samuel reflects this paradigm, as well as its ironic reversal. At the end of the Former Prophets, however, there is no reversal in sight (and the ark has disappeared forever—see further below).

The treaty model is of enduring significance precisely because of its political nature: divine sovereignty trumps all others, even if one of the others is God's appointed leader. Thus the treaty model inherently subverts not only foreign powers (like Assyria), but also one's own nation. No nation or power is inviolable; all are subject to defeat and humiliation. This principle of subversion is at the heart of the prophetic heritage, although it seems that some prophets had trouble

---

16. Cf. Tran, *Vietnam War*, 176: "That America has still no idea of how to remember Vietnam underlines the reality that America has not yet and probably will never come to terms with it, which presages an unenviable future for those who killed in Vietnam."

17. Elie, "Man for All Reasons," 94. As Brueggemann, *Kings*, 500, points out, "It may be that our reading in the U.S. should pay attention not to the destiny of Israel but to the fate of Assyria," which, after all, was one of the "super powers" of its time.

18. Elie, "Man for All Reasons," 96. A recent poll of Americans in their 20s and 30s reveals that forty percent of them do not even know what country we separated from to become the United States of America.

applying it to themselves! Extended to the social or personal level, God's sovereignty also subverts any competing value, ideology, ethnic identity, or lifestyle. This is why I quoted at some length from the sermon by John Winthrop at the outset, for he compares the English colonists arriving in America with ancient Israel, and warns of the corrupting dangers of worshipping "other Gods, our pleasures, and proffitts." Winthrop seemed to be remarkably prescient in anticipating the "other god" that we now call "consumerism."

If the treaty model, along with divine abandonment, provides a healthy dose of self-criticism and humility, however, both create considerable problems, again in relation to the Former Prophets as theodicy. Here we will focus on Israel's covenant theology. A theology with an historically involved God is quite different from a theology in which God is not so involved. The latter often appears in various types of religion that do not like to be called religious, and that focus on individual "spiritual development." Israel's understanding of God as intimately involved in historical, and therefore political, events, inevitably got God into trouble—quite literally. As we have seen, the word (*ra'ah*) that the NRSV sometimes translates as "trouble" literally means "evil" (just so in the RSV). Thus when Nathan tells David that God will "raise up trouble" against him (2 Sam 12:11), we could translate "raise up evil," especially since *God's* action is a *reaction* to *David's* "evil," as previously noted (11:27b). The evil that ensues, of course, includes Amnon's rape of Tamar, Absalom's murder of Amnon, then Absalom's alienation from David, leading to his political revolt, civil war, and Absalom's death, along with the death of twenty thousand soldiers. In effect, this story, contained in 2 Samuel 11–18, is the theodicy of the Former Prophets writ small.

But what exactly is the relationship between David's "evil" and the "evil" that God inflicts upon him and his family? One obvious reading of the story suggests that everything unfolds because of the attitudes and actions of the human characters. We can understand the dynamics in terms of dysfunctional interpersonal relationships, especially involving the members of David's family, without needing to invoke God's involvement. Sometimes the narrator will hint of such a reading, as when telling us that David "would not punish his son Amnon, because he loved him, for he was his firstborn" (2 Sam 13:21; cf. v. 39). In such a reading, what happens is simply a result of human faults (e.g., "permissive" parenting); the "evil" that happens is a consequence of the "evil" things that people do. Thus we have noted the proverb, "The perverse get what their ways deserve" (Prov 14:14). This is simply the way the world works.

On the other hand, the narrator at times will tell us that God is imposing "evil" on the characters as a *punishment* for their wrongdoing. In the case of Nathan's judgment oracle, the narrator clearly thinks that all the "evil" that ensues is *not* simply a consequence of human faults but something enacted by God. Here another proverb operates: God will "repay all according to their deeds" (Prov 24:12).[19] Here "evil" does not simply arise as a result of human interactions; God *raises up* "evil" to *punish* human sin. So insistent is the narrator on this punitive understanding of "evil" that the realism of the psycho-dynamic role of consequences is lost, and it seems that the human characters are *not* acting out of their own free will. Although I have used the incidents with David's family here as an example, we have seen the problem repeatedly and sometimes quite sharply. God is made the subject of all sorts of horrendous acts of "evil," and the difficulty is easily muted when we translate the word as "trouble" or "calamity." Surely the most salient example of the problem occurred in the story of Saul, where *his* troubles were not simply the result of psychological or even spiritual disorders—his jealousy and paranoia, for example—but the result of God's "evil spirit," a phrase that is arresting in its implications (1 Sam 16:14). Less severe, but still creating the same problem, are passages like the narrator's comment on the refusal of Eli's sons to listen to his admonitions and mend their ways, "for it was the will of Yahweh to kill them" (1 Sam 2:25). Similarly, the death of Abimelech happens because "God repaid Abimelech for the crime he committed," just as "God also repaid all the evil of the men of Shechem" (Judg 9:56–57, AT).

In at least some of these situations, the narrator might well respond by saying, the two ostensibly different ways of understanding "evil"-for-"evil" are really simply two sides of the same coin in that act and consequence is a sequence that God makes sure to happen. The Hebrew for the word "repay" in the examples above literally means "to cause to return," suggesting that God is the agent behind the otherwise apparently automatic process in which human acts have their consequences.[20] We say "what goes around comes around," but God is the one who turns the steering wheel. On the other hand, the role of God's "evil spirit" with Saul seems quite different in that it is only loosely connected with Saul's previous alleged offenses. Saul is "driven" and God is the driver.

The ambiguity of "evil"-for-"evil" plays out on the national and international levels as well as the personal level, of course—indeed, this is the heart of the theodicy. The secession of the North is a good example. On the one hand, we saw that we could understand that event in purely political and sociological terms—the North seceded because Rehoboam of Judah would not lighten the load of taxation and forced labor that Solomon had initiated. On the other hand, the narrator frames the secession with God's direct condemnation of

---

19. Literally "he will return to a human (*'adam*) according to his deeds," thus implying that such recompense is not limited to Israel. See below on "return."

20. See Campbell, "God's Anger," 376: "this natural process, the intrinsic link of act and consequence, was understood in the O.T. as part of the dispensation of God's providence, inherent in the order of creation." Cf. more recently, *Of Prophets and Kings*, 166 and n. 49. Here we may repeat a comment by Birch regarding 1 Samuel 4: "the death Hophni and Phinehas *bring upon themselves* is *from God* because God will not rescue them from the *consequences* of *their own sin*" ("1 and Samuel," 989, my italics). Fokkelman, *King David*, 159, compares the Indian understanding of *karma*, "the psychic and spiritual bond of cause and effect in our lives," referring here to David and Bathsheba and all that unfolds following that.

Solomon's sin in marrying foreign women and worshipping their gods; the secession is God's punishment for that sin. Here the treaty model comes prominently to the fore: Solomon has not kept the covenant and its statutes (1 Kgs 11:11). Moreover, that prediction is followed by the scene in which the prophet Ahijah announces to Jeroboam that he will be the agent of God's punishment (11:31). Yet again, the narrator tells us that Rehoboam "did not listen to the people" of the North "because it was a turn of affairs brought about by the Lord," to fulfill the words just spoken by Ahijah (11:15). Rehoboam, like Eli's sons, is deaf because God's hands are over his ears. International events display the same tension. On the one hand, we can easily understand the various conquests and extortions of tribute by powers like the Assyrians as their normal way of operating—this is how aggressive empires work. Just so, Judah and Israel's various submissions and defeats were the consequences of foolish foreign policies (as prophets like Hosea and Jeremiah pointed out). On the other hand, we have the understanding of these political and military actions as punishments inflicted by God, again using the metaphor of the "rod of God's anger."

Clearly, the tension between "evil"-as-consequence and "evil"-as-punishment is inseparable from that between historical events as effected by the human characters and as effected by the will of God—the phenomenon that I have often referred to as "co-operation."[21]

The actions of characters, and, in fact, of nations, seem to take place quite naturally, independent of divine involvement. The book of Ruth displays the clearest example, where the interactions of the characters take place without any intervention from God until Ruth gets pregnant. But other examples abound: Samson pursues his women and brawls with the Philistines; Eli's sons defile their priestly status with greed and lust; Saul swings back and forth between doting admiration and murderous jealousy for David; Absalom's motivations include filial rebellion, political aspirations, fraternal hatred, and a large dose of vanity; Hushai foils Absalom's initial military strategy with shrewdly misleading counsel; Rehoboam foolishly follows the advice of the best and brightest boys, not the wise elder statesmen. Yet, at the same time, the narrator tells us that Samson's amorous desire is "from the Lord," part of a divine plan to defeat the Philistines (Judg 14:4); that Eli's sons are adamant in their recklessness because God wants to kill them (1 Sam 2:25); that Saul's bizarre, bipolar behavior results from God's tortuous, malevolent "evil spirit;" that Absalom's rampage in his family is God's doing, and that Hushai's success is really "ordained" by God (2 Sam 17:14); and finally that Rehoboam's fatal decision is "brought about by the Lord" (1 Kgs 12:15). On the international scene, the Assyrian King Sennacherib boasts of all his mighty acts, but they were all sim-

---

21. For various construals of co-operation, see Gottwald, *Politics*, 251–52 and n. 6; Brueggemann, *Kings*, 391, 586. Referring to David's return from Mahanaim, Fokkelman, *King David*, 187 (cf. 191, 193), says "David's return is entirely the work of God and at the same time entirely the work of David himself . . . Synergism here makes a unity of the two factors."

ply the working out of God's plan (2 Kgs 19:23–25). Even though interpreters have often contrasted the religion of ancient Israel with that of classical Greece by insisting that the notion of "fate" in the latter is missing from the former, such passages as the aforementioned seem to belie the difference. Thus people seem to act out of their own free will, but at the same time people are blamed for doing things that God seems to have made them do. God and people "*co-operate*," even when the people are totally unaware of God's hand at work. Gunn poses the tension in terms of "the tragedy of Fate and the tragedy of the character flaw": while they may seem logically incompatible, they are not so aesthetically; as Scott Fitzgerald said about artists, the biblical author is "one who can hold two irreconcilable views together and still function."[22]

As I have pointed out at numerous places, all of these key texts, and others, raise enormous questions about human freedom vs. fate and the relationship between the human will and God's will. The characters never appear to be mere puppets that God manipulates, and yet, ultimately, it is God who "holds the strings." God is involved in the unfolding events, yet invisibly so, much the way the Psalmist describes God's victorious presence at the Red Sea, but adds "your footprints were unseen" (Ps 77:19). The result is an unresolved tension, but ultimately the two "operators" (as it were) do not enjoy equal control—ultimately, the editors insist that *God* is in control, and that history bends according to God's will. Hamlet would have agreed: "There's a divinity that shapes our ends, / Rough-hew them how we will."[23]

When the editors of the Former Prophets insist that God is in control of history, they are emphasizing the sovereignty of God at the risk of questioning the morality of God. Unfortunately, if God is in control, God has a lot of explaining to do. Many of the examples above illustrate the problem. When God punishes the sons of Eli by means of the Philistine war, there is a lot of collateral damage—i.e., the death of many people for no fault of their own. One of the worst instances is the bloody, fanatical "reform" of Jehu, which the narrator—speaking for God—applauds: "you have done well in carrying out what I consider right, and in accordance with all that was in my heart" (2 Kgs 10:30). One can argue that God does not determine the *means* that bring about God's will, but the examples above show how fine the dividing line can be. Here, as with the horrors of "holy war" in Joshua, we should not smooth over the theological problem, but should be willing to say, God does *not* operate this way.[24]

22. Gunn, *Fate of King Saul*, 31.

23. William Shakespeare, *Hamlet*, V.ii.10–11. Cf. Nelson, *Kings*, 23: "In all that follows, Yahweh will be in complete control of events. The will of God powers the dramatic action of the Book of Kings, and the plan of God shapes the course of its plot."

24. Nelson, *Kings*, 129, can say that: "In some mysterious way, God's will stands behind even such butchers as Jehu and Hazael." "God is in charge even of the dark side" of events (22), and God "brushes aside ethical niceties to effect the divine purpose" (153). "For God (and only God) the ends do justify the means" (153). It does not seem to me that Nelson's appeal to a theology of the cross (22, 206) helps here.

The above discussion of "evil" as consequence or punishment may have left the incorrect impression that it is always obviously one or the other, if not a combination of both. But reality is far messier than that. Often there is no clear reason why "evil" in the sense of "calamity," "trouble," or "disaster," has happened. The problem is particularly acute with respect to individual people when trouble comes to them inexplicably, neither as a consequence of their own fault, nor as a punishment from God for their own sin. It is when bad things happen to good people that theodicy meets its greatest test. Azariah of Judah does everything right (except for preserving the high places) but God strikes him with leprosy (2 Kgs 15:1–5). Jeroboam II did everything wrong (like his namesake, Jeroboam I), but he enjoyed a long reign of prosperity for forty years. Not to be outdone, Manasseh, who excelled everyone in depravity, enjoyed the longest reign of any king!

The problem of undeserved suffering is compounded when people suffer for the sins of someone else, frequently their parents. As we have seen, the Ten Commandments state that God will punish sin to the third and fourth generation, whereas other texts condemn such punishment, at least when meted out by humans (Deut 5:9; 7:10; 24:16; Ezek 18:2). Nevertheless, there are numerous incidences in which God does what humans are forbidden to do. Precedent was set already when Achan's family had to die along with him (Joshua 7). Saul's sons and grandsons have to die to assuage God's anger over Saul's "bloodguilt" (2 Samuel 21). God strikes dead David's and Bathsheba's first child (2 Sam 12:15–18).[25] Gehazi's descendants will have leprosy forever (2 Kgs 5:27). Especially in the books of Kings, the punishment for one king's offenses may be postponed and visited upon his descendants: Rehoboam loses the united monarchy because of Solomon's offenses (1 Kgs 11:12). Ahab, that apparent arch-villain, presents a variation: because he repents after hearing Elijah's oracle of judgment, God postpones the "disaster" (again, literally "evil") to "his sons days" (1 Kgs 21:29). Of course, the entire history of northern Israel is a version of this transference of punishment in that Israel eventually suffers because of the sins of Jeroboam I, a fate which one editor announces before Jeroboam's reign is over (1 Kgs 14:15–16), even though elsewhere the people also are at fault (e.g., 2 Kgs 17:7–18). By far the most awkward example of transferred punishment comes with the premature death of Josiah, whose piety and reforms ought to have earned him a long and happy life (as well as Judah's prosperity), but, instead, his reward looks more like the "wages of sin." The darling of the Deuteronomists dies in a way completely at odds with orthodox Deuteronomic theology, an apparent victim of curse rather than the recipient of blessing.

We have seen two attempts to explain Josiah's death. One editor insists that Josiah's death is the delayed divine punishment for the sins of Manasseh (2 Kgs 23:26–30; 24:3)—Josiah suffered for the sins of his grandfather. The Chronicler escapes the theological prob-

---

25. Campbell, *Joshua to Chronicles*, 164, says of God's killing David's son, "the text's theology explaining it is unspeakable."

lem by blaming Josiah for not obeying "the word of [Pharaoh] Neco from the mouth of God" (2 Chr 35:22).[26] Neither the Manasseh solution ("sour grapes," cf. Ezek 18:2; Jer 31:29) nor the Neco solution ("blame the victim") can bear the weight of Josiah's death. In the end, the system of rewards and punishments that seems to work in theory does not work in practice. The Deuteronomic editors may insist on the truth of the system, especially in the book of Deuteronomy, but they have included within the narrative numerous instances in which the system not only fails, but seems to be reversed—where good things happen to bad people and bad things happen to good people. Reflecting on the problem of Josiah, Nelson puts it this way: "God's ways are more complex than a simple application of the principle that apostasy leads to punishment and reform to reward."[27]

The Chronicler's faulting of Josiah, not just for poor political decisions but for disobeying the word of God, is an example of one voice that simply refuses to see the crack in the system. Such faulting also illustrates the major problem that arises when one moves from the national level to the personal, from the corporate to the individual. We must remember that the covenant model is a political model of God based on ancient Near Eastern treaties between states and rulers. As such it has its strengths (e.g., emphasizing God's sovereignty), but also its weaknesses (as does *every* model).[28] Forcing such a model to apply to an individual person's experience is like fitting a square peg into a round hole. The problem is most evident when "calamity" of any kind is understood to mean that the person has sinned somehow. Other biblical authors will probe the problem in various ways. Job will mount a spirited defense of himself as an innocent sufferer, or at least one whose faults are totally disproportionate to the massive suffering in his life, even though one of his so-called friends will insist that he must have done something wrong to deserve the calamities that have engulfed him. Ecclesiastes will

---

26. The move is the reverse of ascribing David's census idea to "the satan," thereby getting God off the hook (1 Chr 21:1). There is no parallel to the eulogy of 2 Kgs 23:26, although the Chronicler does tell us that he "did what was right in the sight of the Lord, and walked in the ways of his ancestor David; he did not turn aside to the right or to the left," the last phrase also echoing the charge to Joshua (Josh 1:7). We also hear of the prophet Jeremiah composing a lament, and of other public laments (2 Chr 35:25), perhaps a reference to the poem in Jer 22:13–17 noted above.

27. Nelson, *Kings*, 252; cf. 268. Cf. Polzin, *Samuel*, 146: "human repentance, however good and necessary, does not limit God's freedom to act, however mysteriously, in ways that do not correspond to human understandings of mercy" (cf. 141–42, 160, 198).

28. See McFague, *Models of God*, and her other, more recent works, focusing on ecological models, including God as mother, lover, and friend. The parental model works along with the social model of kinship ("brothers"/"sisters"). In his struggle to describe God's grace that overrides God's judgment, Hosea resorted to a parental image, albeit a "holy one" (Hosea 11). Ecological models could help to correct some of the theological problems that have accompanied the exclusive focus on God as one who "acts in history," thus implicitly excluding God from the realm of nature. On this, cf. Smith, *Memoirs*, 162, where he looks at Psalm 104 and its creation language of "ecological balance and harmonious order" as a "sacramental," "nonhierarchical paradigm" for theology.

ask if, in fact, the whole merit system of rewards for the good and punishment for the wicked is simply not the way things are (especially Eccles 8:10–17).

We should not, however, dismiss out of hand the notion of an individual or even an entire nation suffering for the sin of others, especially ancestors, simply because it is universally true. For many people, the connection is most obvious in the setting of the family, where children do, in fact, suffer for the sins of their parents. Some people bear the scars of parental abuse (both physical and verbal) all of their lives. (David and his family are by no means unique!) And on a national level, one need only think of American history and the results of the evil of slavery in perpetual racial animosity and injustice.

> *If we shall suppose that American Slavery is one of those offences which, in the providence of God, must needs come, but which, having continued through His appointed time, He now wills to remove, and that He gives to both North and South, this terrible war, as the woe due to those by whom the offence came, shall we discern therein any departure from those divine attributes which the believers in a Living God always ascribe to Him?*
> —Abraham Lincoln, Second Inaugural Address[29]

> *Don't you see? This whole land, the whole South, is cursed, and all of us who derive from it, whom it ever suckled, white and black both, lie under the curse? Granted that my people [whites] brought the curse on the land: maybe for that reason their descendants alone can—not resist it, not combat it—maybe just endure and outlast it until the curse is lifted.*
> —Ike McCaslin, in William Faulkner's Go Down, Moses[30]

Still, even on the national level, for all the humbling benefits of seeing a nation as under God's judgment as well as enjoying God's grace, any simplistic equation of national disaster with divine punishment is theologically perilous.[31] Most of the examples of this equation in the Former Prophets have been military disasters, the Exile being the most devastating. The same peril appears in the common equation of divine punishment with *natural* disasters such as earthquakes, or drought, or floods. It would be callous as well as

---

29. Quoted in Lundin, *Voices from the Heart*, 175.

30. Modern Library edition, 278. Cf. the remarks of Brueggemann, *Kings*, 182–83 on the effects of slavery in America. Some historians have noted that (at least until Vietnam), the American South was the only part of the country to have experienced defeat and devastation sufficient to require "Reconstruction." Cf. Tran, *Vietnam War*, 238 (on Tony Morrison's *Beloved*): "One may presume slavery simply a thing of the past, a past now dead and buried—a view standard to white *and* black Americans . . . to one's own detriment, because the past refused to submit to our settled arrangements with time, instead invading every present and threatening every future."

31. Cf. Sweeney, *I & II Kings*, 456.

wrong to tell those Haitians with whom we began that they deserved the earthquake because their leaders and their people had sinned against God.³² As for contemporary warfare, it is easy to condemn the Nazi soldiers' use of the phrase "Gott Mit Uns" ("God With Us") on their uniform belts, given the massive evil perpetrated by Hitler; and some may find it easy, on the other hand, to affirm that God was on the side of the Allies. But then there is the firebombing of Dresden and, of course, Hiroshima. Moreover, other conflicts plunge us into even deeper ambiguity. Whose side was God on in the Vietnam War, which many people believe to have been an enormous failure of American foreign policy, if not also an enormously immoral exercise in the use of American power?³³ Contemporary history adds innumerable examples of why the rewards/punishment system either does not make sense or becomes obscene, an unspeakable blaming of the victims—above all, the Holocaust (or the Shoah ["Disaster"], to use its other name).³⁴

Furthermore, in the Former Prophets the criteria for offenses deserving of God's punishment are highly selective. As Halpern points out, the Deuteronomist generally reduces "a welter of concrete motives to that of piety."³⁵ The most serious, of course, is the worshipping of other gods, but closely connected is worship at unauthorized places (e.g., "high places"), the use of various sacramental objects (e.g., *'asherahs*), or heterodox personnel (priests from the "wrong" party, as it were). Virtually all of these offenses were not considered as such at various times earlier than the 9th or 8th centuries. What has been missing all along has been any comparable emphasis on offenses against fellow Israelites—i.e., social injustice.³⁶ Within the books of Kings, the major exception is the story of Ahab and Jezebel and Naboth's vineyard, but there is no reference to that incident or to any

---

32. Earthquakes may be associated with the way in which God created the world, of course, and thus ultimately God's doing as the one who engineered plate tectonics, but that is far different than connecting a particular earthquake with a people's wrongdoing. Drought is a natural disaster that, increasingly, may well be the fault of *humans* due to climate change (or global warming).

33. In discussing the failed military adventure against Moab in 2 Kings 3, Brueggemann, *Kings*, 317-18, draws a parallel to Vietnam: "Surely God has been implicated in the tragedy and the sorrow. As of this late date, we are unable to say how, even as our text does not know how." Cf. Tran, *Vietnam War*, 174: "The Vietnam War continues to be broadly contested because we Americans have yet to figure out how to remember it."

34. See below, especially n. 69. See Sweeney, *I & II Kings*, 389, 458.

35. Halpern, *First Historians*, 229. However, Halpern rightly emphasizes the integrity of the Deuteronomist as an historian who "sincerely believed that the high places and the baals were the causes of Israel's misfortunes; his interest in accurately recalling those misfortunes was sharp" (234).

36. The brief note about the injustice of Samuel's sons is one exception (1 Sam 8:3). The "ways of the king" in 8:10-18 might seem abusive and make the people "cry out" to God, but one can argue that these ways were the normal administrative policies of monarchs. Of course, there are numerous stories of immoral acts throughout the Former Prophets. But even in Judges, when the editor speaks directly to the reader with a negative comment, the concern is exclusively sacerdotal matters.

other social injustice in the summary evaluation of 2 Kings 17. Similarly, the split between North and South under Rehoboam clearly was a result, in large part, of Solomon's oppressive labor and economic policies—a social justice issue (1 Kgs 12:1–5). But the narrator focused the blame for the split on Solomon's theological apostasy (1 Kings 11). It is something like an American historian analyzing the origins of the Civil War and barely mentioning slavery. Furthermore, in the repeated regnal introductory and summary evaluations, there are no references to injustice, with the sole exception of Manasseh's shedding of "innocent blood" (2 Kgs 24:4), which otherwise goes unexplained.[37] There is only one reference to David's adultery and murder (1 Kgs 15:5), but many references that idolize his virtues. The Deuteronomists' criteria for the summaries are almost exclusively sacerdotal matters; not social justice matters. We have to go to the Latter Prophets, almost all of whom are missing from the Former Prophets, to find out about the oppression of the powerless, the abuse of the judiciary, or the ways in which the economic system favored the rich over the poor.[38] We may *infer* such abuses from the narrative (e.g., destitute widows), but the narrator does not *imply* that such abuses occurred, much less explicitly fault the kings or others.

One can argue that the Deuteronomists were concerned about worshipping other gods and liturgical infractions precisely *because* doing so would lead inexorably to the kind of social injustice in the Naboth incident, and that such injustice would lead to God's judgment, again, the curses of the covenant (e.g., Deut 24:10–15).[39] Since much of Israel's social justice legislation is tied to the communal memory of the Exodus, which itself is the ground for the Ten Commandments, the argument makes considerable sense (Deut 5:6; 24:17–18, 21–22). Forgetting or ignoring the community's narrative identity—which is also to say *God's* narrative identity—leads to the corruption of its social ethos. *Not* worshipping Yahweh alone removes the motivation for obeying Yahweh's covenant stipulations. Loving the neighbor is inherently linked to loving God (Deut 10:17–19). However, the editors of the Former Prophets do not make this move, at least certainly not explicitly. We do not see something like, "King X did evil in the eyes of Yahweh by worshipping the Baals and by oppressing the widow, the orphan, and the needy." In fact, had the editors wanted to make that move, they surely had at hand (even aside from Naboth) the perfect example of how not loving Yahweh entailed not loving their neighbors, and they even had the perfect text for such a "sermon,"

---

37. A close analogy would be the report of Menahem's eviscerating pregnant women (2 Kgs 15:16), a horrific act of brutality, although it does not appear in Menahem's regnal summary (15:21).

38. So also Cogan, *I Kings*, 99. Even when there are stories about poor widows, the narrator does not make any overt criticism of the economic system or royal policies.

39. Campbell, "God's Anger," 380, represents a version of this argument: "faith in Yahweh" was the "keystone" to the people's social structure. Apostasy eroded the keystone, and social injustice "weakened the fibre of Israel's national strength," making it even more vulnerable to enemies.

and the text was in their "manual"—the legislation on the release of indentured servants (Deuteronomy 15).

During the reign of Zedekiah, when besieged by the Babylonians, the well-to-do in Jerusalem agreed to "a proclamation of liberty" to "set free their Hebrew slaves," in accordance with Israel's legal traditions. They thought that such an act of justice would earn them God's reward of getting rid of the Babylonians. But when the Babylonians did temporarily lift the siege (they had to deal with the Egyptians, Jer 37:6–11), the well-heeled citizens of Jerusalem promptly canceled their proclamation and forced the victims back into servitude. Jeremiah was not happy (Jer 34:8–22), and his pronounced judgment is full of irony: since they would not release their servants, God was releasing them "to the sword, to pestilence, and to famine," handing over Zedekiah to Nebuchadnezzar, and giving up Jerusalem to be burned with fire (34:17–22; cf. Deut 28:16–24). But we never hear of such an event in the Former Prophets, just as we do not hear anything of Jeremiah himself.[40] Here was a sterling example of social injustice much more recent than Naboth, and one that involved many more villains than just the king. It may not have involved bloodshed, like the apparent injustices of Manasseh, but it certainly involved economic oppression and obvious breach of covenant. Nevertheless, within the Former Prophets, the final defeat and destruction of both Israel and Judah hangs on their failure to worship one God, Yahweh alone, conducted by one party of priests, in the one manner and one place deemed to be liturgically orthodox by the editors, and for other explanations—especially social injustice—one has to look elsewhere.

Except for occasional digressions outside of the Former Prophets, I have tried to stay close to the narrative, honoring its integrity. Here, at the end, however, the only way to explore more deeply the possible reasons for Judah's final defeat and exile is to turn to other sources, of which one is Jeremiah. Here we may simply elaborate on references to him in the preceding pages. We noted Jehoiakim's arrogance in burning the scrolls that contained Jeremiah's message of judgment (Jeremiah 36), and what a striking contrast it makes with the reactions of his father, Josiah, who tore his clothes on hearing "the book of the Torah" (2 Kgs 22:11; no doubt today Jehoiakim would *shred* the document). Jeremiah also contrasts father and son in condemning Jehoiakim's opulent palace renovations for which he used forced laborers (the project resembles that of Solomon). Moreover, Josiah "judged the cause of the poor and needy," whereas Jehoiakim, driven by greed for "dishonest gain," shed "innocent blood" (like Manasseh) and practiced "oppression and violence" (Jer 22:13–17). Coupled with the incident of reneging on the liberation of indentured servants under Zedekiah, Jeremiah's critique thus includes social injustice as a major factor in God's final judgment.

Surely the determinative factor in the destruction of Judah and Jerusalem

---

40. Similarly, Jer 22:13–19 criticizes Josiah's son Jehoiakim for not defending the "cause of the poor and needy" but the narrator of the Former Prophets says nothing about it.

was Zedekiah's foolhardy rebellion against Nebuchadnezzar and his refusal to surrender and pay the usual price of tribute. In short, the critical cause of the disaster was the failure of foreign policy. The deportation of Jehoiachin in 597 proved to be only the first stage in Judah's demise, but there might not have been a second if Zedekiah had not "rebelled against the king of Babylon" (2 Kgs 24:20b). Had he surrendered, as Jeremiah strenuously argued, his life would have been preserved, thereby keeping a Davidic heir on the throne and Jerusalem and the temple intact, however ambiguous the situation with Jehoiachin might have been. Zedekiah would simply have become a dues-paying vassal of Babylonia. It is quite possible that Jerusalem and even the Davidic dynasty would have lasted at least until the next empire came along, in this case, the Persians, whose king, Cyrus, conquered the Babylonians and ruled the area until the Greeks came.[41] But Zedekiah was an exceedingly weak ruler who was cowed by his own advisors, all of whom apparently were "hawks" to whom Jeremiah was not only a "dove" but a traitor. In fact, when they insisted that Jeremiah be imprisoned, the king relented, admitting to them that he was "powerless against you" (Jer 38:5; cf. Excursus 7).

Thus the definitive reason for the fall of Jerusalem was Zedekiah's refusal to surrender to the enemy. One might argue that, again, worshipping other gods was the root cause (cf. 2 Kgs 24:19–20), in that it entailed not trusting in Yahweh "with all his heart." But trusting in Yahweh alone and serving Yahweh alone required also serving the king of Babylon, an equation that Zedekiah apparently found unacceptable. Surrendering would have involved trusting in God's promise of protection as mediated through the prophet Jeremiah. Thus it would have involved precisely the reverse of what was required of Hezekiah a century before. Zedekiah's advisors were arguing the same foreign policy position as had Isaiah! But Zedekiah did not have the courage to resist his advisors and follow Jeremiah's advice instead. Capitulation would have been the act of true courage, the path of honor, the means to security, and to life itself. It was surely as unacceptable then as it is today to speak of the courage to surrender, but failing to surrender was the ultimate cause of the fall of Jerusalem. Paralyzed by his own lack of confidence and fear of his advisors, Zedekiah would not give up. He would not admit defeat. He would not strike the colors and raise the white flag. He would not say "Uncle" to Nebuchadnezzar. He would not "cut and run." The result was disaster, calamity, unmitigated "evil." Zedekiah joins company with those other kings (especially Jeroboam I, Manasseh) whose faults led their nation into the abyss. "Such is the power of one ruler to corrupt a whole people and destroy its destiny."[42]

---

41. It was the Persians who placed Zerubbabel in office; see above.

42. Campbell and O'Brien, *Unfolding*, 380b, regarding Jeroboam I.

> *"I'm not going to be the first American President to lose a war."*
> —President Lyndon Johnson
> November, 1963
>
> *"I can't get out [of Vietnam]. I can't finish it with what I have got. So what the Hell can I do?"*
> —President Johnson
> March, 1965
>
> *Hawks, as militants now began to be called, complained that Johnson had set back the war effort by the pause [in bombing] . . . Doves, as antiwar activists were described, protested against the expansion of an immoral and unwinnable war.*[43]

"Remember, and do not forget" (Deut 9:7)

Why tell a story that ends so negatively and with such ambiguity about the future? To invoke Dickens again, the biblical audience who is in exile might well ask Scrooge's question to the Spirit of the future: "Why show me this, if I am past all hope?" To answer this question we need to explore the rich meaning of memory in ancient Israel's understanding of religious faith: remembering as repentance and revision. We may start with another look at Psalm 137: "By the rivers of Babylon, there we sat down and there we wept, when we remembered Zion." The psalmist then describes how, in exile, their captors taunted them, saying, "Sing us one of the songs of Zion!" But, says the psalmist, "How could we sing the Lord's song in a foreign land?" In many ways this question defines the task faced by the exiles. The Former Prophets begins with the Israelites settling in the Promised Land, the goal that dominates the preceding narrative from Genesis 12, and arguably from Genesis 1. Thus Israel's entire history has come full circle: their ancestors Abraham and Sarah, left "Ur of the Chaldeans to go into the land of Canaan" (Gen 11:31; cf. Josh 24:2), and now the descendants of Abraham and Sarah are exiles in Babylon of the Chaldeans. What is there to sing about? The only genre of psalm appropriate would be a lament (a contemporary musical analogy would be the blues). The exiles might well repeat the words of the King of Israel, besieged by the Arameans, his people starving to death, who said to Elisha, "This trouble ['evil'] is from the Lord! Why should I hope in the Lord any longer?" (2 Kgs 6:33).

Yet the psalmist then says, "If I forget you, O Jerusalem, let my right hand wither! Let my tongue cling to the roof of my mouth, if I do not remember you, if I do not set Jerusalem above my highest joy." Remembering, which at first led only to weeping, now can lead to joy (cf. Psalm 126).[44] Then the psalmist uses the word "remember" one more time, invoking God to "remember" how the Edomites cheered as Jerusalem was destroyed, i.e., invoking God's wrath against them, then closing with the horrific image of Babylonian children bludgeoned to death as "pay back" for those

---

43. Dallek, *Flawed Giant*, 500, 255, 351–52.

44. This psalm may well reflect a post-exilic setting after some of the exiles had returned to Jerusalem. It is the source for the wonderful old hymn, "Bringing in the Sheaves."

Israelite children who died. This is the deleterious dimension of memory—remembering as revenge, surely the most despicable form of "happiness" (v. 9a). It is as human as it is inhumane, an atrocity with countless examples down to the present. We will not dwell here, although (like the atrocities in Joshua and elsewhere), it is healthy to be confronted with it.[45]

What is the process by which memory does not lead to weeping and despair but to joy and hope? And it *is* a *hopeful* joy, not a realized joy. That is, it is a joy experienced in the present in anticipation of a future that has not yet arrived. The psalmist in exile would understand the significance of the title of a novel by Maya Angelou—*I Know Why the Caged Bird Sings*. In referring to the books of Chronicles Mark Smith says that the author used sources "not simply to create a narration presenting the past, but one whose primary function was to celebrate the past as an antecedent to the present."[46] Surely that description fits the Former Prophets as well.

We have discussed above how the Former Prophets is a theodicy, a justification of God's ways in the world with respect to the existence of "evil" (or "calamity"), and in this case demonstrating that God was justified in destroying Israel and Judah and sending them into exile because of the unrelenting sins of the people and their monarchs. Although we have noted theological difficulties with such a theodicy, we have also emphasized how healthy it is for a nation to confront its history, warts and all. The first move toward hope is already present in the theodicy if the ultimate audience—the exiles—*accept it* as valid. That is, the first task of the audience is to acknowledge the truth of the story. To do so is a communal confession of sin, the critical move in the process of repentance. A theodicy that justifies God's judgment against sin calls for the sinner to repent. This is the first dimension of Israel's memory. Remembering is repenting.[47] The opposite of remembering, of course, is forgetting, which, in Deuteronomic parlance, refers to a willful refusal to acknowledge the *significance* of past events.[48] Thus Moses warns Israel to "remember and do not forget" the incident of the golden calf (Deut 9:7), when they came *close* to destruction. Similarly, Deuteronomy 8 presents

---

45. There is a wonderful scene in the film, *Gandhi*, involving the mutual persecution of Muslims and Hindus, when a Hindu man comes to Gandhi utterly distraught with guilt and fearful of hell, saying that he has killed a Muslim child in retaliation for the Muslim's killing his own child. Gandhi says something like this: "There is a way out of hell. Find a Muslim child who is an orphan and take him as your own, and be sure to raise him as a good Muslim." As Volf says, after the evil deed itself, the second victory of evil is "when evil is returned" (*End of Memory*, 9).

46. Smith *Early History*, xxviii. Cf. his comment in *Memoirs*, 137: "to write back through the past is to enable moving through present loss and toward the future."

47. As Volf says (*Memory*, 121), "to obtain this release wrongdoers must receive forgiveness of their misdeeds as just that—*forgiveness*—just as any person must accept a gift for the gift to be given."

48. Cf. Tran, *Vietnam War*, 125: "The call to remember is very much the call to not forget. On the way to redemption, forgetting becomes the greatest temptation because guilt and shame beg for erasure."

an eloquent appeal to *remember* what it was like to live *outside* the fertile land, not to *forget* their absolute dependence on God, and warns that the alternative will be to "perish" "like the nations that the Lord is destroying before you" (8:2, 11, 18–19). Another psalmist suggests how remembering works as repentance: while he refused to acknowledge his sin, he "wasted away," but once he acknowledged and confessed it, God forgave him, leading the psalmist to "be glad in the Lord and rejoice" (Ps 32:3–5, 11). This is the penitential movement of remembering as repentance. The Former Prophets is an extended national confession of sin.[49]

Repentance is only part of the equation leading to hope, of course, namely the human part. The other part is up to God—forgiveness. What assurance does Israel have that God will, in fact, forgive? There are certainly reasons to doubt it. "The Lord will be unwilling to pardon them, for the Lord's anger and passion will smoke against them" (Deut 29:20). Furthermore, another voice in Deuteronomy declares that "all these curses shall come upon you . . . until you are destroyed . . . and they shall be among you and your descendants as a sign and a portent *forever*" (28:45–46). On the other hand, the plot of the Former Prophets, from beginning to end, is a seemingly endless cycle of sin and forgiveness, or at least sin and forbearance. Perhaps the first example was the story of Achan ("Trouble Valley," Joshua 7), in which Achan's sin, once acknowledged and punished, led to the assuaging of God's anger and the survival of the people. Even more programmatically, the book of Judges introduced a cyclical schema of apostasy, punishment, distress cry, and deliverance. Implied also is some degree of periodic reform, for the schema then moves to relapse, and a renewal of the cycle (2:19). Israel has a recidivism problem. The reform appears explicitly at 10:10–16 when Israel confesses "we have sinned" (twice, vv. 10, 15) and they "put away the foreign gods from among them and worshiped the Lord" (v. 16). A similar reform appears after the ark narrative in 1 Samuel 7, with the people "returning to the Lord," putting away "the foreign gods," and confessing "we have sinned against the Lord," appealing to Samuel to intercede for them (vv. 3, 6, 8). In 1 Samuel 12, the anti-monarchical narrator reports that the people concur with Samuel's condemnation, saying "we have added to all our sins the evil of demanding a king," and he promises to continue as their intercessor (vv. 19–23).[50] Saul confesses his sin in not slaughtering Agag in 1 Sam 15:24–30, and David confesses his sin of adultery and murder in 2 Sam 12:13, and his sin in ordering the census in 2 Sam 24:10. In his temple dedication prayer, Solomon asks in advance for God's forgiveness if the people sin, providing a long laundry list (1 Kgs 8:31–53), although he never confesses the sins attributed to him later (e.g., ch. 11). Several kings enact sacerdotal reforms, including Jehoash and Hezekiah of Judah,

---

49. Cf. ibid., 199: "The soul's dark night is not a memory to be forgotten but rather a moment to be confessed in the pilgrim's journey home." Tran argues that such confession is part of what is missing in America's attempt to deal with the Vietnam war.

50. We will look at the significance of v. 22 below.

and Jehu of Israel, even if contemporary readers may find those of Jehu to be more like fanatical persecution. And, of course, Josiah's reform stands out as the Deuteronomic ideal of penitence, torn clothes and all. But Josiah brings us full circle, in that his exemplary repentance came to naught for himself and for Judah. How, then, can exiled Israel expect God to forgive them?

There are several ways to answer that question. Within Deuteronomy, the question does not even appear within the basic covenant structure (chaps. 5-29), but only within the framework, not surprisingly in passages from an exilic editor. Chapter 30 assumes a setting in the exile when "all these things have happened to you, the blessings and the curses," and Israel is scattered "among all the nations."[51] The author employs a play on the Hebrew word *shuv* to describe the mutual effects of Israel's repentance and God's forgiveness. The basic meaning of the word is "return," but it can be used to indicate repetition (doing something the second time), or restoration (restoring something to its previous state), or repentance (changing one's mind). The last connotation can refer to the people's change of heart and renewed faithfulness, or to God's change of mind, in this case, regarding punishment. In vv. 1–10 the word appears seven times, including v. 1 ("call to mind" literally is "return to heart," cf. the expression "come to one's senses"). Thus to paraphrase vv. 1-5: if you return to your senses and return to God then God will return your return (NRSV "restore your fortunes") and return and gather you. "Repentance" is thus the act of returning (or "turning around"), and here *both* Israel and God participate in that act, a kind of spiritual synergy. Sequentially, Israel's repentance seems to initiate the process, but for the audience the author's promise that God will respond favorably provides an assurance grounded in God's grace, a theology of repentance already anticipated in Hosea.[52] Moreover, vv. 11-14 emphasize that Israel has the freedom of will and the capability of returning to obedience.

In addition to repentance there is another possible ground for hope, and that is the promise of an eternal covenant with David. Although its unconditional form underwent considerable qualifications, God never explicitly annulled the covenant. God would punish disobedience, of which the Exile was an extreme example, but God would not withdraw the promise completely (2 Sam 7:14-15; cf. 1 Kgs 11:39). Repeatedly, the editors will emphasize that God's forbearance for Judah in the face of Judah's sin is "for the sake of David,"[53] thus providing a stability and ostensibly a permanence to the Davidic dynasty that the North did not enjoy. Only once is there a report of such forbearance for Israel, rooted in God's "covenant with Abraham, Isaac, and Jacob" that the narrator notes has been in effect "until now" (2 Kgs

---

51. For more discussion see my comments in *Deuteronomy*, 154-58. Cf. also Jer 29:10-14 for similar language.

52. Cf. Wolff, *Hosea*, 201, on Hos 11:8-9: "Hosea lays the foundation for the certainty that Yahweh will never conclusively surrender Israel."

53. E.g., 1 Kgs 9:4; chap. 11 (seven times); 15:4; 2 Kgs 8:19; 19:34; 20:6.

13:23), but it was not to last, of course. Although from a critical perspective the covenant with the ancestors probably is dependent on the Davidic covenant (they are both "dynastic grant" types), canonically the relationship is the reverse: God's promise of an eternal relationship with David is rooted in the promise to Abraham and Sarah. But does the Davidic covenant remain in place at the end of the Former Prophets? At first, the answer to that would seem to depend again on how we read the incident about Jehoiachin, and, as we have seen, the narrator concludes with this Davidic heir still alive, and thus at least the *possibility* that the Davidic covenant continues. But the Davidic covenant did more than insure the permanence of the Davidic dynasty; it also launched something independent of the political institution and far more enduring, namely, the *idea* of the Messiah, to which we will return shortly.

Another exilic Deuteronomic passage combines both repentance and eternal covenant (Deut 4:25–31). Although Moses warns that Israel "will be utterly destroyed," and that God will "scatter" them among the peoples, nevertheless "a few of you will be left." Thus the frequent references to "utter destruction" do not mean annihilation. In exile Israel will "will seek the Lord your God, and you will find him if you search after him with all your heart and soul." "You will return to the Lord your God," Moses says, "*because* the Lord your God is a merciful God, he will neither abandon you nor destroy you; he will not forget the covenant with your ancestors that he swore to them." The conclusion completely reverses the prior warning of destruction. Here Israel's repentance comes first, but it is grounded in the unconditional promise of blessing to the ancestors, and in God's quality of mercy. Here, in effect, Moses ultimately appeals to David! Israel's remembering implicitly derives from God's not forgetting.[54] We should not be surprised by now to hear conflicting voices, one saying that the curses are forever (Deut 28:46), another saying that they are not (4:31; cf. again 1 Kgs 11:39). It is only human to hope that God's "Yes" is greater than God's "No."

There is yet a third way in which the restoration of Israel will occur, according to other sources—God will act unilaterally. In a sense, God will undergo a "change of mind" (another word for "repent"—*naḥam*).[55] God decides to start all over again, initiating a new exodus and a new covenant. Whereas other pictures of restoration assume a point of view from inside Palestine—scattering and gathering (e.g., Deut 30:3)—the new exodus assumes a point of view from outside. Second Isaiah (Isaiah 40–55) champions the new exodus, just as he will revise the figure of David and God's "anointed" (see below). Israel's penalty is more than paid (40:1–2). God, says the prophet, will "blot out your transgressions for my own sake, and I will *not remember* your sins" (43:25). That this unilateral action is for God's own sake, suggests the personal affection

---

54. Cf. God's remembering Noah as the turning point of the flood story, Gen 8:1.

55. Recall the ambiguity of such a notion regarding God's attitude toward Saul, 1 Sam 15:11, 29, 35 ("regret," "change his mind," "was sorry").

that God still holds for Israel (cf. 43:4a). God announces the preparation of a "highway" that leads back to Palestine (40:3–5). Just as the exodus generation passed through the wilderness between Egypt and Canaan, now the exiles will pass through the wilderness between *Babylon* and Canaan (e.g., 43:1–7, 14–21). In the end, God combines the New Exodus with a new Davidic promise: "I will make *with you* an everlasting covenant, my steadfast, sure love for David" (55:3; cf. 54:9–10). The monarchic covenant is now a "democratic" one!

Finally, God can act unilaterally in offering a new covenant, apart from either a new Exodus or David. Deut 30:6–10 seems to contradict both the preceding and following verses that emphasize Israel's capability of repentance: "the Lord your God will circumcise your heart and the heart of your descendants, so that you will love the Lord your God with all your heart" (v. 6). God engages in the surgical procedure that, of course, is the sign of covenant membership (Gen 17:9–10, albeit borne only by males!). The implication, however, is that God will *force* obedience rather than elicit it. Other prophets will use similar metaphors. In Jeremiah, God promises to "write it [the new covenant] on their hearts," "for I will forgive their iniquity, and *remember* their sin no more" (30:31–34). In Ezekiel, God says "a new heart I will give you, and a new spirit I will put within you; and I will remove from your body the heart of stone and give you a heart of flesh" (36:26).[56] God is performing "heart transplant" surgery, saying "[I will] *make* you follow my precepts" (v. 27). There is a chilling feel to these metaphors of divine surgery. On the one hand, here Israel's restoration is attributed solely to the grace of God, not requiring even repentance; on the other hand, that is precisely the problem. Repentance is the *result* of the surgery. This solution to the problem of Israel's restoration has the ring of desperation about it. It seems to deny the moral freedom clearly stated in Deut 30:11–14, and thus to remove the prefix to what we have called "co-operation" between God and humans.[57] Accordingly, Dean McBride once described the "new heart" procedure in Jeremiah as "a lobotomy of the human will."[58]

To summarize some of the discussion above: there are a number of tensions that run throughout the Former Prophets and do not lend themselves to neat either/or conclusions: (1) human freedom and divine will; (2) "calamity" as a consequence of the former and punishment by the latter; (3) forgiveness and restoration as divine grace and as the result of repentance; (4) monism in theology and practice (one God, one people, one temple, one land, one priesthood) vs. pluralism and the freedom of individual conscience (the latter enjoying few defenders in the narrative). The term that I have often used to describe the presentation of historical agents—"co-operation"—would actually apply to (2) and (3) as well. All *four* of the tensions are by no means limited to ancient

---

56. Cf. Ps 51:10–11 and the superscription—David's repentance! This is a traditional text for Ash Wednesday.

57. Note also Deut 10:16: "circumcise, then, the foreskin of your heart"!

58. "Yoke," 302, no. 61.

Israelite religion. In some ways they are the *precedents* for issues that dominate religious history (certainly *Western* religious history), down to the present.

"Do not remember the former things" (Isa 43:18)

We have ventured beyond the literary confines of the Former Prophets to understand the reasons for Israel's defeat and to inquire about the role of repentance and God's unconditional promise of grace. Perhaps we could say that the deepest reconciliation will occur when Israel and God remember each other, or, to put it another way, when God does *not* remember Israel's sin. Another dimension of remembering starts from the etymology of that word: *re* + *memor*, "again" + "mindful." To remember is to be mindful in a new way, to *re*-mind, not in the mere sense of recalling, but of having a *new mind*—rethinking, revisioning, or, to use a word from computer jargon, reconfiguring. I have used the phrase from the exilic prophet, Second Isaiah, to represent the process of revisioning: "do *not* remember the former things," he says, adding that Yahweh was about to do a "new thing," referring specifically to the New Exodus that we outlined above (43:16–21). At first sight, such forgetting might seem to contradict the role of memory in the Former Prophets, but, in fact, Second Isaiah held the two together. He can also say "remember the former things" in arguing that Israel's past holds the proof of the truth of God's promises for the future (49:9). The Former Prophets is a major part of the "former *things*" and quite likely reached its current form simultaneously with Second Isaiah's work. His appeal to "*not* remember" was a way of saying that memory without hope is only "nostalgia"—that wonderful word with the suffix meaning "pain." Healthy remembering would lead to rethinking. Again, we will look briefly outside the Former Prophets to see how themes within it formed the basis for such rethinking in exilic and post-exilic Israel.

Near the end of the Former Prophets, the first appearance in that narrative of a proper name for Israel signals a radical shift in communal identity—the usual "children of Israel" or "Israelites" now become "the Judeans" (NRSV) or "the Jews" (2 Kgs 25:25). This term will be the standard reference to the people who survived the Exile. Although they will still identify themselves with the name "Israel," of course, their primary designation will be "the Jews." Just as name changes signify new identities in other biblical stories (e.g., Abram and Sarai to Abraham and Sarah; Jacob to Israel, etc.), so here a new configuration of the people emerges. We will look at this new configuration in terms of the Davidic covenant (represented by Jehoiachin) and the Mosaic covenant (represented by Josiah).

As we have seen, the concluding scene in which the Babylonian king releases Jehoiachin from prison and honors him with a seat at the royal dining table remains ambiguous—one could read it as a sign of hope or a sign of despair. We have also noted that, beyond the confines of the Former Prophets, Jehoiachin's descendant, Zerubbabel, will disappear from history. But it is obvious that the Davidic ideal does not disappear with him. Like Saul before him, David was "anointed" king of Israel, an act authorized by God. The addition of God's eternal covenant with David introduced the promise of divine blessing that was both politically and theologically stabilizing. By the time we reach the end, however, the extent of David's dynasty has shrunk from all Israel and Judah to Judah alone and then to Jerusalem, and then to a seat at a captor's dining table but no throne. The way was open to reconsider what the promise to David might mean.

In a sense, much of the Former Prophets focuses on the emergence of a new leader to replace a previous one, going all the way back to Joshua replacing Moses (Josh 1:1–6), then the succession of judges, then Samuel, then the first king, then David, and subsequent kings. Samuel seemed to combine political with prophetic leadership (becoming the "prophet like Moses" of Deut 18:15),[59] but the two "offices" diverged with the rise of monarchy. We have seen that the prophets (and sometimes priests) remained a power to reckon with—sometimes running a virtual theocracy that presented its own problems. At the same time, the notion of Israel's "anointed" king of the past increasingly became the expectation of a future king whose title is simply a transliteration of the Hebrew "anointed" (*meshiaḥ*)—the Messiah.[60] Already Isaiah had introduced utopian images of the coming king who would occupy "the throne of David," issuing in "endless peace" (Isa 9:1–7) that would have cosmic dimensions (11:1–9). The companion piece of such prophecy was the exaltation of Zion or Jerusalem, invoking ancient mythic imagery of the cosmic mountain home of the gods. Such passages may originally have functioned as coronation liturgies for royal inaugurations, but the editors of the book of Isaiah introduced framing devices that shifted such Messianic hopes into an undefined future—the "latter days."[61] To use a more technical term, the Messianic hope became "eschatological." For some, the promise to David could be detached from the immediate realm of political power, making the historical dissolution of descendants like Zerubbabel irrelevant. In a sense, the process of reconfiguring is not new; the editors of the Former Prophets often revised prophecies to fit with later reality so that the prophecy/fulfillment scheme held.[62] Now the *disappearance* of a biological Davidic heir did not exclude the future *appearance* of a Messiah. Other prophetic books would have their own idealistic expectations of a coming figure like David,[63] and of a "holy city" of

---

59. The expectation of a future prophetic figure in some ways parallels that of the Messiah, especially in the person of Elijah, who, after all, never died but was taken up into heaven, from whence he could come again (cf. Mal 4:5; Matt 11:14, etc.). The Passover Seder traditionally leaves an empty chair ready for Elijah in case he comes.

60. Cf. Rosenberg, "1 and 2 Samuel," 142: "the house [of David] indeed survived in exile and passed from there into Jewish messianism."

61. E.g., chap. 9 is preceded by a prophecy set in "the latter time" of the future; 11:1–9 is followed by the futurist references "on that day" (vv. 10–11). Cf. Amos 9:11, Hos 2:16–21 "on that day."

62. See Weinfeld, *Deuteronomic School*, 21–26.

63. Jer 23:5–6; 33:14–26; Ezekiel 34.

Jerusalem,[64] sometimes added as conclusions by editors (e.g., Amos 9:11–15). On the other hand, Second Isaiah not only reassigned the Davidic promise to the whole people (see above); he also named the foreign king Cyrus God's "anointed" (45:1)! In a sense, Cyrus became the "carrot of God's grace" to Israel, replacing the "rod of God's anger."

Thus the way was open for both Messiah and Zion to develop in numerous trajectories, one of which, of course, led to the Christian identification of Jesus of Nazareth as the Messiah (Greek *kristos*), but one who eschewed political power and, instead, was a victim of it.[65] In Judaism, the Messiah continued as a future expectation. For all their differences, however, there is a basic similarity expressed by the poignant questions: "The Jews say, the world is so evil, why has the Messiah not come? The Christians say the Messiah has come, why is the world still so evil?"[66] Thus, if historically Jehoiachin was, in effect, the last Davidic king (again, Zerubbabel notwithstanding), he was not the last "Messiah." In fact, *if* the dining table scene is intended to be hopeful, one could argue that Jehoiachin is the last Davidic king but the *first* "Messiah."

Finally, we may look one more time at Josiah, who, of course, could also represent the Messianic trajectory. But his tragic and early death raised the problem of how to reconfigure the covenant tradition that promised blessing for fidelity and warned of curse for infidelity. Recall the eulogistic evaluation in 2 Kings 23:25: "Before him there was no king like him, who turned to the Lord with all his heart, with all his soul, and with all his might, according to all the law of Moses; nor did any like him arise after him." If there was a Josianic edition of the Deuteronomistic history, written before his death, this eulogy would have made a wonderful conclusion, presumably without the last clause.[67] The eulogy for him clearly sees him as the royal paragon of the heart of Deuteronomic theology—quite literally: "you shall love the Lord your God with all your heart, with all your soul, and with all your might" (Deut 6:5). According to some scholarly views, Josiah's reform was the goal already in sight when we first saw Joshua, listening to God's charge to take up the mantle of Moses, to "be strong and very courageous, being careful to act in accordance with all the law that my servant Moses commanded you," not to allow "this book of the law" to "depart out of your mouth," promising him that "I will be with you; I will not fail you or forsake you" (Josh 1:1–9). Josiah did all of that, and yet his violent death suggested that

---

64. Isa 52:1; cf. 40:1–2, 9–11; 44:28; 49:8–26; 52:1–2; chap. 54, especially v. 10; Mic 4:1–4; Ezekiel 40–48 with a (return of the "glory of God" that had departed).

65. Note how Matthew places Jesus within a genealogy that includes David (*and* "the wife of Uriah"!), Matt 1:1–17.

66. The first question (the Jewish one) appears most poignantly in the contemporary Passover reading, composed as a response to the Holocaust: "'I believe with perfect faith in the coming of the Messiah, and though he tarry, nevertheless I believe'" (quoted by Fackenheim, *God's Presence*, 97).

67. Thus this edition would have anticipated the "peaceful death" of the Huldah oracle, 2 Kgs 22:20, just as it hoped for the reforms to prevent the predicted disaster.

God *did* fail and forsake him. For if, as we have seen, neither "sour grapes" nor "blame the victim" could adequately explain it, how else to understand it? One scholar has even suggested that there is "a conspiracy of silence" over Josiah's death "because, given the Old Testament premises, no one could satisfactorily account for it theologically."[68]

In short, the inconsistency between fidelity and "calamity" requires rethinking covenant theology, especially with its system of rewards and punishments, blessings and curses. Why should one love God if that system does not hold? If bad things can happen to good people, why be good? When we put the question this way, the answer already begins to take shape: the primary motivation for being good is not any reward, but the very value of goodness itself. Righteousness is its own reward. We can make the same point with regard to repentance, including that of Josiah. To say that *repentance* has failed to insure God's blessing is to collapse back into the problem of equating *obedience* with rewards. Can we understand the motivation for repentance itself outside that "merit system"?

In covenant terms, the basic motivation for loving God is not the desire to receive a blessing or avoid a punishment. Israel does not love God in anticipation of something to come, although that may happen; rather, Israel loves God out of gratitude for what has already taken place. In the language of Israel's history, Israel loves God because God brought their ancestors out of Egypt and called them to be God's covenant people, a relationship that applies to every subsequent generation. Living with integrity in this relationship is the Jew's deepest joy. Therefore, obedience to God's commandments is also the source of joy, for the commandments provide the structure for the relationship. Psalm 119 is a lengthy poem extolling the Psalmist's love for God through love for the *torah*, i.e., the law: "oh, how I love your law; it is my meditation all day long" (v. 97). The Psalmist even includes times when he is "persecuted without cause," yet has not forsaken God's "precepts" (vv. 86-87), and the Psalmist repeatedly appeals to God for help. But the Torah itself is a source of comfort, even if, in the present, there is only trouble: "I long for your salvation, O Lord, and your law is my delight" (v. 174; cf. v. 92). The deepest significance of fidelity comes from how it defines one's very identity, in this case, to be a Jew. One can be faithful even in the face of undeserved suffering. Indeed, one can be faithful even when it appears that *God* is unfaithful![69]

---

68. Frost, "Death of Josiah," 381.

69. One of the most profound and radical statements of this response to underserved suffering is Emil Fackenheim's *God's Presence in History*, a meditation on the Holocaust. Fackenheim rejects any theodicy based on faulting the victims or declaring them martyrs, any invocations of God as liberator (as in Passover), or God as sufferer (as in the *Shekinah* text cited below). He also rejects Jewish secularism and notions that "God is dead." Instead, he argues that after the Holocaust Jews are *commanded* to remain identifiably Jewish by the God of Sinai, citing Psalm 119: "a commanding Voice without which we, like the Psalmist (Ps. 119:92), would have perished in our affliction" (93; cf. 83). For Fackenheim, such obedience to that Voice is hardly "submissive," in the pejorative sense; rather, it exhibits a "stubbornness" that is the "defining characteristic" of Jewish theology (18). Brueggemann, *Kings*, 608-9 seems to refer to views like

Josiah, then, can become a model for the Jew who is "persecuted without cause," yet clings to the God of the covenant. According to the chronology in 2 Kgs 22:3, Josiah was twenty-six years old when he instigated the reforms, and he died at the age of forty-eight. At the outset, the oracle of Huldah, the prophetess, predicted the fall of Judah as well as Josiah's peaceful death preceding the disaster. Yet Josiah pursued his reforms. Presumably he could have thought, if God is bringing such disaster anyway, why go to the trouble? But such cynicism would be inconsistent with the king who loved Yahweh with all his heart. In this persistence in the face of apparent futility, Josiah resembles the figure of Moses in Deuteronomic tradition, for Moses knew forty years in advance that God would not allow him to enter the Promised Land, yet Moses persisted as Israel's leader—not to mention composing the book of Deuteronomy! Since the Former Prophets addresses exiles (as well as earlier audiences), some of whom did not see how they could have deserved what happened, the message could be this: even though disaster has overcome you, despite your faithfulness, you are still commanded to be faithful, just as Josiah was faithful even in the face of national doom.[70]

If it is possible to reconfigure the cause-and-effect relationship of covenantal fidelity to rewards and punishments, so it is with other parts of the covenant, especially residence in the land of Canaan, sovereignty as a nation, a monarchical government, with a priestly establishment focused on sacrificial worship centered in the Jerusalem temple. Again, the question is one of identity. What does it mean to be a Jew instead of an Israelite? Can one be a Jew and live outside the land? At the beginning and at the end Israel is an outsider ("beyond the Jordan" or in exile). Throughout Israel's entire history, beginning with Abraham and Sarah, the goal was to live in the land that God had granted them (Gen 12:1–2; Exod 3:7–8). Life in the land was part of the covenantal blessing; life outside the land, part of the curse. Many exilic texts express the hope of a return to the land, at times even equating it with God's forgiveness. Just as God had scattered, God would gather.[71] Jeremiah purchased property one year before the fall of Jerusalem, predicting a lively real estate market to come (Jer 32:1–15). Yet

---

Fackenheim's when he says, at the end of his commentary, "Hope, elusive and emancipatory, is a refusal to think that our defeats have in them the defeat of holiness, a refusal as it is more recently said, to give Hitler a posthumous victory."

70. See the previous note. Lohfink, "Das Problem Individuum-Gemeinschaft," 406, suggests something similar: Moses' situation says to the exiles "how one must say Yes to God's will even in such difficult circumstances" (AT). See my study, "Denial of Moses." God determines

that Moses must die before entering the Promised Land. There is a difference in the interpretations of Moses that parallels that of Josiah. The Priestly author blames Moses for his anger in a wilderness incident (when anger was quite appropriate, Num 20:1–13), whereas the Deuteronomist places the blame on the people (Deut 1:37; 3:23–27; 4:21–22). Thus there is a reversal of the "Jeroboam motif" in which the people suffer because of the leader (although the people, finally, are not deemed innocent either). In this context, note that Josiah's repentance is not so much for his own sins as for the sins of the nation.

71. E.g., Deut 30:2–4; Jer 29:14; Ezek 11:17; Neh 1:9. The word for "gather" is the root for the contemporary Hebrew word "kibbutz," referring to a community settlement.

already within the Former Prophets, we can see examples of the possibility of continuing to be Yahweh's people outside the land, even in exile—that is what part of Solomon's prayer presupposes (1 Kgs 8:46–53). Jeremiah (notwithstanding his purchase of land) wrote a letter to the exiles deported with Jehoiachin, telling them to become good citizens of Babylon and not to expect a return until seventy years had passed (Jer 29:7–22).[72] In fact, when Jews *did* return to Palestine under Ezra and Nehemiah, many remained behind, and Babylon became one center of Jewish tradition (eventually producing the commentary called the "Babylonian Talmud").[73] We also know of other outposts, such as Elephantine, and eventually Alexandria, in Egypt. Such communities grew and prospered in the places to which God had "scattered" them, producing the movement known as the Diaspora ("spreading out"). It was possible to be a Jew outside the land.

Indeed, some of the exiles who returned to Israel insisted that only they were the legitimate inheritors of Israel's spiritual heritage—to be a genuine Jew one *had* to have been an exile! Some scholars refer to this as the "myth of the empty land."[74] After all, 2 Kings ends with "the elite of the land" in Babylon, and "all the people" who were not deported to Babylon fleeing to Egypt (24:15; 25:26), which looks indeed like a vacuum.[75] Probably the returnees saw themselves as the "pure" Israel who would now re-occupy the land in the orthodox way it should have happened in the first place! The residents of the North (the Samaritans) already had been marginalized in 2 Kgs 17:24–41. Thus the themes of outsider/insider and exclusivity/inclusiveness that we have seen from the outset appear again. The tension will not go away. Ezra and Nehemiah will enforce the prohibitions against marrying foreign women that we have often seen, and that are enshrined in Deut 7:1–6. On the other hand, some will insist that even "foreigners" and "eunuchs" are welcome within the covenant community, as long as they keep the rules, as it were. Keeping Sabbath will be a hallmark of membership (Isaiah 56).[76]

The point of view of being outside the land and still in full relationship with God pervades various canonical divisions in the Hebrew Bible. In Genesis 12 Abraham and Sarah go into Canaan and right out the other side into Egypt—a brief residence indeed (and by the end of the chapter they are out of Egypt)!

---

72. Jeremiah 24 declares that Jehoiachin and company are "good figs," and Zedekiah and those with him (as well as those who fled to Egypt) are the "bad figs." Jeremiah's prophecy that Zedekiah would die in peace (34:5) hardly seems fitting with what happened to him and his sons.

73. The Talmud and other Rabbinic writings are further examples of how Israel became the "people of the book" (see below).

74. Robert Carroll coined the phrase. See McNutt, *Reconstructing*, 183 and n. 4 for a reference to his work and others; also Smith, *Memoirs*, 69–70.

75. In 24:14 the "poorest of the land" remain; in 25:12 they are designated as vintners and farmers. Presumably the author of 25:26 thinks of all these abandoning the land also. In Lev 26:34, the empty land enjoys the Sabbath rests previously denied it.

76. Strict exclusiveness contradicts more empathetic traditions regarding the stranger, alien, or foreigner, e.g., Deut 26:1–11 (all Israelites are required to act out the role of a newly arrived immigrant once a year); 23:15–16; 24:17–23.

The entire book of Genesis ends with the words "in Egypt." Deuteronomy was composed at various stages, but, as we saw in the Introduction, eventually the Jewish community placed it at the end of the Torah (the "Law") as a conclusion, thereby posing Israel outside the land, looking over the Jordan River, yet with its covenant agreement with God concluded. Again, the last book in the Hebrew Bible is 2 Chronicles, which ends with the words, "go up," referring to those Jews who wish to return to Jerusalem. Canonically, it is as if Israel is perpetually *outside* the land. This "boundary" or "threshold" point of view dominates the liturgical celebration of Passover (the night *before* redemption), with its concluding shout, "Next year, in Jerusalem."[77] For many Jews (down to this day) living in the land of Palestine is essential to being Jewish; for many more, it is not.

The same reconfiguration would take place with the other dimensions of the covenant. The promise to become "a great nation" with a "great name," as numerous as the stars in the sky, sovereign over the whole area between Egypt and Iraq, came true with the establishment of the Davidic empire,[78] but in the end Israel's numbers are decimated; they are left "few in number," and scattered *among* the nations (Deut 4:27). Possessing no sovereign territory, politically they are no longer a nation. But they can still be God's people, a community identified not by territory but by ethos. They are still the people of the covenant, the content of which demonstrates to all other nations their unique relationship to God, and in this they will always be a "great nation" (Deut 4:5–7, with "great nation" three times).

With their king groveling at the table of the king of Babylon, they have no functioning human ruler. For some, as we have seen, the dream of a human monarchy lived on, and fluttered to life under Zerubabbel, only to disappear. For others, the dreams of a just king would coalesce in the figure of the future Messiah. But God has never ceased to be Israel's true king. In fact, for some, the end of the monarchy could mean a return to the ideal theocracy that existed *before* there was a human king (e.g., 1 Sam 12:12). From this perspective, the monarchy was a grand failure.[79] Ironically, it was in the Exile, when Israel had no human king, that the understanding of Yahweh's universal sovereignty, already implied at numerous times throughout the Former Prophets,

---

77. The same theme is present in the Christian Lord's Supper, which is set on the Thursday night before Easter. See my study, "Passover."

78. Gen 12:2; 15:5, 18; 2 Sam 7:9; 1 Kgs 4:20–21.

79. Cf. Birch, *1 and 2 Samuel*, 997. Polzin, *Samuel*, 79, argues that "exilic Israel must reject the monarchy," a view already apparent in 1 Samuel. In fact, "the death of kingship" is what the Former Prophets is all about (218). Cf. Gottwald, *Politics*, 161–62: one reason that exilic and post-exilic communities preserved pre-state (i.e., pre-monarchy) traditions was to give the monarchy "the status of a failed and outmoded enterprise no longer necessary for a religiocultural [sic] community capable of thriving in the absence of Israelite political autonomy." It is possible that an anti-monarchical statement appears in the exilic Priestly author's creation account in Genesis 1, where all of humankind, and not, as usually, a king, is "in the image of God" (1:26). Clearly, such anti-monarchical views stand in tension with the appreciation of the monarchy reflected in the Messianic ideal.

would blossom into the concept of full monotheism, in which Yahweh, as creator of the universe, was the *only* god.[80] Thus, as Smith puts it, "Israel's master narrative about the past, namely, Genesis through Kings, helps to produce a master god."[81]

The figure of the king is closely tied to that of the temple on Mt. Zion, the political establishment tied to the sacerdotal, so that constructing a palace and constructing a temple were symbols of royal power and authority.[82] But both palace and temple lie in ruins. Since the temple provided the means to relate to God through sacrifices (and, for the Deuteronomists, the *only* such place), how could Jews now worship God? Since God had promised to place God's name in the temple in Jerusalem, where *was* God's presence now to be found? Where was "the glory of God" that had descended into the temple? As with the monarchy, the answer was already contained in the tradition. In the exilic context, the words of Samuel to the errant Saul take on new significance: "Has the Lord as great delight in burnt offering and sacrifices, as in obeying the voice of the Lord? Surely, to obey is better than sacrifice, and to heed than the fat of rams" (1 Sam 15:22).[83] Jews could obey God's voice anywhere. The ritual of sacrifice, at the heart of the temple and priesthood, was not necessary to "delight" God, or even to worship God. Although those Jews who returned to Palestine promptly set about rebuilding the temple, the radical departure from the ritual of sacrifice signaled in the old prophet's words had now freed Jews to reconfigure their faith, ultimately in terms of rabbis ("teachers" of the Torah) and synagogues ("assembly" places).[84]

As for the name of God, God had promised to set it in the place that God would choose, but since that place remained undisclosed in Deuteronomy (it had to be without risking blatant anachronism), it meant that other places could qualify. God could be present *anywhere* that God chose. In fact, the mobility of God originally signified the *irrelevance* of a "house" for God (2 Sam 7:1–7).[85] Similarly, just as the glory of God descended into the temple, so it could *ascend* and move elsewhere, a scenario that unfolds in the opening chapters of Ezekiel (ch. 1; 8:1–6; ch. 10). Thus the trajectory of God's glory that began with the Exodus and seemed to

---

80. Note especially Isaiah 45, where the claim that Yahweh is God and there is "no other" appears four times. Not only is the claim based on Yahweh's identity as creator, as elsewhere in Second Isaiah, but here also in Yahweh's "anointing" Cyrus, the Persian King, to take over the Babylonian empire, thus combining Yahweh's acts as both cosmic creator and historical redeemer.

81. Smith, *Memoirs*, 122.

82. Cf. 2 Sam 5:10–12; chs. 6–7; 1 Kings 3–8.

83. Cf. Isa 1:11; Hos 6:6; Amos 5:21–24. Jeremiah 7:21–23 even has God deny ever having required sacrifices, a complete refutation of much of Exodus and Leviticus! In the first century C.E. Rabbi Jochanan referred to Hos 6:6 in responding to the question of fellow Jews who wanted to know how they could worship now that the *second* temple was destroyed by the Romans: God desires mercy, not sacrifice.

84. "Synagogue" is the Greek translation for Hebrew words meaning "assembly" or "congregation."

85. Polzin, *David*, 55–56, adds to his view of the Deuteronomic anti-monarchical stance the likelihood that, "a related purpose may very well have been to speak against Israel's understandable desire to rebuild the temple."

conclude at the temple, has resumed its course, albeit in the strangest way. Indeed, Ezekiel's vision of the departed Glory occurs while he is "among the exiles by the river Chebar" in Babylon (1:1; 10:21)—so the Glory of God, it would seem, has accompanied Israel to Babylon! The theological implications of this movement are truly enormous, but they were already latent in Nathan's oracle to David. Again, there were many who continued to think of a temple as necessary; in fact, Ezekiel has an elaborate vision of the new temple and a return of God's glory at the conclusion of his work (Ezekiel 40–47).[86] Still a precedent for the absence of a temple was set. Much later, the Rabbis would develop the image of God's Shekhinah, or Glory, and say, "'whithersoever Israel was exiled, the Shekhinah, as it were, went into exile with them.'"[87]

Finally, God's promise to the ancestors concluded with blessing: "in you all the families of the earth shall be blessed," or, alternatively, "shall bless themselves" (in either case, the ancestors mediate God's blessing to the world). How can exiled Israel, under the curse, ever be a blessing? In a sense, the answer appears in the preceding paragraphs. The Jews can continue to be God's special people, obedient to God's Torah, the wisdom of which all nations admire; thus the Jews can serve as a model of righteousness (right relations with God and neighbor), and thereby a blessing. Already in the prophecy of Micah, "in days to come" all nations would stream to Zion, seeking to learn Yahweh's ways and live by Yahweh's *torah* (Micah 4:1–4).[88] Thus, for all their drawbacks, the figures of the Davidic king and Jerusalem as the "holy city" that first appear within the Former Prophets have provided a vision of peace and justice that "expands to become inclusive of all human hopes and possibilities."[89] When we began this Conclusion with those Haitians singing the song of the Babylonian exiles, we saw how the ancient blessing on Israel might become a blessing to contemporary people on an island in the Caribbean.

In the end, the Book of the Former Prophets has led us back to the Book of the Torah. "The end of Kings is a gaping hole which, when we peer into it,

---

86. The Glory returns in 43:4–5. However, Ezekiel's description of the new temple sometimes seems paradisiacal. He also envisions new boundaries for the land (47:13–48:29).

87. Quoted by Fackenheim, *God's Presence*, 28, from the text *Mekilta de-Rabbi Ishmael*, I, 114. The word "Shekhinah" is based on the root *shakan*, "to tent, tabernacle." See the discussion of 2 Samuel 7 and 1 Kings 8. The imagery is picked up in the Christian doctrine of incarnation when the "word" "tents" or "tabernacles" in Jesus (John 1:14, NRSV "lived among"). In the apocalyptic book of Revelation, the "heavenly Jerusalem" will have no temple because *God* is the temple (21:22).

88. There is a parallel version in Isa 2:2–4. The setting in Micah is striking in that it follows immediately a prophecy of the destruction of Zion (3:12). Some prophecies of nations coming to Zion were not so benign, e.g., Isa 49:22–26! Cf. Gottwald, *Politics*, 251: "monotheism has encouraged a worldwide vision of peace and justice, while . . . all too easily dividing the world into 'us' and 'them.'"

89. Birch, *1 and 2 Samuel*, 1238. Cf. Miller, *Religion*, 12. For Roberts, "In Defense of the Monarchy," 378, the "messianic hope" should prevent dismissing "the imperialistic theology of the Davidic-Solomonic court as sheer apostasy, as nothing but the progressive paganization of the Yahwistic faith." Cf. Smith, *Early History*, 11, on the development of monotheism.

loops us back to Deuteronomy, to where we stand 'today' before Moses, 'outside', pondering the invitation to enter and participate in a new gift."[90] The Torah provided the foundation for the Former Prophets as a theodicy, spelling out why God was justified in inflicting the curse of the covenant on Israel. In a sense, the canonical collection of *all* the "prophetic" books—Former and Latter—works the same way, in that reading the Latter Prophets will also confirm the divine judgment narrated in the Former. At the same time, the Latter Prophets, as we have seen, interpreted and developed traditions like the Messiah or covenant or repentance in such a way that there was also hope beyond God's judgment. The prophets warned of bad things in good times, but then promised good things in bad times.

The Former Prophets is Israel's memory of at least seven hundred years of its history interpreted through the lens of the Torah. Precisely because it ends with an enormous national failure, it illustrates more eloquently than anything *in* the Torah why the "Great Commandment" of loving Yahweh alone is the center of Israel's identity. All other centers of value have collapsed—national sovereignty, territorial occupation, political power, and religious institutions. The Israelite is now a Jew, *yehudi*, but all that was represented by the name *yehudah* (Judah) is gone. The land is left, of course, but it is now a province of Babylon. Jewish identity must now be defined by the confession, "Yahweh is our God, Yahweh alone," with all that entails. All that the people have is their story. They have become the "people of the book." Remembering now becomes recital—reciting the community's grand story, especially liturgically but also in study and commentary (cf. Exod 13:3, 8–10; Deut 6:6-9; Josh 4:6-7); and remembering remains, as always, reenactment—that is, living in accordance with the story, which is to say righteously (Deut 6:25; 24:17-18). Unlike other ancient civilizations, they will leave no monument in stone—no pyramids, no Parthenon, no Coliseum. There will be a new temple, of course, but it too will not last, and the loss of the first will help to explain the loss of the second. Part of the second will survive the centuries—that part now called the "Wailing Wall"—but when Jews go there they will often have in hand the Torah, the book that shapes who they are and how they shall live more than any masonry can do.

The name of one of the characters in the Former Prophets could easily provide a title for the whole narrative—"Ichabod." He makes only a brief, cameo appearance as the new-born son of the unnamed wife of Phineas, one of Eli's corrupt sons. His mother will die in the process of giving birth to him, but with her last breath, she names him "Ichabod." The name is a question, meaning "where is the glory?" She is referring to the ark captured by the Philistines. However unrealistic such a scene may be (it gives off at least a whiff of male insensitivity), the name takes on deep significance in the light of how the Former Prophets ends, for the narrator explains the meaning of the name as "The glory has gone into exile from Israel" (1 Sam 4:21, AT). The verb (*galah*) will provide the

---

90. Gunn and Fewell, *Narrative*, 172.

noun meaning "exiled person" (*golah*). Of course, the ark eventually returned to Israel, and then David brought it to Jerusalem and placed it in a tent shrine, and then Solomon accomplished what David could not, building a lavish temple, and bringing the ark into the Holy of Holies, surrounded by all that gold. And as the ark entered the temple, the "glory of God" did too. But the ark did not contain that glory, nor did the temple, and when the temple was destroyed, almost half a millennium after Solomon, the ark disappeared forever. This time it did *not* return to Israel, but, for all we know, remained in Babylon among the spoils of war, or was melted down to make gold jewelry. This time the Glory had gone into exile *with* Israel.

Deuteronomic tradition insisted that the most significant function of the ark was not as the numinous throne of Yahweh but as the container for "the two tablets of stone that Moses had placed there at Horeb, where the Lord had made a covenant with the Israelites, when they came out of Egypt" (1 Kgs 8:9). Thus the ark contained the Ten Commandments and the "book of the covenant." (Exod 24:7, 12; Deut 9:9–10). If the ark represented God's Glory, it was because the ark contained God's words. Although we cannot know the historical accuracy of the Deuteronomist's claim, whatever the ark contained must have come to its same end when the temple was burned to the ground. Perhaps the tablets went on display in Babylon, or perhaps they were reduced to dust. What we do know is that, some thirty years or so after the temple's destruction, Ezra read "the book of the law of Moses" to those exiles who had returned to the land of Israel (Neh 8:1), as they stood before "the Water Gate."[91] Scholars continue to debate what that book contained, when it was written, where, and by whom. Certainly it contained much if not all of Deuteronomy. Perhaps copies of the scrolls survived the devastation; it is unlikely that the entire book was rewritten from memory, although we know that oral tradition in such cultures was far more effective in preserving texts than in our own.[92] Eventually, the book of the Torah came to include the books of Genesis through Numbers as well, and much later "the Torah" could refer to the whole of Hebrew Scripture, thereby including the Former Prophets. Mark Smith puts it well: "The Torah, indeed the [Hebrew] Bible as a whole, became part of Israel's portable shrine . . . The texts became the landscape of the places lost in exile, and they captured in words what was lost in time."[93]

---

91. From the perspective of American history, there is a wonderful irony in this scene in that the name of the building in Washington, DC, named the "Watergate" came to symbolize the corruption of the Nixon administration, and subsequently the suffix "-gate" has been used to label all sorts of scandals, real or not (to compound the irony, the "gate" was the "hall of justice" in Israelite towns).

92. In fact, according to Kermode, "The Canon," 601, "The legendary account of the growth of the Bible tells of the destruction of the sacred books during the Babylonian Captivity and their reconstruction by the divinely inspired memory of Ezra."

93. Smith, *Memoirs*, 85. Hoffman, "Principle, Story, and Myth," argues that Jews of today need to reconsider the positive role of myth in their identity, and that ancient Israel set the model: "Israel's biblical mission is to model life in exile, awaiting redemptive homecoming."

Whatever the historical sequence involved, it is clear that the task of remembering Israel's history that ultimately took shape in the Former Prophets played a critical role in mediating the book of the Torah in both its narrow and its widest sense. Together, the Torah and the Former Prophets presented a magnificent "history" of Israel, from the creation of the cosmos to the Exile, but with the hints of a future that lay ahead. Some of those who were involved in the composition of the Former Prophets could never have dreamed of how it would end because they were working long before the fall of Jerusalem. But all those who participated in the composition were witnesses for generations to come. They remembered, and in recording their memories they bequeathed a gift to all those who would hear their story. They taught the world how to "sing the Lord's song" in the poignant, bittersweet harmony of failure and endurance, mourning and rejoicing, despair and hope. Thus the charge to Joshua at the beginning could still be the charge to the Jews everywhere after the Exile, and to those who would identify with their story, even on a Caribbean island in the midst of calamity:

> Only be strong and very courageous, being careful to act in accordance with all the law that my servant Moses commanded you; do not turn from it to the right hand or to the left . . . Do not be frightened or dismayed, for the Lord your God is with you wherever you go.

Glossary

ark of the covenant: The ark was a portable wooden box overlaid with gold, situated in the most holy part of the tabernacle and later temple (Exod 25:10–22; 1 Kgs 8:6–9). The lid of the ark consisted of two fierce cherubim (not to be confused with Valentine cupids), which functioned as an iconic throne protecting the invisible presence of God. In early traditions the ark is associated with Yahweh as Lord of Hosts and functions as a standard or palladium carried in warfare to represent the presence of Yahweh as Holy Warrior (Num 10:35–36; Ps 68:1, 17–18). Deuteronomic tradition emphasizes the ark's other function: it contained the tablets of the Ten Commandments—Israel's covenant with God (hence the term "ark of the covenant"). The ark figures prominently in Joshua 3–5, 1 Samuel 4–6, 2 Samuel 6, and 1 Kings 8.

Asherah: a Canaanite goddess as well as the name for a wooden image (*'asherah*) used in worship, sometimes translated as "sacred pole" in the NRSV; plural usually *'asherim*. See Excursus 4.

Baal: a god in Ugaritic (Canaanite) mythology, a storm deity who competes with Yahweh in providing rain and therefore fertility. See Excursus 4.

ephod: an object used in divination, sometimes described as a kind of priestly vestment, but perhaps taking different shape in other traditions. See Excursus 4.

ḥerem (the ḥ sound is like the *ch* in German *ich* or the Scottish *loch*): the "ban" of warfare in which whole populations are put to death, often constituting (for the modern reader) genocide or "ethnic cleansing."

ḥesed, the Hebrew word often translated as "steadfast love," meaning also "fidelity," "loyalty," "allegiance."

Masoretic Text (abbreviated as "MT"): the Hebrew text of the Bible. "Masora" refers to various kinds of editorial notations.

nagid: "king elect," often translated "prince" in the NRSV

sacerdotal: I use this adjective to refer to various subjects having to do with priestly matters, worship, liturgy, sanctuaries, etc. Often I use the word instead of the common scholarly word "cultic" or "cult" because the latter for many people has the automatic connotation of something weird, unorthodox, and even demonic, even though scholars use "cult" to refer to both orthodox and heterodox matters.

Septuagint (often indicated by the letters LXX). The first Greek translation of the Hebrew Bible, accomplished in Alexandria, Egypt, in the third century BCE.

theophany (adjective "theophanic"): an appearance or manifestation of the divine, ranging from angels to thunderstorms.

Ugarit (adjective, Ugaritic): The ancient city on the coast of Palestine that produced the mythic texts about Baal and other Canaanite deities, along with epic tales about the characters Keret and Aqhat, dating from the end of the fourteenth century.

Yahweh, abbreviated YHWH or Yhwh / "the LORD": The NRSV follows ancient convention in rendering the personal name for God, "Yahweh," with "the LORD." Whenever quoting the NRSV, I follow suit. This gesture of reverence derives from the notion that God's name is too holy to pronounce. Indeed, the tradition is already in the Hebrew Bible, where the name simply appears with the consonants *yhwh* (the "Tetragrammaton") and the *vowels* that are in the word *'adonai* ("lord"; the English invention "Jehovah" follows this tradition, with the *v* interchanging with *w* [as in German]). The name is derived from the verb that means "to be, to become" (*yhwh* from the root *hyh*). Some Jews will not say or even write the full name. In reading the Hebrew text, when they come to the consonants *yhwh* they will say "Adonai" ("lord") or even *hashem* ("the name"). Nevertheless, God does have a personal name, and sometimes it is crucial in understanding the text. "Lord," after all, is a title, not a personal name. People in England, where there still are "lords," will recognize the difference more easily. "Lord" is also masculine, with the feminine being "lady," a title that you will definitely *not* see used for Yahweh. Thus to say "the Lord is God" seems like a tautology, but to say "Yahweh is God" is to make a claim about a specific deity over against other contenders. (Compare "the President is President" over against, say, "Obama is President" and you will see the difference!) With all due respect to Jewish sentiment, in my own translations I will often use the name Yahweh. I appeal to our Taoist friends who, in the *Tao Te Ching*, say at the outset, "The name that can be named / is not the eternal Name. // The unnamable is the eternally real. / Naming is the origin / of all particular things" (translated by Mitchell, *Tao Te Ching*, 1).

Bibliography

Albright, William F. "The Moabite Stone." In *Ancient Near Eastern Texts Relating to the Old Testament*, edited by James B. Pritchard, 320-21. 3rd ed. Princeton: Princeton University Press, 1969.
Allen, Diogenes. *Christian Belief in a Postmodern World*. Louisville: Westminster John Knox, 1989.
Allende, Isabel. Interview regarding her novel *The Island beneath the Sea*. The Lehrer Report: PBS Newshour, 24 May 2010.
Alter, Robert. *The Art of Biblical Narrative*. New York: Basic Books, 1981.
———. *The David Story: A Translation with Commentary of 1 and 2 Samuel*. New York: Norton, 1999.
Anderson, Herbert. *The Family and Pastoral Care*. Theology and Pastoral Care Series. Philadelphia: Fortress, 1984.
Angelou, Maya. *I Know Why the Caged Bird Sings*. London: Virago, 1984.
Auld, A. G. *Joshua Retold: Synoptic Perspectives*. Old Testament Studies. Edinburgh: T. & T. Clark, 1998.
Austin, Richard Cartwright. *Beauty of the Lord: Awakening the Senses*. Environmental Theology 2. Atlanta: John Knox, 1988.
Bal, Mieke. *Lethal Love: Feminist Literary Readings of Biblical Love Stories*. Indiana Studies in Biblical Literature. Bloomington: Indiana University Press, 1987.
Barbour, Ian. *Religion in an Age of Science*. Vol. 1. Gifford Lectures 1989-1990. San Francisco: Harper & Row, 1990.
Bellah, Robert., et al. *Habits of the Heart: Individualism and Commitment in American Life*. New York: Harper & Row, 1985.
——— et al. *Individualism and Commitment in American Life: Readings on the Themes of "Habits of the Heart."* New York: Harper & Row, 1987.
Berlin, Adele, and Marc Zvi Brettler, editors. *The Jewish Study Bible*. Oxford: Oxford University Press, 2004.
Berlin, Adele. "Ruth and the Continuity of Israel." In *Reading Ruth: Contemporary Women Reclaim a Sacred Story*, edited by Judith A. Kates and Gail Twersky Reimer, 255-60. New York: Ballantine, 1994.
Birch, Bruce C. *1 and 2 Samuel*. In *The New Interpreter's Bible* 2:947-1383. Nashville: Abingdon, 1998.
Bird, Phyllis. "The Harlot as Heroine: Narrative Art and Social Presupposition in Three Old Testament Tests." *Semeia* 46 (1989) 119-39.
Blood-Patterson, Peter, editor. *Rise Up Singing*. Bethlehem, PA: Sing Out Corporation, 1988.
Bodner, Keith. *1 Samuel: A Narrative Commentary*. Hebrew Bible Monographs 19. Sheffield: Sheffield Phoenix, 2008.
Brooks, Geraldine. *Year of Wonders: A Novel of the Plague*. New York: Viking, 2001.
Brueggemann, Walter. *1 & 2 Kings*. Smyth & Helwys Bible Commentary 8. Macon, GA: Smyth & Helwys, 2000.
———. *First and Second Samuel*. Interpretation. Louisville: Westminster John Knox, 1990.
Bunker, Nick. *Making Haste from Babylon: The Mayflower Pilgrims and Their World; A New History*. New York: Knopf, 2010.

Calloway Joseph A., and J. Maxwell Miller. "The Settlement in Canaan: The Period of the Judges." In *Ancient Israel: From Abraham to the Roman Destruction of the Temple*, edited by Hershel Shanks, 55–90. Rev. ed. Washington, DC: Biblical Archaeology Society, 1999.

Campbell, Antony F. *From Joshua to Chronicles: An Introduction*. Louisville: Westminster John Knox, 2004.

———. "God's Anger and Our Suffering." *Australasian Catholic Record* 59 (1982) 373–85.

———. *Of Prophets and Kings: A Late Ninth-Century Document (1 Samuel 1–2 Kings 10)*. Catholic Biblical Quarterly Monograph Series 17. Washington DC: Catholic Biblical Association of America, 1986.

Campbell, Antony F., and Mark A. O'Brien, *Unfolding the Deuteronomistic History: Origins, Upgrades, Present Text*. Minneapolis: Fortress, 2000.

Campbell, Edward F., Jr. *Ruth: A New Translation with Introduction, Notes, and Commentary*. Anchor Bible 7. Garden City, NY: Doubleday, 1975.

Carlson, R. A. *David, the Chosen King: A Traditio-historical Approach to the Second Book of Samuel*. Translated by Eric J. Sharpe and Stanley Rudman. Stockholm: Almqvist & Wiksell, 1964.

Childs, Brevard S. *The Book of Exodus: A Critical and Theological Commentary*. Old Testament Library. Philadelphia: Westminster, 1974.

———. *Introduction to the Old Testament as Scripture*. Philadelphia: Fortress, 1979.

Coffin, William Sloane. *Credo*. Louisville: Westminster John Knox, 2004.

Cogan, Mordechai. *I Kings*. Anchor Bible 10. Garden City, NY: Doubleday, 2001.

———, and Hayim Tadmor. *II Kings*. Anchor Bible 11. Garden City, NY: Doubleday, 1988.

Cohen, S "Jordan." In *The Interpreter's Dictionary of the Bible*, edited by George A. Buttrick, 1:973–78. Nashville: Abingdon, 1962.

Collins, John J. "The Bible and the Legitimation of Violence." *Reflections: Yale Divinity School* (Winter 2004) 4–7.

Coogan, Michael David. "Canaanite Origins and Lineage: Reflections on the Religion of Ancient Israel." In *Ancient Israelite Religion: Essays in Honor of Frank Moore Cross*, edited by Patrick D. Miller et al., 115–24. Minneapolis: Fortress, 1987.

———, editor and translator. *Stories from Ancient Canaan*. Philadelphia: Westminster, 1978.

Cook, Roy. "Thanksgiving: A Day of Mourning." Online: http://americanindiansource.com/mourningday.html/.

Coote, Richard B. *The Book of Joshua*. In *The New Interpreter's Bible*, 2:553–719. Nashville: Abingdon, 1998

Cross, Frank Moore, Jr. *Canaanite Myth and Hebrew Epic: Essays in the History of the Religion of Israel*. Cambridge: Harvard University Press, 1973.

Dearman, Andrew, editor. *Studies in the Mesha Inscription and Moab*. Archaeology and Biblical Studies 2. Atlanta: Scholars, 1989.

Dellek, Robert. *Flawed Giant: Lyndon Johnson and His Times, 1961–1973*. New York: Oxford University Press, 1998.

Dever, William C. "The Contribution of Archaeology to the Study of Canaanite and Early Israelite Religion." In *Ancient Israelite Religion: Essays in Honor of Frank Moore Cross*, edited by Patrick D. Miller et al., 209–47. Minneapolis: Fortress, 1987.

———. *Did God Have a Wife? Archaeology and Folk Religion in Ancient Israel*. Grand Rapids: Eerdmans, 2005.

Dickens, Charles. *A Christmas Carol*. New York: Peter Pauper Press, n.d.

Elie, Paul. "A Man for All Reasons." *The Atlantic Monthly*, November 2007, 82–96.

Eskenazi, Tamara Cohn. "Ezra-Nehemiah," In *The Women's Bible Commentary*, edited by Carol A. Newsom and Sharon H. Ringe, 123–30. Expanded ed. Louisville: Westminster John Knox, 1998

Exum, Cheryl. *Plotted, Shot, and Painted: Cultural Representations of Biblical Women*. Journal for the Study of the Old Testament. Supplement Series 215. Gender, Culture, Theory 3. Sheffield: Sheffield Academic, 1996.

Fackenheim, Emil L. *God's Presence in History: Jewish Affirmations and Philosophical Reflections*. New York: Harper, 1970.

Fallows, James. "How America Can Rise Again." *The Atlantic Monthly*, March 2010, 38–55.

Farmer, Kathleen A. Robertson. *The Book of Ruth*. In *The New Interpreter's Bible*, 2:889–946. Nashville: Abingdon, 1998.

Faulkner, William. *Go Down, Moses*. New York: The Modern Library, 1940.
Feiler, Bruce. *Walking the Bible: A Journey by Land through the Five Books of Moses*. New York: Morrow, 2001.
Fewell, Danna Nolan, and David Miller Gunn. *Compromising Redemption: Relating Characters in the Book of Ruth*. Literary Currents in Biblical Interpretation. Louisville: Westminster John Knox, 1990.
Fokkelman, J. P. *Narrative Art and Poetry in the Books of Samuel*. Vol. 1, *King David (II Sam. 9-20 & I Kings 1-2*. Studia Semitica Neerlandica 20. Assen: Van Gorcum, 1981.
———. *Narrative Art and Poetry in the Books of Samuel*. Vol. 2, *The Crossing Fates (1 Sam. 13-31 & II Sam. 1)*. Studia Semitica Neerlandica 23. Assen: Van Gorcum, 1986.
———. *Narrative Art and Poetry in the Books of Samuel*. Vol. 3, *Throne and City (II Sam. 2-8 & 21-24)*. Studia Semitica Neerlandica 27. Assen: Van Gorcum, 1990.
———. *Narrative Art and Poetry in the Books of Samuel*. Vol. 4, *Vow and Desire (I Sam. 1-12)*. Studia Semitica Neerlandica 31. Assen: Van Gorcum, 1993.
Freedman, David Noel. "The Religion of Early Israel." In *Ancient Israelite Religion: Essays in Honor of Frank Moore Cross*, edited by Patrick D. Miller et al., 315-35. Minneapolis: Fortress, 1987.
Fretheim, Terence E. *God and World in the Old Testament: A Relational Theology of Creation*. Nashville: Abingdon, 2005.
Friedman, Richard Elliot. *Who Wrote the Bible?* New York: Harper & Row, 1987.
Goodfriend, Elaine Adler. "Prostitution." In *The Anchor Bible Dictionary*, edited by David Noel Freedman 5:505-10. 6 vols. New York: Doubleday, 1992.
Goodman, Ellen. "Equal Rites Awards 2009." *The Winston-Salem Journal*, August 27, 2009, A9.
Griswold, Eliza. "God's Country." *The Atlantic Monthly*, March 2008, 40-55.
Gottwald, Norman K. *The Politics of Ancient Israel*. Library of Ancient Israel. Louisville: Westminster John Knox, 2001.
Greenstein, Edward L. "Kirta." In *Ugaritic Narrative Poetry*, edited by Simon B. Parker, 9-48. SBL Writings from the Ancient World Series. Atlanta: Scholars, 1997.
Gunn, David M. *The Fate of King Saul: An Interpretation of a Biblical Story*. Journal for the Study of the Old Testament Supplement Series 14. Sheffield: University of Sheffield Department of Biblical Studies, 1980.
———. "Joshua and Judges." In *The Literary Guide to the Bible*, edited by Robert Alter and Frank Kermode, 102-21. Cambridge: Belknap, 1987.
———. *The Story of King David: Genre and Interpretation*. Journal for the Study of the Old Testament Supplement Series 6. Sheffield: University of Sheffield Department of Biblical Studies, 1978.
Gunn, David M., and Dana Nolan Fewell. *Narrative in the Hebrew Bible*. Oxford Bible Series. Oxford: Oxford University Press, 1993.
Hackett, Jo Ann. "1 and 2 Samuel." In *The Women's Bible Commentary*, edited by Carol A. Newsom and Sharon H. Ringe, 91-101. Louisville: Westminster John Knox, 1998.
Hallo, William W., and William Kelly Simpson. *The Ancient Near East: A History*. New York: Harcourt Brace Jovanovich, 1971
Halpern, Baruch. *The First Historians: The Hebrew Bible and History*. San Francisco: Harper & Row, 1988.
Hawk, L. Daniel. *Joshua*. Berit Olam. Collegeville, MN: Liturgical, 2000.
Hay, William Anthony. "Of Storytellers and Statesmen." Review of *Grand Strategies*, by Charles Hill. *The Wall Street Journal* June 12, 2010, W9.
Herzfeld, Noreen. "The Games Kids Play." *The Christian Century* May 4, 2004, 22-23.
Hiebert, Theodore. *The Yahwist's Landscape: Nature and Religion in Early Israel*. New York: Oxford University Press, 1996.
Hitchens, Christopher. "Master of Conventions," *The Atlantic*, September 2008, 113.
Hoffman, Lawrence A. "Principle, Story, and Myth in the Liturgical Search for Identity." *Interpretation* (July 2010) 231-44.
Homer. *The Iliad*. Translated by Samuel Butler. Great Books of the Western World 4. Chicago: Encyclopaedia Britannica, 1952.
Jackson, Kent P. "The Language of the Mesha Inscription." In *Studies in the Mesha Inscription and Moab*, edited by Andrew Dearman, 96-130. Archaeology and Biblical Studies 2. Atlanta: Scholars, 1989.

James, P. D. *The Private Patient*. New York: Knopf, 2008.

Johnson, William Stacy. "God's Ordering, Providing, and Caring for the World: Grace as 'Gift of Death.'" *Theology Today* 54 (1997) 29–42.

Jobling, David. *1 Samuel*. Berit Olam. Collegeville, MN: Liturgical, 1998.

Kapelrud, Arvid S. "Temple Building: A Task for Gods and Kings." *Orientalia* 21 (1963) 56–62.

Kates, Judith A., and Gail Twersky Reimer, editors. *Reading Ruth: Contemporary Women Reclaim a Sacred Story*. New York: Ballantine, 1994.

Kermode, Frank. "The Canon," In *The Literary Guide to the Bible*, edited by Robert Alter and Frank Kermode, 600–610. Cambridge: Belknap, 1987

Kessell, John L. *Spain in the Southwest*. Norman: University of Oklahoma Press, 2002.

King, Martin Luther., Jr. "Letter from Birmingham Jail." In *Why We Can't Wait*, 76–95. New York: Harper & Row, 1963.

Klein, Julia M. "'Ancient Rome & America' in Juxtaposition." *The Wall Street Journal*, April 24, 2010, W9.

Klein, Lillian R. "Bathsheba Revealed." In *Samuel and Kings*, edited by Athalya Brenner, 47–64. Feminist Companion to the Bible, 2nd series, 7. Sheffield: Sheffield Academic, 2000.

Kugel, James L. *How to Read the Bible: A Guide to Scripture, Then and Now*. New York: Free Press, 2007.

Kushner, Harold. *When Bad Things Happen to Good People*. 2nd ed. New York: Schocken, 1989.

Lane, Belden. *The Solace of Fierce Landscapes: Exploring Desert and Mountain Spirituality*. New York: Oxford University Press, 1998

Levenson, Jon D. *Resurrection and the Restoration of Israel: The Ultimate Victory of the God of Life*. New Haven: Yale University Press, 2006.

Levine, Amy-Jill. "Ruth." In *The Women's Bible Commentary*, edited by Carol A. Newsom and Sharon H. Ringe, 84–90. Louisville: Westminster John Knox, 1998.

Linafelt, Tod A. "Ruth." In *Ruth and Esther*, xi–xxv, 1–90. Berit Olam. Collegeville, MN: Liturgical, 1999.

Lloyd, J. B. "Anat and the 'Double' Massacre of KTU 1.3 ii." In *Ugarit, Religion and Culture*, edited by N. Wyatt et al., 151–65. Ugaritisch-biblische Literatur 12. Münster: Ugarit, 1996.

Mann, Thomas W. *The Book of the Torah*. Atlanta: John Knox, 1988.

———. *Deuteronomy*. Louisville: Westminster John Knox, 1995.

———. *Divine Presence and Guidance in Israelite Traditions: The Typology of Exaltation*. Johns Hopkins Near Eastern Studies. Baltimore: Johns Hopkins University Press, 1977.

———. *God of Dirt: Mary Oliver and the Other Book of God*. Boston: Cowley, 2004.

———. "Passover: The Time of Our Lives. *Interpretation* 50 (1996) 240–50.

———. "Stars, Sprouts, and Streams": The Creative Redeemer of Second Isaiah." In *God Who Creates: Essays in Honor of W. Sibley Towner*, edited by William P. Brown and S. Dean McBride, Jr., 135–51. Grand Rapids: Eerdmans, 2000.

———. "Theological Reflections on the Denial of Moses." *Journal of Biblical Literature* 98 (1979) 481–94.

———. *To Taste and See: Exploring Incarnation and the Ambiguities of Faith*. 1992. Reprinted, Eugene, OR: Wipf & Stock, 2008.

Mathews, Donald G. *Religion in the Old South*. Chicago History of American Religion. Chicago: University of Chicago Press, 1977.

Matthews, Victor H. *Judges and Ruth*. New Cambridge Bible Commentary. Cambridge: Cambridge University Press, 2004.

McBride, S. Dean, Jr. "Deuteronomy, Book of." In *The New Interpreter's Dictionary of the Bible*, edited by Katharine Doob Sakenfeld 2:108–17. Nashville: Abingdon, 2006.

———. "The Essence of Orthodoxy: Deuteronomy 5:6–10 and Exodus 20:2–6." *Interpretation* 60 (2006) 133–51.

———. "Polity of the Covenant People: The Book of Deuteronomy," In *Constituting the Community: Studies on the Polity of Ancient Israel in Honor of S. Dean McBride Jr.*, edited by John T. Strong and Steven S. Tuell, 17–33. Winona Lake, IN: Eisenbrauns, 2005.

———. "The Yoke of the Kingdom: An Exposition of Deuteronomy 6:4–5." *Interpretation* 27 (1973) 273–306.

McCarter, P. Kyle, Jr. "Aspects of the Religion in the Israelite Monarchy: Biblical and Epigraphic Data." In *Ancient Israelite Religion: Essays in Honor of Frank Moore Cross*, edited by Patrick D. Miller et al., 137–55. Philadelphia: Fortress, 1987.

———. *I Samuel*. Anchor Bible 8. Garden City, NY: Doubleday, 1980.

———. "Introduction and Annotations to the Books of Samuel." In *TheHarperCollins Study Bible*, edited by Wayne A. Meeks et al., 416–508. New York: HarperCollins, 1993.

———. *II Samuel*. Anchor Bible 9. Garden City, NY: Doubleday, 1984.

McFague, Sallie. *Models of God: Theology for an Ecological, Nuclear Age*. Philadelphia: Fortress, 1987.

McKenzie, John. "Deuteronomistic History." In *The Anchor Bible Dictionary*, edited by David Noel Freedman, 2:160–68. 6 vols. New York: Doubleday, 1992.

McNutt, Paula M. *Reconstructing the Society of Ancient Israel*. Library of Ancient Israel. Louisville: Westminster John Knox, 1999.

Meyers, Carol L. "David as Temple Builder." In *Ancient Israelite Religion: Essays in Honor of Frank Moore Cross*, edited by Patrick D. Miller et al., 357–76. Minneapolis: Fortress, 1987.

———. *The Tabernacle Menorah: A Synthetic Study of a Symbol from the Biblical Cult*. American Schools of Oriental Research Dissertation Series 2. Missoula, MT: Scholars, 1976.

Miller, Patrick D. "Aspects of the Religion of Ugarit," In *Ancient Israelite Religion: Essays in Honor of Frank Moore Cross*, edited by Patrick D. Miller et al., 53–66. Minneapolis: Fortress, 1987.

———, and J. J. M. Roberts. *The Hand of the Lord: A Reassessment of the "Ark Narrative" of 1 Samuel*. Johns Hopkins Near Eastern Studies. Baltimore: Johns Hopkins University Press, 1977.

———. *The Religion of Ancient Israel*. Library of Ancient Israel. Louisville: Westminster John Knox, 2000.

———. *The Ten Commandments*. Interpretation. Louisville: Westminster John Knox, 2009.

Mitchell, Stephen, editor. *Tao Te Ching: A New English Version*. New York: Harper & Row, 1988.

Moran, William L. "The Ancient Near Eastern Background of Love of God in Deuteronomy." *Catholic Biblical Quarterly* 25 (1963) 77–87.

Mueller, E. Aydeet. *The Micah Story: A Morality Tale in the Book of Judges*. Studies in Biblical Literature 34. New York: Lang, 2001.

Nelson, Richard. D. *First and Second Kings*. Interpretation. Atlanta: John Knox, 1987.

———. *Joshua: A Commentary*. Old Testament Library. Louisville: Westminster John Knox, 1997.

———. "Josiah in the Book of Joshua." *Journal of Biblical Literature* 100 (1981) 531–40.

Newman, Murray L. "Rahab and the Conquest." In *Understanding the Word: Essays in Honor of Bernhard W. Anderson*, edited by James T. Butler et al., 167–81. Journal for the Study of the Old Testament Supplement Series 37. Sheffield: JSOT Press, 1985.

Niditch, Susan. *Judges: A Commentary*. Old Testament Library. Louisville: Westminster John Knox, 2008.

———. *War in the Hebrew Bible: A Study in the Ethics of Violence*. New York: Oxford University Press, 1993.

Niebuhr, Reinhold. *The Children of Light and the Children of Darkness: A Vindication of Democracy and a Critique of Its Traditional Defense*. New York: Scribner, 1944.

Nigg, Walter. *The Heretics*. Edited and translated by Richard and Clara Winston. 1949. New York: Knopf, 1962.

Noth, Martin. *The Deuteronomistic History*. 2nd ed. Journal for the Study of the Old Testament Supplement Series 15. Sheffield: JSOT Press, 1991.

O'Brien, Tim. *In the Lake of the Woods*. Boston: Houghton Mifflin, 1994.

Olson, Dennis T. "Judges." In *The New Interpreter's Bible*, edited by Leander E. Keck, 2:723–888. Nashville: Abingdon, 1998.

Pardee, Dennis. *Ritual and Cult at Ugarit*. Edited by Theodore J. Lewis. Writings from the Ancient World 10. Atlanta: Society of Biblical Literature, 2002

Parker, Simon B., editor. "Aqhat." In *Ugaritic Narrative Poetry*, 49–80. Translated by Simon B. Parker. Writings from the Ancient World 9. Atlanta: Scholars, 1997.

———. "The Baal Cycle." In *Ugaritic Narrative Poetry*, 81–180. Translated by Mark S. Smith. Writings from the Ancient World 9. Atlanta: Scholars, 1997.

———. *Ugaritic Narrative Poetry*. Writings from the Ancient World 9. Atlanta: Scholars, 1997.

Penchansky, David. *Twilight of the Gods: Polytheism in the Hebrew Bible*. Louisville: Westminster John Knox, 2005.

Perdue, Leo G. "Introduction and Annotations to the Book of Jeremiah." In *The HarperCollins Study Bible*, edited by Wayne A. Meeks et al., 1110-1207 New York: HarperCollins, 1993.

Pitts, Leonard. "Brutal Act of Bigotry an Outrage to All of Us." *The Winston Salem Journal*, September 16, 2009, A19.

Pritchard, James B., editor. *Ancient Near Eastern Texts Relating to the Old Testament*. 3rd ed. Princeton: Princeton University, 1969.

Polzin, Robert. *David and the Deuteronomist: 2 Samuel*. Indiana Studies in Biblical Literature. Bloomington: Indiana University Press, 1993.

———. *Moses and the Deuteronomist*. New York: Seabury, 1980.

———. *Samuel and the Deuteronomist: A Study of the Deuteronomic History; Part Two, 1 Samuel*. San Francisco: Harper & Row, 1989.

Roberts, J. J. M. "In Defense of the Monarchy." In *Ancient Israelite Religion: Essays in Honor of Frank Moore Cross*, edited by Patrick D. Miller et al., 377-96. Minneapolis: Fortress, 1987.

Rosenberg, Joel. "1 and 2 Samuel." In *The Literary Guide to the Bible*, edited by Robert Alter and Frank Kermode, 122-45. Cambridge: Belknap, 1987.

Robinson, Eugene. "The New Reality for the Black American." *The Winston-Salem Journal* July 22, 2009, A6.

Römer, Thomas. *The So-Called Deuteronomistic History: A Sociological, Historical and Literary Introduction*. London: T. & T. Clark, 2005.

Rubenstein, Suzanne. *Raymond Carver in the Classroom: "A Small Good Thing."* NCTE High School Literature Series. Urbana, IL: National Council of Teachers of English, 2005.

Rubin, Martin. "Matron for a Nation." Review of *The Queen Mother*, by William Shawcross. *Wall Street Journal*, October 31, 2009, W6.

Russell, Robert J. "Does the God Who Acts Really Act?—New Approaches to Divine Action in Light of Science." *Theology Today* 54 (1997) 43-66.

Sakenfeld, Katharine Doob. *Ruth*. Interpretation. Louisville: Westminster John Knox, 1999.

Schneider, Tammi. *Judges*. Berit Olam. Collegeville, MN: Liturgical, 2000.

Schroer, Silvia, and Thomas Staubli. "Saul, David and Jonathan—the Story of a Triangle? A Contribution to the Issue of Homosexuality in the First Testament." In *Samuel and Kings*, edited by Athalya Brenner, 22-36. Feminist Companion to the Bible, 2nd series, 7. Sheffield: Sheffield Academic, 2000.

Sheehy, Gail. *Passages: Predictable Crises of Adult Life*. New York: Dutton, 1976.

Siemon-Netto, Uwe. *The Acquittal of God: A Theology for Vietnam Veterans*. New York: Pilgrim, 1990.

Smith, Mark S. *The Early History of God: Yahweh and the Other Deities of Ancient Israel*. 2nd ed. The Biblical Resource Series. Grand Rapids: Eerdmans, 2002.

———. *The Memoirs of God: History, Memory, and the Experience of the Divine in Ancient Israel*. Minneapolis: Fortress, 2004.

———. *The Origins of Biblical Monotheism: Israel's Polytheistic Background and the Ugaritic Texts*. New York: Oxford University Press, 2001.

Smith, Wilfred Cantwell. "Idolatry." In *The Myth of Christian Uniqueness: Toward a Pluralistic Theology of Religions*, edited by John Hick and Paul F. Knitter, 53-68. Faith Meets Faith. Maryknoll, NY: Orbis, 1987.

Stein, Garth. *The Art of Racing in the Rain: A Novel*. New York: Harper, 2009.

Sternberg, Meir. *The Poetics of Biblical Narrative: Ideological Literature and the Drama of Reading*. The Indiana Literary Biblical Series Bloomington: Indiana University Press, 1985.

Stroup, George W. *Calvin*. Abingdon Pillars of Theology. Nashville: Abingdon, 2009.

Sweeney, Marvin A. *I & II Kings: A Commentary*. Old Testament Library. Louisville: Westminster John Knox, 2007.

———. *King Josiah of Judah: The Lost Messiah of Israel*. Oxford: Oxford University Press, 2001.

Tigay, Jeffrey H. "Israelite Religion: Onomastic and Epigraphic Evidence." In *Ancient Israelite Religion: Essays in Honor of Frank Moore Cross Jr.*, edited by Patrick D. Miller et al., 157-94. Philadelphia: Fortress, 1987.

———. *You Shall Have No Other Gods: Israelite Religion in the Light of Hebrew Inscriptions.* Harvard Semitic Studies 31. Atlanta: Scholars, 1986.

Tillich, Paul. *Dynamics of Faith.* World Perspectives 10. New York: Harper & Row, 1957.

Toorn, Karel van der. "Cultic Prostitution." In *The Anchor Bible Dictionary*, edited by David Noel Freedman, 5:510–13. New York: Doubleday, 1992.

Tran, Jonathan. *The Vietnam War and Theologies of Memory: Time and Eternity in the Far Country.* Challenges in Contemporary Theology. Chichester, UK: Wiley-Blackwell, 2010.

Trible, Phyllis. *God and the Rhetoric of Sexuality.* Overtures to Biblical Theology 2. Philadelphia: Fortress, 1978.

———. *Texts of Terror: Literary-Feminist Readings of Biblical Narratives.* Overtures to Biblical Theology 13. Philadelphia: Fortress, 1984.

Volf, Miroslav. *The End of Memory: Remembering Rightly in a Violent World.* Stob Lectures 2002. Grand Rapids: Eerdmans, 2006.

Webb, Barry G. *The Book of Judges: An Integrated Reading.* Journal for the Study of the Old Testament Supplement Series 46. Sheffield: JSOT Press, 1987.

Weigle, Marta, and Peter White. *The Lore of New Mexico.* Publications of the American Folklore Society, new series. Albuquerque: University of New Mexico Press, 1988.

Weinfeld, Moshe. *Deuteronomy and the Deuteronomic School.* Oxford: Clarendon, 1972.

Wilson, Robert R. "Introduction and Annotations to the Books of Kings." In *TheHarperCollins Study Bible*, edited by Wayne A. Meeks et al., 509–604. New York: HarperCollins, 1993.

———. *Prophecy and Society in Ancient Israel.* Philadelphia: Fortress, 1980.

Winthrop, John. "A Model of Christian Charity." 3 pages. Online: http://www.muhsd.k12.ca.us/.../Winthrop_A_Model_of_Christian_Charity.pdf

Wyatt, Nicolas. *The Mythic Mind: Essays on Cosmology and Religion in Ugaritic and Old Testament Literature.* BibleWorld. London: Equinox, 2005.

———. *Religious Texts from Ugarit.* 2nd ed. Biblical Seminar 53. Sheffield: Sheffield Academic, 2002.

Yee, Gale. "Hosea." In *The Women's Bible Commentary*, edited by Carol A. Newsom and Sharon H. Ringe, 207–15. Expanded ed. Louisville: Westminster John Knox, 1998.

Younger, K. L. *Ancient Conquest Accounts: A Study in Ancient Near Eastern and Biblical History Writing.* Journal for the Study of the Old Testament Supplement Series 98. Sheffield: JSOT Press, 1990.

Zaki, Moheb. "Egypt's Persecuted Christians." *Wall Street Journal* May 18, 2010, A15.

Zinn, Howard. *A People's History of the United States: 1492–Present.* Rev. and updated ed. New York: HarperPerennial, 1995.

Scripture Index

OLD TESTAMENT

Genesis

1	397, 409
1:2	134
1:26	115
2:9	254
2:17	205
2:21	164
2:24	97
3:4–6	205, 254
3:22	205, 254
6:1–4	59
7:11–12	293
8:1	401
8:2	293
9:4	140
9:16	238, 348
12	397, 408
16	75
17:7	238
17:13	238
17:19	238
19	90
20:3	254
20:8–10	5, 74
20:31	254
22	288
25:21–23	113
27–28	188
27	45
28:10–22	302
28:11–22	242
28:13	114, 254
28:18–22	62
28:20–22	208
29:21—30:24	103
29:31	103
30:2	103
30:22	103
31:13	231, 252
31:30–35	62
32	216
32:22–32	297
32:28	38, 59
32:30–31	274
32:30	70, 72
34:7	202
35:7	288
35:11	59
35:18–20	49
38	103
39:2	154
39:6	154
39:23	154
41	293
43:31	135
45:1	135
47:7	254
48–49	45
49–50	248
49	234
49:24	275
50:25	49
50:26	379

Exodus

1	172
1:6–8	54, 64
1:11	98, 257
1:14	98
2:15	301
2:21–24	124
2:23–25	121
2:23	123
2:24	55
2:28	310
3	125
3:1—4:9	71
3:1–6	28
3:1	60, 300
3:2	301
3:7–12	28
3:7–10	121, 127
3:7–8	30, 407
3:9	55
3:11—4:17	128
3:12	128, 260, 300
3:22	117
4	277
4:8–9	128
4:21	146
5:2	327
6:7	327, 344
8:15	146
9:12	272
9:14	151
9:29	151
10:15	309
12:1—13:16	27
12:1–13	27
12:2	28
12:9	331
12:11	30
12:13	241
12:14	28
12:24–27	24
12:25	28, 30
12:26–27	28
12:36	117
12:40–41	28
12:48–49	37
12:48	28
13–14	291
13:1–2	111, 114
13:3	412
13:8–10	412
13:8	28
13:11–16	288
13:14	28
13:21–22	260
13:21	290
13:26	291
14–15	68
14:6–7	66
14:14	151
14:16	28
14:19–20	290
14:21–22	28
14:21	320
14:24–25	40
14:29	28
14:30–31	28, 151
14:31	114, 298
15	68, 180, 256
15:4–16	28
15:4–5	68
15:8–9	290
15:8–10	290
15:11	328
15:15	214
15:18	74
16:2	378
16:22–25a	321
17:8–13	141
19–20	303
19	181
19:1–3	300
19:1	28, 378
19:2	60
19:3–8	123
19:3–4	263
19:4–6	122
19:4–5	312
19:5–6	344
19:5	47
19:6	260
19:9	114, 260, 290, 302
19:10	28, 31
19:12	118
19:16	290
19:16–20	302

19:19	119, 302
19:21	70
19:25	123
20:3	47
20:4	87
20:10	37
20:18–21	302
20:18	290
20:24	259
21:12–14	248
22:21–22	45
22:21	37
22:22	98
22:29b	111
23:14	291
23:20	54
23:23	54
23:29	53, 259
24:7	48, 413
24:10–11	70
24:12	413
24:14–15	302
24:15–16	260
25:8	183
25:10–22	415
25:16	344
25:21	344
25:22	344
25–31	39, 44, 183
25:1–7	366
25:8	262
25:9	260
25:22	115, 275
25:31–40	62
27:1–2	248
28	62
28:6–30	74
28:11–22	242
28:13	114, 254
30:11–16	240
32	275
32:2–4	75
32:4	275
32:11–14	34
32:13	298
32:14	241
32:20	301
33:7–11	184
33:11–23	70
33:11	304
33:19	138
33:21–22	301
34:5	114, 301
34:6	55
34:11–16	20
38:8	112
40	260
40:34	184, 260
40:34–38	290
40:34–35	116

Leviticus

1:1–9	136
7:25	112
13:1–17	328
13:6	328
13:45–46	328
14	328
14:6	328
14:10	328
15:18–19	194
15:18	112
17:10–14	140
18:6–19	100
18:15	226
18:24–30	282
18:24–28	44
18:24–27	122
18:24–25	311
19:9	99
19:31	136
19:33–34	37
20:2–5	354
20:10	198
20:11–12	226
20:17	202
20:24	263
21:3	112
23:22	99
23:33–43	264
24:5–9	157
24:15–16	310
24:22	37
25:1–7	366
25:10	309
25:23	29, 309
25:25–28	309

Leviticus (continued)

26:3–5	291
26:14	291
26:20	291
26:29	332
26:34	408
27:22	309

Numbers

2	240
3:29–31	111
5:11–31	211
6:1–21	81
6:13–20	84
7	270
9:1–10	30
9:15–23	184, 260, 290
10	240
10:11–28	184
10:11–12	28
10:11	260, 378
10:33–36	26, 184
10:33	117
10:35–36	31, 63, 115, 415
10:36	240
11:16–30	129
11:17	320
11:18–20	124
11:25	320
13–14	30, 324
13:1–3	30
13:13–19	34
13:28	41
13:33	41
14:1–25	42
14:24	30
16	118
20:1–13	407
21:2–3	21
21:4–9	371
22–24	96, 234
23:8	60
23:19	60
23:22–23	60
23:22	275
24:3–4	236
24:4	60
24:8	60, 275
24:15–16	236
24:16	60
25	44
25:1–2	96
25:1	97
25:3	288
27:1–12	42
31:7–12	23
35:16–21	205

Deuteronomy

1:7–8	257
1:19–40	30
1:20–21	324
1:21	330, 364
1:22–40	33
1:26–36	324
1:26–28	41
1:28	41
1:37	407
2:9	96
3:11	41
3:22	364
3:23–27	407
3:24	26
4:2	143
4:5–7	409
4:15–20	261
4:15–19	275
4:16–25	87
4:21–22	407
4:25–31	401
4:27	409
4:28	364
4:30–31	18
4:30	118
4:35	264
4:39	26, 264
5:1–6	16
5:2–3	371
5:6–21	312
5:6	394
5:7–9	75
5:7	47, 275, 328
5:8–10	63, 275
5:8	87
5:9	349, 390

Scripture Index 429

5:11	208, 231, 312	10:1–5	36, 258
5:15	54	10:14	263
5:17–18	196	10:15	263
5:18	195	10:16	412
5:20–21	312	10:17–19	394
5:20	196	10:17	44
6:4	252, 261	10:18	98
6:4–7	17	10:24	98
6:4–5	43, 74, 152, 249, 254	11:10	309
		11:13	291
6:5	26, 267, 342, 374, 405	11:14	325
		12:2–4	44
6:6–9	412	12:3	63
6:14	47	12:5–14	276
6:15	279	12:5	185, 188, 262, 373
6:25	412		
7:1–6	26, 40, 53, 122, 308, 311, 418	12:8	86
		12:8–9	87
7:1–5	25, 54	12:10–11	263
7:1–4	58	12:11	185, 262
7:1–2	37	12:13–14	252
7:2	20, 35, 42, 308	12:21	185, 252
7:3–4	45, 266	12:23	140
7:3	55, 82, 96	12:31	80, 288, 354
7:4	21, 44, 47, 58, 371	12:32	48, 143
		13:1–5	299
7:5	63, 85, 282–83, 373	13:11	211
		13:12–18	43, 35
7:6	260	13:16	35
7:7–8	39, 188	13:17	211
7:10	390, 349	14:2	260
7:12	35	15	25, 324, 395
7:17–26	25	16:1–8	374
7:22	359	16:1–6	20
7:25–26	34	16:3	54
7:25	23	16:5–6	373
8	17, 398	16:9–12	291
8:2	54	16:11	373
8:4	40	16:12	54
8:7–9	363	16:15–16	373
8:7	28	16:19	120
8:9	88	16:20	56
8:14	28	16:21–22	48, 68
9–10	40	16:21	61, 73
9:1–5	188	17:6	312
9:7	397–98	17:14–20	14, 103, 122–23, 137, 248, 265
9:9–10	413		
9:18–19	34	17:18–20	370
9:25–29	34	17:18–19	16

Deuteronomy (continued)

Reference	Page
17:18	344
18:1–8	276
18:6–8	373
18:9–19	166, 288
18:9–14	166
18:10	80, 338, 354
18:15–18	134
18:15	300, 404
18:20	279
19:11–13	19
20:1–4	324
20:5–8	72
20:7	95
20:9–14	95
20:10–11	38
20:11	39, 258
20:14–18	33
20:15	38, 20
20:16–20	35
20:16–18	53
20:18	38
20:19–20	323
21:10–15	394
21:14	202
21:22–23	41
22:13	201
21:16	349, 390
22:13–21	201
22:21	202
22:22	198
22:23–25	198
22:28–31	203
23:3	96
23:9–14	240
23:17–18	282
24:17–21	37, 309, 325
24:17	294, 412
24:18	54
24:19	99
24:21–22	313, 394
25:1	207
25:5–10	205
25:9	103
26:1–11	408
26:5	30, 304
26:8–9	28
25:17–19	141
26:15	263
26:16–18	47
26:17–21	325
27:1–13	46
27:2–8	36
27:15	87
27:22	202, 212 230, 293
28:15–68	342
28:15–21	332
28:16–24	395
28:22–24	230
28:22	291, 293
28:36	364
28:46	401
28:53–57	332
28:64	364
29:5	40
29:19	134, 44
29:21	35
29:22–29	264
29:30	399
30:1–10	18
30:10	118
30:14	48
30:19	187
31:24	6
32	2, 214
32:1	236
32:4	236
32:8–9	59
32:8	59–60, 64
31:9	2
31:22	2
31:24	2
33:1	112
33:11–14	46
34:5	177
34:10–12	15, 114, 236

*within the books of the Former Prophets, an asterisk indicates the primary discussion of the literary unit within the narrative chronology

Joshua

1*	15–19
1:1–9	18
1:2	177
1:7–9	248
1:7–8	93
1:7	14, 177, 285
1:8	6
1:12	78
2*	19–27
2	333
2:2	95
2:11	214
2:12	156
3–5*	27–31
3:3–16	320
3:3–4	117
3:13–16	320
3:17	210
4:4–7	54
4:6–7	320, 412
4:10	30
4:24	151
5	322
5:1	214
5:9	28
5:10—12:5	14
5:13–15	28, 54, 214, 254
5:13–14	115
5:14	240
6*	31
6:5	72, 115, 333
6:20	115
6:26	57, 285, 288, 378
7:1—8:29*	31–36
7	296, 327, 345
7:24–26	342
7:25	211
7:26	117, 218
8:1	330
8:3–7	306
8:22	14
8:27	285
8:29	218
8:30–35*	36–37
8:30–35	91, 372
9*	37–40
9	322
9:4	230
9:7	53
9:10	53
9:15	230
9:16	53
9:20	230
9:22	53
9:27	230
10*	40–42
10:4	3, 355
10:10	119
10:12–14	68
10:13	7
10:14	115
10:42	115
11:1	67
11:4	214
11:10	67
13–21*	42–43
13:8–13	78
15:13–19	52
16:10	258
17:18	53
19:47	87
21	274
21:1–15	112
21:14–28	55
22*	43–44
22:7	117
23*	44–46
23:1–14	53
23:3	115
23:6–7	14
23:7	14, 55
23:10	115
23:11	152
23:12	55, 96
23:13	54
23:14	263
23:16	6, 14, 55, 186
24*	46–49
24	372
24:14–24	14
24:14–15	118
24:26	6, 14, 70
24:27	117
24:28	93
24:29	177

Judges

1–2	45	6:2	123
1:1—3:11*	51–65	6:7–10	130
1	53	6:9	347
1:11–15	52	6:12	254
1:16	141	6:13	128
1:19	126	6:17	128, 277
1:28–35	322	6:20–21	61
1:28	258	6:23	364
1:34	872	6:25–35	288
2:1–5	112, 118	6:25	60
2:3	53	6:34	64, 122
2:6	93	7:2–8	305
2:8	177	7:5	177
2:10–11	382	7:12	214
2:11–16	322	7:13–17	119
2:11–13	288	8:22–23	131
2:11	282	8:23	95, 122, 356
2:14	359	8:27	338
2:16	35, 90	8:33	288
2:17	61, 338	9*	75–77
2:18	347	9	119
3:5–6	96, 267	9:1–6	274
3:5	27	9:7–15	350
3:7	282	9:8–15	119, 238
3:7–8	40	9:20–22	258
3:10	122	9:23	147
3:12–30*	65–66	9:45	321
3:12–29	96	9:50–55	196
3:12–25	160	9:56–57	387
3:12	322	10*	77–78
3:19	13	10:2–3	109
3:21–22	227	10:6	61, 13
3:24	160	10:10–16	133, 118
3:27	72	10:12	347
4:1—5:31*	66–69	11:1—12:7*	78–80
4:3	347	11	140
4:14	214	11:1	338
4:15	64, 119	11:29	122, 64
4:21	218	11:30	31
5	68, 79	12:7–14	109
5:4–5	61, 234, 291	13–16*	80–85
5:4	59, 180	13:3	254
5:9	13	13:5–7	109
5:14–18	126	13:6	112
5:20–21	61	13:15	64
5:28	340	14	214
6–8*	69–75	14:2–3	267, 267
		14:4	95, 112, 388
		14:6	122, 13

15:20	109	2:12	238
16:1	338	2:18	74
16:51–31	378	2:25	214, 272, 387–88
17–18*	86–89	2:27–36	104, 198, 250, 285, 372
19–21*	89–93	2:27	274
19:23–24	202	2:28	74
19:31	109	2:30	348
17–21	126, 188	2:34	277
17	252	2:35	172, 270
17:5	62	3:3	48
17:7	95	3:13–14	189
17:16	62	3:19	116
18	51	3:21	254, 285
18:14	62	4–7*	114–19
18:18	62	4	210
18:24	62	4:4	275
19–21	128, 132	4:12–18	207
19	132	4:12–17	218
19:22	238	4:17	217
20:8	132	4:21	412
20:13	238, 132	5:1–5	85
20:48	132	6:19—7:2	181
21:8–25	128	6:19	181
21:10	132	6:20	181
21:15–24	51	6:21	139
		7:2	234
Ruth		7:4	61, 288
1*	96–98	7:8	277
1:4	267	7:9–10	21, 31
2*	98–100	7:10	214, 234, 333
2:20	156	7:12–17	86
3*	100–102	7:16	13
4*	102–6	8*	119–26
4	206	8	186, 238
4:1–6	207	8:3	393
4:18–22	158	8:5	358
		8:7	124
1 Samuel		8:10–18	194, 208
1–3*	109–14	8:10–17	241
1:1	109	8:11–18	186, 257, 308
1:3	48	8:11	207
1:5–6	103	8:14	224
1:11	109	9–11*	126–33
1:19–20	103	9–10	140
2	234	9:1—10:8	3
2:7b	234	9:1	51, 175
2:10	190, 291	9:6–10	279
2:11–36	89	9:6–8	274

1 Samuel (continued)

9:6	112
9:12–26	252
9:12	231
9:16	177, 247, 337
9:21	72
10:6	64
10:26	51
10:27	226
11:11	240
11:12–13	223
11:14–15	208, 222
12*	133–34
12	238
13:1–15*	134–38
13	191
13:3	208
13:5	214
13:13–14	175
13:13	185
13:14	185, 193, 229
13:15b—14:52*	138–41
14:38–44	130
14:50	174–75, 197
15*	141–43
15	172, 307, 372
15:23	166
15:24–26	199
15:26	199
15:38	199
16:1–13*	143–49
16:1–13	8, 179
16:1	337
16:7	229
16:11	185
16:12	206
16:13–14	64, 76, 200
16:14	33, 148
16:18	194
17*	149–52
17	233
18–20*	152–57
18:6–9	216
18:13–16	216
18:16	177, 179
18:17–29	176
18:20–29	177
19:13	62
20:14–17	224
20:15	192
21–22*	157–59
21:5	195, 240
22:1	239
22:6	191
22:18	74
22:20	245
23–24*	159–61
23:2	314
24:6	173
24:14	192
24:21–22	231
25*	161–63
25:7	204
25:11	204
25:28	270
25:30	172, 179
25:36	204
25:44	177
26*	163–64
26:8	175
26:12	214
26:29	173
27*	164–65
27:8–12	186, 235, 255
27:9	193
28*	165–68
28	186, 21
29*	168–69
29	216
29:9	206, 224
30*	169–70
30:7	62, 74, 285
31*	170
31	191
31:11–13	174
31:12–13	232

2 Samuel

1*	172–73
1	7
1:21	293
2–4*	173–78
2–4	156, 172
2	147
2:1	285, 314
2:10b	189

2:23	345	7:16	270
2:26	152	8–10*	190–92
3:1	105	8	3, 96, 411
3:3	45, 154, 267	8:1	85
3:6–8	249	8:5–8	304
3:12–16	154	8:6	140
3:17	170	8:12	140
4:4	297	8:14	140
5–6*	178–82	8:13–14	269
5	108, 143, 172	8:17	250
5:1–3	271	9	244
5:1	170	9:1—10:8	3
5:3	345	10:1	273
5:10–12	410	11–20	144
5:10–11	144	11–18	386
5:10	149, 292	11–12*	192–200
5:11	257	11	105
5:12	375	11:27	148
5:20	288	11:27b	384
6–7	255	12	246, 307
6	115, 259	12:1	33
6:2	259	12:4	148
6:6–11	279	12:11	33, 273, 386
6:7	118	12:14	280
6:8	118, 181	12:15	390
6:12	259	12:24	247
6:17	247	13*	200–205
6:19	246	13:21	246, 386
6:20–23	152	13:30	246
7–11	250	13:39	246, 386
7*	182–90	14*	205–7
7	108, 137, 188–89, 255–57, 259–60, 264, 411	15:1–12*	207–9
		15:13—17:29*	209–16
		15:7	252, 288
7:1–7	410	15:8	231
7:2	259	15:10	338
7:4–7	261	17	53, 273
7:6	110, 261	17:14	125, 148, 272, 388
7:7–11	344		
7:8	179	18:1—19:8*	216–21
7:9	409	18:7	86
7:11–12	248	18:24–32	338
7:11	163, 257	18:27	248
7:13–17	382	19:1–8	246
7:13–16	383	19:9–43*	221–25
7:13	244, 262	20	244
7:14–16	268, 400	20:1–22*	225–29
7:14	356	20:1	388
7:15–16	105, 188	20:24	183, 256, 384

Scripture Index 435

2 Samuel (continued)

21	293
21:1–14*	230–32
21:1–14	34
21:1–4	271
21:1	162
21:15–22*	233
21:19	149
22:1—23:7*	233–39
23:1–7	244
23:1	94
23:2–4	245
23:3–4	255
23:9–39*	239–40
24*	240–42
24:1	399
23:4	173
23:5	348, 356
23:34	195
23:39	195
24	183
24:1	148
24:2	240
25:31	174

1 Kings

1–11	199, 244
1–2*	244–51
1–2	172, 242, 244, 343
1	229, 337
1:1—2:10	228
1:7	231
1:34	208
1:39	208
2	172, 228
2:5–6	218
2:6	224
2:7	216
2:8–9	223
2:12	277
2:21	382
2:27	113, 159, 185
2:35	113, 185, 285
2:46	ix, 190
3–8	410
3:1–28*	251–55
3:1	154
3:2–3	352
3:4	231
3:5	254
3:9	205
3:16–28	205
4–10*	255–65
4:20–20	409
4:25	363
4:32	251
5:1	152
5:3	187
5:4	257
5:21–23	219
6–10	266
7:23–37	355
8	19, 183, 185, 260, 374–75, 411, 415
8:1	259
8:6–9	415
8:9	63, 258, 413
8:16	110
8:10–13	184, 290
8:10–12	302
8:10–11	260
8:12	261
8:22–53	182, 364
8:27	279
8:31–53	399
8:32	293
8:37	230
8:46–53	408
8:48	118
9:3	382
9:4	400
11*	265–71
11	37, 45, 58, 270, 394, 400
11:1–8	308
11:7	324
11:11–13	383
11:11	388
11:13	177
11:23–25	304
11:26	318
11:32–38	177
11:33	324
11:36	375, 383
11:38	163
11:39	400, 401

12–14	244	16:24	278
12:1—16:28*	271–76	16:29—33:40	244
12	174–75, 273, 337, 384	16:29–32	46
12:1–14	8	16:34	57, 321, 378
12:1–5	394	17—2 Kgs 10	58
12:4	123	17–19	61, 234
12:15	125, 215, 285, 388	17–18*	287–300
12:16	226	17:1	230
12:20	345	17:8–16	325
12:22	285	17:17–24	326
12:25—33:9	51	17:17–18	32
12:25–39	370	18	332, 341
12:25	76	18:19	61
12:28	89, 342	18:20–40	72
12:31–32	127, 253	18:30	321
12:31	359	18:40	323, 373
13	373	19*	300–304
13:1–10*	276–77	19:25–28	363
13:1–10	276	19:29–32	45
13:1–3	112	19	59, 258
13:2	369	19:6	100
13:3	113	19:11–12	290
13:11–32*	277–79	19:12	302
13:15–16	369	19:15–17	346
13:24	359	19:15	334
13:33–34	57, 278	19:16	336
14:1—16:23*	279–87	19:26–40	336
14:1–16	214	20*	304–8
14:1–10	337	20	305, 352
14:7–16	372	20:1–6	361
14:11–13	361	20:28	328
14:15–16	11, 390	20:32–36	278
14:16	34, 358	20:35–37	332
14:19	7	20:35	295
14:22–24	354, 358,	20:36	359
14:23	127	20:41	295
14:26	355	21*	308–13
15:4	375, 383, 400	21	46, 158
15:5	255, 394	21:2–5	358
15:13	343	21:19	339
15:14	127, 253	21:21–29	372
15:16–21	355	21:21–24	337
16–19	211	21:21	339
16:4	337	21:29	268, 390
16:7	38, 243	22	147, 357
16:8–20	32	22*	313–17
16:9–13	340	22:1–40	337
		22:4–5	322
		22:19–23	148

1 Kings (continued)

22:25	306
22:38	284
22:43	253

2 Kings

1*	318–19
1	367
1:2	297
2*	319–21
2:2–4	188
2:11	296
2:15–17	288
3	56, 116, 292, 322, 385, 393
3*	321–24
3:27	288
4:1–7*	324–25
4:8–37*	325–26
4:38–41*	326–27
4:42–44*	327
*5:1–19	327–29
5:27	390
6:1–7*	329
6:8—7:20	329–33
6:17	320
6:24	352
6:33	397
8:1–6*	333–34
8:1–6	326
8:7–15*	334–36
8:20–25	349
9–10*	336–43
9–10	62, 86
9:35–37	311
10	108, 311, 418
10:30	389
11*	343–45
11:13–20	369
11:17	356
12*	345–47
12:2–3	253
12:17–18	352
13*	347–49
13:23	401
14:1–22*	349–50
14:23–29*	350–51
15*	351
15:16	394
15:19	352
15:29—16:20	351
16*	354–56
17*	358–60
17	383, 394
17:5–8	17
17:7–18	390
17:7	6
17:9	253
17:11	253
17:13–14	48
17:16	342
17:17	311
17:29	253
17:32	253
18–20*	360–68
18–20	244
18:1–8	57
18:5	6, 249
18:13	362, 366, 367
18:14–16	365
19–20	351
19	307
19:23–25	389
19:25	368
20:20	362, 365
21*	368–69
21:3–7	57
21:4	394
21:6	166
21:19–20	396
21:20b	396
21:24	345
22–23*	369–76
22:2	249
22:3	407
22:4–24	57
22:4–7	371
22:8–13	14
22:8	6
22:10–13	58
22:11	395
22:13–20	166
22:20	405
22:16	6
23	14, 371
23:7	282
23:7b	62

23:10	288, 354
23:13	267
23:15–20	277
23:21–23	14
23:22	291
23:24–26	166
23:24	6, 21
23:25	249, 405
23:26–30	268, 390
23:26	391
23:30	345
22–23	6, 36
24:3	390
24–25	376–79
25:9	264
25:25	403
25:29	192

1 Chronicles

2:7	296
2:12–16	175
6:26	111
8:33	61
9:36	175
21:1	240, 391

2 Chronicles

6:26	136
20:3	310
33:10–13	375
35:22	375, 391
35:25	391

Nehemiah

1:9	407
8	372
8:1	413
9	364
13	21
13:1	96
13:23–27	96

Psalms

2	189, 235
2:2	356
2:6	181
2:7	185, 189, 356
8:5	205
15:1–3	110
18:7–14	302
18:8–15	289
18:10	60
18:13–14	119
18:14	60
19:1	302
20:7	328
23:5	331
27:3	330
29:1	315
29:7	302
48:3	60
51:10–11	402
68:1	115, 415
68:4	60
68:7–8	290
68:16	184
68:17–18	115, 415
68:17	115, 330
68:24–27	115
72	235
72:1–2	205
72:3	173
72:4	271
74:12–15	258
72:12–14	205
73:6	173
73:16	173
76:2	260
77:16–18	258
77:17–20	290
77:19	389
78:1–8	54
80:1	275
81:2	94
82:1	328
88:15	148
89	183
89:9–10	258
89:1–37	235
89:3	345
89:5–7	315
89:6	189
89:17	189
89:26–27	189, 356
89:28	238

Psalms (continued)

89:38–51	188
93:3–4	258
97:1–5	258
97:1–2	261
97:5	123
104:3	60
105:10	238
106:21	275
114:3	290
119:92	406
132	183
132:1–8	115
132:2	275
132:5	275
132:11	176
132:12	188
133:3	214
137:8	47
147:8	291

Proverbs

1:1	251
1:7	237
3:14	289
5:21–22	88
7:6–23	26
14:14	77, 198, 14:14
17:17	152
19:12	214
24:12	77, 198, 387
30:15–16	153
30:18–19	153
30:27	85

Ecclesiastes

1:1	251
2:8–11	259
8:10–17	392

Song of Songs

4:9	202

Isaiah

1:7–8	362
1:11	142, 410
1:21–22	361
2:2–4	366, 411
3:14–15	158
3:16–17	367
5:7	124
5:26–30	352, 363
6:1–5	365
6:1–3	315
6:5	72
6:9	272
6:9–10	48
7–8	197
7	351
7:1—8:15	354
7:4	330
7:5	364
7:11	366
8:18	366
8:19–20	366
9:1–7	404
9:2–7	366
10:5	56, 116, 213, 363, 385
10:15–16	365
10:16	365
10:20–27	363
11:6	278
11:9	366
11:11	363
11:16	363
14:24–27	365
15–16	96
19:6	365
20	211
22:1	365
22:11	368
24:10	134
25:1	365
27:1	59
28–38	360
30:15	365
34:11	134
36–39	360
40–55	125, 236, 401
40	364
40:1–2	405
40:9–11	405
40:9	366
40:12–31	298,

41:1–24	365	6:14	381
42:14	135	7:1–15	377
42:15	365	7:6	311, 369
43:11	235	7:12	89
43:18	403	7:21–23	410, 142
44:8b	235	7:33	311
44:9–20	71	8:13	363
44:27	365	12:5	209
44:28	405	14:3–4	211
45	264, 328, 410	14:12	310
45:1	125, 304	19:10	297
45:5	235	21:1–10	377
45:7	147	21:8–10	363
46:13	366	22:3	369
47:2–3	84	22:11–19	363, 377
49:8–26	405	22:13–19	395
49:22–26	411	22:13–17	391, 395
49:26	275	22:17	369
50:4–5	254	22:18–19	377
51:3	366	23–18	315
51:9	59	23:5–6	404
51:9–11	258	23:9–40	313
51:10–11	59, 237	24	408
51:11	366	27:17	377
51:16	366	27:19	355
52:1–2	405	28:9	316
52:1	405	28:10	314
54	405	29:1–23	378
54:10	405	29:7–22	408
55:3	238	29:10–14	400
56	408	29:14	407
58:6	310	31:29–30	349
64:12	135	31:29	391
		32:1–15	407
		32:16–24	364
		34:8–22	395

Lamentations

2:20	332
4:10	332

34:13–17	17
36	395
36:4–8	310
36:9	310
37:6–11	395
37:11–17	316
38:5	396
38:17	377, 378

Jeremiah

1:4–10	128
1:6	72, 128
1:9	236
2:18–19	357
2:20	354
3:3	291
3:6	354
3:13	354
5:17	363

Ezekiel

1	315, 410
1:1	378

Ezekiel (continued)

1:8	378
3:1–3	236
5:10	332
8:1–6	410
10	410
11:17	407
16:15–17	338
18	199, 349
18:2	268, 313, 390, 391
18:23	112
23:33–36	338
29:7	321
34	404
34:23	382
34:24	270
40–48	405
43:24	321

Amos

1:3—2:3	336
1:3	153
1:4	76
1:6	153
1:9	153
1:10	76
1:12	76
1:12	76
1:13	335
2:5	76
2:6–8	158, 273
2:7	226
4:4	13
4:6–12	17, 237
4:6–11	32, 56
4:6–10	381
4:6	230
4:7	32, 291, 293
5:10–15	207, 273
5:21–24	142, 410
6:4–8	273
7:10–17	198, 296, 351
7:10	338
8:2	358
8:4–6	158, 273
9:7	304
9:11–15	405
9:11	404

Hosea

1	197
1:2	388
1:9–10	344
2:1–13	293
2:2–13	17
2:5	339
2:6	338–39
2:8–9	292
2:8	291
2:10–13	339
2:12	363
2:16–21	414
2:16	61
2:22	292
4:1–3	32, 237
4:12	338
4:13–14	282
4:18	282
5:5–6	275
6:6	142, 410
7:8–13	357
7:14	297
8:8–10	357
11:8–9	400
12:11	13
13:10–11	124
13:16	335

Micah

2:1–5	324
2:1–2	158
3:1–4	124
3:9–11	369
4:1–4	405, 411
4:4	256, 363
5:2	104
6	197
6:8	26, 156

Malachi

4:5	404

NEW TESTAMENT

Matthew

1:1–17	105, 405
1:5	25, 26
7:12	3
10:25	297, 319
10:34–39	304
11:14	404
22:36–40	17
29:52	198

Luke

16:16	3

Romans

3:21	3
5:10	188

James

2:25	25, 26

Revelation

21:22	411

www.ingramcontent.com/pod-product-compliance
Lightning Source LLC
Chambersburg PA
CBHW060302010526
44108CB00042B/2609